DB2 Universal Database and SAP® R/3® Version 4

IBM DB2 Certification Guide Series

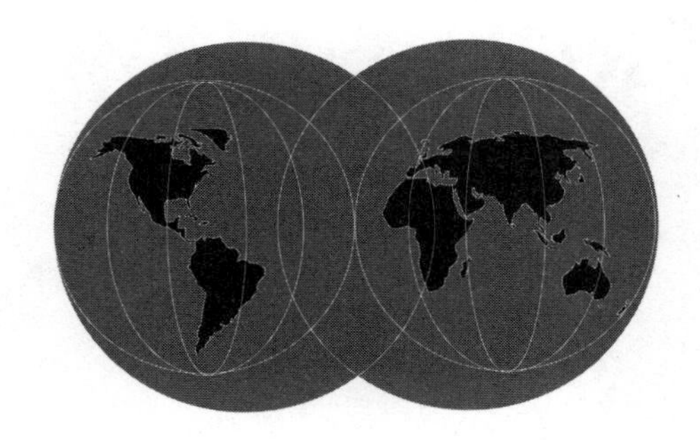

DB2 Universal Database Certification Guide, Second Edition
edited by Janacek and Snow

DB2 Cluster Certification Guide
by Cook, Janacek, and Snow

DB2 Universal DRDA Certification Guide
by Brandl, Bullock, Cook, Harbus, Janacek, and Le

DB2 Replication Certification Guide
by Cook and Harbus

DB2 Universal Database and SAP R/3 Version 4
by Bullock, Cook, Deedes-Vincke, Harbus, Nardone, and Neuhaus

Universal Guide to DB2 for Windows NT
by Cook, Harbus, and Snow

DB2 Universal Database and SAP® R/3® Version 4

DIANE BULLOCK ■ JONATHAN COOK ■ STEPHEN DEEDES-VINCKE
ROBERT HARBUS ■ LUKE NARDONE ■ RODOLFO NEUHAUS

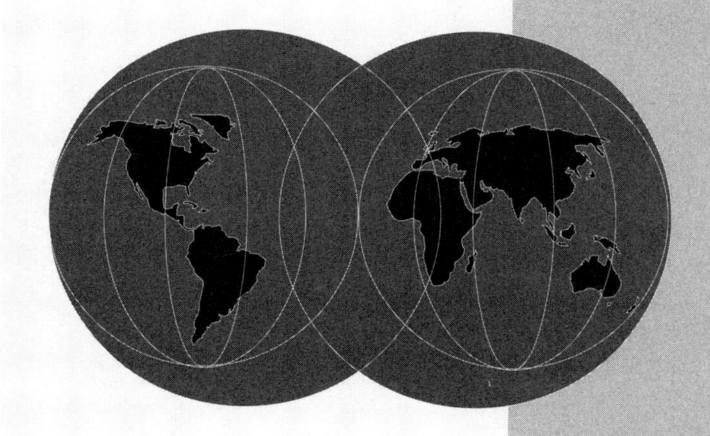

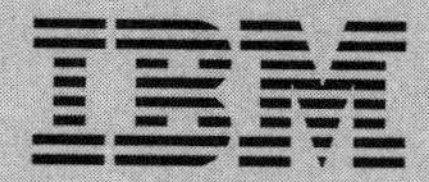

International Technical Support Organization
Austin, Texas 78758

PRENTICE HALL PTR, UPPER SADDLE RIVER, NEW JERSEY 07458
http://www.phptr.com

Editorial/production supervision: *Jane Bonnell*
Cover design director: *Jayne Conte*
Cover designer: *Bruce Kenselaar*
Manufacturing manager: *Pat Brown*
Marketing manager: *Kaylie Smith*
Acquisitions editor: *Michael Meehan*
Editorial assistant: *Bart Blanken*

Published by Prentice Hall PTR
Prentice-Hall, Inc.
Upper Saddle River, NJ 07458

Prentice Hall books are widely used by corporations and government agencies for training, marketing, and resale.
The publisher offers discounts on this book when ordered in bulk quantities.
For more information, contact
Corporate Sales Department,
Phone 800-382-3419; FAX: 201-236-7141
E-mail (Internet): corpsales@prenhall.com
Or Write: Prentice Hall PTR
Corporate Sales Department
One Lake Street
Upper Saddle River, NJ 07458

DB2 information on the Internet—http://www.software.ibm.com/data/db2
DB2 certification information on the Internet—http://www.ibm.com/certify

Printed in the United States of America
10 9 8 7 6 5 4 3 2 1

ISBN 0-13-082426-7

Prentice-Hall International (UK) Limited, *London*
Prentice-Hall of Australia Pty. Limited, *Sydney*
Prentice-Hall Canada Inc., *Toronto*
Prentice-Hall Hispanoamericana, S.A., *Mexico*
Prentice-Hall of India Private Limited, *New Delhi*
Prentice-Hall of Japan, Inc., *Tokyo*
Simon & Schuster Asia Pte. Ltd., *Singapore*
Editora Prentice-Hall do Brasil, Ltda., *Rio de Janeiro*

Contents

Figures

Tables

Preface

This book is intended to provide guidance to the new administrator of an SAP R/3 installation using DB2 Universal Database (DB2 UDB) as the database management system. It is designed to be very task-oriented and focused on bridging the gap between the R/3 and DB2 worlds. This book is not intended to replace SAP R/3 and DB2 Universal Database education.

This book will help you install and configure SAP R/3 using DB2 Universal Database as the database manager on the AIX and Windows NT platforms. It will also provide a broad understanding of the R/3 and DB2 Universal Database architecture.

You should understand that the installation chapters of this book only reflect the activities involved in the implementation of R/3 version 4.0B and DB2 UDB version 5.0. Please refer to the current SAP supplied installation documentation and OSS Notes to generate your own installation plan. This book is not intended to eliminate the need for a certified SAP R/3 consultant when installing SAP R/3 for the first time.

Chapter 1 contains an introduction to the R/3 and DB2 Universal Database architecture and facilities. The subsequent chapters will assist you in the planning, installation, administration, maintenance and tuning of your new R/3 and DB2 UDB environment. The installation chapters will be especially useful during the initial planning and preparation phases of your R/3 and DB2 implementation.

The Team That Wrote This Book

This book was produced by a team of specialists from around the world working at the International Technical Support Organization Austin Center.

Jonathan Cook is the DB2 Project Leader at the International Technical Support Organization (ITSO), Austin Center. He has ten years of experience as a database specialist working in the areas of application development and database administration. He has been with IBM since 1992, working in both the United Kingdom and France before joining the Austin ITSO. He writes extensively and teaches IBM classes worldwide on DB2 for the UNIX and Intel platforms.

Diane DeVere Bullock has been a Database Specialist since 1986 working with both DB2 and IMS, and has been with IBM Global Service for 4 years.

Diane provides consulting services internationally in the areas of database tuning, query tuning, cross platform data replication, and DRDA connectivity.

Stephen Deedes-Vincke is a Database Specialist in the United Kingdom. He has been working with DB2 on most platforms for the last 5 years. This is the second book he has worked on, having previously contributed to the *SQL/DS V3 R4 Performance Guide* GG24-4047-00.

Robert Harbus is the DB2 Universal Database Certification and Education coordinator at the IBM Toronto Lab. A member of the DB2 UDB team since its inception in 1991, Robert provided Technical Marketing and electronic customer support and direct customer support most recently as a member of the DB2 Universal Database Enterprise - Extended Edition (EEE) support team. Robert is currently responsible for the DB2 UDB certification program and testing, and works with the ITSO and Education & Training to ensure that DB2 UDB education courses, training and material are available to meet the needs of DB2 UDB users. Robert teaches DB2 internals and certification courses worldwide and is involved in producing certification guides and redbooks.

Luke Nardone is an SAP Certified Technical Consultant for IBM Poughkeepsie, N.Y. He has been supporting IBM's SAP effort for the last 4 years. For the 5 years previous to his SAP assignment Luke was responsible for AIX support on workstations as well as 9076/SP2 systems.

Rodolfo F. Neuhaus is a professional service specialist from IBM Peru. He is a SAP R/3 Basis consultant and a DB2 technical consultant on the VM, MVS, OS2 and AIX platforms. He is currently working as a SAP Basis technical architect for Andean companies. His primary responsibilities are to provide SAP Basis consultant and technical support for customers running SAP R/3 on the IBM RS/6000.

We would like to thank the following people for their help in verifying the technical content of this book:

Katherine Frogley
IBM Toronto Lab

Thinh Hong
IBM/SAP Integration Center

Nadim Khoury
IBM/SAP Integration Center

Jeorg Nalik
IBM/SAP Integration Center

Yeong Soong
IBM/SAP Integration Center

Joyce Taylor
IBM/SAP Integration Center

Darrin E. Woodard
IBM Toronto Lab

Liwen Yeow
IBM Toronto Lab

Thanks to the IBM Netfinity group for the loan of equipment used during this project.

The following people made invaluable contributions to this project:

Edgar Heirsekorn
Add On Consulting of Germany

David Theissen
International Technical Support Organization, Austin Center

Steve Gardner
International Technical Support Organization, Austin Center

Carmelo Longordo
IBM Southbury US

The IBM Southbury Technology Center
IBM US

Robert A. Johnson
IBM Raleigh US

Charles Greene
IBM Raleigh US

Theresa Mangine
IBM Southbury US

Melanie Stopfer
IBM US - DB2 UDB Developer /Instructor

Kim Solsky
IBM US - SAP Education

Marie Wilson of Atlanta, GA
IBM US - Education and Training

Calene Janacek
IBM Austin

Jim Geeslin
IBM Atlanta US

Catherine Cook
IBM France

A special thanks goes to the following people without whose help this project would have never been completed:

Annie Bullock, Brandy Nardone, and Eugene Koerner.

Chapter 1. Introduction

In this chapter we discuss the architecture of SAP R/3 as implemented with DB2 Universal Database on the Windows NT and AIX platforms. The software versions used here are DB2 Universal Database Version 5 and SAP R/3 Version 4.0B, hence to be referred to as DB2 and R/3 respectively.

1.1 What Will SAP R/3 Do For Me?

SAP R/3 is a comprehensive business application system providing a vast array of integrated enterprise-wide software solutions that has come to be the standard information processing system for organizations around the world.

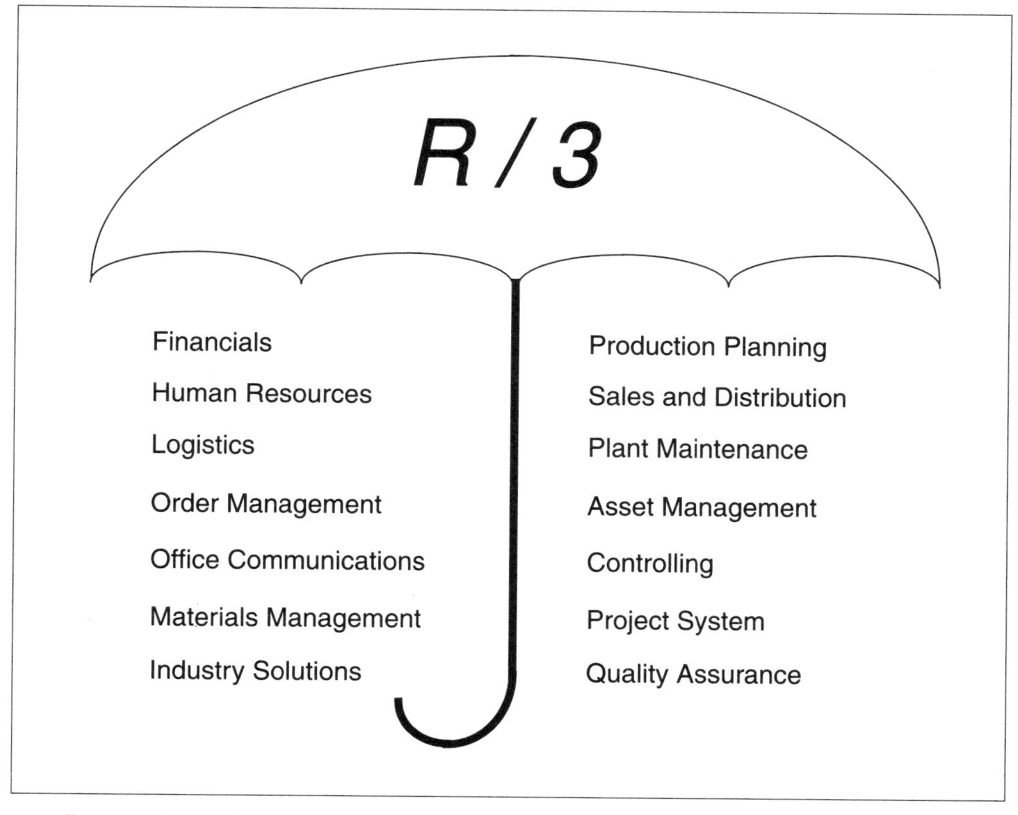

Figure 1. R/3 Umbrella of Integrated Business Applications

The R/3 business systems form an integrated information processing environment that spans the entire organization. In addition to the fully customizable R/3 business systems, R/3 offers a variety of pre-configured industry solutions that incorporate industry standard terminology and provide for a more rapid implementation of R/3. One such solution is the new Ready to Run program from IBM and SAP utilizing the IBM Netfinity server series; for further information on Ready to Run, refer to the web site listed in Appendix D of this book.

SAP offers on-line access through which the R/3 customer may communicate electronically with the R/3 support staff. This on-line interface is known as the On-line System Service (OSS). Through OSS, the R/3 customer may search for solutions to situations encountered in executing their own R/3 system as well as report problems to SAP, obtain new OSS user ids, and register programmers.

SAP also provides a Remote Consulting Service through which you may obtain support from an R/3 consultant. The consultant may provide technical, specific application, or upgrade assistance.

Once you have completed your initial application development cycle and have installed R/3 in production, SAP has a facility known as Early Watch to assist in tuning your production implementation. Early Watch can assist you in problem determination, operating system and database performance tuning.

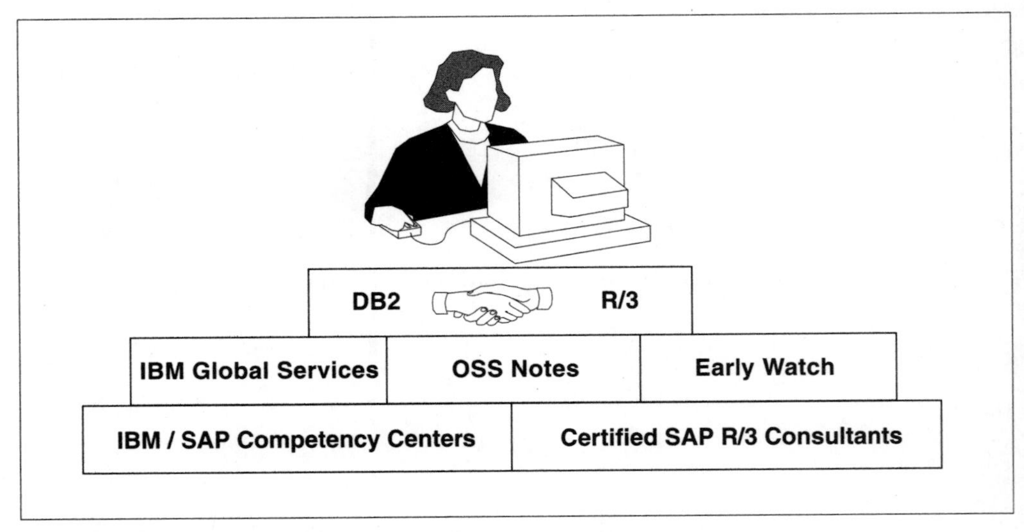

Figure 2. Partnership Between DB2 UDB and SAP R/3

IBM and SAP have teamed to form Competency Centers that can help you with your initial planning and installation as well as performance tuning and problem determination. The IBM/SAP Competency Centers may be contacted via the internet. See Appendix D, “IBM and SAP Web Sites” on page 505 for a list of useful web sites.

You will find that the terminology used in the SAP R/3 environment is similar to that of other data processing environments, but that the meaning of some of the terms is sometimes quite different. For example, the term *client*, when used in reference to R/3 means the customer’s collection of data. When the term *client* is used in conjunction with DB2, it refers to a hardware configuration in which one machine, the *client*, requests that a server machine perform a specific task. Which is correct? Both. We will discuss the variations in the terminology later as we transition from the discussion of DB2 UDB to the discussion of R/3.

In addition to the applications that fall under the R/3 umbrella, R/3 also provides an entire suite of administration tools interfaces through which not only application administration, but operating system and database monitoring may be performed. These interfaces are provided to assist your staff in monitoring and maintaining your R/3 system.

1.2 DB2 Universal Database (DB2 UDB)

DB2 Universal Database is IBM’s highly scalable relational database product. DB2 UDB Version 5 enables the database manager to exploit the multiprocessor capability available in many of the new UNIX and Intel based servers. This additional functionality expands the workload that may be processed and improves performance.

DB2 UDB is supported on a wide variety of systems. The smallest system, an Intel-based laptop PC running DB2 UDB Personal Edition serves the individual user’s needs. The second level is the Intel-based server system running DB2 UDB Workgroup Edition that supports groups of local end users accessing the server from a variety of client platforms. The third level is DB2 UDB Enterprise Edition which may be run on Intel-based servers or UNIX-based platforms. The fourth and final level is DB2 UDB Enterprise-Extended Edition which supports massively parallel processors. This allows a database to be physically partitioned across multiple independent machines, while providing a single logical database interface. DB2 Enterprise-Extended Edition is supported on Intel-based machines running Windows NT (such as the Netfinity Server series), or UNIX machines (such as IBM RS/6000 SP systems).

The beauty of DB2 is that you may move from the lower-end Intel platforms such as laptops to the higher end UNIX platforms such as the RS/6000 SP without necessarily modifying your application; the database manager has not changed, but has grown with you and your application requirements. DB2 Enterprise Edition is currently the only DB2 server edition supported to work with SAP R/3 Version 4.

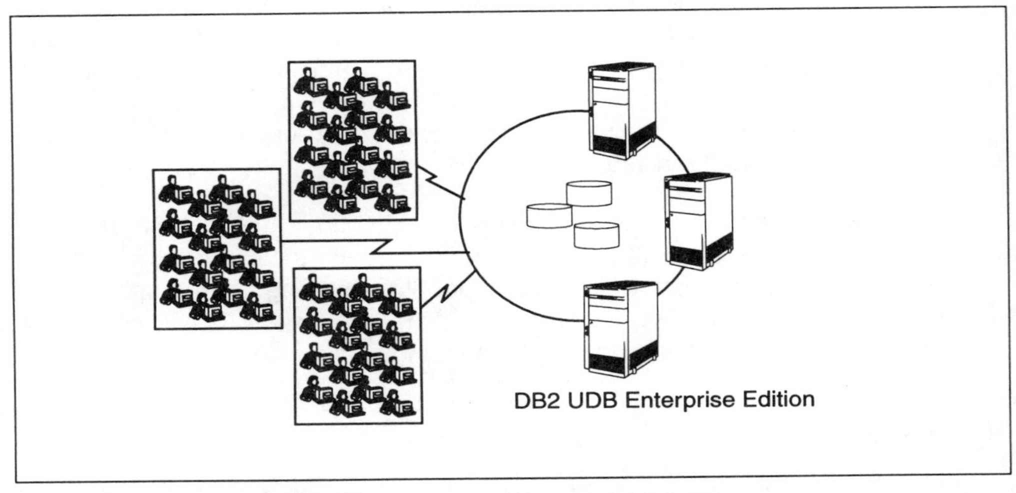

Figure 3. DB2 Universal Database Products Supported with SAP R/3 Version 4

In addition to DB2 Enterprise Edition, DB2 Client Application Enabler (DB2 CAE) is also supported to work with SAP R/3. The Client Application Enabler is needed on any administrator workstation to give access to the DB2 functions necessary to perform their job. DB2 CAE provides the ability to issue SQL statements from the client machine to the remote DB2 UDB database server machine.

While all three product packages, DB2 Workgroup Edition, DB2 Enterprise Edition and DB2 CAE are delivered by SAP when you purchase the DB2 version of R/3 for Windows NT or AIX, only the DB2 CAE and DB2 Enterprise Edition are certified by SAP.

Note

DB2 Workgroup Edition is **not** SAP certified and should not be installed.

The licensing fee for these products is handled by SAP and not directly by IBM. For your SAP installation, you should only use the DB2 installation code provided to you by SAP.

If you wish to use DB2 UDB as your database manager for applications other than SAP R/3, please contact IBM Sales at 1-800-IBM-4YOU or http://www.ibm.com. Additional IBM web sites are referenced in Appendix D of this book.

1.2.1 DB2 UDB Enterprise Edition

DB2 Universal Database Enterprise Edition is a superset of DB2 UDB Workgroup Edition. The Workgroup Edition is supported only on the Intel platform and is intended for use in a LAN environment. DB2 Universal Database Enterprise Edition provides more functionality and platform support. Not only is Enterprise Edition additionally available for the UNIX platforms, it enables access host databases such as DB2 for OS/390, DB2 for AS/400, and DB2 Server for VSE/VM Version 5.1. Access to the SAP database via an interface outside of SAP is not recommended; however, with DB2 UDB Enterprise Edition, access to legacy host database systems is simplified with the DRDA support between the platforms. This data may be of vital use to the implementation and the integration of SAP into your corporate data processing environment.

DB2 UDB Enterprise Edition is supported on Windows NT, OS/2, AIX, HP-UX and Sun Solaris.

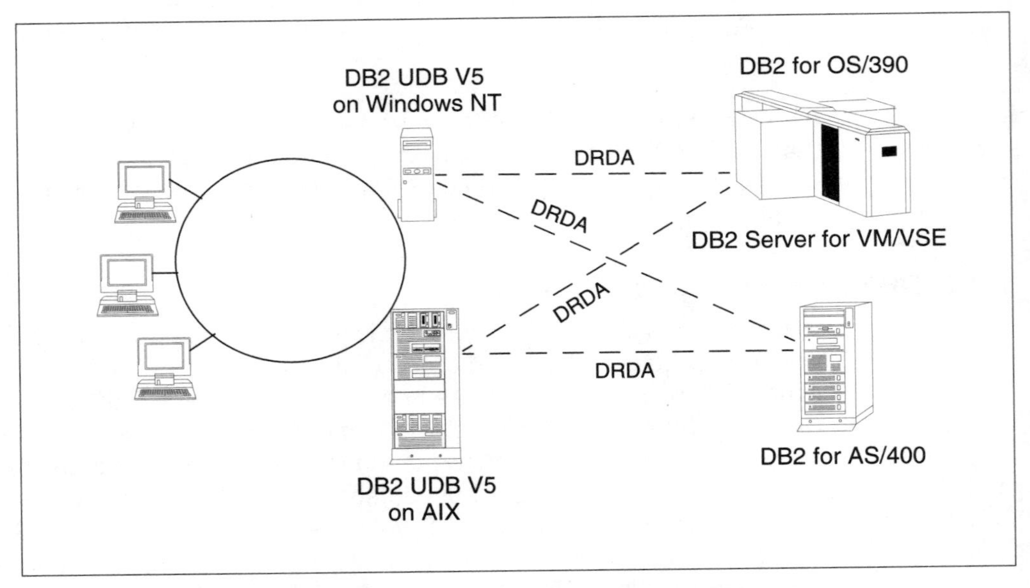

Figure 4. DB2 UDB Enterprise Edition Servers Connecting to Host Systems

DB2 UDB Enterprise Edition is supported on both single processor systems and multiprocessor systems, thus making the database scalable as your organization and information requirements expand.

Normally, there are specific licensing tiers for DB2 UDB Enterprise Edition that are based on the number of processors and the number of users accessing the database. When purchased via SAP R/3, these licensing tiers are not negotiated with IBM, but are included in the price of your SAP system software.

1.3 DB2 UDB Components

DB2 UDB consists of a collection of processes (UNIX-based systems) or processes and threads (Intel-based systems). These processes/threads work together to perform the functions requested by the user and to maintain database integrity. They include:

- Communication listeners that wait for connection requests
- The system controller that performs database functions
- Agents that act as coordinators on behalf of the user requests
- Prefetchers that read the data from the database tables

- Page cleaners that write data back to the database tables
- A transaction logger that records the before and after images of each table modification
- A deadlock detector that manages lock contention
- A number of database server processes/threads that handle various internal database tasks

These processes/threads are allocated at various levels - some at the connection level, others at the database level or at the instance level. Many of these processes/threads are governed by parameters set in the database manager configuration or in the database configuration. Modifications to these configuration parameters may be made through the DB2 Control Center.

1.3.1 DB2 UDB Control Center

The DB2 Universal Database Control Center is a graphical user interface used to administer DB2 UDB databases. The Control Center provides the tools necessary to perform common database administration tasks.

The Control Center provides a visual system overview. From a single Control Center, you may administer multiple DB2 servers, whether they are local or remote.

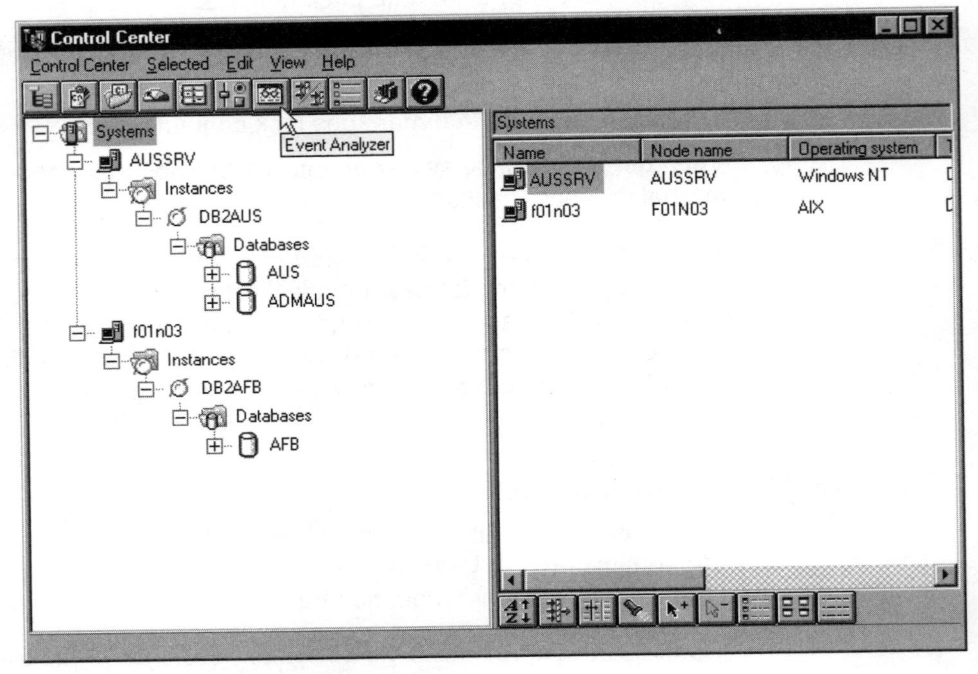

Figure 5. DB2 Control Center with Hover Help

Figure 5 shows the Control Center. From this display you can see both the DB2 UDB SAP R/3 databases on our Netfinity Server running Windows NT as well as the DB2 UDB SAP R/3 database on our IBM RS/6000 SP running AIX. Because the **Systems** icon is highlighted within the tree structure on the left, the system names, Node name and Operating system are displayed in the Contents Pane on the right. Within the Contents Pane on the right is a separate tool bar that may be used to customize the view within the Contents Pane.

The figure above also shows the Hover Help feature of the Control Center. Notice the box on the left side of the screen that displays the word, **Event Analyzer**. Hover help is available for all of the icons on the Control Center tool bar as well as the Contents Pane tool bar.

Although many of the database administration functions such as table, index and view definitions are handled within the R/3 data dictionary, the DB2 Control Center is still an invaluable tool in the administration of your SAP R/3 environment. Extensions to the DB2 Control Center such as log file management and user password management have been added to assist specifically with the management of an SAP R/3 environment. These extensions are delivered in the SAP R/3 installation. It is recommended that you only administer your DB2 UDB systems for SAP R/3 through the Control Center and not through any of the other provided interfaces such as the Command Line Processor.

1.3.1.1 Smart Guides

The Control Center also provides a number of Smart Guides to assist you in managing your DB2 UDB environment. Smart Guides provide step by step assistance for complicated tasks such as performance tuning and so on. These facilities are quite helpful to the newcomer to DB2 UDB as well as to seasoned professionals.

1.3.2 DB2 Command Line Processor (CLP)

The Command Line Processor may be used as a native interface to DB2 UDB. It is provided with both Intel and UNIX DB2 products. From the Command Line Processor (CLP), you may issue SQL statements or native DB2 commands.

```
db2 ==> list applications
```

Although this text-based interface exists, the Control Center provides similar functionality via a graphical user interface without the worry of command syntax or typographical errors.

It is recommended that you do not use the Command Line Processor to interface with your R/3 system. Certain database administration functions have been disabled in the Control Center to protect the R/3 environment; these functions have not been removed from the Command Line Processor interface.

1.3.3 DB2 UDB Monitoring and Windows NT Performance Monitor

DB2 monitors are used to collect detailed resource usage information. Monitoring activity may be performed from a DB2 client or a DB2 server. The monitor interface can be invoked using the graphical interface, the DB2 Command Line processor commands, or monitoring API calls. In addition, you can register DB2 UDB counters with the Windows NT Performance Monitor to tightly integrate DB2 monitoring into Windows NT.

DB2 UDB provides two methods of monitoring, which differ in the way the monitored data is gathered:

- Event Monitoring
- Snapshot Monitoring

The **Event Monitor** records the occurrence of specific milestones of DB2 events. This allows you to collect information about transient events such as deadlocks, connections, and SQL statements. By specifying the type of database activity desired in the monitor definition, the event monitor is able to collect the data, and store it on disk so that the **Event Analyzer** may be used to present to the user, at a later time, the data collected.

The **Snapshot Monitor** provides information regarding database activity at a specific point in time. The amount of data returned to the user when the snapshot is taken is determined using DB2 UDB monitor switches. These switches can be set at the instance or application levels. For example, you can use the Snapshot Monitor to determine connection information at a given point-in-time, monitor I/O activity, review buffer pool statistics, and so on.

In addition, you can use the Windows NT Performance Monitor to monitor DB2 counters.

The DB2 snapshot monitors are fully integrated in the SAP R/3 environment within the R/3 Computing Center Management System (CCMS), providing ease of use for your administrators.

1.3.4 DB2 UDB Cost-Based Optimizer

DB2 UDB includes a cost-based optimizer. This facility formulates the various access plans which could be used to execute the SQL statement, determines the cost of executing these plans and chooses the plan with the least expensive cost for obtaining the information.

For example, assume we have a table, MARA, and index, MARAIX1 defined on the MATNR column of the MARA table.

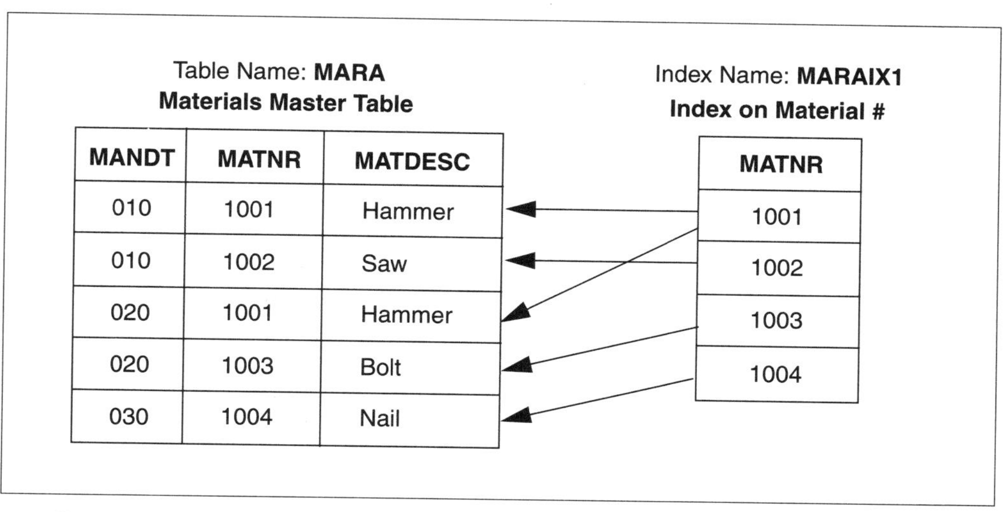

Figure 6. The DB2 Optimizer

The following SQL statement is issued:

```
select * from MARA where MATNR = 1002
```

The requested data may be obtained in one of two ways. The entire MARA table may be read with the data matching the stated criteria being output as it is found. The alternative is to scan the index, MARAIX1, for the specified value and then directly access just the specific records that match the selection criteria. Assuming that the MARA table is significantly larger than depicted in the above example, it may be much more efficient and less costly, in terms of time, effort and resources, to scan the index instead of the reading all rows and columns from the entire MARA table.

1.3.5 DB2 UDB Configuration Files

A DB2 UDB installation has several configuration files that provide the user with the ability to configure both the DB2 instance and each database within that instance. These configuration files are maintained through the Control Center interface and the physical files are stored within the DB2 directories. These DB2 configuration files are similar in concept to SAP R/3 profiles.

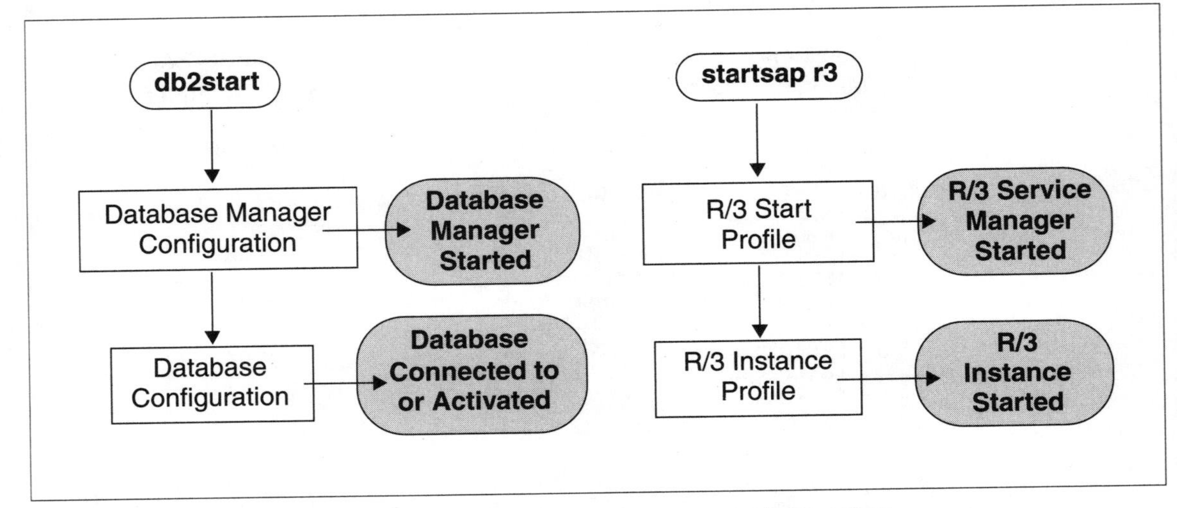

Figure 7. Comparison of DB2 Start-Up Process and R/3 Start-Up Process

1.3.5.1 Database Manager Configuration

The *Database Manager Configuration* is a collection of parameters that relate to the DB2 UDB instance. Most of the parameters either affect the amount of system resources that will be allocated to a single instance of the database manager, or they configure the settings of the database manager and the different communications subsystems based on environmental considerations. In addition, there are other parameters that serve informative purposes only and cannot be changed. All of these parameters have global applicability independent of any single database stored under that instance of the database manager. The database manager configuration is stored in a file named **db2systm.** The database manager configuration is similar in concept to the SAP R/3 Start profile.

The database manager configuration file should never be modified using any method other than the Control Center or the Command Line Processor. As you can see in Figure 8, there is one database manager configuration file for each database instance.

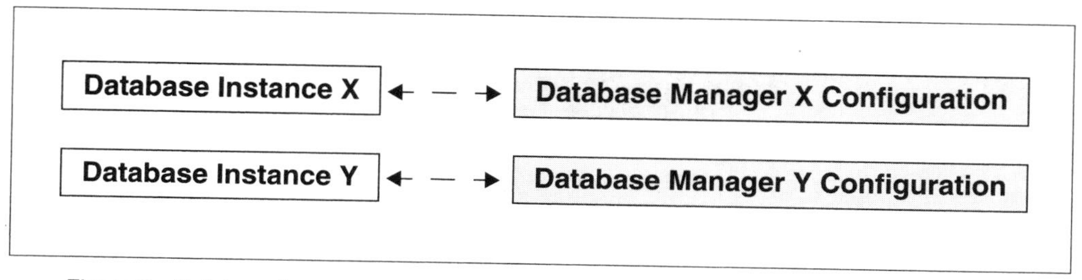

Figure 8. Database Instances and Database Manager Configurations

1.3.5.2 Database Configuration

The *Database Configuration* is the collection of parameters associated with an individual database. The database configuration file is named SQLDBCON and is stored in the SQLnnnnn directory associated with the particular database. Primarily, the database configuration file contains parameters that influence the amount of resources allocated to the database.

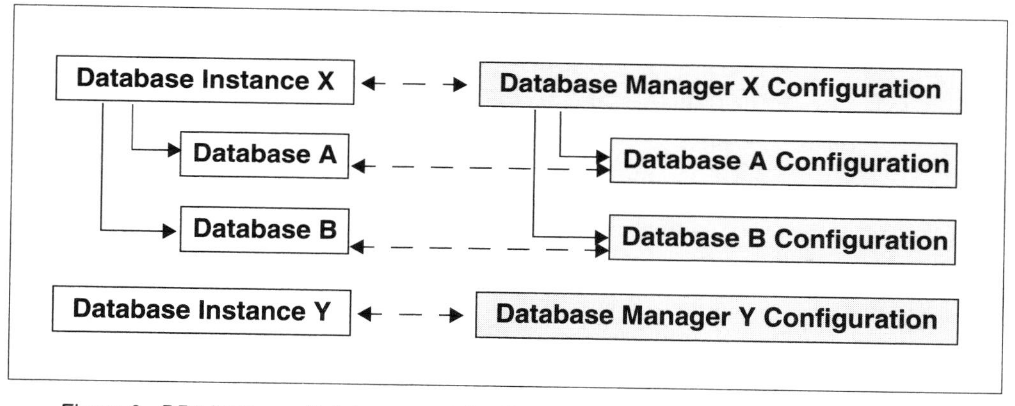

Figure 9. DB2 Instance, Databases and Configuration Files

Figure 9 depicts the relationship between the DB2 configuration files and DB2 instance and databases. On a system, there may be one or more database instances. Within each instance, there may be one or more databases. Associated with the database instance is one, and only one, database manager configuration. For each database within a database instance, there is one, and only one, database configuration.

A typical configuration of an SAP R/3 4.0B system which uses DB2 UDB is one database instance per R/3 system. The database instance typically consists of 2 databases, an R/3 database and an administration database.

1.3.6 DB2 UDB Logging

In order to provide database recoverability, DB2 has a logging facility that tracks all changes made to the database. These logs, in conjunction with a backup of the database, may be used to recover the database. A recoverable database is one in which the log retain parameter is turned on and/or the userexit parameter is turned on.

The active logs are used by DB2 to recover a database should a system crash occur (this recovery is known as crash recovery). In this case, all committed units of work that have not been physically written out to disk are written during the crash recovery. Any changes that have not been committed are rolled back. As a result of these two actions, the database is left in a consistent state and database integrity is maintained.

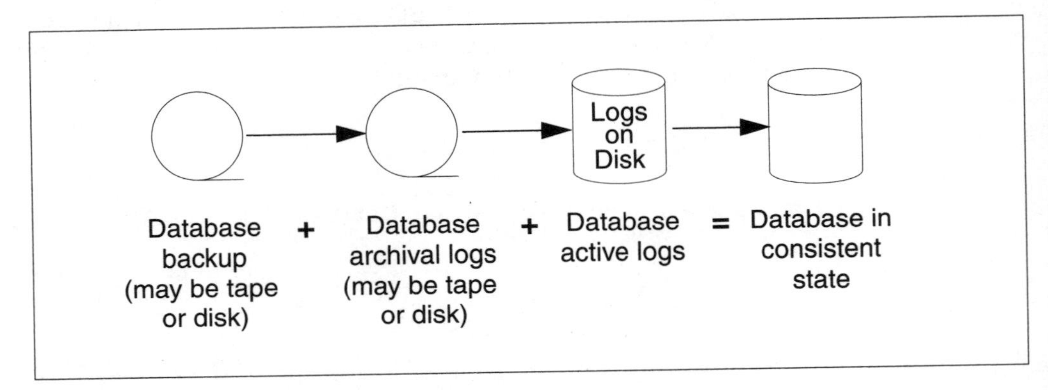

Figure 10. Roll Forward Database Recovery

Another method of recovery is roll-forward recovery, which is depicted in Figure 10. Roll forward recovery is accomplished by restoring a valid backup of the database and then applying the log files (both archived and active) which were created after the backup was taken. You have the choice of rolling forward to the end of the logs or a specific point in time. The restore of a database backup and the application of the database logs also leaves the database in a consistent state and integrity is once again maintained.

Database backups, in combination with the logging of database changes, provide a recovery path that prevents the loss of vital data in the event that a crash situation occurs.

In addition to these DB2 facilities, SAP R/3 provides another restart facility for the asynchronous updates that are performed as batch background jobs. This facility must also be used after a crash occurs and those asynchronous updates that have terminated abnormally must be restarted via the SAP interface. This will be discussed in further detail in "R/3 Database Maintenance" on page 327.

1.3.7 DB2 UDB Security

Security within DB2 UDB is achieved in a number of ways. The first is via *authentication* of DB2 UDB users on the Windows NT and UNIX platforms. Authentication is the process of determining that the user is who they say they are and is performed by the operating system or a separate product, not within DB2. Once the user is authenticated, the tasks that the user may perform are determined by the permissions that the user has within the database manager and the database itself. The setting and verification of these user permissions is done through DB2 UDB itself. These permissions are stored either in the database manager configuration file or in the database itself.

There are two separate types of permissions established within DB2:

- Authority levels
- Privileges

An *authority level* is a set of rights to create or access database manager resources or perform database manager or database level tasks. These rights are assigned to a group of users. Predefined groups within DB2 UDB which can group users and categorize their rights are: SYSADM, SYSCTRL, SYSMAINT and DBADM. Note that the first three (SYSADM, SYSCTRL, and SYSMAINT) are controlled outside of DB2 and are recorded in the database manager configuration file, while DBADM is controlled within DB2 through the SQL GRANT statement and the SQL REVOKE statement.

A *privilege* is the right of a particular user or group to create or access a database resource and is stored within the database itself. There are three types of privileges: Ownership, Individual, and Implicit.

1. **Ownership or control privileges**. For most objects, the user or group who creates the object has full access to that object. Control privilege is automatically granted to the creator of an object. There are some database objects, such as views, that are exceptions to this rule. Having control privilege is like having ownership of the object. You have the right to access the object and grant access to others. Privileges are controlled by users with ownership or administrative privileges. They provide other users with access using the SQL GRANT statement.
2. **Individual privileges**. These are privileges that allow you to perform a specific action. These privileges include select, delete and insert, and are granted by a user with ownership or control privileges.

3. **Implicit privileges**. An implicit privilege is one that is granted to a user automatically when that user is explicitly granted certain higher level privileges. These privileges are not revoked when the higher level privileges are explicitly revoked.

In the case of SAP R/3 and DB2 UDB, all access to data in the SAP R/3 tables is performed via the user SAPR3. This user is granted the appropriate privileges and authority levels by the SAP installation program. Most security constraints are managed by SAP R/3 at the application level.

1.4 SAP R/3 V4

In this section we begin the discussion of the SAP R/3 architecture. We examine the logical architecture as well as the physical architecture of R/3.

As mentioned earlier in this book, we are addressing R/3 Version 4 and DB2 Universal Database Version 5. SAP AG delivers the DB2 UDB database manager with the R/3 code. You must only use the version of DB2 delivered by SAP. You must obtain database updates from SAP, not IBM; the database updates are referred to as a *service pack* by SAP.

Periodically, SAP will distribute CD-ROMs with a collection of R/3 related fixes; this collection of fixes is known as a *Hot Package*. These are all generally available via OSS and SAPnet.

1.4.1 Logical Architecture of R/3

The logical architecture of R/3 is implemented in a layered manner:

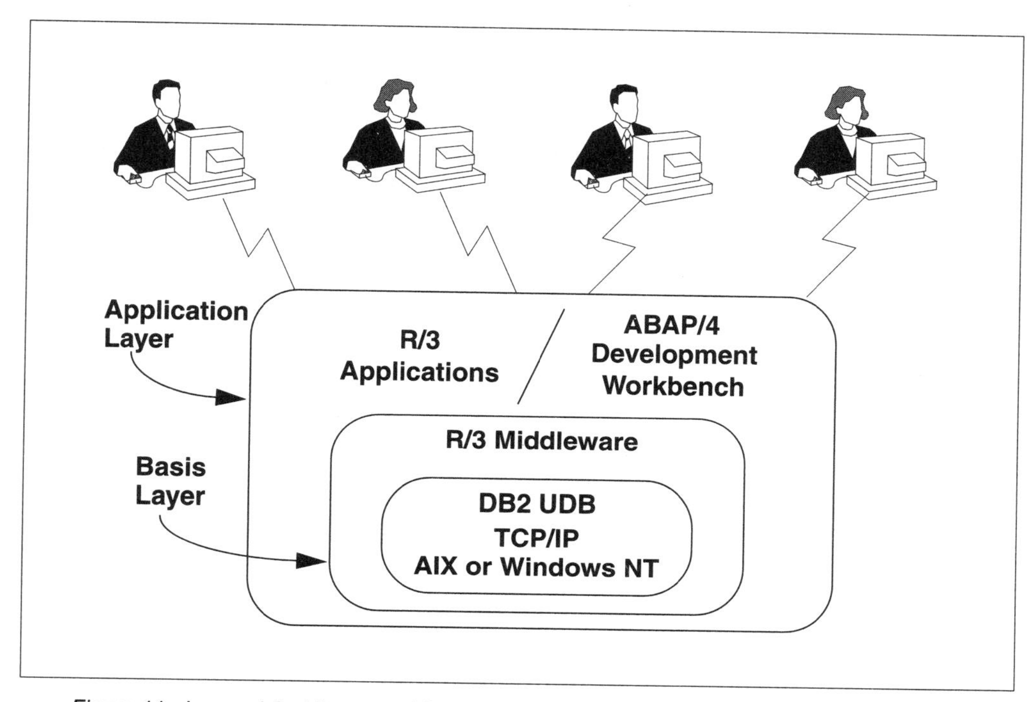

Figure 11. Layered Architecture of SAP R/3

The R/3 application layer is the outer layer and consists of the R/3 applications and the ABAP/4 Development Workbench. ABAP/4 is a fourth generation programming language that is used exclusively with the SAP R/3 product.

The R/3 basis layer is the next layer which consists of the R/3 middleware. The basis layer directly interfaces with the inner layer that consists of the operating system (UNIX or Windows NT), database manager (DB2 UDB) and the communications protocol stack (TCP/IP).

The R/3 middleware overlays the operating system layer, thereby making the R/3 applications independent of the operating system and database manager. As a result, the ABAP/4 programs are portable between different database managers and operating systems.

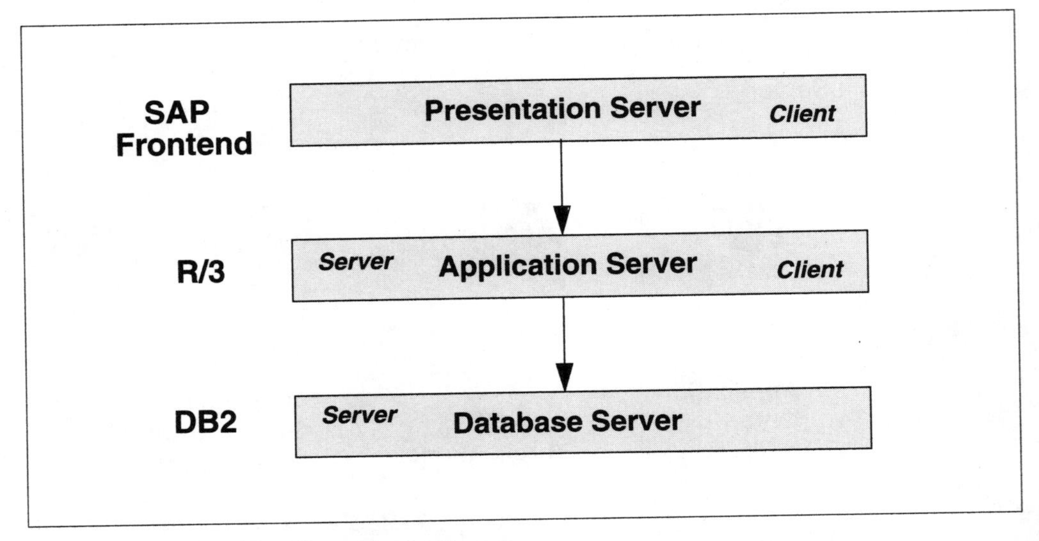

Figure 12. R/3 Client/Server Logical Layers

Another way to visualize the R/3 layers is to divide the SAP environment into three layers, Presentation Server, Application Server, and Database Server.

The *Presentation Server* layer refers to the SAP user interface program that must be installed on the user's workstation. The SAP user interface program is known as the SAP Frontend or SAP GUI. The workstation operating system platform may be Windows 3.1/3.11, Windows 95, Windows NT, OS/2, HP-UX, Sun Solaris and AIX. This layer serves as the logical client of the Application Server layer of SAP.

The *Application Server* layer refers to the server system where the R/3 work processes execute. *Work Processes* perform various tasks as assigned by the Dispatcher work process. The *Dispatcher* is the work process that interfaces with the SAP Frontend and funnels the end-user requests to the appropriate work process. This layer acts as the server for the Presentation Server.

The Application Server may be one or more physical computers and may be a Windows NT server or a UNIX server. Please refer to URL http://www.r3onnt.com for further information on certified Windows NT server platforms. Please refer to the SAP documentation for the UNIX platform requirements. In this book, we will be working on the AIX operating system.

The *Database Server* layer refers to the server where DB2 Universal Database resides. The Application Server interfaces with the database server to access the R/3 applications and the application data. The DB2 UDB database manager performs all data manipulations as instructed by the requests delivered by the ABAP/4 programs. In this scenario, the Application Server acts as a client of the database server.

1.4.2 R/3 Instance

There are two different types of R/3 instances, the Central Instance and the Dialog Instance. The type of instance determines the type of processes that will execute within the instance.

The *Central Instance* is always the instance that is installed first. The Central Instance runs the Enqueue process and the Message Server process, both of which are critical work processes.

The *Dialog Instance* is an R/3 application server instance that was installed after the Central Instance was installed. The Dialog instances execute the Batch and Update processes. The machine where a Dialog Instance runs is referred to as a *Dialog Server* or an *Application Server.*

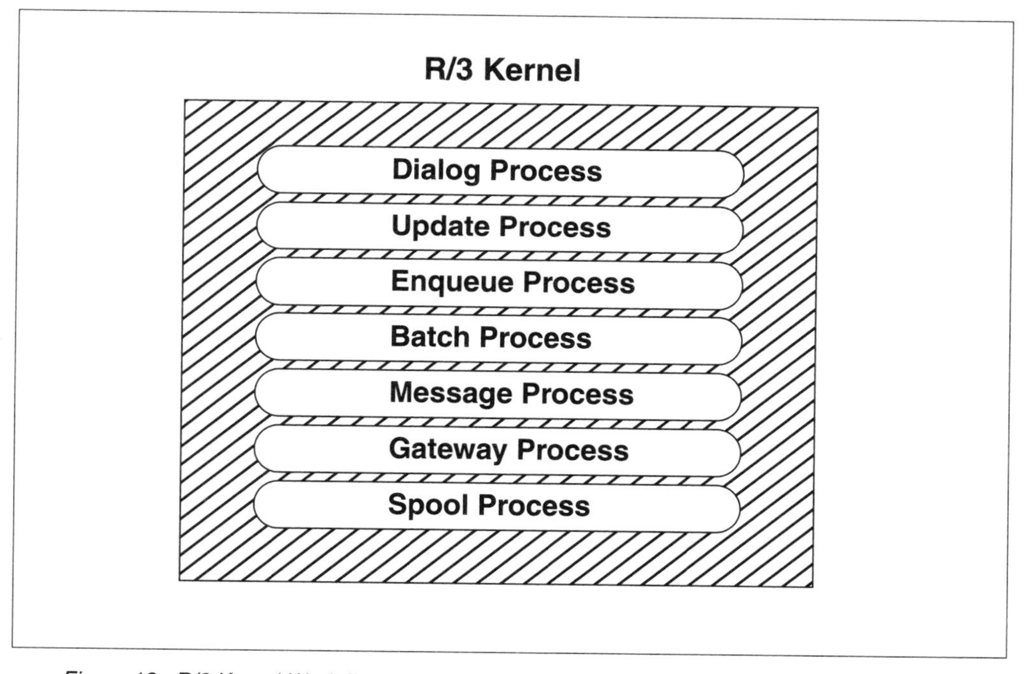

Figure 13. R/3 Kernel Work Processes

The R/3 kernel is essentially a collection of parallel processes. These processes consist of the dispatcher and work processes. There are 7 different types of processes:

- **D** - Dialog Process
- **V** - Update Process
- **E** - Enqueue Process
- **B** - Batch Process
- **M** - Message Process
- **G** - Gateway Process
- **S** - Spool Process

These work processes are collectively referred to as **DVEBMGS**.

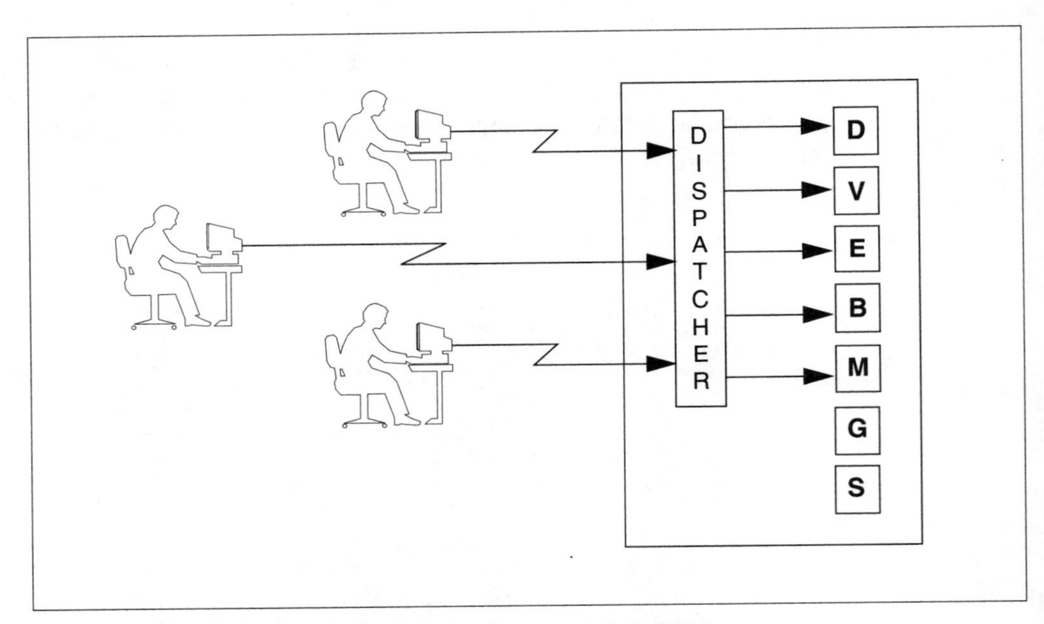

Figure 14. Interaction between R/3 Dispatcher and Work Processes

A *Dispatcher* resides on each Dialog Server and the Central Instance. The dispatcher manages the communication between the SAP Frontend and the Dialog servers and distributes the incoming work packages among the various work processes based on the type of work required (with the exception of the Gateway and the Message processes). The work processes are configured based upon the complexity of your system's workload and the physical resources available.

The *Dialog* work processes manage the requests from the end-user sessions. There are a minimum of two Dialog work processes per R/3 system. Multiple user sessions are associated with each Dialog work process. The dispatcher assigns the user requests to the least busy Dialog work process.

The *Update* work processes perform the asynchronous updates to the database. A portion of the R/3 database changes are performed synchronously via the Dialog work processes and another portion are performed asynchronously by the Update work process.

The *Enqueue* work process is fundamental to the management of the R/3 system's internal locking. The R/3 system does not rely on DB2 to manage locks; it handles the locks on its own via the Enqueue work process. The Enqueue process uses a lock table that is stored in main memory. Because of the critical function that it performs, if there is more than one Enqueue work process, all of those processes must execute on the same instance.

The *Batch* work process performs the execution of the ABAP/4 reports and the batch R/3 programs that can be executed in the background. Typically, batch programs execute at a lower priority than the interactive users associated with the Dialog work processes. By running the Batch work processes at a lower priority, contention with the interactive users is avoided.

The *Message Server* work process manages communication between application servers in a distributed R/3 system. It is critical to the processing of an R/3 system. The Message Server is used by the application servers to exchange data and to send internal messages.

The *Gateway* work process handles the communication between SAP R/3 and external applications. The Gateway is responsible for processing CPIC and RFC (Remote Function Call) requests. It is generally used for moving large quantities of application data.

The *Spool* work process manages all of the print requests by interfacing with the spooler for the operating system.

1.4.3 R/3 Application Database Interface

Within an R/3 application is a database interface that intercepts all R/3 program requests for data and transforms the requests into the appropriate SQL statements for accessing the R/3 tables managed by DB2 UDB. The interface may be invoked from any Dialog instance as well as the Central instance. The R/3 database interface eliminates the need for application developers to code SQL statements in their ABAP/4 programs. The database interface does not prevent access the R/3 tables via SQL; however, direct access to tables via SQL is not recommended, as it does not adhere to internal R/3 application security or take advantage of the data held within the R/3 table buffers.

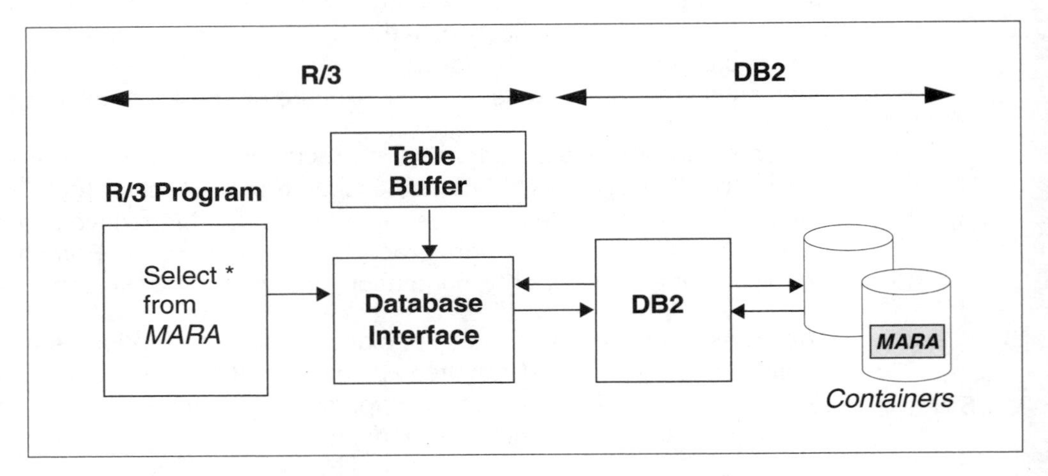

Figure 15. R/3 Database Interface

1.4.4 R/3 Table Buffering

R/3 provides its own table buffering facility. By buffering heavily accessed tables, you can improve your on-line performance since the data you require will be held in memory instead of having to access the database manager. You may specify which tables are to be buffered, but you should choose ones that are primarily read-only. Table buffering can become a performance issue if you buffer tables that are not relatively static. When updates occur to tables that are buffered, the updates must be propagated to all of the other R/3 application servers.

The following is an example of how table buffering may be used. The request for all rows in the MARA table is issued by the ABAP/4 program. The R/3 buffer manager first determines if the MARA table is buffered. If it is, it will use the buffered table instead of going to the database to satisfy the request.

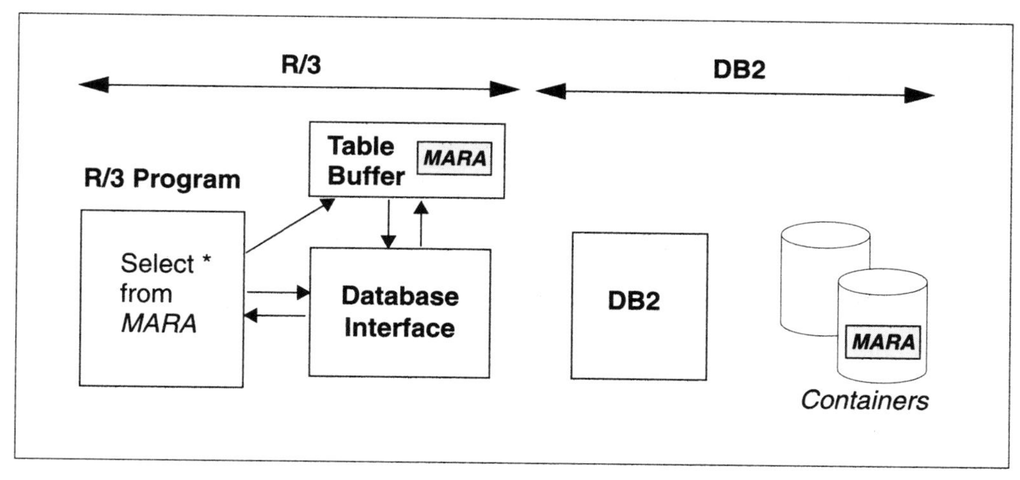

Figure 16. R/3 Table Buffers

Determining which tables are buffered is a customer decision and should be done on a per installation basis. SAP delivers some tables with the flag set for table buffering. Do not change the table buffering as delivered by SAP without the consent of SAP. Synchronization across dialog instances occurs once each minute; this is an interval established by SAP and should not be changed.

1.4.5 High Availability

Because R/3 applications support many of the critical functions associated with a business, high availability for R/3 production systems is frequently a priority. Typically, such systems should be able to perform a takeover should one of the critical production machines fail.

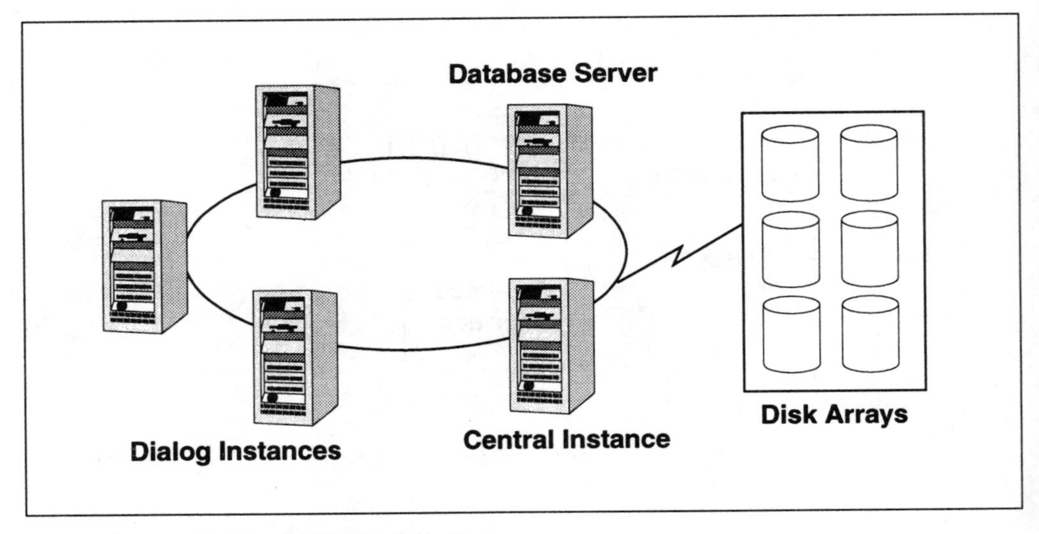

Figure 17. High Availability Configuration

Figure 17 shows an example of a high availability configuration for an R/3 system. In this example, the database server is on one system and the R/3 central instance is on another system. If the database server fails, the database server may be restarted on the central instance server. If the central instance fails, then it may be restarted on the database server. In either case, the dialog servers do not have to be restarted; they will attempt to reconnect. The R/3 profiles on each system must be maintained and synchronized. Uncommitted transactions must be rolled back during the takeover to ensure database consistency. (At time of writing, SAP R/3 did not support Microsoft Cluster Server (MSCS). It is expected that this support will be forthcoming.)

1.4.6 R/3 Client Concept

Within an R/3 system, the data for one or more companies may be stored and treated as separate logical installations. The way this is accomplished is via SAP clients. Essentially, each SAP client corresponds to a SAP customer and contains the data associated with a specific business entity. One or more clients may exist within the same R/3 instance. The data associated with a client contains the:

- Customizations
- Transaction data
- Master data
- User master records

Although the data for all clients in an R/3 instance is stored within the same database tables, the data is segregated within the tables via a three digit client number assigned to each client. The client number is attached to each record in the SAP system that belongs to a specific client. By differentiating data associated with one client from that of another via the client number, the data from one business entity is protected from access by another business entity.

Table Name: **MARA**
Materials Master Table

MANDT	MATNR	MATDESC
010	1001	Hammer
010	1002	Saw
020	1001	Hammer
020	1003	Bolt
030	1004	Nail

Figure 18. Client Number Stored in Each Record

In the example above, a user is accessing client 010. This user has issued the following SQL statement that is imbedded in an ABAP/4 program. The SQL statement has requested all records in the Materials Master Table (MARA).

```
select * from MARA
```

This SQL statement is intercepted and converted to the following SQL statement:

```
select MATNR, MATDESC from MARA where MANDT = '010'
```

As a result, the program returns only 2 records; those associated with client 010 as demonstrated in Figure 18.

In the same example, the other user is accessing client 030. The user has also called the same ABAP/4 program that issues the same SQL statement requesting all records in the MARA table. The SQL statement is converted to the following SQL statement for the user accessing client 030:

```
select MATNR, MATDESC from MARA where MANDT = '030'
```

The user receives only one record as demonstrated in Figure 18 on page 25. The results differ because the R/3 database interface intercepts the SQL statement and returns only the records associated with the client that the user is currently accessing.

1.4.7 Client Dependent and Client Independent

Some portions of the R/3 system are considered to be client independent, and other portions are considered to be client dependent. The base R/3 programs and reports are considered to be client independent (the same programs are used no matter which client you are using). Physical hardware such as printers are also client independent. Data is considered to be client dependent. Customizations may be either client dependent or client independent.

1.4.8 System Landscapes

The philosophy of R/3 implementation also incorporates a development methodology and it is advisable that you follow this methodology. After performing the initial installation of R/3, you will want to establish your Development Client, Quality Assurance / System Test Client, Master Client, and Production Client. Together these clients are referred to as the System Landscape.

While all of these may be defined on the same R/3 system, it is not advisable. For security purposes, you should isolate your production client on a separate system.

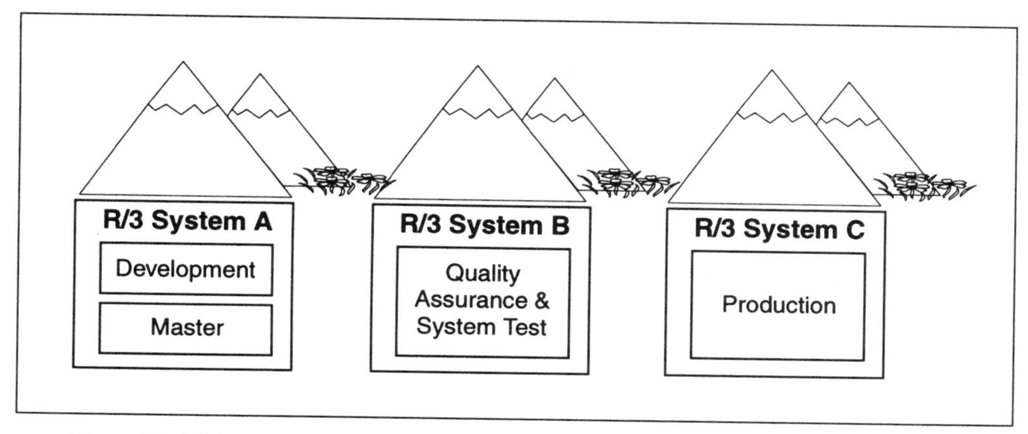

Figure 19. Minimum Recommended R/3 System Landscape

1.4.9 Application Link Enabling

Application Link Enabling (ALE) is used by large companies to further enhance the distribution of their business processes. ALE is an interface that allows different SAP systems to be linked together. By linking the SAP systems together, the central business office may gather data from all of the distributed systems to gain a consolidated view of the business.

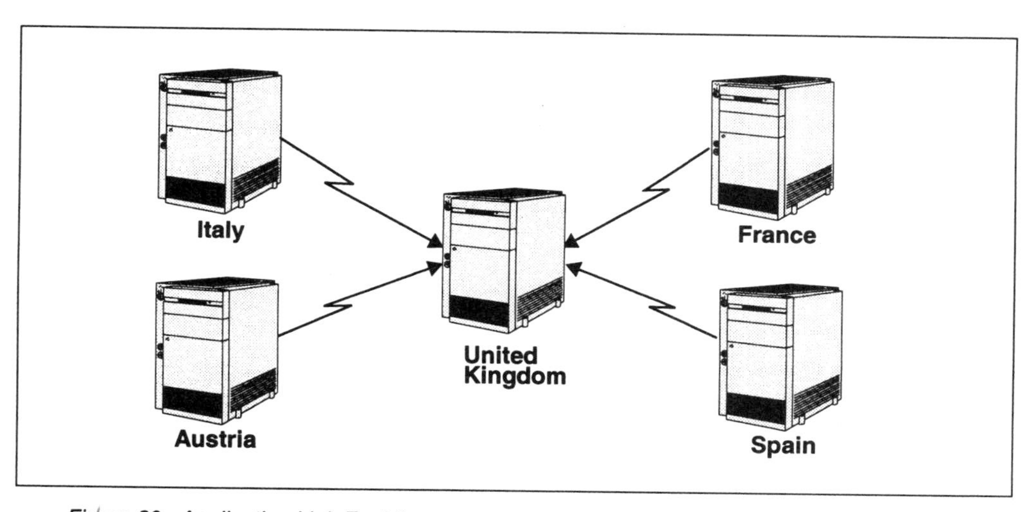

Figure 20. Application Link Enabling

1.4.10 Transports

Transports are used to migrate objects and data from one R/3 system to another. There are two types of transports that may be performed in the R/3 system: client transport and change request.

Client transports are used to migrate one client on one R/3 system to another. A Client transport will move all R/3 objects associated with one client on the source R/3 system to the target R/3 system. The objects migrated include the client dependent and client independent customizations, the user master data, and the application-related data.

Change requests are also used to migrate objects between R/3 systems. They are the vehicle used to migrate a smaller collection of objects between clients on different R/3 systems. They are usually used to migrate application enhancements and fixes from the R/3 Test, to R/3 Master, to Quality Assurance and finally Production.

1.4.11 Client Copies

Client copies are used to migrate client objects between clients on the same R/3 system. In a client copy, all objects related to the customization of the source client are copied to the target client. Client copies are used to generate the initial client from the R/3 delivered clients.

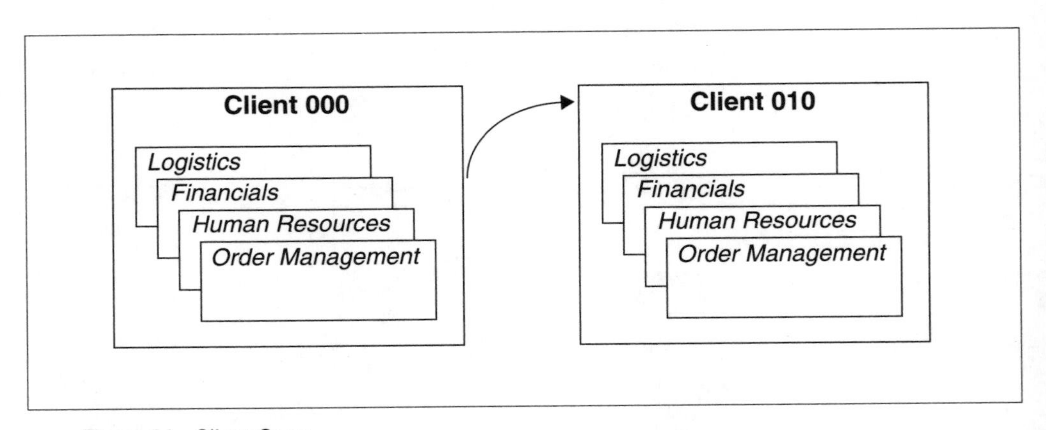

Figure 21. Client Copy

SAP delivers three clients during the initial R/3 install: 000, 001, and 066. Within each of the delivered clients is the master copy of the R/3 client specific data. These clients should never be changed. Client 000 is the base client and should be copied using a client copy to generate all new clients.

1.4.12 Basis Transactions

As an administrator of an SAP R/3 system, you may access the SAP supplied administration functions in two different ways. You may use the pull-down menus that are available from the initial SAP menu, or you may issue SAP transaction codes.

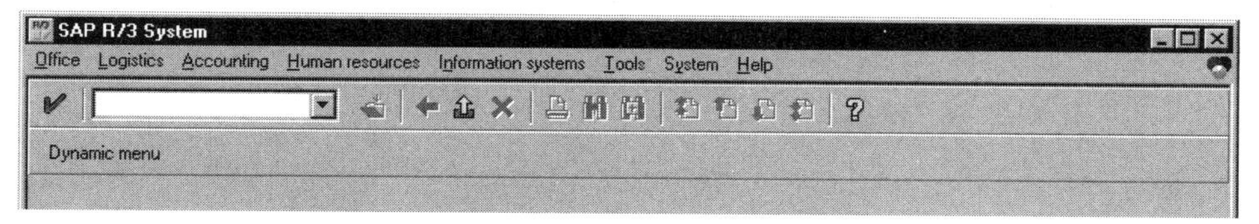

Figure 22. SAP R/3 Frontend Initial Menu

Most of the R/3 administration tools may be found under the **System** and **Tools** menu items on the initial R/3 menu. As an alternative, you may enter the four character transaction code into the pulldown window at the top left of each R/3 screen. Most of the four character transaction codes begin with the characters AL*, RZ*, or S*. The R/3 transactions are nested in a tree structure. By prefacing the R/3 transaction code with /N, you will avoid any transaction problems that might occur due to your position in a transaction tree. The /N allows you to go directly to the transaction entered. If you prefer to open a new SAP R/3 session, you may preface your command with /O (the letter, not a zero) which will open a new R/3 session.

As you become more familiar with the systems, you will want to memorize the various transactions that you commonly use. To determine the transaction name, you may go to the **System->Status** menu item:

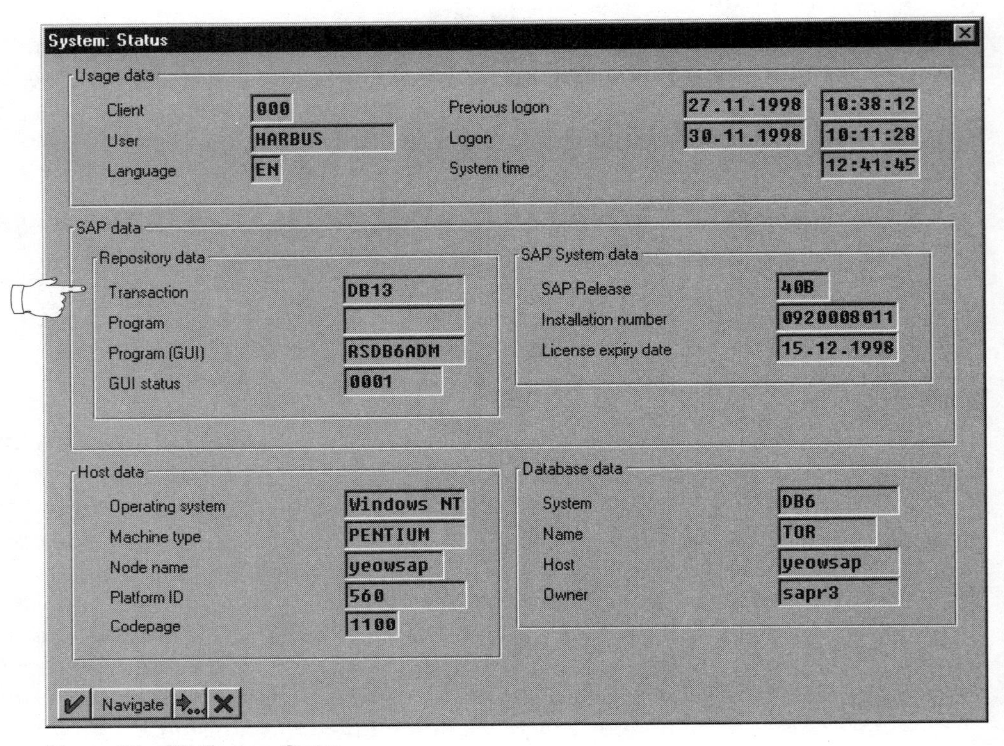

Figure 23. R/3 System Status

Here you see the name of the current transaction. You can get a list of all R/3 transactions using the **SM01** transaction or by using the pull-down **Tools->Administration, Administration->Tcode Administration**. You can also view the R/3 table TSTC.

1.4.13 Operation Modes

The operation mode facility within the R/3 product is used to define the processes allocated for the R/3 instance. It may also be used to define normal operations, as well as alternative work schedules in the event of a system outage, a holiday, or for seasonal needs such as year end. Typically, a day operation mode and a night operation mode are defined.

For example, let's assume that the majority of the on-line users access the R/3 system during the hours of 9 AM until 5 PM and the rest of the time is spent processing background jobs. We have a total of 6 processes to allocate to Dialog and Background processes.

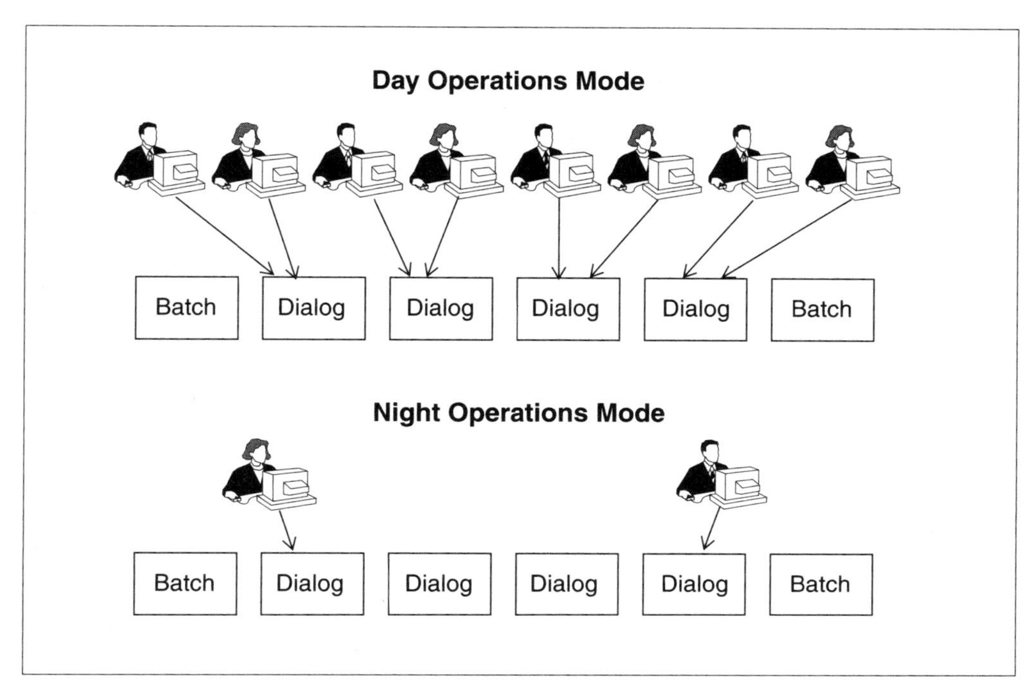

Figure 24. Operation Modes

In this case, you would probably want to establish a day operation mode that allocates 4 dialog processes and only 2 batch background processes during the time frame of 9 AM until 5 PM. By allocating the majority of the processes as dialog processes, we have established an on-line environment with an appropriate amount of available resources to support the users during the day.

Additionally, you would want to create a night operation mode that allocates 2 dialog processes and 4 batch background processes. By shifting 2 of the dialog processes to batch background processes, we have provided ample resources to support the batch workload.

These two operation modes would be defined as the normal operation modes for the production R/3 instance. By manipulating the allocation of the processes available, we have made effective use of the resources available.

1.4.14 Users

R/3 does not depend upon the operating system for user profile administration. R/3 application-level user profiles are required for all users.

There is no direct relationship between R/3 user profiles and operating system user profiles. In other words, a user may logon to their workstation with one id, then use a separate id to logon to the R/3 system.

Figure 25. Same User Logging on to Workstation and SAP R/3

1.4.15 Logon Groups

The R/3 system offers a facility that allows the user workload to be spread across multiple application servers; this facility is known as *logon groups*. Logon groups are defined by an R/3 administrator on each R/3 system and are used for performance and not security. Users who perform the same functions are grouped together in various logon groups. The end user then uses *Saplogon* to connect to their R/3 system.

Saplogon connects the user to the message server. The message server takes a snapshot of the work load on all of the application servers and connects the user to the least utilized application server. The message server does not look at the actual work load volume, but at the number of users connected.

As an example, let's say a customer has several application servers and each one is used by specific groups of users (MM, SD, FI, and so on). The buffers on each application server contain specific tables for those application areas. When an MM user logs on, that user is pointed to the application server that contains the MM specific buffer, because the user is part of the MM logon group which is pointing to the MM application server. This improves the user's response time because the application server the user is logged on to will contain the main tables that the user will most probably need in the buffer. This is also called logon load balancing. (If the server initially pointed to is fully used, then the user will be pointed to another application server.)

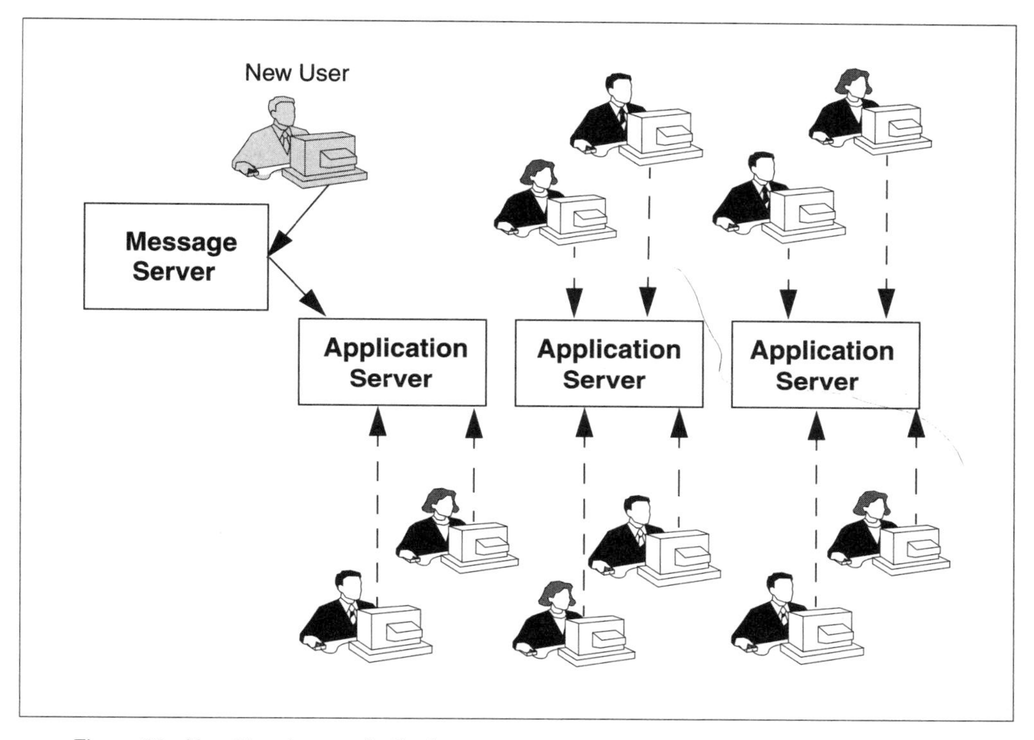

Figure 26. New User Logon via Saplogon

1.4.16 Authorizations

In R/3 applications, user access to application objects and functions is managed internally via *authorization profiles*. An authorization profile is a collection of authorizations. R/3 authorities are never explicitly defined for an individual user, but are assigned via authorization profiles. A user may be assigned one or more authorization profiles.

The SAP authorization profiles are related to application function and do not address access to the database tables, indexes and views; in this sense, the SAP R/3 use of authorizations is somewhat different from that of a typical DB2 application. In most DB2 applications, the authority is granted via DB2 SQL statements that GRANT authority to users or groups. The DB2 level authorities are stored in DB2 UDB system catalog tables.

In the R/3 application, all R/3 database access is executed via a connect to the DB2 UDB database under the SAPR3 user id. This user id has DB2 System Control authority and may perform any function within the database without limitation.

1.4.17 RFC Groups

Remote Function Calls are supported in the R/3 environment. This expands the functionality of R/3 and the ABAP/4 programming environment. SAP provides an RFC generator that may be used by external applications to call ABAP/4 function modules. RFCs may also be imbedded in ABAP/4 programs to access information stored in other R/3 systems or other external applications.

1.4.18 R/3 Profiles

Your SAP R/3 system has several profiles that control the activation of the components of the R/3 system. These profiles are maintained through an R/3 interface and the profiles are stored within the R/3 database.

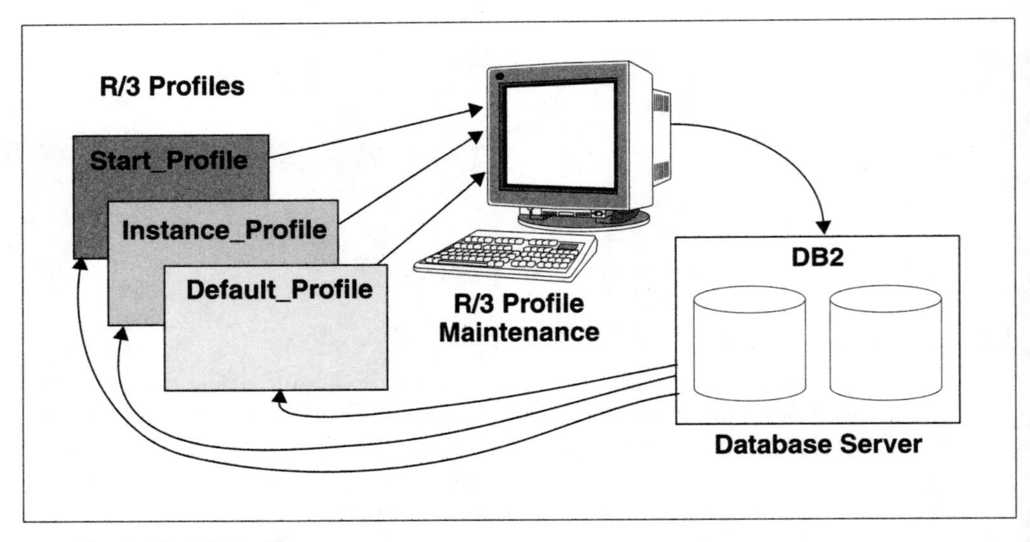

Figure 27. R/3 Profiles

When the SAP Service Manager initiates the start of your R/3 system, it reads the *Start Profile.* The Start Profile contains the list of services that are to be started.

Once the SAP service manager starts the dispatcher, the dispatcher reads the *instance profile* and the *default profile* to determine which work processes need to be started. Each of these profiles contains a set of parameters that determine which work processes are to be started, the shared memory allocations, and the buffer pools for the specific instance. The default profile is generated upon the creation of the new instance. The instance profile is used to override the parameters set in the default profile. The instance profile always takes precedence.

1.4.19 R/3 Physical Client/Server Architecture

One of the main advantages of the implementation of the SAP R/3 architecture with DB2 Universal Database is the flexibility inherent in both products. R/3 with DB2 UDB may be installed in a two or three tier client/server configuration. While you might start with a relatively simple two-tier implementation initially, you have the ability to expand to additional servers, thereby enhancing your capacity without having to worry about application incompatibilities or database constraints.

The simplest implementation of an R/3 system is the Central Instance. In this configuration, the Application server and the database server reside on the same host. The R/3 instance performs all of the dialog instance tasks such as handling user requests and executing batch jobs.

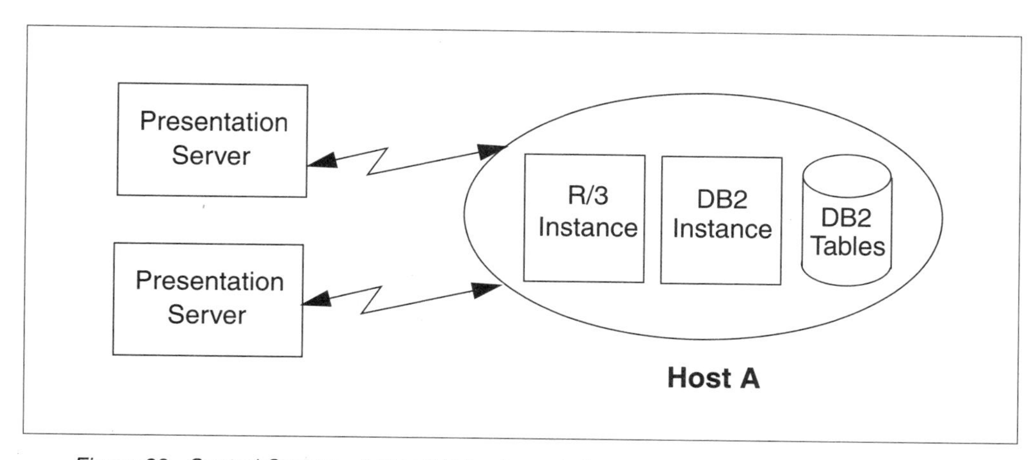

Figure 28. Central System - 2 Tier R/3 Implementation

While this configuration may be effective in a small R/3 installation or in an initial implementation, over time this may not be the optimal solution. With some applications and databases, it might be difficult to expand beyond the central system configuration; however with R/3 and DB2 UDB, you have a variety of options.

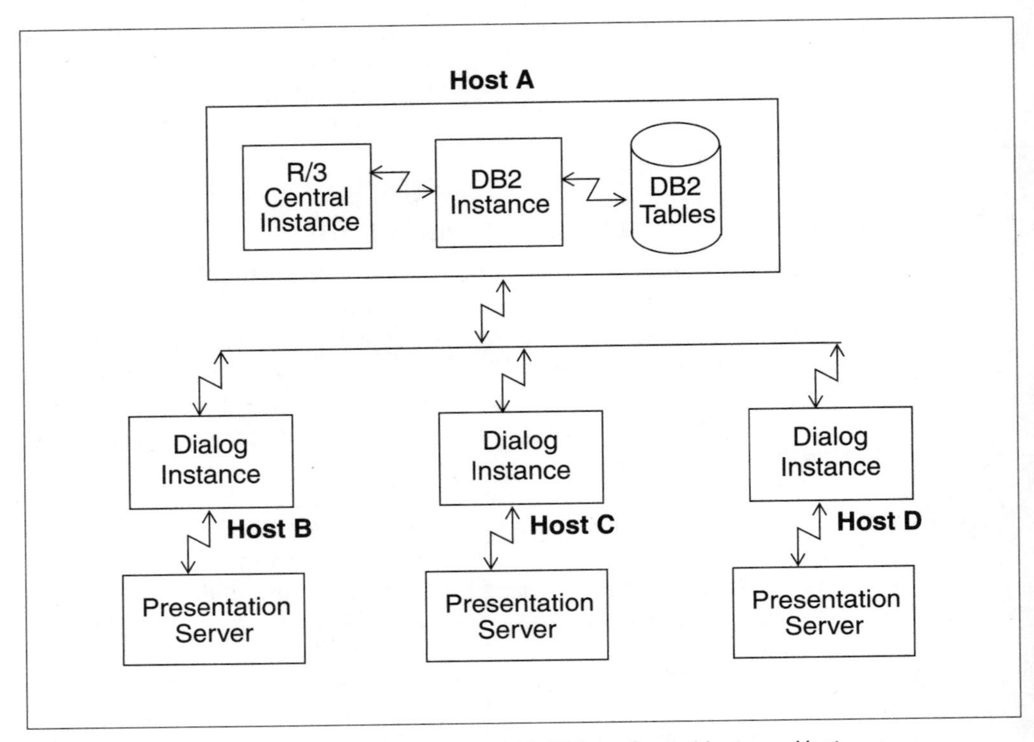

Figure 29. Three Tier R/3 Implementation with DB2 on Central Instance Host

If you need to be able to support more end users and have not exceeded the capacity of your central instance host, you may add additional dialog instances. Dialog instances can be added or deleted dynamically without needing to restart either R/3 or DB2 UDB. In Figure 29 on page 36, you see an example of a three tier R/3 implementation in which the database instance and the R/3 instance reside on the same server. The dialog instances in this example are all on different systems. Please note that the number of dialog instances is not limited to three.

As your R/3 system grows and you have higher availability requirements, you may move to a fully distributed R/3 environment. In Figure 30 on page 37, the R/3 central instance still resides on the initial host, but the database instance has been moved to a separate host system. This configuration offers the greatest flexibility and the most recovery options.

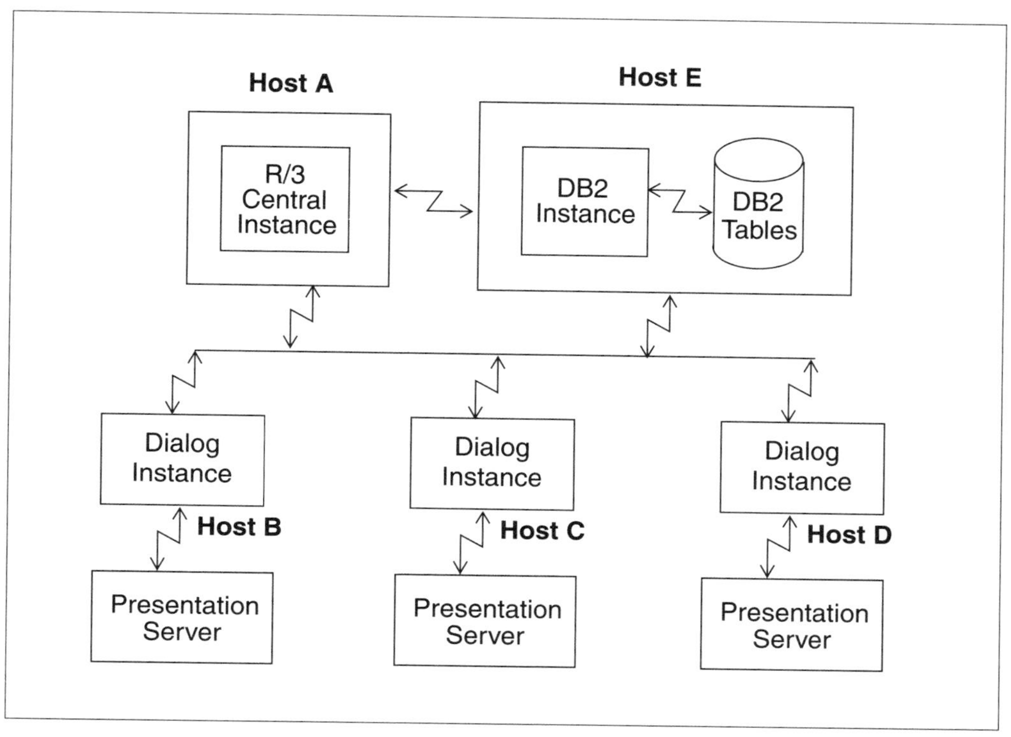

Figure 30. Three Tiered R/3 Implementation with Separate Server for DB2

As you can see from the three sample R/3 configurations, there is a great deal of flexibility in the types of environments that can support an R/3 installation. The generic hosts depicted in these diagrams may be RS/6000s, Netfinity Servers, OS/390, or AS/400s.

Chapter 2. Pre-Installation Planning and Preparation

The purpose of this chapter is to assist you in planning and preparing for your SAP R/3 V4 and DB2 Universal Database installation. Included are steps that must be performed, such as determining hardware and software requirements, reviewing R/3 installation documentation, obtaining release notes, and creating a check list of procedures before you start the installation of DB2 UDB and R/3.

2.1 Pre-Installation Activities

We begin by discussing how to determine your hardware capacity requirements, reviewing the SAP R/3 documentation delivered, and obtaining release notes.

2.1.1 Hardware Capacity Requirements

In the supplied SAP R/3 documentation, SAP outlines the minimum hardware requirements for your installation. This does not, however, address the sizing requirements for your specific needs. Since SAP R/3 may be installed on a variety of platforms, the platform partners of SAP R/3 have developed their own tools and questionnaires to help customers determine the hardware requirements for:

- CPU Capacity
- Memory Size
- Disk Space Size

Based on your answers to this questionnaire, the platform partner will be able to assist you in sizing an environment based on your current and future business requirements.

As an alternative, SAP, in close cooperation with all platform partners, has developed an internet-based tool to make sizing easier and faster. This tool is named **Quick Sizer**. It is available on the Internet[1] for all R/3 customers who have their own OSS user identification[2]. The Quick Sizer contains a series of business related questions that must be answered. Once you have responded to all of the questions, the tool will return a report to you that contains the Quick Sizer's estimates for the CPU capacity, disk, and memory required to support your planned SAP R/3 system landscape.

[1] The Internet Address is: URL http://sapnet.sap-ag-de. Select the Quick Sizing' from the Quick Find window.
[2] The OSS user identification is obtained after applying an OSS User Registration form.

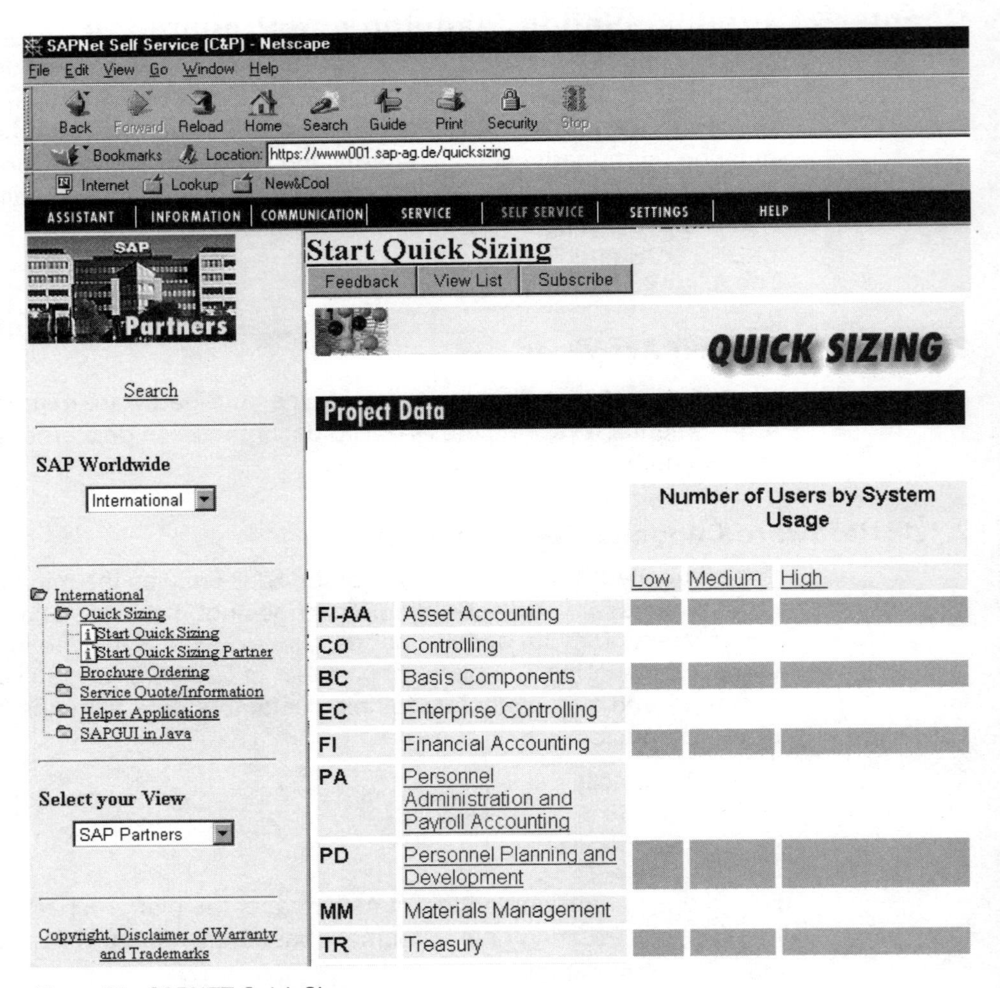

Figure 31. SAPNET Quick Sizer

The results from the Quick Sizer will help you estimate the size of the system necessary to run your required workload. This information may be useful in initial budget planning. Your Quick Sizer report can be used by your hardware vendor to determine hardware sizing based on entering the information into the vendor's own sizing tool.

2.1.2 R/3 Installation Documentation

SAP delivers R/3 in a box with the following items to customers:

- CD-ROMs
- Installation Documents
- Checklists
- Fax Forms
- Business Notes

The following documents should be read before you start your installation planning:

1. Cover Letter: *First Installation Release R/3 4.0B*
2. Check List - Installation Requirements.
3. *R/3 Installation on UNIX/Windows NT* (depending on the operating system you have chosen)
4. *R/3 Installation on UNIX - OS Dependencies* (if you are installing on a UNIX based platform)
5. *Check List - Installation Requirements: Frontends*

All of these documents are also available in PDF format on the CD *Database Export 1*.

2.1.3 Obtaining R/3 Notes from OSS

OSS is an important and useful source of information which contains release specific notes that are vital in preparing for your SAP R/3 and DB2 UDB installation.

There are three ways to obtain R/3 notes from OSS:

1. If you do not have your own OSS user id, then complete form 1350 - 02/98 that was delivered in your R/3 installation box and fax to: +49 (0) 180 / 53 43 430 (or the telephone number indicated on the form).
2. If you have already obtained your own OSS id, use your web browser to connect to internet address http://sapnet.sap-ag.de/notes to download the required notes. You can then search for the required notes:

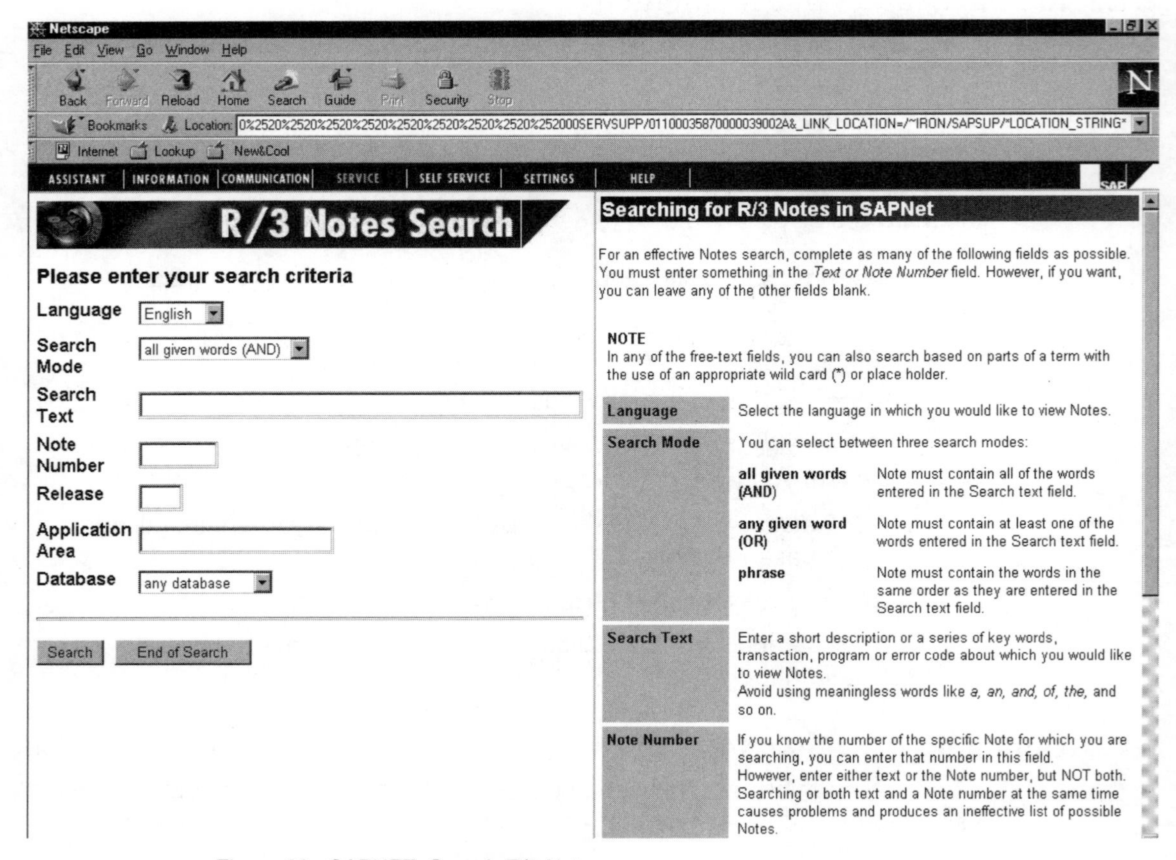

Figure 32. SAPNET: Search R/3 Notes

3. Obtain the R/3 Notes via the R/3 Frontend, SAPGUI[3]. To do this, your customer site must have the network infrastructure to connect to the OSS Message Server. You also require an OSS user ID that has been registered previously. For more details, see “OSS” on page 71.

Using one of these methods, please read the following notes prior to proceeding with your planning activities:

For AIX installations:

- Note 015023: Initializing table TCPDB
- Note 033525: Important information about Hot Packages
- Note 100125: 4.0B R/3 Installation on UNIX - OS Dependencies

[3] SAPGUI : SAP Graphical User Interface, R/3 client program.

- Note 101315: 4.0B R/3 Installation on UNIX
- Note 101316: 4.0B R/3 Installation on UNIX - DB2 Common Server

For Windows NT installations:

- Note 033525: Important information about Hot Packages
- Note 098711: 4.0B Installation on Windows NT
- Note 098717: 4.0B R/3 Installation on Windows NT: DB2/CS
- Note 109413: DB2/CS on NT: Installation of fix pack US9044
- Note 112329: DB6INSTALLADMIN: error when changing directory (NT)
- Note 113799: DB2/CS: Statement exceeded at db limit

Note

This is not a complete list of all the OSS Notes available on SAP R/3 Version 4.0B with DB2 Universal Database. Once you obtain an OSS Notes user ID, consult OSS for the most up-to-date list of notes at the time of your installation planning.

Here is an example OSS note:

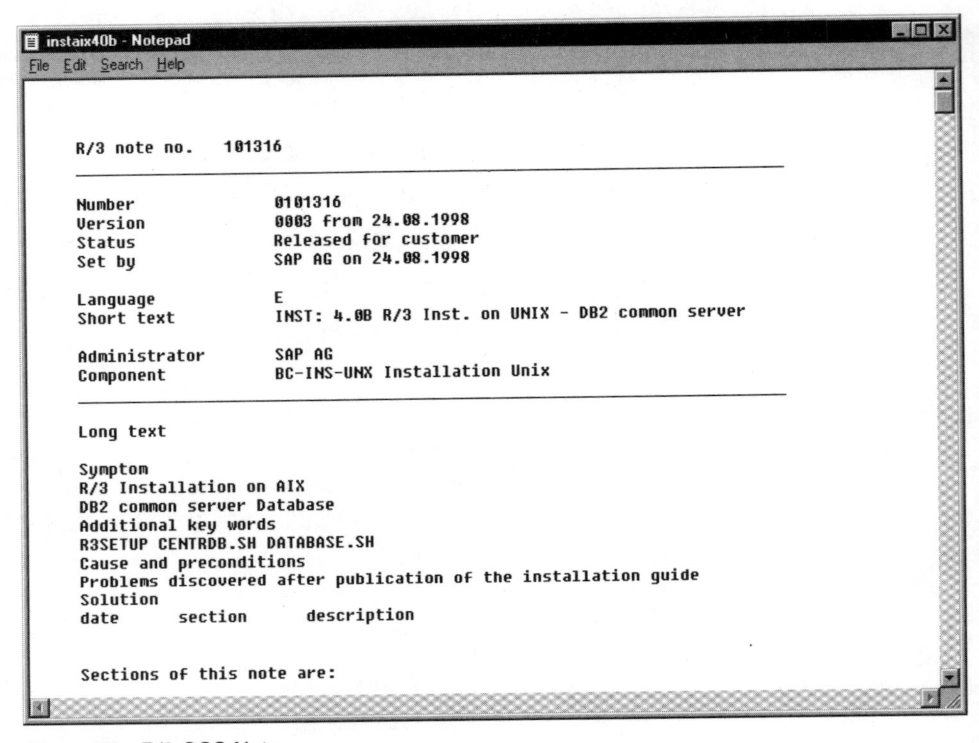
instaix40b - Notepad

File Edit Search Help

```
R/3 note no.   101316

Number              0101316
Version             0003 from 24.08.1998
Status              Released for customer
Set by              SAP AG on 24.08.1998

Language            E
Short text          INST: 4.0B R/3 Inst. on UNIX - DB2 common server

Administrator       SAP AG
Component           BC-INS-UNX Installation Unix

Long text

Symptom
R/3 Installation on AIX
DB2 common server Database
Additional key words
R3SETUP CENTRDB.SH DATABASE.SH
Cause and preconditions
Problems discovered after publication of the installation guide
Solution
date      section      description


Sections of this note are:
```

Figure 33. R/3 OSS Note

This OSS Note (Figure 33) was obtained directly from OSS through the SAP Frontend using a search on SAP R/3 V4.0B with DB2 UDB installation.

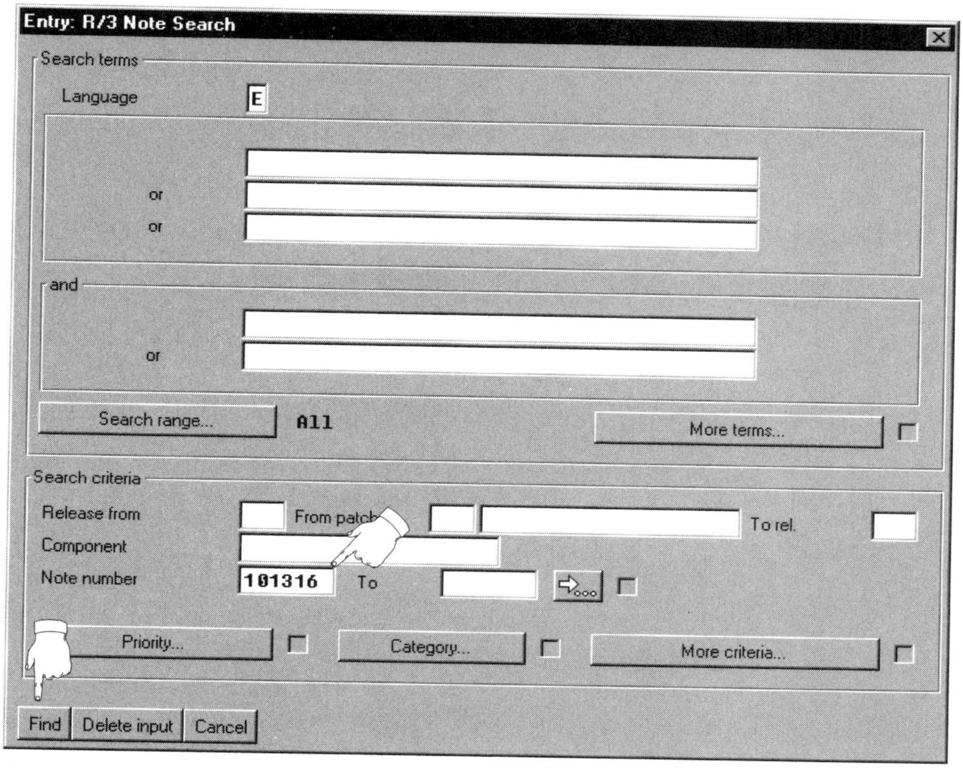

Entry: R/3 Note Search

Search terms

Language E

or

or

and

or

Search range... All

More terms...

Search criteria

Release from

From patch

To rel.

Component

Note number 101316 To

Priority...

Category...

More criteria...

Find Delete input Cancel

Figure 34. Entry : R/3 Note Search

Figure 34 shows an example of the OSS Notes search facility. To display this screen after logging into OSS from the main menu, click on **Gen. Functions**. We entered note number 101316 in the Note number field of the R/3 Note Search screen. To search for this note, click on **Find**, and the following screen is displayed:

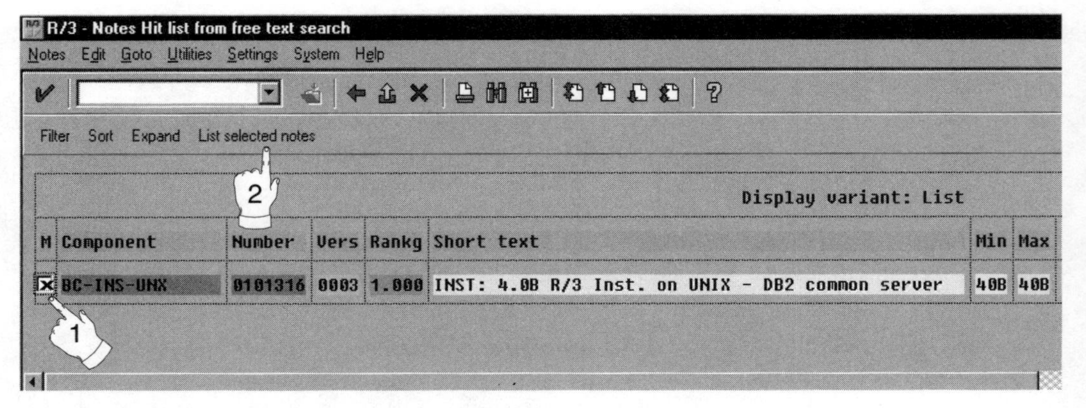

Figure 35. R/3 - Notes Hit List from Free Text Search

In this screen (Figure 35), check the box next to the note that you wish to download, and then click on **List selected notes** in the tool bar.

> **Note**
>
> It is very important to read all required notes and also download any required patches before starting the R/3 installation.

2.1.4 Installation Requirements Checklists

SAP provides two installation requirement checklists with the R/3 software. These checklists vary based on the operating system.

The two installation checklists for Unix are:

- Check list - Installation Requirements: DB2 common server
- Check list - Installation Requirements: Frontends

The two installation checklists for Windows NT are:

- Check list - Installation Requirements: Windows NT
- Check list - Installation Requirements: Frontends

> **Note**
>
> The hardware and software requirements detailed in these checklists will play an important part in your pre-installation planning.

2.2 R/3 Installation Hardware Requirements

This section describes the hardware requirements to install an R/3 system on Windows NT or on AIX.

2.2.1 Disk Requirements

There are a number of factors that influence the amount of disk space needed to run R/3.

2.2.1.1 Variables Affecting Disk Space Requirements

The variable factors and how these factors affect disk utilization are as follows:

Table 1. Variables Affecting Disk Space Requirements

Factor	Disk Space Utilized
Number of users accessing R/3	Disk space for paging
Number of R/3 modules used	Disk space for database
Number of business operations	Disk space for database
Data retention requirements	Disk space for database
Degree of hardware recoverability required	Disk space for RAID-1 or RAID-5 for database and database logs
Level of performance required	Disk space for RAID-1 for database and database logs
Amount of application programming development	Disk space for database and R/3 base code
Number of languages installed	Disk space for database

The minimum disk space required to complete an R/3 installation is 11 GB. It is strongly recommended to have at least 13 GB, or 30% additional disk space, in order to have some free space available after copying one client.

2.2.1.2 Additional Factors Affecting Disk Space Requirements

The configuration that you choose for your R/3 environment also affects the disk space requirements for your installation. The following table details the space (in MB) required for a central instance and a dialog instance, by operating system. These are just the basic disk requirements for a single instance, so if you plan to configure several dialog instances, you will need to multiply the values below by the number of dialog instances you intend to support. Remember that you need to plan for your entire system landscape.

Table 2. Disk Space Requirements

Configuration	Disk Space for AIX	Disk Space for NT
Central Instance	300 MB	1150 MB
Dialog Instance	250 MB	700 MB

2.2.1.3 Virtual Memory Requirements

The amount of virtual memory (RAM + paging space) required for SAP R/3 varies by operating system and by instance type. SAP R/3 uses the virtual memory for paging space. In the table below, we have outlined the minimum requirements for virtual memory, as well as a formula to assist you in calculating the memory requirements for your installation. It is suggested that you choose the greater of the two values for your configuration.

Table 3. Virtual Memory Requirements

Configuration	Virtual memory Required: Windows NT	Virtual Memory Required: AIX
Central Instance	1 GB (minimum) or 3 * RAM + 500 MB	1.2 GB (minimum) or 3 * RAM + 500 MB
Dialog Instance	1 GB (minimum) or 3 * RAM + 500 MB	1.2 GB (minimum) or 3 * RAM + 500 MB

2.2.1.4 Example Disk Layout Using Disk Mirroring

In order to provide a high degree of data protection in an SAP R/3 environment, it is recommend that you use either operating system controlled logical volume mirroring or RAID -1 in your different R/3 environments (development, quality assurance and production landscapes).

Figure 36 on page 49 shows an example disk layout that may be implemented on either Windows NT or AIX:

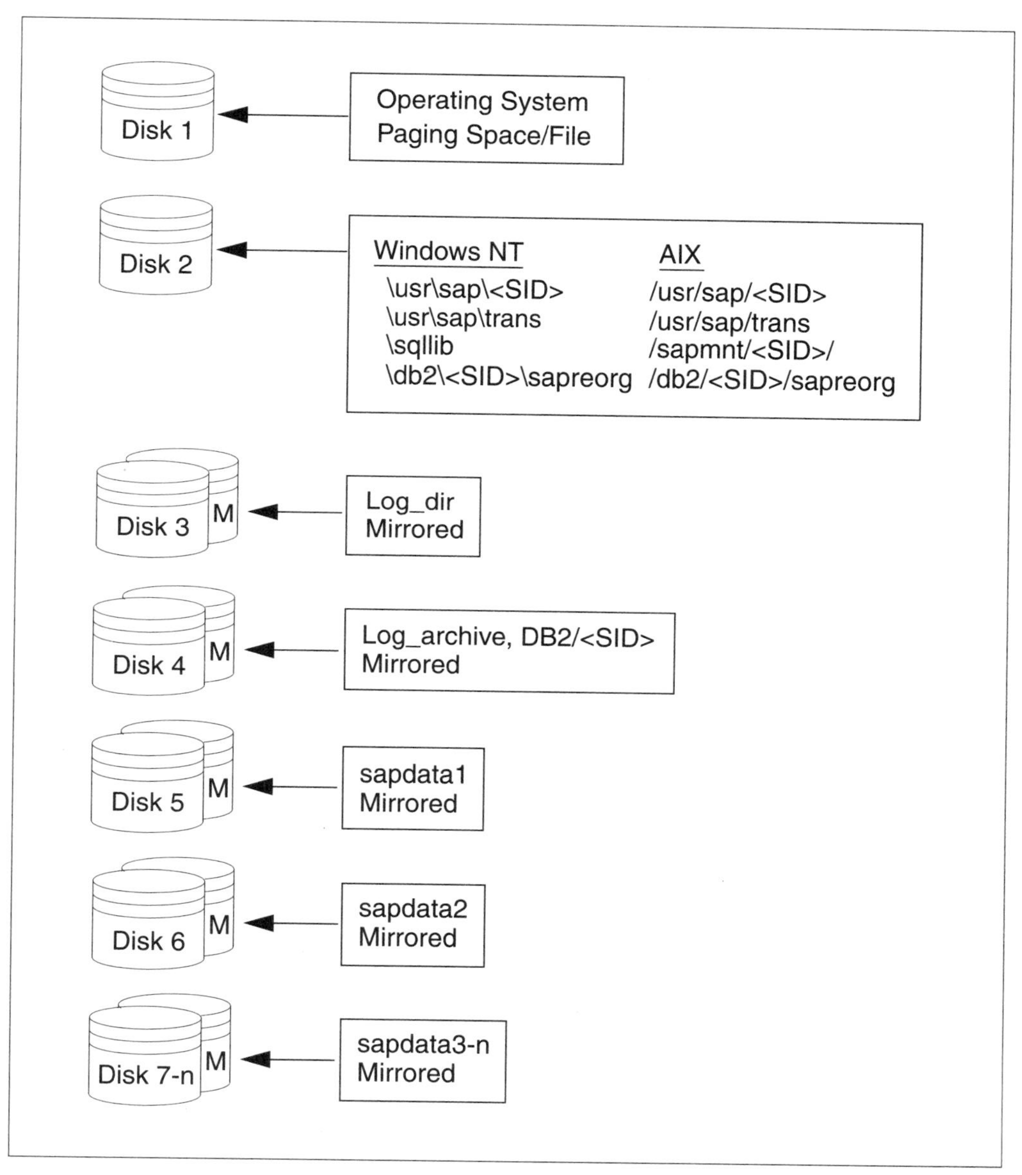

Figure 36. Example Disk Layout

The above example uses RAID-1 to mirror the disks containing log_dir, log_archive, and sapdata1-n. The database can be mirrored by logical volume mirroring, RAID-1 or RAID-5. RAID-1 mirroring offers the best recoverability with logical volume mirroring running a close second. RAID-1 and logical volume mirroring also offer better performance than RAID-5. RAID-5 is the least expensive mirroring alternative, but does not perform as well as RAID-1. Many customers choose RAID-5 for cost reasons. It is recommended to use RAID-1 for your log directory.

If RAID is implemented at the hardware level, this considerably reduces the load on the CPU and it will also be transparent to the operating system.

Note

The instance directory \db2\<SID> (/db2/<SID> on UNIX) should be mirrored because it contains important information for DB2 crash recovery. <SID> refers to SAP System ID, which is discussed later.

2.2.1.5 Database Logging

The directory where the on-line and retained active log files are stored (*log_dir*) must be mirrored to ensure data integrity. This can be done by hardware or by the operating system. These logs provide you with the ability to recover your system in the event of a system crash. They contain a record of all database changes made since the last backup.

DB2 UDB roll-forward recovery provides the ability to recover lost transactions and data due to media failure, such as a disk crash. Roll-forward applies the log file information to your restored database.

In a production environment, the log retention and user exit switch parameters must be activated in order to allow the R/3 version of the DB2 UDB userexit to move on-line retained log files from the on-line log directory, *log_dir,* to the off-line directory, *log_archive.* When DB2 is installed, the user exit parameter is set to OFF and logging is set to circular logging by default. You must set these parameters manually through the DB2 Control Center after installation is complete. This topic is covered in detail in “R/3 Database Maintenance” on page 327.

2.2.1.6 Archive Logs

When a log file becomes full, the log file is moved from the active log directory *log_dir* to the archive log directory *log_archive.* The space used in the archive log directory will grow over time. You must plan for the archive log directory to be large enough to hold up to two backup intervals worth of logs. This value is dependent upon your application environment. Reasonable values are 300 MB for a low activity system and over 5 GB for a high activity system.

2.2.1.7 Database Files

The database files are distributed across multiple subdirectories, *sapdata1* through *sapdatan* where n is a sequential number starting from 1. SAP R/3 is delivered with six sapdata subdirectories. If you wish to increase the number of sapdata directories prior to install, you should edit the R/3 delivered files, DATABASE.R3S or CENTRDB.R3S, before installing R/3. Modify DATABASE.R3S if you are installing a database instance or CENTRDB.R3S if you are installing a Central Instance. See "R/3 Table Space Sizes" on page 61 for more details.

2.2.1.8 Disk Layout Recommendations

As part of your system planning, consider the following recommendations:

1. The DB2 UDB on-line and archive log files should be mirrored in an R/3 production system for availability and performance reasons. The mirroring can be done either by hardware or operating system software. Hardware mirroring is done by RAID (AIX and NT) and software mirroring is only available in AIX.
2. Avoid installing the log files on the same disk as the database files. Should you experience a media failure, you will lose any changes that have been made since the last backup, unless disk recovery is successful. This may cause many hours of programming or on-line data entry to be lost. You must weigh the cost of hardware against the value of data to your day-to-day business.
3. In an R/3 production system, you must keep the archived on-line log files on a separate disk from the active log files.

For performance reasons, you should follow these guidelines:

1. Do not place any non-DB2 files on the same physical disk as the DB2 data files. For example, do not place any operating system paging spaces or swap files on the same volume as a sapdata directory.
2. The on-line log files are very I/O intensive. It is very desirable to place these on a small, fast, dedicated disk (between 500 MB and 1 GB).
3. The data and index table spaces should not reside on the same physical disk.
4. If a table space has more than one container, it is recommended that the containers all be the same size.

5. There are several table spaces in R/3 that tend to grow very quickly because they contain the bulk of the application data. These table spaces are listed below:

   - PSAPSTABD/I
   - PSAPBTABD/I
   - PSAPCLUD/I

   You should consider spreading these table spaces over multiple containers on separate physical devices.

2.2.1.9 Main Memory

The amount of main memory (RAM) required is dependent upon the number of end users accessing your R/3 system and the various R/3 components being actively used.

The minimum recommended main memory size is 256 MB for both a central instance and application instance configuration on either Windows NT or AIX. In addition, the stand alone database instance needs a minimum of 128 MB for either operating system.

2.2.1.10 CD-ROM Drive

A CD-ROM drive is needed to install R/3 and DB2 UDB. It must be ISO9660 compatible.

2.2.1.11 Tape Drive

A tape drive is recommended for backups. The speed and capacity must be in accordance with the size of the database and the window of time allocated for taking backups.You should consider multiple tape devices for redundancy purposes. Please note, that while a tape drive is recommended, you may also perform backups to both a disk or ADSM.

2.3 Operating System Software

SAP publishes a certified software version matrix. You use this matrix to determine which version of the operating system is compatible with the version of R/3 you intend to install. When you receive your copy of SAP R/3, it includes the DB2 UDB code, so you don't have to worry about the version of DB2 UDB.

2.3.1 AIX Operating System

The SAP-certified version of the AIX operating system that is compatible with R/3 4.0B is as follows. Please be sure to apply the latest system patches for the operating system.

- Version 4.2.x, where x is equal to or greater than 1
- Version 4.3.y, where y is equal or greater than 0

Additional software products and their versions include:

- NFS is required for a client/server configuration.
- C Set++ for AIX Application Runtime Version 3.1.4.8. APAR IX67978, PTF U447884 is required only for AIX Version 4.2.1. See OSS note 100125.
- Motif/X11 Version 1.2 with X11R5 is needed if you want to install the UNIX front end.
- For languages different than English and German, you must install:
  - The necessary fonts/code pages and NLS
  - The locale foreign code
- Performance Agent server and tools.

2.3.2 Windows NT Operating System

The SAP certified version of the Windows NT operating system that is compatible with R/3 4.0B is as follows:

- Windows NT Server Version 4.0, Build 1381, English (international) version. Service Pack 3 is highly recommended.

It is also recommended that you install the Windows NT Resource Kit.

2.4 SAP R/3 and DB2 UDB Directories

This section lists the important SAP R/3 and DB2 UDB directories that are created when you perform a default R/3 Central Instance Database installation. We include the directories for both AIX and Windows NT environments.

2.4.1 Directories Created at R/3 Installation (AIX)

The following directories are created by the R/3 installation tool on the AIX platform.

Table 4. SAP Directory Tree (AIX)

Root	Sub directory	Description
/sapmnt/	<SID>/profile	R/3 profile files
	<SID>/global	R/3 global files
	<SID>/exe	R/3 executables
/usr/	sap/trans	Used as a temporary repository generated by the control transport system within the R/3 system landscape
	sap/<SID>/SYS/	R/3 system sub directory
	sap/<SID>/SYS/exe/run/	R/3 executables
	sap/<SID>/SYS/exe/dbg/	R/3 executable debug files
	sap/<SID>/SYS/exe/opt/	R/3 optional executable files
	sap/<SID>/SYS/profile	R/3 profile information
	sap/<SID>/<INS><nbr>/	R/3 central instance directory
	sap/<SID>/<INS><nbr>/log/	System log for R/3 instance
	sap/<SID>/<INS><nbr>/work/	R/3 instance work directory
	sap/<SID>/<INS><nbr>/data/	R/3 instance data
	sap/put/	Used only during R/3 upgrades

The abbreviation <INS> refers to R/3 instance name and <nbr> to R/3 instance number. For example, our R/3 instance name is DVEBMGS, our R/3 instance number is 00, and our SID is AFB (the SID is the SAP system identifier); therefore the R/3 instance directory is /usr/sap/AFB/DVEBMGS00.

2.4.1.1 DB2 UDB Directories (AIX)

The following directories are created during DB2 installation. These directories contain the DB2 UDB executable code and other DB2 UDB files:

Table 5. DB2 UDB Directory Tree (AIX)

Root	Sub directory	Description
/db2/<SID>/	sqllib/	Installation and upgrade directory for the database software; specified and created during the installation of the DB2 UDB software
	sqllib/.netls/	NetLS licensing files used with DB2
	sqllib/Readme/	DB2 Readme files
	sqllib/adm/	DB2 utility and system executables local to the instance
	sqllib/adsm/	ADSTAR Distributed Storage Manager files
	sqllib/bin/	DB2 shared executable files
	sqllib/bnd/	DB2 bind files
	sqllib/cfg/	Default system configuration files
	sqllib/conv/	DBCS conversion tables
	sqllib/db2dump/	Diagnostic and alert logs and files and userexit log
	sqllib/doc/	Documentation
	sqllib/function/	Stored procedures, UDFs and related files
	sqllib/include/	Include files
	sqllib/java/	Java interface code
	sqllib/lib/	DB2 libraries
	sqllib/map/	Map files for DB2 Connect
	sqllib/misc/	Utilities and tools
	sqllib/msg/	Message files
	sqllib/odbclib/	ODBC related configuration and other files
	sqllib/samples/	Sample files
	sqllib/sqldbdir/	DB2 system database directory files
	sqllib/sqlnodir/	DB2 node directory files

Root	Sub directory	Description
/db2/<SID>/	sqllib/tmp/	Work directory

The following directories are created for the R/3 database during the installation process. DB2 UDB uses these directories to manage the R/3 database:

Table 6. DB2 UDB and SAP R/3 Data Directories (AIX)

Root	Sub directory	Description
/db2/<SID>/	sapdata1/	R/3 data containers
	sapdata2/	R/3 data containers
	sapdata3/	R/3 data containers
	sapdata4/	R/3 data containers
	sapdata5/	R/3 data containers
	sapdata6/	R/3 data containers
	saprest/	Protocol files for restoring the archived log files
	saparch/	Protocol files for recording the archived log files
	sapreorg/	Used for DB2 import and export files
	log_dir	On-line log file
	log_retrieve	DB2 log files retrieved from BRDB6RST
	log_archive/	Off-line archived log files
	errors/	Error log of ADSM application
	db2<sid>/	DB2 UDB database root directory used by the instance
	db2<sid>/NODE000n/ sqldbdir/	DB2 local database directory files
	db2<sid>/NODE000n/ SQL0000n/	R/3 DB2 UDB database files
	db2<sid>/NODE000n/ SQL0000n+1/	R/3 DB2 UDB Administration database files

The character *n* as a suffix on the above directories refers to a sequential number starting at 0.

The following directory is used for the DB2 UDB Database Administration Server instance (DAS):

Table 7. DAS Instance Directory

Directory	Sub directory	Description
/db2/db2as/	sqllib/	DB2 UDB Database Administration server instance directory

2.4.2 Directories Created at R/3 Installation (Windows NT)

The following directories are created by the R/3 installation tool on the Windows NT platform.

Table 8. SAP Directory Tree (Windows NT)

Root	Sub directory	Description
<drive>:\usr\	sap\trans\	It is used as a temporary repository by the control transport system within the R/3 landscape system.
	sap\<SID>\SYS\	R/3 system sub directory
	sap\<SID>\SYS\exe\run\	R/3 executables
	sap\<SID>\SYS\exe\dbg\	R/3 executable debug files
	sap\<SID>\SYS\exe\opt\	R/3 optional executable files
	sap\<SID>\SYS\global\	R/3 global files
	sap\<SID>\SYS\profile\	R/3 profile files
	sap\<SID>\<INS><nbr>\	R/3 central instance directory
	sap\<SID>\<INS><nbr>\log	System Logs from R/3 landscape
	sap\<SID>\<INS><nbr>\work\	Instance working directory
	sap\<SID>\<INS><nbr>\data\	Instance data information
	sap\put\	Used only during upgrades

The abbreviation <INS> refers to R/3 instance name and <nbr> to R/3 instance number. For example, our R/3 instance name is DVEBMGS, our R/3 instance number is 00, and our SID is AUS (the SID is the SAP system identifier); therefore the R/3 instance directory is d:\usr\sap\AUS\DVEBMGS00.

2.4.2.1 DB2 UDB Directories (Windows NT)

The following directories are created during DB2 installation. These directories contain the DB2 UDB executable code and other DB2 UDB files. Note that the default DB2 instance directories are not listed here:

Table 9. DB2 UDB Directory Structure (Windows NT)

Root	Sub directory	Description
<drive>:\sqllib\		Installation and upgrade directory for the database software; specified and created during the installation of the DB2 UDB software
	adsm\	ADSTAR Distributed Storage Manager files
	art	DB2 Software Registration
	bin\	DB2 executable files
	bnd\	DB2 bind files
	cfg\	DB2 default system configuration files
	conv\	DBCS conversion tables
	DB2<sid>\	DB2 instance directory created during SAP R/3 instance creation
	DB2<sid>\log\	Default directory for DB2 system logs for this instance
	DB2<sid>\security\	DB2 instance security related files
	DB2<sid>\sqldbdir\	DB2 R/3 system database directory
	DB2<sid>\sqlnodir\	DB2 node directory files
	DB2<sid>\tmp\	DB2 R/3 temporary work directory
	DB2das00\	DB2 Administration Server related files
	doc	DB2 UDB documentation
	function\	Stored procedures and related files
	help\	Help files
	java\	Java-related files for DB2 UDB
	map\	Map files for DB2 Connect
	misc\	Utilities and examples
	msg\	Messages files

Root	Sub directory	Description
	samples\	Sample files
	msodbc16\	ODBC related files

The following directories are created for the R/3 database during the installation process. DB2 UDB uses these directories to manage the R/3 database:

Table 10. DB2 UDB and SAP R/3 Data Directories (Windows NT)

Root	Sub directory	Description
<drive>:\db2\<SID>\	sapdata1\	R/3 data
	sapdata2\	R/3 data
	sapdata3\	R/3 data
	sapdata4\	R/3 data
	sapdata5\	R/3 data
	sapdata6\	R/3 data
	sapreorg\	Used for DB2 import and export files
	log_dir	On-line log file
	log_archive	Off-line archived log files
	db2dump	Diagnostic and alert logs and files
<drive>:\db2<sid>\		DB2 UDB root database file directory for the instance
	\NODE000n\SQLDBDIR\	DB2 local database directory files
	\errors\	Error log of ADSM application
	db2UserExit/	DB2 user exit programs
	NODE000n\SQL0000n\	DB2 UDB R/3 database files
	NODE000n\SQL0000n+1\	DB2 UDB R/3 Administration database files

The character *n* as suffix on the above directories refers to a sequential number starting from 0.

2.5 Table Spaces

Table spaces exist in DB2 UDB to provide you with a logical layer between your data and storage devices. All DB2 tables reside in a table space. This enables you to control where your data is stored.You can place table spaces on different kinds of devices. This gives you the ability to create a detailed physical database design to fit your particular environment. For example, you can choose slower disks to store less frequently accessed data and faster disks to store indexes or frequently accessed data.

For more details about table spaces in DB2 UDB, see "DB2 UDB Storage Methods" on page 301.

2.5.1 R/3 Table Spaces

When R/3 is installed, a number of R/3 table spaces are created to store the R/3 applications and data. The R/3 table spaces are generated in pairs; one table space contains the data and the other contains the indexes. There are other table spaces in the R/3 database which belong to DB2 and are used for system catalog tables and temporary table spaces.

Table 11. R/3 Table Spaces

Table Space Type	Table Space Name	Description
DB2	SYSCATSPACE	DB2 UDB System Catalog tables
DB2	PSAPTEMP	Temporary Table Space
R/3 Basis	PSAPLOADD/I	Dynpro+Report loads
R/3 Basis	PSAPSOURCED/I	Dynpro+Report Sources
R/3 Basis	PSAPDDICD/I	R/3 Data Dictionary
R/3 Basis	PSAPPROTD/I	Spool, Protocols, Converter
R/3 Basis	PSAPES40BD/I	Repository Source
R/3 Basis	PSAPEL40BD/I	Repository Load
R/3 Application	PSAPCLUD/I	Cluster Tables
R/3 Application	PSAPPOOLD/I	Pool Tables
R/3 Application	PSAPPOL2D/I	Additional Pool Tables
R/3 Application	PSAPSTABD/I	Master Data
R/3 Application	PSAPBTABD/I	Transaction data

Table Space Type	Table Space Name	Description
R/3 Application	PSAPDOCUD/I	Documentation, SAP Script
R/3 Customer Application Tables	PSAPUSER1D/I	Customer Tables

Note

The table space names, PSAPES40BD/I and PSAPEL40BD/I are dependent on the release of R/3.

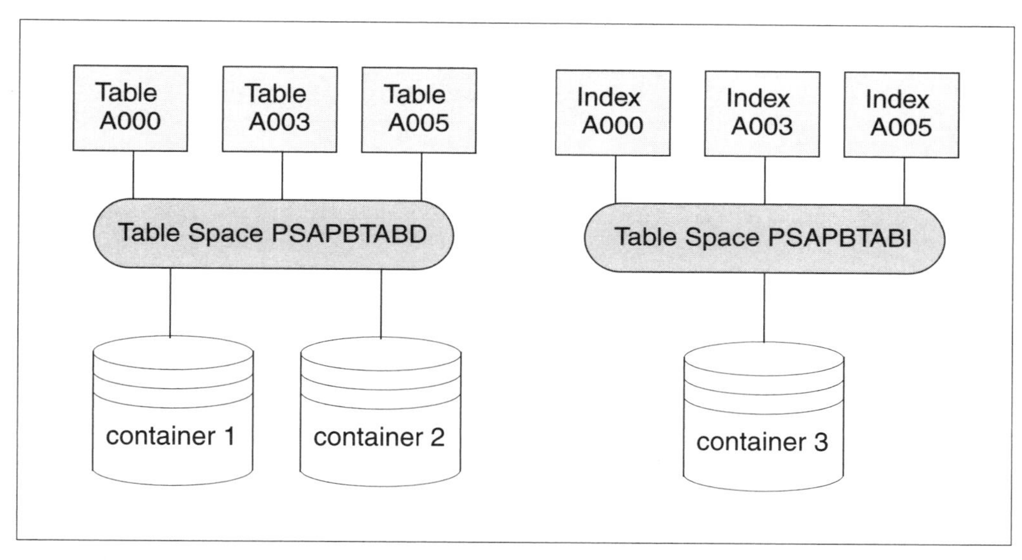

Figure 37. SAP R/3 Table Spaces, Tables, Indexes and Containers

2.5.2 R/3 Table Space Sizes

The files that contain the table space creation parameters differ depending on whether you are installing a central instance with database or a stand alone database server. The files are named as follows:

- DATABASE.R3S: Database instance
- CENTRDB.R3S: Central instance with database

If you believe that you need to change the definitions of the default table spaces, then you can modify the table space definitions in the DATABASE.R3S or CENTRDB.R3S file. For example, you should do this if you want to increase the size of a table space, or if you want to increase the number of containers in a table space.

The files contain a list of SAP data directories named *sapdatan*, where *n* is a sequential number starting at 1. Each of these SAP data directories contains several table spaces. The size of the directory is the sum of the size of the table spaces assigned to that directory.

The default R/3 table space sizes are shown in the following table:

Table 12. R/3 Table Space Sizes

Table Space Name	Subdirectory	Size (MB)	Number of containers	Extent Size
SYSCATSPACE	SAPDATA1	80	3	32
PSAPBTABD	SAPDATA1	600	1	16
PSAPBTABI	SAPDATA2	300	1	8
PSAPCLUD	SAPDATA1	100	1	64
PSAPCLUI	SAPDATA2	20	1	32
PSAPDICCD	SAPDATA1	280	1	16
PSAPDICCI	SAPDATA2	150	1	16
PSAPDOCUD	SAPDATA1	60	1	16
PSAPDOCUI	SAPDATA2	50	1	32
PSAPEL40BD	SAPDATA1	500	1	32
PSAPEL40BI	SAPDATA2	50	1	16
PSAPES40BD	SAPDATA5	550	5	16
PSAPES40BI	SAPDATA6	400	2	16
PSAPLOADD	SAPDATA1	40	1	64
PSAPLOADI	SAPDATA2	40	1	32
PSAPPOL2D	SAPDATA3	500	1	8
PSAPPOL2I	SAPDATA4	400	1	8
PSAPPOOLD	SAPDATA3	500	1	8
PSAPPOOLI	SAPDATA4	400	1	8
PSAPPROTD	SAPDATA1	80	1	32

Table Space Name	Subdirectory	Size (MB)	Number of containers	Extent Size
PSAPPROTI	SAPDATA2	50	1	16
PSAPSOURCED	SAPDATA3	100	1	64
PSAPSOURCEI	SAPDATA4	100	1	32
PSAPSTABD	SAPDATA3	600	1	8
PSAPSTABI	SAPDATA4	400	1	8
PSAPTEMP	SAPDATA1	128	1	32
PSAPUSER1D	SAPDATA2	5	1	16
PSAPUSER1I	SAPDATA1	5	1	8

2.6 R/3 Naming Conventions

SAP has standard naming conventions for R/3 objects. It is important that you comply with the R/3 naming conventions in order to avoid any problems with your R/3 installation and subsequent use of the R/3 product.

2.6.1 Hostname of R/3 Central Instance Machine

The TCP/IP hostname of the machine which runs the R/3 central instance must comply with the following format:

```
ynnnnnnn
```

Where:

- **y** is an alphabetic character
- **nnnnnnn** is a string of up to 7 additional alphanumeric characters. This string of characters may not contain any special characters such as dashes or underscores.

If you do not comply with these standards, unpredictable problems may arise during installation or while using the R/3 system (especially the R/3 transport system).

2.6.2 SAP System ID

There must be a unique SAP System ID for each R/3 installation in your company's system landscape. The SAP System ID, also known as SAP SID or <SID>, is used to identify the instance that owns the R/3 objects.

The SAP SID must conform to the following format:

Where:

- **Y** is a single upper-case alphabetic character.
- **NN** is a pair of upper-case alphanumeric characters.
- The composite name may not be one of the names that SAP has placed on the restricted names list provided in the most current SAP documentation.

The list of restricted names includes the following: ADD, ALL, AND, ANY, ASC, B20, B30, BCO, BIN, COM, DBA, END, EPS, FOR, GID, INT, KEY, LOG, MON, NOT, OFF, OMS, P30, RAW, ROW, SAP, SET, SGA, SHG, SID, UID or VAR. You should review your most current SAP documentation for the latest list of restricted system names.

2.6.3 R/3 Table Space Names

All of the R/3 table spaces comply with the following naming standard:

PSAP	nnnn	D/I

Where:

- **PSAP** is a constant indicating that the table space belongs to the R/3 SAP system.
- **nnnn** is the short name for the table space indicating its usage. Note that the number of characters is not limited to four.
- **D/I** is the suffix of the name where:
  - **D** indicates that the table space contains tables.
  - **I** indicates that the table space contains indexes.

Using this standard, a table space named PSAPPROTD is the SAP table space containing protocol tables; PROT being the short name for Protocols.

2.6.4 R/3 Container Names

This section describes the naming conventions of R/3 containers. SAP uses two types of DB2 containers for table spaces, raw device containers and file containers.

2.6.4.1 R/3 File Container Names

Each R/3 file container follows this naming standard:

PSAP	nnnn	D/I	.container	zzz

Where:

- **PSAPnnnnD/I** is the table space name.
- **.container** is a constant indicating that the file is a container for the indicated table space
- ***zzz*** is a number ranging from 000 through 999, indicating the container number; container numbers are assigned sequentially.

Assume that you are using AIX and that your transaction data table space has multiple containers. In this case, the first container would be named PSAPBTABD.container000, the second container would be named PSAPBTABD.container001, and so on.

2.6.4.2 R/3 Raw Device Container Names

Each R/3 raw device container uses the following naming standard:

r	PSAP	nnnn	D/I	_	zzz

Where:

- **r** is a constant and indicates that it is a raw device.
- **PSAPnnnnD/I** is the table space name.
- _ is constant.
- **zzz** is a sequential number ranging from 000 through 999.

For example, on AIX, if the table space PSAPSTABD uses a single raw device container, then the container name would be /<devicepath>/rPSAPSTABD_000.

2.6.5 R/3 Instance Names

The instance name is used to identify the type of R/3 instance. There is a separate naming standard for the central instance and the dialog instance.

2.6.5.1 Central Instance Names

The central instance process name complies with the following format:

D	V	E	B	M	G	S	nn

Where:

- **D** represents the *dialog work process*. This is an interactive process that handles input/output between the Application Server and the SAPGUI.
- **V** represents the *update work process*.
- **E** represents the *enqueue work process*. This is a special work process that is responsible for handling the special locking requirements of R/3.
- **B** represents the *batch work process*.
- **M** represents the *message server process*. This is a special process in a Central Instance responsible for facilitating communication between instances within the same R/3 system and for identifying services in the R/3 system to processes outside the SAP system.
- **G** represents the *gateway work process*. This process is responsible for communication between an instance and processes outside of the instance.
- **S** represents the *spool work process*.
- **nn** represents the number of the central instance ranging from 00 to 99.

The central instance name is composed of the single character associated with each of the seven work processes available in an R/3 system followed by a two digit suffix. The numeric suffix of the central instance name allows more than one R/3 system to run on the same machine.

2.6.5.2 Dialog Instance Names

The dialog instance name complies with the following format:

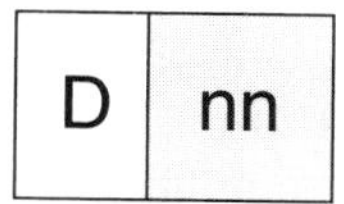

Where:

- **D** represents the dialog instance.
- **nn** represents the number of the dialog instance ranging from 00 to 99 and should be the same as the central instance numeric suffix, unless more than one dialog instance is executing on the same machine.

The figure below shows an example of the different instance names. On computer Host1, there is a central instance process, DVEBMGS00. On Host2 and Host3, there is a dialog instance, D00. The dialog instance numeric suffixes are the same as the central instance suffix, 00.

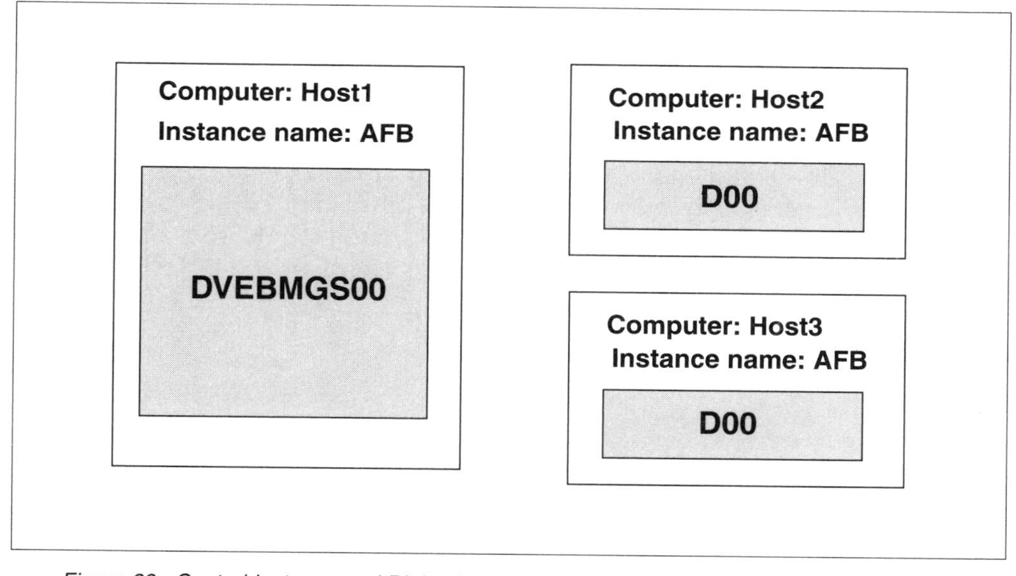

Figure 38. Central Instance and Dialog Instance Names

2.7 Communications Requirements

The SAP R/3 system is based on the client/server architecture; therefore, inter-system communication is critical to the functionality of your SAP R/3 environment.

Your communications requirements vary depending on whether you are considering the communication between the workstation and the application server, between the workstation and database server or between the database server and the external interfaces.

SAP provides information regarding your communications requirements in this document: *System R/3, SAP System Requirements for networks, frontends and communication interfaces.* Here you will find information on the required level of communication software for each operating system. The details for Frontends, web browsers, CPIC, RFC, and network communications are all included.

2.7.1 Protocols

R/3 uses one protocol, TCP/IP, to communicate between database instances and application instances. TCP/IP is also used between application instances and front end workstations by the SAPGUI program. The front end workstation may need a protocol other than TCP/IP to share R/3 front end code and on-line documentation among clients from a file server. The supported protocols are NetBIOS, NetBEUI and IPX/SPX.

2.7.2 Network Considerations

When choosing the topology of the network for your R/3 system, you must consider the number of users who will be accessing the R/3 system, and the workload on your existing network.

Figure 39 shows an example of a small R/3 environment in which one LAN is shared by all machines in the R/3 environment:

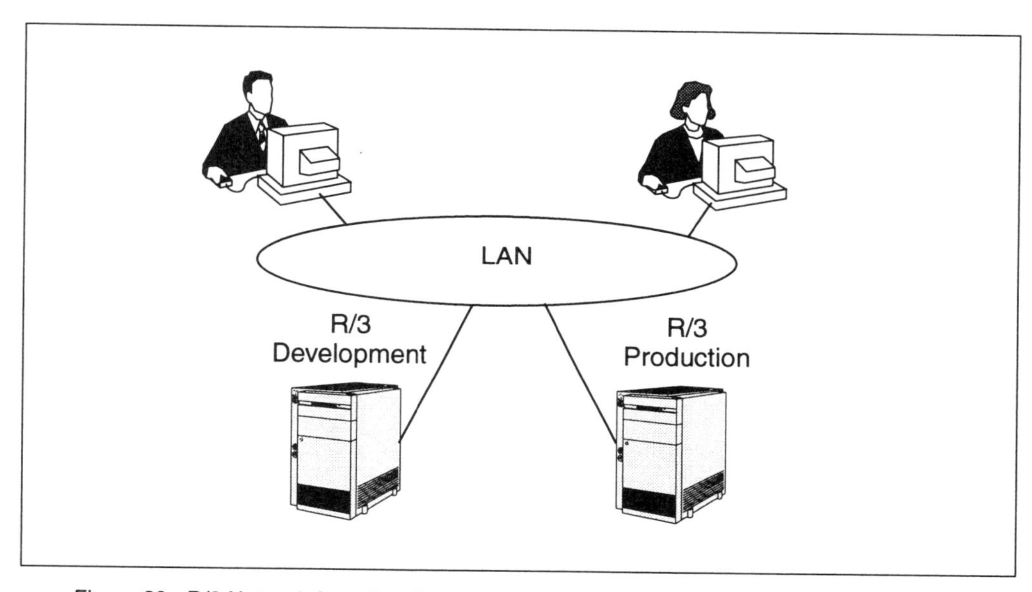

Figure 39. R/3 Network for a Small Installation

The next example depicts a larger R/3 installation which is using an already congested local area network:

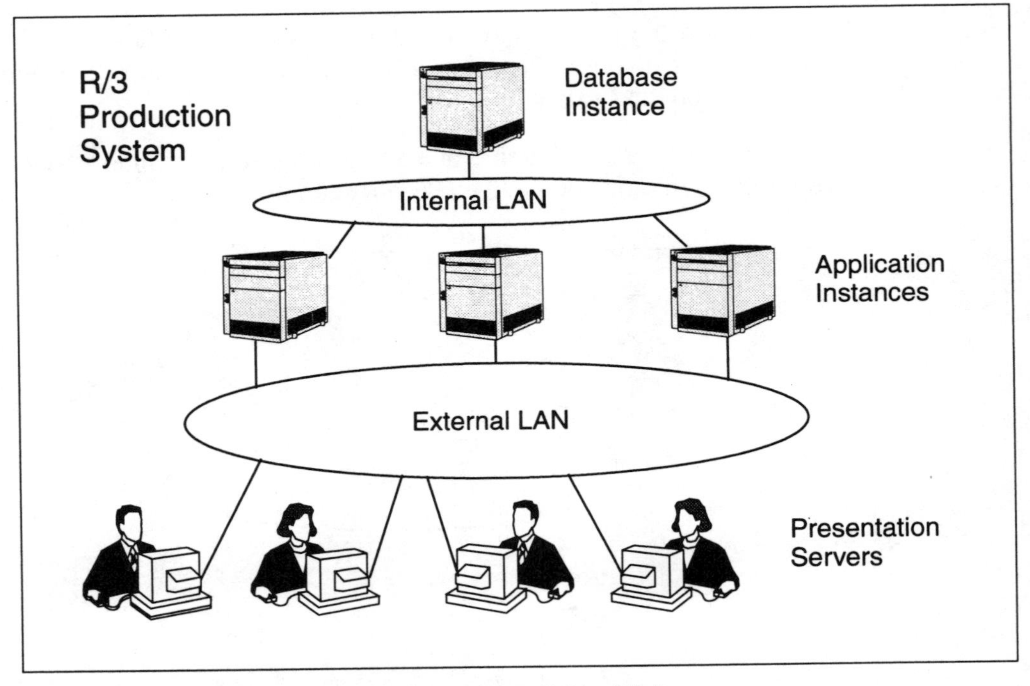

Figure 40. R/3 Network for a Medium to Large R/3 Installation

Figure 40 shows two separate networks, one internal and one external. The communication between the database instance and the application instances causes much more traffic to occur than between the application instance and the presentation servers. The internal network should be high speed such as FDDI, ATM or an SP High Performance Switch (HPS). The external network may be Ethernet 10/100 MB or Token Ring 4/16 MB.

2.8 Presentation Servers

The presentation servers must be able to run the SAP Frontend GUI and communicate with an R/3 application server. This section will discuss the minimum requirements for configuring a machine as an R/3 presentation server.

2.8.1 Supported Operating Systems

The SAP Frontend GUI interface runs on any of the following operating systems at the specified versions:

- Windows 3.1/ 3.11

- Windows 95
- Windows NT
- OS/2 Warp Version 3 or higher
- UNIX:
  - AIX
  - NCR
  - Digital Unix
  - HP-UX
  - ReliantUNIX
  - Solaris
  - Sequent Dynix/ptx

2.8.2 Hardware and Software Requirements

For detailed information about the Frontend requirements and the installation process, review the following SAP documents:

- Check list - Installation requirements: Frontends
- Installing SAP Frontend Software for PC

2.9 OSS

Access to OSS is vital to the success of your SAP R/3 environment. Through OSS, you can send questions directly to SAP as well as search the SAP notes database for solutions to problems. Also, through your OSS connection, the SAP support team can connect to your R/3 system to perform a variety of services such as diagnostic analysis, monitoring, remote consulting, and problem determination and resolution.

To determine the network requirements for accessing OSS from your existing network, you need to perform the steps listed below.

2.9.1 Connecting to OSS

To fully take advantage of OSS, you need to establish a remote connection between your R/3 installation and one of SAP's support servers. Based on your LAN environment, your production systems, and your telecommunications environment (transmission mode, available concentrator connections, and available connections to PBX, and wide area interfaces), you should analyze the possible ways to integrate an OSS router into your existing network topology.

2.9.1.1 Mode of Transmission

The fundamental requirement for remote connection to SAP is a suitable transmission mode. SAP supports different transmission modes via various service providers, such as:

- X.25
- Frame Relay
- ISDN

You should choose the most effective mode of transmission based on your expected usage and existing telecommunications infrastructure.

2.9.1.2 SAP Network Providers

The network provider that you use to connect to SAP depends on where your installation is located. You should check the OSS note related to your region to obtain the information related to carriers and modes of transmission as well as the required application forms. Procedures may vary by region. The following table lists some OSS notes at the time of writing:

Table 13. SAP Network Providers

Region	**Network provider**
Asia (except Japan)	*See OSS note 37946*
Australia	*See OSS note 102414*
Europe	*See OSS note 33953*
Japan	*See OSS note 39894*
North America	*See OSS note 40739*

2.9.2 Communication Hardware

Your system will communicate with SAP's support server via a routed TCP/IP connection. Routing is a function which provides a path for transmission of data packets between different logical and physical networks.

The configuration of hardware depends on your security requirements, your network topology, and your present infrastructure.

2.9.2.1 Hardware Requirements

SAP recommends a dedicated router to ensure better security, high availability, and flexibility. The minimum communication hardware requirement is:

- One computer to be used as a communications server.

- One network card for internal network communication. The internal network card may be one of:
  - Token Ring
  - Ethernet
- One modem or a network card for external network connection. The external network card may be any of the following and is connected to a router or a virtual private network:
  - X.25
  - ISDN
  - Frame Relay
  - Token Ring
  - Ethernet
- One router, if an external network card is used.

The following diagram shows an example configuration:

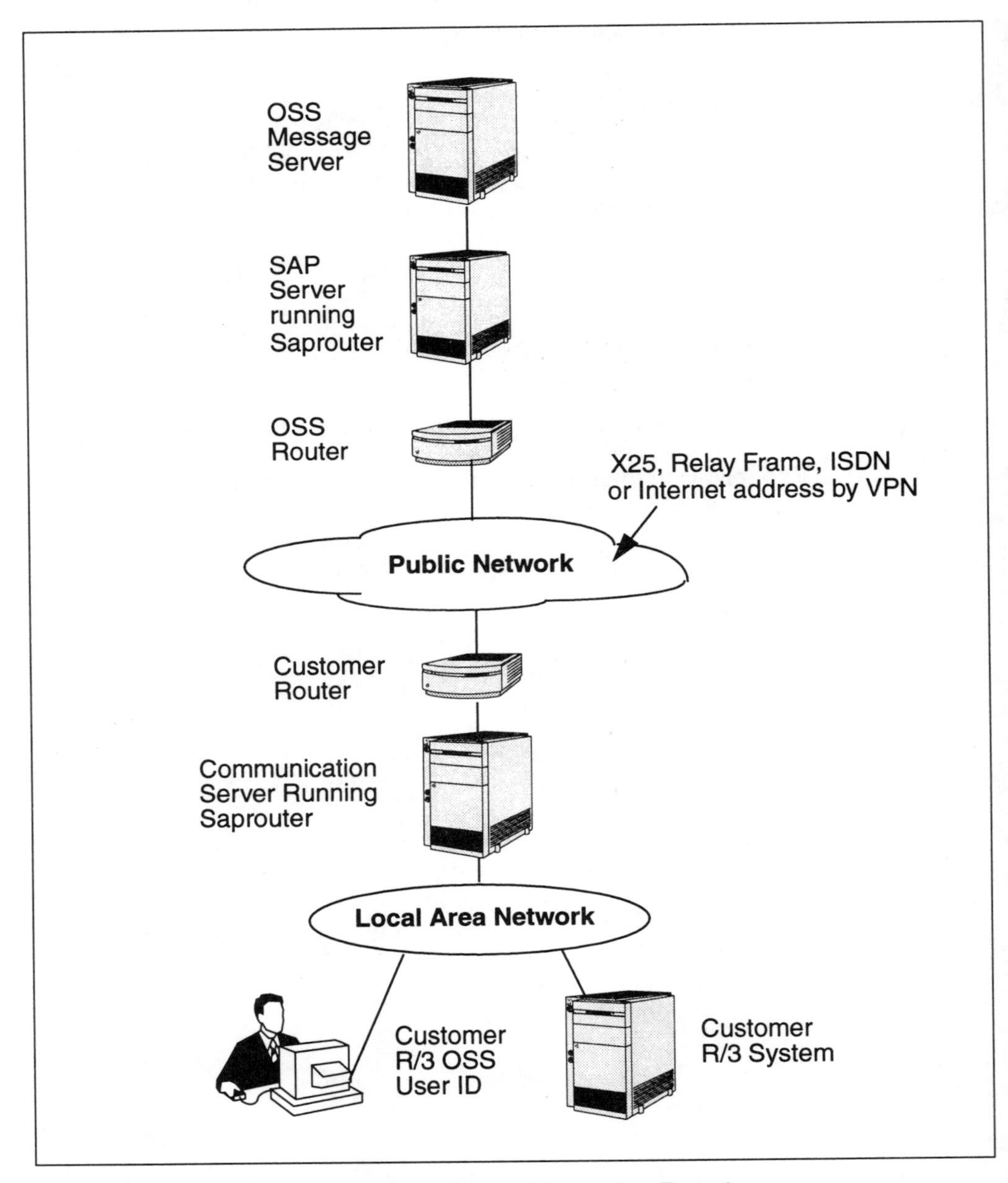

Figure 41. OSS Remote Connection Network Infrastructure Example

2.9.2.2 Obtaining an Official TCP/IP Address

Communication via TCP/IP requires unique addressing within the entire TCP/IP network. Because of the large number of users in SAP's support network, it is necessary to use an officially assigned and registered TCP/IP address. Your remote connection requires that you install the SAProuter communication software at your site. This becomes the only entry and exit point of your network to the SAP network. Since there is only one entry and exit point, only one address is required for the network card on the machine that has the SAProuter communication software installed.

SAP provides a form, *Remote Connection Data Sheet*, in the SAP booklet, *Remote Connection to R/3 Online Service and Support* to request this address:

```
remote_connection - Notepad
File  Edit  Search  Help

                    Remote Connection Data Sheet

Company ______________________________________________

Customer no.: ____________  Customer info no. (2): __________

SAPGUI release: __________  Message number (3): ____________

R/3 system administrator: ______________________________

Tel.: _____________________     Fax: _____________________

Network specialist _____________________________________

Tel.: _____________________     Fax: _____________________

Information on the network connection (4):

( ) X.25 connection

X.25 number (5): _____________________________________

IP address of the X.25 connection (6): _______________

( ) ISDN connection (protocol PPP with CHAP is required)

IP address of the ISDN connection: ___________________

User name for CHAP: __________________________________

Password for CHAP: ___________________________________

( ) Frame Relay connection

Frame Relay provider (name): _________________________

Frame Relay DLCI: ____________________________________

IP address of the Frame Relay connection: ____________
```

Figure 42. OSS Remote Connection Data Sheet

Alternately, you may obtain OSS note 28976, provide the required information such as TCP/IP address, and fax the form to your SAP office. You will receive in return from SAP:

- Notification of approval to connect to SAP servers.
- The TCP/IP address of the SAP support server assigned to your SAP installation.
- The SAP router TCP/IP address.
- Technical details about X.25, ISDN, and so on.

Once you receive the required information from SAP, you must configure the SAProuter program and the technical parameters for accessing OSS. To test your OSS connection from the SAPGUI, you also need an OSS user ID.

2.9.3 Obtaining an OSS User ID

You must obtain an OSS user ID in order to communicate with SAP via the OSS interface. You should request the OSS user ID as soon as you receive your R/3 installation kit. The form used to request an OSS user ID is included in the SAP document, *The Online Service System (OSS) User Guide*. You may also obtain this form by requesting OSS note 18554, *Registration form: New OSS users*, from SAP if you have not established connectivity with an SAP server. SAP will send you one OSS user ID that is an administrator ID with the authority to create additional user IDs for your company.

2.9.4 Programmer Registration

In order to create or modify an ABAP/4 program, you need to be a registered SAP programmer listed in the SAP Software Change Registration (SSCR). Programmer registration is required if you plan to create new ABAP/4 programs or make changes to the SAP supplied R/3 source modules or data dictionary objects. SAP matchcodes and tuning measures such as the setup of database indexes and buffers are excluded from the registration.

The registration of a programmer in SSCR is done only once, prior to the start of any modifications to any R/3 object. Programmer registration does not expire and is valid even through release upgrades.

You need to know your installation number to perform the registration. To locate your installation number, choose **System->Status** from the primary GUI panel. The following screen is displayed:

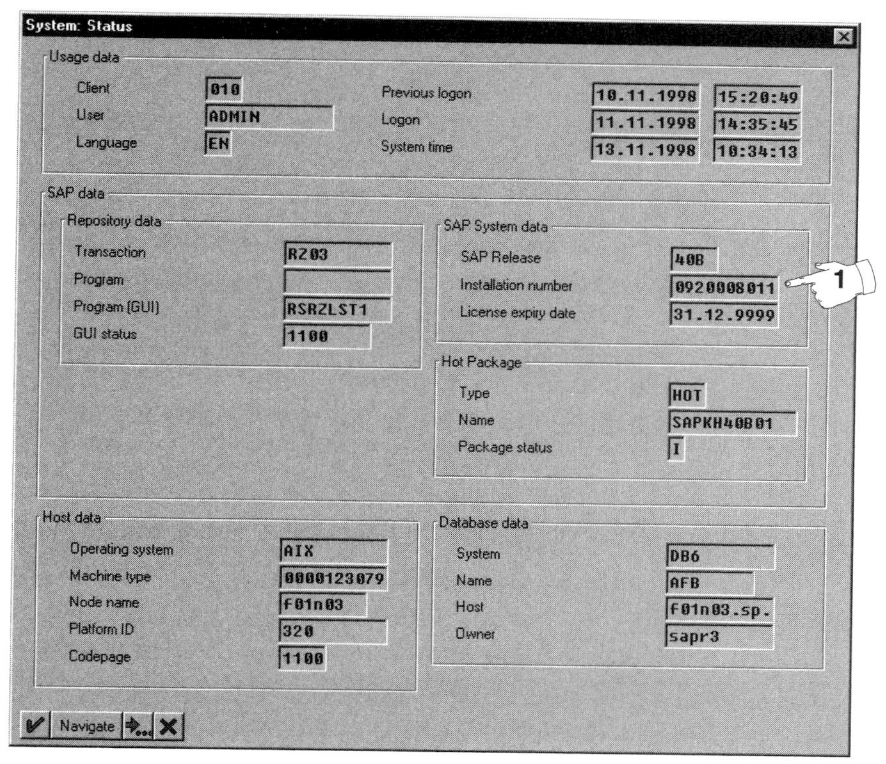

Figure 43. System Status

The Installation number is found in the SAP System box (1 in Figure 43).

The registration procedure is as follows:

1. Log on to OSS. The OSS inbox is displayed:

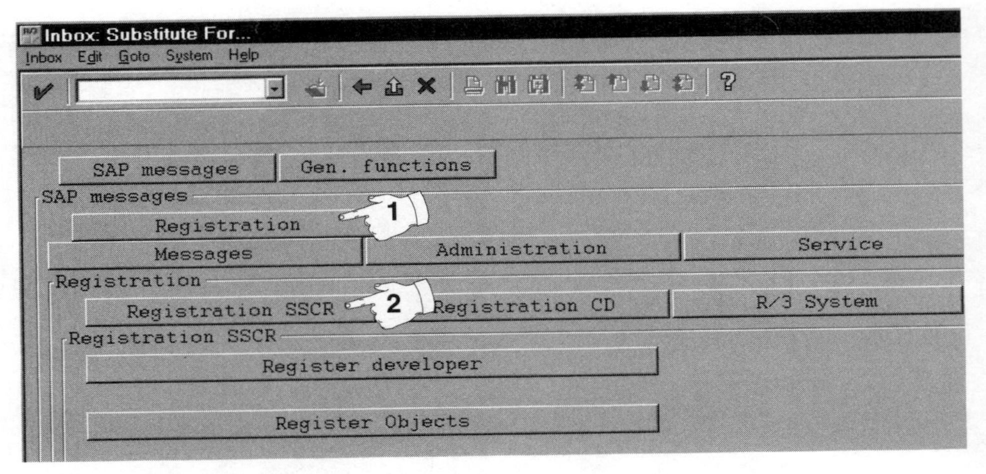

Figure 44. OSS Registration

2. In the OSS Inbox, click on **Registration** (1 in Figure 44).
3. Click on **Registration SCCR** (2 in Figure 44). The following screen is displayed:

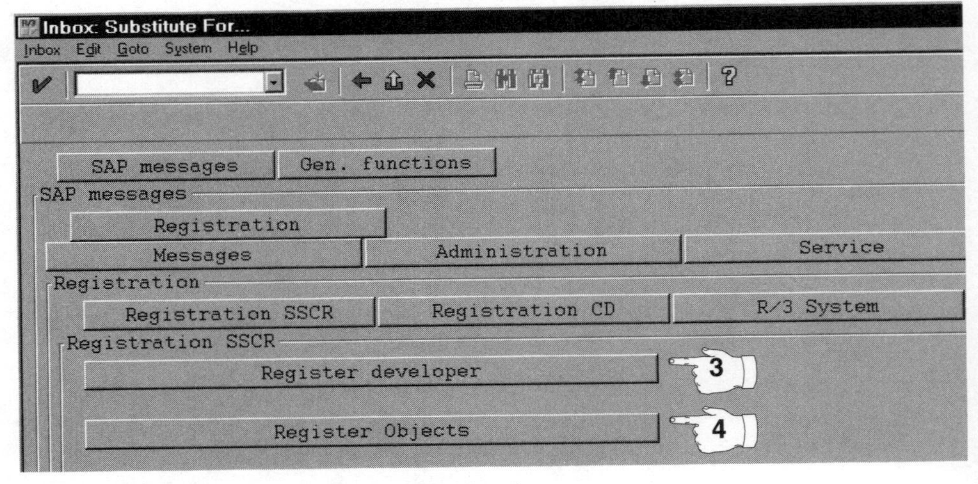

Figure 45. SSCR Developer and Object Registration

4. Click on **Register Developer** (3 in Figure 45) to register the R/3 user who will be modifying the R/3 source code.
5. Click on **Register Objects** (4 in Figure 45) to notify SAP of your intent to modify an R/3 module.

To register an object in SCCR, you need the fully qualified object name. To find the object name, you will need to go into the ABAP/4 Editor using transaction **SE38**. Enter the name of the object you wish to modify, and click either **Change** or **Create**. The following screen will be displayed:

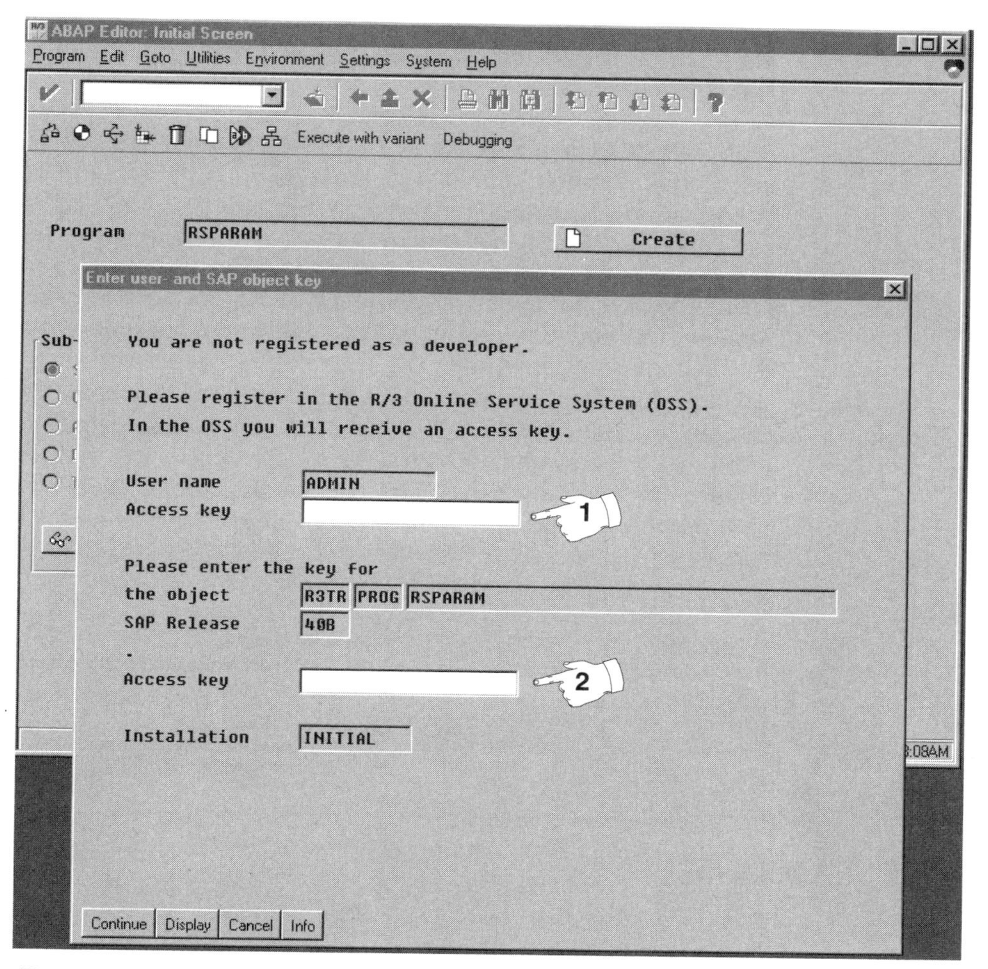

Figure 46. User and Object Access Key Entry Screen for Object Modifications

This screen shows the *fully qualified SAP object name* for the object specified in the ABAP/4 Editor Initial Screen. Use the fully qualified SAP object name from this panel in the SSCR registration panel.

Once you have the keys for the developer and the object, you can enter them in the screen shown in Figure 46. Click **Continue** and you will now be allowed to modify the object.

Often an object that you assume is an ABAP/4 report turns out to be an R/3 function module. Therefore, when registering objects in SSCR via OSS, always enter the name specified in the *Enter user- and SAP object key* screen. In our example above, the object key for the program, RSPARAM, is: R3TR PROG RSPARAM. While this seems to be a fairly straight forward naming convention, it will not hold true in all cases. For example, it you attempt to change the program, LCTBIF01, the object key for this program is R3TR FUGR CTBI.

An SSCR developer key is made up of the developer's R/3 user ID plus the installation number. This user ID must be correctly entered in the SSCR developer registration; it must match the user ID on the R/3 System corresponding to the installation number referenced.

If R/3 user IDs containing country-specific characters are registered, problems occur when validating the keys if you use different code pages in the customer system and in OSS. The OSS system converts all external entries (user entries in popups) to the codepage that is used internally (1100). The generated SSCR keys are based on the converted R/3 user IDs. If the customer system uses a different codepage, the keys will not match. Ensure that you only use R/3 user IDs which do not contain special characters.The following table contains some examples of valid and invalid R/3 user IDs:

Table 14. R/3 User IDs

Valid User ID	Invalid User ID
NAME	$NAME#
Andre	André
Nunez	Nuñez

2.9.5 Hot Packages

A Hot Package is a collection of corrections for errors in the ABAP/4 repository. Hot Packages can be obtained via OSS and are imported in a fixed sequence. Hot Packages are obtained after R/3 is installed since they are only applied by direct communication between your R/3 system and OSS server. You should plan to download the latest hot packages after you complete your R/3 installation. Normally, the Hot Package collection for the current R/3 release are supplied on CDs in the R/3 box delivered to customers.

If you have an OSS user id, you can download Hot Packages in one of two ways. You can either download the Hot Packages over the internet by connecting to URL http://sapnet.sap-ag.de/ocs or over the connection between your R/3 system and the OSS Server.

2.9.5.1 Obtaining Hot Packages over the Internet

The following figure shows the SAP web site for Hot Packages:

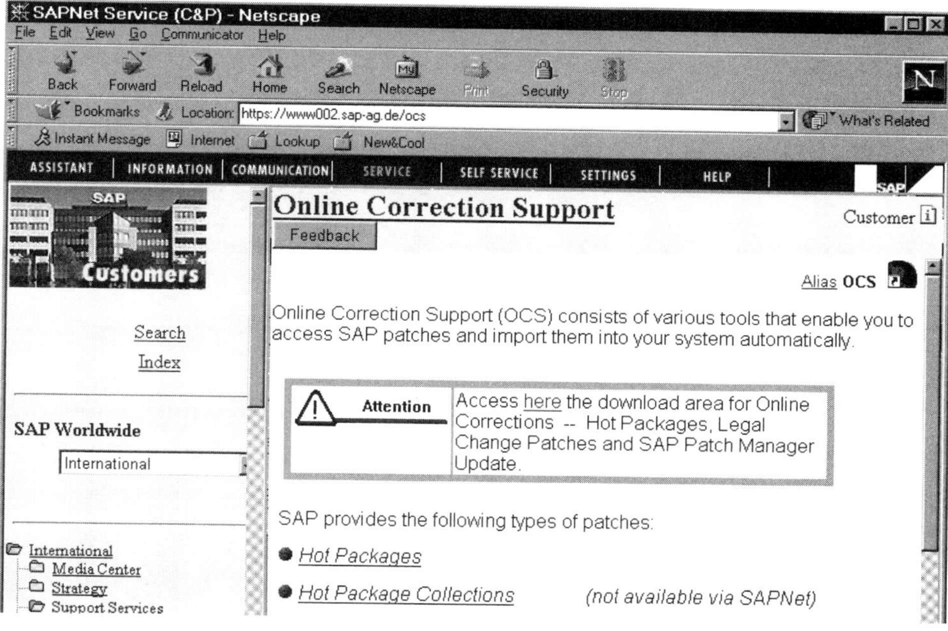

Figure 47. SAPNET: On-line Correction Support Via the Internet

From this page, you can download Hot Packages using the hypertext links and obtain information on Hot Package Collections.

2.9.5.2 Obtaining Hot Packages Using OSS

To request a Hot Package using OSS:

1. Log on to OSS. The OSS inbox is displayed:

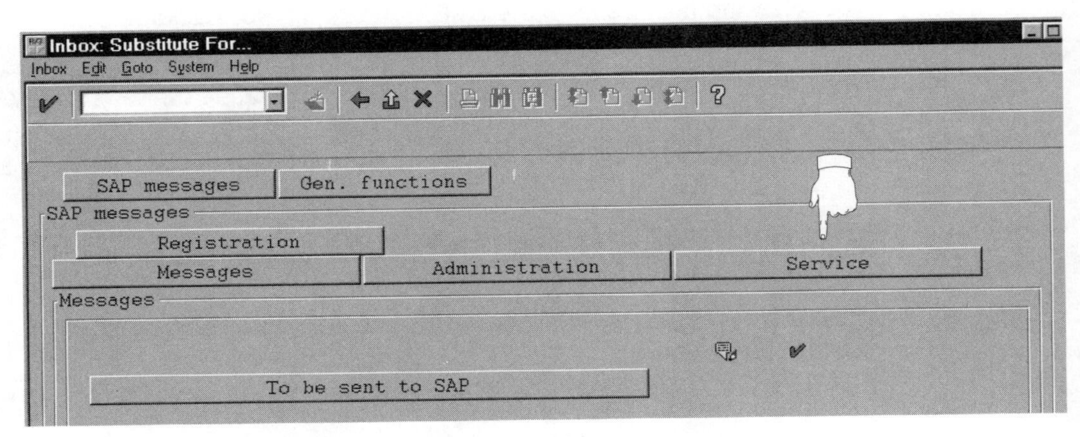

Figure 48. Requesting Hot Package Via OSS

2. Click on **Service** (shown in Figure 48).
3. Click on **SAP Patch Service**.

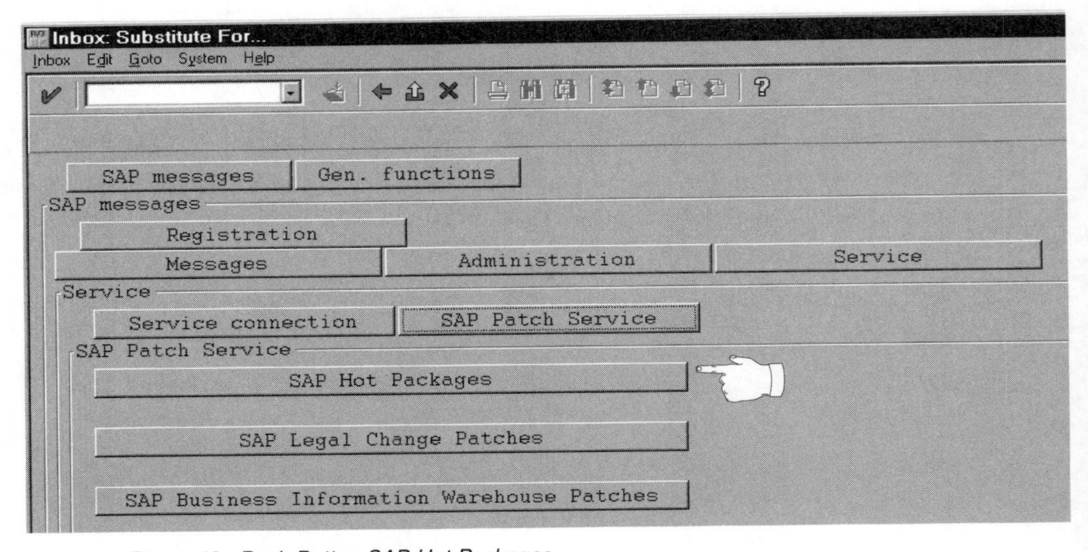

Figure 49. Push Button SAP Hot Packages

4. Click on **SAP Hot Packages** (shown in Figure 49). The screen entitled **List of SAP R/3 Hot Packages** is displayed:

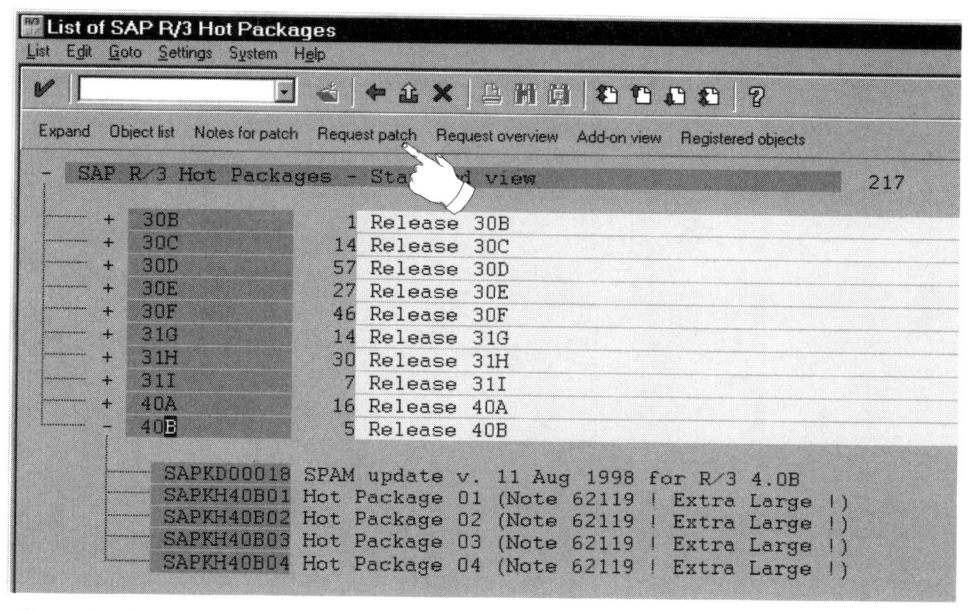

Figure 50. List of SAP R/3 Hot Packages for Selected Release

5. Double click on the **+** next to the appropriate release level of R/3. A list of the available fixes for the selected release is displayed. Select the Hot Packages you wish to obtain and click on **Request patch**.
6. Select the SAP system which will be receiving the Hot Package and enter the system ID before the installation number.
7. Click **Continue**.

You can now log on to your R/3 System, download the Hot Package and apply it to your system.

Detailed documentation is available in the *OSS note 33525* and in the OSS documentation, *OSS User Guide*, about the steps that must be followed during the application of Hot Packages by the SAP Patch Manager using the transaction **SPAM**. You may also access the SAP Patch Manager (SPAM) by choosing the following menu path: **Tools->ABAP Workbench, Utilities-> Maintenance->Patches**. The SAP Patch Manager screen is displayed:

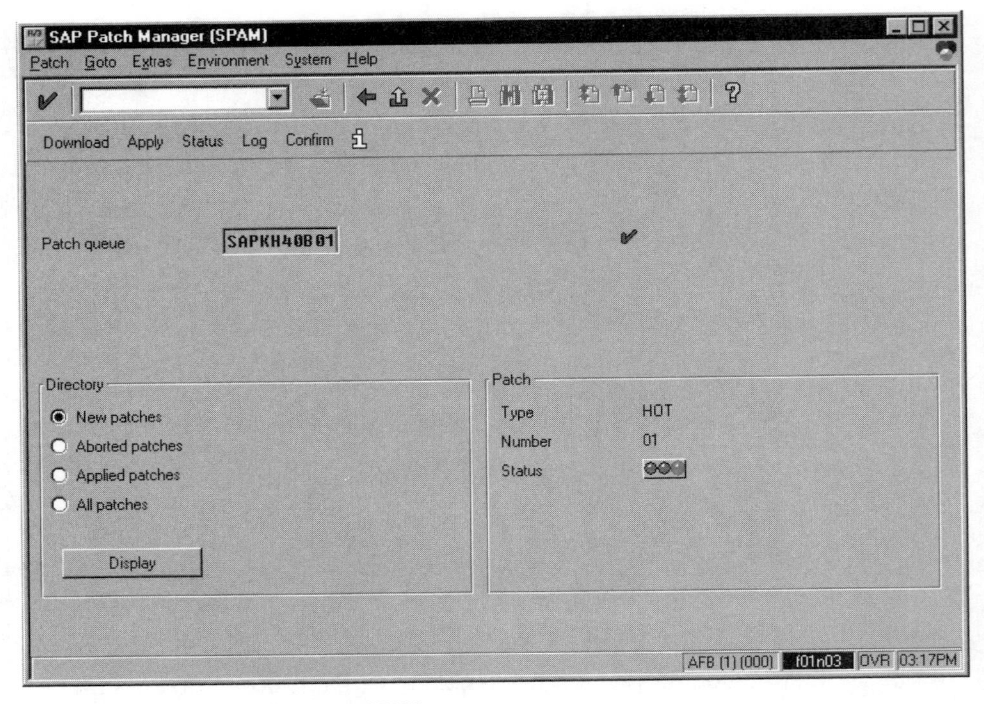

Figure 51. SAP Patch Manager - SPAM

If you do not download patches from OSS, SAP will periodically send a Hot Package Collection which contains all Hot Packages available at that time. It is automatically sent to every customer with a correction release.

2.9.6 R/3 Kernel Patches

Similar to the Hot Package, the creation of a new sub-version is carried out during a kernel release; every error which leads to a kernel patch being created raises what is known as the patch level. The patch level is output together with the kernel update level.

For every patch level, an explanatory line is stated in the output with reference to an OSS note. Since the patch level counter is raised across platforms, it may happen that some kernel changes do not affect your platform. To import a new kernel patch proceed according to the OSS *note 19466*.

A kernel fix patch may be obtained via FTP to any SAP FTP server. The server, sapserv3, is the master SAP server. Objects on sapserv3 are replicated regularly to all of the other SAP servers. The update is generally done once a day.

To be able to FTP to any SAP FTP server, you must have the TCP/IP infrastructure and permissions to connect to OSS. You must also know the TCP/IP address of the SAP FTP server.

The following table contains a list of the available SAP FTP servers, the regions supported, and the server location:

Table 15. List of SAP FTP Servers, Primary Geography, and Server Locations

SAP FTP Server	Primary Geography	Location of SAP FTP Server
sapserv3	Europe and Africa	Waldorf, Germany
sapserv4	America	Foster City, USA
sapserv5	Asia - Japan	Tokyo, Japan
sapserv6	Asia - Australia	Sydney, Australia
sapserv7	Asia	Singapore, Singapore

Figure 52 depicts the contents of the sapserv3 FTP server:

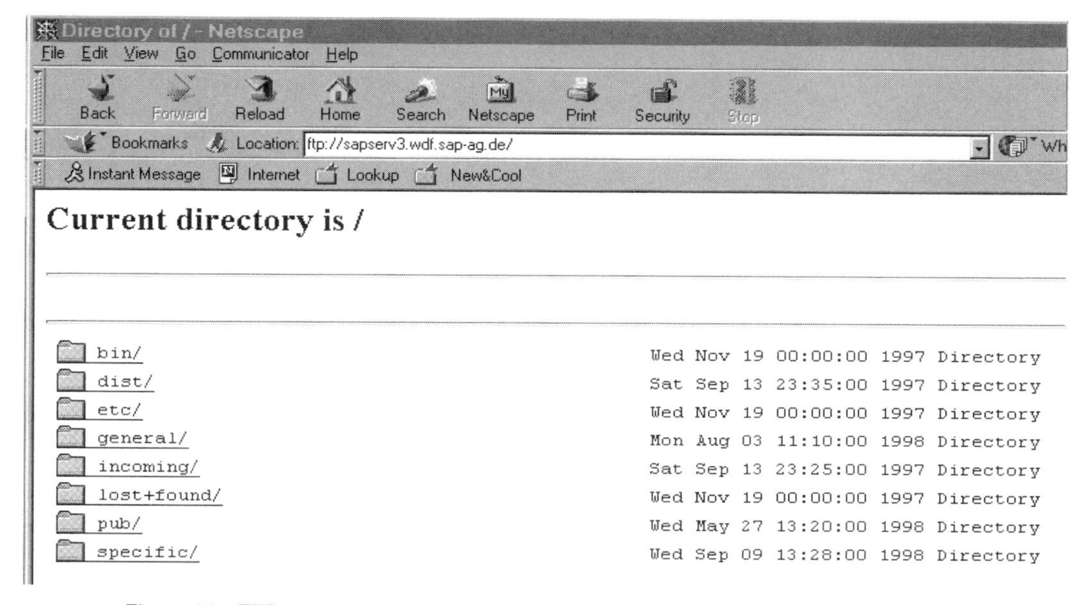

Figure 52. FTP to sapserv3.wdf.sap-ag.de

Once you connect to the sapserv FTP server, select the appropriate directory, locate the desired patches, and download them to your SAP R/3 system. For further details about downloading a Kernel fix patch from an SAP FTP server, read the OSS note 19466 and refer to “Applying Hot Packages” on page 246.

Chapter 3. Installing and Configuring R/3 and DB2 UDB on AIX

This chapter details the tasks necessary to install and configure DB2 UDB Version 5 and SAP R/3 4.0B on AIX 4.2.1. It also covers the creation of the AIX Journaled File Systems (JFS) needed for the installation. It is assumed that AIX has already been installed by your local AIX support group responsible for this activity.

3.1 Operating System Prerequisites

It is very important to review the manual supplied with the R/3 installation kit entitled *R/3 Installation on UNIX OS Dependencies*. The steps it outlines need to be performed prior to any attempt at installation. The installation kit also includes a *Check List of Installation Requirements* that should be reviewed. You should also download the OSS notes mentioned in the Installation Guide and review them. They may contain important changes to installation procedures and any known problems.

3.1.1 Hardware Requirements

Before you start the installation, ensure that the following hardware is available:

1. A CD-ROM drive.
2. A tape drive or access to IBM ADSTAR Distributed Storage Manager (ADSM).
3. At least 256 MB of RAM. This can be checked by entering either of the following two commands. Note that the first command may not show you the size on some systems. If this is the case on your system, use the second command.

```
lscfg | grep mem
lsattr -l sys0 -E | grep realmem
```

4. At least 16 GB of external disk space. SAP recommends that 8 physical disks should be used for optimum installation.
5. Disk space for swap space equal to 3 times RAM plus 500MB. If possible, this should be allocated from internal disk space.

3.1.2 Software Requirements

You should also ensure that the following software is installed:

1. The minimum AIX level for SAP R/3 V4.0B is AIX 4.2.1 or higher (AIX 4.3.0 may be used). The level can be checked using the command:

```
oslevel
```

2. AIX requires a language library for each language installed and used by SAP. A locale must be installed for each language you run.
3. Verify that the en_US locale is installed using one of the two commands below. The first command checks specifically for the en_US locale, and the second lists all installed locales. You also need to ensure that you have the German locale installed.

```
lslpp -l bos.loc.iso.en_US
locale -a
```

4. Verify that C SET++ is installed at level 3.1.4.8 or higher using this command:

```
lslpp -l xlC.rte
```

5. Verify that NFS is installed using this command:

```
lslpp -l bos.net.nfs.*
```

6. The AIX performance product perfagent is required by the SAP statistics program, saposcol. Verify perfagent is installed using this command:

```
lslpp -l perfagent.server
```

If any of these software products are not installed, you should request that your AIX support organization install them.

3.2 Installing DB2 UDB

Install the DB2 UDB code provided in the SAP installation kit from the CD entitled DB2 Common Server. You must be logged in as the root user to perform this task.

1. The installation of this product requires about 150MB of space in /usr/lpp/db2_05_00. You should verify that you have ample space available in the rootvg volume group or the /usr filesystem. To check the space, enter one of these commands:

```
lsvg rootvg
df -k /usr
```

   Check the FREE PPs field if using the lsvg command (Figure 53). Check the Free column value if using the df command.

```
f01n06:/ > lsvg rootvg
VOLUME GROUP:     rootvg          VG IDENTIFIER:    000203627ecde456
VG STATE:         active          PP SIZE:          4 megabyte(s)
VG PERMISSION:    read/write      TOTAL PPs:        267 (1068 megabytes)
MAX LVs:          256             FREE PPs:         2 (8 megabytes)
LVs:              11              USED PPs:         265 (1060 megabytes)
OPEN LVs:         10              QUORUM:           2
TOTAL PVs:        1               VG DESCRIPTORS:   2
STALE PVs:        0               STALE PPs         0
ACTIVE PVs:       1               AUTO ON:          yes
f01n06:/ >
```

Figure 53. Using lsvg to Check for Space

2. The database software must be unpacked to a temporary file system for installation. Create a file system of 500 MB called /tmp/DB2. If required, see section “Creating Filesystems” on page 100 for more details on how to create filesystems.
3. Change directory to /tmp/DB2.

4. Assuming that the DB2 Common Server CD is mounted on /sapcd, enter this command:

```
/sapcd/unix/aix/car -xvf /sapcd/unix/aix/db2aix.car
```

This command will create the directories DBSW and FIXPACK in /tmp/DB2.

5. Change directory to /tmp/DB2/DBSW.
6. To start the DB2 UDB for AIX installation process, issue this command:

```
./db2setup
```

The initial screen of the DB2 Installer is displayed:

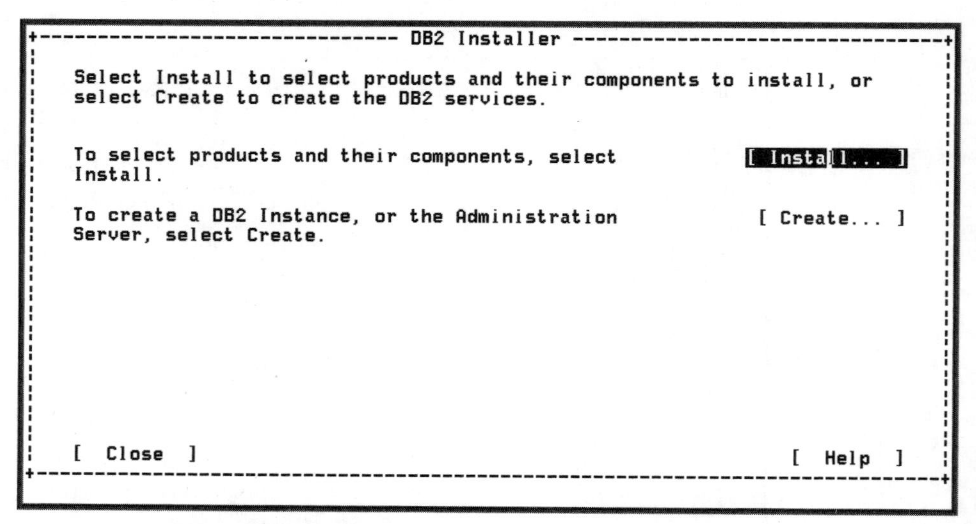

Figure 54. DB2 Installer - Initial Screen

7. Press **Enter** when your cursor is over the **Install** option. The Install DB2 V5 screen is displayed:

```
+------------------------------ Install DB2 V5 -------------------------------+
:                                                                             :
:  Select the products you are licensed to install. Your Proof of             :
:  Entitlement and License Information booklet identify the products for      :
:  which you are licensed.                                                    :
:                                                                             :
:  To see the preselected components or customize the selection, select       :
:  Customize for the product.                                                 :
:  [ ] DB2 Client Application Enabler                       : Customize... :  :
:  : : DB2 UDB Workgroup Edition                            : Customize... :  :
:  [*] DB2 UDB Enterprise Edition                           [ Customize... ]  :
:  : : DB2 Connect Enterprise Edition                       : Customize... :  :
:  : : DB2 UDB Extended Enterprise Edition                  : Customize... :  :
:  : : DB2 Software Developer's Kit                         : Customize... :  :
:                                                                             :
:  To choose a language for the following components, select Customize for    :
:  the product.                                                               :
:      DB2 Product Messages                                 [ Customize... ]  :
:      DB2 Product Library                                  [ Customize... ]  :
:                                                                             :
:  [   OK   ]                 [ Cancel ]                        [  Help  ]    :
+-----------------------------------------------------------------------------+
```

Figure 55. Install DB2 V5 on AIX

8. Select **DB2 UDB Enterprise Edition** by moving your cursor to the appropriate box and pressing **Enter**. The enter key selects and deselects items in this screen.
9. Tab to **OK** and press **Enter**. The Create DB2 Services screen is displayed:

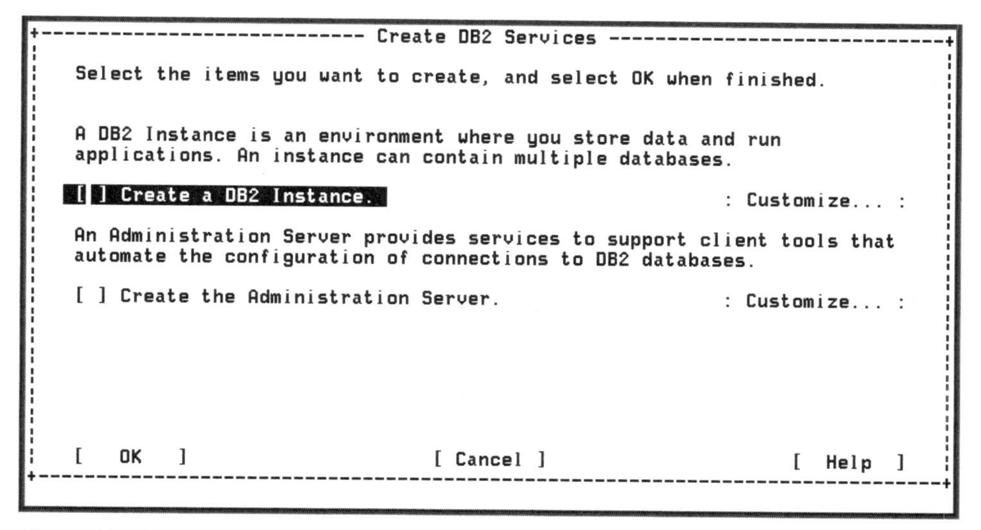
Create DB2 Services
Select the items you want to create, and select OK when finished.
A DB2 Instance is an environment where you store data and run applications. An instance can contain multiple databases.
[ ] Create a DB2 Instance.
: Customize... :
An Administration Server provides services to support client tools that automate the configuration of connections to DB2 databases.
[ ] Create the Administration Server.
: Customize... :
[OK]
[Cancel]
[Help]

Figure 56. Create DB2 Services

10. You do not need to create either the DB2 instance or the Administration Server (DAS) instance at this stage. Tab to **OK** and press **Enter** to

continue. Press **Enter** when you see the warning messages about the creation of the DB2 and DAS instances.The list of product components to be installed is displayed:

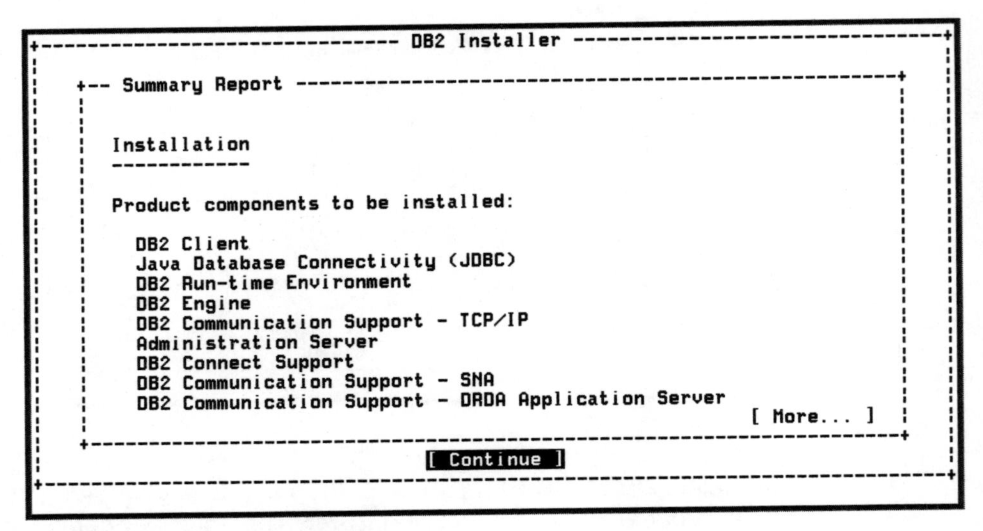
```
+------------------------------ DB2 Installer ------------------------------+
|                                                                           |
|  +-- Summary Report ---------------------------------------------------+  |
|  |                                                                     |  |
|  |                                                                     |  |
|  |  Installation                                                       |  |
|  |  ------------                                                       |  |
|  |                                                                     |  |
|  |  Product components to be installed:                                |  |
|  |                                                                     |  |
|  |    DB2 Client                                                       |  |
|  |    Java Database Connectivity (JDBC)                                |  |
|  |    DB2 Run-time Environment                                         |  |
|  |    DB2 Engine                                                       |  |
|  |    DB2 Communication Support - TCP/IP                               |  |
|  |    Administration Server                                            |  |
|  |    DB2 Connect Support                                              |  |
|  |    DB2 Communication Support - SNA                                  |  |
|  |    DB2 Communication Support - DRDA Application Server              |  |
|  |                                                      [ More... ]    |  |
|  +---------------------------------------------------------------------+  |
|                               [ Continue ]                                |
+---------------------------------------------------------------------------+
```

Figure 57. DB2 Installer - Summary Report

11.Tab to **Continue** and press **Enter**. A pop-up panel is displayed which gives you an option to cancel. Press **Enter** to start the installation. As each component is installed, a popup panel is displayed with the name of the component. When the installation has completed, a pop-up panel tells you if the installation was successful or not. Press **Enter** to display the status report:

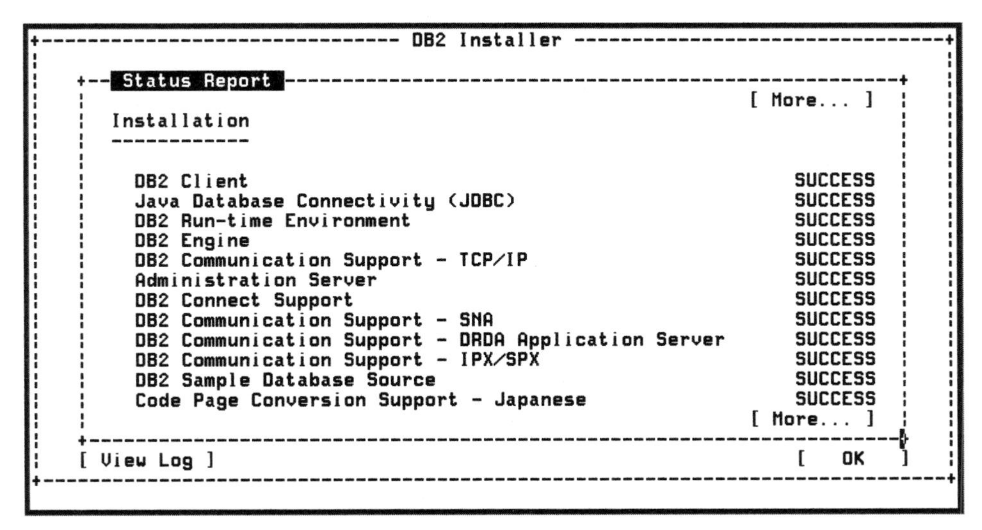

Figure 58. DB2 Installer - Status Report

12. If the installation was not successful, you should tab to **View Log** and press **Enter** to display the log of the installation.

13. If there were no errors, tab to **OK** and press **Enter**. This should bring you back to the main DB2 Installer screen where you can continue the installation.

3.2.1 Installing DB2 HTML Documentation

You may now install the DB2 HTML documentation if you wish.

1. From the DB2 Installer initial screen, tab to **Install** and press **Enter**:

```
+------------------------------ Install DB2 V5 -------------------------------+
|                                                                             |
|   Select the products you are licensed to install. Your Proof of            |
|   Entitlement and License Information booklet identify the products for     |
|   which you are licensed.                                                   |
|                                                                             |
|   To see the preselected components or customize the selection, select     |
|   Customize for the product.                                                |
|   :*: DB2 Client Application Enabler                    [ Customize... ]    |
|   : : DB2 UDB Workgroup Edition                         : Customize... :    |
|   [ ] DB2 UDB Enterprise Edition                        : Customize... :    |
|   : : DB2 Connect Enterprise Edition                    : Customize... :    |
|   : : DB2 UDB Extended Enterprise Edition               : Customize... :    |
|   : : DB2 Software Developer's Kit                      : Customize... :    |
|                                                                             |
|   To choose a language for the following components, select Customize for  |
|   the product.                                                              |
|       DB2 Product Messages                              [ Customize... ]    |
|       DB2 Product Library                               [ Customize... ]    |
|                                                                             |
|                                                                             |
|   [   OK   ]                 [ Cancel ]                     [  Help  ]      |
+-----------------------------------------------------------------------------+
```

Figure 59. Install DB2 V5 HTML documentation

2. Tab to the **Customize** entry next to **DB2 Product Library** and press **Enter**. A pop-up panel is displayed:

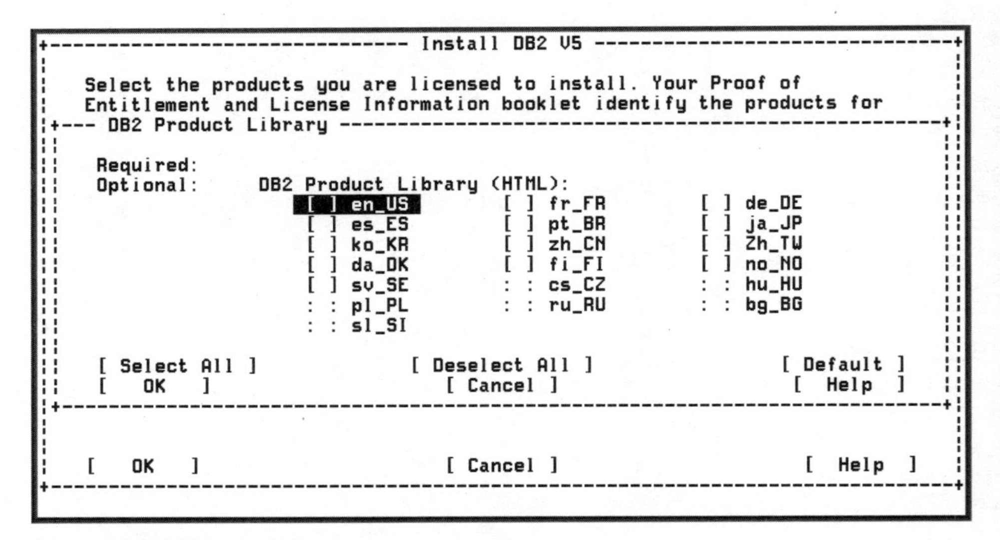

```
+------------------------------ Install DB2 V5 -------------------------------+
|                                                                             |
|   Select the products you are licensed to install. Your Proof of            |
|   Entitlement and License Information booklet identify the products for     |
|+--- DB2 Product Library ---------------------------------------------------+|
||                                                                          ||
||   Required:                                                              ||
||   Optional:      DB2 Product Library (HTML):                             ||
||                     [ ] en_US          [ ] fr_FR          [ ] de_DE      ||
||                     [ ] es_ES          [ ] pt_BR          [ ] ja_JP      ||
||                     [ ] ko_KR          [ ] zh_CN          [ ] Zh_TW      ||
||                     [ ] da_DK          [ ] fi_FI          [ ] no_NO      ||
||                     [ ] sv_SE          : : cs_CZ          : : hu_HU      ||
||                     : : pl_PL          : : ru_RU          : : bg_BG      ||
||                     : : sl_SI                                            ||
||                                                                          ||
||   [ Select All ]            [ Deselect All ]              [ Default ]    ||
||   [    OK    ]                [ Cancel ]                  [  Help  ]     ||
|+--------------------------------------------------------------------------+|
|                                                                             |
|                                                                             |
|   [   OK   ]                 [ Cancel ]                     [  Help  ]      |
+-----------------------------------------------------------------------------+
```

Figure 60. DB2 Product Library

3. Tab to the entry for your required language and press **Enter**. Tab to **OK** and press **Enter** to take you back to the Install DB2 V5 screen.
4. Tab to **OK** and press **Enter** to display the summary report:

```
+-------------------------------- DB2 Installer --------------------------------+
|                                                                                 |
|  +-- Summary Report ---------------------------------------------------+      |
|  |                                                                      |      |
|  |                                                                      |      |
|  | Installation                                                         |      |
|  | ------------                                                         |      |
|  |                                                                      |      |
|  | Product components to be installed:                                  |      |
|  |                                                                      |      |
|  |   DB2 Product Library (HTML) -- English                              |      |
|  |   Uncompress DB2 Product Library (HTML) -- English                   |      |
|  |                                                                      |      |
|  | Note:                                                                |      |
|  |                                                                      |      |
|  | * The log file is in /tmp/db2setup.log.                              |      |
|  |                                                                      |      |
|  |                                                                      |      |
|  +----------------------------------------------------------------------+      |
|                               [ Continue ]                                      |
+---------------------------------------------------------------------------------+
```

Figure 61. DB2 Installer - Summary Report

5. When you press **Enter** to continue, a pop-up panel is displayed which gives you an option to cancel. Press **Enter** to start the installation.

3.2.2 Verifying the DB2 License

You should verify that the DB2 license (nodelock file) is correctly installed. There should be a symbolic link from the actual nodelock file location in /var/ifor to /usr/lib/netls/conf. You can check that this link is created using the `ls -l` command on the file in /usr/lib/netls/conf. If this symbolic link has not been created for you, create it now using the following command:

```
ln -s /var/ifor/nodelock /usr/lib/netls/conf/nodelock
```

3.2.3 Installing the DB2 Service Pack

The final step in the DB2 UDB installation process is to install any fixes for DB2 provided on the CDs contained in the SAP installation kit. These fixes, if present, should be installed before using DB2 UDB. You should always use the fixes provided by SAP.

To install a DB2 UDB for AIX service pack, you need to be logged in as root. These are the steps to follow:

1. From smitty, choose:

   Software Installation and Maintenance
   ->Install and Update Software
   ->Install and Update from LATEST Available Software

2. In the field: INPUT device / directory for software, enter **/tmp/DB2/FIXPAK**.

3. In the field: SOFTWARE to install, press **F4** to display a list of software. Select the following entries:

   - DB2 Connect
   - DB2 Communications Support for TCP/IP
   - Administration Server
   - DB2 Engine
   - DB2 Run-time Environment
   - License Support for DB2 UDB Enterprise Edition

3.2.4 Installing DB2 UDB as a Database Client Only

You only need to install DB2 as a database client if you are installing a system which will:

- Only host the Central Instance and not the DB2 database instance, or
- Only host a dialog instance

Use the same procedure to install DB2, but select DB2 Client Application Enabler. You also use the same procedure to apply the Service Pack, but only select the **DB2 Client Application Enabler** from the software list.

3.3 Filesystems and AIX Configuration

The next step is to configure some filesystems on your AIX system. We also cover other AIX configuration tasks, such as user characteristics and Portable Streams Environment (PSE).

3.3.1 Configuring Paging Space

You must setup enough paging space for the SAP/DB2 environment. Although we cover the basic steps here, it is advisable to have an AIX system administrator do this work for you.

1. First determine the memory installed on your system by using one of the following two commands:

```
lscfg | grep mem
lsattr -l sys0 -E | grep realmem
```

The first command (**lscfg**) may not show anything in the memory field on some AIX systems; in this case use the second command (**lsattr**). The results for an **lscfg** command are shown here:

```
f01n03:/ > lscfg | grep mem
+ mem9                00-0A              32 MB Memory Card
+ mem3                00-0B              32 MB Memory Card
+ mem8                00-0C              32 MB Memory Card
+ mem2                00-0D              32 MB Memory Card
+ mem7                00-0E              32 MB Memory Card
+ mem1                00-0F              32 MB Memory Card
+ mem6                00-0G              32 MB Memory Card
+ mem0                00-0H              32 MB Memory Card
f01n03:/ >
```

Figure 62. Check Installed Memory

2. Next display the amount of paging space currently on your system using this command:

```
lsps -a
```

Here is an example of the output from this command:

```
f01n06:/ > lsps -a
Page Space  Physical Volume   Volume Group    Size   %Used  Active  Auto  Type
paging04    hdisk1            notesvg        100MB      24     yes   yes    lv
paging03    hdisk0            rootvg         100MB      24     yes   yes    lv
paging00    hdisk1            notesvg         80MB      34     yes   yes    lv
paging01    hdisk1            notesvg        120MB      23     yes   yes    lv
paging02    hdisk0            rootvg          64MB      43     yes   yes    lv
hd6         hdisk0            rootvg          80MB      52     yes   yes    lv
f01n06:/ >
```

Figure 63. Checking Paging Space

3. The total space allocated to paging should be set to at least 3 times RAM plus 500 MB. If you need to increase the total paging space, use the smitty utility. You may wish to confer with your AIX system administrator regarding any specific policies on paging space creation.
4. To add a paging space, enter **`smitty lvm`**, then select **Paging Space ->Add Another Paging Space**.
5. Choose the volume group to be used for the paging space.The following screen is displayed:

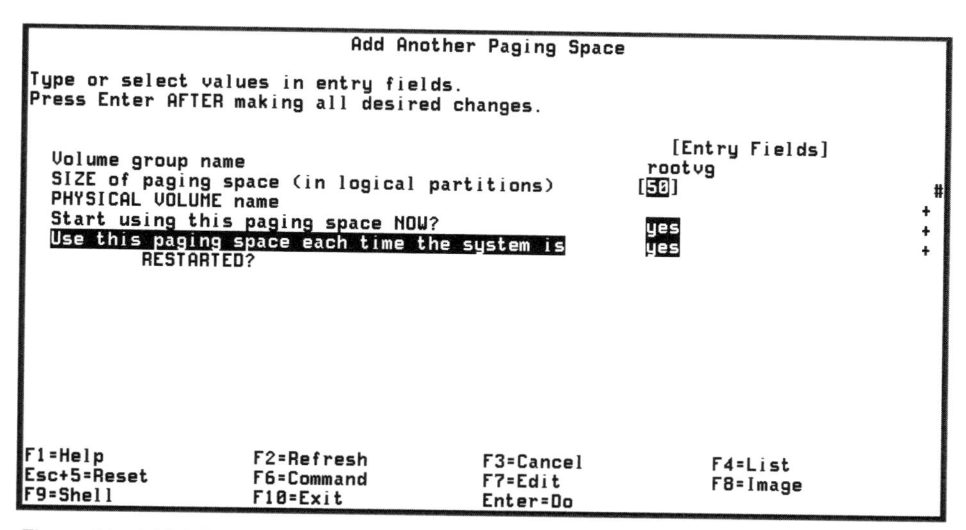

Figure 64. Add A Paging Space

6. Fill in the size in physical partitions (not MB) of your paging space. To determine the amount of space available for your use, you can use the lsvg <vgname> command on the volume group you want to use for this paging space.
7. If required, choose the disk to use for your paging space.
8. For the field: Start using this paging space now, select **yes**.
9. For the field: Use this paging space each time the system is restarted, select **yes**.

3.3.2 Changing User Characteristics

The next step is to ensure that the characteristics of some of the primary users required for this installation are correct. You need to make sure the user parameters of root, <SID>adm, sapr3 and <DB2>adm, and db2as are set to suggested values as given in the *OS Dependencies* manual. The root id should be adjusted before the installation is started. The SAP and DB2 userids are created during the installation of R/3. At the point in the installation just prior to the start of the database load, the characteristics of these userids may be changed. To make this change, proceed as follows:

1. Enter `smitty users`, then select **Change/Show Characteristics of A User**.
2. Enter the User Name in the field provided and press **Enter**.

3. Page down until you see the field: Soft FILE size. Enter values as shown here:

```
                    Change / Show Characteristics of a User

Type or select values in entry fields.
Press Enter AFTER making all desired changes.

                                                       [Entry Fields]
[MORE...33]
  Password MIN. DIFFERENT characters                [0]                  #
  Password REGISTRY                                 []
  Soft FILE size                                    [4194302]            #
  Soft CPU time                                     [-1]
  Soft DATA segment                                 [524288]             #
  Soft STACK size                                   [512000]             #
  Soft CORE file size                               [100000]             #
  Hard FILE size                                    [4194302]            #
  Hard CPU time                                     [-1]
  Hard DATA segment                                 [524288]             #
  Hard STACK size                                   [512000]             #
  Hard CORE file size                               [100000]             #
  File creation UMASK                               [022]
[MORE...4]

F1=Help             F2=Refresh          F3=Cancel           F4=List
Esc+5=Reset         F6=Command          F7=Edit             F8=Image
F9=Shell            F10=Exit            Enter=Do
```

Figure 65. Change/Show User Characteristics

It is very important to set the umask setting of root to **022**. This is the last field in Figure 65. This will allow for the proper mount point permissions of the SAP and DB2 directories. Serious problems can result if permissions are too restrictive.

3.3.3 Creating Filesystems

There are a number of steps involved in creating the Journaled File Systems needed for the installation. Although we will cover the basic steps to accomplish this task it is advisable to have your AIX system administrator do this work.

A description of these filesystems can be found in the following locations:

- For the sapdata filesystem, look in the db tpl file on the SAP Kernel CD.
- For all other filesystems, refer to the *R/3 Installation on Unix* manual.

3.3.3.1 Creating Volume Group(s)

It is assumed that enough external disk space is attached to your system to install and run SAP. You should have at least eight external disks to install a base system that will perform well. These disks need to be included in a volume group. You can include all disks in 1 volume group or split them over several volume groups. The important point to remember is that there is a limit of 32 disks per volume group so it is advisable to create multiple volume groups to allow for future growth.

For our example, we will put 1 disk in the sapvg volume group as follows:

1. Enter `smitty vg`, then select **Add A Volume Group**.
2. Enter the Volume group name.
3. Choose the Physical Partition size using the tab key. When choosing the Physical Partition size, you should make the value large enough for any future disks that you may add to this volume group. If you need more information, contact your AIX administrator. You can also get information by pressing the F1 key when your cursor is positioned at this entry field.
4. Choose your Physical Volume Name. You can use the F4 key to generate a list.

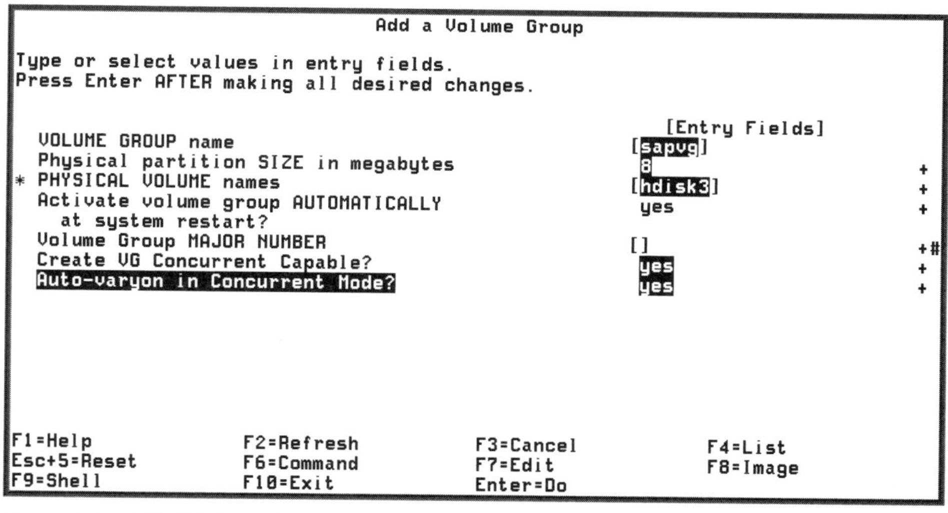

Figure 66. Add A Volume Group

5. Press **Enter** to create the volume group.

3.3.3.2 Creating Logical Volumes

For each filesystem that you wish to create, a corresponding logical volume should be created to enable the filesystem to be placed on specific disks in the volume group. The AIX Logical Volume Manager also allows the setup of logical volume mirroring (managed by the operating system) to support redundancy of critical data. It is critical that at least the on-line DB2 logs are mirrored and this will be accomplished in this step. Note that by creating the logical volumes to be used later, the administrator can control how the data is spread over multiple disks.

To create logical volumes:

1. Enter `smitty lvm`, then select **Logical Volumes ->Add A Logical Volume**.
2. Enter the volume group name. You can use F4 to generate a list.
3. Enter a logical volume name.
4. Enter the required number of logical partitions. This is calculated by the dividing the filesystem size by the physical partition size.
5. Enter a physical volume name or names. You can use F4 to generate a list.
6. Enter the number of copies for each logical partition. If you wish to mirror the logical volume, this value should be 2.

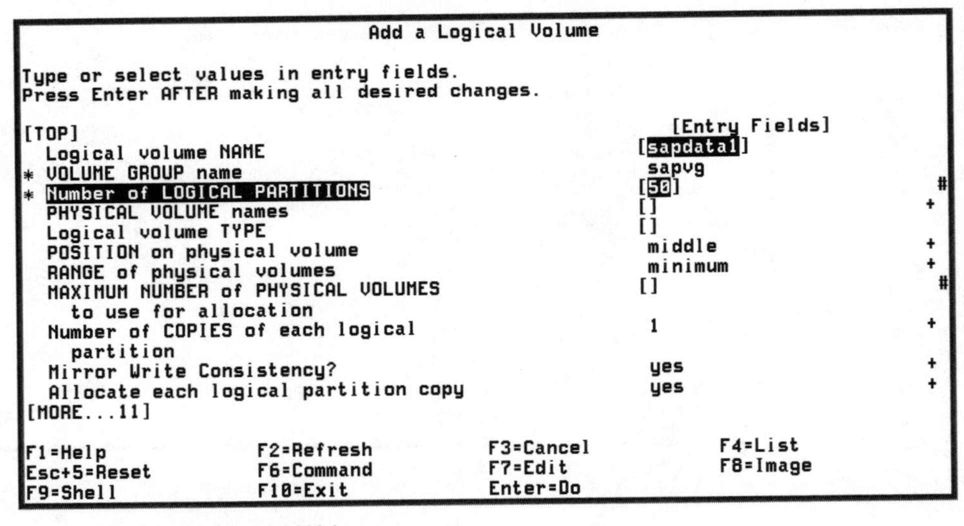

Figure 67. Create A Logical Volume

7. Repeat these steps for each logical volume you need to create.

3.3.3.3 Creating Filesystems

You are now ready to create the filesystems corresponding to the logical volumes you have just created. You should always refer to the Installation Guide provided in your SAP installation kit for information about required filesystems, as they can change between releases.

To create the filesystems, proceed as follows:

1. Enter **`smitty jfs`**, then select **Add a Journaled File System to Previously Defined Logical Volume-> Add a Standard Journaled File System**.

> **Note**
>
> If you are creating the JFS for /db2/<SID>/log_archive, choose the **Add a Compressed Journaled File System** option instead.

2. Use F4 to generate a list of logical volumes names and then choose one from this list.
3. Enter the path to use as the mount point.
4. For the field: mount automatically at system restart, select **yes** by using the tab key.

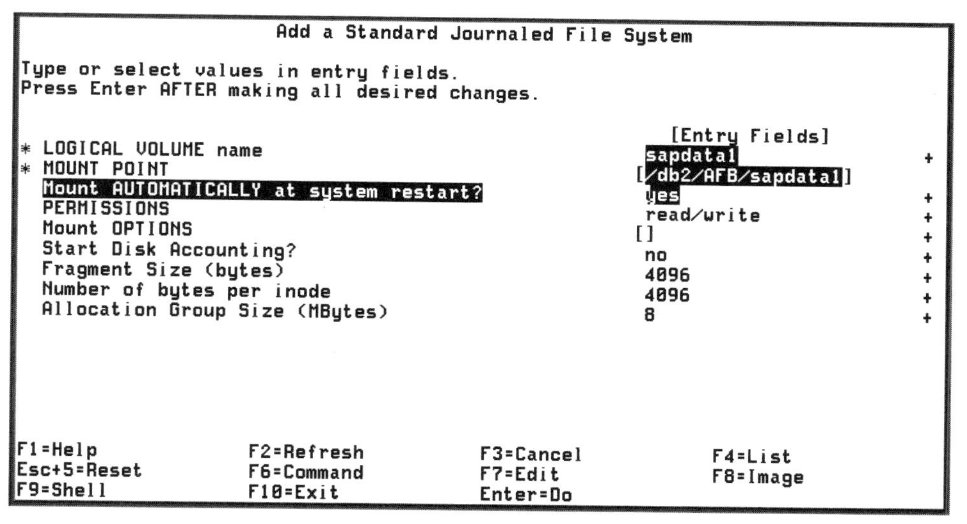

Figure 68. Create a JFS File System

5. Press **Enter** to create the filesystem.
6. Repeat the above steps for each filesystem to be created.
7. To make these filesystems available immediately, you should mount them manually. Enter **`smitty fs`**, then select **Mount a File System** for each file system.

A typical installation will have the following filesystems configured. The sizes indicated are suggestions and were used in this example installation. These sizes vary by release and also depend on your installation requirements. It is important to only use these as a guideline for a minimal system and refer to the aforementioned documentation when you perform an installation.

Table 16. R/3 Filesystems

Filesystem	**Size (MB)**
/tmp/install	50
/usr/sap/<SID>	500
/sapmnt/<SID>	400
/usr/sap/trans	500
/db2/<SID>	400
/db2/db2as	200
/db2/<SID>/log_dir	100
/db2/<SID>/log_archive	200
/db2/<SID>/log_retrieve	200
/db2/<SID>/sapdata1	250
/db2/<SID>/sapdata2	100
/db2/<SID>/sapdata3	100
/db2/<SID>/sapdata4	200
/db2/<SID>/sapdata5	300
/db2/<SID>/sapdata6	100

3.3.4 Enabling Portable Streams Environment (PSE)

PSE, a Streams Device Driver used by LAN devices as a communication protocol, is required by SAP.

To enable it at system start-up, run the command:

```
mkitab strload:2:once:/usr/sbin/strload
```

This will insert an entry in the /etc/inittab file that is read at system start-up. You can check the entry using the command:

```
lsitab strload
```

The output should be:

```
strload:2:once:/usr/sbin/strload
```

3.4 Installing SAP R/3 on AIX

There are two methods to install SAP R/3 on AIX:

1. Using a command line interface.
2. Using a graphical interface. This enables remote installation.

We will cover both methods in the following discussion beginning with the command line method.

3.4.1 Installing SAP R/3 Using a Command Line Interface

The following steps take you through an installation from the command line:

1. Mount the CD labeled SAP KERNEL.

   In our case the CD mount point was /sapcd.

2. Change directory to the install directory /tmp/install.

   The next step is to run the shell script that will copy the required installation code from the CD to the /tmp/install directory. The script that you run depends on the type of installation you wish to perform. There are five possible selections:

   - Central instance: /sapcd/UNIX/CENTRAL.SH
   - Central instance with database: /sapcd/UNIX/CENTRDB.SH
   - Dialog Instance: /sapcd/UNIX/DIALOG.SH
   - Database Instance: /sapcd/UNIX/DATABASE.SH
   - You may also install a Stand-alone Gateway but this requires the CD labeled PRESENTATION to be mounted. The script is /sapcd/UNIX/GATEWAY.SH.

In this example, we have chosen to install a central instance and database on the same physical machine. We proceed as follows:

3. Execute the appropriate script:

```
/sapcd/UNIX/CENTRDB.SH
```

This shell script copies the contents of the CD directory to the install directory /tmp/install. The following screen appears:

```
f01n03:/tmp/install > /sapcd/UNIX/CENTRDB.SH

   Welcome to CENTRDB instance installation.

   Please do first the preparations found in the manual
   'R/3 Installation on UNIX'

   All information needed for the installation is requested before
   the real setup is started. This script fills out the most important keys
   in the installation command file (express setup). After entering the
   requested values you have the possibility to customize the installation
   command file.

   The current directory is used as the installation directory.
   The following files will be copied into this directory:
   CENTRDB.TPL    : installation profile
   R3SETUP        : installation program

   Please answer the following questions. You can savely abort this script
   at any time with ^C and restart later.

Generating installation command file CENTRDB.R3S...
This can take some time.
```

Figure 69. Centrdb.Sh

4. When the script finishes the copy, it will ask if the installation should be continued. Answer **NO** as you will start the installation manually.

5. To begin the installation enter the command:

```
./R3SETUP -f CENTRDB.R3S
```

Note

If the installation aborts at any point you should refer to the CENTRDB.log in /tmp/install for error messages. After correcting the problem, you can then force R3SETUP to repeat the step by editing the file /tmp/install/CENTRDB.R3S. Locate the step where the failure occurred. In the field that says ACTION= type in **FORCEDDO**. This will force R3SETUP to re-do that step even though it had a previous error. If you wish to skip steps you may use **ACTION=SKIP**. Please be aware that you should not skip a step to resolve an error. This will cause problems later in the install. To restart R3SETUP issue the command string that you began your install with.

Answer the following prompts:

6. For the SAP system name, enter the three character name in **UPPER** case. Press **Enter**. Do **NOT** choose SAP for your name.
7. For the two-digit SAP system number, enter **00** and press **Enter**. If you already had another SAP system running on the same physical hardware you would use 01.
8. For the SAP mount directory, accept the default: **/sapmnt/<SID>** and press **Enter** to confirm.
9. For the hostname of the R/3 central instance machine, the default hostname is displayed. Press **Enter** if this is correct; otherwise enter the correct hostname.

Note

Make sure that your hostname is **NOT** longer than 8 characters. SAP will truncate the name if it is longer and the installation will fail.

10. For the hostname of the R/3 database server machine, the default hostname is displayed. Press **Enter** if this is correct; otherwise enter the correct hostname.
11. For DB2DB6EKEY, the default is <SID>hostname. In our example, this is AFBf01n03. Press **Enter**.
12. For the password of db2<sid>, enter a password and press **Enter**.
13. For the Installation working directory (keyword INSTALL_PATH), use **/tmp/install** and press **Enter**.

14.For the password of <SID>adm, enter a password and press **Enter**.

15.For the port number for the message server, the default value of **3600** is displayed. Check that the /etc/services file has no conflicting entries for port 3600 and press **Enter**.

16.For the group id (gid) of the sapsys group:

- If you want the R/3 installation program to create the R/3 related groups and users, press **Enter** to accept the defaults.
- If you have already created the R/3 related groups and users, enter the group id (gid) that you used and press **Enter**.

17.For the password of db2as, enter a password and press **Enter**.

18.For the password of sapr3, enter a password and press **Enter**.

19.For the user id (uid) of the <SID>adm user, press **Enter**.

20.If you wish to use raw devices for the database containers, answer yes to the next prompt. The default is [NO]. Press **Enter**.

21.If you need to use the R/2 connection facility, answer yes to the next prompt. The default is [NO]. Press **Enter**

22.Specify the amount of memory in MB to use for the R/3 Central Instance. This does not include memory for the database. The default is 128. Press **Enter**.

23.For DB6DBSERVICES_IND_DB6 and key: PORT [5912], press **Enter**.

24.For DB6PATH [/usr/lpp/db2_05_00/instance], press **Enter**.

25.For the empty directory to which the CD_ROM is to be copied, accept the default: /db2/<SID>/log_archive/CD4_DIR and press **Enter**. This directory will be created by R3SETUP. The program will copy the EXPORT CD1 to disk so that the database load does not have to stop to have CDs changed.

26.For the number of parallel R/3 load processes [3], press **Enter** to accept the value of 3.

27.For Valid platform [AIX], press **Enter**.

The installation program will now:

- Create subdirectories
- Extract executables
- Create the instance profile
- Complete the creation of users and groups

After the user creation is complete you should alter the user settings of the <SID>adm, sapr3, db2<SID> and db2as users as described in "Changing User Characteristics" on page 99.

The installation continues and you are prompted as follows:

28. Mount the CD labeled DB EXPORT CD1 and enter the CD mount point or press **Enter** to accept the default.

    The installation process will copy the contents of DB EXPORT CD 1 to the directory /db2/<SID>/log_archive/CD4_DIR.

> **Note**
>
> If you only have one CD drive to use during installation, the R3SETUP program will complete the copy of the CD and look for the SAP Kernel CD again. It will **NOT** find the SAP Kernel CD and will abort the install. You must remount the CD and restart R3SETUP.

The program will now create the DB2 instance and all table spaces. At the completion of the table space creation it will ask for the CD EXPORT CD2.

29. Insert the EXPORT CD 2. When the CD is accessible enter the CD path, or press **Enter** to accept the default.

    The load phase will now begin. This may take 8 to 16 hours depending on the hardware being used.

30. After the load is completed insert the Report Load CD. When the CD is accessible, enter the CD mount point, or press **Enter** to accept the default.

    This phase will generate all system objects. Following successful generation, you are then asked about the language used.

31. The next step concerns updating the MNLS Tables. If you use a language other than English, German or Western European, you should update the tables as per OSS note 045619. Press **Enter**.

This ends the R3SETUP installation processing.

At the completion of the installation, you must add the following profile parameters to the DEFAULT.PFL profile:

- zcsa/system_languages = E
- zcsa/installed_languages = DE or your installed languages
- login/system_client = xxx (your default client)

Transaction **RZ10** is used to maintain profile data. Refer to “Adjusting SAP R/3 Profiles after Installation” on page 131 for an example. You should also proceed to this example if you wish to skip over the next section, which covers installing SAP R/3 using the graphical interface.

3.4.2 Installing SAP R/3 Using a Graphical Interface

This installation method allows you to install SAP R/3 remotely. There are two components:

- INSTGUI - This graphical interface tool runs on a machine from which you control the installation.
- R3SETUP- This command line tool runs on the machine where SAP R/3 is to be installed.

These two components communicate over a TCP/IP port.

The INSTGUI Tool

There are 4 options that you can use when starting INSTGUI:

- -port <number>

  This is the port used to communicate with R3SETUP. 61312 is the default.
- -docupath <path>

  This is the path used for the on-line help. The default is ./doc
- -fontsize <size>

  This is the font size of 8 to 14, with 8 being the default.
- -help

The INSTGUI program must be started before R3SETUP. There are 2 views that INSTGUI may be started with.

1. STEP VIEW

   This Monitors each installation step and what it does. You may choose **HELP** for on-line help or **LOGS** for the log view.
2. LOG VIEW

   This Displays all R3SETUP messages written to the log file. You may choose **HELP** for on-line help or **Back** to change back to the step view.

3.4.2.1 Preparing to Use INSTGUI

To use INSTGUI, you must first copy the INSTGUI code onto the machine that will control the installation, and unpack the online help.

On **AIX**, perform the following steps:

1. Create an install directory or use /tmp/install.
2. Copy INSTGUI for the SAP Kernel CD to /tmp/install.
3. To unpack the on-line help, change directory to /tmp/install and enter this command:

```
/<CD>/UNIX/AIX/CAR -xvf /<CD>/DOCU/R3S_DOC.CAR
```

On **Windows NT/9x** machines, perform the following steps:

1. Create an install directory <DRIVE>:\tmp\install.
2. Copy INSTGUI for the SAP Kernel CD into <DRIVE>:\tmp\install
3. To unpack the on-line help, enter this command:

```
/<DRIVE>:\NT\<Platform>\CAR -xvf <DRIVE>:\DOCU\R3S_DOC.CAR
```

In "Installing a SAP Dialog Instance" on page 118, we cover an example of running the INSTGUI tool. Before doing this, you must complete some preparation tasks which are covered in the following section.

3.4.3 Preparing to Install a Dialog Instance

Some directories need to be shared between the central instance and dialog instance (or application server) machines. Make the following three NFS mounts on the dialog instance machine:

1. Mount /usr/sap/trans from the Central Instance machine on mount point /usr/sap/trans.
2. Mount /sapmnt/<SID> from the Central Instance machine on mount point /sapmnt/<SID>.
3. Mount /tmp/DB2 from the database machine (or Central Instance if they are on the same machine) on mount point /tmp/DB2.

3.4.3.1 Creating NFS Mounts and Paging Spaces

To create the NFS mounts:

1. Grant permission from the Central Instance/Database Machine (where the filesystems involved physically reside) to the Application Server machine that will NFS mount them.

Enter **smitty nfs**, then select **Network File System (NFS)->Add A Directory to Exports List**.

If an export already exists, choose the **Change/Show Attributes of an Exported Directory** option instead.

Fill in the required information as shown in the following figure and press **Enter**.

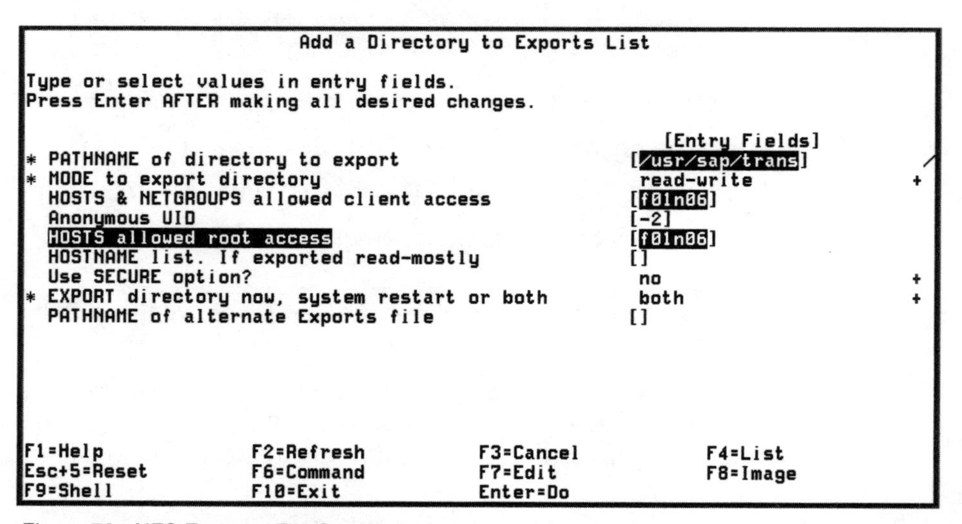

```
                         Add a Directory to Exports List

Type or select values in entry fields.
Press Enter AFTER making all desired changes.

                                                         [Entry Fields]
* PATHNAME of directory to export                      [/usr/sap/trans]
* MODE to export directory                              read-write          +
  HOSTS & NETGROUPS allowed client access              [f01n06]
  Anonymous UID                                        [-2]
  HOSTS allowed root access                            [f01n06]
  HOSTNAME list. If exported read-mostly               []
  Use SECURE option?                                    no                  +
* EXPORT directory now, system restart or both          both                +
  PATHNAME of alternate Exports file                   []

F1=Help            F2=Refresh          F3=Cancel           F4=List
Esc+5=Reset        F6=Command          F7=Edit             F8=Image
F9=Shell           F10=Exit            Enter=Do
```

Figure 70. NFS Export a File System

2. After you have exported the required filesystems, you must mount them to the machine that will be used as the Application Server as follows:

   Enter **smitty nfs**, then select **Network File System (NFS)->Add a Filesystem for mounting**.

   Fill in the required information as shown in the figure below and press **Enter**.

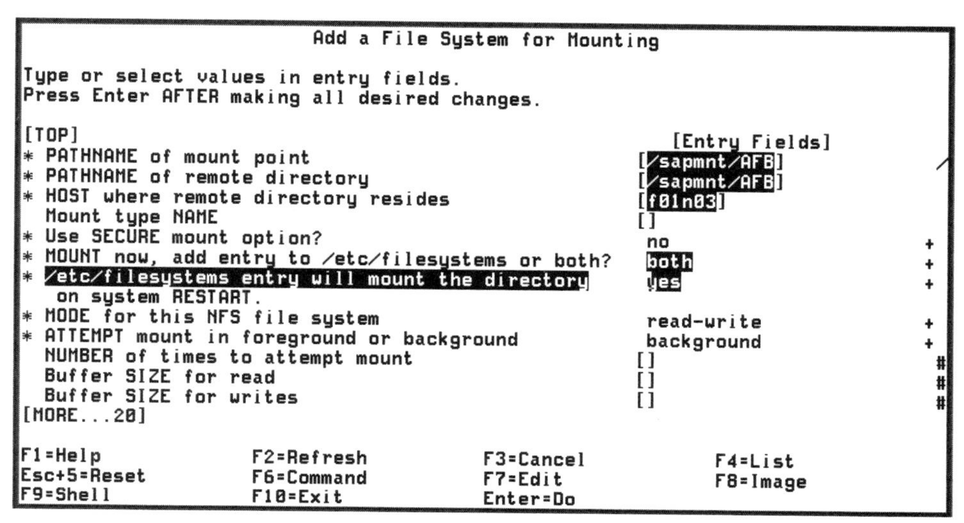

Add a File System for Mounting
Type or select values in entry fields.
Press Enter AFTER making all desired changes.
[TOP] [Entry Fields]
* PATHNAME of mount point [/sapmnt/AFB]
* PATHNAME of remote directory [/sapmnt/AFB]
* HOST where remote directory resides [f01n03]
Mount type NAME []
* Use SECURE mount option? no +
* MOUNT now, add entry to /etc/filesystems or both? both +
* /etc/filesystems entry will mount the directory on system RESTART. yes +
* MODE for this NFS file system read-write +
* ATTEMPT mount in foreground or background background +
NUMBER of times to attempt mount [] #
Buffer SIZE for read [] #
Buffer SIZE for writes [] #
[MORE...20]
F1=Help F2=Refresh F3=Cancel F4=List
Esc+5=Reset F6=Command F7=Edit F8=Image
F9=Shell F10=Exit Enter=Do

Figure 71. Mount an NFS File System

3. Create the following local Journaled File Systems:
   - /usr/sap/<SID> of size 400 MB
   - /db2/<SID> of size 400 MB
   - /tmp/install of size 50 MB

   If you need more details about creating filesystems, see “Creating Filesystems” on page 100.

4. Check the memory and paging space requirements as indicated “Hardware Requirements” on page 87.

3.4.3.2 Creating Groups and Users

To avoid problems with the dialog server installation, the required groups and users should be created manually. Be sure that the definitions exactly match those that were created at the Central/Database instance (verify the uid and gid values before creation). Also be sure that the file system permissions for the NFS mounted directory /sapmnt/<SID> are 755.

The groups to create are:

- sapsys
- db2asgrp
- sysadm
- sysctrl

The users to create are:

- <SID>adm
- db2<SID>

Use the following paths to create these groups and users:

- Enter `smitty users`, then select **Add a User**.
- Enter `smitty groups`, then select **Add a Group**.

To check that the uid and gid are correct, use these commands:

```
grep <username> /etc/passwd
grep <groupname> /etc/group
```

3.4.3.3 Installing DB2 Client Application Enabler

To install the DB2 CAE, use a similar procedure as for DB2 Enterprise Edition (“Installing DB2 UDB” on page 89):

1. Select DB2 Client Application Enabler by pressing **Enter** in the appropriate box:

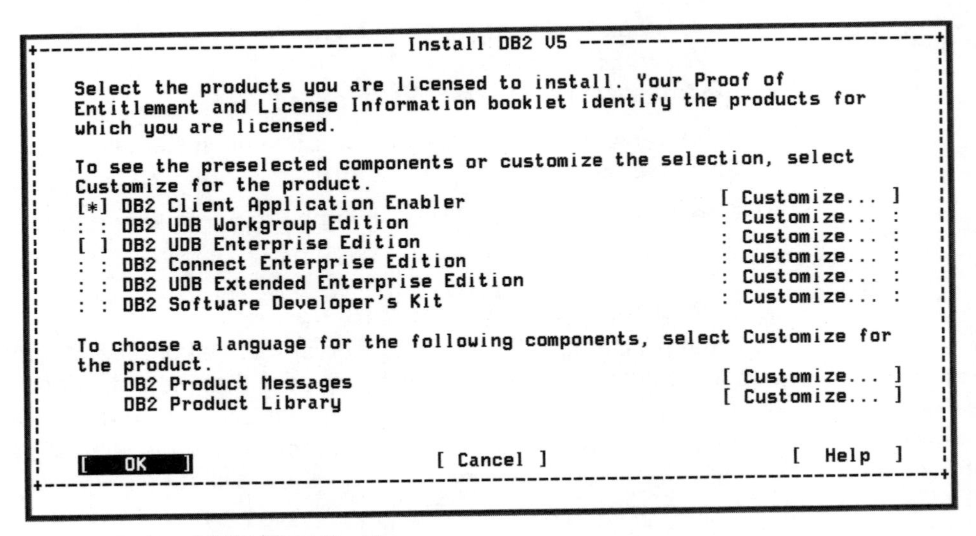

Figure 72. Install DB2 Client Enabler

2. Tab to **OK** and press **Enter**.

3. In the next panel, do **NOT** select Create a Database instance or the Administration Server:

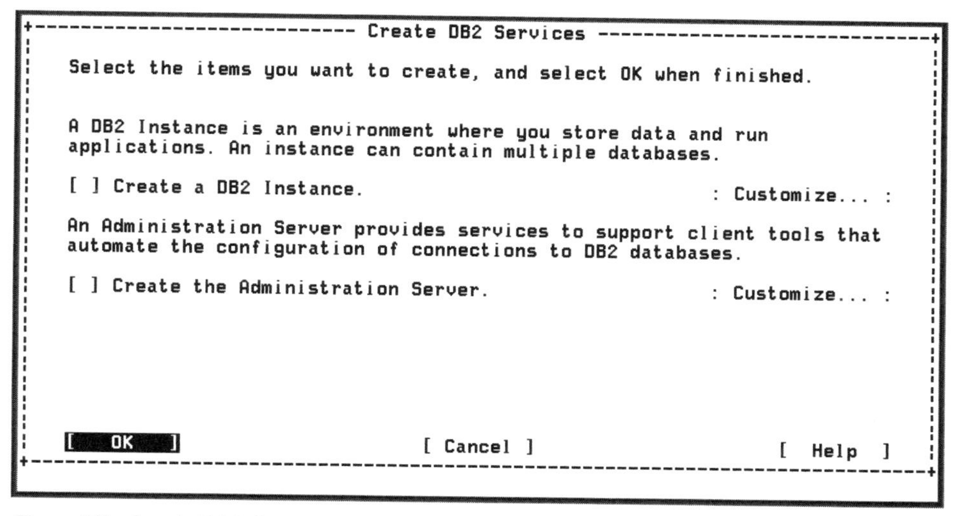

Create DB2 Services
Select the items you want to create, and select OK when finished.
A DB2 Instance is an environment where you store data and run applications. An instance can contain multiple databases.
[ ] Create a DB2 Instance.
: Customize... :
An Administration Server provides services to support client tools that automate the configuration of connections to DB2 databases.
[ ] Create the Administration Server.
: Customize... :
[OK]
[Cancel]
[Help]

Figure 73. Create DB2 Services Screen

4. Tab to **OK** and press **Enter**.

5. A warning message pops up which notifies you that an INSTANCE has not been created:

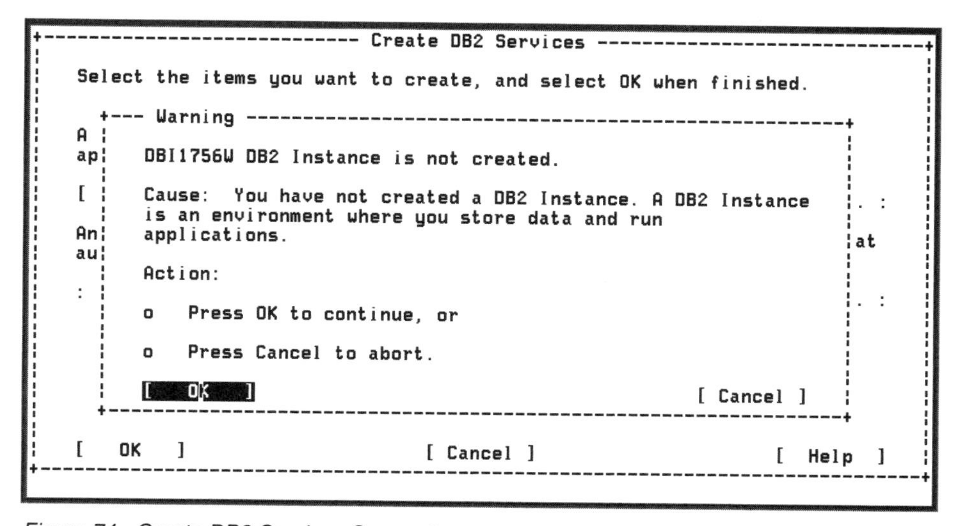

Create DB2 Services
Select the items you want to create, and select OK when finished.
Warning
DBI1756W DB2 Instance is not created.
Cause: You have not created a DB2 Instance. A DB2 Instance is an environment where you store data and run applications.
Action:
o Press OK to continue, or
o Press Cancel to abort.
[OK]
[Cancel]
[OK]
[Cancel]
[Help]

Figure 74. Create DB2 Services Screen 2

6. Tab to **OK** and press **Enter**.

7. The DB2 components are installed.
8. The Service Pack must now be installed by entering `smitty`**-> Software Installation and Maintenance ->Install and Update Software -> Install and Update from LATEST Available Software**.
9. In the field: INPUT device / Install directory for software, enter **/tmp/DB2/FIXPAK**.
10. Use F4 to display a list of components, and then select **Client Application Enabler** from the list.
11. Press **OK**. A message indicating success will be displayed when installation is complete.

3.4.3.4 Configuring DB2 Parameters

You should configure these DB2 parameters according to your needs:

- MAXAPPLS - A database configuration (db cfg) parameter
- MAXAGENTS - A database manager configuration (dbm cfg) parameter

Each SAP process that runs creates a DB2 agent on the database server. To determine the number of DB2 agents you might need on the database server system itself, enter the following command logged in as db2<sid> when the SAP system is up and running:

```
db2 list application for database <SID>
```

The output will be similar to this:

```
f01n03:db2afb 14> db2 list application for database afb

Auth Id  Application    Appl.      Application Id                 DB       # of
         Name           Handle                                    Name     Agents
-------- -------------- ---------- ------------------------------ -------- -----
SAPR3    disp+work      34         *LOCAL.db2afb.980910015044     AFB      1
SAPR3    disp+work      38         *LOCAL.db2afb.980910015050     AFB      1
SAPR3    disp+work      37         *LOCAL.db2afb.980910015049     AFB      1
SAPR3    disp+work      35         *LOCAL.db2afb.980910015046     AFB      1
SAPR3    disp+work      39         *LOCAL.db2afb.980910015051     AFB      1
SAPR3    disp+work      36         *LOCAL.db2afb.980910015048     AFB      1
SAPR3    disp+work      40         *LOCAL.db2afb.980910015052     AFB      1

f01n03:db2afb 15>
```

Figure 75. DB2 List Applications

Count the number of agents and then, for each additional application server, add 5-8 agents. The total should be less than or equal to MAXAPPLS or MAXAGENTS.

To check the current setting of MAXAPPLS:

```
db2 get db cfg for <SID> | grep MAXAPPLS
```

To check the current setting for MAXAGENTS:

```
db2 get dbm cfg | grep MAXAGENTS
```

If required, update MAXAGENTS or MAXAPPLS to a new value:

```
db2 update db cfg for <SID> using MAXAPPLS xx
```

```
db2 update dbm cfg using MAXAGENTS xx
```

You must stop and start the DB2 instance for the changes to take effect.

3.4.4 Installing a SAP Dialog Instance

To perform the installation of the SAP Dialog instance, follow these steps:

1. Mount the SAP KERNEL CDROM on mount point /sapcd.
2. Change directory to /tmp/install and enter this command:

```
/sapcd/UNIX/DIALOG.SH
```

The code will be copied from the CD-ROM to the /tmp/install directory:

```
f01n01:/tmp/install > /sapcd/UNIX/DIALOG.SH

Welcome to DIALOG instance installation.

Please do first the preparations found in the manual
'R/3 Installation on UNIX', section 'Installing an R/3 Instance'

The current directory is used as the installation directory
and some files will be copied into this directory.
This can take some time.


Generating installation command file DIALOG.R3S...
This can take some time.
Generation successfull.

You can start the installation with:
./R3SETUP -f DIALOG.R3S
The log file will be DIALOG.log.
In some (non standard) cases you need to customize the command file.

Should the installation be started? (yes or no)
[default is 'no']:
```

Figure 76. DIALOG.SH

3. As the graphical tools will be used to perform the installation, accept the default 'no' response to the 'Should the installation be started ?' prompt. Press **Enter** to exit the installation script.
4. In this example, we will install the dialog instance on an AIX machine using a Windows NT machine to control the installation. To start INSTGUI on the Windows NT machine, change directory to <drive>\tmp\install and enter:

```
INSTGUI
```

This will display the main INSTGUI screen:

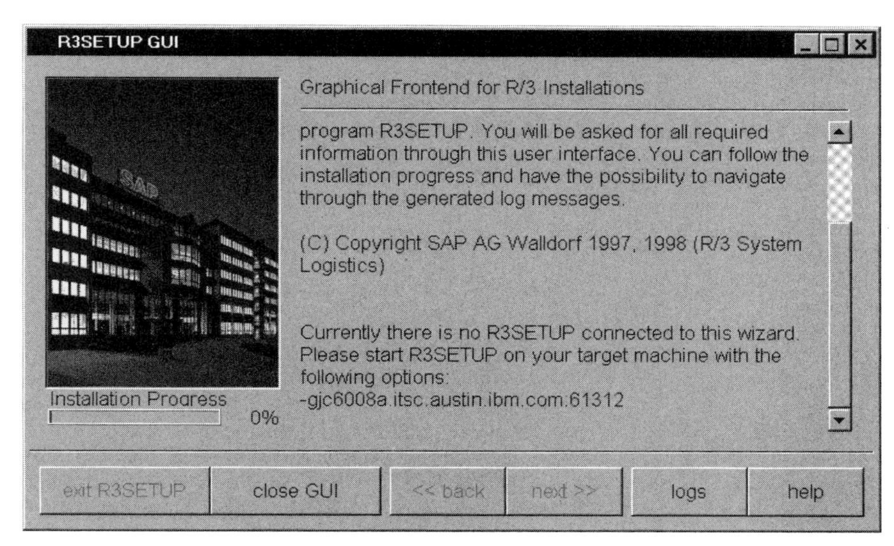

Figure 77. INSTGUI Main Screen

5. On the AIX machine where the dialog server is to be installed, change directory to /tmp/install and issue this command:

```
./R3SETUP -f DIALOG.R3S -g<hostname>:61312
```

INSTGUI listens on port 61312 and connects when R3SETUP starts. The installation will now be controlled from the INSTGUI screen on the Windows NT machine.

Note

If INSTGUI fails because port 61312 is already in use, use a different port. The port is specified in the following ways:

- INSTGUI: Using the -port option
- R3SETUP: Using the -g<hostname>:<port> option

6. Using INSTGUI on the Windows NT machine, enter or confirm your 3-character SAP system name (SID) and press **next>>**:

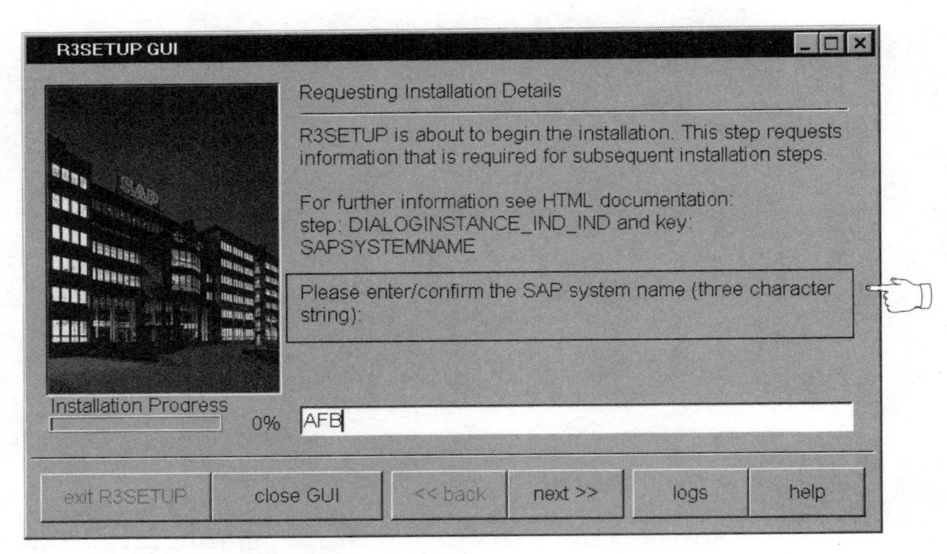

Figure 78. Enter Three Digit SID

Make sure you read the important boxed part of the screen, as highlighted in Figure 78.

7. Enter/confirm your 2-digit SAP system number and press **next>>**:

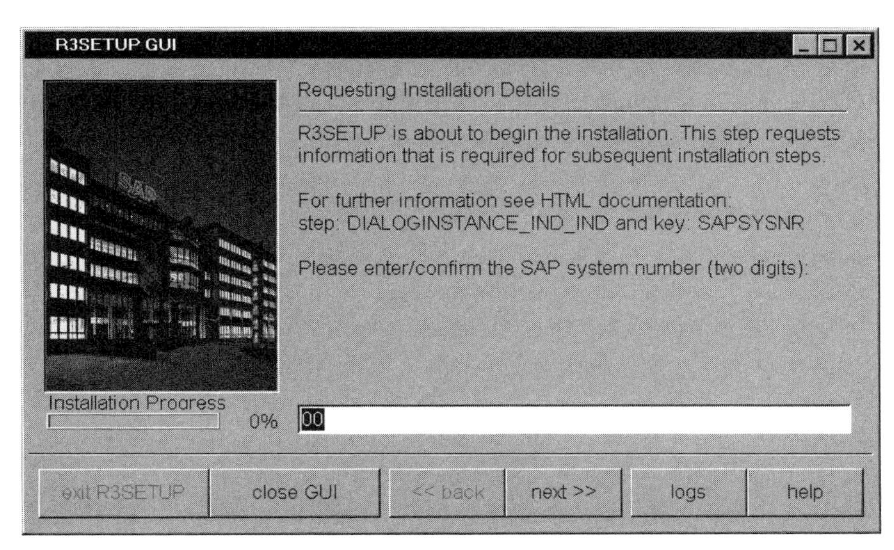

Figure 79. Enter Instance Number

8. Enter/confirm the SAPMOUNT directory (always /sapmnt/<SID>) and press **next>>**:

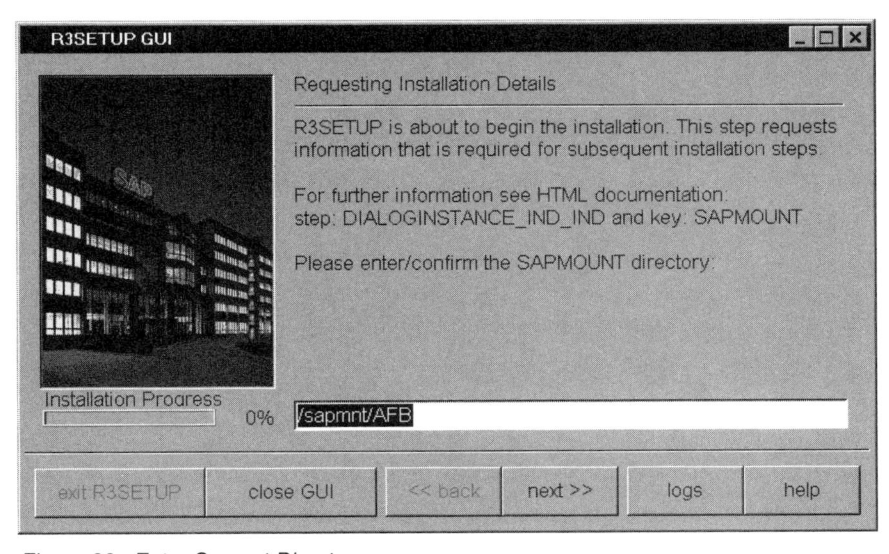

Figure 80. Enter Sapmnt Directory

9. Enter/confirm the hostname of the Central Instance and press **next>>**:

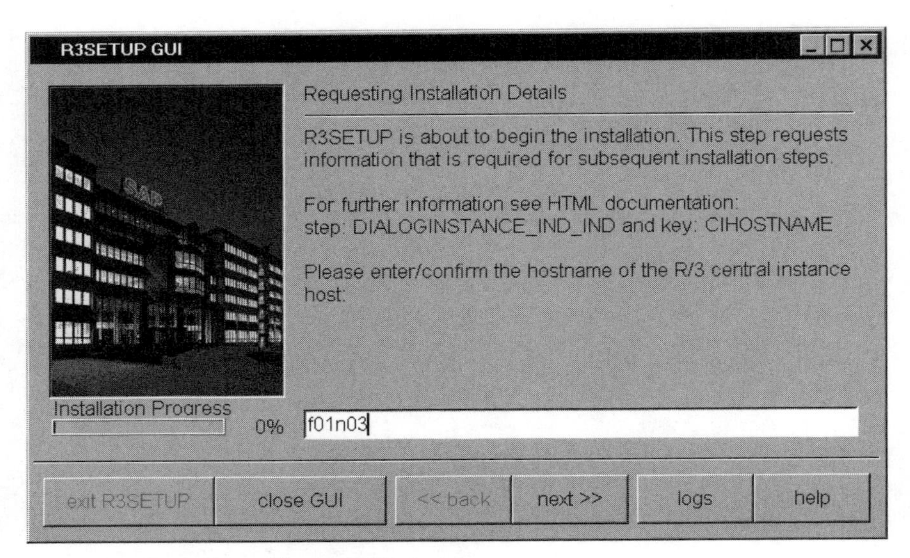

Figure 81. Enter Central Instance Hostname

10. Enter/confirm the hostname of the DB2 database server and press **next>>**:

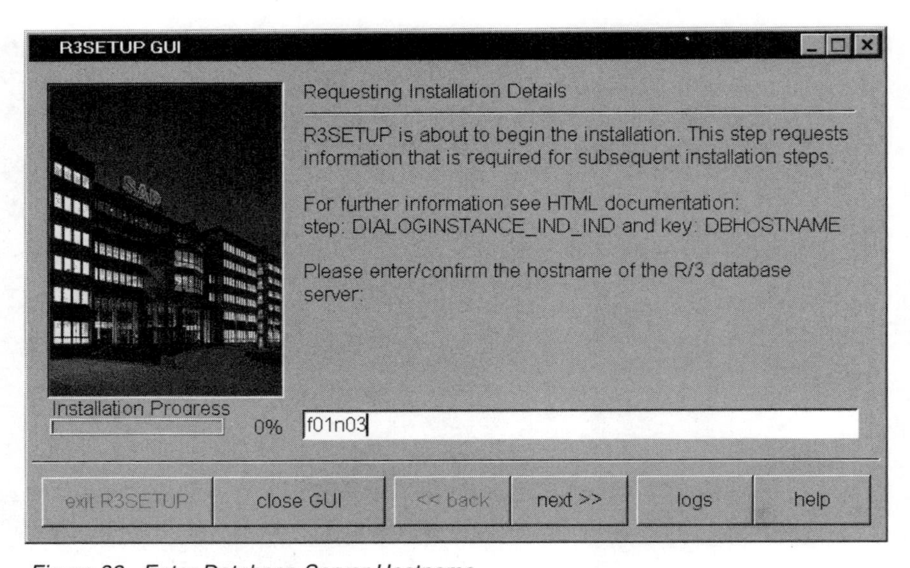

Figure 82. Enter Database Server Hostname

11.Enter/confirm the SAP system number of the Central Instance and press **next>>**:

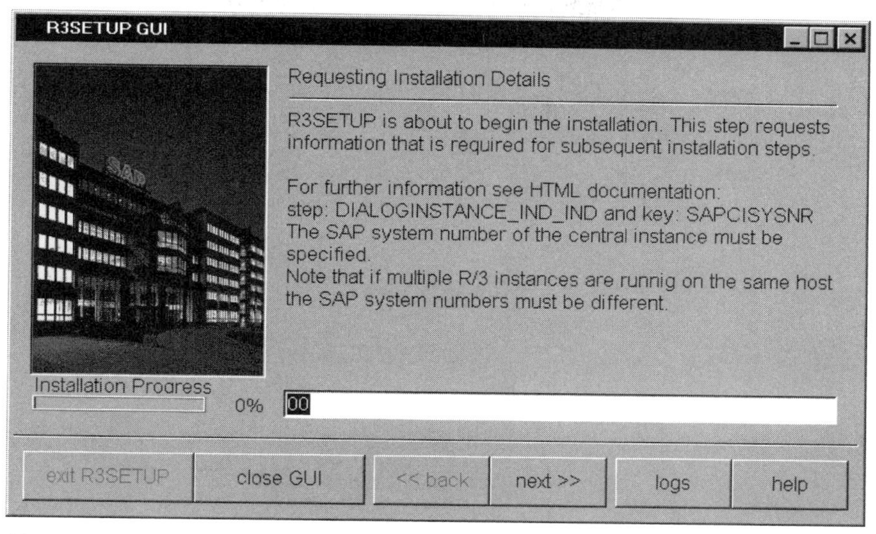

Figure 83. Enter SAP System Number

12.Enter/confirm the DB2DB6EKEY and press **next>>**. This value is <SID>hostname, where hostname is your database server hostname. In our example it is AFBf01n03:

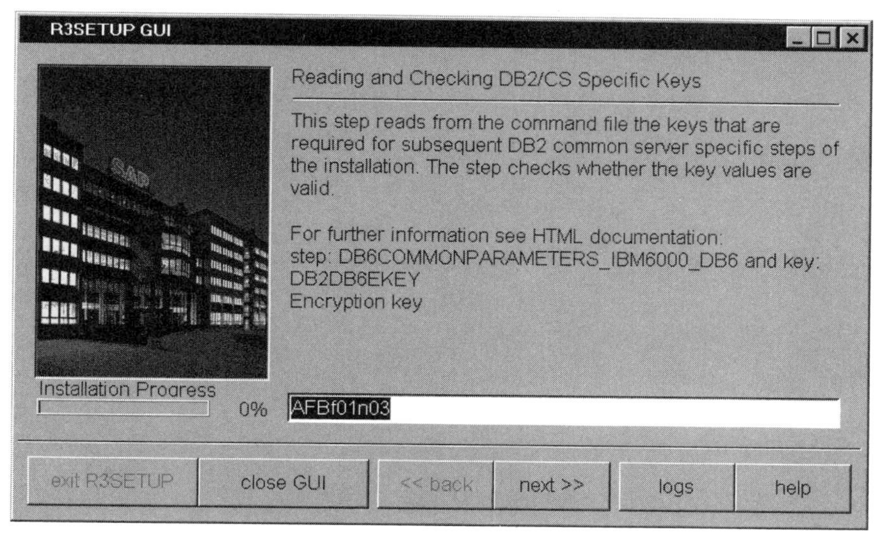

Figure 84. Enter DB2DB6EKEY

13.Enter/confirm the password of the db2<sapsid> user and press **next>>**:

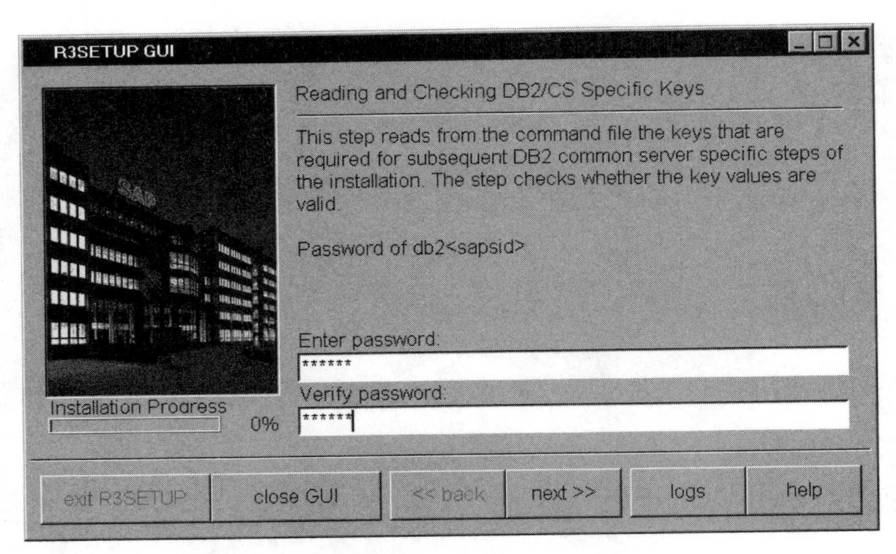

Figure 85. Enter db2<sapsid> Password

14.Enter/confirm the Installation working directory and press **next>>**. This should be **/tmp/install**:

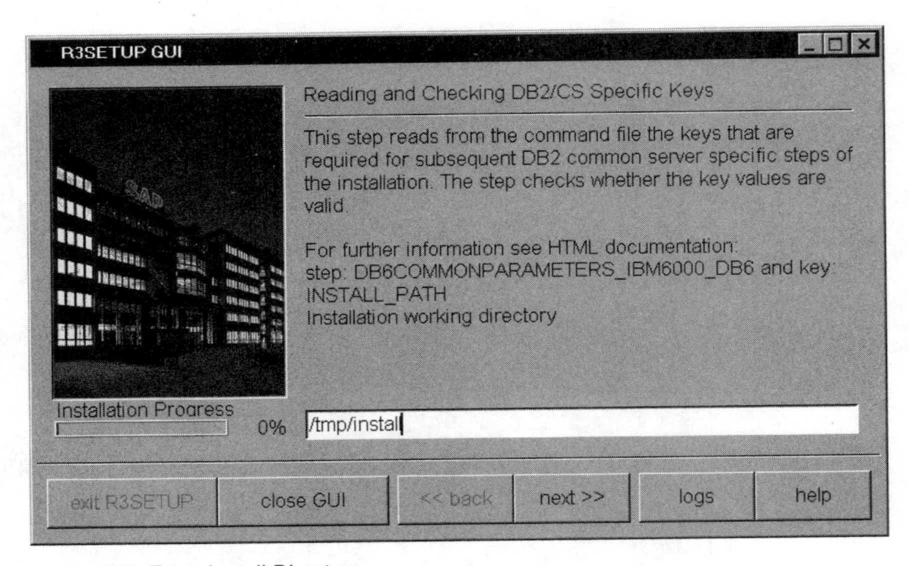

Figure 86. Enter Install Directory

15.Enter/confirm the password for <sapsid>adm and press **next>>**:

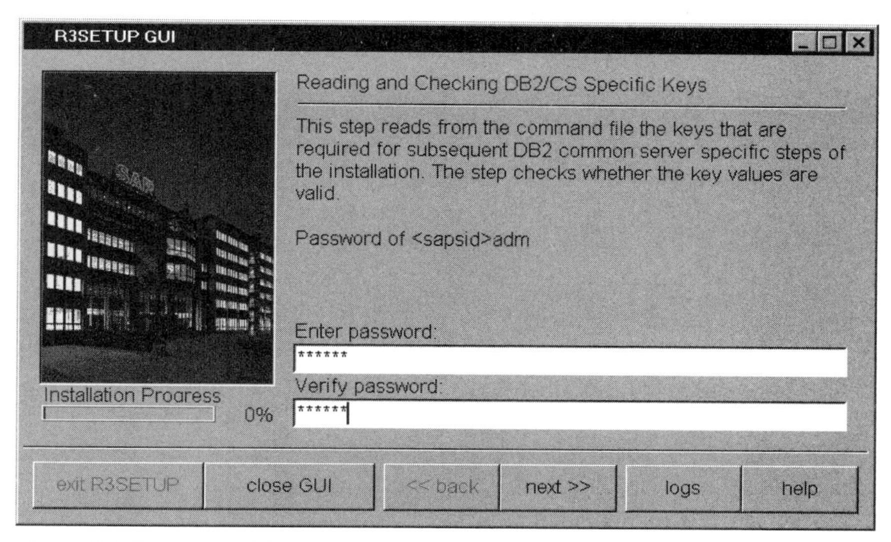

Figure 87. Enter <sapsid>adm Password

16.Enter/confirm your CD mount point and press **next>>**:

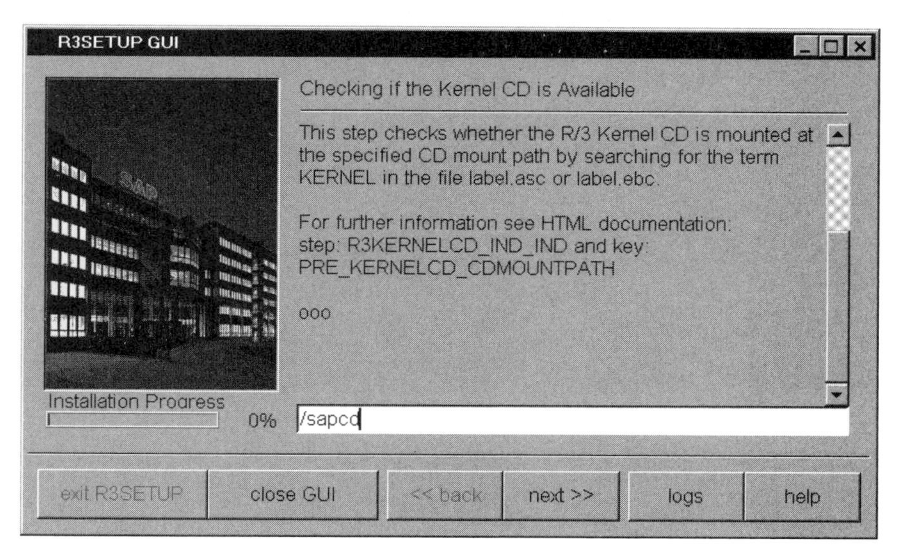

Figure 88. Enter CD Mount Point

17.Enter/confirm the Message Server Port Number and press **next>>**. Port number **3600** should be used on the Central Instance and all application servers:

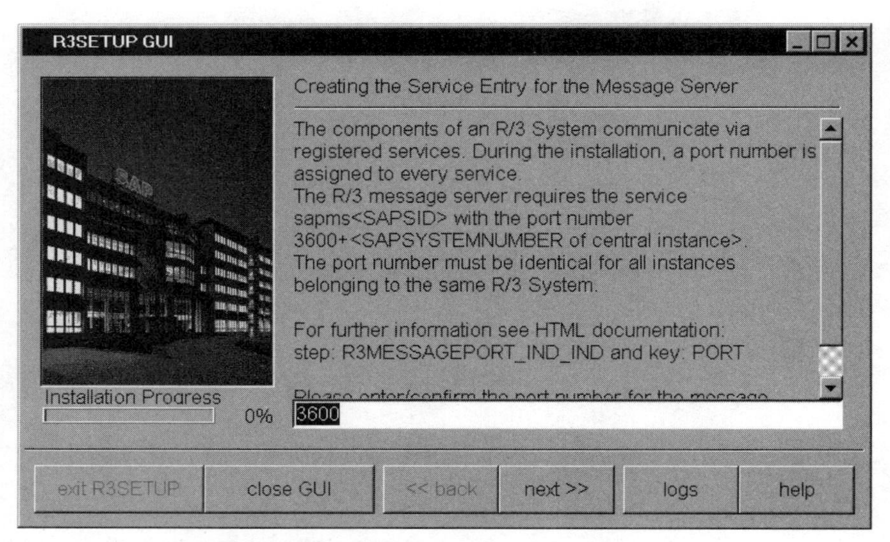

Figure 89. Enter Message Server Port Number

18.Enter/confirm the DB2 Client Service Port and press **next>>**. Port number **5912** should be used on the database server and all application servers:

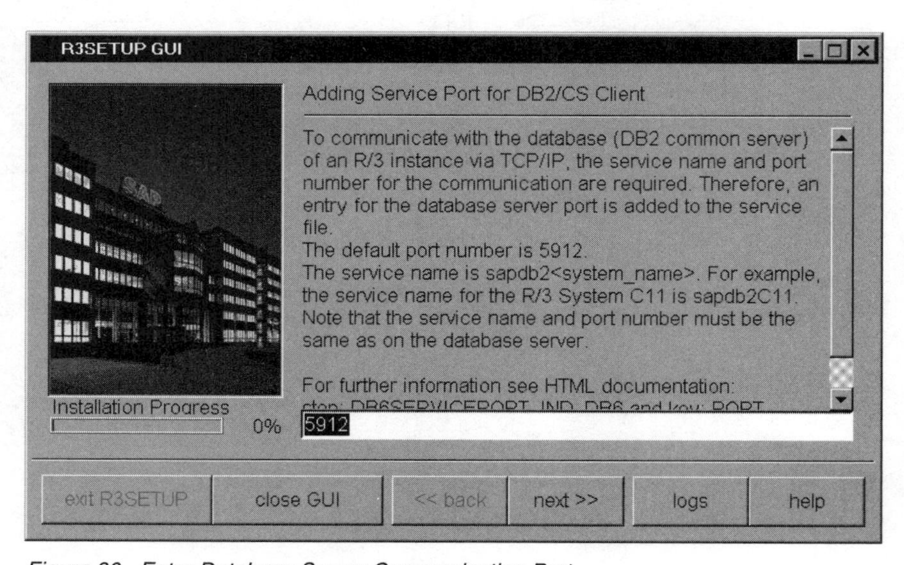

Figure 90. Enter Database Server Communication Port

19.Enter/confirm the Group ID of the sapsys group and press **next>>**. You can check this by using the following command:

```
grep sapsys /etc/group
```

The gid should be the same on the Central Instance and all application servers.

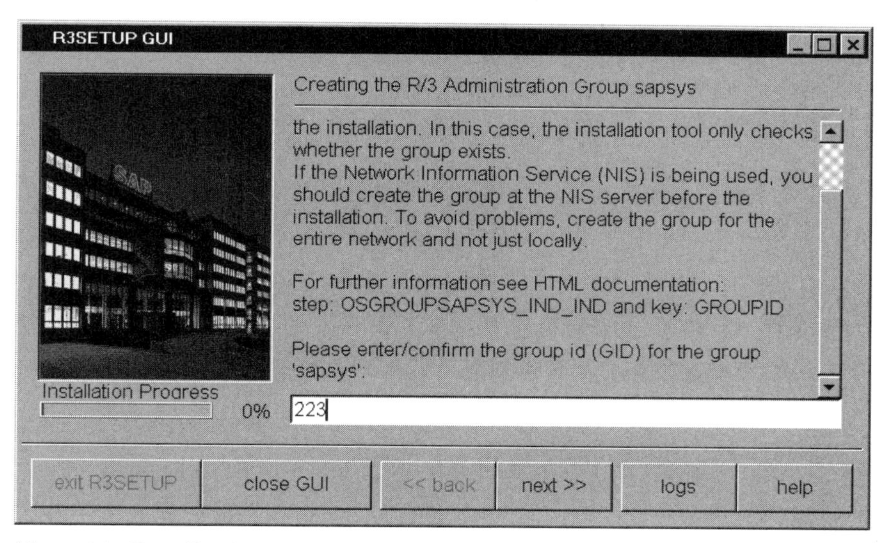

Figure 91. Enter/Confirm sapsys Group

20. Enter/confirm the user ID of the <SID>adm user and press **next>>**. You can check this by using the following command:

```
grep <SID>adm /etc/password
```

The uid should be the same on the Central Instance and all application servers.

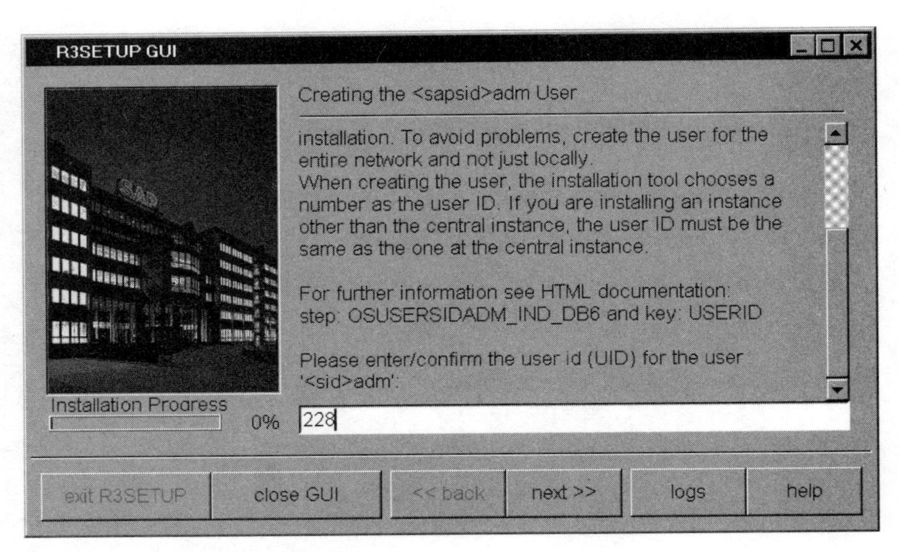

Figure 92. Confirm <sid>adm uid

21. Select if you wish to use the SAP Gateway as an interface for R/2 systems and press **next>>**. The default is no:

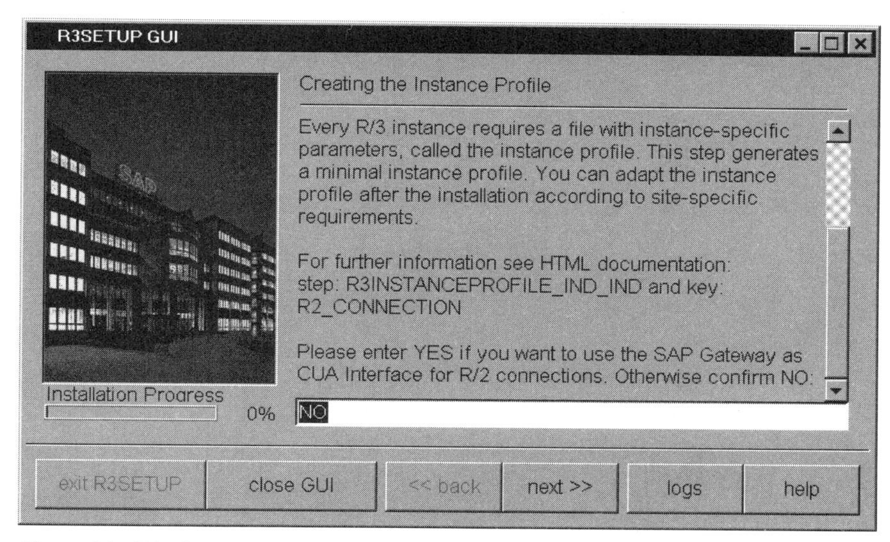

Figure 93. R/2 Connection

22. Enter the amount of memory you wish to use for your R/3 Instance and press **next>>**:

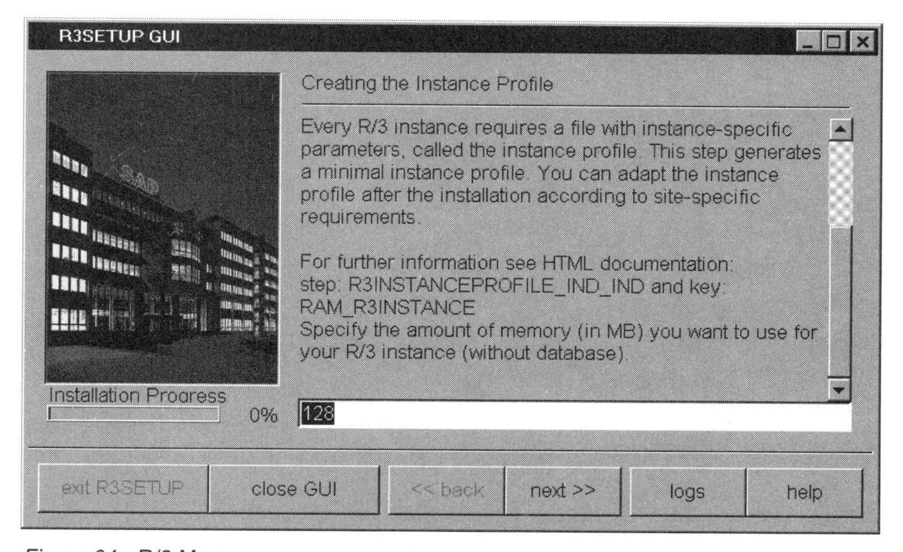

Figure 94. R/3 Memory

23.Confirm the directory where the DB2 executable db2icrt is located and press **next>>**. This will always be **/usr/lpp/db2_05_00/instance**.

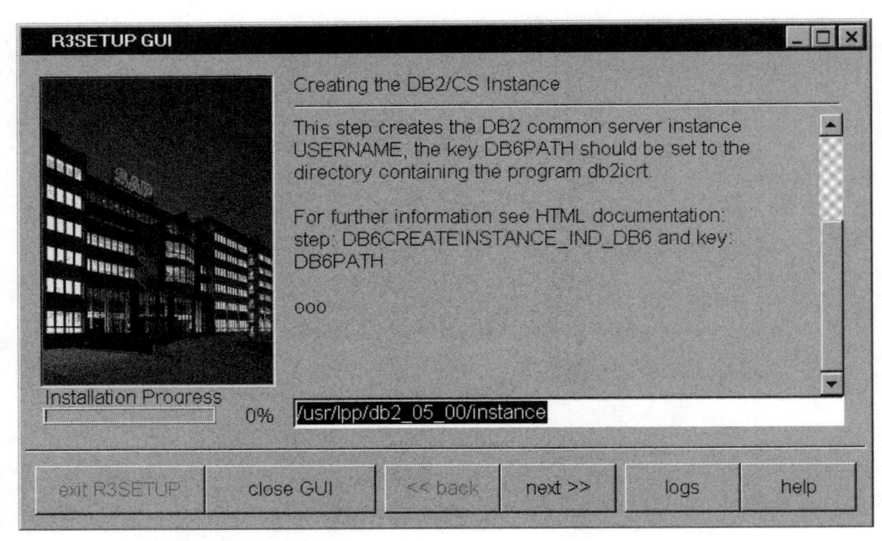

Figure 95. Confirm DB2 Instance Directory

24.The installation processing now starts and status messages are displayed in the INSTGUI panel. When this has finished, the message **`./R3SETUP finished`** is displayed:

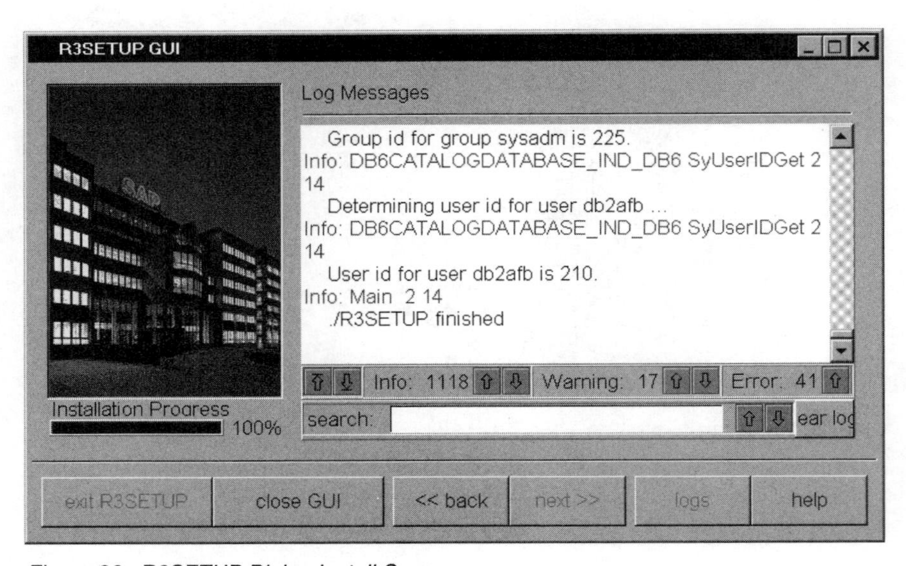

Figure 96. R3SETUP Dialog Install Success

3.4.5 Adjusting SAP R/3 Profiles after Installation

During the application server installation, the default profile is updated automatically by the R3SETUP program.The parameter rdisp/bufrefmode is set to sendon,exeauto to allow buffer refreshes on the dialog server.

You must manually add the following parameter to the default profile:

- rslg/send_daemon/talk_port = 3801

You must also manually add the following parameters to the dialog instance profile or the DEFAULT.PFL profile on each application server:

- zcsa/system_language = E
- zcsa/installed_languages = DE
- rdisp/btcname = $(rdisp/myname)

To update the profiles use transaction **RZ10** or menu path **Tools->CCMS, Configuration->Profile Maintenance**.

Proceed as follows to make a profile change using **RZ10**:

1. Select **Utilities->Import profiles->Of active servers** from the menu bar:

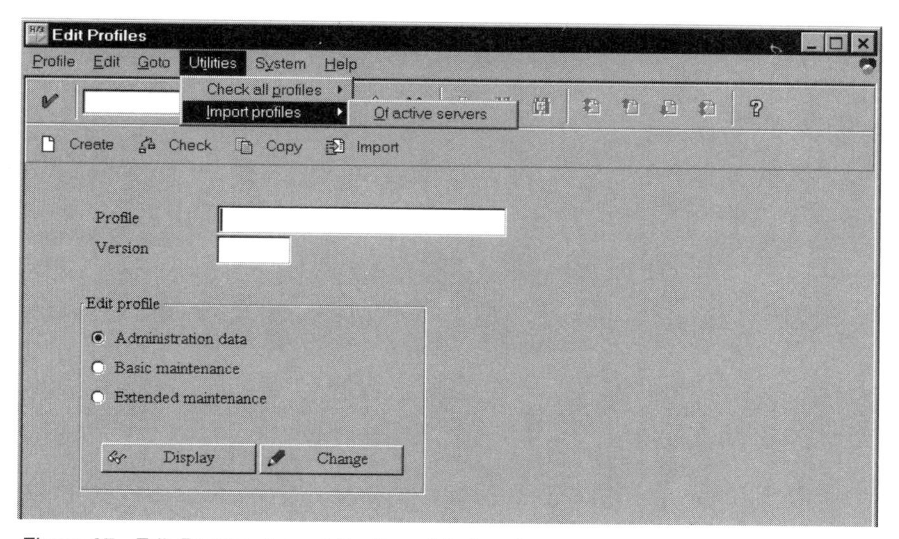

Figure 97. Edit Profiles: Import Profiles of Active Servers

2. Click the pull-down in the Profile selection area to display active profiles:

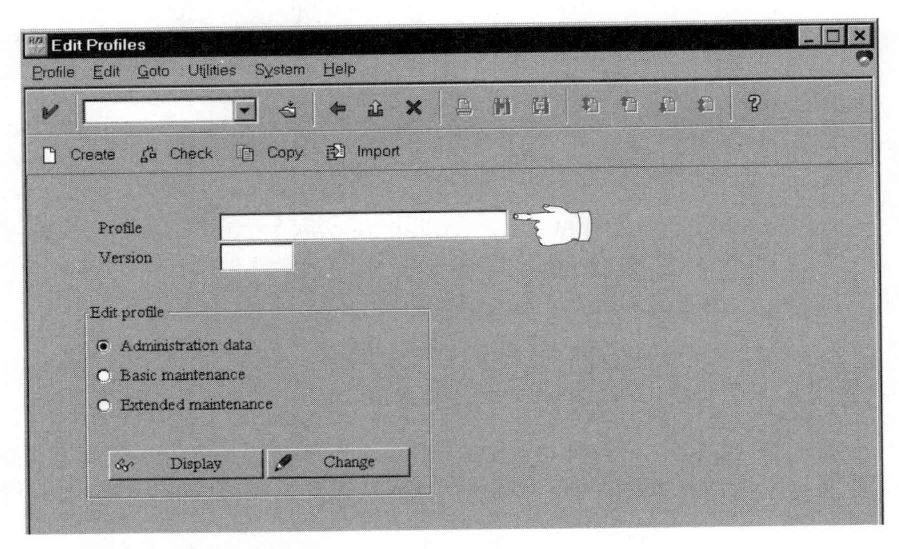

Figure 98. Edit Profiles

3. You will see the output below:

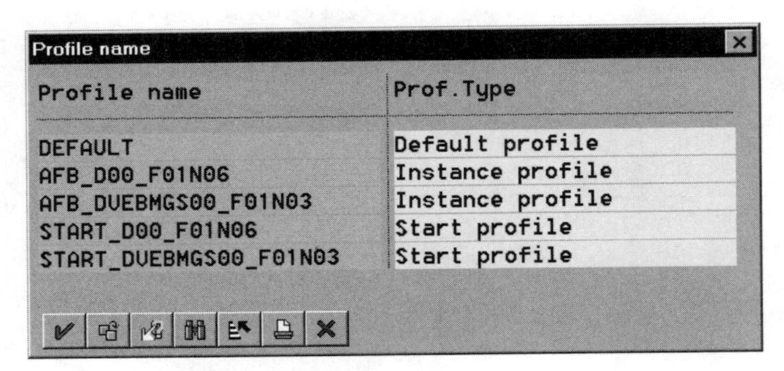

Figure 99. Imported Profiles Screen

4. Select the Profile to be changed. In this case we chose the Instance profile AFB_D00_F01N06 owned by our Dialog Server.

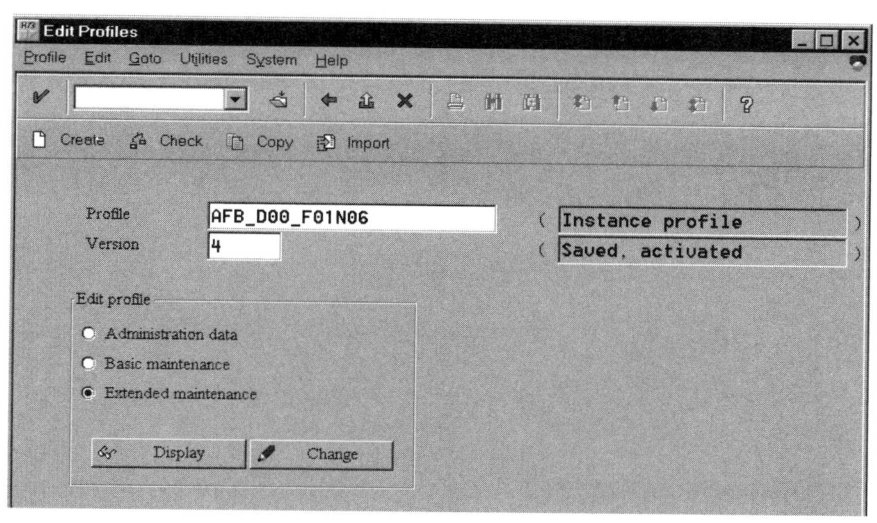

Figure 100. Edit Profile of Dialog Server

5. Click on **Extended maintenance** then click on **Change**.
6. In the next screen, click on **Create Parameter** in the tool bar:

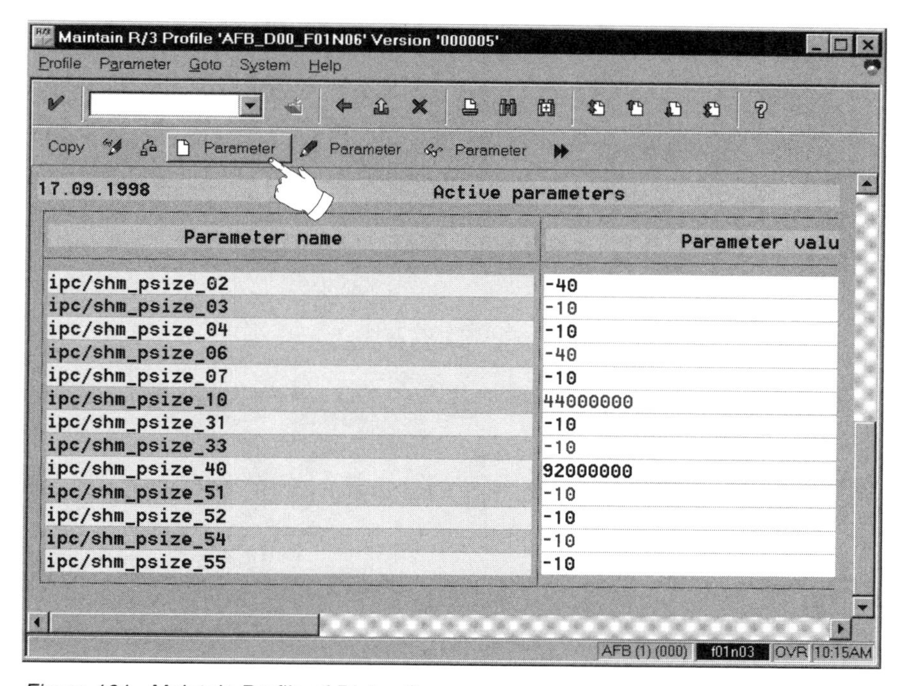

Figure 101. Maintain Profile of Dialog Server

7. Enter the parameter name and value that you wish to add:

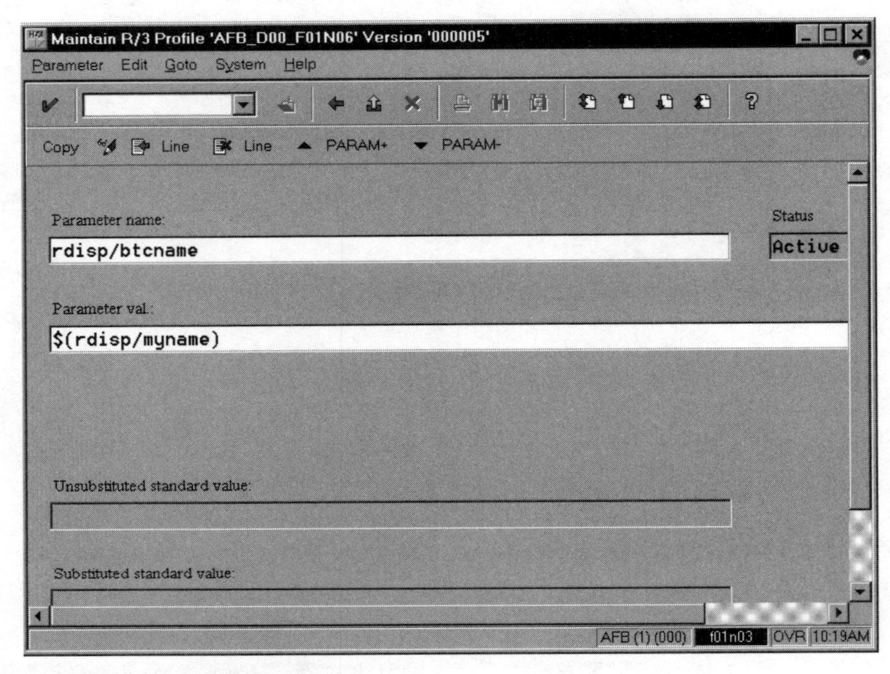

Figure 102. Add Profile Parameter

8. Click **Copy**.
9. Click on the **Back** icon in the tool bar.
10. Click **Copy**.
11. Click on the **Back** icon in the tool bar.
12. Click on the **Save** icon in the tool bar.
13. Click **Yes** to activate the profile:

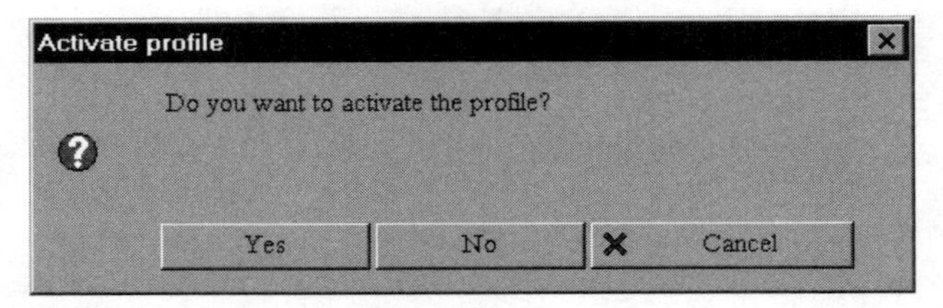

Figure 103. Activate Profile Pop-Up

14.Click the check icon on the information pop-up:

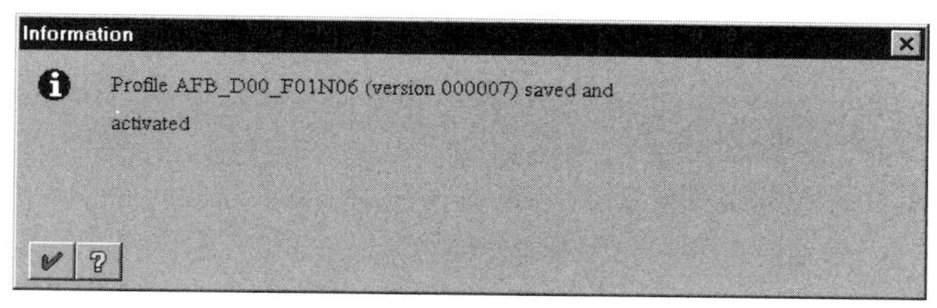

Figure 104. Profile Activation Conformation Pop-Up

15.Click the check icon on the warning screen:

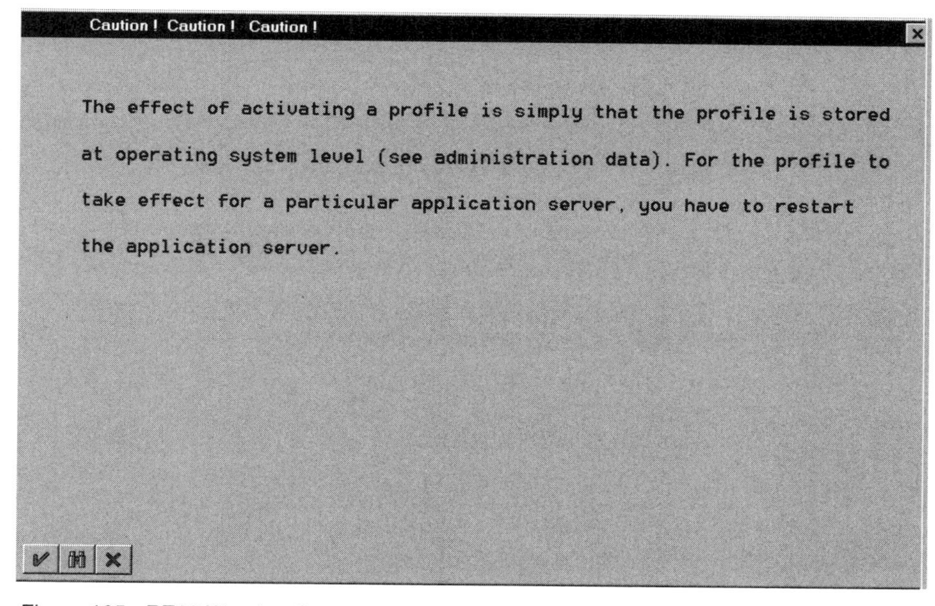

Figure 105. RZ10 Warning Screen

16.You must restart the Dialog server to activate the actual changes to the running system even though they were activated in the profiles.

3.5 Configuring the DB2 Administration Server

After you have completed the R/3 and DB2 installation on AIX, you must configure the DB2 administration server in order to gain access from the Control Center and other graphical tools on your remote clients You also need to ensure that the DB2 instance itself will be able to listen for remote requests.

1. Check the entries in the /etc/services file. They should look similar to the entries in this figure:

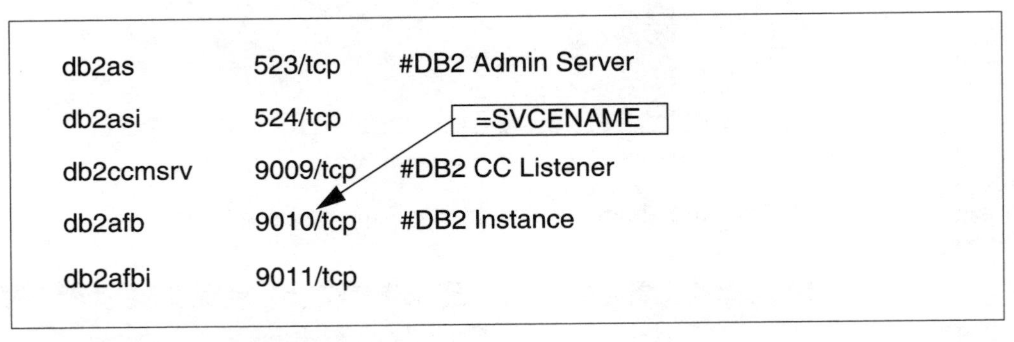

Figure 106. AIX etc/services file

   - The DB2 Administration Server should be set to 523.
   - There should be an entry for db2ccmsrv.
   - Make a note of the DB2 instance port number.

2. Update the database manager configuration file for the DB2 instance and set the service name (SVCENAME) to the port number corresponding to the DB2 instance shown in Figure 106.

```
db2 update dbm cfg using svcename 9010
```

3. Check that the DB2 Administration Server Instance is available and working:

   - Login as the Administration Server owner.
   - Set up the instance owner environment by copying the .profile from /db2/<SID> to /home/db2as
   - Issue the **db2set** command. This should confirm what the Administration Server is set to.

```
DB2DIR/bin/db2set -g DB2ADMINSERVER
```

   Where DB2DIR is /usr/lpp/db2_05_00.

4. Start-up the Administration Server. If it is already started you will simply get an information message indicating that the server is already started. Otherwise it will start the server.

```
db2admin start
```

5. Set up the DB2 Control Center daemon listener.

   • The listener daemon requires a predefined named port. The named port must be called db2ccmsrv and must be defined in the /etc/services.

   • Change the permissions for db2cclst to 4755.

   • Switch user to db2as.

   • Issue the following command:

```
db2cclst
```

6. You should set up the db2cclst daemon to start at machine reboot time. You can do this by changing the /etc/inittab file as follows:

```
mkitab "db2cclst:2:once:/db2/db2as/sqllib/bin/db2cclst
```

7. To see if the daemon is running, issue the following command:

```
ps -aef | grep db2cclst
```

   Error information for the db2cclst daemon is returned to the syslog file. Errors are written to this file, instead of the db2diag.log file, because the daemon runs independent from the instance.

8. Check your DB2 environment variables with the **db2set** command. The output should be similar to this:

```
f01n03:/db2/db2as > db2set  -all
[i] DB2COMM=tcpip
[g] DB2SYSTEM=f01n03
[g] DB2ADMINSERVER=db2as
```

For further information about the DB2 administration server refer to the DB2 UDB manuals, in particular, *Quick Beginnings for Unix*.

3.6 Installing SAP R/3 UNIX Frontend

To install the UNIX R/3 Frontend in order to access SAP from an AIX system proceed as follows:

1. Mount the Presentation CD. In this example, the mount point is /sapcd.
2. Change directory to the install directory /tmp/install.
3. Enter this command:

```
/sapcd/GUI/GUI.SH
```

   This will unpack the Frontend code in /tmp/install.

4. Enter **YES** to install.
5. Enter the SAP System Name <SID>.

Chapter 4. Installing SAP R/3 and DB2 UDB on Windows NT

This chapter specifically deals with the installation of SAP R/3 V4.0B on the Windows NT operating system. See "Installing and Configuring R/3 and DB2 UDB on AIX" on page 87 for details about the installation of SAP R/3 V4.0B on AIX. Pre-installation issues are discussed in "Pre-Installation Planning and Preparation" on page 39. The installation procedures that are *common* to both Windows NT and AIX installation environments are discussed in the next chapter, "Installation Procedures Common to Both NT and AIX" on page 171.

This chapter not only covers the necessary steps required for the installation but also includes advice on problem determination, as well as tips on how to avoid common installation problems. The chapter is split into the following sections:

- Windows NT setup and configuration
- DB2 UDB installation:
    - DB2 UDB Enterprise Edition
    - DB2 UDB Service Pack
- SAP R/3 installation:
    - Central Instance and DB2 Instance

A complete Central System installation (that is, the central instance is running on the same host as the database server) is covered in this chapter. While installing a Dialog Instance for Windows NT is not covered, the installation would be done in a similar fashion using the *SAP R/3 setup* panel.

In Appendix B, "R/3 and DB2 Installation Checklist" on page 499, there is a checklist which can be used as a guide when following the installation process.

Note

The load of the tables in the R/3 database takes a considerable amount of time (8-16 hours depending on your hardware). Try to schedule this part of the installation procedure to be run overnight.

4.1 Windows NT Setup and Configuration

Although it is not the purpose of this book to explain in detail Windows NT administration procedures, certain Windows NT configuration tasks should be performed before installing SAP R/3.

4.1.1 Verifying the Windows NT Version

Ensure that you are running Windows NT Server Version 4.00, Build 1381 with the English (United States) Language option.

To check the version:

1. Select **Start->Settings->Control Panel**.
2. Select the **System** icon. The version is displayed under the **General** tab.

There are two possible methods to check the language. The first is for a system on which DB2 has not yet been installed. The second can be used once you have installed DB2 UDB.

The first method uses the Windows NT Registry to check the Windows NT codepage and the OEM code page:

1. From the Windows NT command prompt, start the registry editor by entering `REGEDT32`.
2. Select the **HKEY_LOCAL_MACHINE** panel.
3. Expand the **System** folder, then **CurrentControlSet, Control,** then **NLS,** and finally **CodePage**.
4. In the right-hand pane at the bottom of the list you will see entries for **ACP** and **OEMCP**. ACP is for the Windows NT codepage and should be by default 1252. The OEMCP should show the value of 437.

If you have already installed DB2 UDB for Windows NT, you can also check the language as follows:

1. Select **Start->Settings->Control Panel**.

2. Then select the **System** icon. The language is displayed under the **Environment** tab.

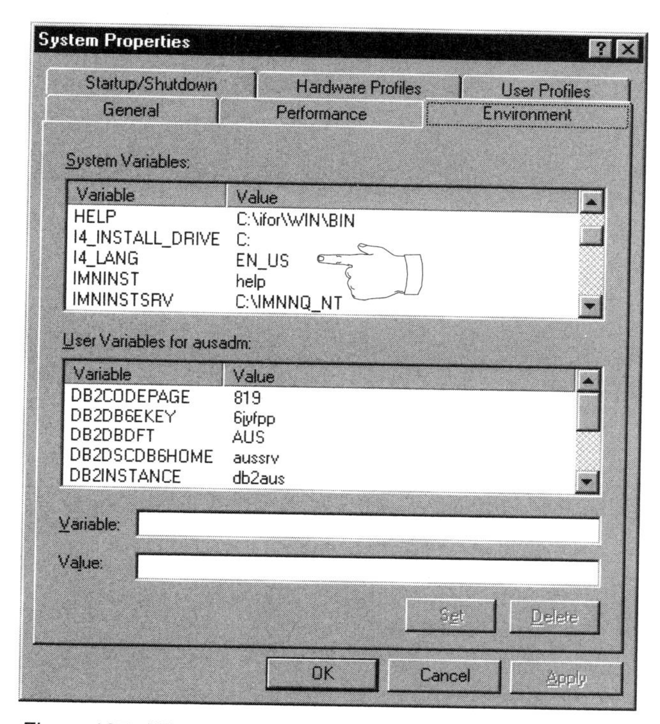

Figure 107. Windows NT Language Settings

4.1.2 Creating Windows NT User Accounts

There are two user accounts related to the SAP R/3 installation:

- <sapsid>adm - This user must be created before running the installation process.
- SAPService<sapsid> - If you wish, you can create this user manually. However the installation process will create this for you if it is not defined.

For the purpose of this book the abbreviation *aus* (for Austin) is used as the <sapsid>. Be aware that the two abbreviations <sapsid> and <sid> are used to refer to the SAP System ID. For more details about users, refer to Appendix A, “R/3 and DB2 Userids” on page 497.

4.1.2.1 The <sapsid>adm User

The installation of the Central Instance and DB2 Instance are carried out under the <sapsid>adm userid. This userid must be created and added to the

Administrators, the **Domain Admins** and **Domain Users** groups. Logoff and logon as the newly created <sapsid>adm user. In this example, the <sapsid>adm is *ausadm*.

4.1.2.2 The SAPService<sapsid> User

As an optional step, this userid can be created manually. If you choose to do this, then this user should be put in the following groups: **Administrators**, **Domain Admins** and **Domain Users**. In this example, the SAPService<sapsid> is *SAPServiceaus.*

4.1.3 Windows NT User Rights

The final step in the setup of user accounts involves setting the correct Windows NT Advanced User Rights.

1. Select **Start**->**Programs**->**Administrative Tools**(**Common**)->**User Manager for Domains**.
2. Select **Policies** from the menu bar and then **User Rights**.
3. Click on **Show Advanced User rights**.

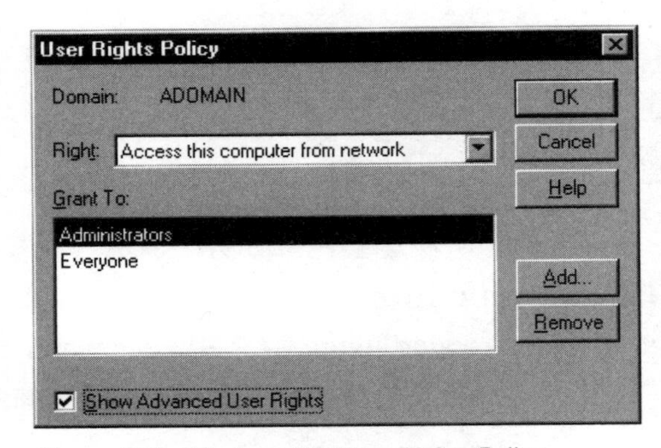

Figure 108. Windows NT User Rights Policy

4. From the pull-down menu box labelled **Right**, select **Act as part of the operating system** and click on **Add**.

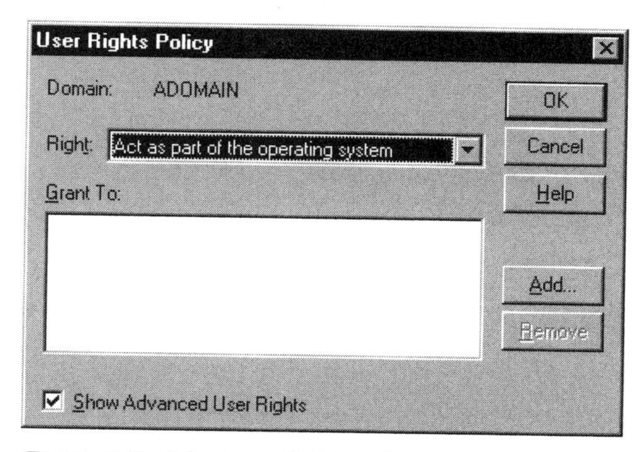

Figure 109. Windows NT User Rights Policy - Add

5. Click on **Show Users**, select <sapsid>adm (*ausadm* in this example) and then click on **Add**.

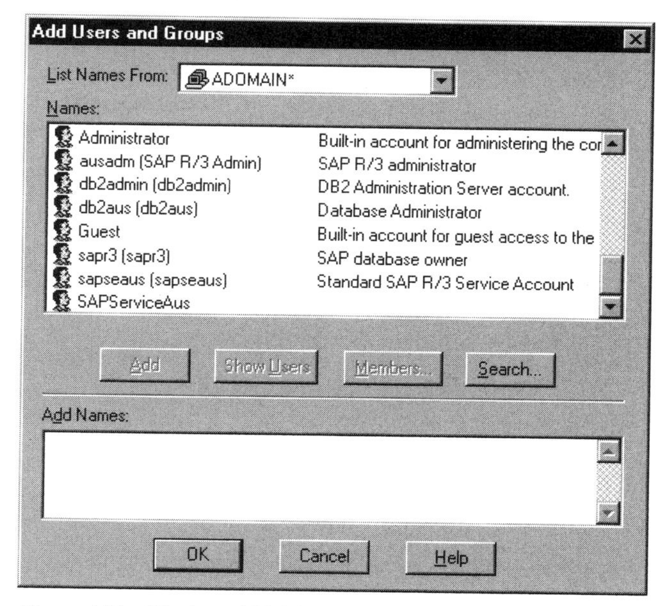

Figure 110. Windows NT Add Users and Groups (User Rights Policy)

6. Repeat the above steps for the following Rights:
   - Log on as a service.
   - Replace a process level token.
   - Increase quotas

Logoff your current session and logon once again to have the new settings take effect.

4.1.4 Choosing the Hostname

You should be careful when choosing a hostname as it is difficult to change after R/3 has been installed.

Note

The hostname must not be more than 8 characters and must not contain any special characters such as an underscore.

You must also make sure there is an entry in the Windows NT hosts file (C:\winnt\system32\drivers\etc\hosts) which matches the hostname in the TCP/IP network configuration panel. In this example, the name chosen for the hostname was *aussrv*.

4.1.5 Verifying the Windows NT Partitions

Check that the disks intended to be used for the installation are available, partitioned and formatted. They should be formatted using the NTFS option.

1. To verify this, select **Start**->**Programs**->**Administrative Tools(Common)** ->**Disk Administrator**.
2. Select **View**->**Disk Configuration**.

This will display the current disk setup on the SAP R/3 Windows NT server:

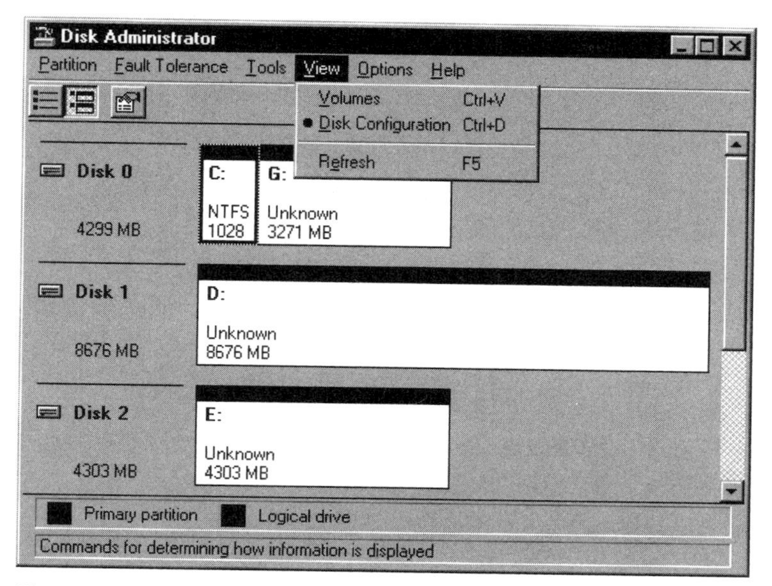

Figure 111. Windows NT Disk Administrator

3. To format a partition, right-click on the required partition to display a menu of formatting options.

In addition, you should make sure that all the partitions have the authorization: Full control (All) (All) assigned to Everyone.

1. To do this, right-click on the partition, then click on **Properties**. Select the **Security** tab followed by the **Permissions** button. This will display the permissions for this partition:

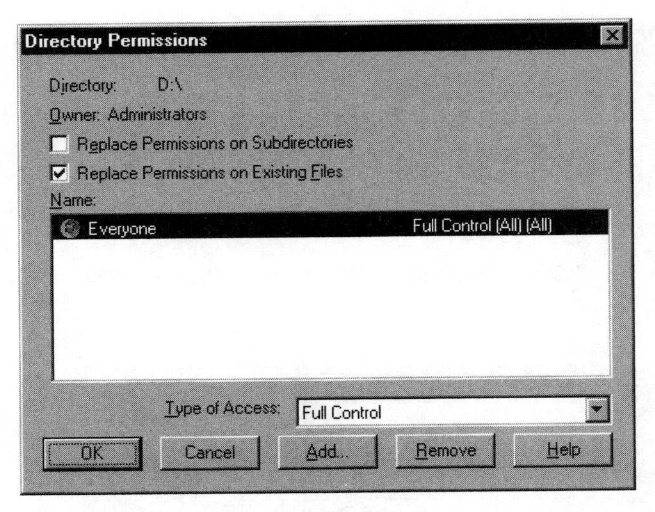

Figure 112. Windows NT Permissions

4.1.6 Windows NT Virtual Memory

The virtual memory of the server should be adjusted to a size as recommended in "Pre-Installation Planning and Preparation" on page 39. As a rough guide, multiply the amount of RAM by 3 and add 500 MB.

In order to make adjustments to the virtual memory in Windows NT, execute the following steps:

1. Select **Start->Settings->Control Panel**. Select the **System** icon.
2. Select the **Performance** tab.
3. Click on the **Change** button in the Virtual Memory section to change the paging file size.
4. Do not reboot your machine at this time as this will be done in the following section when changes are made to the server's network properties.

4.1.7 Optimizing Windows NT Network Services for SAP R/3

The Windows NT Network Services should be configured to optimize performance on the server for SAP R/3.

1. Select **Start->Settings->Control Panel**. Select the **Network** icon.
2. Select the **Services** page.
3. Select the **Server** entry and click on **Properties**.
4. Activate the **Maximum Throughput for Network Applications** button.

5. Select **Close** and select **Yes** to reboot the machine.

4.2 Installing DB2 UDB

This section describes the steps required to install DB2 UDB and the appropriate Service Pack. There are two possible installation methods, as shown in Figure 113. The method you use depends on whether you are installing DB2 UDB on a SAP R/3 Server, or on an Administrator Workstation. The Administrator Workstation installation is dealt with in the following chapter “Installation Procedures Common to Both NT and AIX” on page 171.

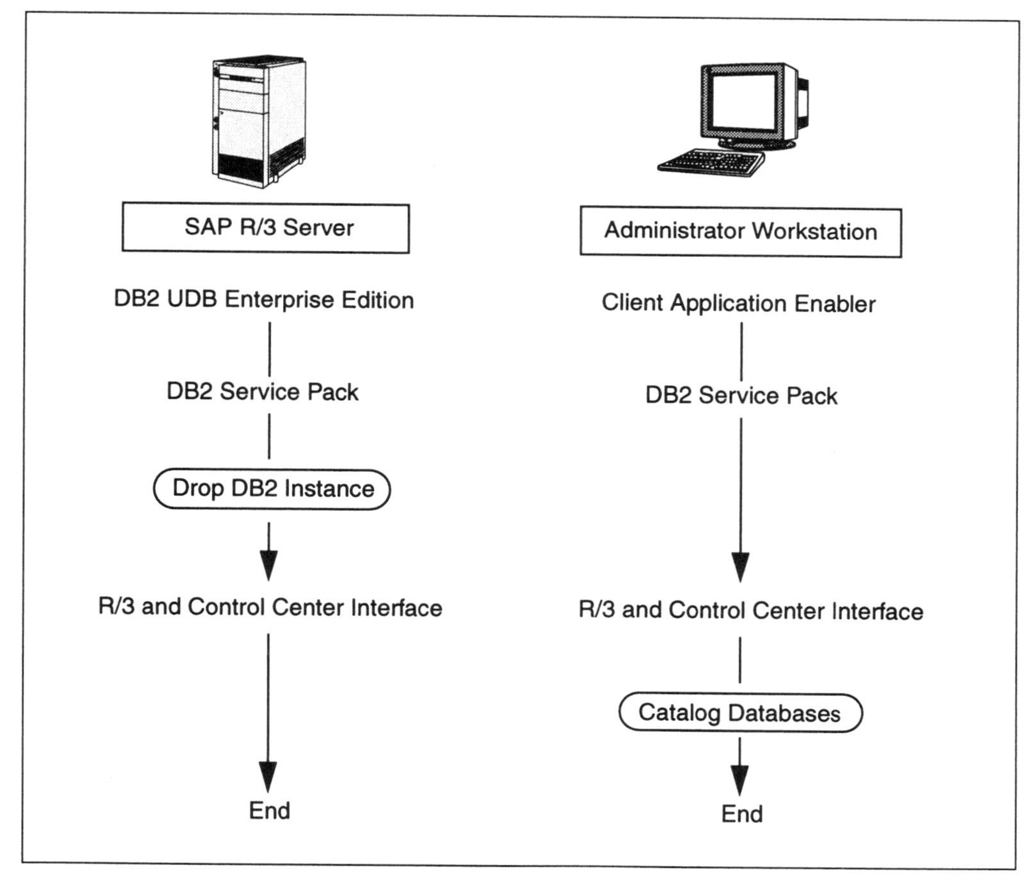

Figure 113. DB2 UDB Installation Methods

Further information on DB2 Universal Database for Windows NT is available in the *IBM DB2 Universal Database for Windows NT Quick Beginnings*,

Appendix A: Obtaining Information. This manual is available in HTML format on the SAP R/3 CD labelled *DB2 common Server/RDBMS 5.0.0.17* under the directory: nt_i386\Doc\En\Html\db2i6. Open the file db2i6.htm with your web browser.

4.2.1 Installing DB2 UDB Database Server

To install DB2 UDB on a SAP R/3 Server (known as a Central System):

1. Logon as <sapsid>adm (in this example, ausadm).
2. Insert the CD labelled: *DB2 Common Server/RDBMS 5.0.0.17.*
3. Select **Start** ->**Run**, and enter **<X>:\NT_I386\DBSW\Setup.exe** (where X is the CD-ROM drive) and click on **OK**. The Welcome screen is displayed:

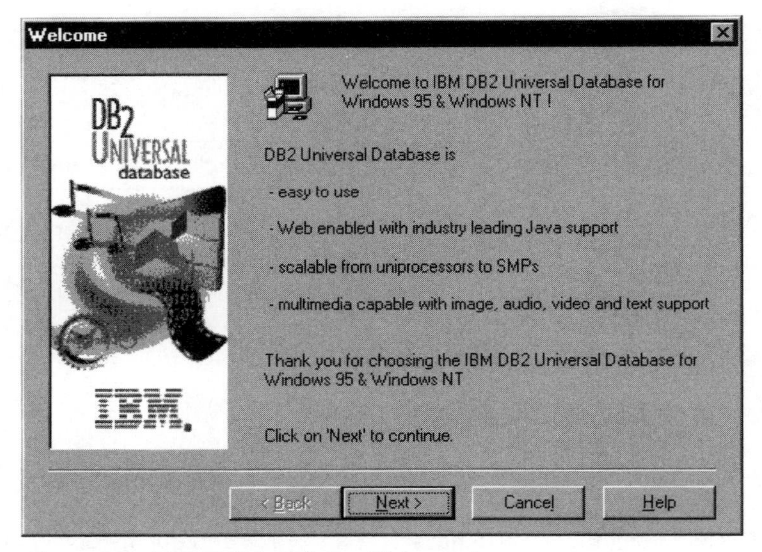

Figure 114. DB2 UDB Installation Welcome Screen

4. Select **Next** on the Welcome screen. The Select Products screen is displayed:

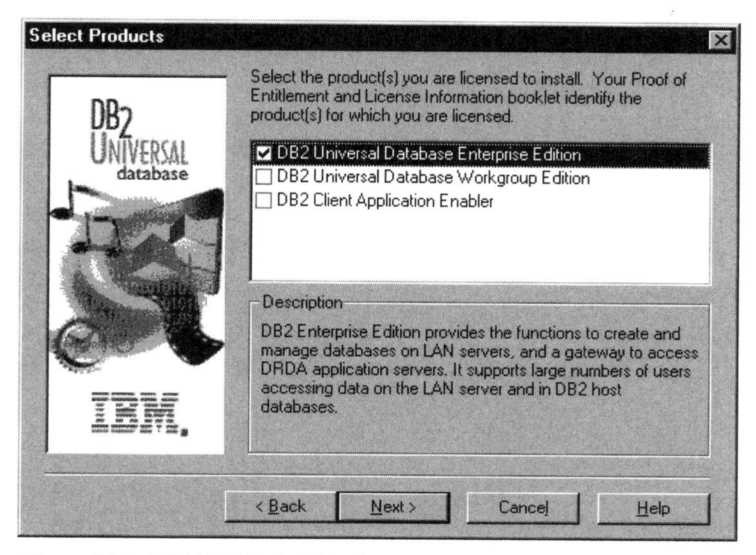

Figure 115. DB2 UDB Select Products

5. At the Select Products screen, select **DB2 Universal Database Enterprise Edition** by clicking in the tick box. Click on **Next**.

   There is no need to select the DB2 Client Application Enabler (CAE) even if you intend to logon to the another DB2 server from this machine. By selecting DB2 Universal Database Enterprise Edition, the CAE elements are automatically included. The process for installing the CAE on a workstation is documented in "Installing DB2 UDB Client Application Enabler (CAE)" on page 173.

6. Select **Typical** at the Select Installation Type screen. You will need about 124 MB of space available for the software install (based on version 5.0 of DB2 UDB and assuming an NTFS partition). The Select Destination Directory screen is displayed:

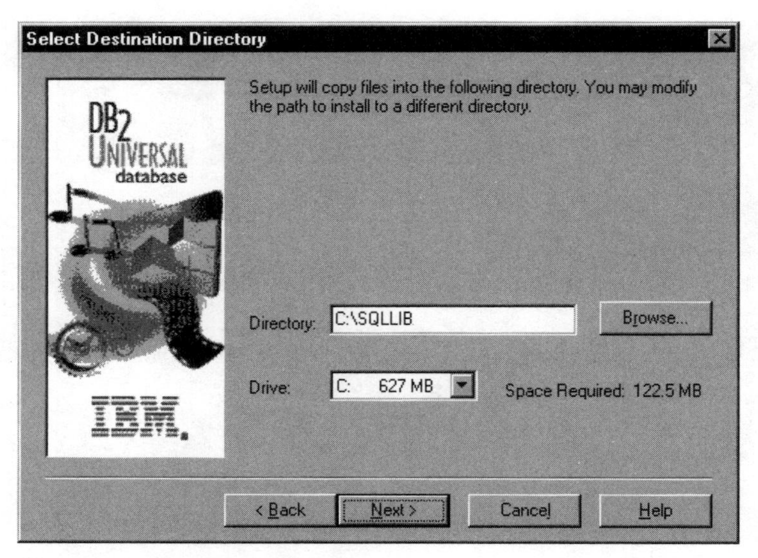

Figure 116. DB2 UDB Select Directory

7. Select the installation directory you wish to use for the DB2 UDB software and click on **Next**. The Enter Username and Password screen is displayed:

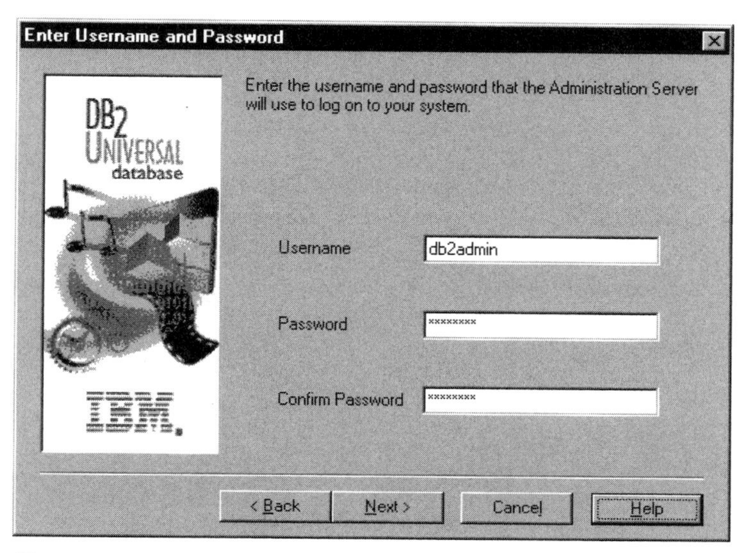

Figure 117. DB2 UDB Enter Username and Password

8. Accept the default of db2admin, enter a password for this userid and select **Next**.

   The setup program will check to see if the username specified for the administration server exists, if it does not, it will be created. If it does exist, the setup program will:

   • Verify that the username is a member of the Administrators group.
   • Verify that the password is valid; provided that the username used to install DB2 has the "Act as part of the operating system" advanced user right.

   The Start Copying Files screen is displayed:

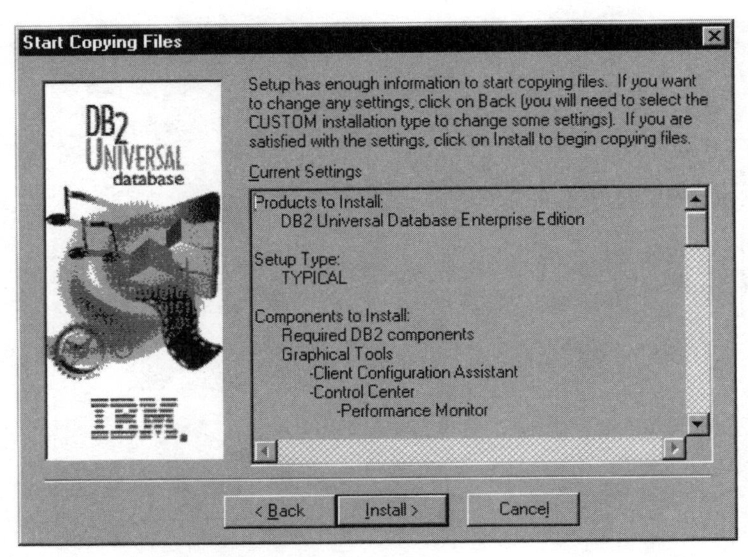

Figure 118. DB2 UDB Start Copying Files

9. Select **Install**. Note that within the Current Settings window, the Graphical Tool components have automatically been selected for installation.

10. After the files have been copied, the Complete Setup screen will be displayed. You should reboot your system after installing DB2 UDB for Windows NT. You should not install the Service Pack prior to rebooting. Select **Yes, I want to restart my computer now**. Click on **Finish**.

This completes the installation of the DB2 UDB server software. You must now install the DB2 UDB Service Pack.

4.2.1.1 Installing the DB2 UDB Service Pack

To install the DB2 UDB Service Pack, perform the following steps:

> **Note**
>
> Note that the DB2 UDB Service Packs supplied by SAP are not the same as the DB2 UDB Service Packs supplied by IBM. You should not install DB2 UDB Service Packs supplied by IBM on a machine in an SAP R/3 system.

1. Logon as <sapsid>adm.

2. Insert the CD labelled: *DB2 Common Server/RDBMS 5.0.0.17*. This CD should already be inserted since the service pack is installed immediately after the DB2 UDB server as described in the previous section.
3. Select **Start**->**Run**, enter `<X>:\NT_I386\FIXPAK\Setup.exe` (where **x** is the CDROM drive) and click on **OK**.
4. The Welcome screen is displayed again. Click on **Next**.
5. In the next screen, the Destination Directory **must** be the same as the original install directory. As a result, you are not allowed to change it at this point. Click on **Next**.
6. The Select Start Options screen is then displayed:

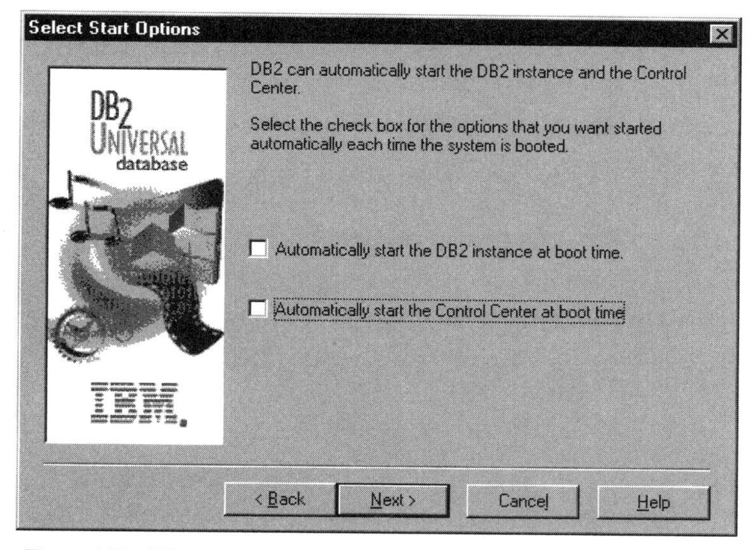

Figure 119. DB2 UDB Select Start Options

Ensure that neither option is selected and click on **Next**.

You should not select the option to have the DB2 instance start automatically at boot time, as the SAP R/3 Service Manager will control the database startup procedures. More information on starting up DB2 and SAP R/3 is discussed in "Administration in the R/3 DB2 UDB Environment" on page 257.

Starting the DB2 UDB Control Center automatically at boot time is a personal choice; however, we recommend that the Control Center should not be started automatically.

7. At the next screen, Start Copying Files, select **Install**.

8. After the installation process has completed successfully, select **Yes, I want to restart my computer now**. Remove the CD and choose **Finish**.

After system has rebooted, the installation of the DB2 UDB Service Pack is complete.

4.2.2 Dropping the DB2 Instance

After you have successfully rebooted and logged on again, close the DB2 First Steps window. The final step is to drop the existing DB2 instance before running the SAP R/3 Setup utility which will create its own database instance.

Note

Do not drop the DB2 instance if you are installing DB2 on an Administrator Workstation, as shown in Figure 113 on page 147.

From a command prompt, type

```
db2idrop DB2
```

You must reboot your computer at this point.

4.2.3 Installing the SAP R/3 Interface to the DB2 Control Center

The DB2 UDB Control Center needs to have an additional interface installed for use with R/3. This interface enables you to carry out R/3-related administrative tasks from the Control Center.

1. Logon to the computer where you will run the Control Center.

   This will either be an Administrator Workstation or the SAP R/3 server itself. The workstation setup is discussed in "Installation Procedures Common to Both NT and AIX" on page 171.

2. Insert the CD labelled: *DB2 Common Server/RDBMS 5.0.0.17*. This CD should already be inserted.

3. Select **Start** -> **Run**, and enter `<X>:\NT_I386\ADMIN\GUI\Db2ainst.exe` , where `x` is the CD-ROM drive, and click on **OK**.

4. At this point, you should see a command window as shown here:

```
E:\NT_I386\ADMIN\GUI>db2ainst
==================================================
Getting TEMP ...
        Ok.
Opening log file C:\TEMP\db2admin.log ...
        Ok.
Start of installation of DB2admin utilities GUI.
Determining DB2HOME ...
        found: C:\SQLLIB
        Ok.
Checking existence of directory C:\SQLLIB\bin ...
        Ok.
Unpacking files from E:\NT_I386\ADMIN\GUI to C:\SQLLIB\bin
        with car
----------------
Start log of car.
x CPPWOT3.DLL XXXXXXXXXXXXX
x db6achpw.exe XXXXXXXXXXXXXXXXXXXXXXXXXXXXXXXXXXX
x db6algfl.exe XXXXXXXXXXXXXXXXXXXXXXXXXXXXXXXXXXXXXXXXXXXXXX
x db6aopt.exe XXXXXXXXXXXXXXXXXXXXXXXXXXXXXXXXXXXXXXXXXX
x db6ar3db.exe XXXXXXXXXXXXXXXXXXXXXXXXXXXXXXXXXXXXX
x db6atape.exe XXXXXXXXXXXXXXXXXXXXXXXXXXXXXXXXXXXXXXXXXXXX
x sapact.dll XXXXXXXXXXXXXXXXXXXXXXXXXXXXXXXXX
x sapact.hlp
       XXXXXXXXXXXXXXXXXXXXXXXXXXXXXXXXXXXXXXXXXXXXXXXXXX
x sapdef.dll XXXXXXXXXXXXXXXXXXXXXXXXXXX
x sddb6wfm.dll X
End log of car.
----------------
        Ok.
DB2admin utilities GUI successfully installed.
```

5. After the command has completed successfully, the command window should close down automatically. If it does not, close down the command window after the utilities are successfully installed. This completes the installation of the SAP R/3 interface to the DB2 UDB Control Center.

4.3 Installing SAP R/3

This section takes you through the steps to install SAP R/3 on a Windows NT machine which hosts both the Central Instance and the Database Instance.

> **Note**
>
> Before running the R3SETUP GUI, you must have a frames-enabled web browser installed. This is required for the on-line help. You may use:
>
> - Netscape Navigator 3.0 or higher
> - Microsoft Internet Explorer 3.0 or higher

4.3.1 Installing R3SETUP

The first step is to install the R3SETUP GUI on your hard disk by running the R3SETUP.BAT program from the CD. This will copy some files to your computer. As a later step, you will run the R3SETUP GUI to perform the R/3 installation procedure.

1. Make sure you are still logged on as the <sapsid>adm userid (in this example, this is ausadm).
2. Check that the TEMP environment variable has been set. This is normally c:\temp. You can check this by typing the **set** command at a command prompt:

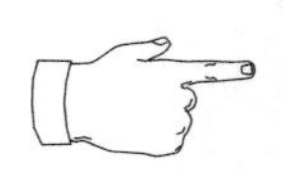

```
C:\WINDOWS>set
TMP=C:\WINDOWS\TEMP
TEMP=C:\TEMP
PROMPT=$p$g
winbootdir=C:\WINDOWS
COMSPEC=C:\COMMAND.COM
IMNINSTSRV=C:\IMNNQ_95
IMNINST=help
PATH=C:\PROGRA~1\PERSON~1;C:\WINDOWS;C:\WINDOWS\
:\CARDWORK;C:\SQLLIB\BIN;C:\SQLLIB\FUNCTION;C:\S
P;C:\IMNNQ_95
LIB=C:\SQLLIB\LIB
INCLUDE=C:\SQLLIB\INCLUDE
DB2INSTANCE=DB2
DB2PATH=C:\SQLLIB
windir=C:\WINDOWS
BLASTER=A220 I5 D1 T4
```

Note

It is advisable to clear out the TEMP directory of any other files and make sure that you have at least 40 MB of free space in this directory.

3. Insert the CD labelled *Release 4.0B/SAP Kernel*.
4. Select **Start** -> **Run**, then enter `<X>:\NT\COMMON\R3setup.bat`, where **x** is the CDROM drive) and click on **OK**.
5. Enter **c:\temp** as the name of the temporary directory and click on **Next**:

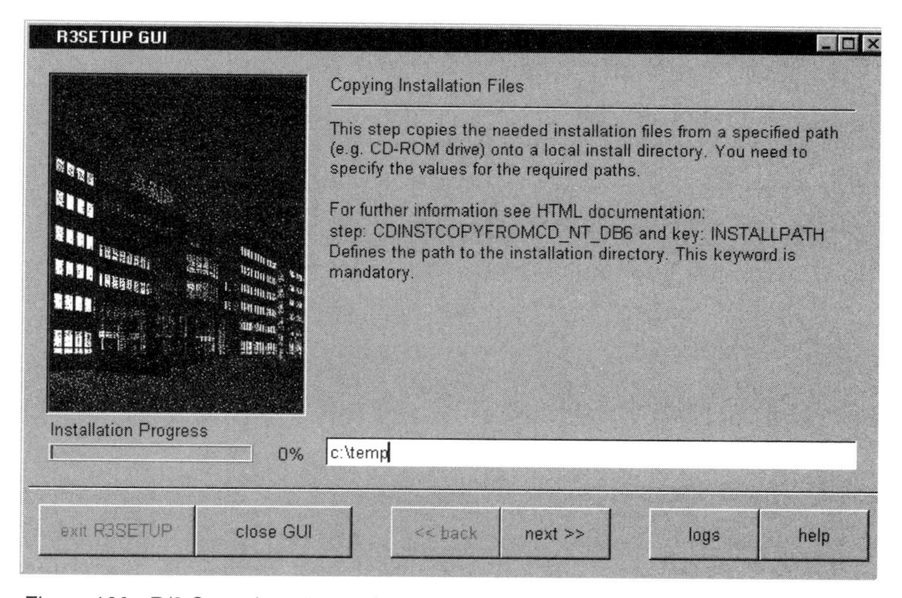

Figure 120. R/3 Setup Installation GUI

6. In the next screen, enter the name of your R/3 System (also known as the <sapsid> or <sid>) and click on **Next**. In this example, we used AUS.

Note

You must enter the name of the <sapsid> in UPPER CASE.

The program will now copy the initial installation files on to your hard disk and will add options to the Windows NT Programs menu.

7. When the copying is complete, you are prompted to logoff the system. Enter **YES** (the default) and click on **Next**.

You should now logon to the system again using the <sapsid>adm userid. This completes the initial setup and copying of files to your computer prior to the installation of R/3.

4.3.2 Installing R/3 Central and Database Instances

The previous steps copied several files to the c:\temp directory, including some instance templates which contain the default sizes of the table spaces used by the R/3 database. If you want to change these sizes, you can edit the template before executing the R3SETUP installation utility.

Note

For the remainder of this installation, it is very important to verify that you are entering the correct values as the installation program does minimal verification.

The template files are:

- **centrdb.r3s** - Used for the installation/configuration of a system which will host both the central and database instances, as in this example.
- **database.r3s** - Used for the installation/configuration of a database instance system only.

Here is an example of the layout of some template entries:

```
[Z_DB6CREATETSP]
PSAPBTABD=@Z_SAPDATAPATH=SAPDATA1@;600;1;16
PSAPBTABI=@Z_SAPDATAPATH=SAPDATA2@;300;1;8
PSAPCLUD=@Z_SAPDATAPATH=SAPDATA1@;100;1;64
PSAPCLUI=@Z_SAPDATAPATH=SAPDATA2@;20;1;32
PSAPDDICD=@Z_SAPDATAPATH=SAPDATA1@;280;1;16
PSAPDDICI=@Z_SAPDATAPATH=SAPDATA2@;150;1;16
```

The first parameter, Z_SAPDATAPATH, describes the path which is set during the creation process. The second parameter refers to the size of the table space (in MB), followed by the number of table space containers. The last parameter refers to the extent size to use. Based on these entries, it is possible to calculate the total amount of space needed during the database load, and then allocate sufficient disk space.

Note

In addition, two variables in the r3s files must be changed as explained in the most recent OSS notes. At the time of writing, these changes were:

- In Section [DB6USERDB2SIDENVIRONMENT_NT_DB6]
  - Replace @RUN_AS_SIDADM@ with @RUN_AS_DB2SID@
  - Replace @SIDADM_PWD@ with @DB2SID_PWD@

4.3.2.1 Running R3SETUP

This section goes through a complete installation of R/3 with a Central Instance and Database Instance, together with a database load. During the installation, an Installation Progress bar is displayed. This is not based on the elapsed time, but on the number of tasks completed. Even though the progress bar may show 88% complete, you may find that the next few tasks may take several hours (for example, table loads and updating the database statistics).

1. Start the installation by selecting **Start**->**Programs**->**SAP R/3 Setup**-> **Central Instance and Database Instance**. This screen is displayed:

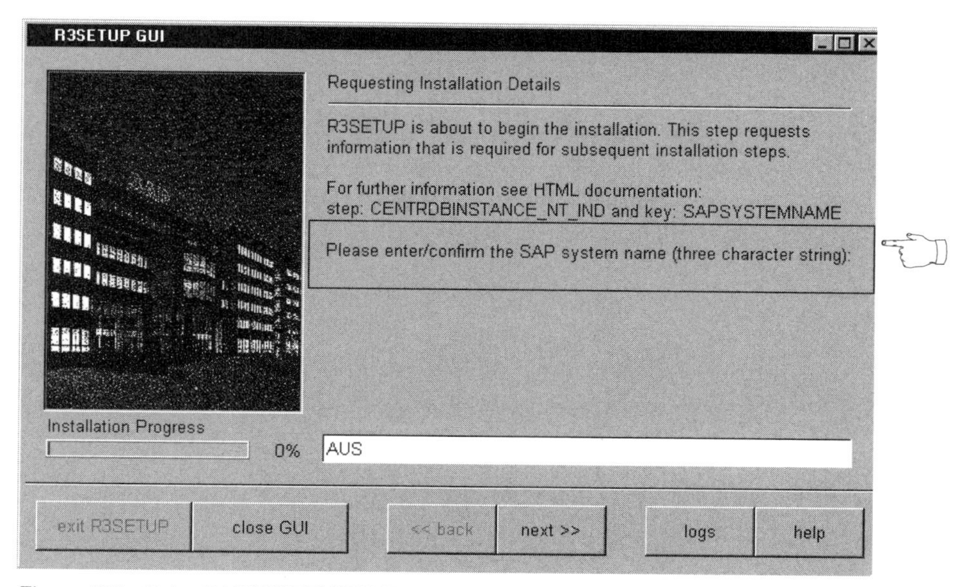

Figure 121. Enter SAPSYSTEMNAME

2. Enter the <sapsid> in upper case and select **Next**. Make sure you read the important boxed part of the screen, as highlighted in Figure 121.

Note

At any point in time, you can press the **help** button which will give you information about what is required at each prompt.

You can also select the **logs** button, which will display the current status of the R3SETUP installation, plus any warnings or error messages.

While the R3SETUP program is running, there is also a command window running in the background. It is useful to check this from time to time.

If the installation fails at any of the following stages, use these sources of information as well as the database.log or centrdb.log log files stored in the c:\temp directory to aid in problem determination.

3. The next prompt is for the SAP system number. If this is your first R/3 system on this server, enter **00** and **enter** or select **next**.
4. Enter the drive where the R/3 code will be installed, and select **next**.

Note

Enter the drive in uppercase followed by a colon (for example, D:)

5. The R3SETUP requires the name of the Windows NT domain of the R/3 System. In this example, we used the name ADOMAIN. Enter the domain name and select **next**.
6. The following SAP Transport screen is displayed:

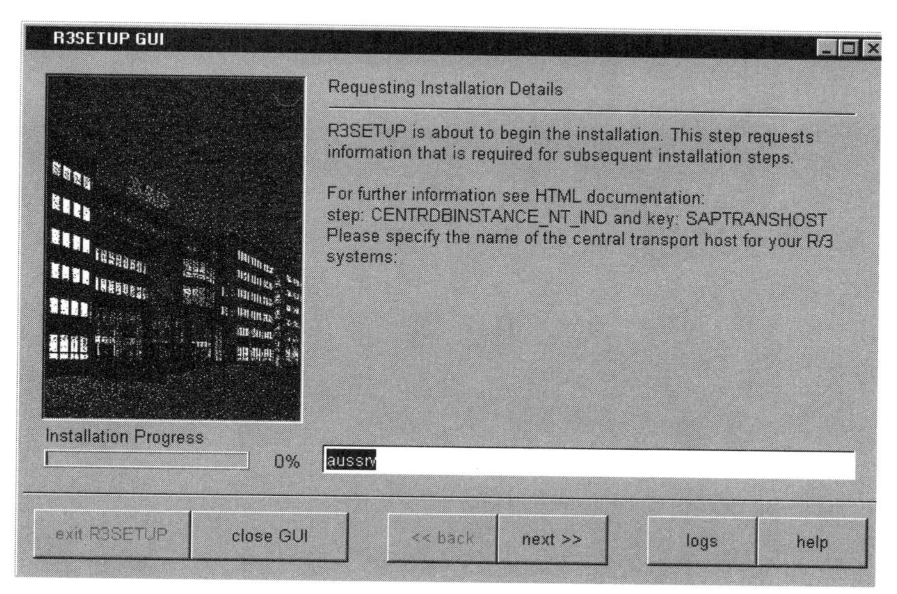

Figure 122. Enter SAPTRANSHOST

This is relevant in a Development, Test and Production landscape where R/3 Transports play an important role in the controlled movement of code. In this example, we used `aussrv` (the hostname of the system), since this is a single system environment. Enter the appropriate information for your environment and select **next**.

7. The next screen prompts you for the DB2 encryption key:

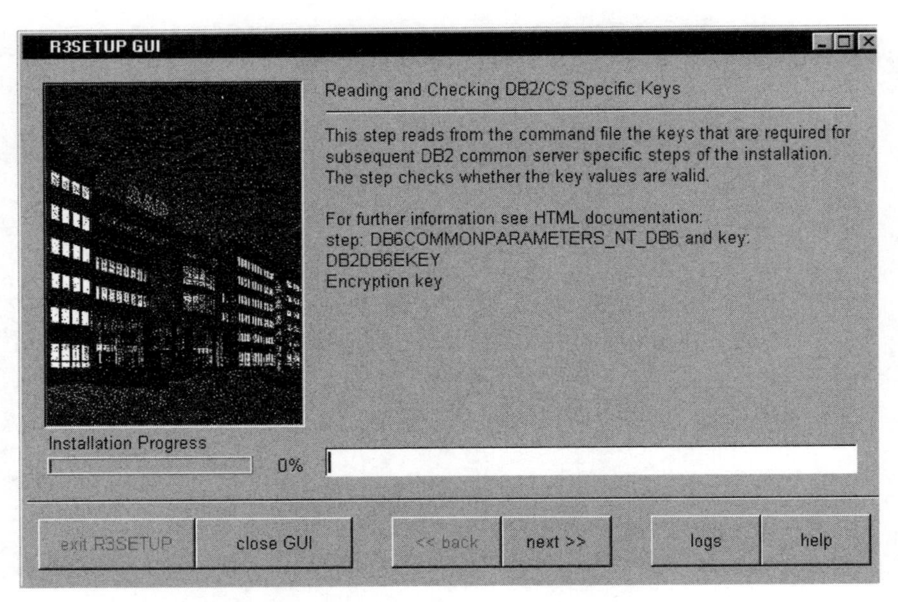

Figure 123. Enter DB2 Encryption Key

This is the license or nodelock key supplied with DB2 UDB. To get the value of this key, (assuming you have successfully installed DB2 UDB) follow these steps without exiting from the installation program:

1. Select **Start**->**Programs**->**License Use Runtime**->**Nodelock Administration Tool.**
2. Highlight the database product and click on **Selected->Open**. This screen is displayed:

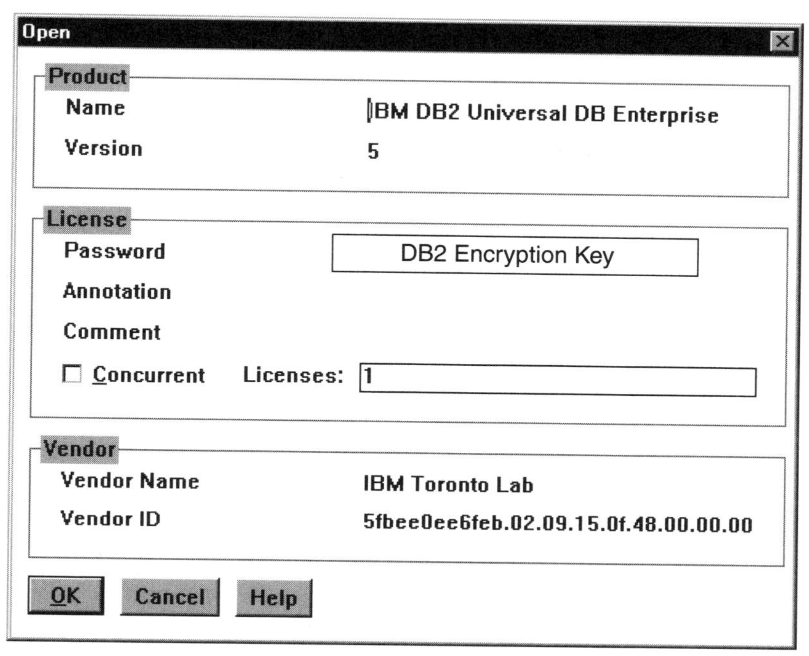

Figure 124. DB2 UDB Encryption Key

3. Highlight the key, and then cut and paste the key into the field in the R3SETUP program.

4. Close the Nodelock Administration Tool program.

Once the key has been entered in the R3SETUP screen, click on **next**.

8. Back in R3SETUP, the next screen requests a password for the db2<sapsid> userid. If this userid does not exist, it is created by the installation program. Enter a password. It is strongly recommended that you make a note of this password.

9. Enter the password of the <sapsid>adm userid. This userid already exists and should be the same userid as the one you have used to log onto Windows NT for this installation process.

10. Enter the database default installation path (DFTDBPATH).

Note

Make sure that the value for DFTDBPATH is in **upper case** followed by a **colon**. The DFTDBPATH is requested at various points during the installation — make sure you use the same path every time.

The installation program now prompts you for information about the disks you will use for the database setup. Enter the appropriate disks depending on the hardware configuration of your R/3 server. See the recommendations as discussed in "Pre-Installation Planning and Preparation" on page 39. In each case, enter the drive letter in upper case followed by a colon.

11. Enter the DB2 diagnostic file drive (DBDIAGPATH).
12. Enter the DB2 log drive.
13. Enter the DB2 log archive drive.
14. Enter the SAP reorganization drive.
15. Enter the drives for SAPDATA1 through SAPDATA6.
16. Enter a password for the userid sapr3. The userid will be created if it does not exist.
17. Enter the DB2 default path (DFTDBPATH). This parameter *must* the same as the DB2 default path you entered at the previous prompt (step 10).
18. For the SAP TCP/IP message port, accept the default value **3600**. Use the default unless you have a specific reason not to do so.
19. For the SAP TCP/IP service port, use the default value **5912**. As with the above entry, accept the default unless you have a different TCP/IP port already setup.
20. Enter the password for the SAPService<sapsid> userid.
21. The R3SETUP installation program now prompt you to mount various CDs, starting with the *SAP KERNEL* CD. Enter the CD and click on **next**.
22. The next prompt concerns SAP R/2 connections. If you do not require to setup a connection between R/2 and R/3 servers, you should choose **NO**. If you do require this kind of connection, enter **YES** and consult your SAP documentation for more details.

23. For the next prompt concerning the amount of memory on your system, enter **0** to make the installation program detect the amount of memory on your system.

24. You are prompted to insert the CD labelled: *DB Export CD 1*. The following screen is displayed:

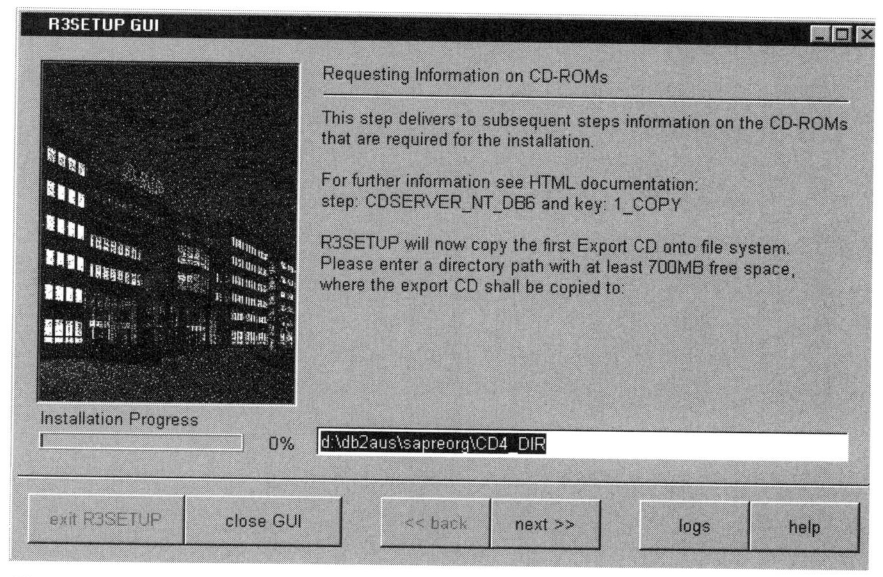

Figure 125. Enter Export CD Copy Path

25. Enter a directory where the *DB Export CD 1* is to be copied, then click **Next**.

Note

Make sure that this directory path has at least 700 MB of free space. Note that, by default, a directory under the SAP reorganization drive (see step 14) is used.

26. Insert the CD labelled: *DB2 Export CD 2*, and enter the appropriate drive letter in uppercase followed by a colon.

27. Insert the CD labelled: *Report Load CD Installation* and enter the appropriate drive letter in uppercase followed by a colon.

Note

After you have replied to the Report Load Installation prompt and have selected **next** to move to the next screen, remove the CD labelled *Report Load Installation* and replace it with the *SAP Kernel* CD.

28. The following prompt requests the number of parallel processes available for the DB2 load. Depending on your hardware setup, you may wish to increase the default. With only one processor, you should accept the default value of 3. If in doubt, accept the default value.

29. For the next prompt (platform specific), enter **NT** and press **enter** or select **next**.

30. For the DB2 default drive (DFTDBPATH), enter the same value that you entered in the previous prompts (steps 10 and 17). At this point, double-check that you have the *SAP Kernel CD* inserted.

31. R3SETUP will again prompt you for the DB2 default drive (DFTDBPATH). Enter the same value as in the previous prompt.

    There will be some disk activity as files are copied on to the hard disk.

32. You are prompted to insert the CD labelled: *DB2 Export CD 1*, and then enter the appropriate drive letter in uppercase followed by a colon.

33. You are prompted to insert the CD labelled: *DB2 Export CD 2*, and then enter the appropriate drive letter in uppercase followed by a colon.

    At this point, the R3SETUP process begins the load. Depending on the hardware you are using, this can take 8-16 hours. You may wish to activate the command window called: *SAP R3 setup* in order to monitor progress. Be careful not to close the R3SETUP GUI in the process. You will be prompted for further information towards the end of the installation process. The following figure shows an extract of the command window output.

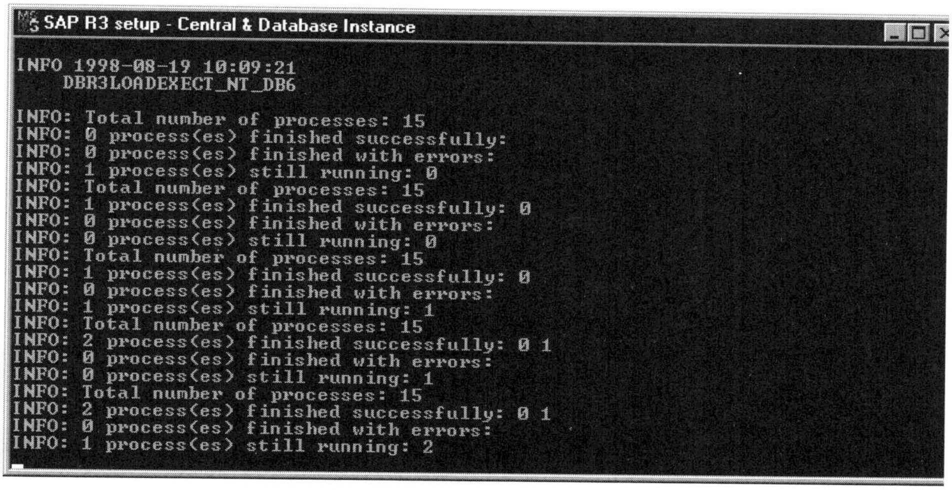

SAP R3 setup - Central & Database Instance

```
INFO 1998-08-19 10:09:21
    DBR3LOADEXECT_NT_DB6

INFO: Total number of processes: 15
INFO: 0 process(es) finished successfully:
INFO: 0 process(es) finished with errors:
INFO: 1 process(es) still running: 0
INFO: Total number of processes: 15
INFO: 1 process(es) finished successfully: 0
INFO: 0 process(es) finished with errors:
INFO: 0 process(es) still running: 0
INFO: Total number of processes: 15
INFO: 1 process(es) finished successfully: 0
INFO: 0 process(es) finished with errors:
INFO: 1 process(es) still running: 1
INFO: Total number of processes: 15
INFO: 2 process(es) finished successfully: 0 1
INFO: 0 process(es) finished with errors:
INFO: 0 process(es) still running: 1
INFO: Total number of processes: 15
INFO: 2 process(es) finished successfully: 0 1
INFO: 0 process(es) finished with errors:
INFO: 1 process(es) still running: 2
```

Figure 126. SAP R/3 Setup Command Window

34. When the progress bar reaches about 88%, you will be prompted to insert the *Report Load CD* and confirm the drive. These ABAP/4 report loads are CPU-dependent and are therefore not included in the initial DB2 Export 1 and 2 CDs.

    At approximately 94%, the data load completes and the R3SETUP program starts to generate statistics.

Note

On some systems, you may get a failure at 94%, relating to section DB6INSTALLADMIN_NT_DB6. This error is caused by the program sddb6ins.exe not being able to change directory to \\<hostname>\sapmnt\<sid>\sys\exe\run. If this occurs, you will need to download a new version of sddb6ins.exe from the SAP sapserv machine. Look in this directory:

/general/R3Server/patches/rel40B/NT/I386/DB6/sddb6ins_1.CAR.

Once downloaded, unpack the CAR file and replace the original version located in \usr\sap\<sid>\SYS\exe\run.

You will also need to update the Windows NT registry. Use REGEDT32 and go to **HKEY_LOCAL_MACHINE->SYSTEM->CurrentControlSet->Services->LanmanServer->Parameters**. You want to add a new value using **Edit->Add Value**. Enter a new value of IRPstackSize with a data type of REG_DWORD. Enter a value of 7 Decimal.

35. After the successful completion of the statistics generation, there is a panel requesting whether you plan to import languages other than Latin-1. If you require other language support, you will have to exit at this point and execute the appropriate MNLS programs [1]. You must however re-run the R3SETUP program to complete the installation.

Note

To support additional languages, before you rerun R3SETUP above, use transaction **RZ10** to change:

- zcsa/table_buffer_area from 600000 (default) to 25000000.
- rtbb/buffer_length from 2000 (default) to 25000.
- rdisp/bufrefmode to sendoff/exeauto. Change it back to sendoff/exeauto when the language load is done.

This will reduce generic key and single record table buffer swapping.

[1] See the most recent OSS NOTES on additional language support. At the time of writing these were OSS Notes 15023 and 45619

Note

If at any point in time you need to restart R3SETUP, it will continue from where it last terminated; whether because of a system error or because the user has explicitly terminated the program.

If you have selected **No** to the above prompt, the R3SETUP will complete successfully.

36. The final step after the R3SETUP has completed is to install the latest Dynamic Link Libraries. Insert the *SAP Kernal* CD ROM. Select **Start-> Run** and enter `<X>:\NT\i386\NTPATCH\r3dllins.exe`, where `x` is the CD-ROM drive, and click on **OK**. Reboot after the successful installation of the new DLLs.

This completes the SAP R/3 installation on Windows NT. You should now install the SAP Frontend as described in the next chapter.

Chapter 5. Installation Procedures Common to Both NT and AIX

This chapter covers the installation procedures that are common to both a Windows NT and AIX R/3 DB2 UDB environment. For the purposes of this book, these procedures are performed on Windows NT. In particular, we examine the setup of an administrator workstation, the installation of the SAP Frontend, and the installation of the SAP On-line Documentation. Both the SAP Frontend and the SAP On-line Documentation can be installed on either the R/3 server, in the case of the Windows NT server, or on an administration workstation. The chapter is divided into the following sections:

- DB2 on the Administration Workstation:
    - Installing the DB2 Client Application Enabler
    - Installing the DB2 UDB Service Pack
    - Installing the SAP R/3 interface to the DB2 UDB Control Center
    - Cataloging the database to be administered
- Installing the R/3 Frontend
- Installing the R/3 On-line Documentation

You can also refer to Appendix B, “R/3 and DB2 Installation Checklist” on page 499 to help you follow all the necessary installation steps. This chapter follows the steps as indicated in Figure 127 on page 172 (below) under the section Administrator Workstation, as well as the installation of the R/3 Frontend and On-line Documentation for both the server and the workstation.

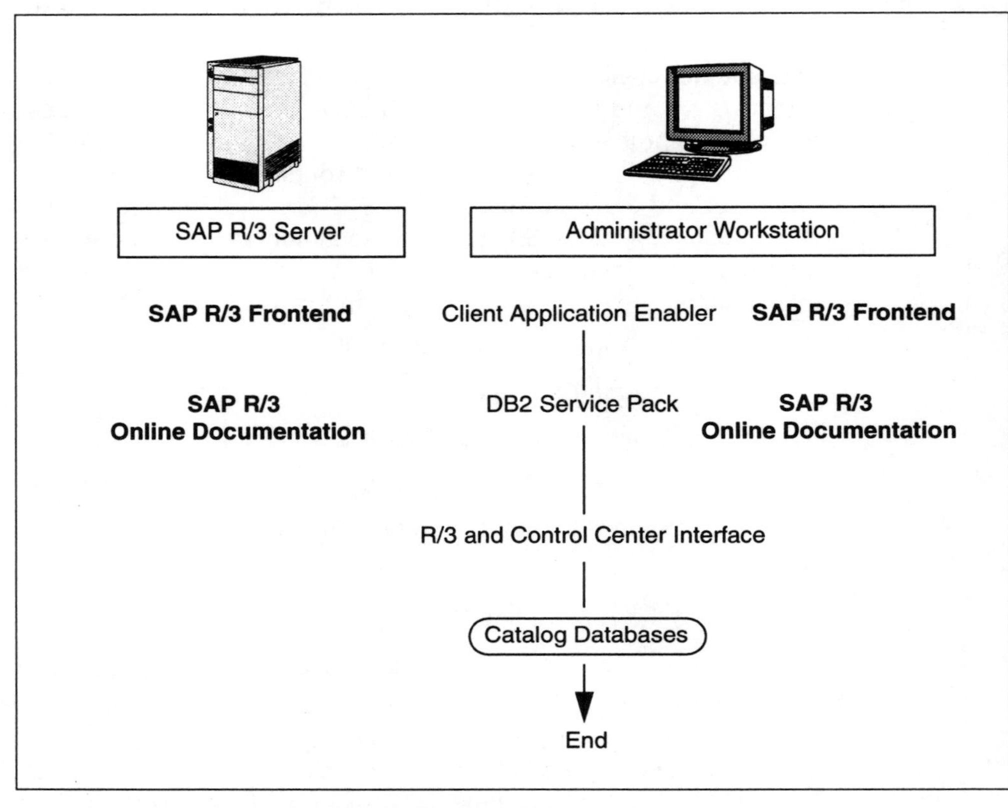

Figure 127. DB2 UDB and R/3 Software Installation Path

Further information on DB2 UDB is available in the *IBM DB2 Universal Database for Windows NT Quick Beginnings* in Appendix A: Obtaining Information. It is available in HTML format on the SAP R/3 CD labelled *DB2 common Server/RDBMS 5.0.0.17* under the directory \Doc\En\Html\Db2i6. Open the file DB2I6.HTM with your web browser.

5.1 DB2 on the Administrator Workstation

You should setup at least one administrator workstation to administer your DB2 UDB environment. You will install the DB2 Client Application Enabler (CAE) on this machine. If you setup more than one administrator workstation, you can perform administration tasks for your entire R/3 and DB2 landscape from any one of these workstations.

5.1.1 Installing DB2 UDB Client Application Enabler (CAE)

The CAE may be installed on any Intel client from which you wish to administer the R/3 DB2 UDB environment. The CAE will give you access to the DB2 Control Center, the command line interface to DB2, as well as the Client Configuration Assistant and Information Center.

> **Note**
>
> It is not necessary to install the CAE on the Windows NT R/3 server as this is included in the DB2 UDB Enterprise Edition installation.

To install the CAE on the administrator workstation:

1. Logon to the workstation.
2. Insert the CD labelled: *DB2 Common Server/RDBMS 5.0.0.17*.
3. Select **Start**->**Run**, then enter `<X>:\NT_I386\DBSW\Setup.exe`, where `x` is the CDROM drive, and click on **OK**.
4. The Welcome screen is displayed. Select **Next**.
5. The Select Products screen is displayed:

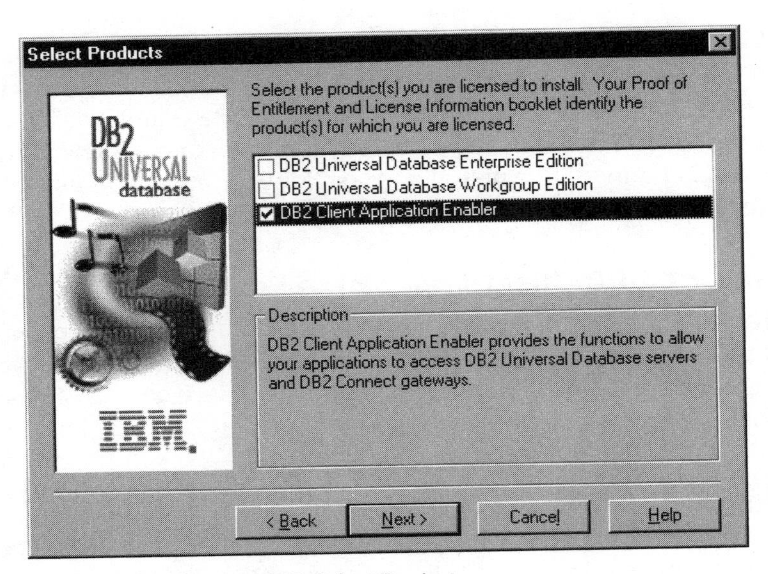

Figure 128. DB2 UDB CAE Select Products

Select DB2 Client Application Enabler and click on **Next**.

6. The Enable Remote Administration screen is displayed:

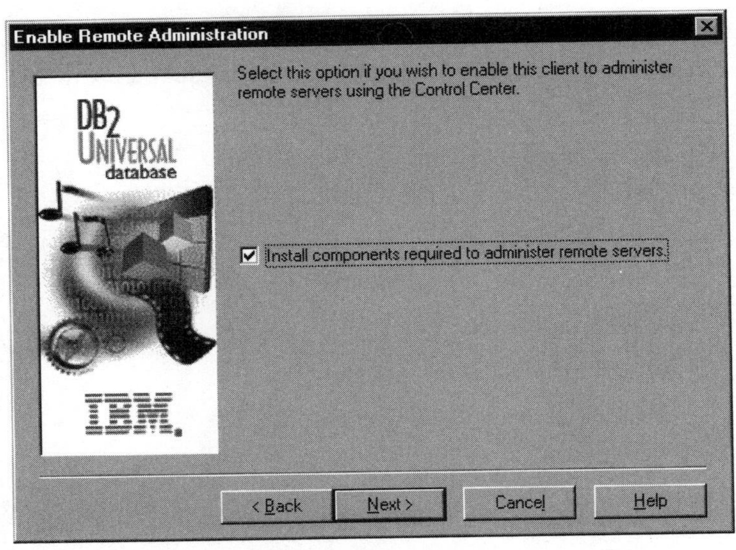

Figure 129. DB2 UDB CAE Enable Remote Administration

Select the option to install components required to administer remote databases and click on **Next**.

7. The Select Installation Type screen is then displayed. Select **Typical**.
8. In the next screen, select an appropriate destination directory and click on **Next**.

> **Note**
>
> You must have about 100 MB of free space on the selected partition before you install the CAE.

9. The Start Copying Files screen is displayed. Within this screen, there is a window which displays your current settings and which options will be installed. Select **Install**.

   The installation process will now copy the appropriate files onto your computer.

10. The Complete Setup screen is displayed. Select **Reboot only** (Manually start the Client Configuration Assistant at a later time) and click on the **Finish** button.

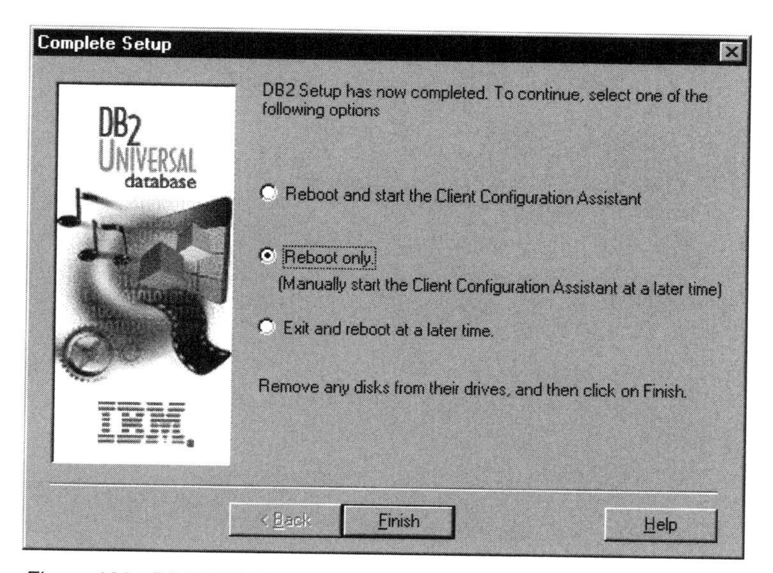

Figure 130. DB2 UDB CAE Complete Setup

After your computer reboots, logon and you will see the DB2 Control Center started automatically. This happens because the installation process adds an icon for the Control Center in the Windows NT Startup folder. When you install the DB2 UDB Service Pack in the next step, you can change the Control Center autostart settings.

There is an another entry in the StartUp folder called Start HTML Server. This is required for the DB2 Information Center, and should not be removed from the StartUp folder.

5.1.2 Installing the DB2 UDB Service Pack

To install the DB2 UDB Service Pack, perform the following steps:

> **Note**
>
> Note that the DB2 UDB Service Packs supplied by SAP are not the same as the DB2 UDB Service Packs supplied by IBM. You should not install DB2 UDB Service Packs supplied by IBM on a machine in an SAP R/3 system.

1. Logon to your workstation and ensure that your Windows NT userid has administrative authority.
2. Insert the CD labelled *DB2 Common Server/RDBMS 5.0.0.17.*
3. Select **Start** ->**Run**, then enter `<X>:\NT_I386\FIXPAK\Setup.exe` (where **x** is the CDROM drive) and click on **OK**.
4. The Welcome screen is displayed. Select **Next**.
5. At the following screen, select the destination directory and click on **Next**.
6. The Select Start Options screen is then displayed:

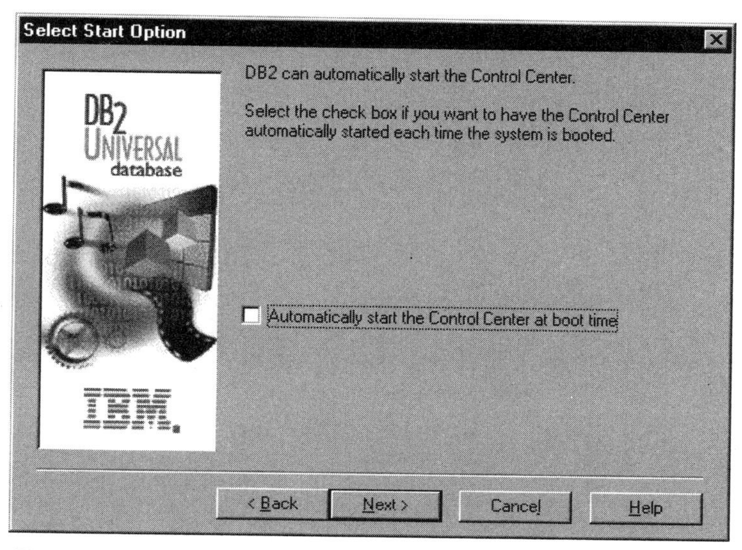

Figure 131. DB2 UDB CAE Select Start Option

Ensure that the option to automatically start the DB2 UDB Control Center is *not* selected and click on **Next**.

While the option to automatically start the DB2 UDB Control Center at system start time is a personal choice, we recommend that the Control Center not be started automatically.

7. At the next screen, Start Copying Files, select **Install**.
8. After the install has completed successfully select **Reboot only** (Manually start the Client Application Enabler at a later time). Remove the CD and choose **Finish**.

The system will now reboot and the installation is complete.

5.1.3 Installing the R/3 Interface to the DB2 UDB Control Center

For the R/3 environment, you now should install an additional interface to the DB2 UDB Control Center. This interface enables you to carry out R/3 administrative tasks from the Control Center.

1. Logon to the computer where you will run Control Center. This will either be an administrator workstation or the R/3 server (Windows NT only) itself.
2. Insert the CD labelled *DB2 Common Server/RDBMS 5.0.0.17.*
3. Select **Start** ->**Run**, then enter `<X>:\NT_I386\ADMIN\GUI\Db2ainst.exe` (where `x` is the CD-ROM drive) nd click on **OK**.

The following command window should be displayed:

```
E:\NT_I386\ADMIN\GUI>db2ainst
==================================================
Getting TEMP ...
        Ok.
Opening log file C:\WINDOWS\TEMP\db2admin.log ...
        Ok.
Start of installation of DB2admin utilities GUI.
Determining DB2HOME ...
        found: C:\SQLLIB
        Ok.
Checking existence of directory C:\SQLLIB\bin ...
        Ok.
Unpacking files from E:\NT_I386\ADMIN\GUI to C:\SQLLIB\bin
        with car
-----------------
Start log of car.
x CPPWOT3.DLL XXXXXXXXXXXXX
x db6achpw.exe XXXXXXXXXXXXXXXXXXXXXXXXXXXXXXXXXXX
x db6algfl.exe XXXXXXXXXXXXXXXXXXXXXXXXXXXXXXXXXXXXXXXXXXXXXX
x db6aopt.exe XXXXXXXXXXXXXXXXXXXXXXXXXXXXXXXXXXXXXXXXXX
x db6ar3db.exe XXXXXXXXXXXXXXXXXXXXXXXXXXXXXXXXXXXXX
x db6atape.exe XXXXXXXXXXXXXXXXXXXXXXXXXXXXXXXXXXXXXXXXXXXX
x sapact.dll XXXXXXXXXXXXXXXXXXXXXXXXXXXXXXXXX
x sapact.hlp
        XXXXXXXXXXXXXXXXXXXXXXXXXXXXXXXXXXXXXXXXXXXXXXXX
x sapdef.dll XXXXXXXXXXXXXXXXXXXXXXXXXXX
x sddb6wfm.dll X
End log of car.
-----------------
        Ok.
DB2admin utilities GUI successfully installed.
```

After the command has completed successfully, close down the command window (if it does not automatically close down). This completes the installation of the R/3 interface to the DB2 UDB Control Center.

5.1.4 Cataloging the Remote R/3 Database

After you have installed the CAE on a workstation, you will need to catalog (or add) the server, the DB2 Instance and the databases at the workstation before you can start using the DB2 administration utilities.

1. To start the Control Center, select **Start**->**Programs**-> **DB2 for Windows NT**->**Administration Tools**->**Control Center**.

2. To add the remote system, right-click on the **System** icon In the left hand panel and choose **Add**. A popup window is displayed:

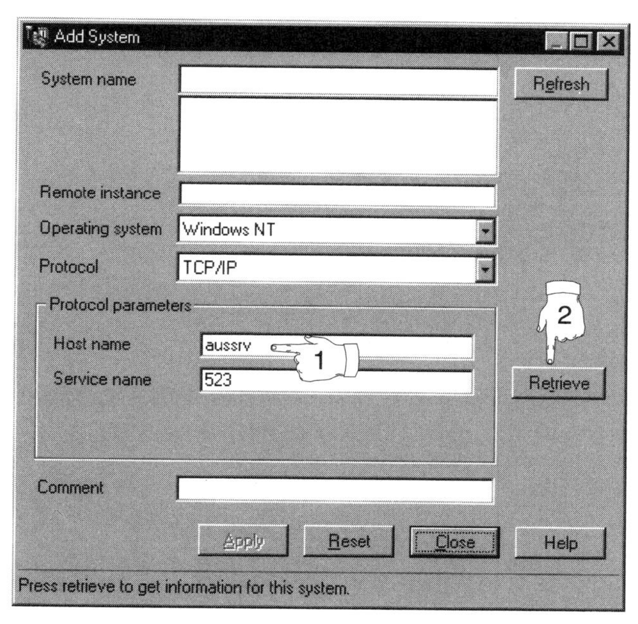

Figure 132. DB2 Control Center Add System

Enter the **Host name** (1) and click on the **Retrieve** (2) button. After the details have been displayed, add a **Comment** if you wish and click on **Apply** followed by **Close**. If the details are not displayed ensure that the DB2 Administration Server at your remote DB2 system is running.

3. To add the remote instance, click on the **+** against the newly added system to expand the tree. Right click on the **Instance** icon for the system you just added and select **Add**. Select **Refresh.** You will be presented with a list of instances on the remote system. Using the pulldown on the remote instance entry field, choose the remote instance to catalog, add a comment, **Apply** and **Close**.

4. To add a remote database, click on the + character to expand the tree under the new instance name. Right click on the **database** icon and select **Add**. Select **Refresh**, choose the database desired from the pulldown list, add a comment, **Apply** and **Close**.

There are two databases associated with the SAP R/3 system, called <sapsid> and adm<sapsid>. The <sapsid> database holds most of the R/3 data and the adm<sapsid> holds a small amount of administrative data. This completes the cataloging of the databases using the DB2 UDB Control Center.

In order to confirm that you have successfully installed the R/3 DB2 administration tools, right click on the <sapsid> database icon and you should be presented with these R/3 specific options:

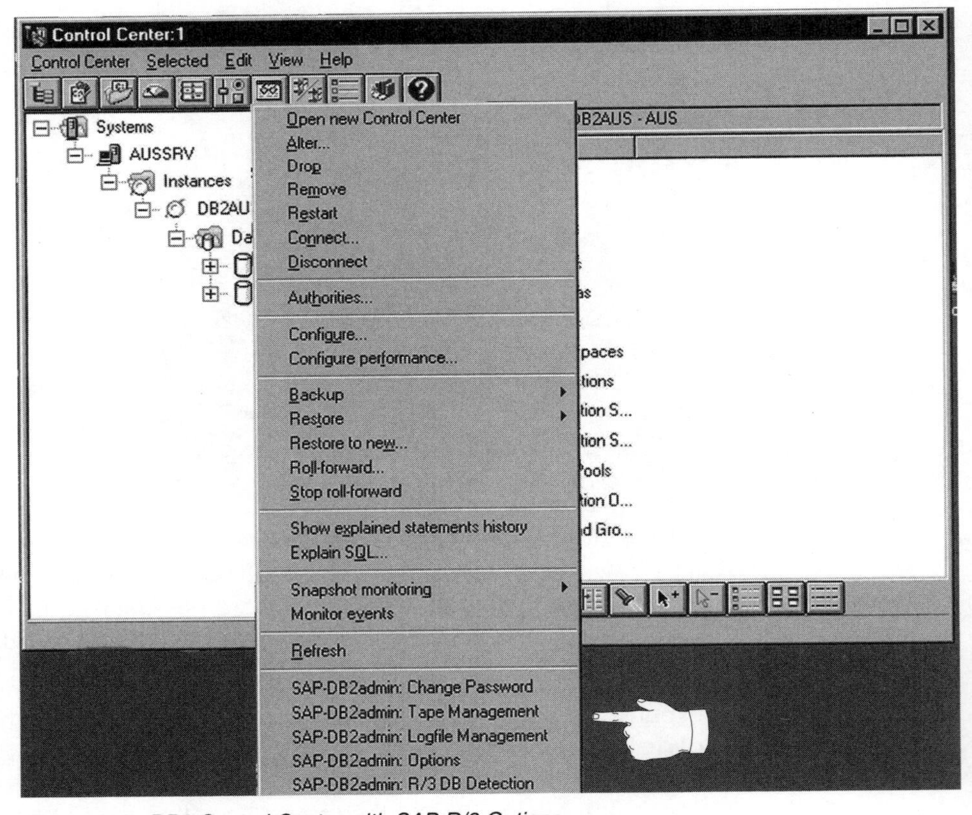

Figure 133. DB2 Control Center with SAP R/3 Options

5.2 Installing the SAP R/3 Frontend

This section describes the installation steps required to install the R/3 Frontend. This GUI enables the user to connect to the R/3 system and run applications or perform administrative tasks such as managing users or databases. The SAP Frontend can be installed on the R/3 server as well as on the workstation. It is not automatically installed as part of the Central Instance installation. You will need to go through these steps to install it on the SAP R/3 server.

There are various scenarios for the installation of the SAP Frontend software. You can set up a PC as an installation server from which many PC's can install the SAP Frontend or simply install the code directly onto the computer you wish to work from.

This section describes a local client installation also known as a standard installation. For details about other available scenarios, see the installation documentation entitled *Installing SAP Frontend Software for PCs.*

1. Insert the CD labelled *Presentation.*
2. Select **Start**->**Run**, enter **<X>:\GUI\WINDOWS\WIN32**[1]**\Sapsetup.exe** (where **x** is the CDROM drive) and click on **OK**.
3. The SAP Frontend welcome screen is displayed. Select **Next**.

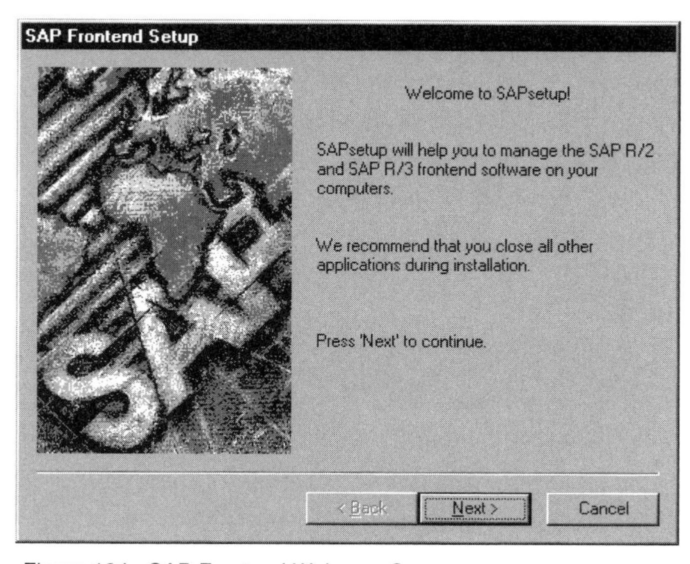

Figure 134. SAP Frontend Welcome Screen

[1] This directory structure is dependent on which operating system you are running on.

4. At the next several prompts, enter **Next** to move forward through the installation:
   - Select **Client Installation**.
   - Select **Individual installation**.
   - Select the appropriate components - **SAPGUI** and **SAPLOGON**.

   You may wish to add further components to your environment other than just SAPGUI and SAPLOGON.
   - Select **Local Installation**.
   - Leave the installation directory to default if you have enough disk space for the installation or provide a directory which does have the required disk space.
   - Select the language.
   - Leave the directory to default.
5. At this point you are presented with the panel asking you for application server information:

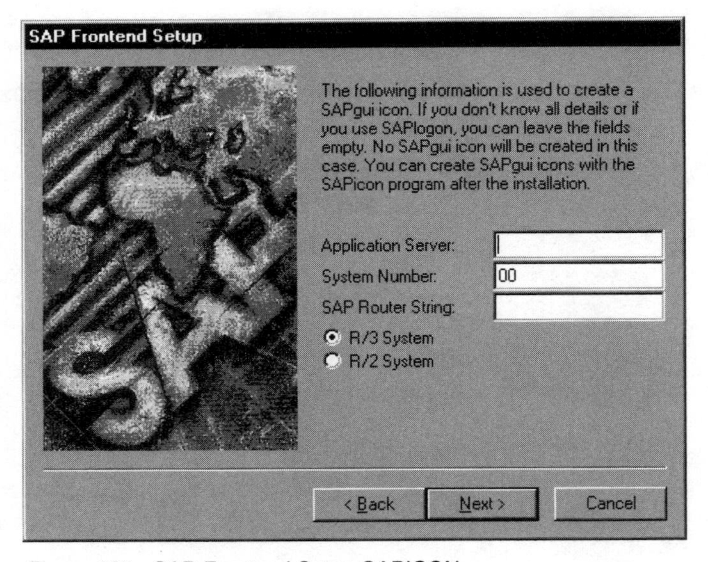

Figure 135. SAP Frontend Setup SAPICON

For Application Server, enter the hostname or IP address of the R/3 server. Normally the System Number is 00.

You can also configure the SAP Frontend at a later stage by using the SAPicon utility or the SAPLogon utility. Once you fill in this panel, press **Next**.

6. At the next panel, enter the path of the CD. Leave the Program Group information as default.

The program will now copy the files from the CD to your computer. The amount of disk space will vary on the options selected. After the copying has finished, the installation is complete. To startup the SAP Frontend, select **Start**->**Programs**->**SAP Frontend 4.0B**. This will take you to your SAPLogon item(s) as well as any previously configured SAPicons. You can use either of these to start your Frontend and connect to your SAP R/3 system.

5.3 Installing the R/3 On-line Documentation

This section details how to install the R/3 On-line Documentation using the HtmlHelpFile setup. There are other possible scenarios available and should one of these options be more suitable then you should refer to the separate documentation as supplied with the SAP software, *Installing the Online Documentation.* The various options exist to meet the requirements and exploit the potential different SAP installations and Frontend platforms.

The different installation types differ primarily in their file format and in the way in which they access the documents. The following types are available:

PlainHtmlHttp — Standard HTML files accessed via a web server, available on all Frontend platforms.

PlainHtmlFile — Standard HTML files accessed via a file server, available on all frontend platforms except for Windows 16 bit.

HtmlHelpFile — Compressed HTML files accessed via a file server, available on Windows NT 4.0 and Windows 95.

5.3.1 Features of HtmlHelpFile

This version of the R/3 On-line Documentation is in Compressed HTML format (CHM), developed by Microsoft. The following features are available:

- Only available from Windows 95 and Windows NT 4.0 Frontend platforms.
- Documents are stored on a file server of your choice.
- Documents are displayed with Microsoft HTML Help Viewer 1.1. This is an extension to Microsoft Internet Explorer.

- Browsing in defined structures, such as using a table of contents and along hypertext links.
- Full text search.
- Keyword search on all documents.
- Printing of single documents.

5.3.2 Installing HtmlHelpFile

To install the HtmlHelpFile files:

> **Note**
>
> You can either copy the files over from the CD to a hard disk, or access the help and online documentation directly from the CD.

1. First, you should install Microsoft Internet Explorer 3.2:
   - Insert CD *R/3 Online Documentation (English)*.
   - Select **Start->Run** and enter `<X>\htmlhelp\setup\ie302\nt4_en\msie302.exe`, where `x` is the CDROM drive.
   - Allow the installation to complete and reboot your system.
2. Install the HtmlHelp interface facility. Use Windows NT Explorer to locate the Htmlhelp.inf file on the CD, which is in the \Htmlhelp\Setup\Hh11 directory, then right-click on the file and click **Install**:

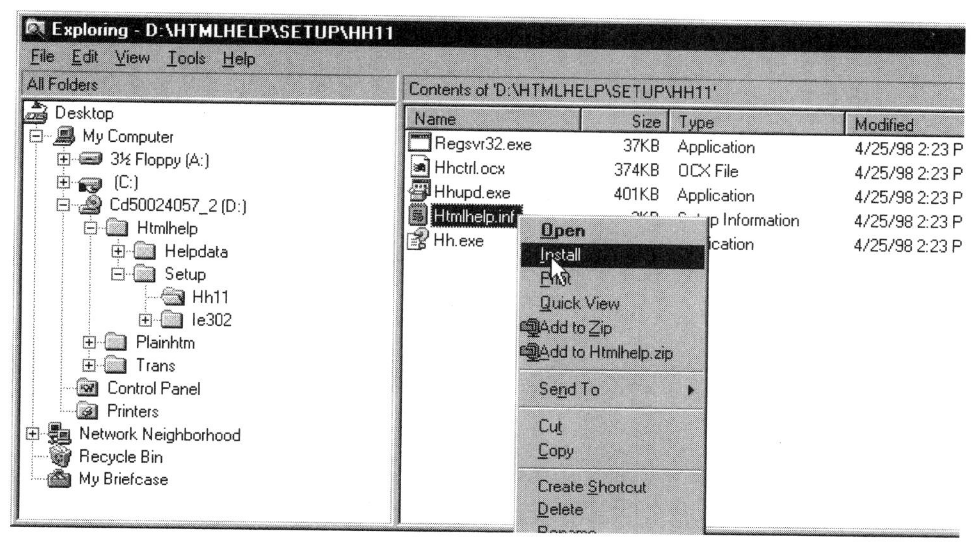

Figure 136. Installing the Htmlhelp.inf file

3. Update the Windows NT program interface. Use Windows NT Explorer to locate the Hh40b-en.inf file on the CD, which is in the \Htmlhelp\Helpdata\En directory, then right-click on this file and click **Install**:

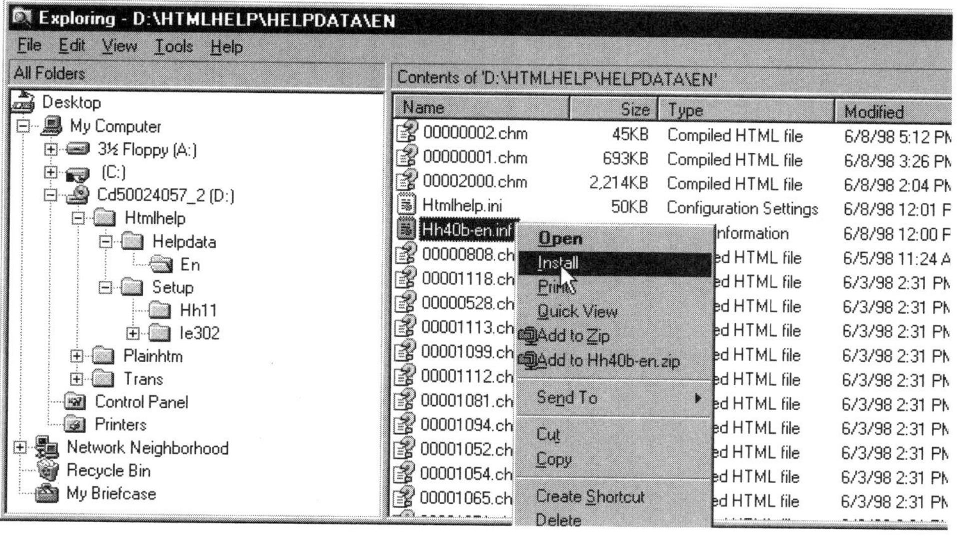

Figure 137. Installing Hh40b-en.inf

In order to access the online documentation, select **Start->Programs->SAP Online Help 4.0B (HtmlHelp)**. You then have the following choices:

- Getting started
- Glossary
- Implementation Guide
- Library
- Release Notes

You can select any of the options and will be presented with a screen similar to this one:

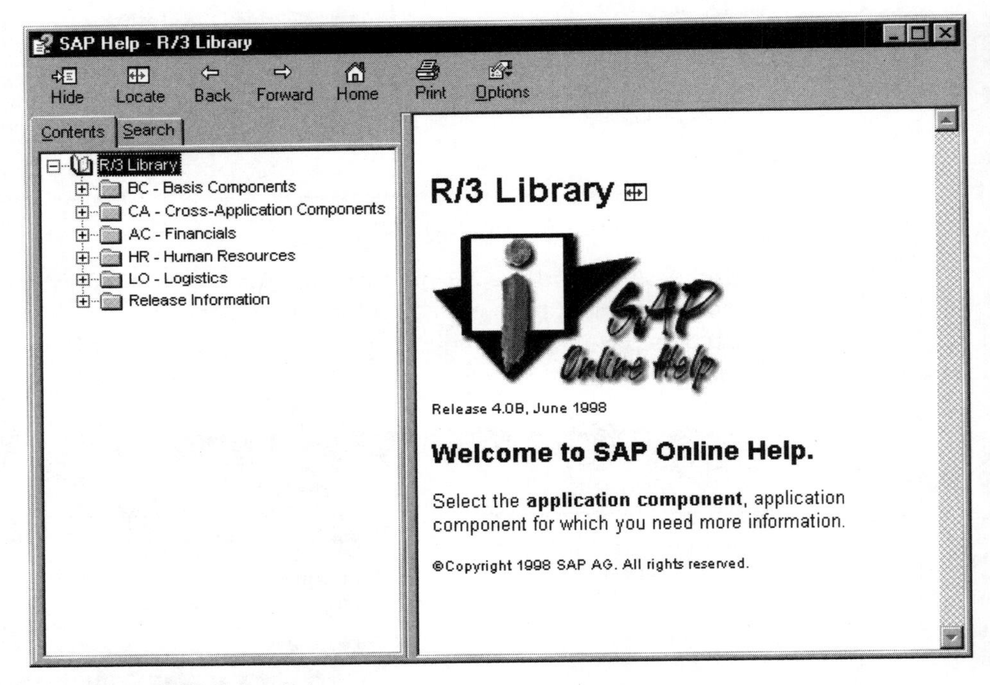

Figure 138. SAP Online Help

This completes the installation procedure for the R/3 On-line Documentation in the Windows NT environment.

To have access to the help and online documentation from within the R/3 Frontend, you also need to configure the R/3 instance profile. Edit the following three parameters using transaction **RZ10**:

eu/iwb/help_type	5
eu/iwb/installed_languages	List one letter (for example, E)
eu/iwb/path_win32	Name of the path where the compressed HTML files are stored

Save and reload the instance profile.

Chapter 6. Post-Installation Tasks

This chapter details the tasks that must be performed after the installation of SAP R/3 to make the system usable to the customer. Failure to complete these tasks could result in an unusable SAP system; or may cause a large amount of reconfiguration at a later date.

The post installation tasks are the same for both the AIX and Windows NT operating systems. The commands to accomplish them may vary, and these differences will be noted in the chapter.

It is also important to review the *R/3 Installation Guide* which applies to your level of SAP as well as for the operating system that you will use. There may be special steps that are level specific.

6.1 Installing a SAP License

The SAP product requires a license to allow you to access your system.

A 30 day temporary license is installed with the initial setup. The permanent key must be obtained from SAP by supplying the hardware key for your system. SAP provides a tool called SAPLICENSE to install, check, and delete the license key.

6.1.1 Using Saplicense

The user must be logged in as <SID>adm to run the saplicense tool.

To show the options, enter **saplicense** from a command prompt. The following functions are available:

```
-delete                 delete installed license
-get                    get customer key (hardware key)
-help [option]          display help information
option: get/install/temp/show/test
-install                install license key
-number                 get installation number
-show                   show license table
-temp                   install temporary license
-test                   test license
-version                show version of saplicense
[ ... ]       optional SAP command line parameters
              e.g. NAME=<SID>  TRACE=2  pf=<profile
```

6.1.2 Displaying the Hardware Key

To display the hardware key of your system, type:

```
saplicense -get
```

A response similar to the one below is displayed:

```
saplicense: CUSTOMER KEY = M055899026
```

6.1.3 Requesting A Permanent Key

To obtain the permanent key, there are two methods that can you can use:

1. Fax the hardware key to SAP using the fax number supplied in your installation kit.
2. Submit the key using OSS if you already have an OSS account.

   The procedure to do this is as follows:

1. Log on to OSS via transaction **OSS1**.

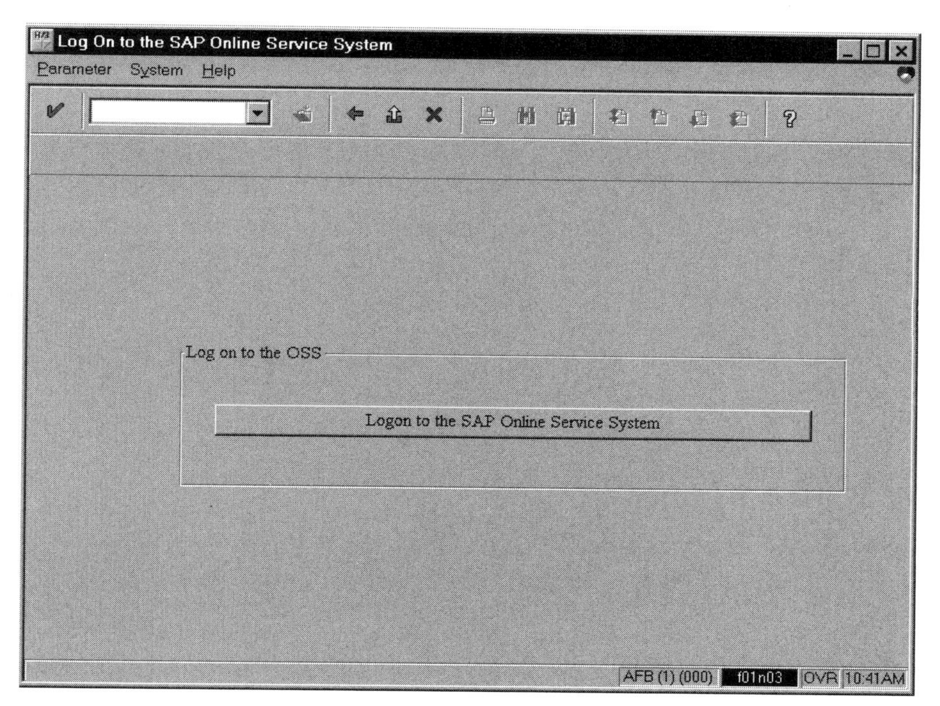

Figure 139. OSS Logon Screen

2. Click the Logon Button.

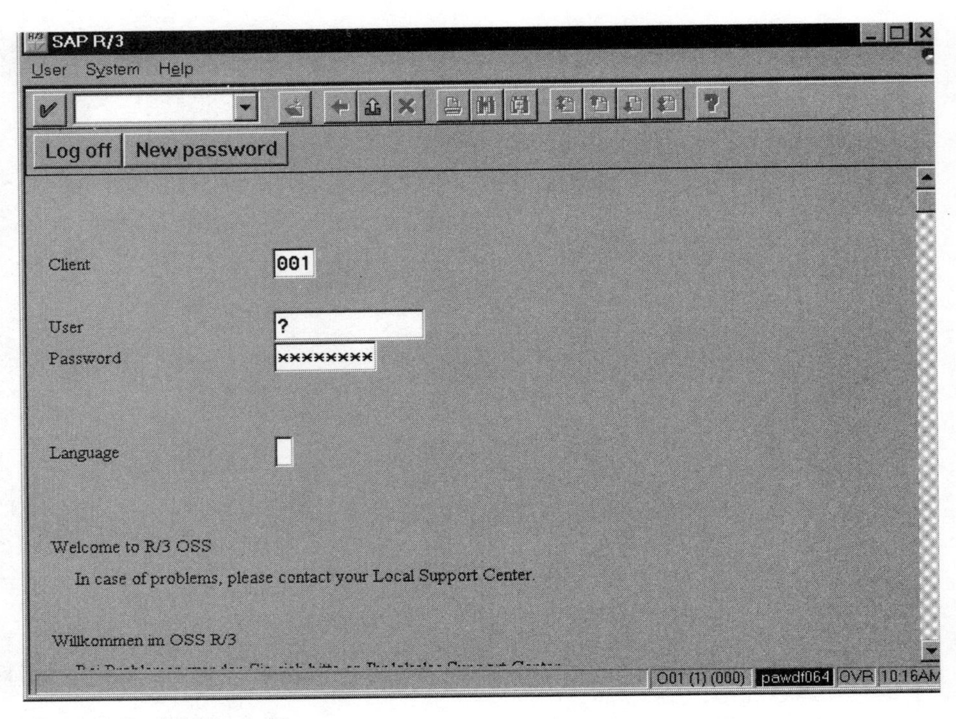

Figure 140. OSS Login Menu

3. Enter your ID and Password and press **Enter**. The OSS Main Menu is displayed:

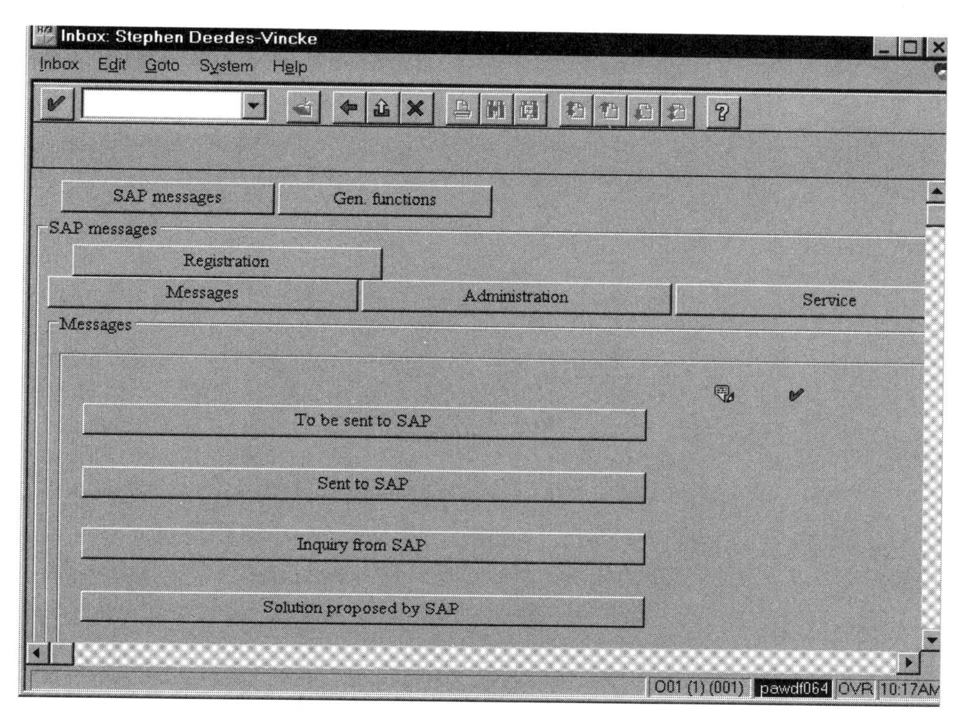

Figure 141. OSS Main Menu

4. Click **Registration,** followed by **R/3 System**.

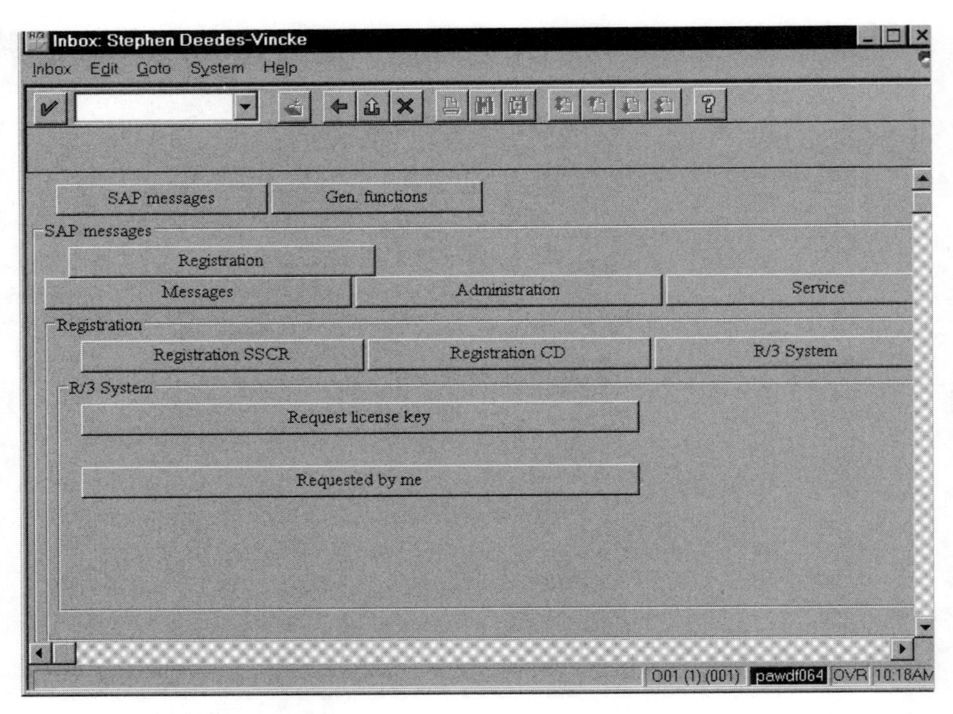

Figure 142. OSS Request License Key

5. Click **Request License Key**. The panel to request your key is displayed:

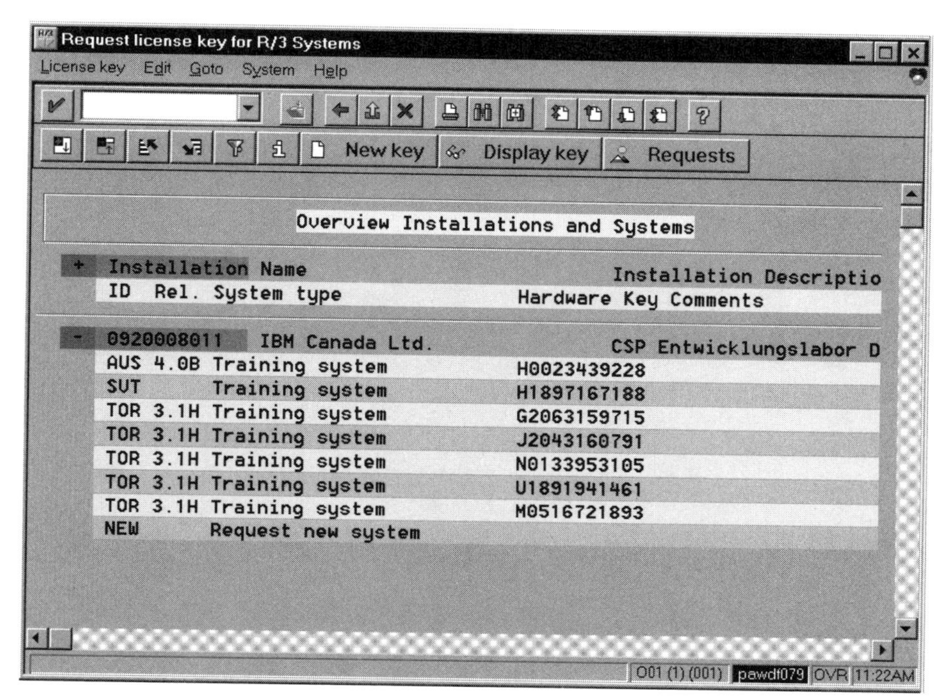

Figure 143. Request License Key for R/3 Systems

6. Select your installation number.

- Click on **New Key**.

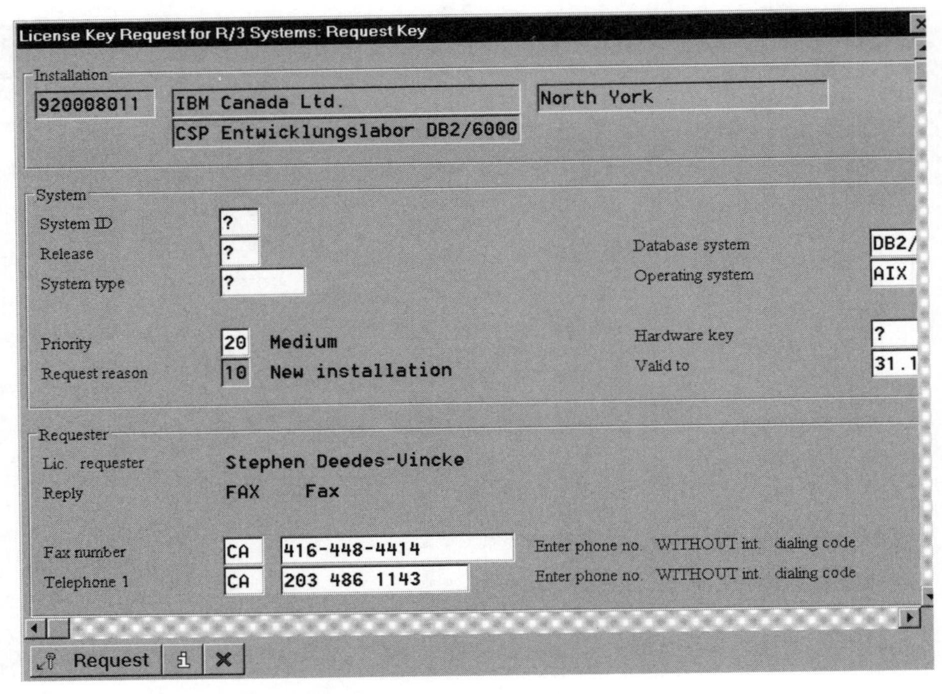

Figure 144. Request Key: Detail Screen

7. Fill in your details for your site.
   - Click **Request** at the bottom left of the above panel.

To check the status of your requests, or to see the key when it is generated:

- From the request screen shown in Figure 142 on page 194, click on **Requests**.
- To look at the key, select the installation number and hardware key and click **Display Key**.

You should record *both* the license key and the expiration date when the license generation is completed, as both these pieces of information are required to install this permanent license.

6.1.4 Installing the Permanent License

When you receive the key from SAP, you can install it by entering:

```
saplicense -install
```

You will need your:

- SAP System ID or <sapsid>.
- Your customer key - you can get this by using **saplicense -get**.
- Your installation number.
- The expiration date of the license key.
- The license key.

Be careful when entering these values. Leading zeroes should be included, as shown in the example below for the installation number:

```
C:\>SAPLICENSE -install
Specify your SAP System ID:
SAP SYSTEM ID = AUS
Specify your customer key:
CUSTOMER KEY = H0023439228
Specify your installation number:
INSTALLATION NO = 0920008011
Specify your expiration date:
EXPIRATION_DATE [YYYYMMDD] = 99991231
Specify your license key:
LICENSE_KEY   1...5....0....5....0...4
LICENSE_KEY = 4NBPS2H2QOG4NG6G1GLT1GLT
saplicense: License successfully installed

C:\>_
```

Figure 145. SAPLICENSE -install

6.2 SAP Administration Users

At the completion of an SAP installation there are two administration users in Client 000 with the authority to perform any function within the system. These users are **SAP*** and **DDIC**. These userids are very important for the administration of the system and should not be deleted or altered. The default password should be changed for security reasons.

A copy of the user SAP* should be created for system administration purposes and the SAP* id should be locked. This copied user should contain the user profile **SAP_ALL** which confers all administrator authority. Additional user ids can be created at a later date as job responsibilities and separation of duties are established. These users will contain profiles that contain only authorizations for the particular job responsibility.

It is advisable that the security administrator responsible for user id and profile administration attend the *SAP AUTHORIZATION CONCEPTS* class, *CA010*.

Note

The DDIC user should never be locked in Client 000, as it is used during the import of client independent objects. If DDIC is locked these imports will fail, causing system problems.

6.2.1 Creating a New Administration User

To create a new administration user:

1. From the SAP Frontend, enter transaction **SU01** or select menu path **Tools ->Administration**, **User maintenance-> Users**.

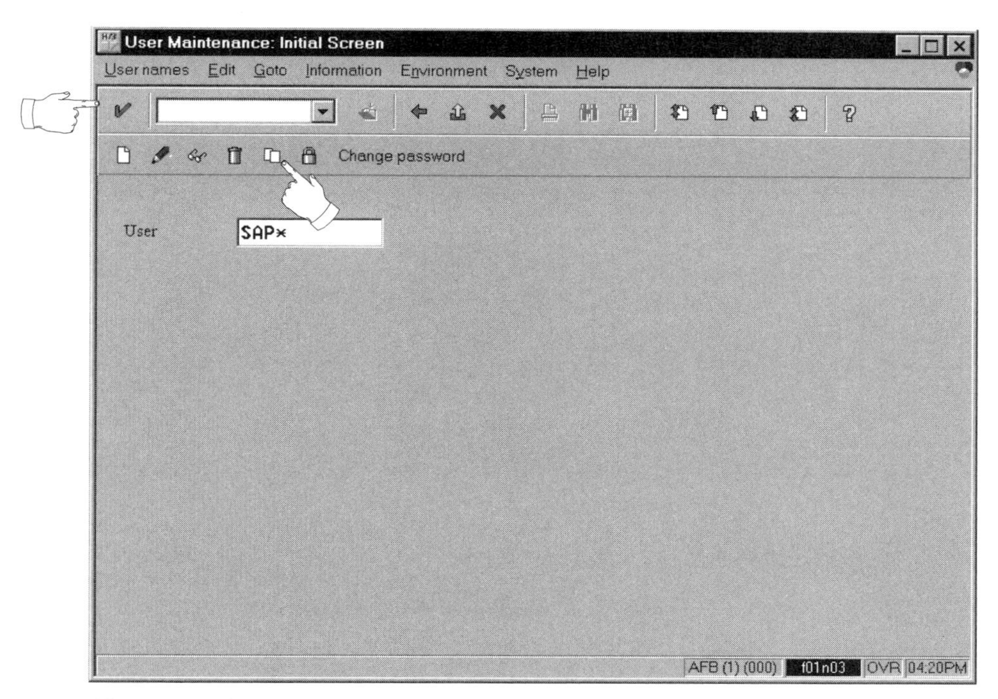

Figure 146. User Maintenance: Initial Screen

2. Enter **SAP*** for the source user to be copied.

- Click the check mark, followed by the double box across the top of the panel.
- This takes you to the Copy Users panel:

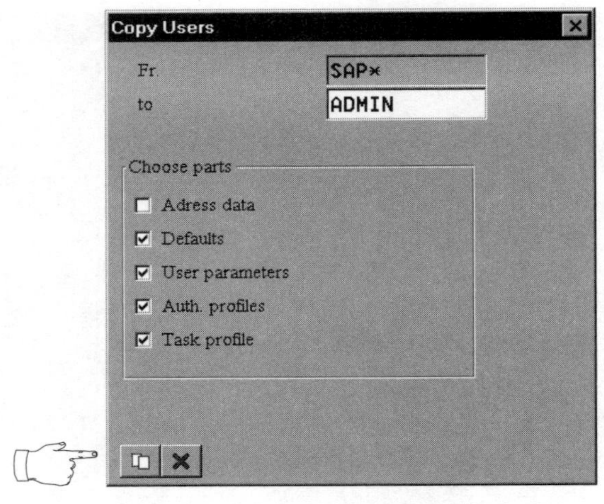

Figure 147. Copy User Pop-Up Screen

3. Enter the the new user name (in this example, ADMIN).

- Click the double box as shown above.
- The Maintain User screen is displayed:

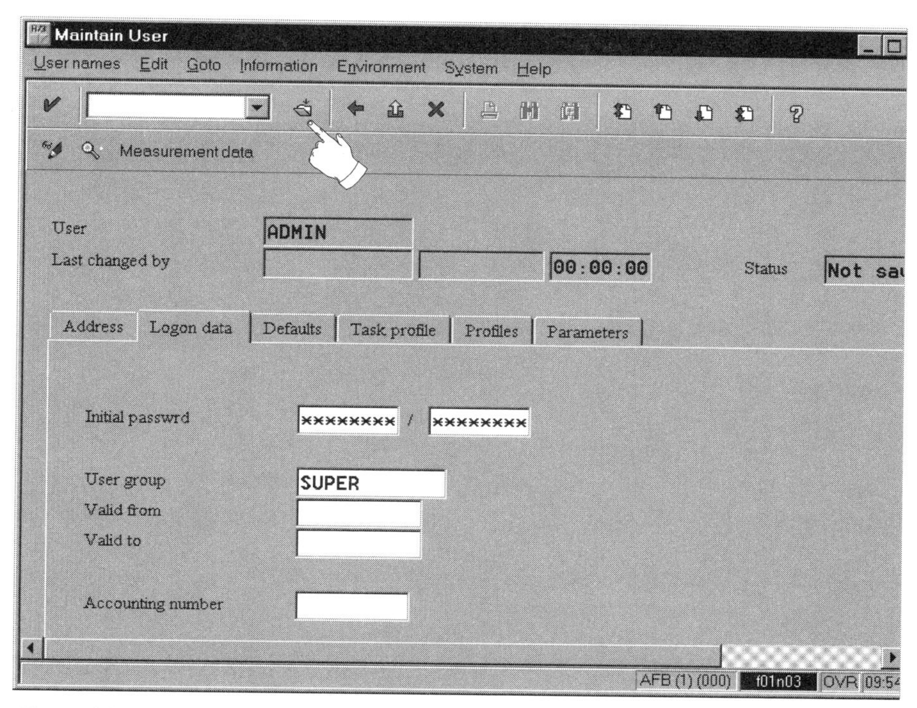

Figure 148. Maintain User: Password Screen

4. Enter the initial password in the two fields. You must change this password at the first login.
5. When the SAP* user is copied, its profiles are copied to the new user.
   - To check the profiles to be copied, click on the **Profiles** tab:

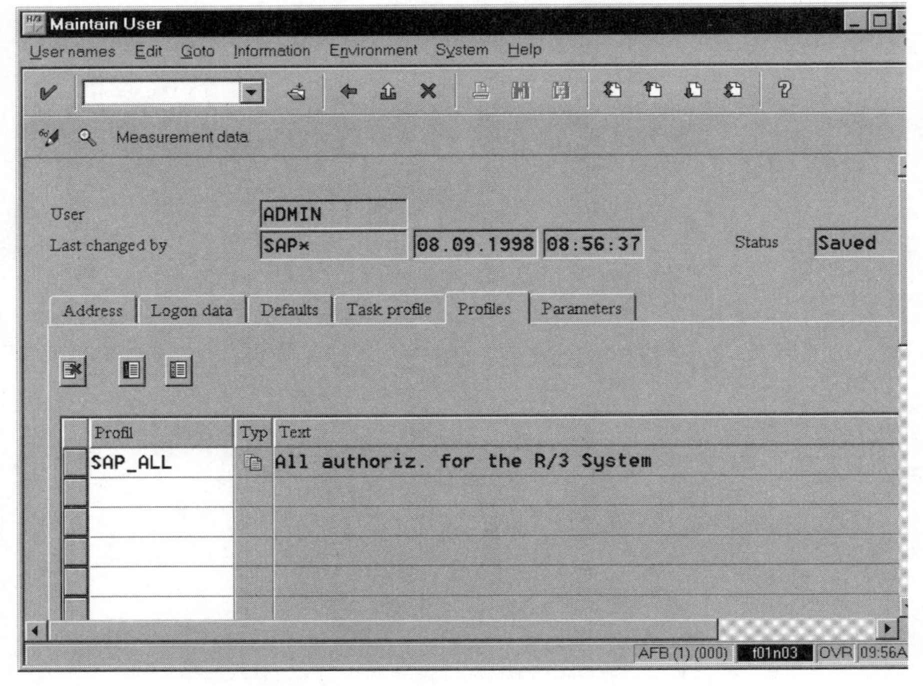

Figure 149. Maintain User: Profile Screen

6. You can add or delete profiles in this screen as needed.
   - Click on the save icon.

6.2.2 Changing the Password of SAP* and DDIC

After you have created a new administration user, you should change the default passwords of the **SAP*** and **DDIC** users. It is also advisable to lock the SAP* user id. To change these passwords:

1. Enter transaction **SU01** or select menu path **Tools** -> **Administration**, **User maintenance->Users**.

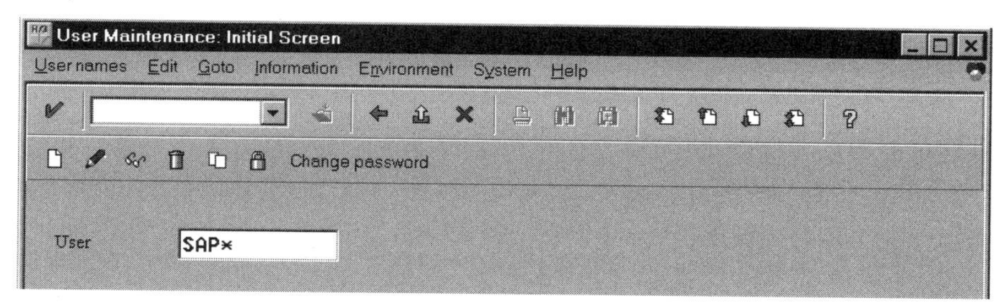

Figure 150. User Maintenance: Initial Screen

2. Enter the user and select **Change Password**. The following panel is displayed:

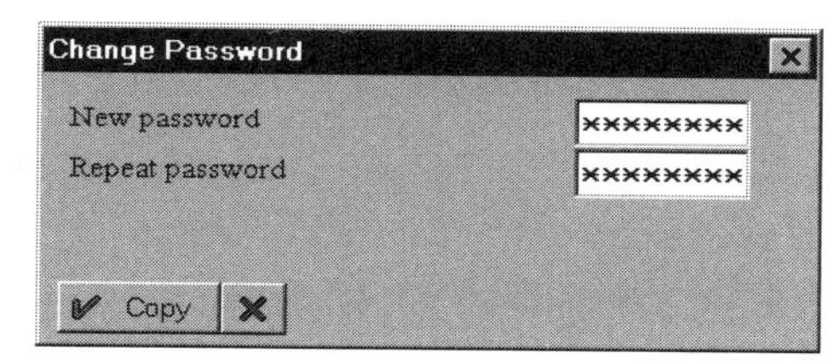

Figure 151. Change Password Pop-Up Screen

3. Enter the new password in both fields.
 - Click **Copy**.

6.2.3 Locking the SAP* User

To lock the SAP* user:

1. From the *User Maintenance: Initial Screen* (shown in Figure 150 on page 203), enter SAP* for the user.
 - Click the lock icon in the tool bar.

Figure 152. Lock/Unlock Pop-Up Screen

2. In the pop-up, click on the lock icon.

To unlock the user, click the lock icon again in the *User Maintenance: Initial Screen*.

6.3 Configuring the Transport System

The Transport system is necessary to move code, configuration and client information across the system landscape. The Work Bench Organizer must be initialized for the Transport system to function correctly. In this example we show the AIX scenario.

6.3.1 Initialize Work Bench Organizer

To initialize the Work Bench Organizer, copy /usr/sap/trans/bin/TPPARAM.TPL to TPPARAM using these commands:

```
cd /usr/sap/trans/bin
cp -p TPPARAM.TPL TPPARAM
```

6.3.2 Configure the Transport Domain Controller

The next step is to configure the Transport Domain Controller:

1. From the SAP Frontend, choose the menu path **Tools->Administration, Transports->Transport Management System** or enter transaction **STMS**. The configuration steps will automatically populate the tables required for the Work Bench Organizer. This panel is displayed:

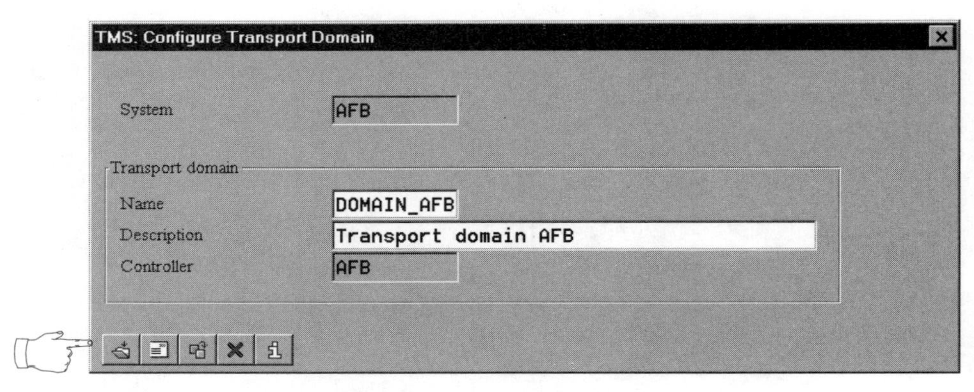

Figure 153. Configure Transport Domain Screen

2. The first time **STMS** is run it will attempt to configure the Transport Domain Controller.

- Enter your system Name and Description. If you already have a Transport Domain Controller, enter that name.
- Click on the save icon.

Saving will configure the Transport Domain and perform the following actions:

- SAP User TMSADM is created in client 000.
- RFC Destinations for the Transport Management System are generated.
- The TMS configuration is stored in /usr/sap/trans/bin as DOMAIN.CFG

The main Transport Management Screen will now display the Transport Domain. All other configuration in the TMS system now stems from this screen:

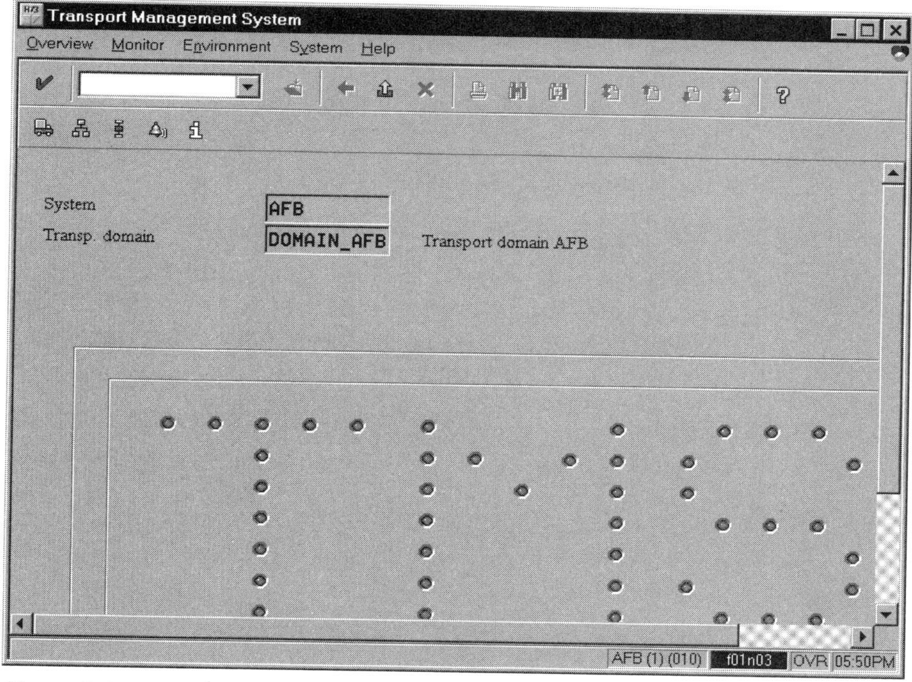

Figure 154. MAIN TMS Screen

6.3.3 Configuring a Virtual System

A virtual system should now be set up for a consolidation/test system that is not yet physically installed. This will allow the Work Bench Organizer to configure a downstream destination for all transports released from the development system. If this step is not performed, all objects will become local and it will be very difficult to transport them at a later date when the physical test system is installed. You should therefore map your system landscape and assign system names or <SID>s to each one before this step is completed.

1. From the Transport Management System main screen, choose **Overview->Systems, R/3 System->Create->Virtual System**. This panel is displayed:

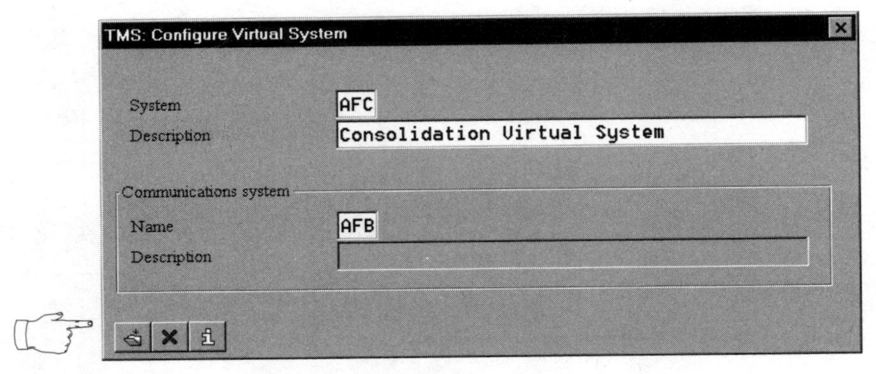

Figure 155. Configure Virtual System

2. Enter the name and description, and click the save icon.
3. At this point you need to create a **Transport Layer**. This definition is the default route that a transport request and associated tasks will be assigned. It will automatically target the released transport to be stored in the buffer of the consolidation system which is AFC in our example.
   • Choose menu path **Overview->Transport routes** from the primary TMS panel:

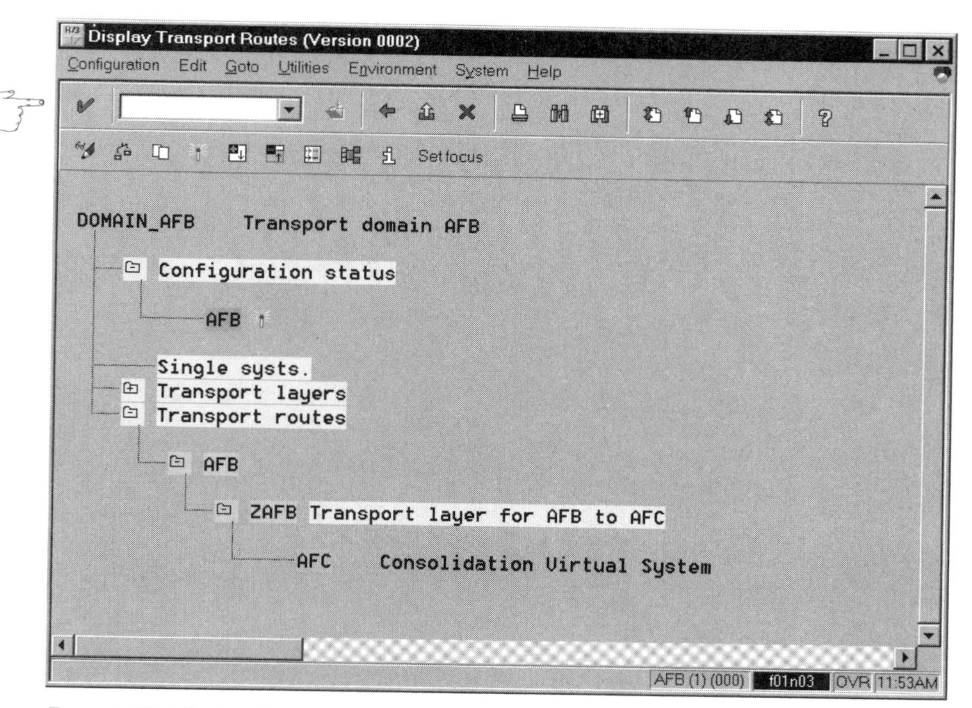

Figure 156. Display Transport Routes

4. Click the pencil pointed to in the above figure above to change to write mode.
   - Select pulldown **Configuration->Transport Layer->Create.**

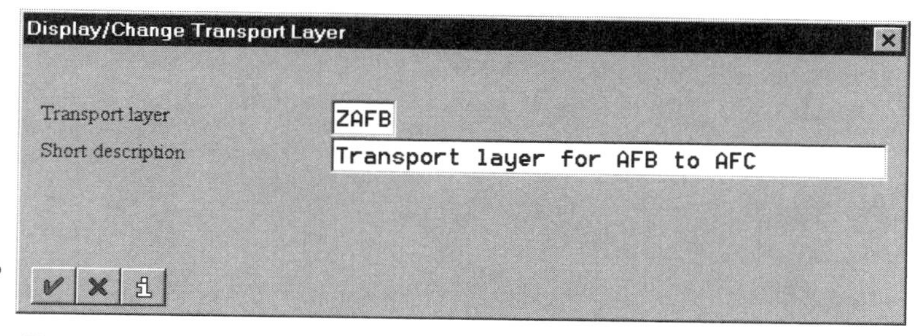

Figure 157. Display/Change Transport Layer

5. Enter the name for the Transport Layer.

   A meaningful convention such as Z<SID> or ZAFB in our example is a good choice. The SAP naming convention for customer objects and names is to begin them with the letter Z. This will prevent them from being overlaid when any upgrade activity is conducted as SAP does not modify any Z objects It is **very important** that you adhere to this standard, otherwise this can cause problems at a later date.

- Click the check mark which will take you back to the Display Transport Routes screen shown in Figure 156 on page 207.
- Click the save icon at the top of the screen.

6. Now you will need to create a Transport Route.

- From the Display Transport Routes screen, select pulldown **Configuration->Transport Route->Create**:

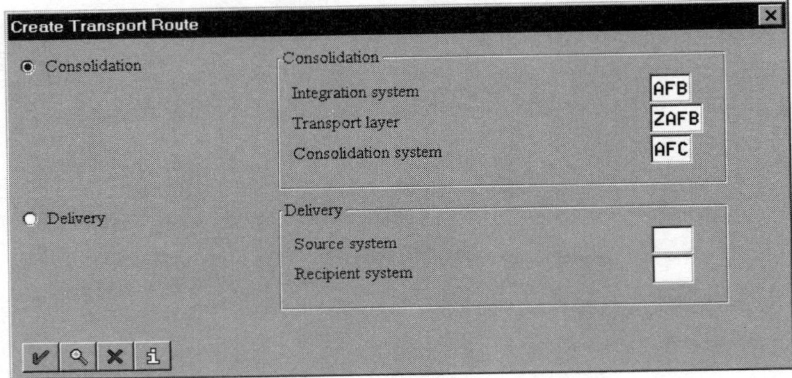

Figure 158. Create Transport Route Screen

7. Enter your Integration system.

- Enter your Transport Layer.
- Enter your Consolidation system.
- Click the check mark.
- You will now be taken back to the Change Transports Routes screen shown in Figure 156 on page 207. Click the save icon to save.

8. Select the pulldown **Configuration**:

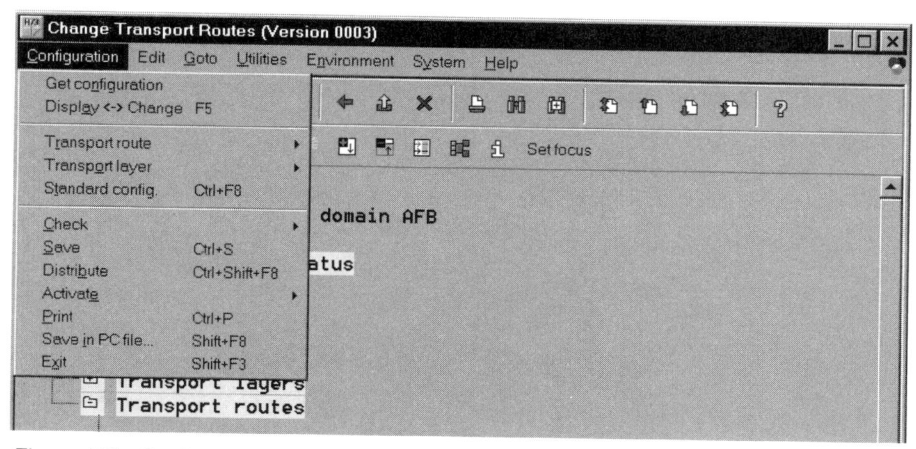

Figure 159. Configuration Pulldown

9. Click **Activate** to activate the configuration.
   - Click **Distribute** to distribute the configuration to all systems in the landscape.
10. You may now display the configured system by selecting **Environment->System Overview**:

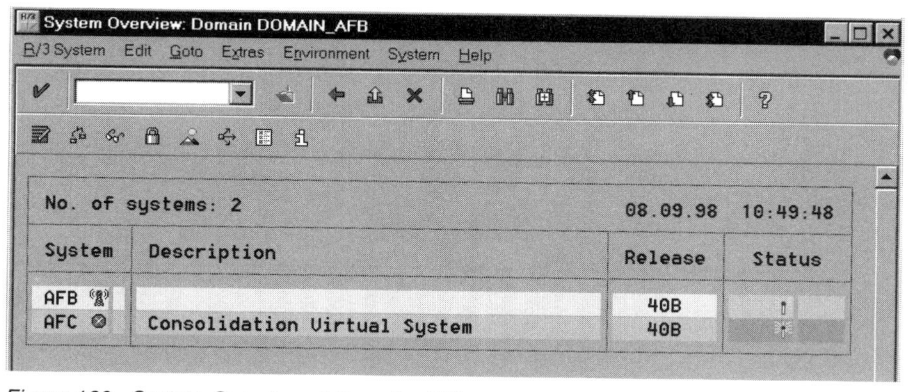

Figure 160. System Overview of Domain_AFB

6.3.4 Setting the System Change Options

The system change options must be set at this point. These change option settings control what data can or cannot be modified in the R/3 system. To do this:

1. Enter transaction **SE06**:

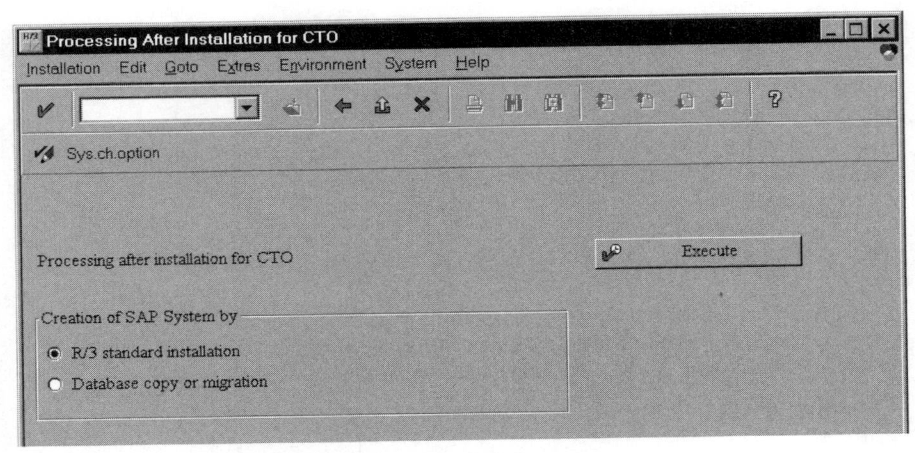

Figure 161. Processing After Installation for CTO Screen

2. Click in the **Sys.ch.option** button to display the default and current change option settings:

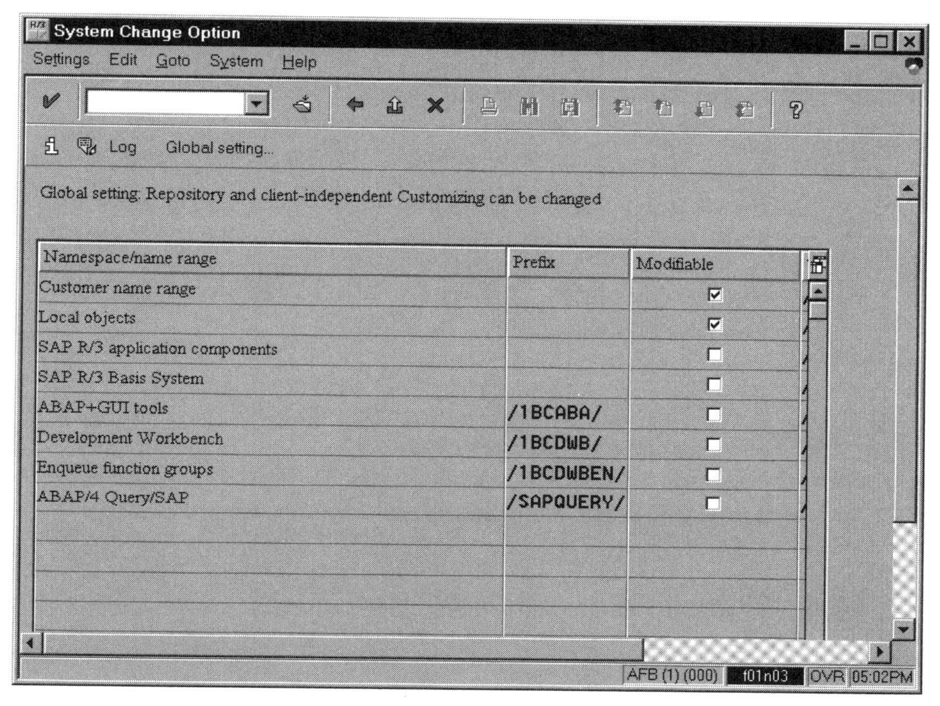

Figure 162. System Change Options (1)

3. You will note that at this point, Repository and Client-Independent Customizing is allowed.

   • Click the **Global Setting** button. The setting is currently Modifiable:

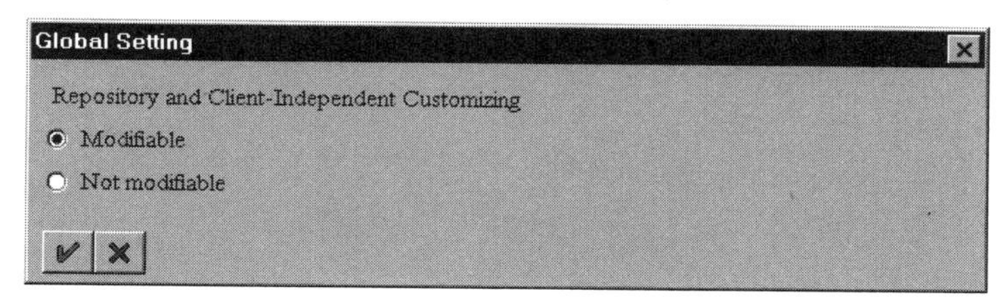

Figure 163. Global Settings (1)

4. Click on **Not modifiable** to change the settings:

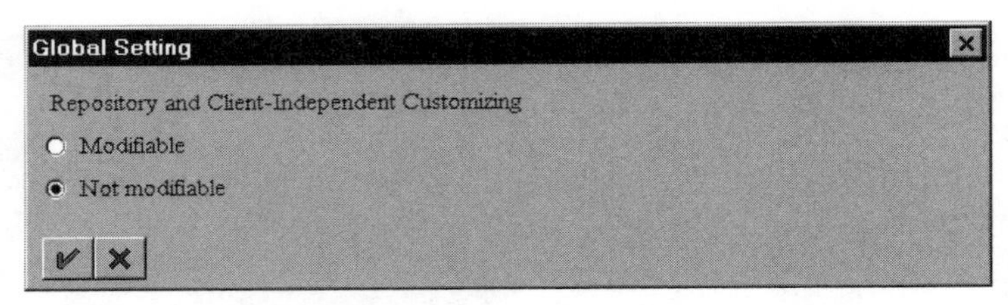

Figure 164. Global Settings (2)

5. Click the check mark, and then click the save icon in the System Change Option screen.

You will now see that the Global Settings have been changed to Repository and Client-Independent Customizing cannot be changed.This setting would be used for a production system where you do not want changes allowed.

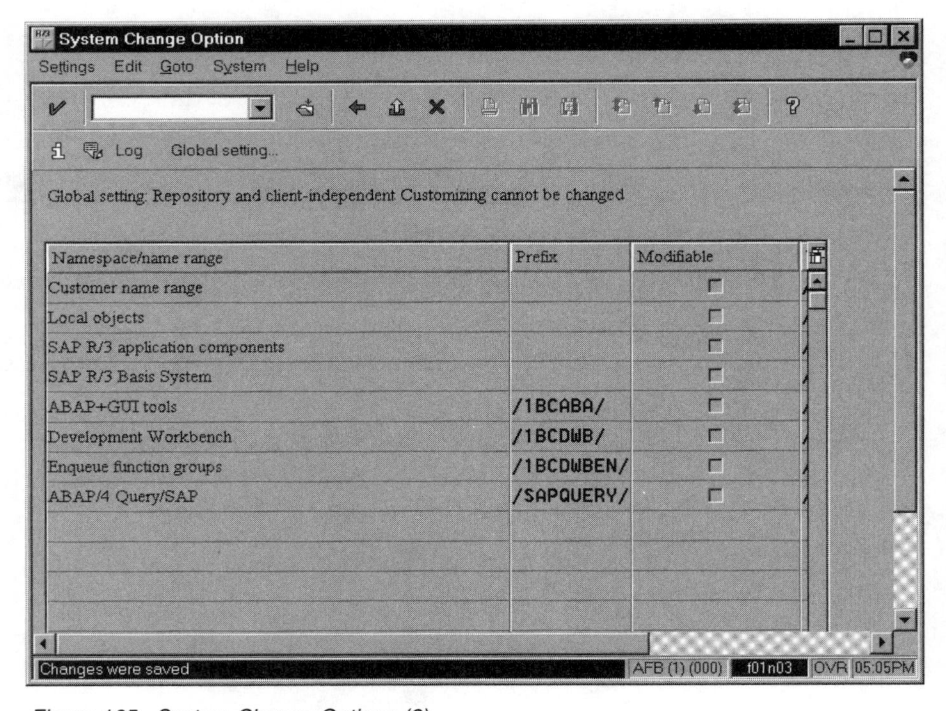

Figure 165. System Change Options (2)

There are eight categories as shown above that can be selected for modification. Remember that these flags are system wide. The selections you choose depend on the requirements of your project.

6.4 Enabling DB2 UDB Archival Logging

At this point, archival logging should be enabled in DB2 UDB. The default logging method after installation is circular logging, where the system log files are overwritten in a circular fashion, first to last. No R/3 DB2 UDB system should be run in this mode as roll-forward recovery is not possible in the event of a system failure. To enable archival logging:

1. For the database <sid>, set the DB2 database configuration parameters **LOGRETAIN** and **USEREXIT** to **YES.**

   • These settings can be changed via the DB2 Control Center or using the DB2 Command Line Processor. For example, from the DB2 CLP:

```
db2 update db cfg for AUS using logretain yes
db2 update db cfg for AUS using userexit yes
```

   To have these parameters become active, all users and applications must disconnect from the database.

2. Once active, the user exit moves log files that are no longer active or needed for crash recovery from the active log directory to the archive directory.

   The active log directory is:

   - /db2/<SID>/log_dir (AIX)
   - \db2\<SID\log_dir (Windows NT)

   The archive log directory is:

   - /db2/<SID>/log_archive (AIX)
   - \db2\<SID>\log_archive (Windows NT)

Note

A full offline backup must be done after enabling archival logging. The SAP system will not start if a backup is not successfully completed.

6.4.1 Backing Up the DB2 UDB database

A full off-line backup can be scheduled from the DB2 Control Center. Please refer to “Offline Backups” on page 353 for details about how to do this. To take a backup using the DB2 CLP, refer to the *DB2 UDB Command Reference*.

6.5 Setting up a New Client

Before any work can begin in the system, a new client must be created. SAP delivers clients 000 and 001 which should never be deleted or changed. The new working client should be created by making a copy of client 000.

6.5.1 Creating a New Client

To create a new client:

1. An entry must be created for the new client in table **T000** using transaction **OY25** or menu path **Tools -> Administration, Administration->Client Admin.->Client Maintenance**:

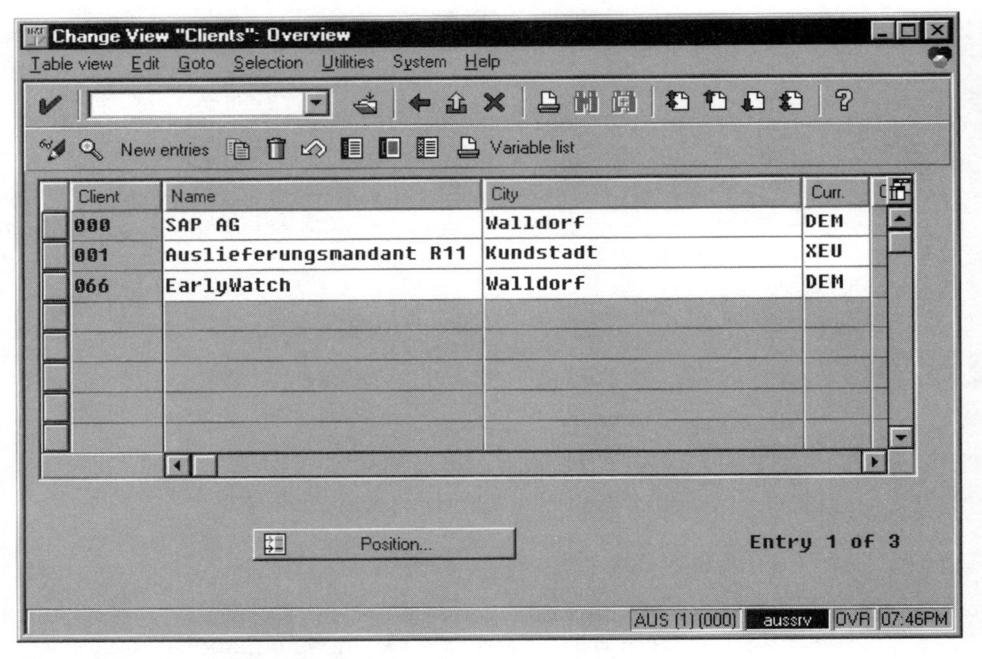

Figure 166. Change View "Clients": Overview

2. Click on **New Entries**.

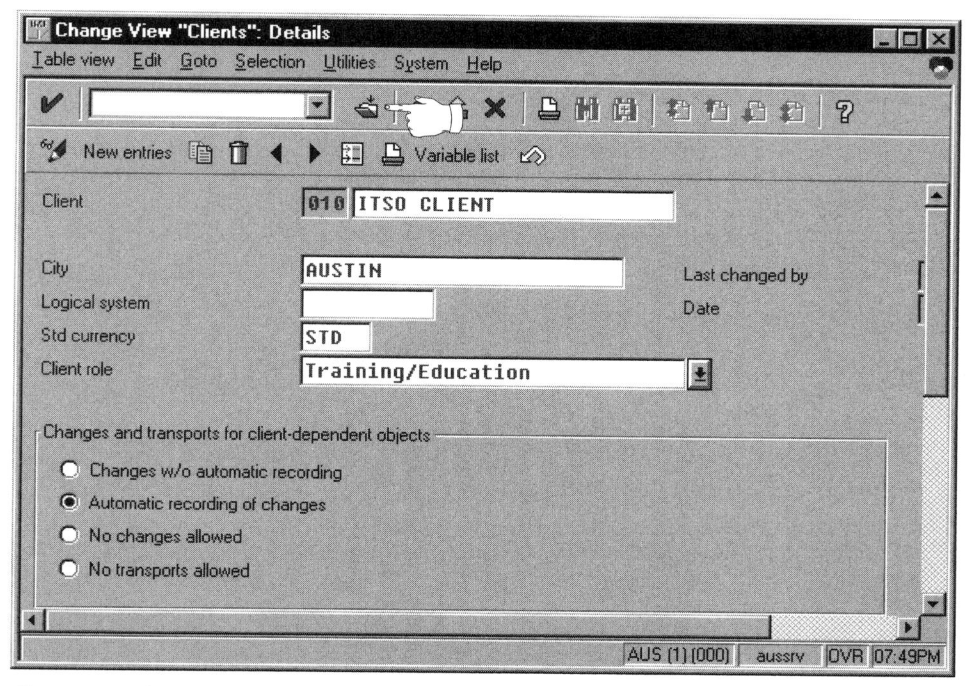

Figure 167. Change View "Clients": Details

3. Choose a selection for the box entitled: *Changes and transports for client-dependent objects*.

   There are four choices for *Changes and transports for client dependent objects*. The choice you make will depend on the system being configured.

   - *Changes w/o automatic recording* will prevent you from transporting any work or configuration that you have done, to another system. This option will require a full client export/import to accomplish that move.
   - *Automatic recording of changes* is the best option as it will record all work in transports that can be moved from system to system. It also creates a version of your work that you can revert back to if needed.
   - The *No changes allowed* option would be used in a production system or pristine client that you do not want changed.
   - *No transports allowed* will not allow any changes to be transported into the system. This would also be useful in a production system since if all is running smoothly you would not want any transports into the system. If at a later time you need updates transported, you will need to change

this setting, allow the transports to occur, then change this setting back to No transports allowed.

- Save the new client by clicking the save icon in the screen above.

6.5.2 Executing the Client Copy

The next step is to execute the client copy:

1. Log into the new client with user **SAP*** and password **pass**.
2. Enter the transaction **SCCL** or select menu path **Tools->Administration, Administration->Client admin.->Client copy->Local copy**:

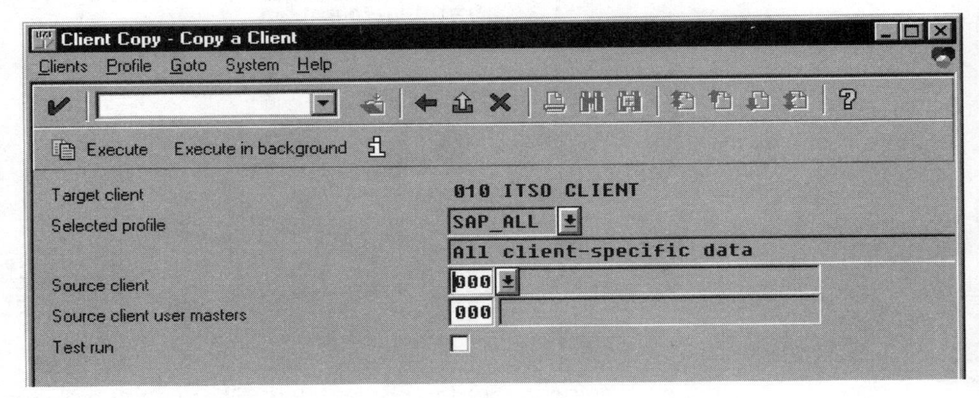

Figure 168. Client Copy

3. Select the profile to copy.
   - Enter the source client.
   - Enter the user master source client.

   The copy should be submitted in the background as it will run for several hours. Be sure that you have ample space in the DB2 archive directory as a copy will cause a large number of logs to be generated.

   - Click on **Execute in background.** A verification screen will pop-up:

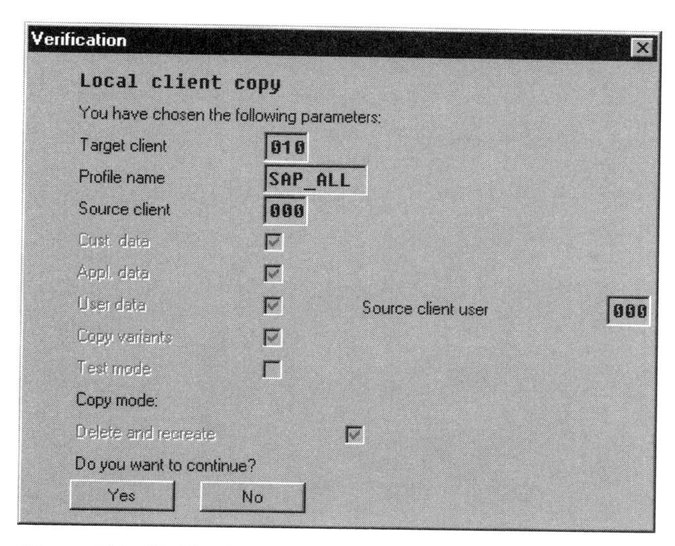

Figure 169. Verification

4. Click **Yes**. The Start Time screen is displayed:

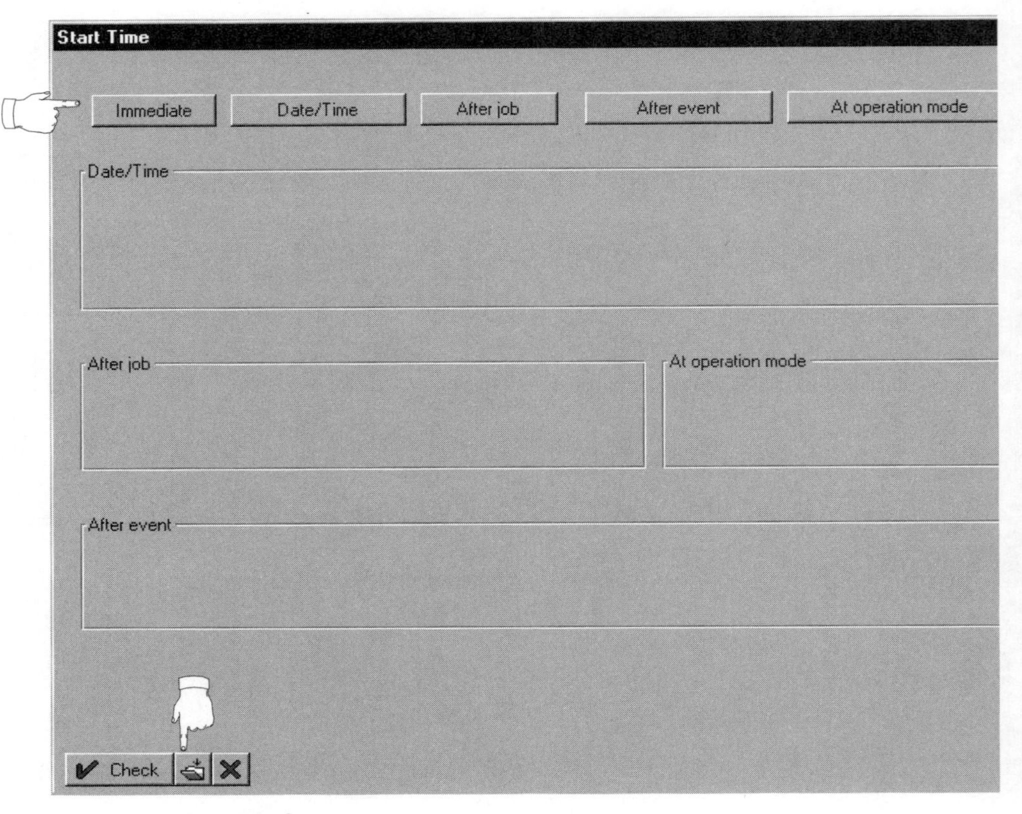

Figure 170. Schedule Copy

5. Click **Immediate**, and then click the save icon.
6. Use transaction **SCC3** to check the copy progress:

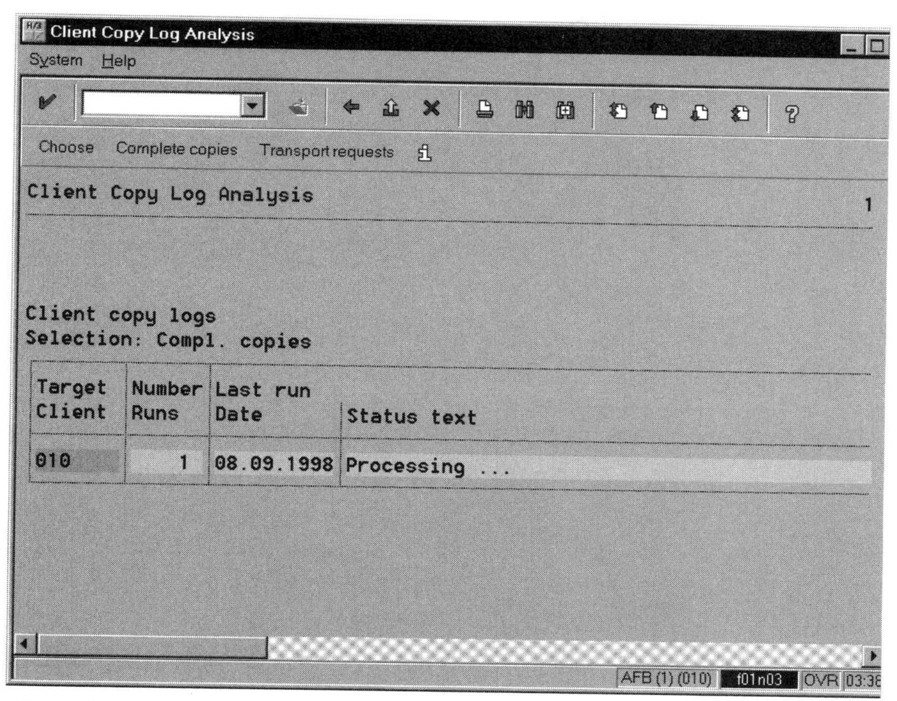

Figure 171. Client Copy Log Analysis

7. Select the client you wish to view, and choose **Log Analysis**:

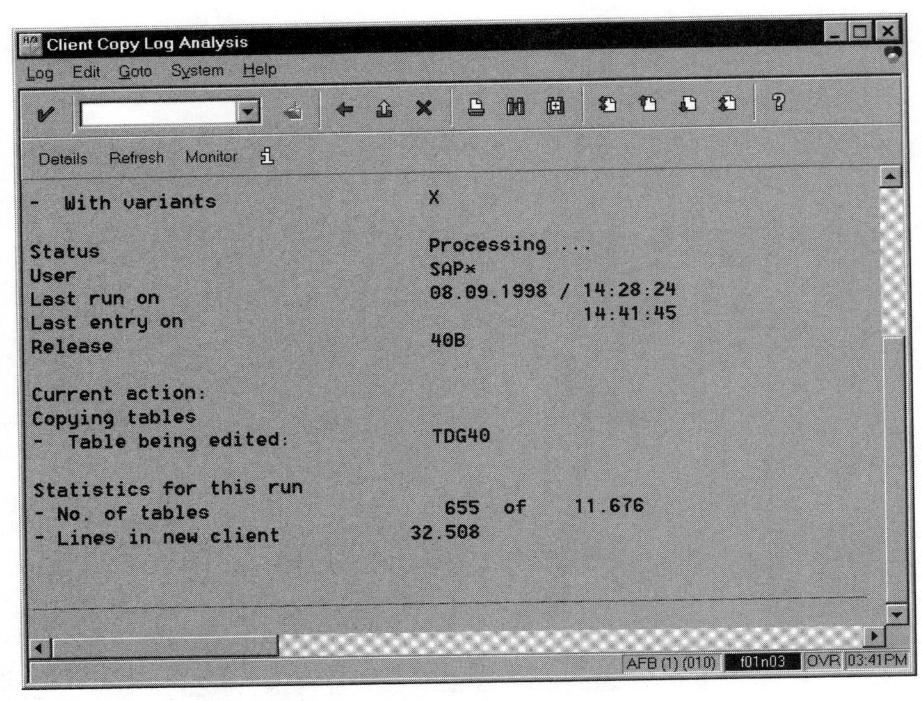

Figure 172. Client Copy Log Analysis

8. When the copy is complete, it will have the same userids and passwords as the client you copied from. You may login in using one of these userids.

6.6 Printing from SAP

You should now set up at least one printer to ensure that you can print from SAP. There are a number of methods that can be used depending on the operating system platform you are using. We cover the methods for Windows NT and AIX in this section.

6.6.1 Configuring a Printer in Windows NT

The most commonly used method for printing in Windows NT is a remote PC connection. In this configuration, the spool data is transferred to the Windows NT Print Manager via the **SAPLPD** program running on the SAP Central Instance. The Print Manager then handles transfer over the network to the server that has the printer attached.

You must be able to print to this printer from your Windows NT Print Manager before it can be defined to SAP. To set up a Windows NT network printer, follow these steps:

1. Open **My Computer**, then open **Printers**:

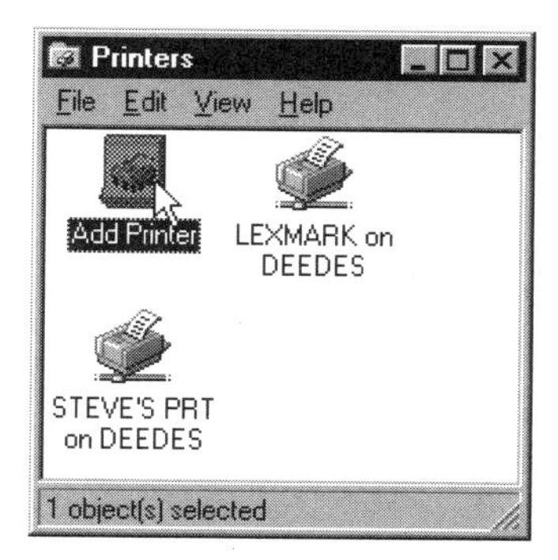

Figure 173. Printers Screen

2. Open **Add Printer**. The Add Printer Wizard panel is displayed:

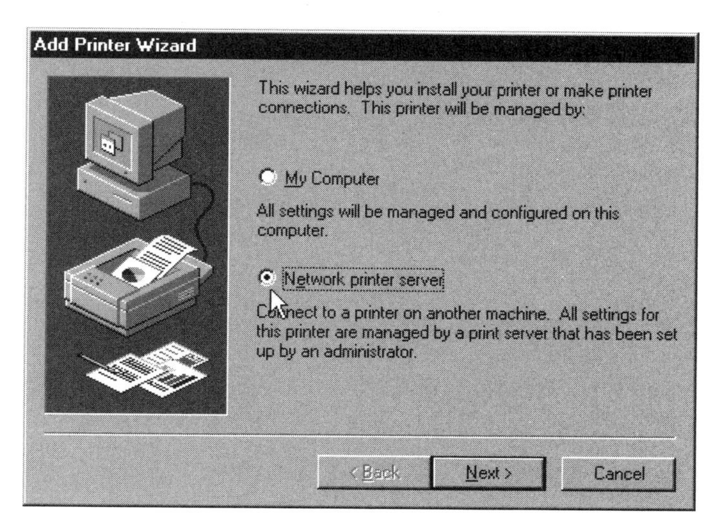

Figure 174. Add Printer Wizard

3. Click Network Printer Server, and **Next**.

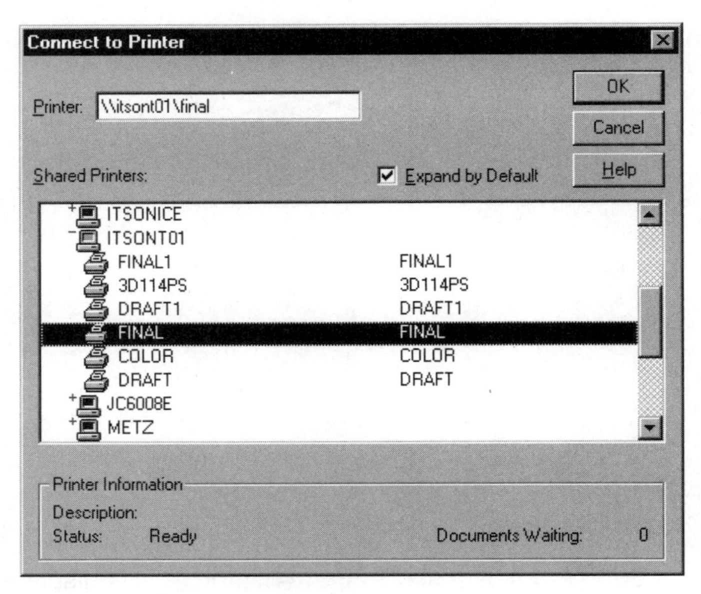

Figure 175. Connect To Printer Screen

4. Fill in your printer name, and click **OK**.

Figure 176. Add a Printer Wizard

5. Click **Yes** to make this printer the default, then click **Next**.

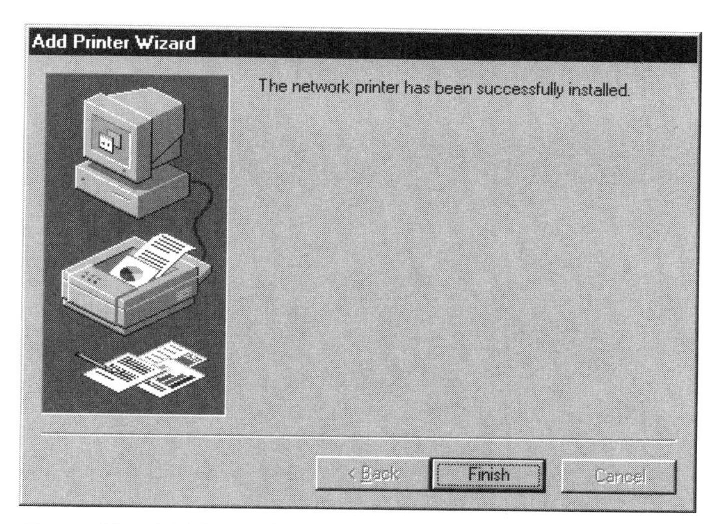

Figure 177. Add Printer Wizard Screen

6. Click **Finish** in the success screen

SAPLPD is installed when the SAP Frontend GUI is installed. To have SAPLPD start at system boot proceed as follows:

1. Select **Start->Settings->Taskbar->Start Menu Programs** to display this panel:

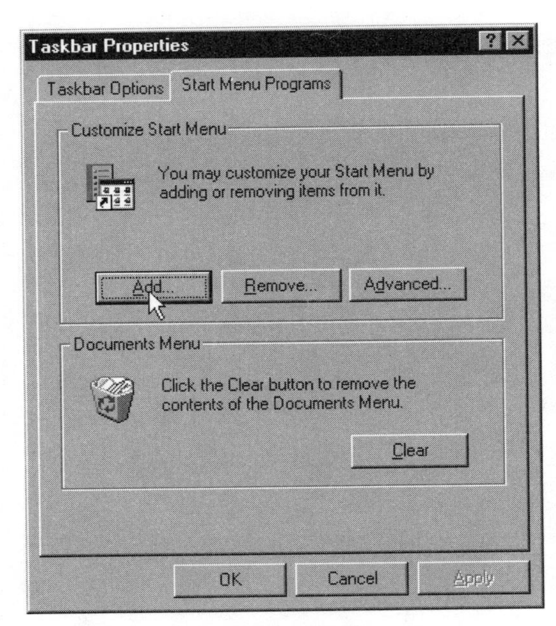

Figure 178. Taskbar Properties Screen

2. Click **Add**.

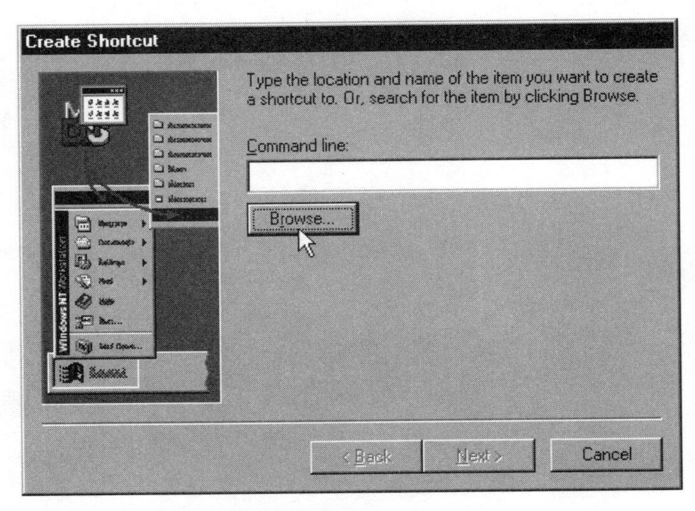

Figure 179. Create Shortcut Screen

3. Click **Browse**, and locate the SAPLPD executable on your Windows NT system. In our system, its full pathname is:

C:\Program Files\SAPpc\SAPGUI\SAPlpd\Saplpd.exe. When you have located the executable, click on **Open**.

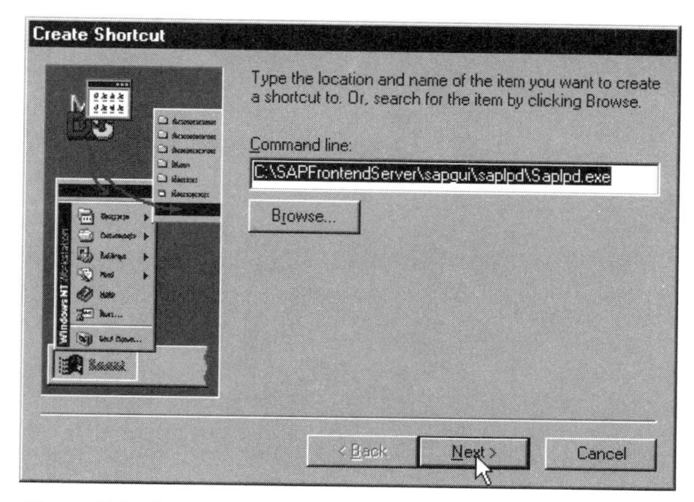

Figure 180. Create Shortcut

4. Click **Next**.

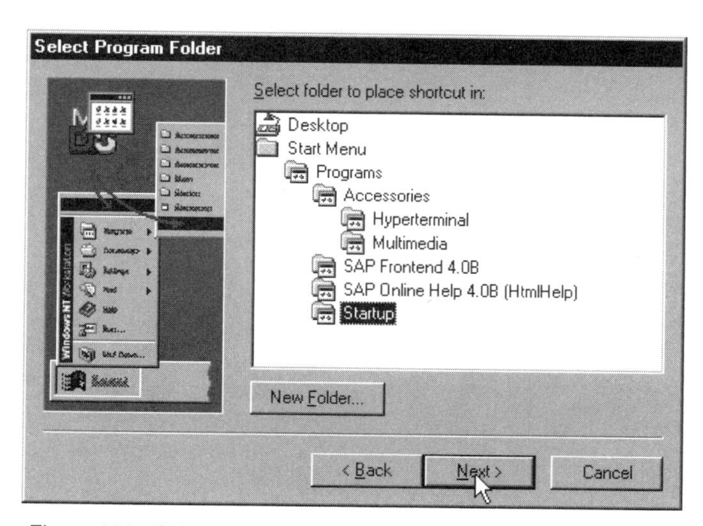

Figure 181. Select Program Folder

5. Select **Startup** as the folder to place the executable in, and click **Next**.

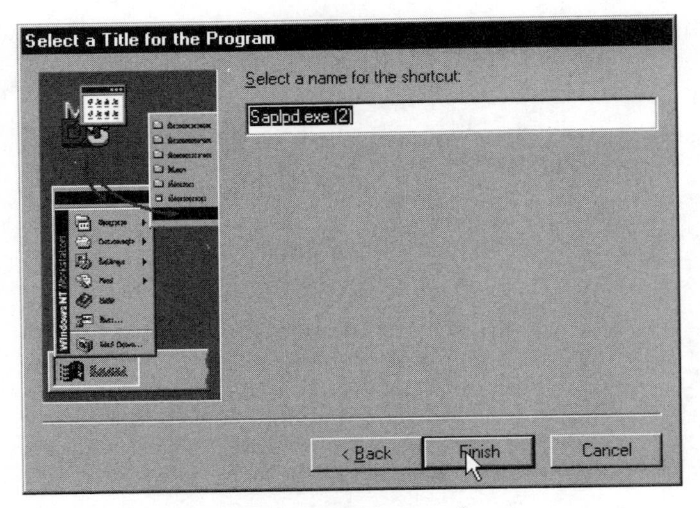

Figure 182. Select a Title For the Program Screen

6. Click **Finish**.

6.6.1.1 Adding the Printer in SAP

To add this printer to SAP:

1. From the SAP Frontend, enter the transaction **SPAD** or select **Tools->CCMS, Spool->Spool Administration**:

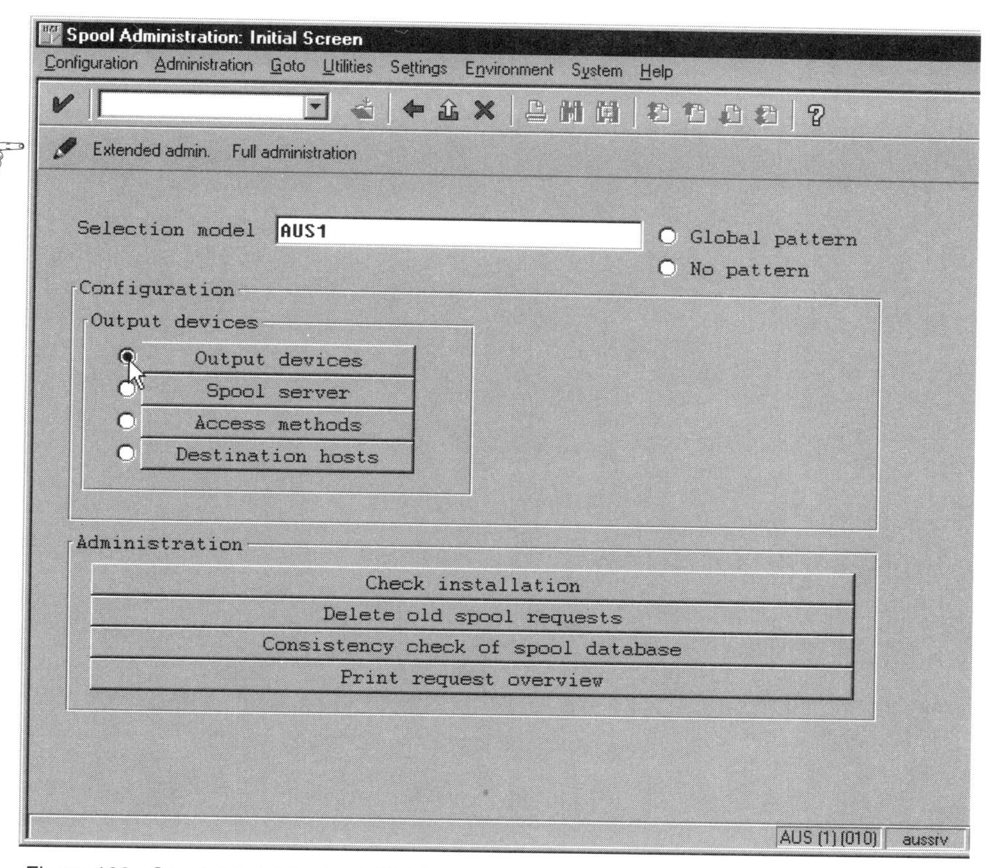

Figure 183. Spool Administration Initial Screen

2. Enter the name of the printer to create in the **Selection model** field.
   - Click the pencil for write mode as pointed to above.
   - Select the pulldown **Configuration->Output Devices, Output device->Create**.

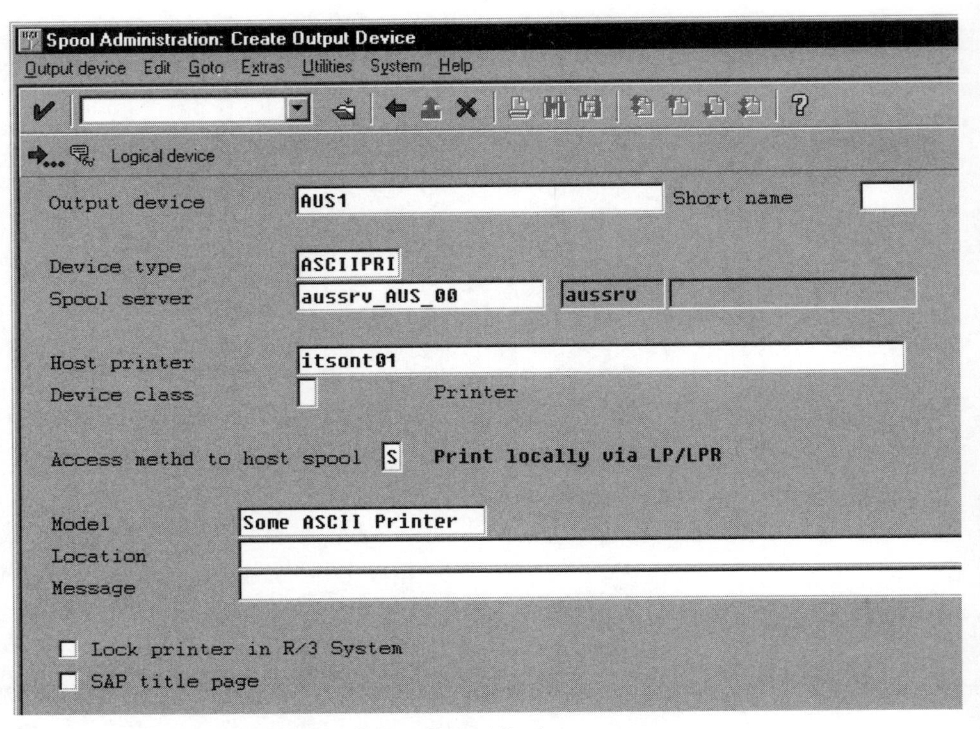

Figure 184. Spool Administration Create Output Device

3. Select a device type for your printer from the pulldown.
   - Enter the Host printer name which is the name of the network printer that you defined to Windows NT.
   - For the **Access method** select **S** for *Print on LPDHOST via SAP protocol.*
   - Press **Enter**. Note that some of the entry fields are changed as you have selected to print remotely:

Spool Administration: Create Output Device

Output device Edit Goto Extras Utilities System Help

Logical device

Output device AUS1 Short name

Device type ASCIIPRI Some generic ASCII printer

Spool server aussrv_AUS_00 aussrv

Destination hosts itson1 Conn.Setup time

Port no. Response time

Host printer itsont01

Device class Printer

Access methd to host spool S Print on LPDHOST via SAP protocol

Model Some ASCII Printer

Location

Message

Lock printer in R/3 System

SAP title page

Figure 185. Spool Administration Create Output Device

4. Enter the name of the machine that the network printer is attached to in the Destination hosts field.
   - Save by clicking the save icon as pointed to in the above figure.
   - Click on the back icon, and the list of output devices will now be displayed in the *Spool Administration: List of Output Devices* panel:

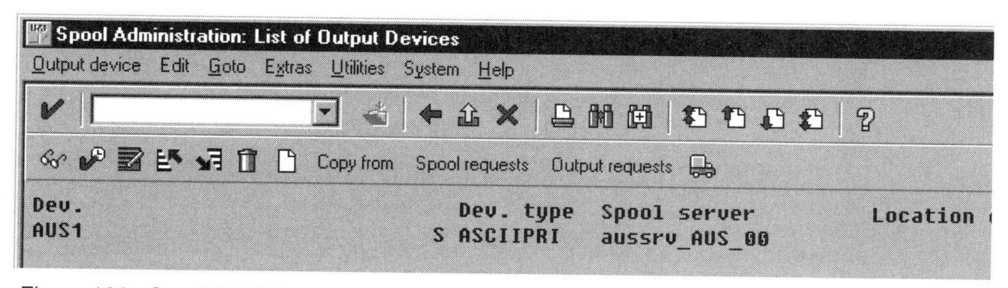

Figure 186. Spool Administration: List of Output Devices

6.6.2 Configuring a Printer in AIX

There are two methods you can use used to print from SAP on an AIX system:

- Print on **LPDHOST** via Berkley Protocol. This method reads the **THOST** table for the printer host and IP address and will send spool files directly to the printer queue on that host.
- Print **Locally via LP/LPR.** For this method an AIX remote printer queue is required on the SAP system where the spool process runs. SAP will complete its print routine and spool the print requests on the remote AIX queue. The operating system will then handle the printing to the AIX system that has the printer locally attached.

6.6.2.1 Printing Using LPDHOST

To setup printing using LPDHOST:

1. From the SAP Frontend, enter the transaction **SPAD** or select **Tools->CCMS, Spool->Spool Administration**.

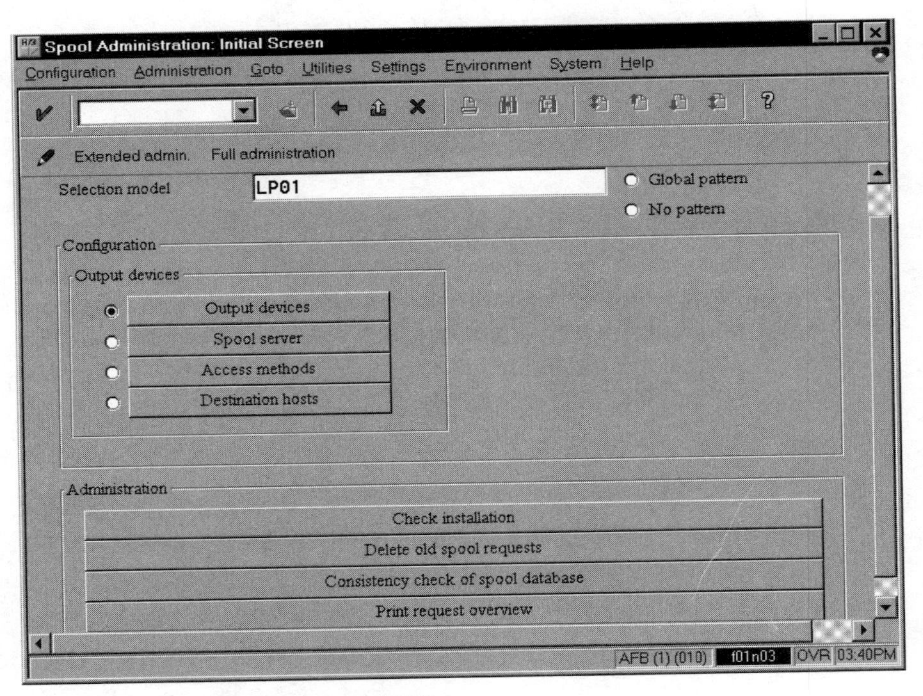

Figure 187. Spool Administration Initial Screen

2. First click on the pencil to be able to change and create a new entry.

- Enter the name of the printer to create in the **Selection model** field.
- Check the **Output Devices** button.
- Using the pulldown, select **Configuration->Output Devices**, followed by the pulldown **Output Device->Create**.

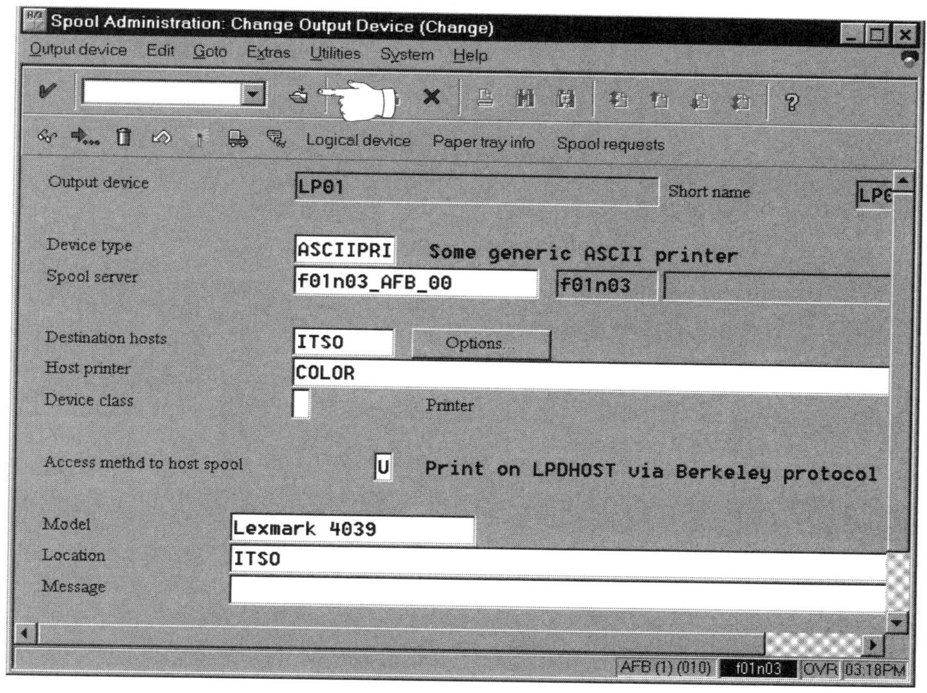

Figure 188. Spool Administration: Change Output Device

3. Enter your printer name in the Host printer field.
   - Select **U** for Access method *Print on LPDHOST via Berkeley protocol* .
   - Complete other required fields and press **Enter**.
   - Add the name of the host that physically owns the printer in the Destination hosts field.
   - After you have completed the required entries click the save icon pointed to above.
4. Now you must add a THOST entry via Transaction **SM55**:

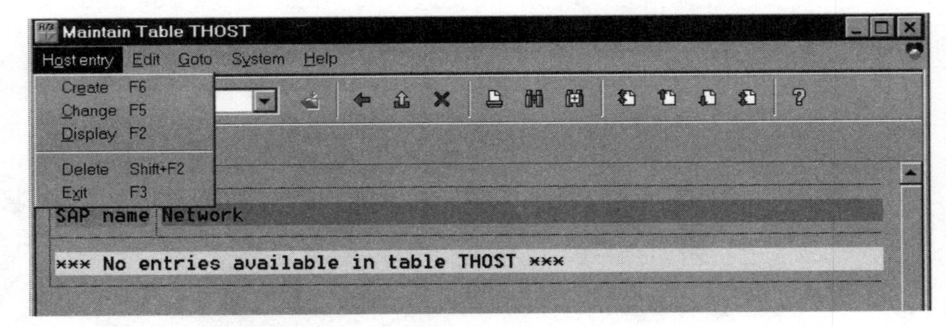

Figure 189. Maintain Table THOST

5. Select pull down **Host entry->Create**.

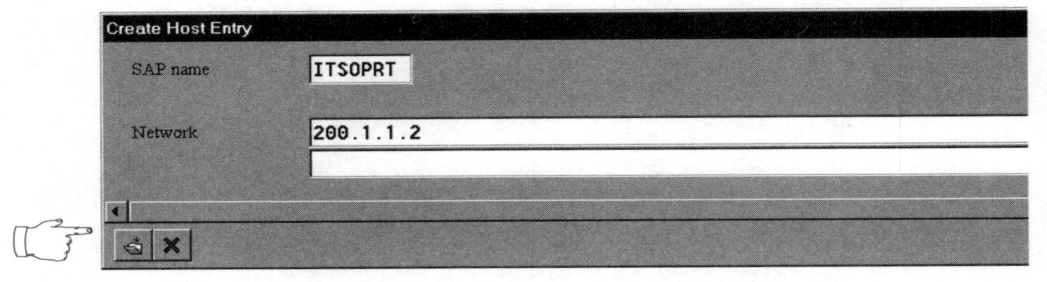

Figure 190. Create Host Entry

6. Enter the print host name in the SAP name field.
   - Enter the associated IP address.
   - Click the save icon.

6.6.2.2 Printing Using LP/LPR

To setup printing using LP/LPR:

1. Determine the remote AIX machine and print queue that you will use.
2. Define a remote print queue on your AIX system running the spool process.
   - Enter **smitty->Print Spooling->Add a Print Queue->remote->Standard Processing**:

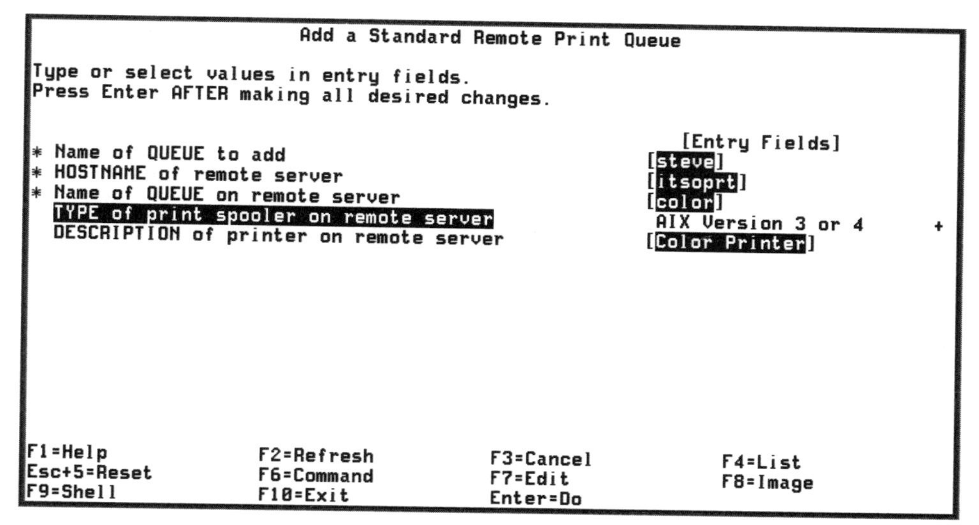

Figure 191. Create AIX Remote Queue

3. Fill in the values as shown for your installation and press **Enter**.
4. Check that the queue was created using the **lpstat** command:

```
f01n03:/ > lpstat
Queue   Dev   Status    Job Files              User       PP %  Blks  Cp Rnk
------- ----- --------- --- ------------------ ---------- ---- -- ----- --- ---
steve   @prt3 READY
steve   color READY
f01n03:/ >
```

Figure 192. Run lpstat

5. Test that you can print to the queue from your AIX system using the **enq** command:

```
enq -P <queuename> <filetoprint>
```

6. To define your printer to SAP, from the SAP Frontend, enter transaction **SPAD** or select **Tools->CCMS, Spool->Spool Administration**.

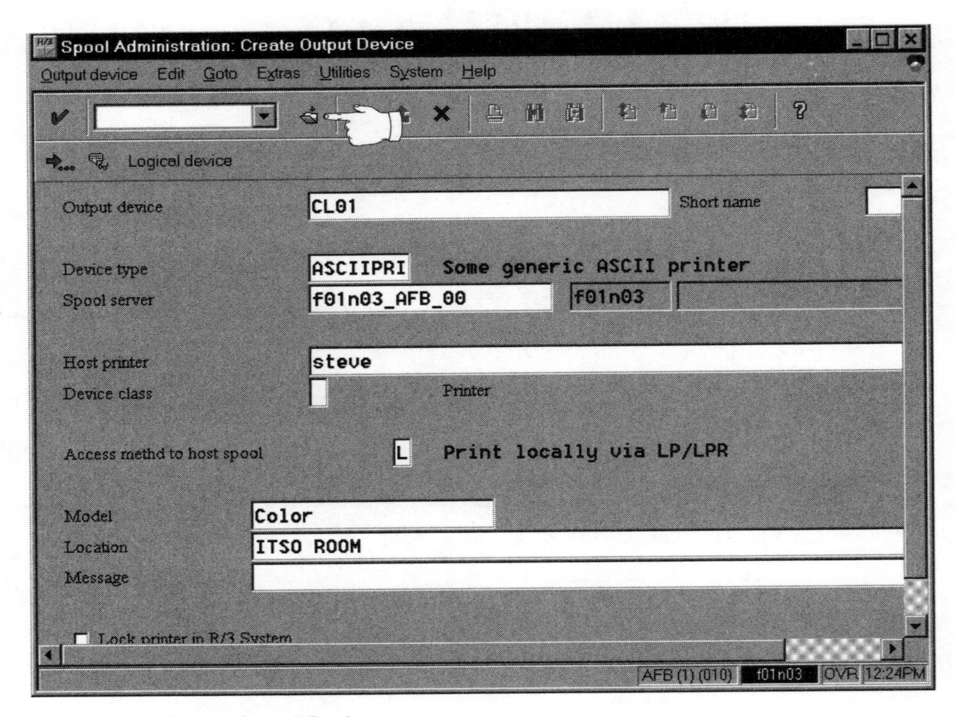

Figure 193. Create Output Device

7. Use the same procedure to define this printer as detailed in “Printing Using LPDHOST” on page 230 with the following exceptions:
   - For Access method, Select **L** for *Print locally via LP/LPR.*
   - You need only enter the printer name in the Host printer field. Because the AIX remote queue will handle the spooling to the remote host you do not need to enter the Destination host.
   - Save the entry by clicking the save icon.
   - Test that you can print.

6.7 Connecting to OSS Using SAProuter

A connection to OSS, the SAP on-line help system, needs to be setup to allow you to work efficiently with your R/3 system.

A utility called **SAProuter** is supplied with the installation software. It must be configured to allow secure OSS and EARLYWATCH connections to your system. You can install SAProuter as follows:

6.7.1 Configuring SAProuter on Windows NT

To configure SAProuter on Windows NT:

1. From an MS-DOS Prompt, create a subdirectory called saprouter in directory <DRIVE>:\usr\sap.
2. Enter the following commands:

```
ntscmgr install SAProuter -b
<DRIVE>:\usr\sap\<SID>\sys\exe\run\saprouter.exe -p service
-r -R
<DRIVE>:\usr\sap\<SID>\sys\exe\run\saprt
```

3. To start the SAPpad editor, enter the following command:

```
<DRIVE>:\usr\sap\<SID>\sys\exe\run\sappad
```

The following screen is displayed:

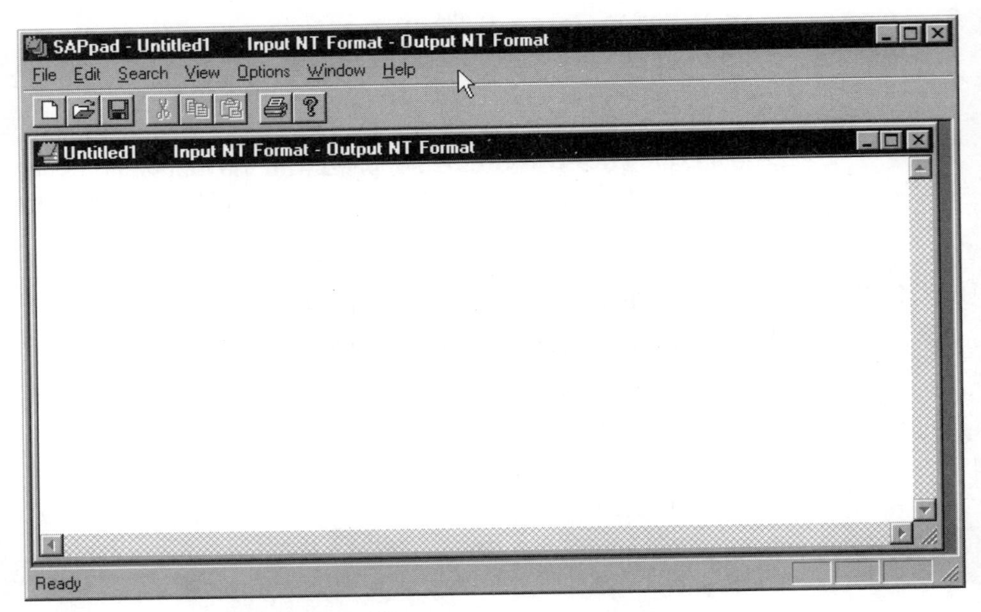

Figure 194. SAPpad on Windows NT

4. Maximize the smaller window, and enter the router path IP addresses for your system and the SAProuter at SAP as shown here:

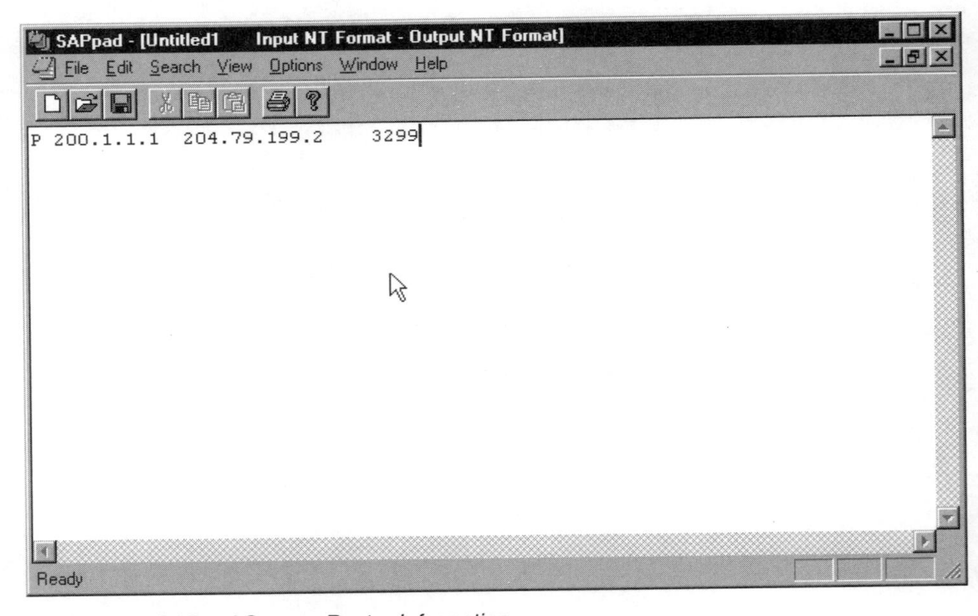

Figure 195. SAPpad Screen: Router Information

5. Save the line as a file called as **saprt**.
6. Now you must add two parameters to SAProuter to suppress the message 'The description for Event ID(0)' in the Windows NT event log. Enter the command **regedt32** in a Command Window and follow the path down to **HKEY_LOCAL_MACHINE->SYSTEM->CurrentControlSet->Services->EventLog->Applications** as shown here:

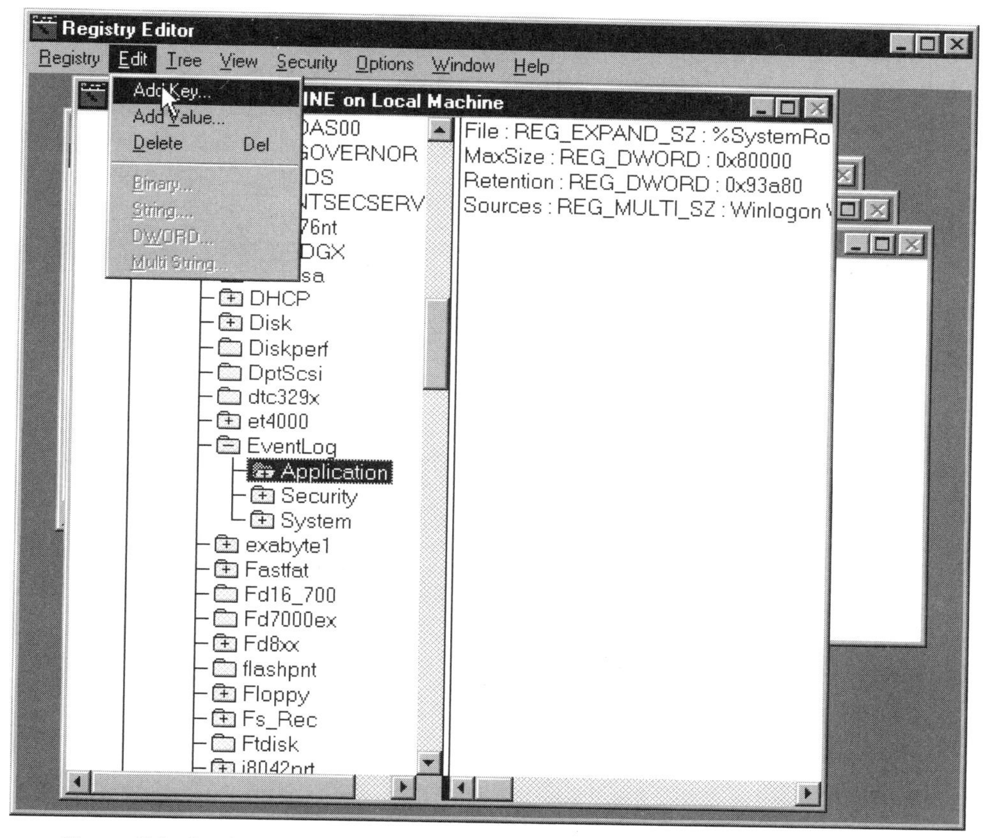

Figure 196. Registry Add Key Menu

7. Select **Edit->Add Key**:

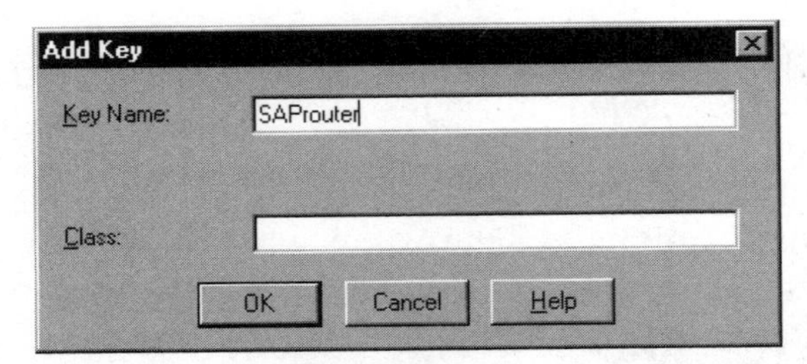

Figure 197. Add Key Pop-Up

8. Enter SAProuter in the Key Name field and click **OK**. A new entry named SAProuter will be added to the registry. Now click on the new SAProuter entry:

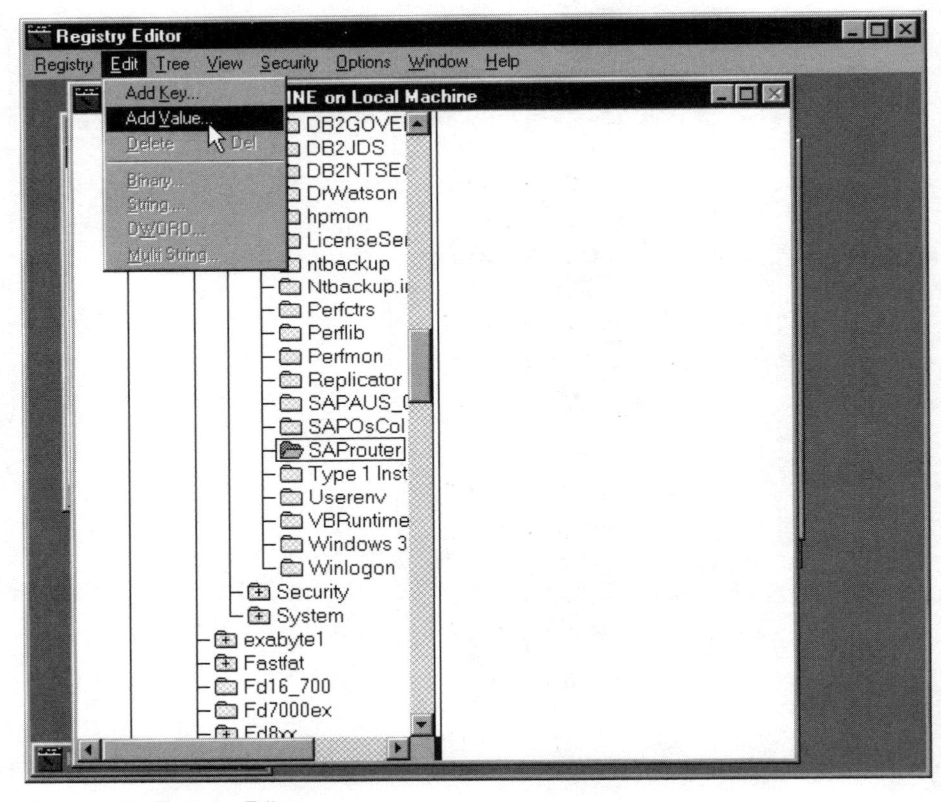

Figure 198. Registry Editor

9. Select **Edit->Add Value**:

Figure 199. Add Value Pop-Up

10.Enter EventMessageFile for the Value and Click **OK**.

11.Switch to a Command Window, and enter the following command:

```
<DRIVE>:\usr\sap\<SID>\sys\exe\run\sapntstartdb.exe
```

12.This will pop up the string editor with the string below. Click **OK**.

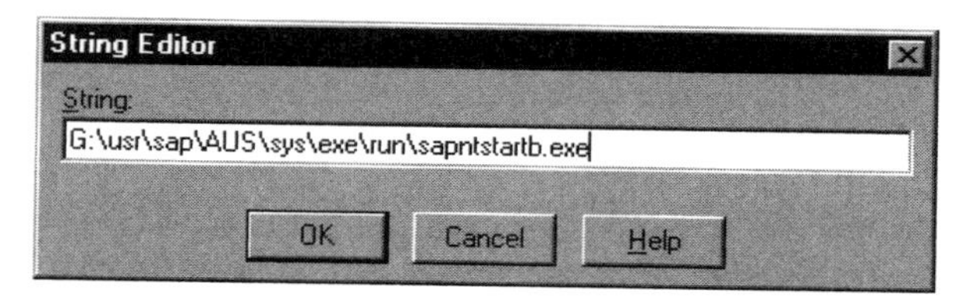

Figure 200. String Editor Pop-Up

13.Back in the registry editor, select **Edit->Add Value** for the SAProuter key field.

14.Enter the string **Types Supported** in the Value Name field.

15.Select **Reg_Dword** from the pulldown for the type, and click **OK**:

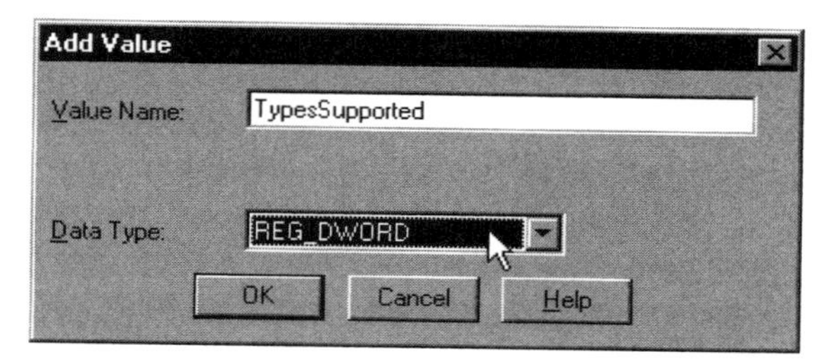

Figure 201. Add Value Pop-Up

16.Enter the value **7**, check **Hex**, and click **OK**:

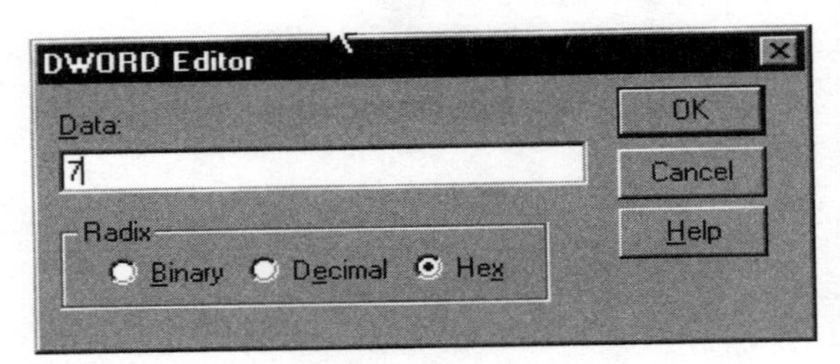

Figure 202. Add Value Popup

17.To start SAProuter, exit the registry, and from the Windows NT Control Panel, select the **Services** icon. You should see that the saprouter entry has been added and that the startup is manual at this point.

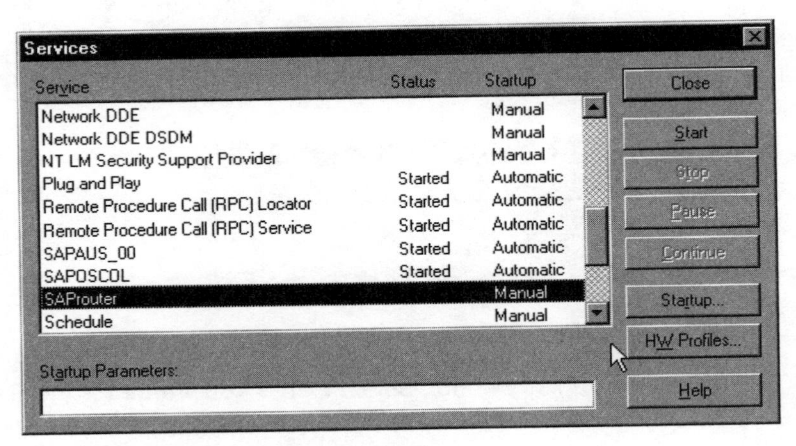

Figure 203. Windows NT Services Display

18.Click on the SAProuter entry, and click on **Startup**:

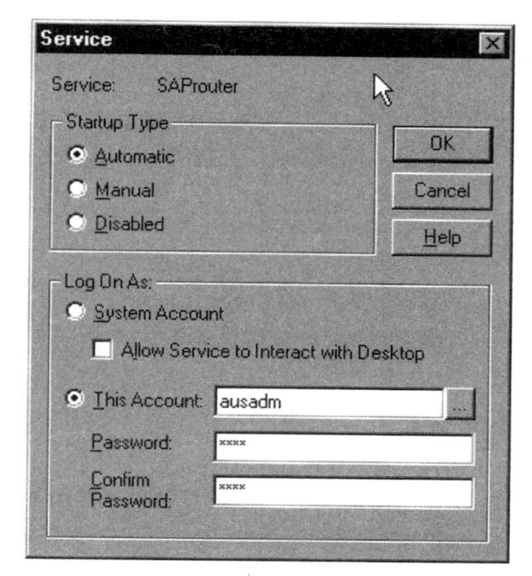

Figure 204. Windows NT Services Edit Screen

19. Select **Automatic**, then Select **This Account.** Enter the <sid>adm account and password, and click **OK**.

20. The services startup column for this entry should now show as automatic. Click **Start** to start Saprouter now. The SAProuter will also automatically start at system boot.

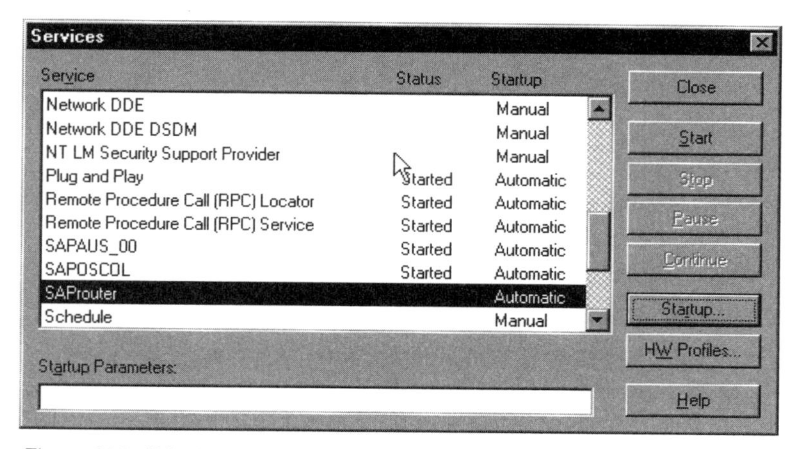

Figure 205. Windows NT Services Display

6.7.2 Configuring SAProuter on AIX

To configure SAProuter on AIX:

1. Create a saprouter directory in /usr/sap.
2. Copy the programs **saprouter** and **niping** from /sapmnt/<SID>/exe to /usr/sap/saprouter as follows:

```
cd /usr/sap/saprouter
cp -p /sapmnt/<SID>/exe/saprouter saprouter
cp -p /sapmnt/<SID>/exe/niping niping
```

3. Change the ownerships via these commands:

```
chown <SID>adm:sapsys saprouter
chown <SID>adm:sapsys niping
```

4. Create a shell script containing the following lines to start the saprouter daemon. This script should be executed when the AIX system is started.

```
#Start saprouter
#
SRDIR=/usr/sap/saprouter
LOGFILE=/usr/sap/saprouter/saprouter.log
echo "\nStarting saprouter Daemon" | tee -a $LOGFILE
echo "----------------------------------" | tee -a $LOGFILE
$SRDIR/saprouter -r -W 30000 -R $SRDIR/saprouttab | tee -a
        $LOGFILE &
```

5. You now need to construct a saprouttab file that will contain the IP addresses of the systems that will use your saprouter. The format is:

```
# P/D <source-host> <dest-host> <service> <password>
#
P     9.32.143.5   9.3.16.243  3200      password
```

   The P/D in the first column are abbrevations for Permit and Deny.

6. Include an entry in /etc/inittab to run your script. In our example we used **saprouter.sh** for the script name. Add the /etc/inittab entry as follows:

```
mkitab saprouter:2:once:/usr/sap/saprouter/saprouter.sh
```

7. To check this entry, use this command:

```
lsitab saprouter
```

The output should be:

```
saprouter:2:once:/usr/sap/saprouter/saprouter.sh
```

6.7.2.1 Configuring OSS Technical Settings

After SAProuter is running on your system, you must enter the information that will allow you to connect to OSS. This is accomplished by maintaining the technical settings on the OSS screen.

1. Add the following entry to the services file on your system:

```
sapdpw99 3399/tcp
```

2. From your SAP GUI, enter transaction **OSS1**. From the main screen, select **Parameter->Technical Settings**:

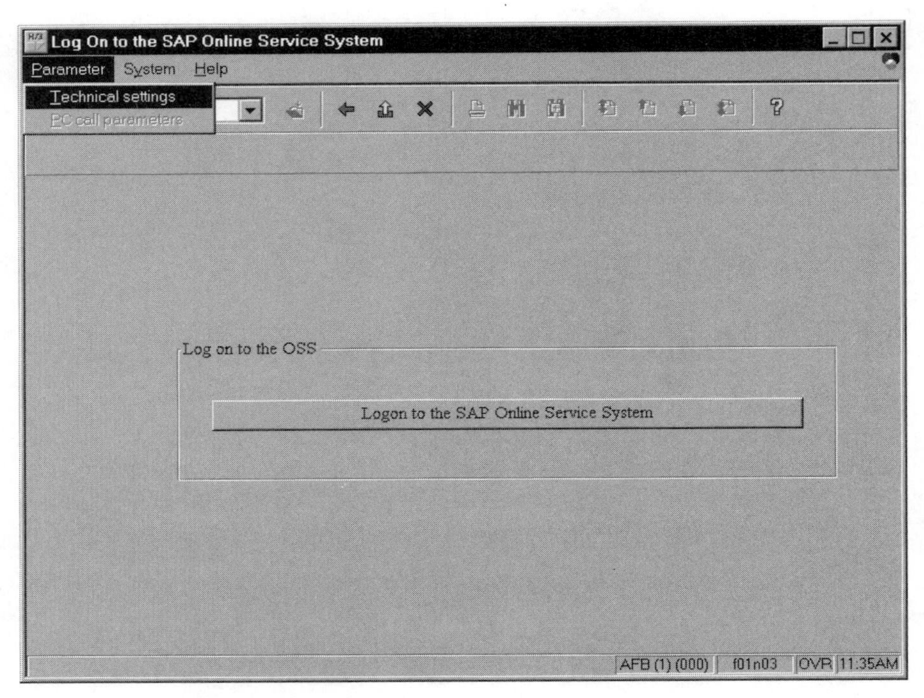

Figure 206. OSS Main Screen

3. Now fill in the appropriate information for you SAProuter setup.

   If your company has a firewall router, you will need its IP address and need to have its routing tables updated to allow access from the saprouter you have set up. That machine would most likely be administered by your company networking group.

4. Here is an example screen showing router data:

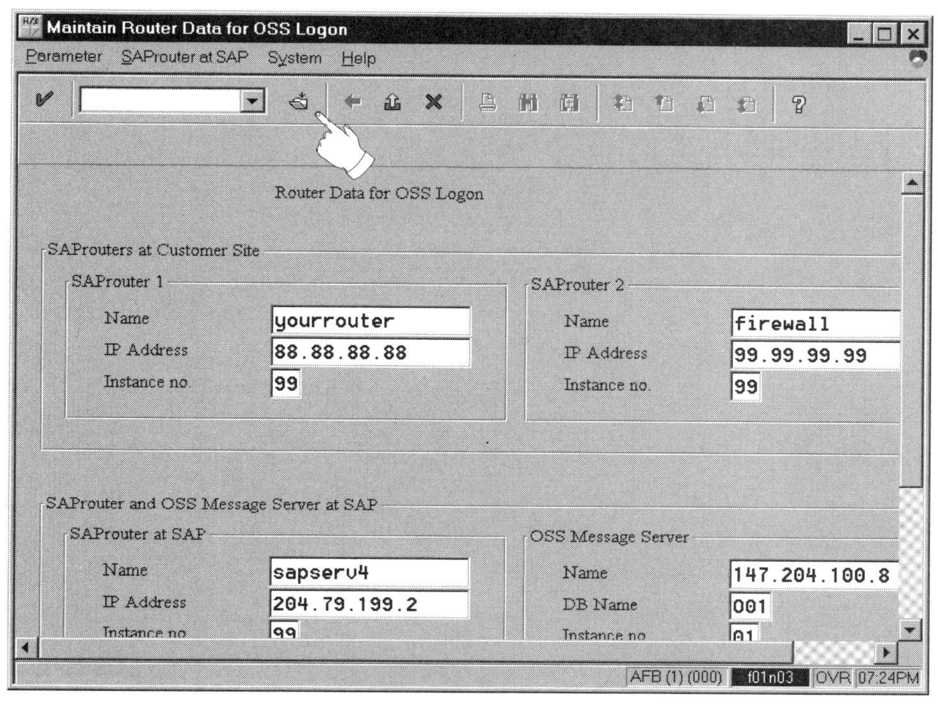

Figure 207. Maintain Router Data for OSS Logon

The saprouter at SAP and the OSS Message server values are the actual ones being used for a connection to SAP in Foster City, California. The saprouter 1 and saprouter 2 values are examples only.

5. When you have entered your parameters, save your configuration by clicking the save icon pointed to above.

6. At this point you can test the connection by logging on to OSS. Click the logon button on the main panel of the **OSS1** transaction.

6.8 Applying Hot Packages

Hot Packages are a collection of fixes or OSS notes that are packaged for ease of installation. These packages can be applied from CD-ROM or downloaded from OSS. Hot Packages on CD-ROM are typically released at intervals, while the latest Hot Packages are available from OSS. In this example, we will apply both from CD-ROM and OSS.

> **Note**
>
> When applying Hot Packages, you should increase the **abap/buffersize** value from 25000 (the default) to 250000.

6.8.1 Applying Hot Packages from CD-ROM

To apply Hot Packages from CD-ROM:

1. Mount the CD on your system. You must be the <SID>adm user for both AIX and Windows NT.
2. Change directories and execute the commands as follows:

```
G:\usr\sap\trans>cd \usr\sap\trans

G:\usr\sap\trans>CAR -xvf H:\Hot_40b\Kh40b01.car
x EPS/in/CSS0120024545_0000657.PAT

G:\usr\sap\trans>CAR -xvf H:\Hot_40b\Kd00018.car
x EPS/in/CSS0120024545_0000654.PAT

G:\usr\sap\trans>
```

Figure 208. Windows NT Command String

   This will unpack the files into the **trans** directory. This example shows the commands for NT. Similar commands exist for AIX.

3. From the SAP Frontend, issue transaction **SPAM**. Select the pulldown **Patch->Upload**:

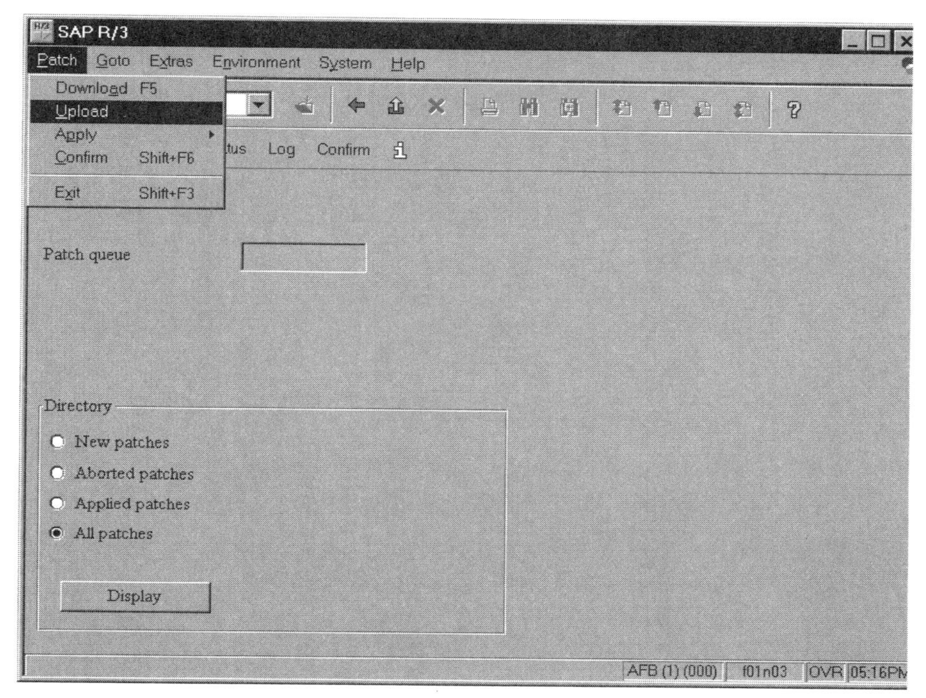

Figure 209. SPAM Screen Upload Patch

4. Click the check mark in the pop-up below:

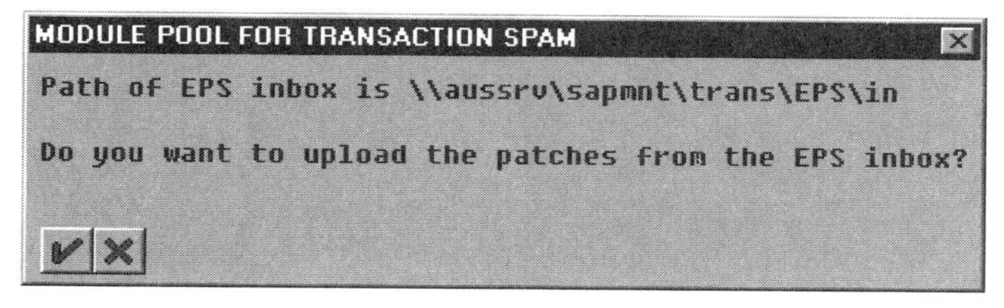

Figure 210. SPAM Verification Popup

5. At this point, a success window should pop up with the packages uploaded as shown below:

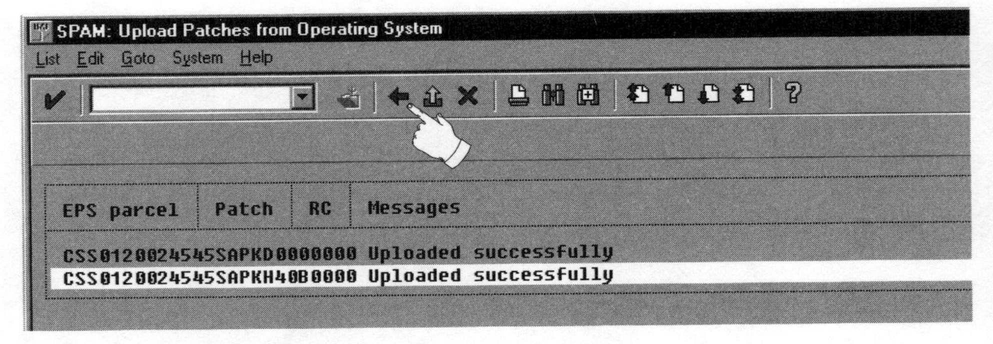

Figure 211. Patch Upload Screen

6. Now click the arrow to go back to the main **SPAM** menu.
7. Before you apply the actual Hot Packages you first need to apply the **SPAM** update. From the main **SPAM** menu, select **Patch->Apply->SPAM update**.

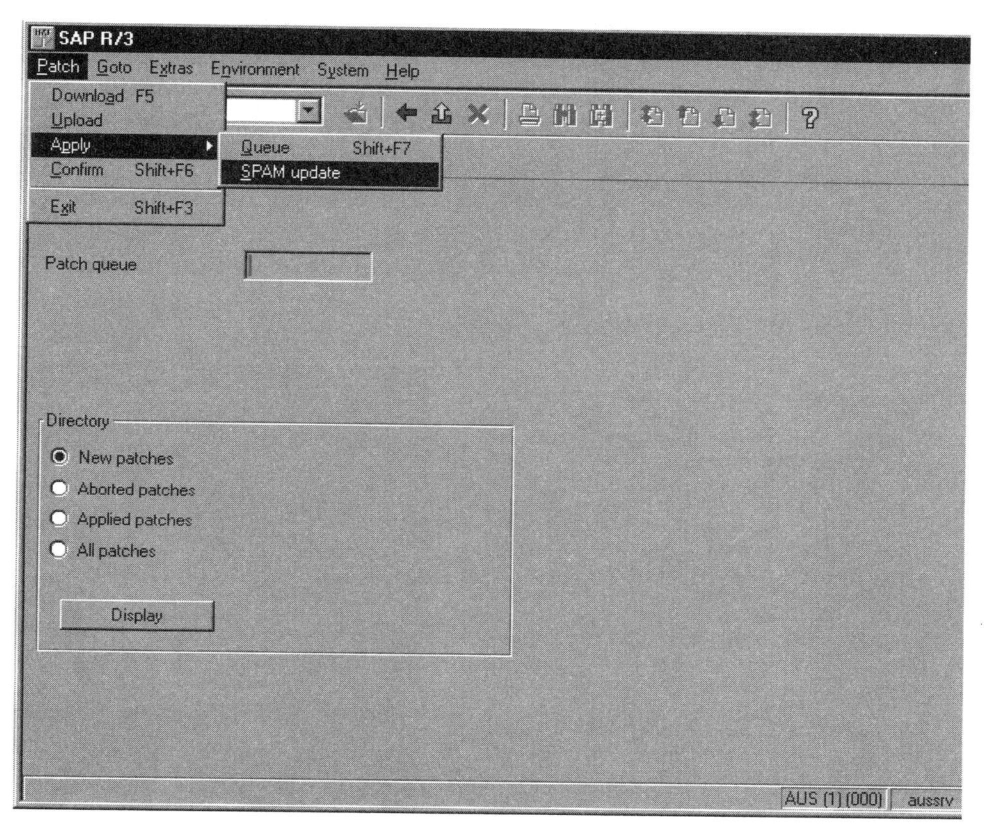

Figure 212. Spam Update Screen

8. New patches is selected by default. Click **Yes** to apply.
9. Click the check to confirm once the patch is applied:

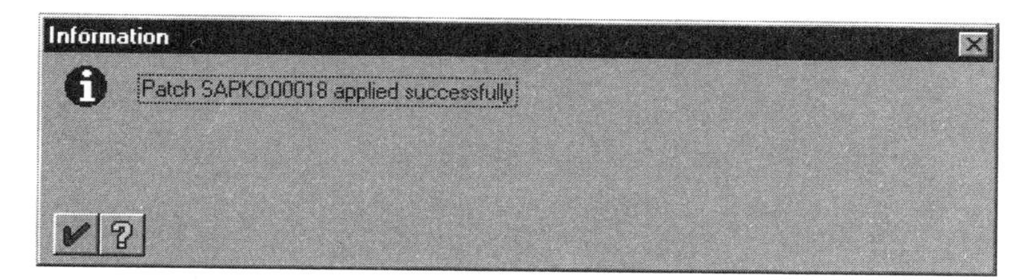

Figure 213. Information Screen

10. Now click the arrow at the top to go back to the main **SPAM** menu.
11. Issue the **SPAM** transaction one more time to generate the newly applied objects.

12.The system is now ready for the Hot Packages to be applied. Place your cursor in the patch queue box and hit **F4**. The Patch Queue will pop up:

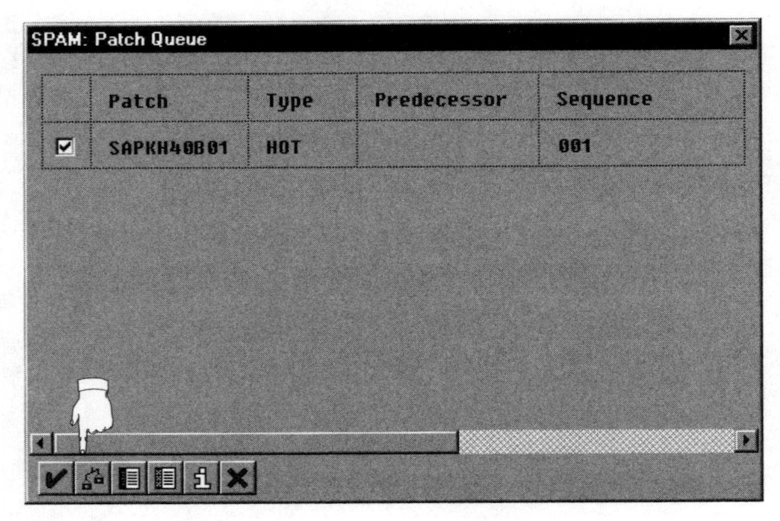

Figure 214. Patch Queue

13.Click the check queue icon pointed to above.

14.Click the check mark shown above and the queue will be generated. A confirmation message is displayed:

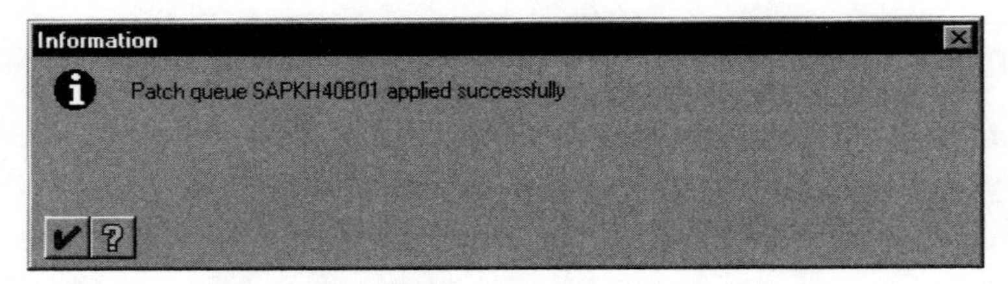

Figure 215. Information Screen

15.Click the check mark, and you are taken back to the SPAM main screen:

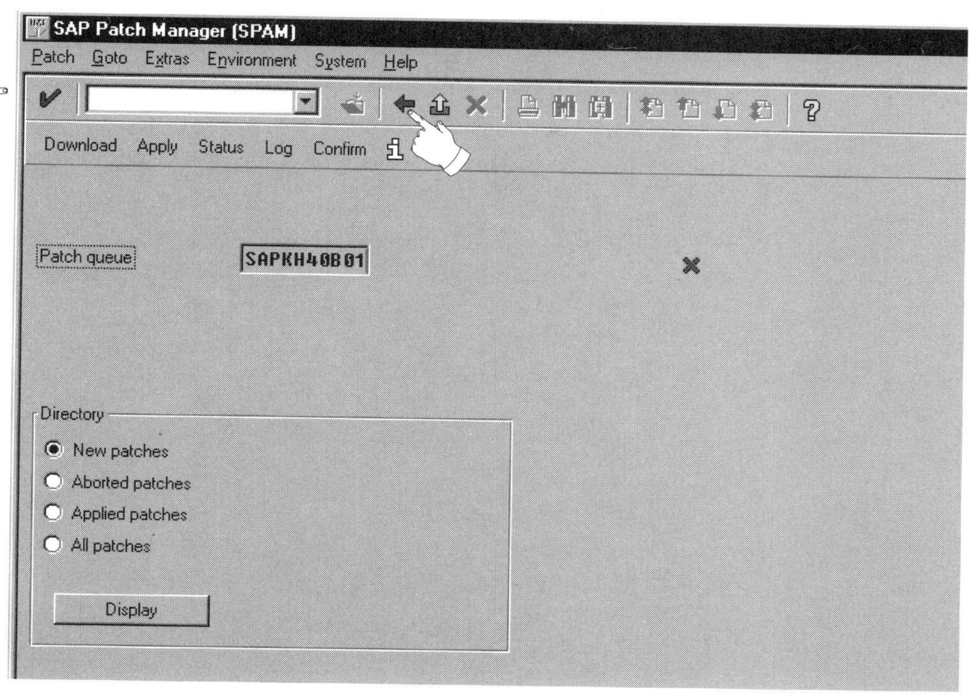

Figure 216. SAP Patch Manager Screen

16.Click the green Back arrow.

17.Click the check mark.

18.Now click **Apply** in the tool bar to actually apply the patches.

19.After the Hot Packages have been applied, the **SPAM** screen status will show yellow. You must click **Confirm** and the status will turn green:

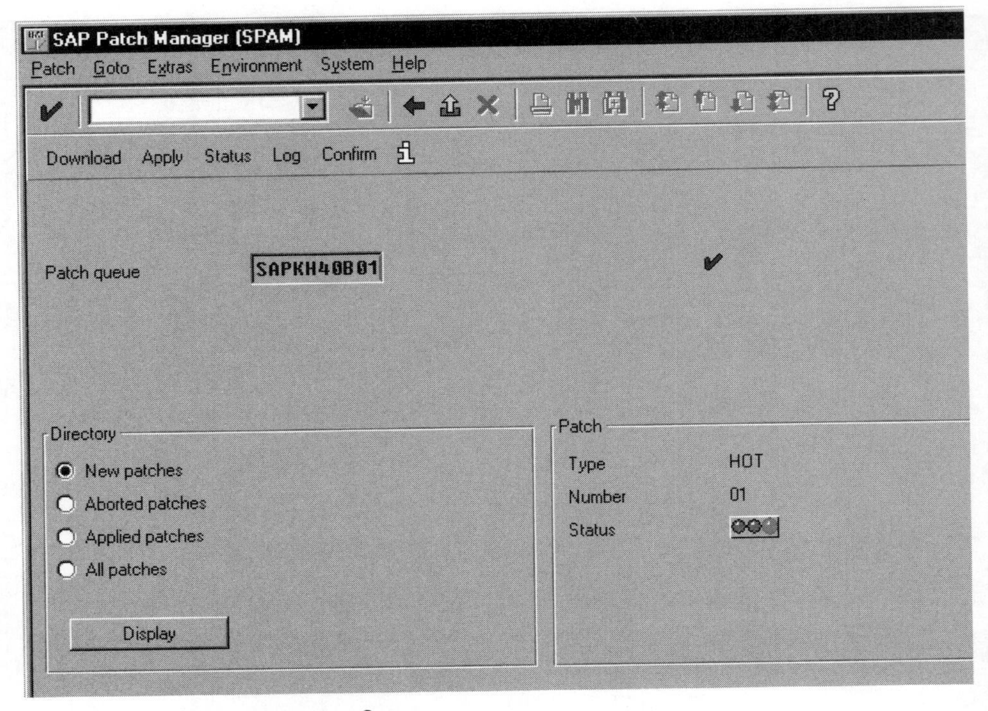

Figure 217. SAP Patch Manager Screen

6.8.2 Downloading Hot Packages From OSS

To apply Hot Packages from OSS, you must first download them.

1. Log onto OSS with your OSS ID.
2. From the main screen, click **SERVICE->SAP Patch Service->SAP Hot Packages**:

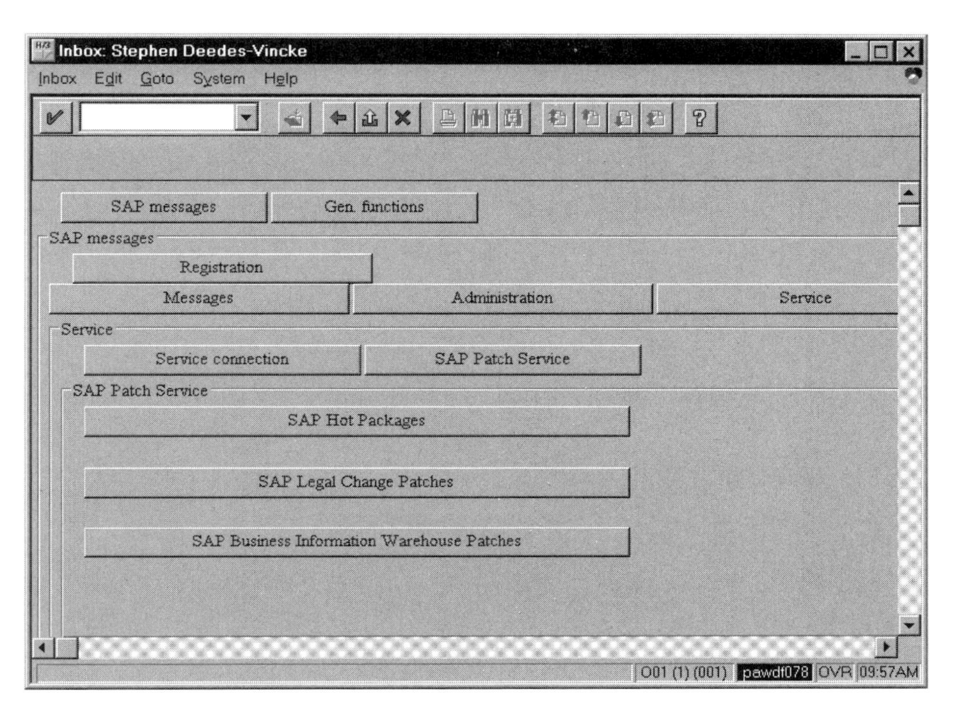

Figure 218. OSS Hot Package Screen

The List of Hot Packages is displayed:

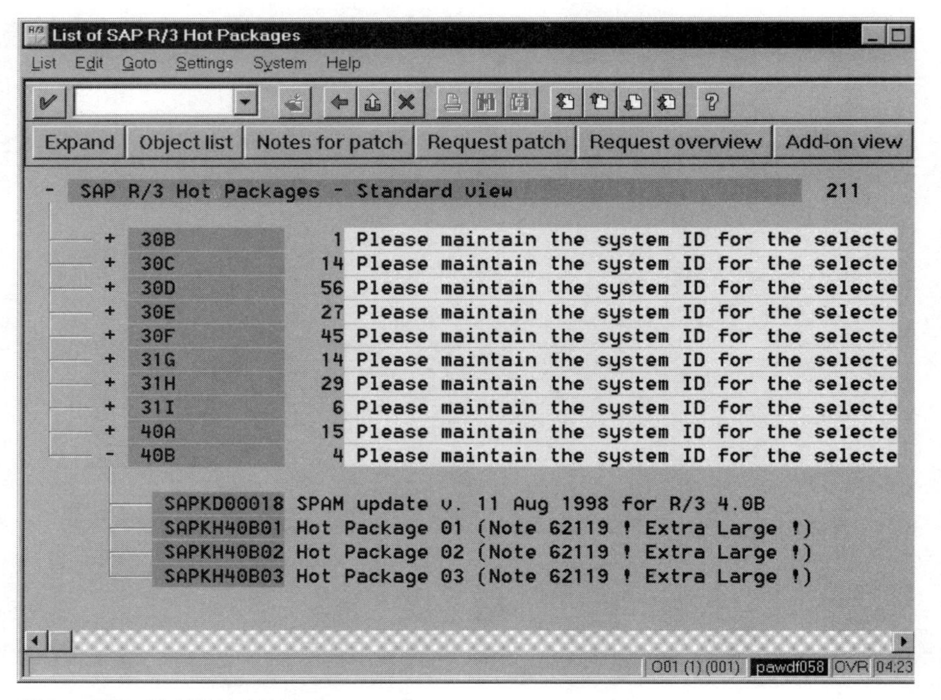

Figure 219. List Of Hot Packages.

3. Double click on the level you wish to select. In our case, we selected 4.0B.
4. Click on the patch you need to download.
5. Click **Request patch**. The Request Patch popup is displayed:

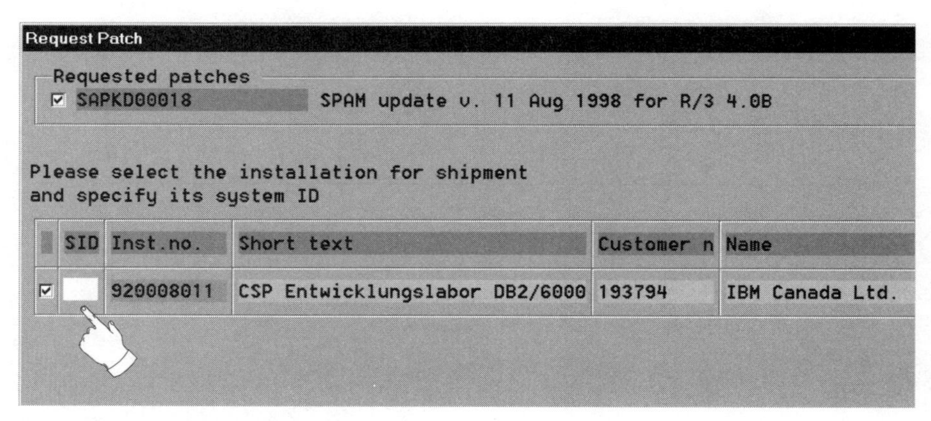

Figure 220. Request Patch

6. Enter your 3 character <SID>, and click **Continue** to download.
7. The confirm the status of the patch, click **Request Overview** in the List of Hot Packages (Figure 219 on page 254).
8. When the patches are downloaded, proceed as explained in “Applying Hot Packages from CD-ROM” on page 246 to apply them.

Chapter 7. Administration in the R/3 DB2 UDB Environment

This chapter provides an overview of some of the administrative tasks in an R/3 environment which use DB2 UDB as its database management system. It covers the starting and stopping of both DB2 UDB and R/3, DB2 storage concepts, user maintenance and security.

7.1 Starting the db2<sid> DB2 Instance

The DB2 instance created during R/3 installation is called db2<sid>. Within this instance is the R/3 database, called <sid>. The startup of the db2<sid> DB2 instance can be performed:

- Automatically, either at R/3 startup or at reboot time
- Manually, by the system administrator before the initialization of SAP R/3

Note that for clarity, we refer to the starting of the db2<sid> DB2 instance as *starting DB2* or *starting the DB2 instance* in this chapter. This is based on the fact that R/3 only uses this one DB2 instance.

7.1.1 Starting DB2 Automatically at R/3 Startup

When you start R/3, it will check to see if the DB2 instance is started. If it is not started, then R/3 will start it. The R/3 startup process differs somewhat between AIX and Windows NT. The differences by operating system are as follows:

- On the Windows NT platform, the SAP Service manager calls the R/3 instance control, <SID>_<instance number>, which in turn will call the R/3 command, **sapntstartdb.exe**. This command will test the availability of the R/3 database by using the R/3 command, **r3trans.exe**, before attempting to invoke the R/3 command, **strdbs.cmd**. The command strdbs.cmd will use the NET START command to start the DB2 instance.
- On the AIX platform, the R/3 command, **startsap**, calls the R/3 command, **R3trans**, to determine if the R/3 database is available or not. If it is, the DB2 instance startup process is skipped; otherwise, startsap will call the DB2 instance startup command, **db2start**.

More details about starting R/3 are given in “Starting R/3” on page 272.

7.1.2 Starting DB2 at Reboot

When you install DB2 UDB, you are given the option to have the DB2 instance started at reboot time. See “Installing DB2 UDB” on page 89 for details of this procedure on AIX, and “Installing DB2 UDB” on page 147 for more details on Windows NT.

7.1.3 Starting DB2 Manually

Starting the DB2 instance on AIX requires that you be logged in as a user that is part of either the SYSADM_GROUP, SYSCTRL_GROUP or SYSMAINT_GROUP. For example, the db2<sid> user or the <sid>adm user will meet this criterion.

On Windows NT, starting up the DB2 instance launches a Windows NT service. As such, a user attempting to start DB2 must meet Windows NT’s requirements for starting a service. Specifically, the user account must satisfy *either* of the following criteria:

- The user must be a Windows NT administrator.
- The user must be part of either the SYSADM_GROUP, SYSCTRL_GROUP or SYSMAINT_GROUP as defined in the database manager configuration file *and* also have the right to start a Windows NT service (by being a member of the Administrators, Server Operators or Power Users group on Windows NT).

DB2 can be started by using either the DB2 Control Center, the Windows NT Services panel (if on Windows NT), or from an operating system command prompt. To start DB2 from the Control Center:

1. Select **Start->Programs->DB2 for Windows NT->Administration Tools->Control Center**.
2. Expand the system tree to the instance level.
3. Right-click on the DB2<SID> instance, then select **Start** as shown in Figure 221.

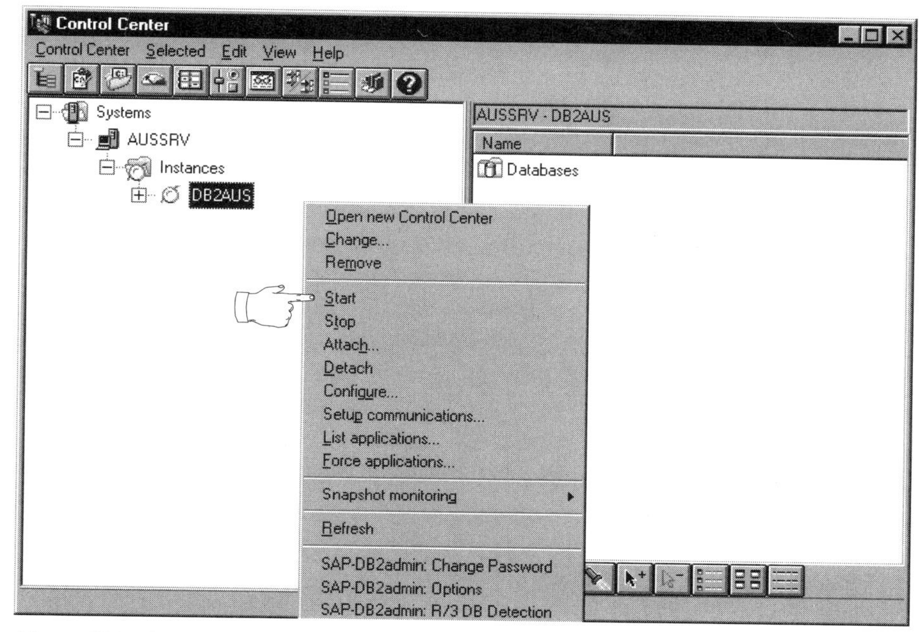

Figure 221. Starting DB2 from the Control Center

To start DB2 from the Windows NT Services panel, select the DB2 - DB2<SID> service, and click **Start**.

To start DB2 from a command line, first make sure that the environment variable DB2INSTANCE is set to DB2<SID>, then issue the **db2start** command. On the Windows NT platform, you can also issue **net start DB2<SID>**.

7.1.4 Verifying that DB2 Has Started

On Windows NT, you can check that DB2 has started from the Windows NT Services panel:

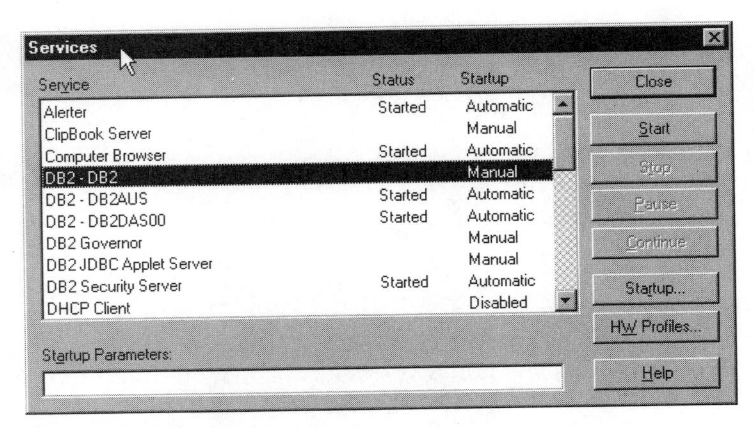

Figure 222. DB2 Services

DB2 is started if the service named DB2-DB2<sid> is started. You can also check in the Windows NT Task Manager for any processes whose names start with db2. To start the Task Manager:

- Press **Ctrl + Alt + Delete**.
- Click **Task Manager**.

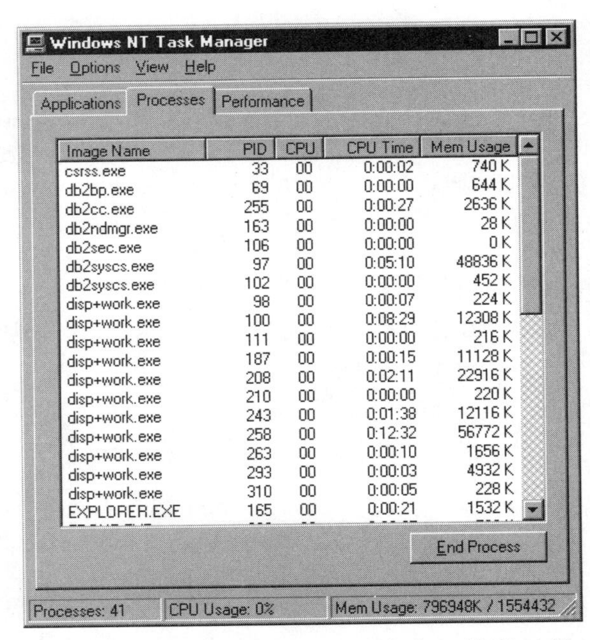

Figure 223. DB2 Processes in the Windows NT Task Manager

- Click the **Processes** tab.
- To sort the processes by name, click twice on the **Image Name** column heading.

On AIX, the following command may be issued to verify that DB2 has been started:

```
ps -ef | grep db2 | more
```

If there are no processes whose name begins with db2, then DB2 has not been started (specifically you are looking for the process **db2sysc**).

7.1.5 DB2 Startup Problem Determination

If DB2 does not start or an error message is displayed during start up, you should check the following points:

- On Windows NT

  1. Check the Windows NT Services panel for any DB2 services that have not been started by clicking: **Start->Settings->Control Panel,** and selecting the **Services** icon.

  - If some of the services are missing or not started, start the Windows NT Event Viewer by clicking **Start->Programs->Administrative Tools->Event Viewer.**
  - Find the event associated with the error encountered during DB2 startup.
  - Click on the event and press enter to display the event details.

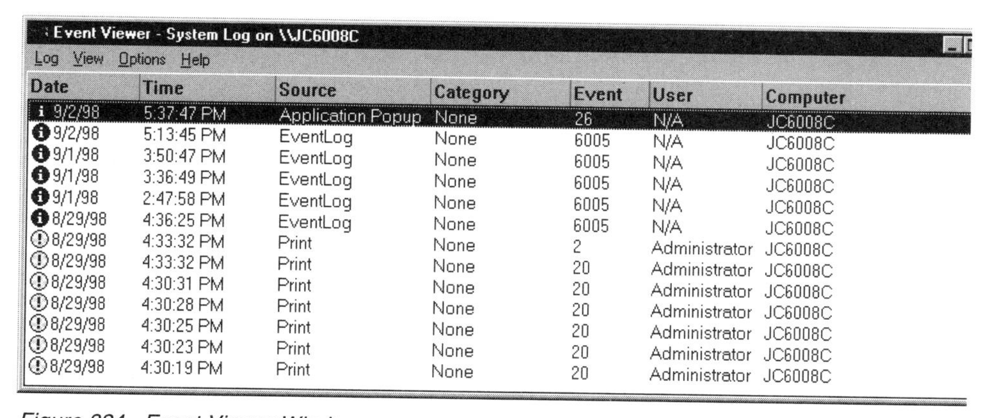

Figure 224. Event Viewer Window

2. If the event log shows no information about the database startup problems, check the DB2 diagnostic log file, db2diag.log, under the directory \db2\<SID>\db2dump for further information.

- On AIX:
  1. If DB2 was started by R/3 and an error message has been displayed, check the startdb.log file in the <sid>adm home directory.
  2. If the startdb.log does not provide enough information about the start up problem, check the DB2 diagnostic log file, db2diag.log, in the /db2/<SID>/sqllib/db2dump directory.

7.1.6 Causes of DB2 Startup Problems

There are many factors that can prevent DB2 from starting. The following is a list of some of the most common causes for startup failure.

- DB2 environment variables are not set correctly.
- DB2 services are not running.
- Loss of some database objects such as a control files, containers, or on-line logs as the result of disk crash or the object being removed by a user.
- The user trying to start DB2 has insufficient authority to do so.

7.2 Stopping DB2

There are times when DB2 needs to be stopped in order to perform database maintenance, such as to upgrade the version of DB2. To stop DB2, you must be logged in as a user that has the DB2 authority SYSADM, SYSCTRL, or SYSMAINT, for example, the db2<sid> user or the <sid>adm user. With Windows NT, since stopping the DB2 instance also implies stopping a service, the userid must also have the ability to start and stop a service.

To stop DB2 using the Control Center:

1. Start the Control Center by selecting **Start->Programs->DB2 for Windows NT->Administration Tools->Control Center**.
2. Expand the Systems tree until you reach the database instance level.
3. Right click on the DB2<SID> instance. The following menu will be displayed.

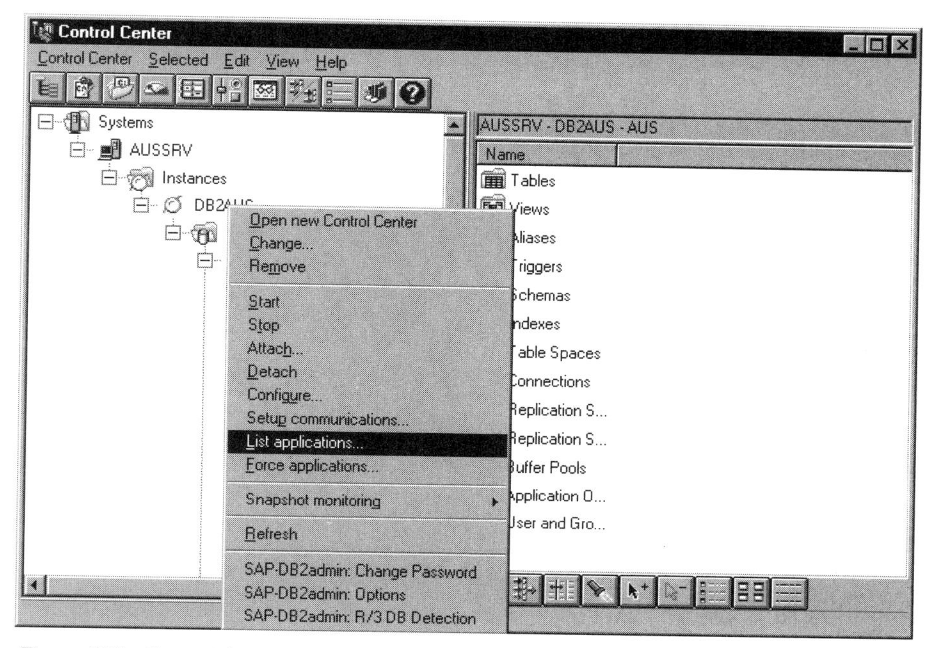

Figure 225. Control Center DB2 Instance Menu

4. Before stopping the DB2 instance, you must first ensure that there are no applications running in the instance. To do this, click **List applications**. The following screen will be displayed.

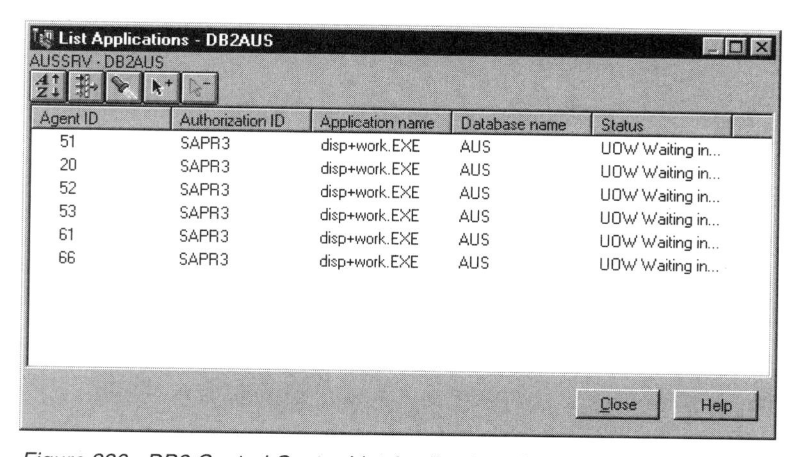

Figure 226. DB2 Control Center List Applications Screen

5. This screen displays all applications and users that are connected to databases in the instance you have chosen.

6. Once you determine that it is safe to end all applications or no applications are connected to your instance or instance database, return to the DB2 instance menu and click **Stop** to stop the database instance. The following window will be displayed.

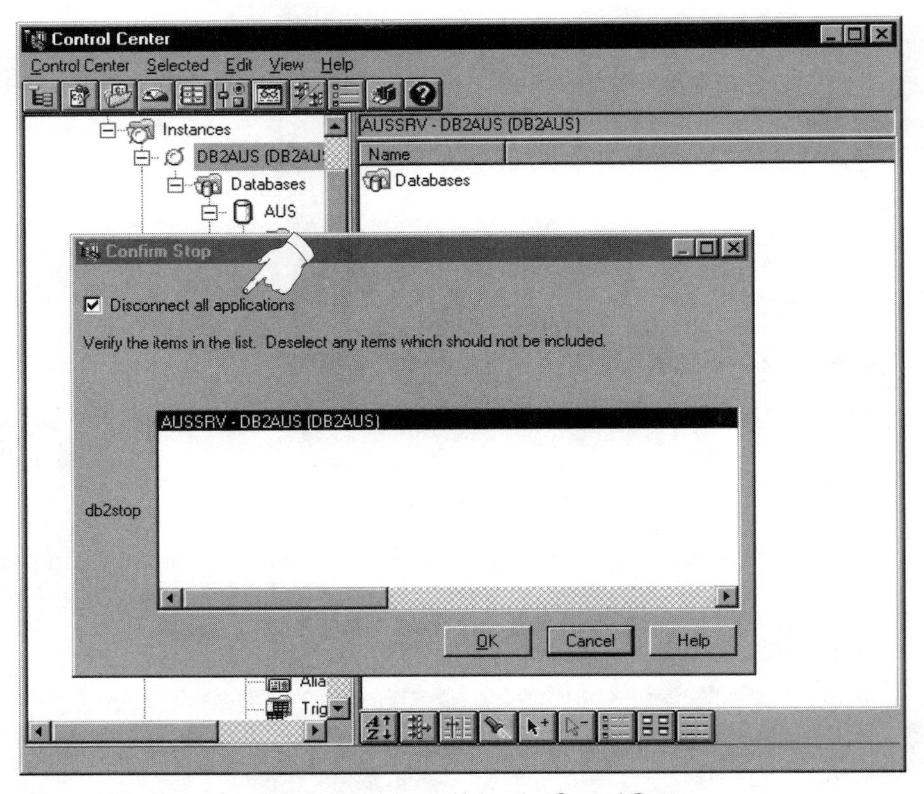

Figure 227. Stopping a Database Instance Using the Control Center

7. Select **Disconnect all applications** in the Confirm Stop panel.
8. Click **OK** to complete the shut down of the instance.

7.2.1 DB2 Shutdown Problem Determination

If DB2 is still running after issuing the stop command against the database instance from the Control Center and waiting a reasonable amount of time, you should check the following:

1. From the Control Center, check to see if any applications are still active by right-clicking on the database instance and then clicking the List applications option from the pop-up menu. If there are still some

applications displayed, return to the DB2 Instance menu and click on the Force applications option as shown in Figure 228.

2. After waiting for a period of time to let the Force request to take effect, return to the DB2 instance menu and click **Stop** to stop the database instance

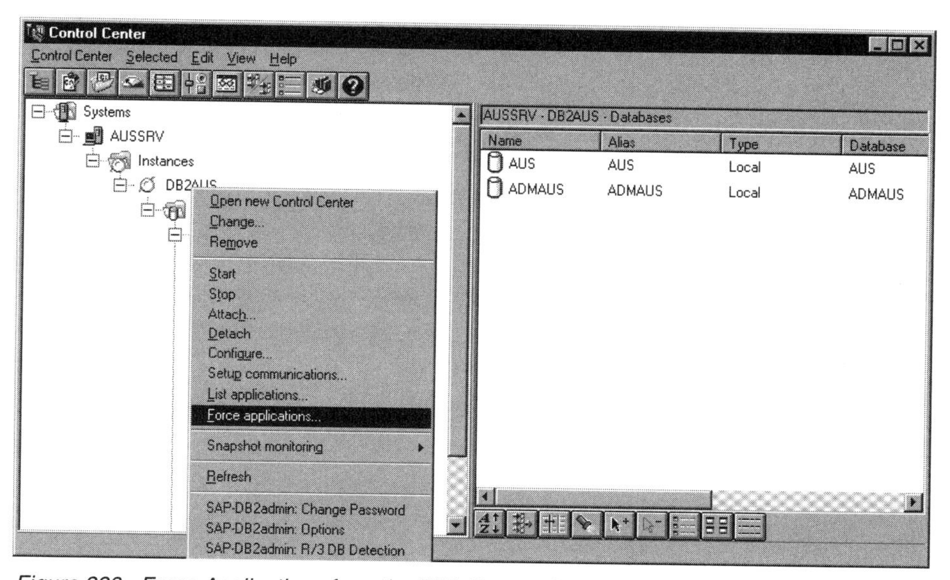

Figure 228. Force Applications from the DB2 Control Center Instance Menu

If you still have problems stopping the DB2 instance, you may also try the two methods listed below. Under no circumstances should you ever manually terminate a DB2 process using either the Windows NT Task Manager or the kill command on AIX.

- Use the DB2STOP FORCE command from an operating system prompt.
- On the Windows NT platform, you may use the Windows NT Services panel to stop the DB2 instance. Click **Start->Settings->Control Panel,** and choose the **Services** icon. Highlight the instance service by clicking on the service, then clicking **Stop** as is depicted in Figure 229:

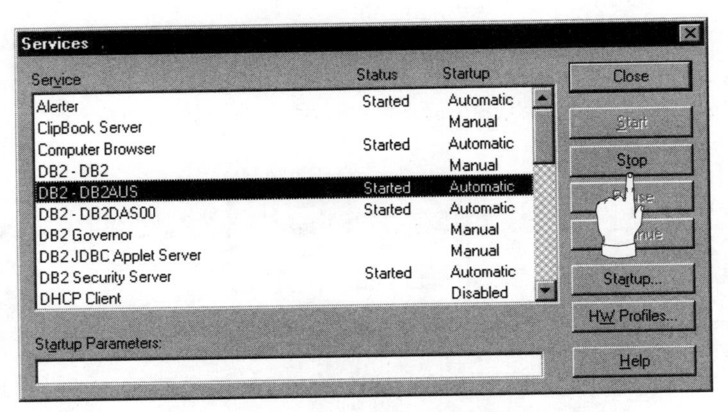

Figure 229. Stop DB2 Instance from Windows NT Services Menu

7.3 The DB2 Process Model

When DB2 starts, a number of processes (AIX) or processes/threads (Windows NT) are started. When the first connection is made to the R/3 database, some more processes/threads are started (Figure 230):

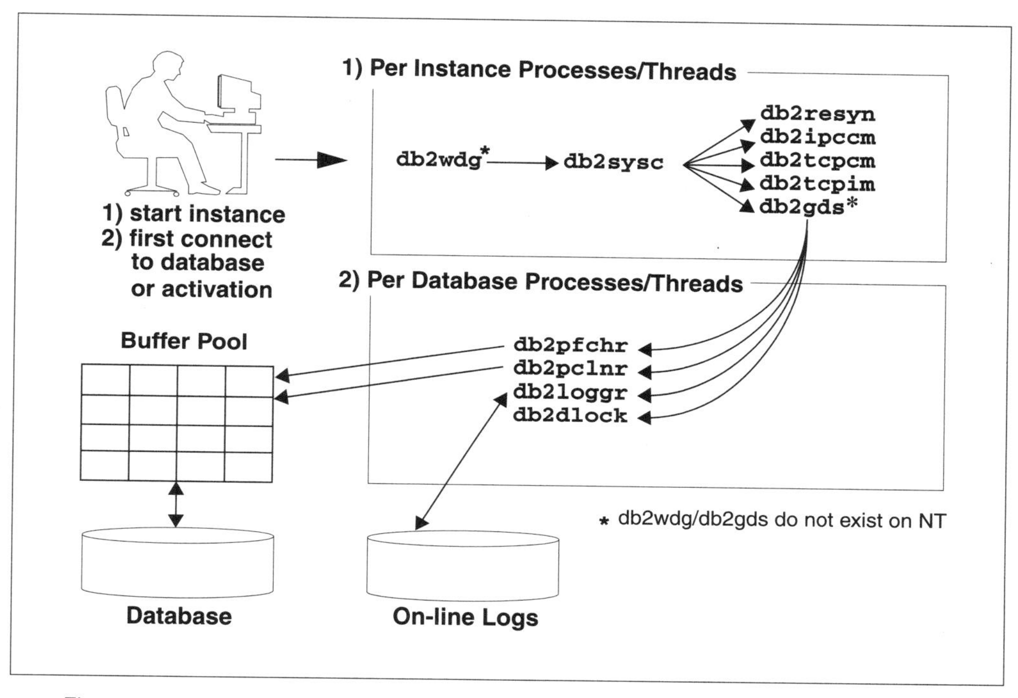

Figure 230. DB2 Processes/Threads

The **db2start** command on both operating systems (AIX and Windows NT) starts all per-instance processes or threads. The database manager is initiated to allocate operating system resources for the database. Once the database manager is started, the listener processes listen at the network / inter-process communications (IPC) ports for inbound connection requests.

When R/3 starts, the R/3 dispatcher is activated and a connection is sent from the R/3 application to the DB2 instance containing the R/3 database. The first connection triggers the initialization of the DB2 database bufferpool and memory heaps and a db2agent is created to service the request of the dispatcher agent. When the dispatcher programs connect, a remote listener (or IPC listener) allocates a coordinating agent (db2agent) to represent the user's application within the database manager. The coordinating agent will perform any work or arrange for another process or thread to perform the work on its behalf. All data and return code information is passed back to the user's application via the coordinating agent.

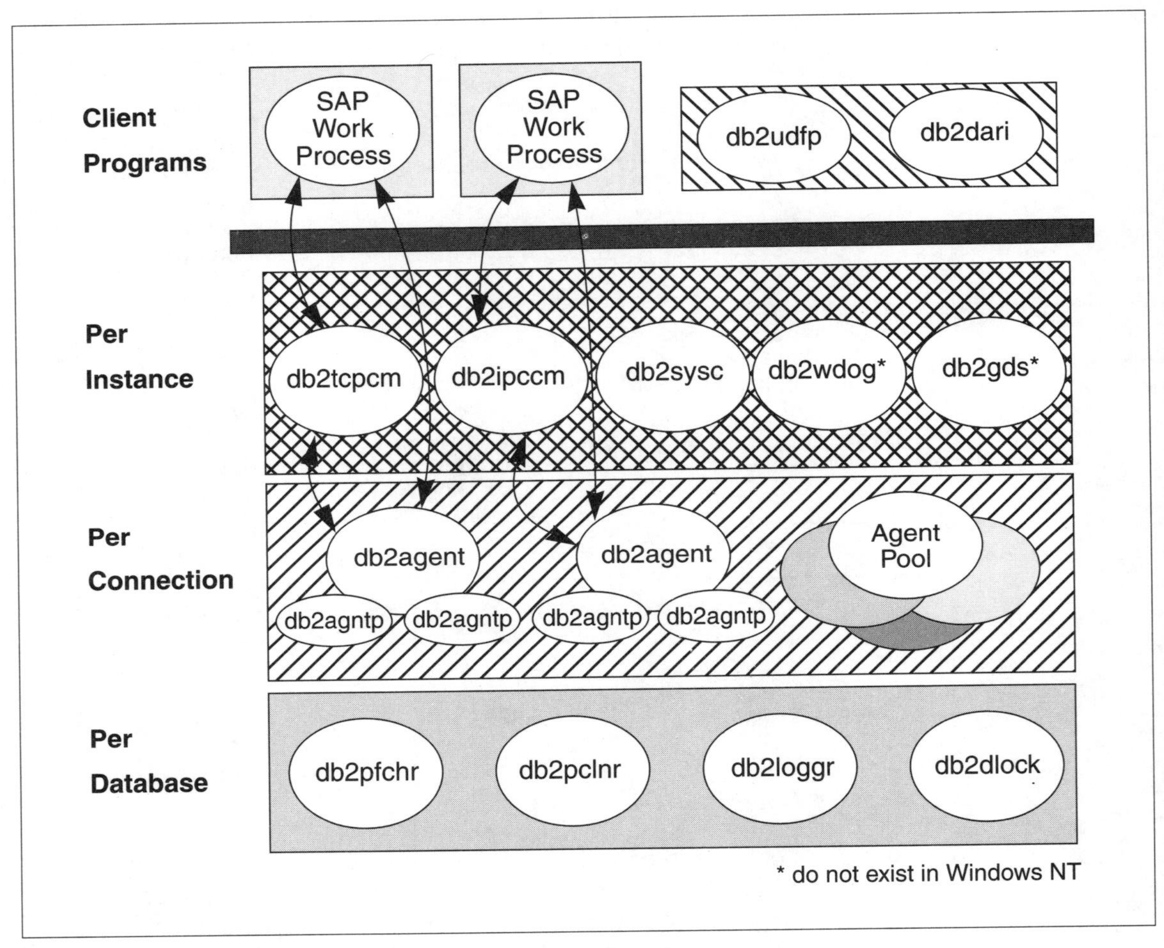

Figure 231. DB2 UDB Process Model with SAP R/3

As shown in Figure 231, there is a pool of spare or idle agents kept by DB2 to allow for the rapid allocation of new agents for an application. When SQL requests are passed to the coordinating agent which may involve parallel execution the coordinating agent will pass the work out to a number of subagents (db2agntp) to perform this work on its behalf. Since each subagent is a separate process or thread, they can be executing simultaneously.

Each database has a group of input/output agents, these include:

- Buffer pool cleaners (db2pclnr) which are used to asynchronously write changed pages from the bufferpool to the disk.
- Prefetchers (db2pfchr) are in charge of asynchronous retrieval of data pages into the bufferpool from the tables on disk.
- The DB2 logger (db2loggr) writes the database transaction information to the log files and handles transaction processing and recovery
- The deadlock detector (db2dlock) is responsible for determining that a deadlock has occurred and for resolving the deadlock.

The process model used by all DB2 servers facilitates the communication that occurs between database servers and client and local applications. It also ensures that database applications are isolated from resources such as database control blocks and critical database files.

UNIX-based environments, such as AIX, use an architecture based on processes. Intel operating systems, such as Windows NT, use an architecture based on threads.

In this section we use the term process/thread to represent either processes or threads, and process model to represent the model for DB2 processes and/or threads.

For each database manager or database being accessed, various processes/threads are started to deal with the various tasks such as logging, prefetching, communication, and so on.

Each process/thread of a client application has a single coordinator agent that operates on a database. The coordinator agent works on behalf of the requesting application, and communicates to other agents using inter-process communications (IPC) or remote communication protocols.

The DB2 architecture also provides a firewall so that user applications must run in a separate address space from DB2. The firewall protects the database and the database manager from user applications, application stored procedures, and user-defined functions (UDFs). A firewall maintains the integrity of the data in the databases, because an application programming error cannot overwrite an internal buffer or file of the database manager. It also improves reliability, because an application programming error cannot crash the database manager.

7.3.1 Application Client Programs

Client programs, such as the SAP R/3 work processes, can run remotely or on the same machine as the database server. They make their first contact with the database manager through a DB2 listener. A coordinator agent (db2agent) is then assigned to them.

Client programs, such as SAP R/3 work processes, db2udfp (fenced user-defined functions (UDFs)), and db2dari (fenced stored procedures) all run outside of the firewall.

7.3.2 DB2 Listeners

Client application programs make initial contact with communication listeners, which are started when DB2 is started. There is a listener for each configured communication protocol, and an inter-process communications (IPC) listener (db2ipccm) for local client programs. Listeners include:

- db2ipccm, for local client connections
- db2tcpcm, for TCP/IP connections
- db2snacm, for APPC connections
- db2tcpdm, for TCP/IP discovery requests

7.3.3 DB2 Agents

All connection requests from client applications, whether they are local or remote, are allocated a corresponding coordinator agent (db2agent). When the coordinator agent is created, it performs all database requests on behalf of the application.

In symmetric multiprocessor (SMP) environments, partitioned database environments, and non-partitioned database environments in which the intra_parallel database manager configuration parameter is enabled, the coordinator agent may distribute the database requests to subagents (db2agntp), and these agents perform the requests for the application.

A coordinator agent may be:

- Connected to the database with an alias. For example, db2agent (AUS) is connected to the database alias AUS.
- An idle agent residing in an agent pool. These agents are available for requests from coordinator agents operating on behalf of client programs, or from subagents operating on behalf of existing coordinator agents. The number of available agents is dependent on the database manager configuration parameter NUM_POOLAGENTS.

7.3.4 Database Threads/Processes

The following list includes some of the important threads/processes used by each database:

- db2pfchr: Performs prefetching of database pages into the buffer pool.
- db2pclnr: Performs buffer pool page cleaning by writing dirty pages from the buffer pool to disk.
- db2loggr: writes the database transaction information to the log files and handles transaction processing and recovery
- db2dlock: Detects and resolves deadlock situations.
- db2sysc: The system controller (db2sysc) must exist in order for the database server to function. Also, the following threads/processes may be started to carry out various tasks:
  - db2resyn: the resynchronization agent.
  - db2gds: the generic daemon spawner on UNIX-based systems that starts new processes
  - db2wdog: the watchdog on UNIX-based systems that handles abnormal program terminations

7.3.5 DB2 UDB on Intel Compared to DB2 UDB on UNIX

The Intel systems supported by DB2 on Windows operating systems differ from UNIX-based environments in that the database engine is multi-threaded. In the Intel systems, each of the dispatchable units on the agent side of the firewall is a thread under the process db2sysc, allowing the database engine to let the operating system perform task-switching at the thread level and not the process level. For each database being accessed, there are other threads started to deal with database tasks such as logging, prefetching, page cleaning, and so on.

Another difference is in the handling of abnormal terminations. There is no need for a watchdog process in Intel systems, because the Intel systems manage the cleanup of all the allocated resources after an abnormal termination. The equivalent of the db2wdog is buried within the operating system and is not a required DB2 thread. In addition, a db2gds thread also is not needed on the Intel systems, because the Intel systems have their own mechanisms for generating new threads.

7.4 Starting R/3

This section looks at what is involved in starting an R/3 instance. We will discuss the processes that are started during the startup of the R/3 instance. The processes that are started depend on the type of R/3 instance (central or dialog/application). The R/3 administrative user is the only user authorized to start R/3. The R/3 startup procedure differs slightly between AIX and Windows NT platforms.

7.4.1 Overview of R/3 Startup on AIX

Starting R/3 on the AIX platform is performed using the **startsap** command logged in as <sid>adm, the R/3 Administrative user. This startsap script is an alias to a script called startsap_<hostname>_<instance number>, which is found in the home directory of <sid>adm. This script performs the following functions in this order:

1. Starts the saposcol process. This is the statistics collector program which collects information about the operating system.
2. Checks that the DB2 instance, DB2<SID> is running. If this DB2 instance is not running, it is started.
3. Determines if the R/3 Service Manager is active. If it is not active, R/3 services and work processes are started:
   - Based on the startup profile, DEFAULT.PFL, the collector daemon and send daemon services are started. The message work process and disp+work work processes are also started.
   - Based on the instance profile, <SID>_<INSTANCE NAME><instance number>_<hostname>, the dialog, batch, spool, gateway, enqueue, and update work processes are started.

7.4.1.1 Starting R/3 on AIX

To start R/3 on AIX, perform the following steps:

1. Logon to AIX as the R/3 administrator userid, <sid>adm, on a machine where an R/3 central instance or application instance runs.
2. Run the **startsap** command. This command can be invoked as follows:
   - **startsap all** - This starts saposcol, DB2 and R/3. The **all** can also be in upper case (**ALL**). The startsap command with no parameters defaults to this behavior.
   - **startsap R3** - This starts only R/3. The **R3** can also be in lower case (**r3**).

3. Check the messages in the startup log file in order to make sure that R/3 is running.

```
f01n03:afbadm 4> startsap

Starting SAP-Collector Daemon
------------------------------
Collector already running ... don't launch
 saposcol already running

Checking SAP R/3 AFB Database
------------------------------
 Database is not available via /usr/sap/AFB/SYS/exe/run/R3trans -d -w

Starting SAP R/3 AFB Database
------------------------------
 Startup-Log is written to /home/afbadm/startdb.log
 Database started

Checking SAP R/3 AFB Database
------------------------------
 Database is running

Starting SAP R/3 Instance
------------------------------
 Startup-Log is written to /home/afbadm/startsap_f01n03_00.log
 Instance on host f01n03 started

f01n03:afbadm 5> █
```

Figure 232. Startsap Messages

There are two other ways to check that R/3 has started:

1. Look for the R/3 work processes using the AIX **ps** command:

   ps -ef | grep sap | more

2. Check for the presence of the file kill.sap under the directory: /usr/sap/<sid>/<instance name><instance number>/work. If it is not there, then R/3 has probably not yet started.

4. If there are application servers running on other machines in the R/3 system, there are several ways to start these application servers:

   1. Logon as operating system R/3 administrator <sid>adm and invoke the command, **startsap**, at each machine which hosts an application instance.

   2. Customize the shell script called startsap_<hostname>_<instance number> by adding a command to start up each application instance. The following are several command examples; choose only one to include in the startsap shell script:

```
rsh hostname -l user startsap
rexec -n hostname startsap
su - hostname -c startsap
```

3. Run the SAP Frontend and logon as an R/3 administrator user (for example: SAP*). Use the transaction **RZ03** or use the menu path **Tools->CCMS, Control/Monitoring->Control Panel, Control->Start SAP Instance** to start R/3 from the control panel under the Computing Center Management System (CCMS) menu. This only works when any instance (central instance or application instance) has been defined with at least one dialog work process.

7.4.1.2 R/3 Startup Problem Determination on AIX

If the R/3 instance does not start or there is an error message returned from the `startsap` command:

1. Check the file sapstart_<hostname>_<instance number>.log for any error messages.
2. Check the file, startdb.log, in the home directory of the <sid>adm user. If this log file contains any errors, you can check for further error details in the db2diag.log file in /db2/<SID>/sqllib/db2dump.
3. Look for any error messages in the most recently created files in the directory /usr/sap/<sid>/<instance name><instance number>/work. The instance name varies depending on the R/3 configuration. The central instance is called: DVEBMGS<nn> and the dialog instance is called D<nn> where nn is the instance number. Check the following developer trace files with the most recent time stamps:

   - dev_disp
   - dev_digr
   - dev_ms
   - dev_rd
   - dev_rfc*
   - dev_w*
   - stderr*

   where the * is a wildcard.

7.4.1.3 Typical Causes of R/3 Startup Problems on AIX

Here are several typical causes of startup problems with R/3 on AIX:

1. The user is logged on to the operating system with insufficient permissions and has attempted to start R/3. The only user that can start SAP R/3 is <sid>adm.

2. A filesystem is full. Verify that you have enough space in the on-line log filesystem, the archive log filesystem and the SAP filesystem.
3. The database has not yet started or it has encountered problems in start up. For additional details about the DB2 start process, see Section 7.1.5, "DB2 Startup Problem Determination" on page 261.
4. R/3 environment variables are not correctly initialized.
5. The database is running an off-line backup or in the process of recovery.
6. The passwords of sapr3 or <sid>adm have been changed via the operating system and not using the DB2 Control Center and are now out of synchronization. This will prevent R/3 from connecting to the database and the R/3 startup will fail.

7.4.2 Overview of R/3 Startup on Windows NT

Windows NT has a somewhat different R/3 startup procedure than AIX. First, the Windows NT administrator should check in the Windows NT Services panel that the following two services are started:

- **SAPOSCOL**: SAP R/3 operating system collector data program.
- **SAP<SID>_<instance_number>**: SAP R/3 control instance. In our example, the control instance would be named SAPAUS_00.

It is recommended to configure these services to start automatically at reboot time. To do so,

1. From the Windows NT Services panel, click on the name of the service (for example, SAPAUS_00).
2. Click on the **Startup** button to display the following window:

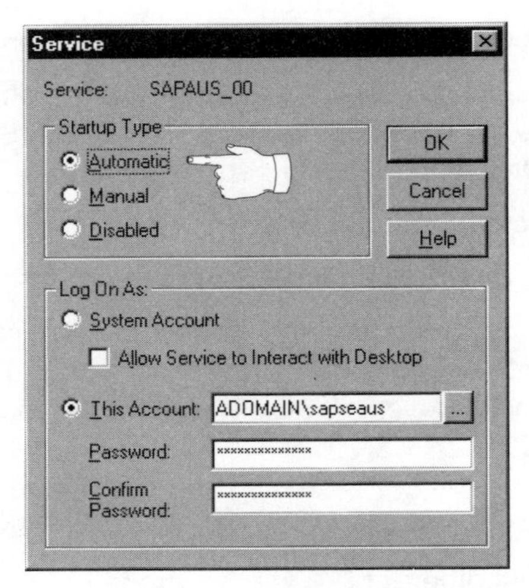

Figure 233. Change SAP Service to Start Automatically

3. Click **Automatic** in the Startup Type section, then click **OK**.

The next time the system is rebooted, this service will be started automatically.

Once these two services are started, the SAP Service Manager should be started. To do this:

1. Logon as R/3 administrator userid, <sid>adm, and select **Start->Programs->SAP R3->SAP R3 Servicemanager <SID>_<instance number>** as shown in Figure 234:

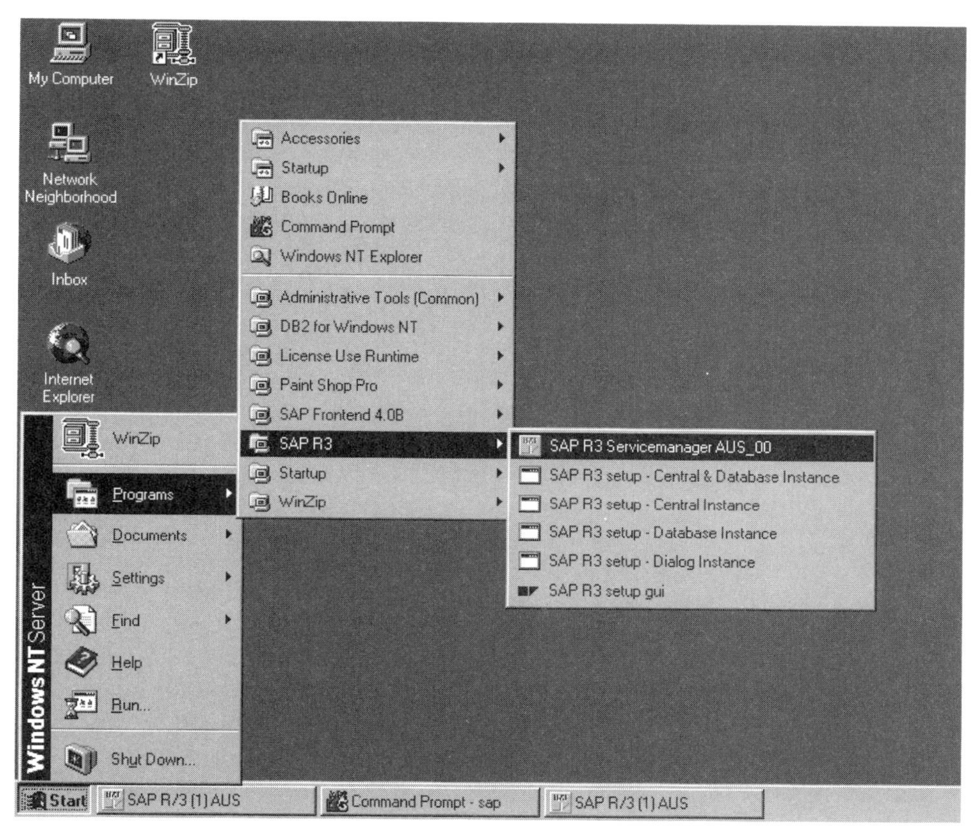

Figure 234. Starting the SAP R/3 Service Manager

2. The SAP Service Manager is displayed:

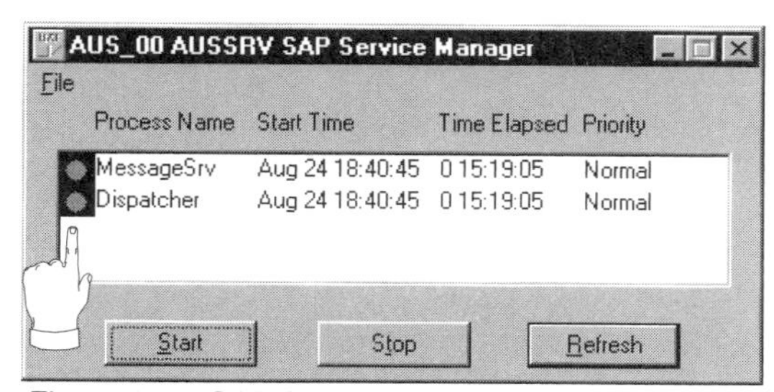

Figure 235. SAP Service Manager Window

3. Click **Start** in the SAP Service Manager window.

The SAP Service Manager sends a message through a named pipe to the SAP R/3 Control Instance to start the database. If the database is already running, the database start up process is skipped.

The SAP R/3 control instance, after the successful database startup, will read the start profile, START_<INSTANCE NAME><instance number>_<hostname>, under the directory, drive:\usr\sap\<SID>\sys\profile, and start the appropriate services:

- The message service and disp+work services are started by the SAP R/3 control Instance.
- The R/3 dispatcher will read the instance profile, <SID>_<INSTANCE NAME><instance number>_<hostname>, and default profile, DEFAULT.PDF, from the R/3 profile directory. From these profiles, the R/3 dispatcher will determine which work processes and how many of each process are to be started. The work processes include the dialog, batch, spool, enqueue, update and gateway work process.

If your SAP R/3 configuration includes other application servers, the Windows NT SAP Service Manager will start the rest of the application instances.

7.4.2.1 Verifying that R/3 Has Started on Windows NT

You should check in the Process window of the Windows NT Task Manager to determine if DB2 and R/3 are active. As a minimum, the following DB2 and R/3 processes should appear in the Task Manager Process list:

DB2 process:

- db2syscs.exe

R/3 processes:

- saposcol.exe
- sapntstartdb.exe
- gwrd.exe
- msg_server.exe
- disp+work.exe

If any of these processes are not found in the process list, a problem of some sort has occurred. If R/3 is stopped, the last three R/3 processes do not appear in the Task Manager Process list.

7.4.2.2 R/3 Problem Startup Determination on Windows NT

The following steps should be followed if R/3 does not start or the SAP Service Manager shows a red traffic light:

1. Check that the Windows NT Services related to SAP are running. Select **Start->Programs->Administrative Tools->Windows NT Diagnostics->Services** and verify that the following services are active:
   - SAPSOCOL
   - <SID>_<instance number>
   - DB2 <SID>

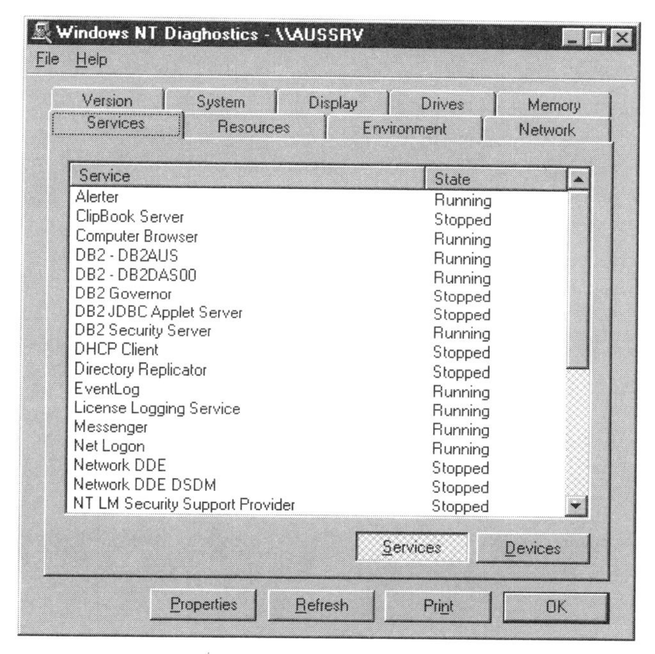

Figure 236. Verifying that all SAP Related Windows NT Services are Started

   If one of these services is not active, investigate the cause of this failure before starting it again. Check the Windows NT Event Viewer for problems related to the service. If the DB2<SID> service is not running, refer to “DB2 Startup Problem Determination” on page 261.

2. Check the contents of the sapstart.log and sapstart.trc files in the SAP instance work directory, <drive>:\usr\sap\<SID>\DVEBMGS<instance number>\work as shown in Figure 237:

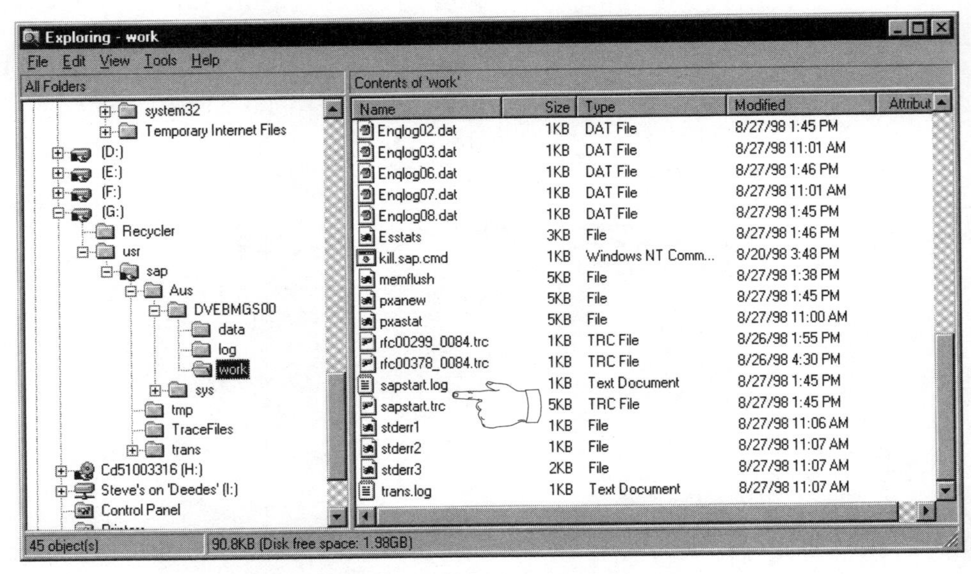

Figure 237. Log and Trace Files in the SAP Instance Work Directory

3. For more information about DB2 startup, check in the db2diag.log file in directory, <drive>:\db2\<SID>\db2dump directory:

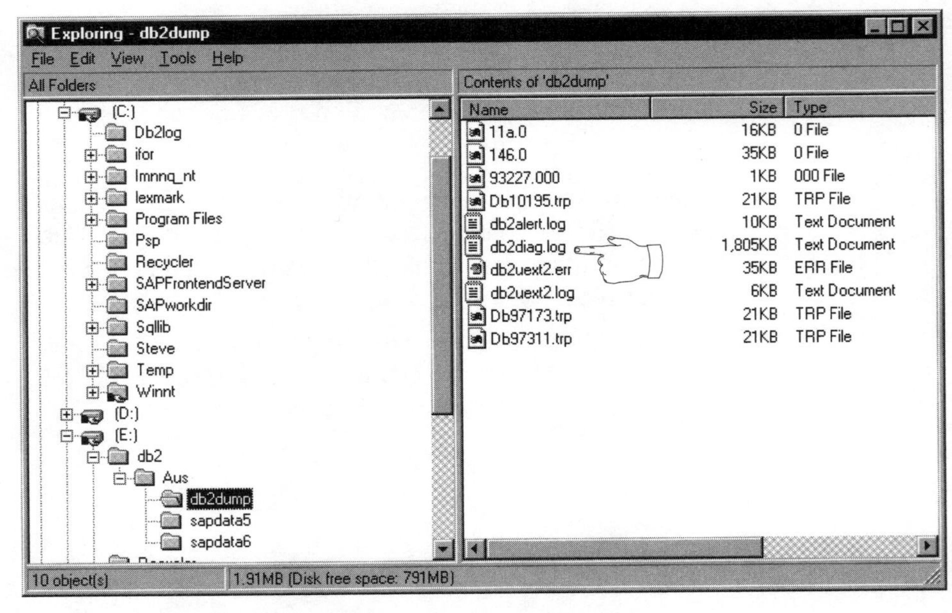

Figure 238. DB2 Diagnostic Log File in the db2dump Directory

4. Check for error messages in the most recently created developer trace files in the instance work subdirectory, <drive>:\usr\sap\<sid>\<instance name><instance number>\work. The instance name can vary depending upon to the R/3 configuration. The central instance is named DVEBMGS<nn> and the dialog instance is named D<nn> with nn being the instance number.

   In this example, the central instance name is DVEBMGS00:

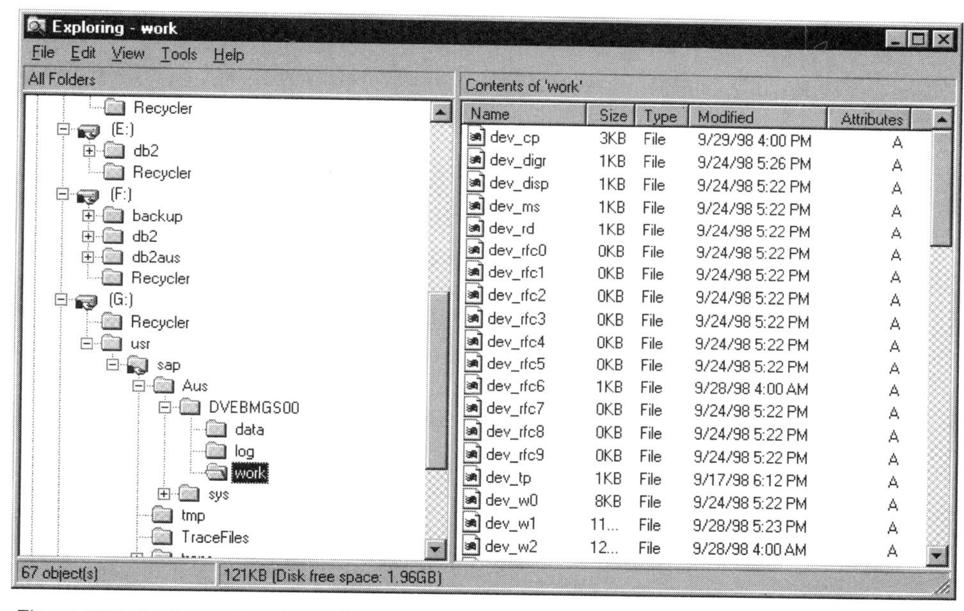

Figure 239. Instance Developer Traces in the Instance Work Directory

   Review the developer trace files indicated below with the most current time stamps (the * is a wildcard):

   - dev_disp
   - dev_digr
   - dev_ms
   - dev_rd
   - dev_rfc*
   - dev_w*
   - stderr*

7.4.3 Causes of R/3 Startup Problems on Windows NT

There are several possible causes of R/3 startup problems:

1. The user is logged on to the operating system with insufficient permissions. The only user that can start R/3 is <sid>adm.
2. A drive is full. Check all drives, especially the ones containing the directory for archival logs, the directory for instance working storage and the directory for database error diagnostics. These directories are:
   - <drive>:\db2\<SID>\log_dir
   - <drive>:\usr\sap\<SID>\<INSTANCE NAME><instance number>\work
   - <drive>:\db2\<SID>\db2dump
3. The TCP/IP address for the local host has no entries in the hosts file under the directory, <drive>:\winnt\system32\drivers\etc.
4. R/3 environment variables are not correctly initialized.
5. The database has not yet started or it has problems in starting up.
6. The database is running an off-line backup or a recovery.

7.5 Stopping SAP R/3

You need to stop R/3 to perform certain tasks related to maintenance of R/3 itself, DB2 or the operating system. To stop R/3 cleanly, the R/3 administrator should coordinate an acceptable time with the R/3 users. The general order of tasks to be done before stopping are:

1. Check to see if there are any active R/3 background or triggered jobs. Enter the transaction **SM37** (Select Background Jobs) into the R/3 transaction pull-down window on the tool bar or choose menu path, **System->Services->Jobs->Job Overview**:

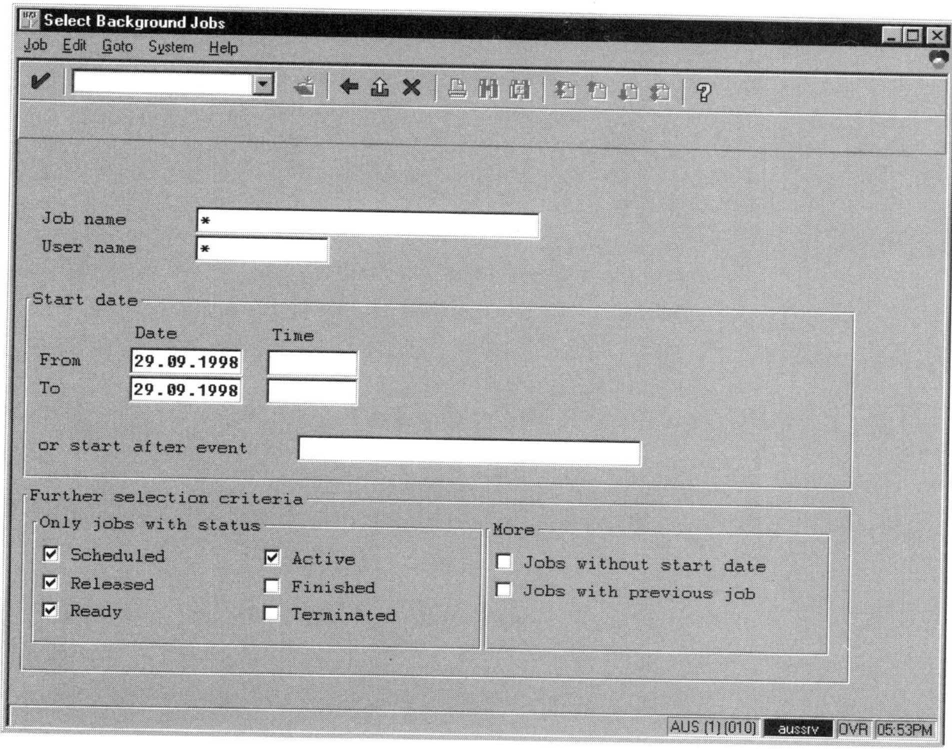

Figure 240. R/3 Transaction SM37 - Select Background Jobs

2. Enter a * in the Job name field and the User name fields. Deselect the **Finished** and **Terminated** options in the *Only jobs with status section*, as shown in Figure 240. Press **Enter** and look for any active jobs.
3. Check if there is any active batch input. Enter the R/3 transaction **SM35** (Batch Input: Initial Screen) into the transaction pulldown window on the tool bar or choose menu path, **System->Services->Batch input->Edit:**

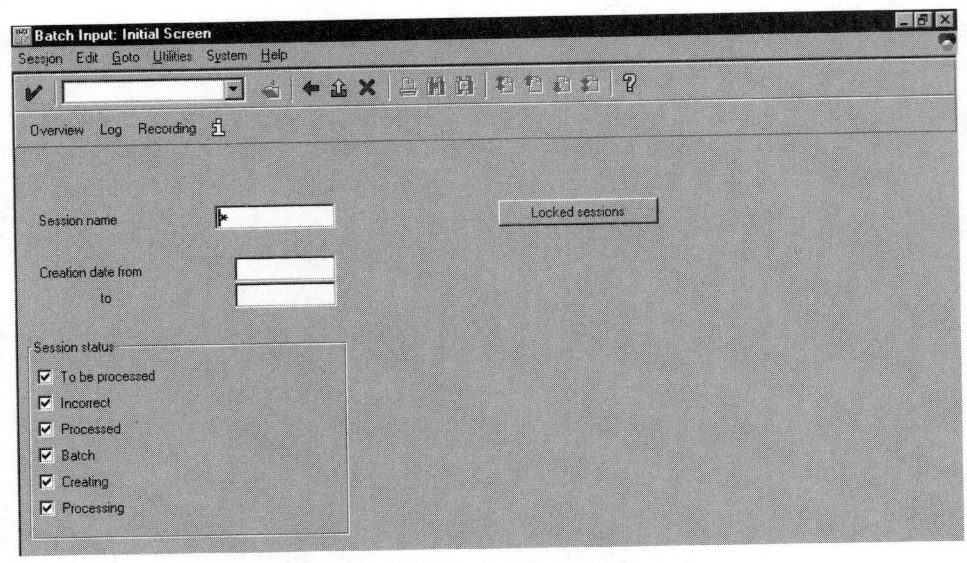

Figure 241. R/3 Transaction SM35 - Batch input: Initial Screen

4. Press the **Overview** button. Press **Enter** and any active sessions will be displayed.

5. Check to see if any jobs are running. Enter the R/3 transaction **SM50** (Process Overview) into the transaction pulldown window on the tool bar or choose menu path, **Tools->Administration, Monitor->System Monitoring->Process Overview**:

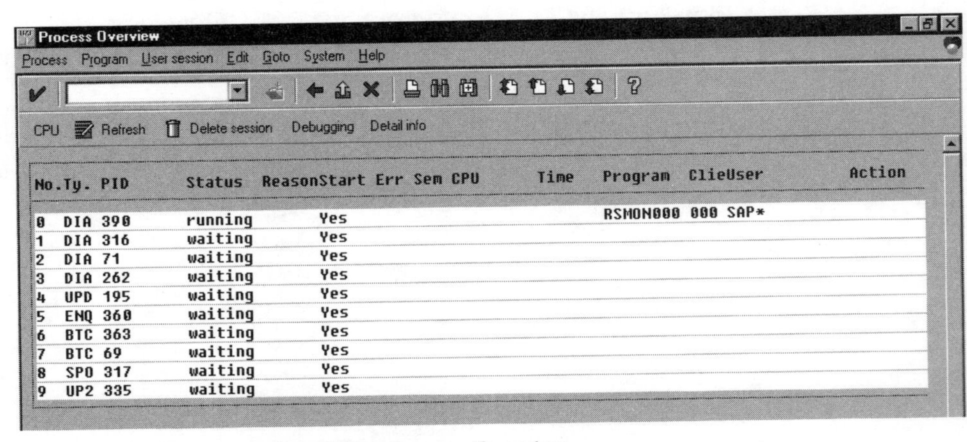

No.	Ty.	PID	Status	Reason	Start	Err	Sem	CPU	Time	Program	Clie	User	Action
0	DIA	390	running		Yes					RSMON000	000	SAP*	
1	DIA	316	waiting		Yes								
2	DIA	71	waiting		Yes								
3	DIA	262	waiting		Yes								
4	UPD	195	waiting		Yes								
5	ENQ	360	waiting		Yes								
6	BTC	363	waiting		Yes								
7	BTC	69	waiting		Yes								
8	SPO	317	waiting		Yes								
9	UP2	335	waiting		Yes								

Figure 242. R/3 Transaction SM50 - Process Overview

6. Check to see if there are any open update records. Enter the R/3 transaction **SM13** (Update Record: Main Menu) into the transaction pulldown window on the tool bar or choose menu path, **Tools->Administration, Monitor->Update** and press **enter** (Figure 243).

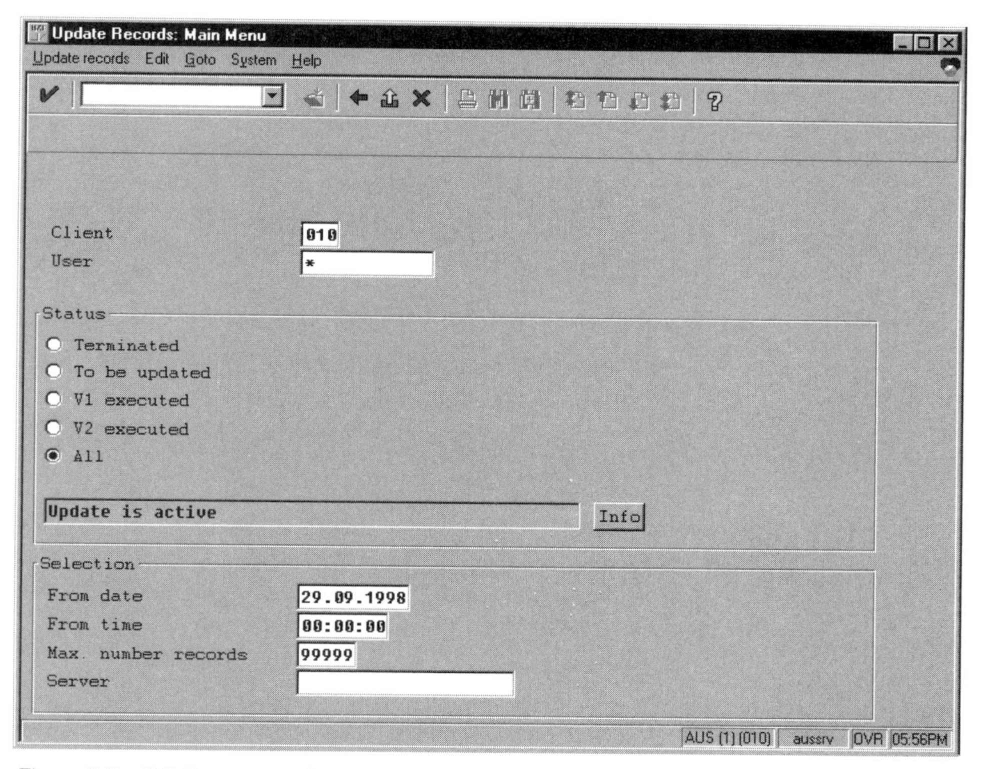

Figure 243. R/3 Transaction SM13 - Update Records: Main Menu

7. Check to see if there are any external interfaces. This can be done through transaction **SM37** (Job overview) or transaction **SM50** (Process overview).

8. Check to see if any users are logged on so that you may notify them prior to stopping R/3. Enter the R/3 transaction **SM04** (Overview of users) into the transaction pulldown window on the tool bar or choose menu path, **Tools->Administration, Monitor->System Monitoring->User Overview** (Figure 244). The user notification can be done by phone or by sending an R/3 general message by using the R/3 transaction, **SM02**.

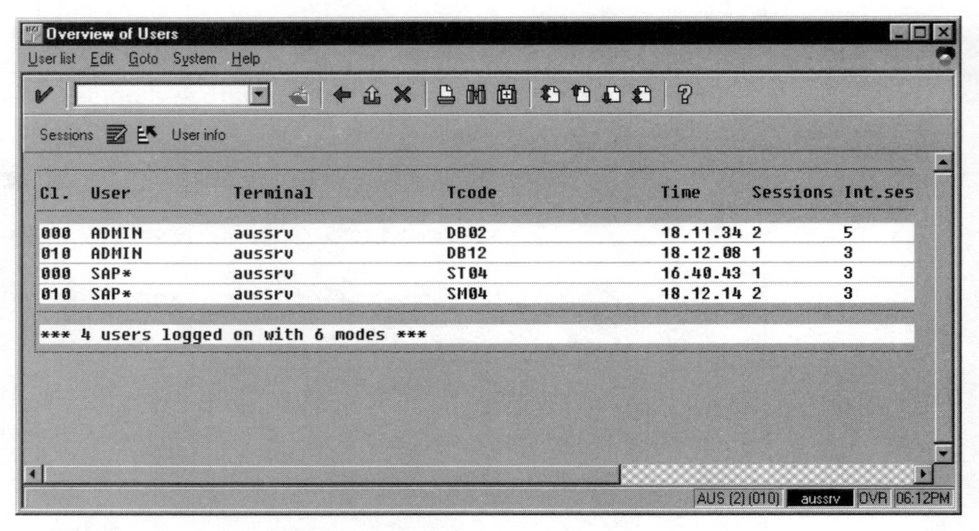

Figure 244. R/3 Transaction SM04 - Overview of Users

Note

There is no need to stop the R/3 system during a database off-line backup. R/3 may continue to be active while the database off-line backup executes. R/3 will continue trying to connect to the database at a frequency determined by the R/3 parameters:

- rsdb/reco_trials = n (Number of attempts)
- rsdb/reco_sleep_time = s (Number of seconds to sleep in between attempts).

See “R/3 Database Maintenance” on page 327 for more details about backing up the R/3 database.

7.5.1 Stopping R/3 on the AIX Platform

R/3 will use the information in the kill.sap file in the instance work directory, /db2/<sid>/<instance name>/work, in order to end all work processes such as dispatcher, message server, collector, send daemon and gateway. The softlinks to each work process created during R/3 startup are removed.

To stop R/3, perform the following steps:

1. Logon to a Central instance or Application server as the R/3 administrator userid <sid>adm.

2. Run the **stopsap** command. This command can be invoked as follows:

   - **stopsap all** - This stops DB2 and R/3. The **all** can also be in upper case (**ALL**). The stopsap command with no parameters defaults to this behavior.
   - **stopsap R3** - this stops only R/3. The **R3** can also be in lower case (**r3**).

   The stopsap command in the <sid>adm home directory is an alias to:

   stopsap_<hostname>_<instance number>.

   Check the messages that are displayed to make sure that R/3 has been stopped.

3. If your R/3 landscape involves Application servers on other machines, there are several ways to stop the Application servers:

   - Logon to each Application server as <sid>adm and invoke the stopsap command on each Application server.
   - Customize the shell script: stopsap_<hostname>_<instance number> by adding a stopsap command to stop each Application server. Here are some example commands:

     ```
     rsh hostname -l user stopsap
     rexec -n hostname stopsap
     su - hostname -c stopsap
     ```

   - To stop R/3 using CCMS, logon to R/3 as the R/3 administrator and enter the transaction **RZ03** (CCMS Control Panel: Display Server Statuses and Alerts) into the transaction pulldown window on the tool bar or choose menu path, **Tools->CCMS, Control/Monitoring->Control Panel**, then choose **Control->Stop SAP Instance** (Figure 245). This only works when the Central instance and Application server(s) have defined at least one dialog work process.

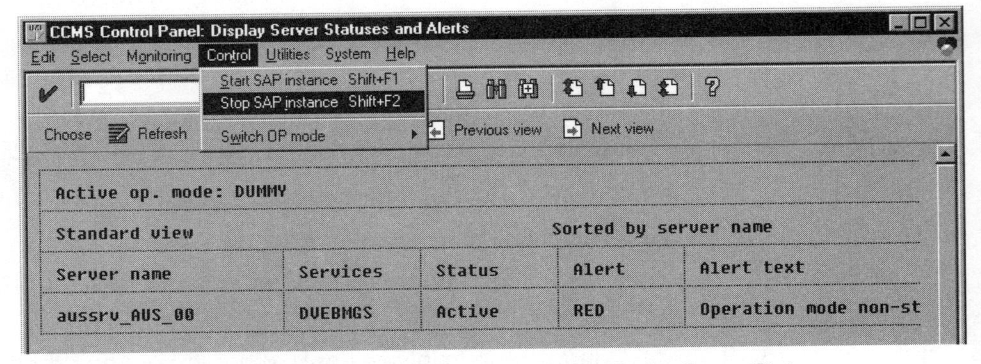

Figure 245. R/3 Transaction RZ03 - CCMS Control Panel: Display Server Status

7.5.1.1 R/3 Shutdown Problem Determination on AIX

If R/3 does not stop or the messages displayed during the stopsap command execution indicate that an error has occurred, follow these steps:

1. Check the sapstop_<hostname>_<instance number>.log file for any error messages. This file is in the home directory of the <sid>adm user.
2. Check the stopdb.log file in the home directory of <sid>adm user. If this log contains any errors, check the db2diag.log file in the directory /db2/<SID>/sqllib/db2dump for additional details.
3. There may be additional error messages in the most recently created developer trace files in the instance work subdirectory, /usr/sap/<sid>/<instance name><instance number>/work. The instance name can vary depending on the R/3 configuration. The Central instance is named DVEBMGS<nn> and the Dialog instance will be D<nn> where nn is the instance number. In our example, the Central instance name is DVEBMGS00, so the developer trace files will be in the /usr/sap/AUS/DVEBMGS00/work directory.

   Review the developer trace files indicated below with the most current time stamps (the * is a wildcard):

   - dev_disp
   - dev_digr
   - dev_ms
   - dev_rd
   - dev_rfc*
   - dev_w*
   - stderr*

7.5.1.2 Causes of R/3 Shutdown Problems on AIX

Problems encountered when stopping R/3 are most likely caused by:

1. The user is logged on to the operating system with insufficient permissions. The only user that can stop R/3 is <sid>adm.
2. R/3 was not stopped via the `stopsap` command but by some other method.

7.5.2 R/3 Shutdown on the Windows NT Platform

Windows NT has a different R/3 stop procedure. On Windows NT, when R/3 is stopped, the SAP Service Manager issues a message through a named pipe to the SAP control instance, (implemented as an Windows NT service called SAP<SID>_<instance number>) to stop the R/3 instance locally by killing all R/3 work processes such as the dispatcher, gateway and message server.

The SAP services will remain operative until the R/3 Administrator stops the services explicitly from the Windows NT Services window. Database services are not stopped by the SAP Service Manager. The SAP Services that remain active after R/3 has stopped are:

1. **SAPOSCOL**: The SAP operating system collector data program.
2. **SAP<SID>_<instance_number>**: SAP control instance.

To stop R/3, perform the following steps:

1. Logon to the operating system as <sid>adm, the R/3 administrator, and select **Start->Program->SAP R3->SAP R3 Servicemanager <SID>_<instance number>** as shown in Figure 246:

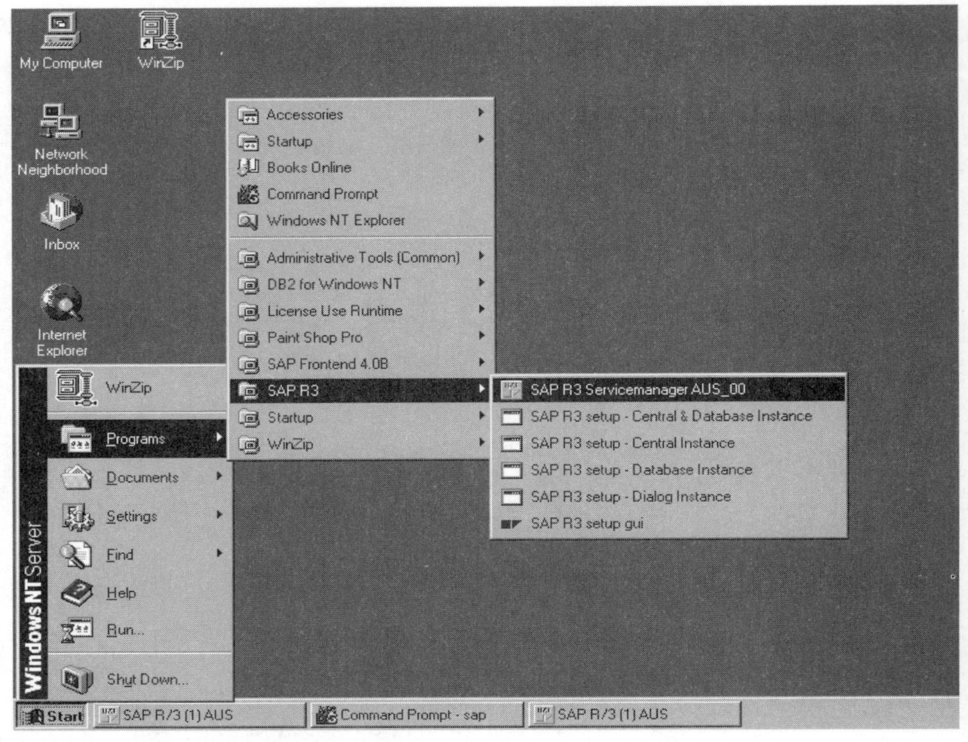

Figure 246. SAP R3 Service Manager

2. Click on **Stop** in the SAP Service Manager Window:

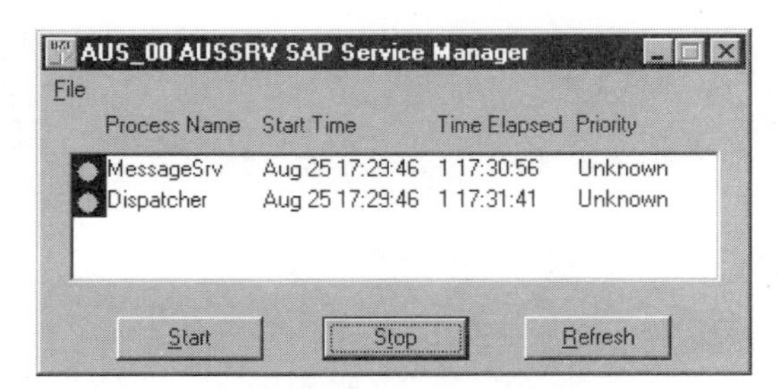

Figure 247. SAP Service Manager

3. When the traffic light has turned red for both the Message Server and Dispatcher, all the R/3 work processes have been stopped.

4. Optionally, you can also stop the two SAP services, SAPOSCOL and SAP<SID>_<instance_number> by performing a stop for each service from the Windows NT Services panel.

7.5.2.1 R/3 Shutdown Problem Determination on Windows NT

If R/3 does not shut down or if the SAP Service Manager does not display a red light for the both the Message Server and the Dispatcher:

1. Check the R/3 work processes in the Windows NT Task Manager. Look for any R/3 work processes that are still not stopped.
2. Check for errors in the db2diag.log file in directory \db2\<SID>\db2dump.
3. There may be additional error messages in the most recently created developer trace files in the instance work subdirectory, \usr\sap\<sid>\<instance name><instance number>\work. The instance name can vary depending on the R/3 configuration. The Central instance is named DVEBMGS<nn> and the Dialog instance will be D<nn> where nn is the instance number. In our example, the Central instance name is DVEBMGS00, so the developer trace files will be in the \usr\sap\AUS\DVEBMGS00\work directory.

   Review the developer trace files indicated below with the most current time stamps (the * is a wildcard):

   - dev_disp
   - dev_digr
   - dev_ms
   - dev_rd
   - dev_rfc*
   - dev_w*
   - stderr*

7.5.2.2 Causes of R/3 Shutdown Problems on Windows NT

Problems encountered during the shutdown of R/3 can be caused by:

1. The user is logged on to the operating system with insufficient permissions. The only user that can stop R/3 is <sid>adm.
2. R/3 was not stopped using the SAP Service Manager, but by some other method.

7.6 R/3 Work Processes

The R/3 work processes are special programs that are responsible for executing R/3 application tasks. Each work process acts as a specialized system service. Using client/server architecture terminology, a work process is a service offered by a server and requested by a client.

The R/3 dispatcher manages the information exchange between the SAPGUIs and the work processes, enabling users to share the different work processes available. From the point of view of the operating system, a group of parallel R/3 work processes make up the R/3 runtime system. R/3 work processes execute dialog steps for the end users. These steps generally relate to the processing or display of a single screen, which means that right after one work process completes the execution of a dialog step for a user session, the work process is immediately available for use by another user session.

The number of available work processes per application server is configured using the appropriate SAP system profile parameters. See "Configuring Work Processes" on page 299 for more details.

There are several types of R/3 work processes: dialog, background, update, enqueue, and spool. Additionally, the R/3 runtime system includes three other special types of services: message, gateway and the system log collector (AIX only).

Since the R/3 work processes are responsible for executing ABAP/4 programs and applications, the dispatcher and a set of work processes is referred to as an Application server.

7.6.1 R/3 Instance Configuration

Each type of R/3 work process has a specific purpose. These work processes are combined to build different instance configurations.

In R/3 terminology, you can consider the term instance to be equivalent to a server. An instance is an administrative unit.

- The components of an R/3 system application server are allocated to an instance.
- The components belonging to an instance are started and stopped simultaneously.

The R/3 system consists of the following seven types of work processes:

- D - Dialog
- V - Update
- E - Enqueue
- B - Batch
- M - Message
- G - Gateway
- S - Spool

See "R/3 Instance" on page 19 for a description of these work processes.

The acronym DVEBMGS (seen in various R/3 names) is made up of the first letter of each one of the types of work process.

An R/3 instance can be one of three types:

1. The Central Instance: this may or may not include the database.
2. An Application Instance, or Dialog instance. The database does not reside on an Application instance.
3. The database instance, which consists of the database manager and its associated processes/threads and provides database services to the R/3 system.

It is possible to configure several instances belonging to the same R/3 system on one computer. However, separate instances are often installed on separate computers. The following figures represent three instance configuration examples.

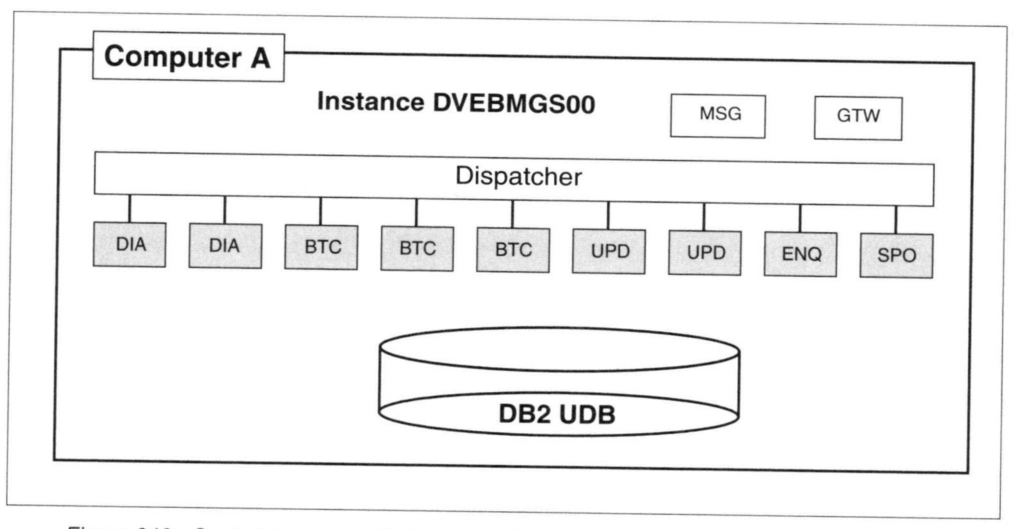

Figure 248. Central Instance with Database Configuration

In Figure 248, a single computer supports all R/3 services and the DB2 database. This is known as a *central instance with database configuration*. This configuration requires minimal hardware and is generally only used by smaller businesses or test systems.

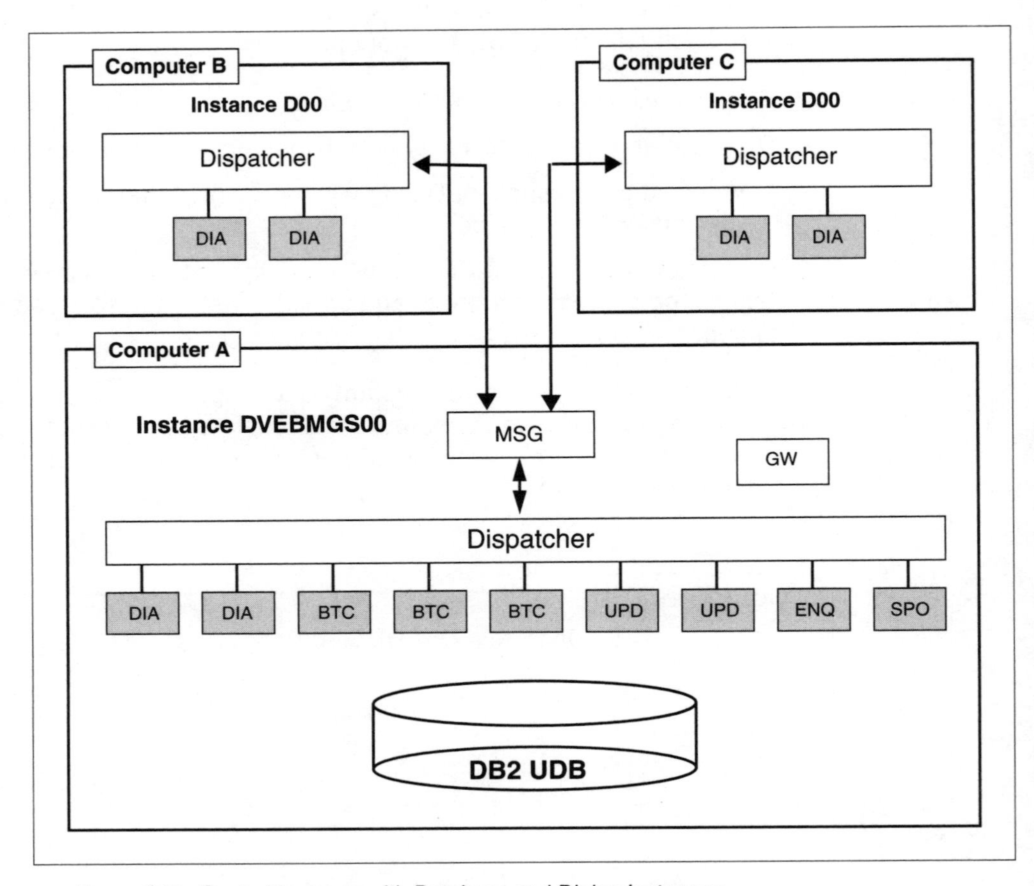

Figure 249. Central Instance with Database and Dialog Instances

Figure 249 shows the second example. The central instance is configured on Computer A and a dialog instance (or application instance) is configured on Computers B and C. This is known as a *distributed R/3 system*, and is suitable for medium to large business requirements.

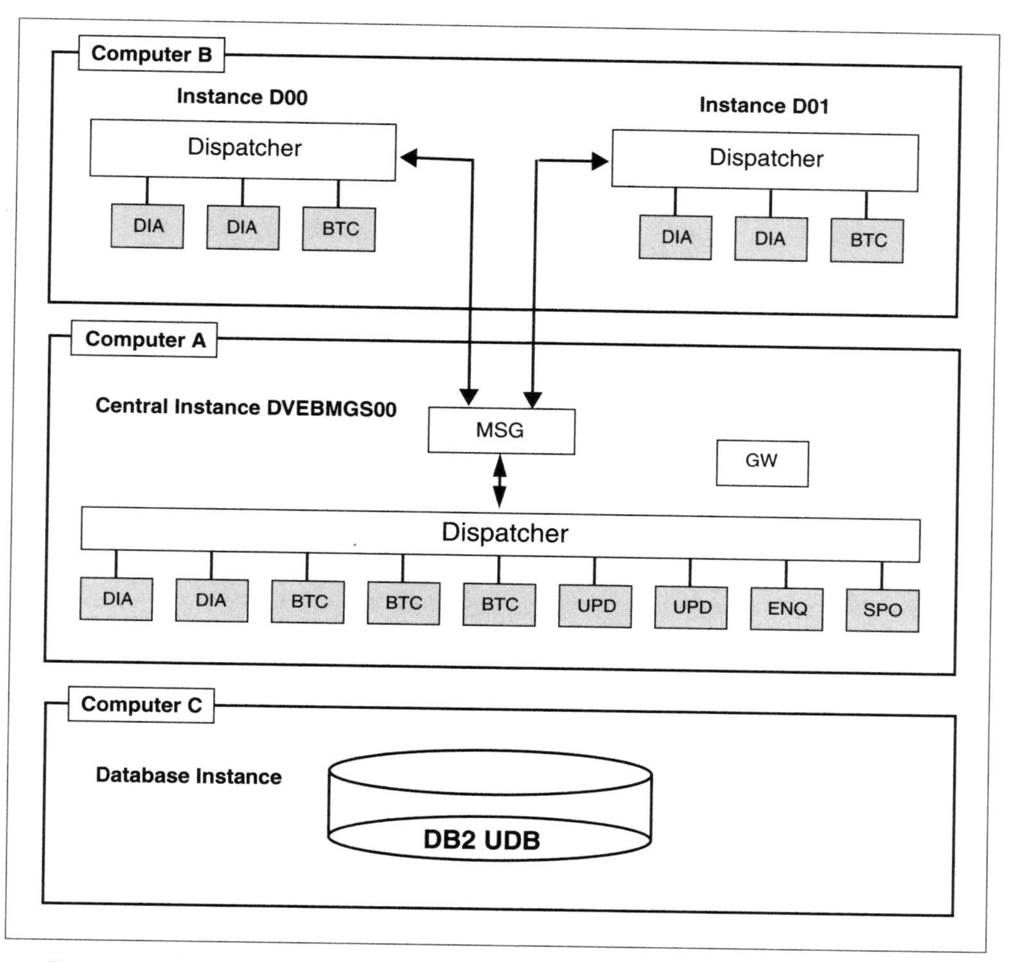

Figure 250. Central Instance, Database Instance and Dialog Instances

Figure 250 shows the third example configuration. This is another type of distributed R/3 system. The central instance is configured on Computer A, with two dialog instances, D00 and D01, configured on Computer B. In this case, Computer B can be referred to as an application server with two dialog instances. The database instance is configured on another machine, Computer C.

7.6.1.1 Configuring the Work Processes

The following table gives certain rules and guidelines about configuring work processes:

Table 17. SAP R/3 Work Processes

Work Process	R/3 System	R/3 Instance	Comments
Dialog	2-n	2-n	Each dialog work process should serve between 5 - 7 users.
Update	1-n	1-n	Several update servers are permissible per instance.
Update 2	0-n	0-n	If there are UP2 processes in the system, U2 update (update low priority) is only possible in these processes; the UPD processes are then reserved for U1 (update high priority). If there are no UP2 processes, the UPD processes take over both U1 and U2. Hence, UP2 processes do not have to exist. However, delays can occur for the U1 update if there are no UP2 processes. Therefore, at least one UP2 process should be scheduled.
Batch	2-n	0-n	Number of processes: at least 2 in each system. Reservation of processes for job class A: If n background processes are running, a maximum of n-1 processes may be reserved for class A jobs, as jobs with class B and C would otherwise be blocked.
Enqueue	1-n	0-n	Number of servers: there is exactly one enqueue server in the system. Number of processes: One ENQ process must be running on the enqueue server. Only in certain special cases (extremely large systems) can it make sense to have more than one ENQ process running.
Spool	1-n	0-n	Spool processes cannot be switched on and off when switching operation modes.
Gateway	1-n		It is configured only on a central instance.You can only have 1.
Message	1	0-1	It is advisable to put this work process along with update and enqueue on the central instance due to their high communication traffic.

Based on these rules, the following theoretical minimum configurations result:

- Central instance: 2 DIA, 1 UPD, 2 BTC, 1 ENQ, 1 SPO, 1 GTW, 1 MSG
- Dialog Instance: 2 DIA

Here are some considerations to bear in mind when configuring work processes:

1. If there are too few processes of one type (dialog, update, batch), then end user requests must wait for free work processes. The ideal is a configuration in which at least one work process is always free.
2. If too many processes are configured then virtual memory is wasted, and the system will become slower due to operating system paging. Thus, if you have limited memory resources it may make sense to keep the number of work processes low.
3. If the machine is very powerful, it may be a good idea to install several instances rather than one.
4. As the demands on a server can vary, it often makes sense to define different operation modes for the entire system. For example, during the day, you may need many dialog processes, while at night the requirement is for many batch processes. Note that the total number of work processes does not change during the switch from day to night operation; this applies to every server. The number of spool processes must also remain constant.

7.6.1.2 Checking the Running Work Processes

To see which work processes are running, there are two views; one at a local level, and one at a system level.

To see the work processes locally, use the transaction **SM50** or from the menu, select **Tools -> Administration, Monitor -> System monitoring ->Process Overview**:

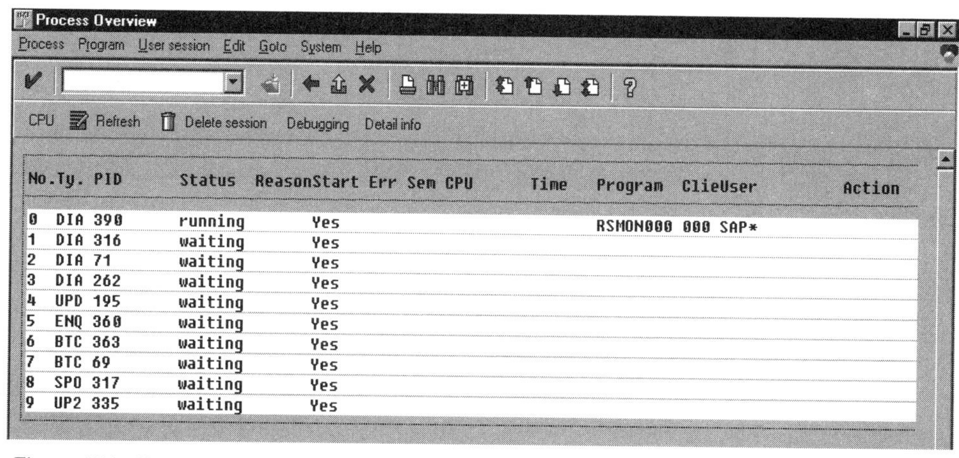

Figure 251. Process Overview - Transaction: SM50

This screen displays the various active R/3 work processes along with their process ID (PID). The PID is associated with a process/thread in the operating system. The Ty column of the **Process Overview** screen indicates the type of work process associated with each process/thread.

To see the work processes globally, use the transaction **SM51** or from the menu, select **Tools -> Administration, Monitor -> System monitoring -> Servers**.

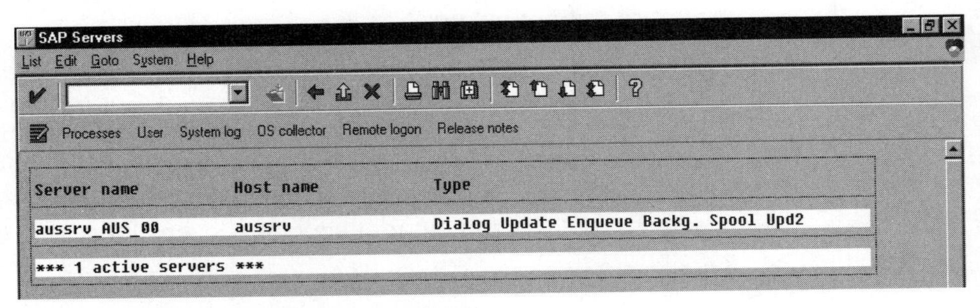

Figure 252. SAP Servers (Transaction: SM51)

Alternatively, you can use transaction **SM66** or from the menu, select **Tools -> CCMS, Control/Monitoring -> All Work processes**:

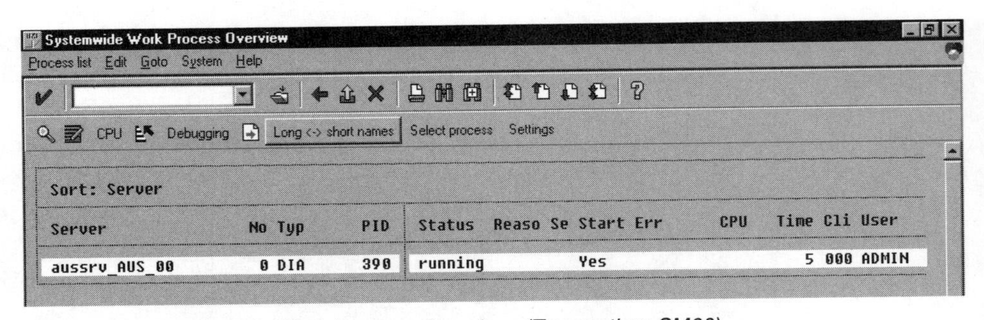

Figure 253. Systemwide Work Process Overview: (Transaction: SM66)

To see the utilization of the services, use the transaction **ST03** or from the menu, select **Tools-> CCMS, Control/Monitoring->Performance MenuMonitor, Workload->Analysis.**

Then select the Application server (**Choose for Analysis**) and click on the **check mark**. Choose a period for reporting on and click the **check mark**. Finally, click on **Transaction profile**.

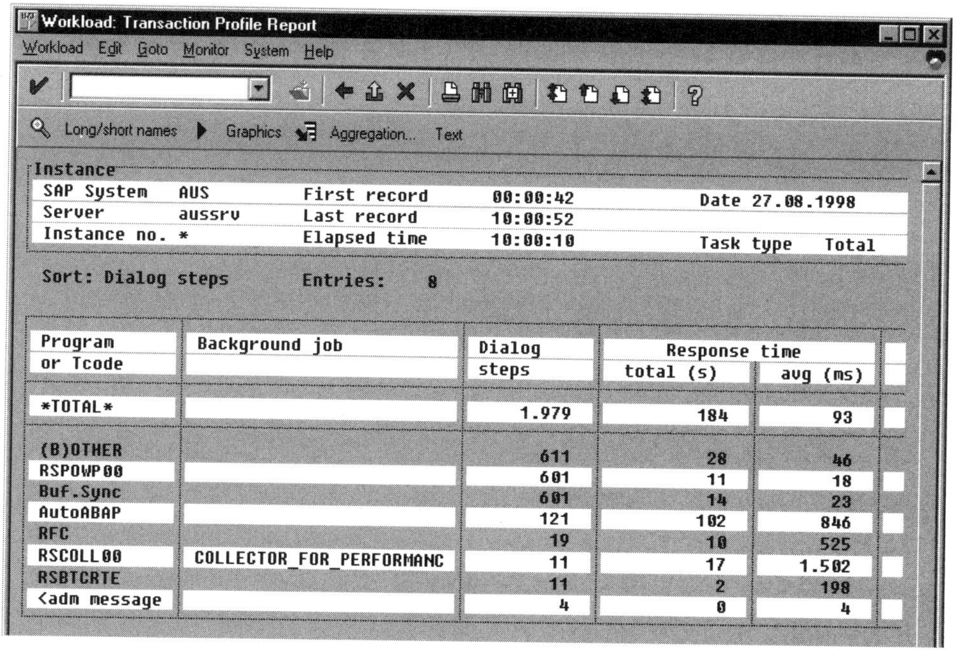

Figure 254. Workload Transaction Profile Report Screen

Move the screen right until you see the column Wait Time and look for transactions or programs having a long wait time. This is an indication that there is an insufficient number of dialog or batch work processes.

7.6.2 Configuring Work Processes

To view the work process configuration for an R/3 system, look in the instance profile, <SID>_<INSTANCE NAME><instance number>_<host>, in the R/3 system profile directory, /usr/sap/<SID>/SYS/profile (on AIX for example). This profile is unique for each server. The system parameters in the instance profile that are used to establish the number of work processes for each type of service are described in the following table:

Table 18. *Work Process Configuration Parameters*

SAP Parameter	Description
rdisp/wp_no_dia	Dialog
rdisp/wp_no_btc	Background
rdisp/wp_no_vb	Update
rdisp/wp_no_vb2	Update 2
rdisp/wp_no_enq	Enqueue
rdisp/wp_no_spo	Spool

By defining operating modes, you can dynamically change the distribution of work processes allocated to various services.

The message server and the gateway are defined in the default R/3 profile file named DEFAULT.PDF. There is only one message server and one gateway per R/3 system. The DEFAULT.PDF is also located in R/3 system instance profile directory, /usr/sap/<SID>/SYS/profile (on AIX for example). The profile parameters for these two services are as listed in the following table.

Table 19. *Message and Gateway Parameters*

SAP Parameter	Description
rdisp/mshost	Message
rdisp/sna_gateway	Gateway

The default instance profile also provides information about the server instance profile and includes the parameters that define the number of enqueue, update and batch work processes for the R/3 system.

7.7 DB2 UDB Storage Methods

This section discusses the methods DB2 uses to store data. Understanding these methods will help you to decide how to store your data and how you can improve access to that data. We cover the following:

- Table spaces
- Containers
- Buffer pools

You are not required to create a table space, container, or buffer pool to be able to add data to tables in a database. You can accept the default definitions for table spaces, containers, and buffer pools when you install R/3. However, if you are interested in tuning database access in your environment, you may find the following descriptions useful.

7.7.1 Table Spaces

Table spaces exist in DB2 to provide you with a logical layer between your data and the storage devices. They define where table data is physically stored on disk. All DB2 tables reside in table spaces. You can use different kinds of table spaces to store different portions of a table, such as the data and the index. This gives you the ability to control the assignment of database objects to storage devices. For example, you can choose slower disks to store less frequently accessed data and faster disks to store indexes or frequently accessed data. You can also specify a particular table space for the system catalog tables, user tables or temporary tables.

Table Space Backup and Recovery

Backup and recovery operations can be made at the table space level. However in an R/3 environment, these operations are not recommended since R/3 has its own referential integrity.

7.7.2 Containers

A container is a generic term used to describe the allocation of physical space.

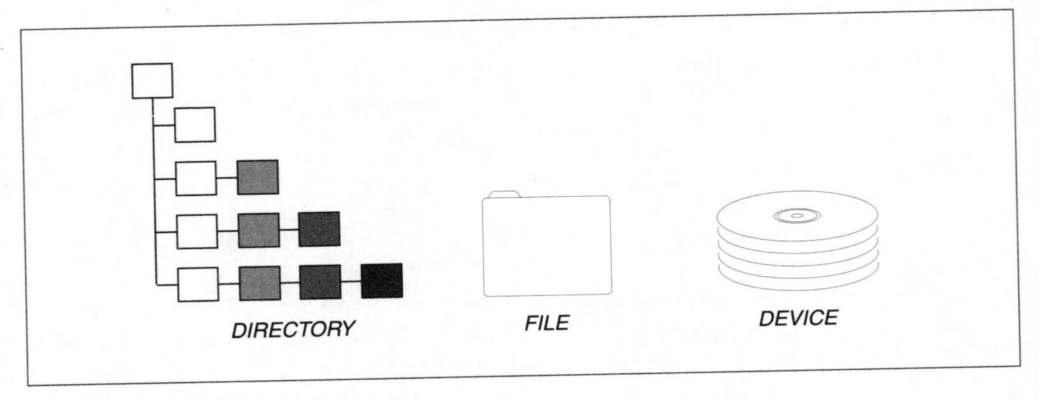

Figure 255. DB2 Containers

As shown is Figure 255, a container can be any of the following:

- Directory
- File
- Device

The type of container depends on the type of table space and the operating system being used. For example, in AIX, a logical volume can be used as a device container. In this next section, we detail the relationship between table spaces and containers.

7.7.3 The Relationship between Table Spaces and Containers

There is a one-to-many relationship between table spaces and containers. Multiple containers may be defined for a single table space. However, a container can only be assigned to one table space. Figure 256 shows this one-to-many relationship.

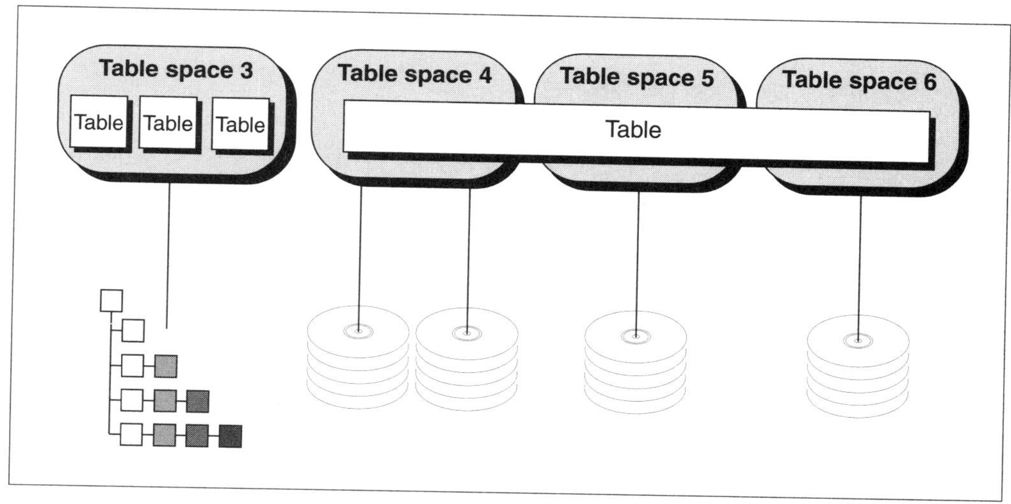

Figure 256. Table Spaces and Containers.

Table space 3 has only one container assigned to it, a directory container. Table space 4 has two containers assigned to it. The containers for table space 4, table space 5 and table space 6 are devices. A mixture of containers is possible within a database. You may also mix container types and sizes within a table space, though it is not recommended for performance reasons. For example, if you use a mixture of fast and slow disks as the containers of a single table space, performance will be constrained by the slower disks. Notice that a table can use multiple table spaces. In Figure 256, one table uses table space 4, table space 5 and table space 6 to store its data.

7.7.4 Types of DB2 Tables Spaces

DB2 supports two kinds of table spaces:

- System Managed Storage (SMS) table spaces
- Database Managed Storage (DMS) table spaces

Note

SAP only uses DMS table spaces and the containers associated with them.

Both types of table spaces may be used in the same database. SMS table spaces are called System Managed because the operating system's file system manages the containers. With DMS table spaces, DB2 itself manages the container access and space allocation.

7.7.4.1 SMS Table Spaces

System Managed Storage table spaces are based on the storage model where storage is acquired as needed. The space for the data of the tables created within an SMS table space is managed by the operating system.

SMS table spaces have the following characteristics:

- An SMS table space can only use directory containers. It cannot use file or raw/device containers.
- A container in an SMS table space does not pre-allocate its storage. A small amount of space is allocated during table space creation.
- Containers cannot be dynamically added to an SMS table space after the table space is created.
- The total number of containers in an SMS table space must be specified when creating the table space.

7.7.4.2 DMS Table Spaces

Database Managed Storage (DMS) table spaces are characterized by table spaces that are built on pre-allocated portions of storage. These areas of storage, known as containers, can be either raw devices or files. The space for the data of the tables created within a DMS table space is managed by the database manager.

The database manager controls the storage space and allocates all the space when the container is created. When working with DMS table space containers, the following statements apply:

- If the container is a file, it is created when the table space is created and dropped when the table space is dropped.
- If the container is a device, such as a logical volume in AIX, the logical volume must exist before creating the table space. After dropping the table space, the device still exists and must be removed manually.
- Disk storage is pre-allocated to a container when a container is created.
- Containers can be added to a DMS table space after the table space is created.

7.7.4.3 Comparing the Types of Table Spaces

It is important to understand the benefits and restrictions of the two types of table spaces.

Let's first take a look at the benefits of using DMS table spaces:

- You can distribute a table across several table spaces. This may give you a performance benefit:

  One of the biggest advantages of using DMS table spaces, compared to SMS table spaces, is the ability to span a table over multiple table spaces. When creating a table in a DMS table space, you can decide to place certain table objects in different table spaces. DMS table spaces give you the flexibility to store data, indexes, and long/large object data in separate table spaces. This leads to more flexibility in administration tasks such as backup and restore operations. For example, if you have a certain amount of static data, you can place this data in a separate table space, and back it up much less frequently than the rest of the database.

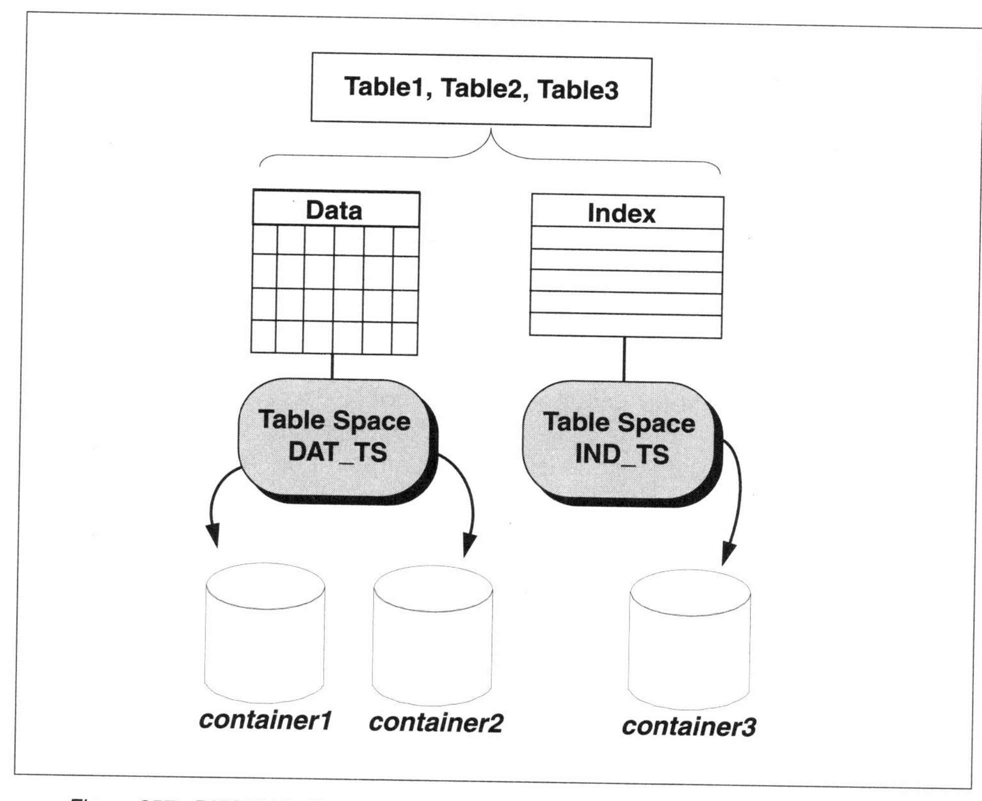

Figure 257. DMS Table Spaces

Figure 257 shows an example of three tables using two DMS table spaces. The regular table data is placed in the table space DAT_TS. Indexes for these tables are placed in the table space IND_TS. We can see from

Figure 257 that the table space DAT_TS is created with two containers. These containers do not have to be on separate disks. However, for performance reasons, it is better to assign the containers to different physical devices if you can.

- DMS table spaces can be expanded by adding new containers while the table space is being used.
- There may be performance benefits in using DMS table spaces because DB2 has more knowledge of the placement of the data. In addition, if you are using raw device containers, you can avoid the overhead of using the operating system's file system.
- When you create a DMS table space, you specify the size of the containers and the necessary disk space is pre-allocated. After this, the database manager does not have to compete with other applications for this disk space.

SMS tables spaces may be more suitable in the following cases:

- You have very small tables where even the smallest possible extent size (2 pages) would involve wasting space
- You are doing tests where the optimum performance is not required.
- To store temporary data.

7.7.5 Buffer Pools

A buffer pool is an area of memory used as a cache for the database manager for data and index pages. DB2 supports multiple buffer pools. Each buffer pool can have one or many table spaces assigned to it, but a table space can only be associated with one buffer pool.

Let's first look at how to manage buffer pools. All table spaces are assigned to a buffer pool. This assignment can be made with the **`create tablespace`** or **`alter tablespace`** SQL statements or via the Control Center. A buffer pool must exist in order to be referenced in the **`create tablespace`** or **`alter tablespace`** statements.

If during the creation of a table space a buffer pool is not specified, then the default buffer pool IBMDEFAULTBP is used. The default buffer pool definition is specified for each database partition, with the capability to override the size on specific database partitions. During database creation, the three system-defined table spaces that are created (SYSCATSPACE, USERSPACE1 and TEMPSPACE1) are assigned to the IBMDEFAULTBP buffer pool.

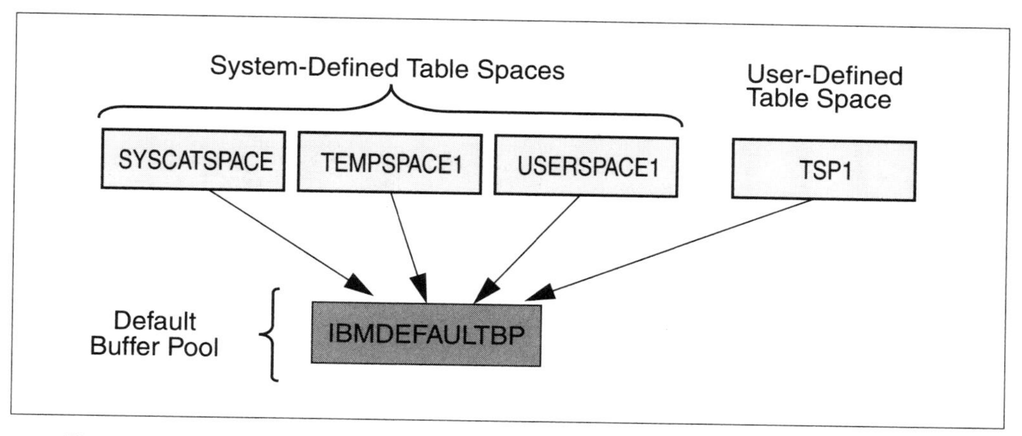

Figure 258. IBMDEFAULTBP Buffer Pool

Figure 258 shows that the three system-defined table spaces are associated with the default buffer pool, IBMDEFAULTBP. There is also a user-defined table space, called TSP1, that is also using the default buffer pool because when creating TSP1, no buffer pool was specified. This example also illustrates that the relationship between buffer pools and table spaces is one-to-many.

During the creation of a table space, you can specify that a user-defined buffer pool be used instead of the default IBMDEFAULTBP.

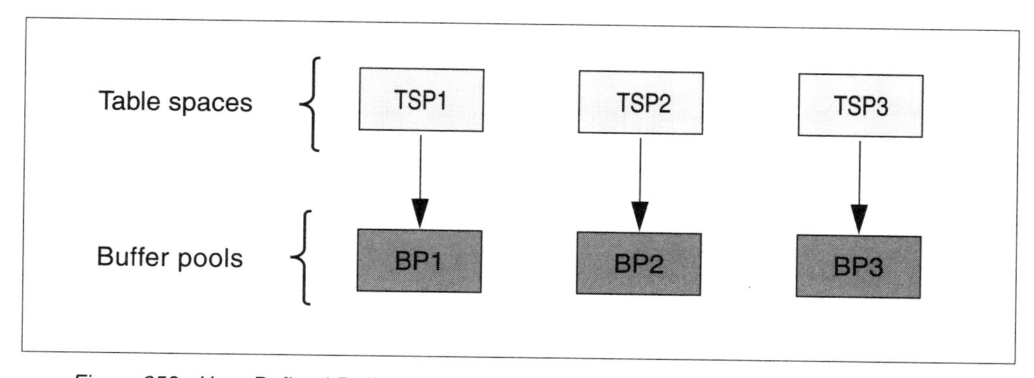

Figure 259. User-Defined Buffer Pools

Figure 259 shows three user-defined buffer pools (BP1, BP2 and BP3) each associated with a table space (TSP1, TSP2 and TSP3).

If a table space is dropped, the buffer pool to which it was assigned remains as an object within the database. This is true even if no table spaces are now assigned to this buffer pool. The memory remains allocated for the buffer pool. You must explicitly drop the buffer pool to free up this memory.

7.7.5.1 Performance Improvements Using Multiple Buffer Pools

The use of multiple buffer pools can lead to performance improvements in your system. Here are some actions you can take in order to exploit multiple buffer pools:

- Allocate separate buffer pools for tables and indexes.

  In an environment such as OLTP, where a number of key tables and indexes can be identified, the performance of the application may benefit from assigning the data portion of a table and the index portion of certain tables to different buffer pools. It may then be possible, for example, to provide enough space in the index buffer pool to have a vital index permanently in memory once it has been accessed. Since this is the only object in the database assigned to this area of memory, it will not be flushed out of memory by other application activity.

- Isolate memory for important transaction tables.

  If the application performance in your environment is heavily dependent on the use of one or more key tables, then these tables can be defined in table spaces that are linked to their own exclusive buffer pool. This will provide an area of memory exclusively dedicated to the processing of objects defined within the table space.

- Limit temporary table spaces to prevent ad-hoc queries affecting more critical applications.

  A large ad-hoc query may typically require large temporary work tables for sorting during its processing. This can result in the flushing from the buffer pool of repeatedly used memory pages. By assigning temporary table spaces to their own buffer pools, you can prevent this happening. By isolating the temporary table space from memory used by tables critical to OLTP-type applications, the impact of such ad-hoc activities on the more predictable application activities can be reduced.

- Limit bufferpools on large tables with random access patterns.

  In an environment where random access patterns occur, such as a data warehousing application, the benefits of defining a large table to its own buffer pool will be minimal. This is because the likelihood of the buffer pool containing information for reuse without disk I/O are low. In this type of scenario, a smaller buffer pool should be assigned to reduce the impact on other more predictable system activity and conserve memory for other performance gains.

7.8 User Maintenance and Security

This section looks at the different users that exist in a typical R/3 system. Users and their configuration information are stored in the operating system or in R/3 itself. DB2 makes use of the users defined in the operating system; it does not store any users itself. The creation of users in the operating system and R/3 is usually performed by the R/3 installation tool, R3SETUP.

7.8.1 Operating System Users and Groups

Prior to starting the installation, you can manually create the operating system users for R/3 and DB2 or let the installation program create them automatically. The following sections will describe the different ways to create and maintain these users.

7.8.1.1 AIX Users and Groups

The following AIX **users** are created by R3SETUP if they do not already exist:

- <sid>adm: R/3 administrator
- sapr3: R/3 database object owner
- db2<sid>: DB2 instance owner
- db2as: DB2 DAS instance owner. The DAS instance is a special instance used by DB2 for administration purposes.

Where <sid> refers to R/3 System name in lower case.

The following AIX **groups** are created by R3SETUP if they do not already exist:

- sapsys: R/3 system group
- sysctrl: R/3 system control group
- sysadm: DB2 instance group
- db2asgrp: DB2 DAS instance group

The relationship between these users and groups is the following:

User	Group
<sid>adm	(*) sapsys, sysctrl
sapr3	(*) sapsys
db2<sid>	(*) sysadm
db2as	(*) db2asgrp

Where (*) indicates the primary group.

Note

The user ID (uid) and group ID (gid) of R/3 users and groups must be identical for all servers belonging to any R/3 system. After installation, it is very important to note the uid and gid of all R/3 users and groups in case any of them need to be recreated.

7.8.1.2 AIX Users and Groups Maintenance

The maintenance of AIX users can be done in two ways:

1. The AIX smit tool. Run **`smitty users`** to go directly to user maintenance. You can list, add, remove or change users attributes:
2. The following AIX commands can also be used:
   - **`lsuser`** - to list users
   - **`mkuser`** - to create users
   - **`rmuser`** - to remove users
   - **`chuser`** - to change user characteristics

   To get more information about these commands, enter the command with no parameters or refer to your AIX documentation.

Similarly, the maintenance of AIX groups can be done in two ways:

1. The AIX smit tool. Run **`smitty groups`** to go directly to group maintenance. You can list, add, remove or change group attributes:
2. The following AIX commands can also be used:
   - **`lsgroup`** - to list groups
   - **`mkgroup`** - to create groups
   - **`rmgroup`** - to remove groups

- `chgroup` - to change group characteristics

7.8.2 Windows NT Users and Groups

The following Windows NT **user** must be created before running R3SETUP:

- <sid>adm: R/3 Administrator

The following Windows NT **users** are created by R3SETUP if they do not already exist:

- sapr3: Owner of R/3 database objects
- sapse<sid>: Standard R/3 service account
- SAPService<Sid>: R/3 service instance
- db2<adm>: DB2 instance owner
- db2admin: DB2 DAS instance owner

The following Windows NT **groups** are created by R3SETUP if they do not already exist:

- sysctrl: R/3 system control group
- SAP_<SID>_GlobalAdmin: R/3 global administration group
- SAP_<SID>_LocalAdmin: R/3 local administration group
- sysadm: DB2 instance group

The relationship between these users and groups (and their user rights) is the following:

User	Group	User Rights
<sid>adm	Administrator Domain Administrator Domain Users SAP_<SID>_GlobalAdmin SYSCTRL	Access this computer from network Act as part of the operating system Increase quotas Log on as a service Replace a process level token
db2<sid>	Administrator Domain Users SYSADM	Access this computer from network Act as part of the operating system Log on as a service Replace a process level token
db2admin	Administrator Domain Users	Increase quotas Log on as a service Replace a process level token

User	Group	User Rights
sapr3	Domain Users Users	
sapse<sid>	Administrator Domain Users SAP_<SID>_GlobalAdmin SYSCTRL	Access this computer from network Log on as a service
SAPService<Sid>	Administrator Domain Administrator Domain Users	

7.8.2.1 Maintenance of Windows NT Users and Groups

The Windows NT User Manager tool is used to maintain users and groups. To run User Manager, select **Start -> Programs -> Administrative Tools (common) -> User Manager for Domains** as shown in Figure 260:

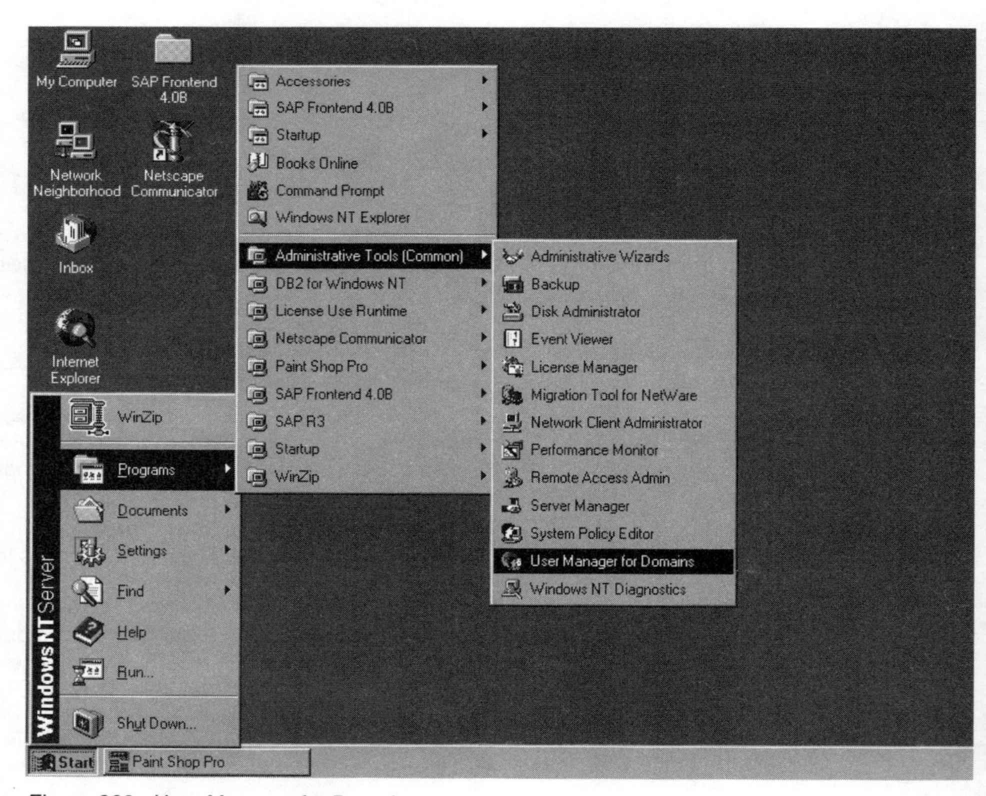

Figure 260. User Manager for Domains

The main panel of the User Manager is displayed:

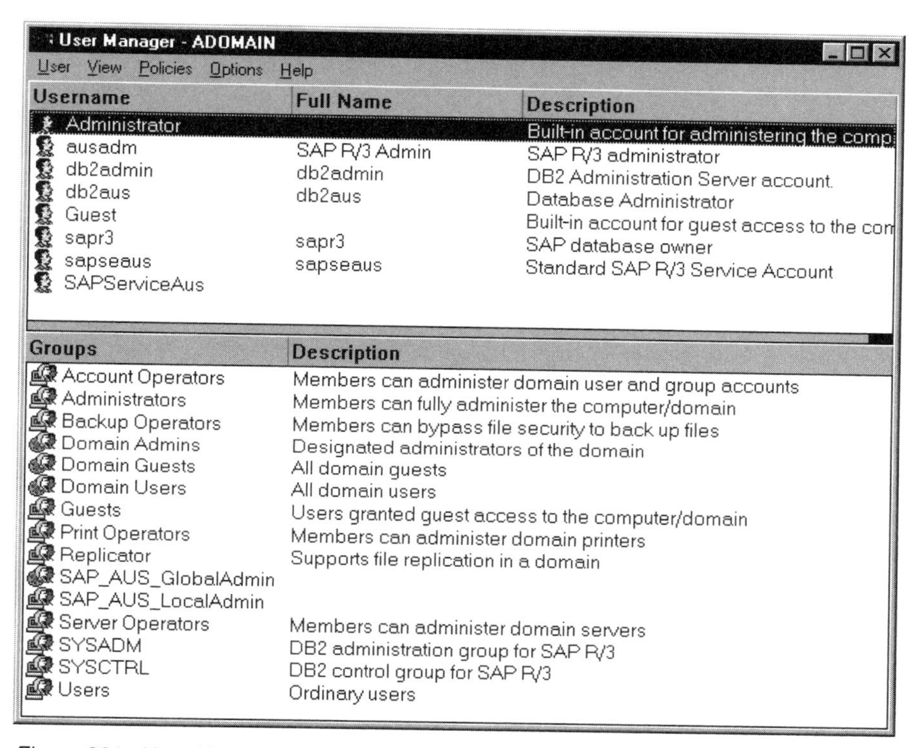

Figure 261. User Manager Main Panel

To maintain users or groups, select **User** from the menu bar. You can then choose to create/remove users or create global/local groups. To change a user's characteristics, you can double-click on the user.

For example, if we double-click on the user **ausadm**, the following screen is displayed:

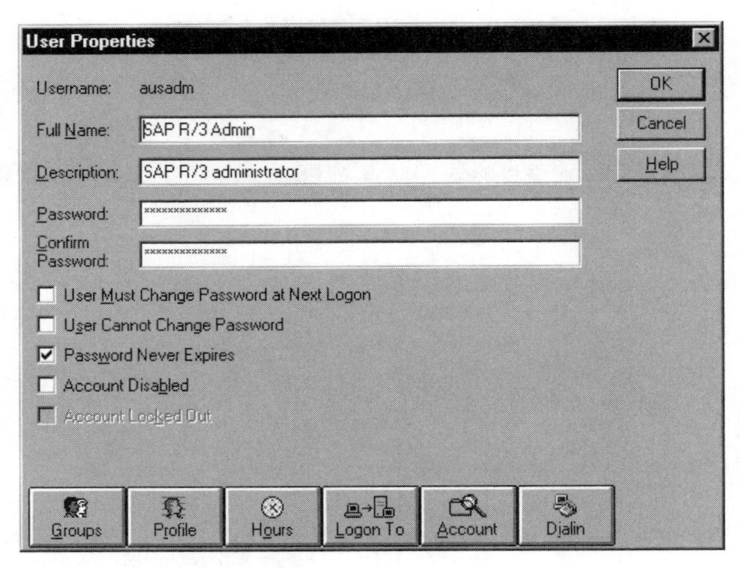

Figure 262. User Properties

To assign this user to a group or to check which groups this user is a member of, click **Groups** to display the Group Memberships panel:

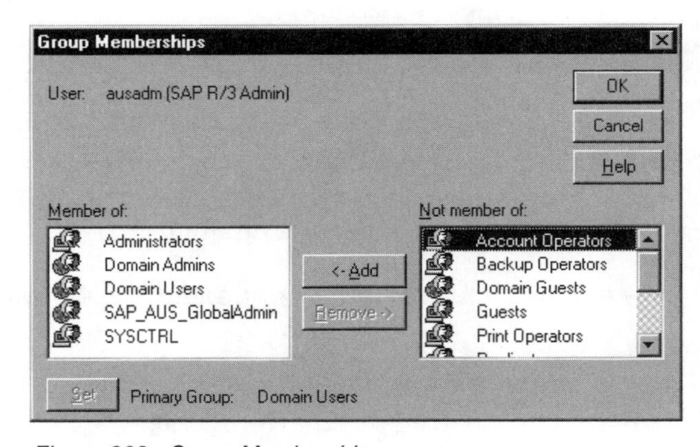

Figure 263. Group Memberships

You can use the Add and Remove selection buttons to add or remove a group from the set of groups of which this user is a member.

In Windows NT, rights can be assigned to users or groups. These rights give the user the permission to perform a particular task, such as backing up the system. The User Rights panel is reached by selecting **Policies->User Rights** from the User manager main panel, as shown in Figure 264:

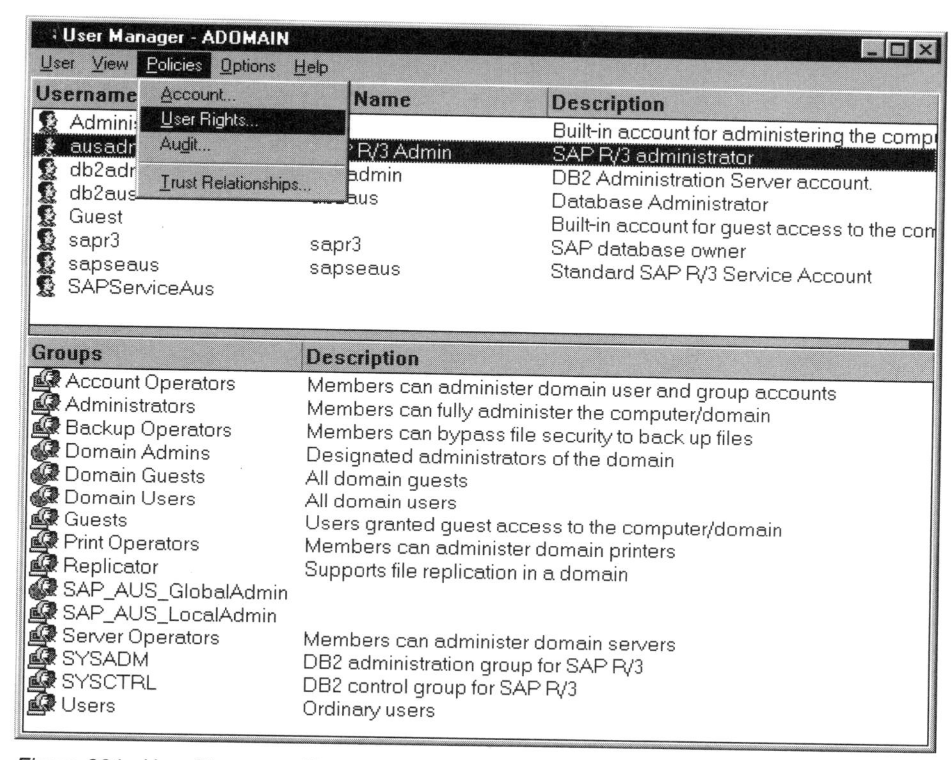

Figure 264. User Manager - User Rights

The next screen shows user rights panel. You should click the **Show Advanced User Rights** box to display all the rights.

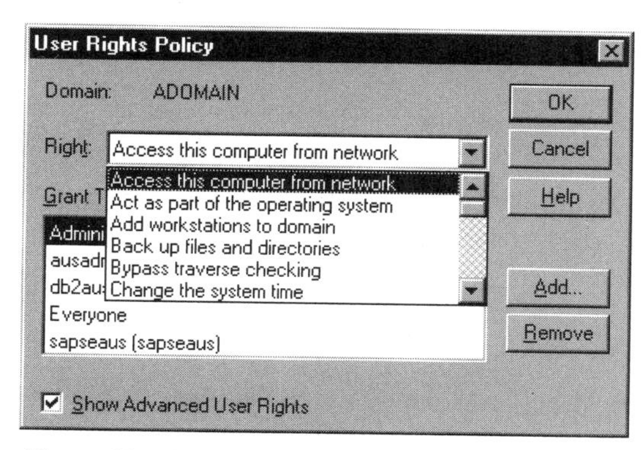

Figure 265. Windows NT User Rights

You can assign a right to a user or group by first selecting the right, then clicking **Add**.

7.8.2.2 Passwords

After installation, especially in a production quality assurance and/or production environment, the passwords of the users related to R/3 should be changed. Some users' passwords can be changed by the operating system tools and others should only be changed by using the special R/3 options in the DB2 Control Center.

The following users can be changed by the operating system tools or commands:

- db2<sid>: AIX and Windows NT
- db2as: Only AIX
- db2admin: Only Windows NT
- sapse<sid>: Only Windows NT

To change the password of the following users, you should use the DB2 Control Center:

1. <sid>adm: AIX and Windows NT
2. sapr3: AIX and Windows NT

The reason for this last requirement is that the passwords are not only stored in the operating system but also in an operating system file. This file holds the passwords in encrypted format to be used by R/3. If you change the passwords for these R/3 users using the operating system tools, the changed passwords will not be passed on to this file and you will not be able to connect to the database with R/3.

7.8.2.3 Password Maintenance

To maintain passwords, the tools you use depend on the operating system. Use these tools to change the passwords of all the R/3 related users apart from the <sid>adm and sapr3 users.

AIX

Password maintenance can be done in two ways:

1. Using the AIX smit tool. Enter `smitty passwords` to go directly to the password maintenance panel.

2. Using the AIX `passwd` command. Enter `passwd username` to change the password for a user. The command will prompt twice asking for the same password.

Windows NT

To maintain the operating system passwords, you use the User Manager tool.

Select **Start->Program->Administrative Tools->User Manager for Domains** then double-click on the user and enter the new password in the Password and Confirm Password fields (assuming you have the necessary rights to do this). The new password will take effect the next time the user tries to log on the operating system.

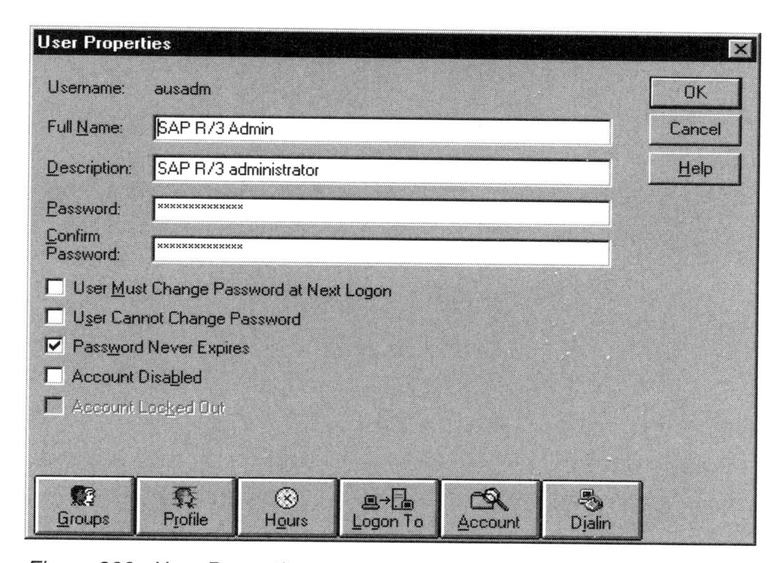

Figure 266. User Properties

Using the DB2 Control Center to Change Passwords

To change the passwords for the <sid>adm and sapr3 users using the DB2 Control Center, select **Start->Program->DB2 for Windows NT->Administration Tools->Control Center**. Expand the tree in the left panel until you see your database. Right-click on the <sid> database and choose **SAP-DB2admin: Change Password**:

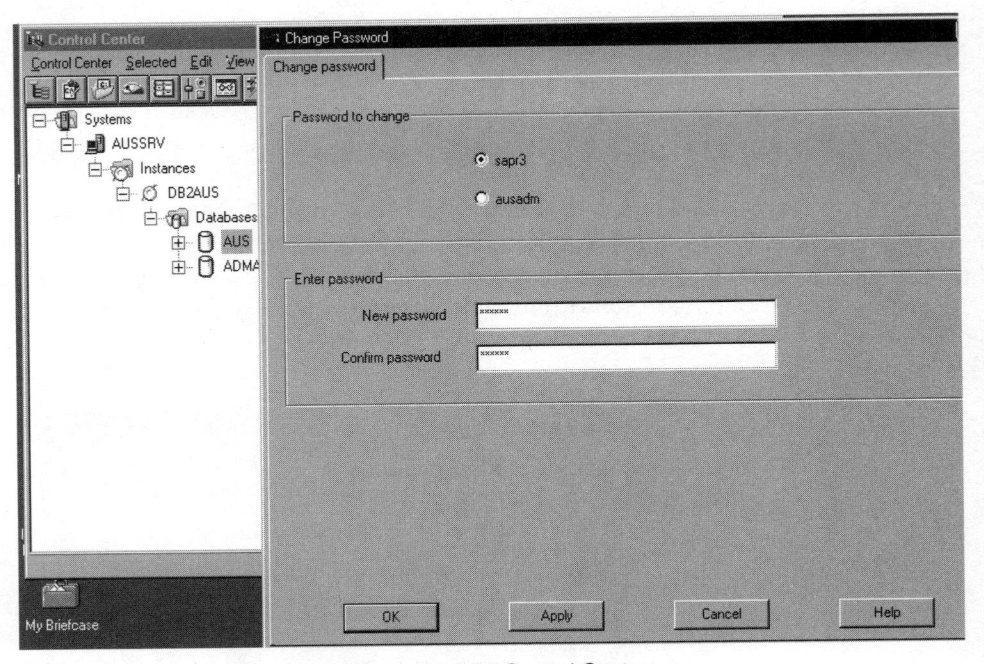

Figure 267. Change Password through the DB2 Control Center

After changing the password, click on **Apply** then **OK**.

7.8.3 DB2 Authorizations and Privileges

DB2 does not store any users or passwords itself. It relies on the operating system to authenticate a user. The functions that a user can perform in DB2 depends on the authorization level of the user, and the user's privileges.

7.8.3.1 DB2 Authorization Levels

Authorization levels in DB2 provide you with the hierarchy for the database administration capabilities. An authority is a set of privileges covering a set of database objects and activities. These authorities are assigned to a group of users. Each member of the group has the same DB2 authority, unless they are explicitly removed from the user. Two of the DB2 UDB authorization levels are SYSADM and SYSCTRL. SYSADM is at the top of the hierarchy and is the DB2 system administrator. SYSADM is able to perform any of the DB2 administration operations as well as select any information from the database. SYSADM is the only authorization level able to make changes to the database manager configuration file.

System control (SYSCTRL) provides the ability to perform almost any administration command within DB2. For example, SYSCTRL in R/3 can start the database instance. That is why the R/3 administrator can start the database manager. However, a user with SYSCTRL authorization does not have the authority to access user information or modify the database manager configuration. This user will get almost complete control of database objects defined in the DB2 instance, but cannot access user data directly, unless granted the privilege to do so. A user with this authority, or higher, can perform the following functions within DB2:

- Update the database, node and DCS directory entries.
- Update database configuration parameters (but not database manager configuration parameters without SYSADM authorization).
- Force applications using the DB2 force application command.
- Run the RESTORE/BACKUP/ROLLFORWARD commands within DB2.
- Create or drop a table space.

The group authorities are also related to the security mechanisms of the operating system. For example, a user who is placed in the sysctrl group has their access controlled within DB2 according to the SYSCTRL authority.

As part of the R/3 installation, the two groups which relate to these authorization levels are created. The group for SYSADM is sysadm. The group that is created during R/3 installation for SYSCTRL is sysctrl. If you place a user in the sysadm or sysctrl groups, the user will inherit the relevant DB2 authorization. Ensure that you understand the implications of such a move. For example, you might want a user to be able to run the BACKUP and RESTORE utilities. However, before placing a user in the sysadm group, make sure that you know all the functions that a user with the SYSADM authorization level can perform within DB2 before doing so.

7.8.3.2 DB2 Privileges

A privilege in DB2 is the right to create or access a database resource. Both DB2 authorities and privileges on database objects are hierarchical in nature.There are three types of privileges: Ownership, Individual, and Implicit.

1. **Ownership or control privileges**. For most objects, the user or group who creates the object has full access to that object. Control privilege is automatically granted to the creator of an object. There are some database objects, such as views, that are exceptions to this rule. Having control privilege is like having ownership of the object. You have the right to access the object and grant access to others. Privileges are controlled

by users with ownership or administrative privileges. They provide other users with access using the SQL `GRANT` statement.

2. **Individual privileges**. These are privileges that allow you to perform a specific action. These privileges include select, delete and insert, and are granted by a user with ownership or control privileges.
3. **Implicit privileges**. An implicit privilege is one that is granted to a user automatically when that user is explicitly granted certain higher level privileges. These privileges are not revoked when the higher level privileges are explicitly revoked.

Information about privileges is maintained in four system catalog views:

- SYSCAT.DBAUTH. Contains database privileges
- SYSCAT.TABAUTH. Contains table and view privileges
- SYSCAT.PACKAGEAUTH. Contains package privileges
- SYSCAT.INDEXAUTH. Contains index privileges

Let us look at all the database privileges assigned to the <sid>adm user. From the DB2 Control Center, click on the **<sid>** database and then select **User and Group Objects->DB Users**. Then right-click on the **<sid>** user in the Objects Pane and select **Change** to display the panel shown in Figure 268 on page 321:

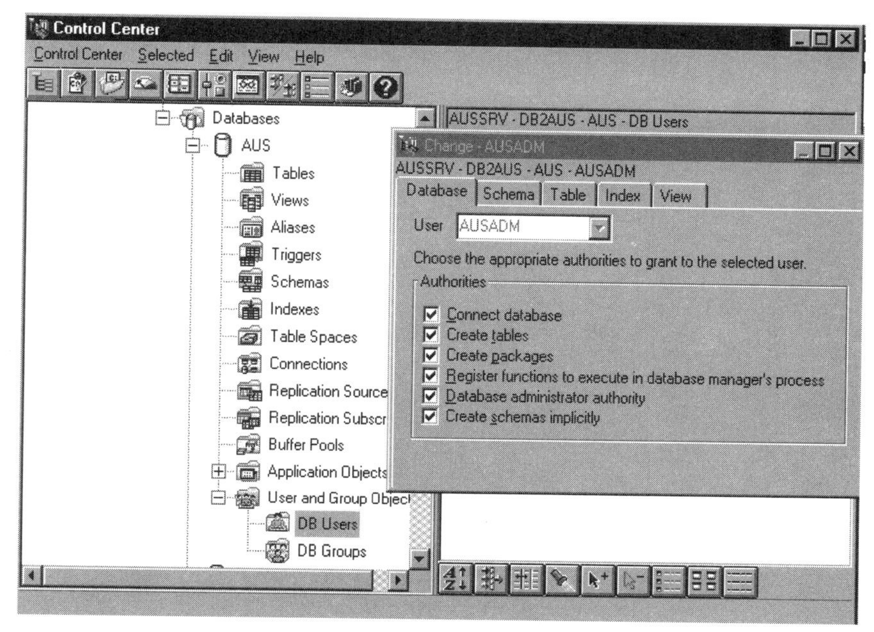

Figure 268. Database Privileges

Alternatively, you can execute an SQL statement from the DB2 Command Center or Command Line Processor (CLP). For example, Figure 269 shows the SQL statement to use from the DB2 Command Center:

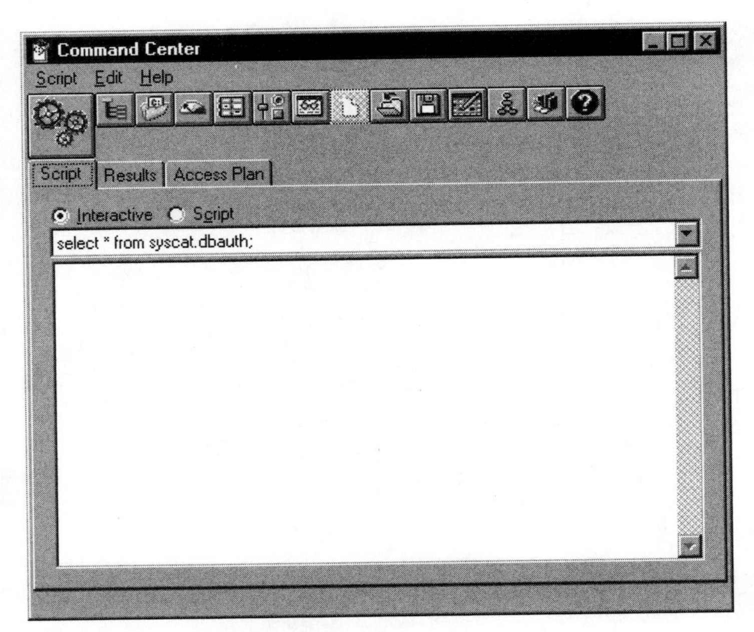

Figure 269. Command Center - Database Privileges

The output would be similar to the following:

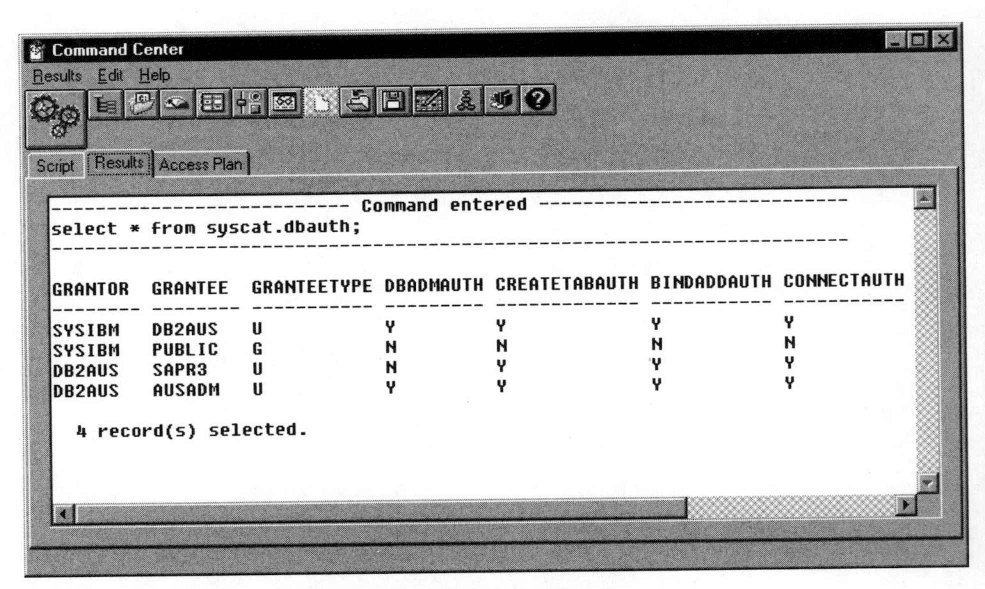

Figure 270. Command Center - Database Privileges Results

From the output, we can see for example that there are two users who have been granted database administrator (DBADM) authority: DB2AUS and AUSADM. The user SAPR3 can perform various database activities such as connect to the database and create tables within the database. You will not see the associations to the SYSADM and SYSCTRL groups in the DB2 catalog tables as these associations are held outside of DB2.

7.8.4 The R/3 Security System

The R/3 system has user control access to protect business data. The R/3 security system is composed of these objects:

- User master records
- Authorization profiles
- Authorizations
- Authorization objects and fields

R/3 security is very flexible since it permits the administrator to select which R/3 entity and its field values and what type of access is granted to the user. In this section, we discuss user master records, authorization profiles and authorizations. Authorization objects and fields are only relevant to ABAP/4 programmers.

7.8.4.1 R/3 Authorization General Concepts

The system administrator creates authorizations, which are assigned to individual users in collections called profiles. Generally speaking, profiles are created using the Profile Generator, although they can also be generated manually after assigning an authorizations object to the profile. The authorization object has a group of authorizations related to a business specific object. The authorization is the next level from authorization object and it is the lowest level of access authorization. Each one can group up to 10 fields and they are tested with AND logic in programs to see if a user has the authorization to carry out an action.

Let's look at an example which illustrates the authorization components and explains their relationship. This example concerns personnel files and who is allowed to view or update them.

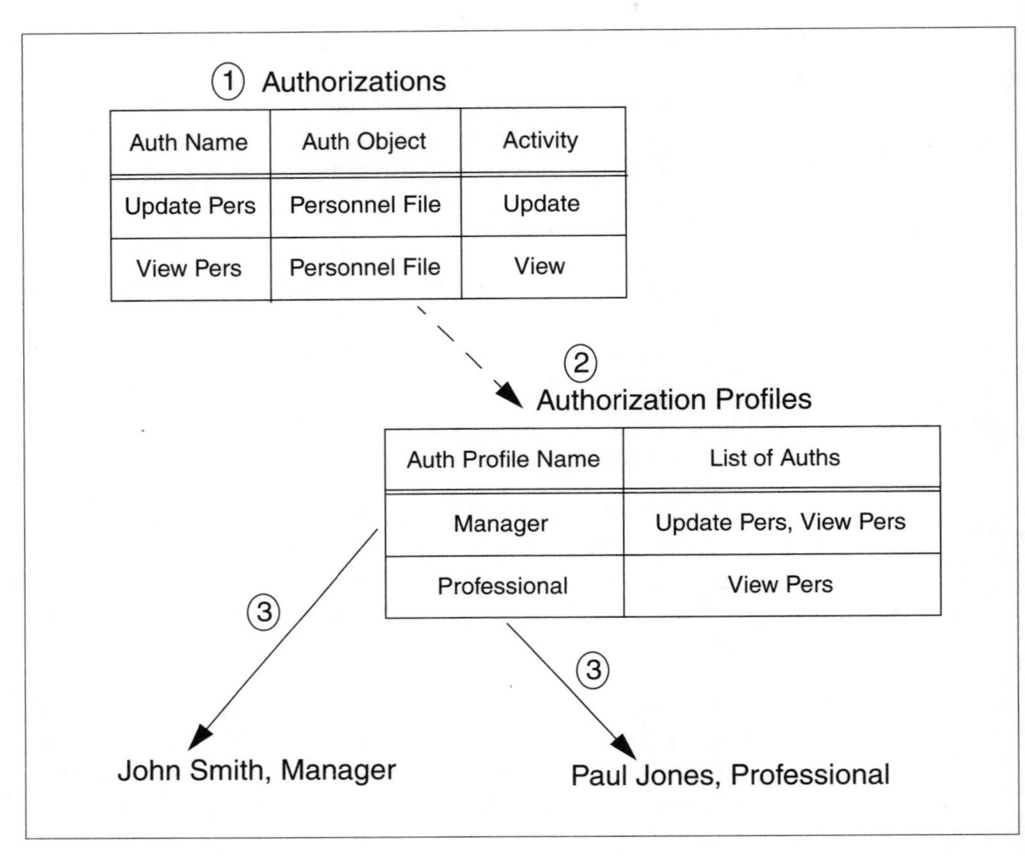

Figure 271. R/3 Authorizations Example

In this example:

1. The *authorizations* define which activity can be performed against which object. In this case, there are two activities, update and view, that can be performed against a personnel file.
2. The *authorization profiles* allow the administrator to group together a set of authorizations into one profile. In this case, a manager is allowed to update or view a personnel file, whereas a professional can only view the file.
3. Users are assigned authorization profiles. In this case, John Smith is a manager and Paul Jones is a professional.

7.8.4.2 User Master Records

These enable the user to log onto the R/3 system and allow access to the functions and objects in it within the limits of the specified authorization profiles. Changes only take effect when the user next logs on. Users who are logged on when the change takes place are not affected in their current session.

7.8.4.3 Authorization Profiles

As a rule, user authorizations are not assigned directly to user master records, but grouped together in the form of authorization profiles. The system administrator can either create authorization profiles manually or automatically using the Profile Generator.

The R/3 system contains a large number of predefined profiles for the Basis System and the work areas in the R/3 System. This makes it considerably easier for the system administrator to create profiles.

The following different types of profiles exist:

- Single profiles
  - Specify authorizations in user master records.
  - Contain specific access rights, identified by an object name and a corresponding authorization name.
- Composite Profiles (Manual maintenance only)
  - Specify a group of authorization profiles in the user master record.
  - Contain the names of single and composite profiles as well as individual authorizations.

Changes affect all users to whom this profile is assigned. Changes only take effect when the user next logs on. Users who are logged on when the change takes place are not affected in their current session.

7.8.4.4 Authorizations

An authorization enables you to execute a particular activity within the R/3 system, based on a set of values for the individual fields within an authorization object. The R/3 system administrator can maintain authorizations using the Profile Generator or manually. Changes take effect for all users as soon as the authorization is activated.

7.8.4.5 Assigning Authorizations

The R/3 system administrator or a designated sub-administrator is responsible for assigning authorizations.

By assigning authorizations, the administrator determines (within the range of possibilities defined by the programmer) which functions a user may execute or which objects he or she may access.

As an administrator, you are responsible for the following actions in the recommended sequence:

1. Maintaining authorizations for each authorization object:

   From the R/3 GUI select: **Tools->Administration, User Maintenance->Authorization**. Alternatively, type the transaction code **SU03** in the command input field.

   An authorization is the combination of permissible values in each authorization field of an authorization object.

2. Generating authorization profiles:

   Authorizations are grouped in authorization profiles in such a way that the profiles describe work centers, for example, flight reservation clerk.

   The system administrator can create authorization profiles in two ways:

   - Automatically, based on activity group maintenance (**Tools->Administration, User maintenance->Activity groups)**, using the Profile Generator or type the code transaction: **PFCG** in the command input field.
   - Manually, by choosing **Tools->Administration->User maintenance->Profiles** or type the transaction code **SU02** in the command input field.

   You can combine profiles and single authorizations to form composite profiles using the manual maintenance tool. Composite profiles are not strictly necessary, but they do make system administration easier.

3. Assigning authorization profiles to a user master record:

   This is done during the creation or maintenance of a user master record by following the selection: **Tools->Administration, User Maintenance->Users** or by typing the transaction code **SU01** in the command input field.

   You assign one or more authorization profiles (work centers) to a user master record.

When an authorization check takes place, the system compares the values entered by the system administrator in the authorization profile with those required by the program for the user to execute a certain activity.

Chapter 8. R/3 Database Maintenance

This chapter deals with the maintenance of the R/3 database in terms of backup and recovery, data reorganizations and statistics generation. It also investigates the tools available to the database administrator to help in performing these tasks.

We also take a look at the R/3 system database architecture with particular reference to the SAP-DB2admin interface in the DB2 Control Center. A brief overview of the Control Center is also included in this chapter.

The chapter is split into the following three main sections:

1. R/3 Database Architecture
   - SAP-DB2admin Control Center
   - adm<sid> Database
2. Backup and Recovery
   - Initial Backups
   - Database Logging
   - Recovery
3. Data Maintenance
   - RUNSTATS, REORGCHK and REORG utilities
   - Table space maintenance

A summary of these tasks is given in Appendix C, "R/3 and DB2 Control Center Tasks" on page 503. In cases where it is possible to use more than one method to perform a task, we give recommendations as to which one is the most appropriate.

Throughout the chapter, the following symbols are used:

DB2's Control Center together with the SAP-DB2admin interface

SAP R/3 interface, menus and tasks

8.1 R/3 Database Maintenance Architecture

Many database maintenance tasks in an R/3 system which uses DB2 UDB are performed using the DB2 Control Center.

8.1.1 DB2 UDB Control Center

The Control Center interface shown in Figure 272 has five elements that help you define and manage the R/3 databases.

- **Menu bar**. Use the menu bar to work with objects in the Control Center.
- **Toolbar icons**. Use the toolbar icons above the object tree to access other functions, such as setting preferences and alerts and viewing job status, logs, and messages. These functions can also be selected in the View menu bar item.
- **Object tree**. Use the object tree to display and work with system and database objects.

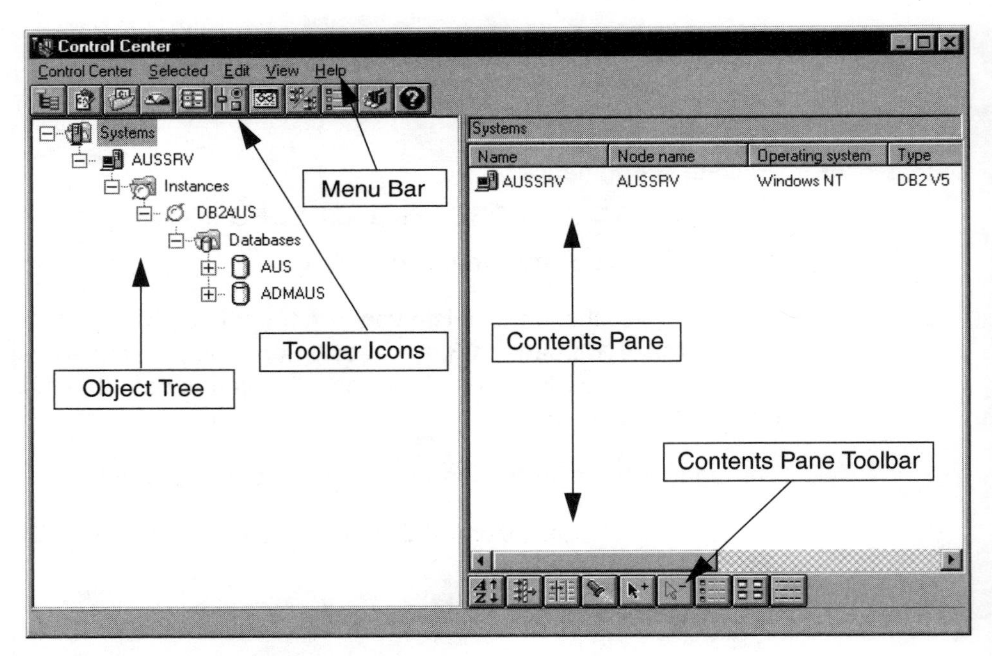

Figure 272. DB2 Control Center Features

- **Contents pane**. Use the contents pane to display and work with system and database objects. The contents pane displays those objects that make up the contents of the object that is selected in the object tree.

- **Contents pane toolbar**. Use the toolbar below the contents pane to tailor the view of objects and information in the contents pane to suit your needs. These toolbar functions can also be selected in the Edit menu and the View menu items.

8.1.2 SAP-DB2admin Interface

The DB2 UDB Control Center supplied with the SAP R/3 software has been enhanced to include some specific R/3 functions such as log file management and password management.

In addition, there are certain features within the Control Center environment which have in been disabled in order to prevent accidental damage to the R/3 database. An example of this is the fact that you can not drop an index on database <sid>. Details on index maintenance are given in "Index Maintenance" on page 384. In addition, performing database administration tasks on the R/3 database from a DB2 Command Line interface is *not* recommended.

Figure 273 on page 330 illustrates the SAP-DB2admin architecture. The numbers in the figure represent the following:

1. The Control Center GUI is invoked and the appropriate SAP-DB2admin function is selected by calling sapdef.dll.
2. The available actions are returned, for example, **SAP-DB2admin: Change Password.**
3. After completing the dialog, the sapact.dll is called. This interfaces with the DB2admin Work and Feedback Manager (DWFM).
4. The DWFM initiates the task and calls the SDDB6DAS stored procedure, thus bypassing the normal Control Center administration environment.
5. Status information such as the success or failure of the original request is then returned to the Control Center.

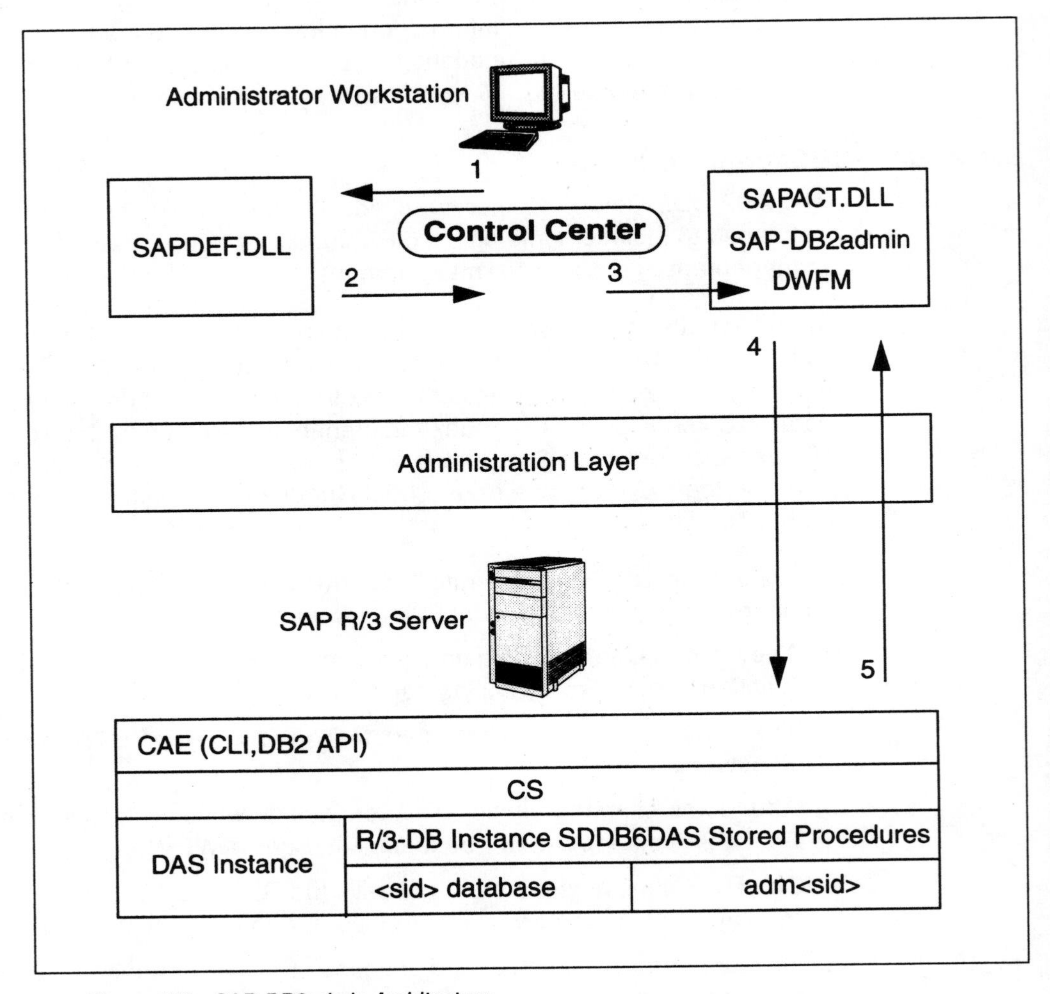

Figure 273. SAP-DB2admin Architecture

8.1.3 The adm<sid> Database

After completing the R/3 installation process on a Windows NT or AIX server, you will find that two databases have been generated.

- **<sid>** - The R/3 database.
- **adm<sid>** -The administration management database.

All administration activity is logged in the adm<sid> database and then mirrored to the R/3 database on a regular basis. For this reason it is not essential that you backup the adm<sid> database, however you may wish to do this.

The CCMS interface enables you to monitor all external and internal database maintenance. In order for this to happen however, the activities logged in the adm<sid> database must be transferred to the <sid> database. This process is known as mirroring. It is recommended that you mirror the adm<sid> database on an hourly basis using the following procedure:

1. Use transaction **SM36** to schedule a job called **ADMIN_MIRROR** to run once an hour, specifying a Job class of **C** and entering the name of the database host for the Target Host.

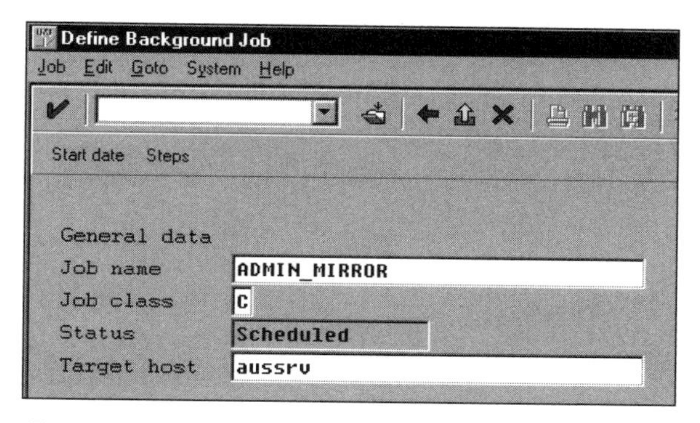

Figure 274. R/3 Mirroring Define Background Job

2. Click on **Start Date** in the tool bar to display the *Start Time* panel.
3. Click on **Immediate**, select the **Periodic** check-box and click on **Period Values** to display the following popup:

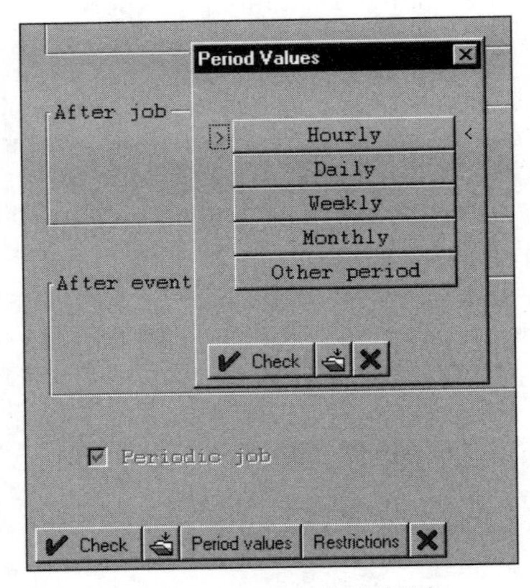

Figure 275. R/3 Mirroring Period Values

4. Click on **Hourly** and then click on the save icon. Click on the save icon again to return to the *Define Background Jobs* screen (Figure 274 on page 331).

5. Click on **Steps** in the tool bar, and then select **External Program**. This scheduled job should call an external program `sddb6mir` with the parameters `-m <sid>`. Enter the following values:

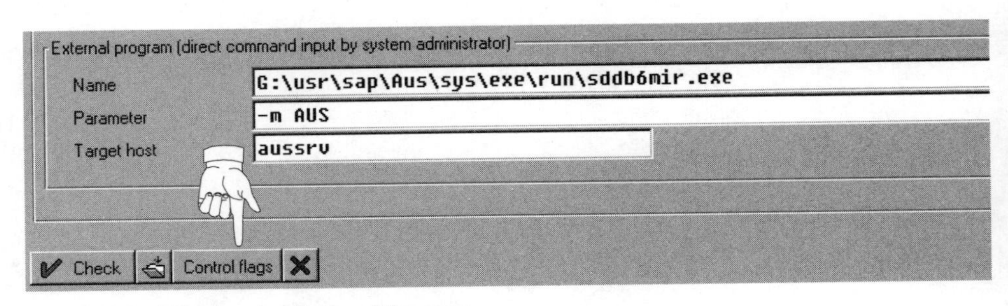

Figure 276. R/3 Mirroring External Program

6. Select **Control flags**. The field called: Job to wait for ext.program to end should be set to **no**.

7. Click on the save icon to return. Click again on the save icon.

8. You can check that the job has run successfully using transaction **SM37**.

The command **sddb6mir** can also be run from a command window with the appropriate parameters.

```
sddb6mir -m <sid>
```

The **-m** option transfers new administration data from adm<sid> to the <sid> database.

You can use the **-r** option together with **-p** and the path name to rebuild the administration database. The **-p** option refers to a path where temporary data is stored. These files will be removed after the successful data transfer.

```
sddb6mir -r adm<sid> -p path
```

8.1.4 SAP-DB2admin Functions

The following functions are available with the SAP-DB2admin environment and are discussed in the appropriate sections of this chapter.

- At the DB2 instance level:
  - SAP-DB2admin: Change password
  - SAP-DB2admin: Options
  - SAP-DB2admin: R/3 DB Detection
- At the DB2 database level:
  - SAP-DB2admin: Change password
  - SAP-DB2admin: Tape Management
  - SAP-DB2admin: Log File Management
  - SAP-DB2admin: Options
  - SAP-DB2admin: R/3 DB Detection

These options are illustrated in Figure 277:

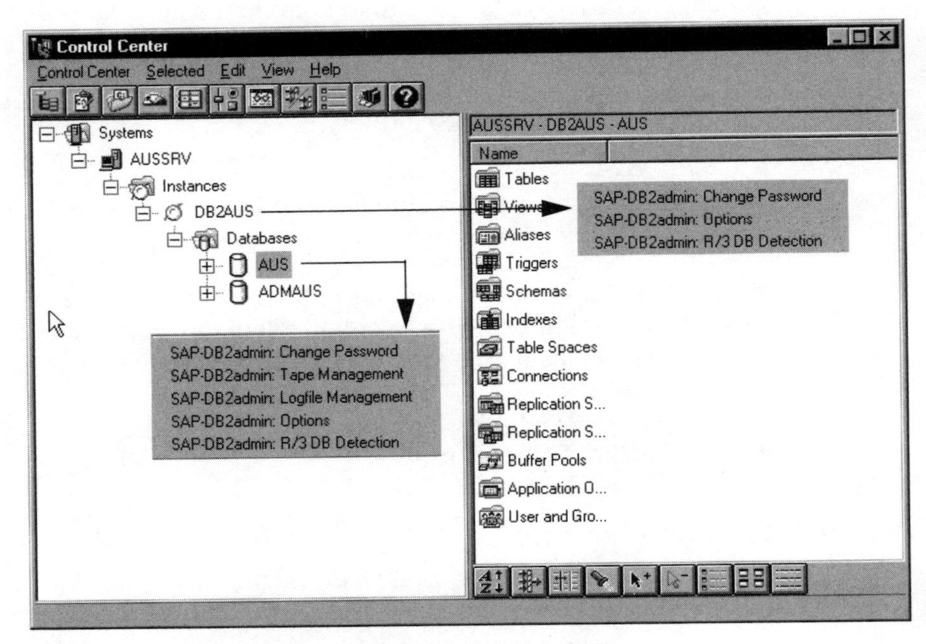

Figure 277. DB2 Control Center SAP-DB2admin Interface

> **Note**
>
> Whenever one of the SAP-DB2admin functions is invoked from the Control Center, the new window will appear minimized.

8.1.5 R/3 Database Detection

Since not all databases being administered from a single workstation are R/3 databases it is necessary to make sure that the SAP-DB2admin Control Center tool is used for R/3 databases only.

For this reason, there are two ways that R/3 can differentiate between R/3 and non-R/3 databases:

1. R/3 checks for the following criteria:
   - The instance name is 6 characters long and starts with DB2.
   - The database name is 3 characters long and corresponds to the last 3 characters of the instance name.

   Based on the above criteria, the R/3 system will assume it is an R/3 database.

2. Alternatively, R/3 can identify an R/3 database by using a configuration file.

This file is located in the \sqllib\bin directory (on Windows NT for example) and is named r3db.db2. The entry in the r3db.db2 file in our environment looks like this:

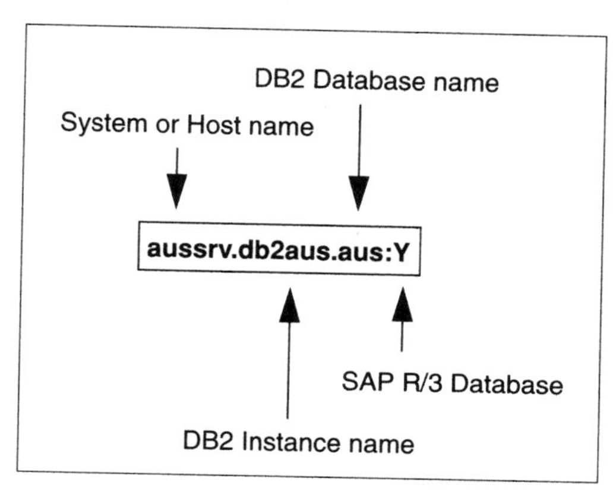

Figure 278. SAP-DB2admin r3db.db2 file

To update this file from within the Control Center environment follow these steps:

1. Select the **R/3 DB Detection** option by right clicking on the database.

Note

You must install the SAP-DB2admin interface after having installed DB2's Client Application Enabler on your workstation. See "Installing the R/3 Interface to the DB2 UDB Control Center" on page 177.

2. Fill in the 4 fields as illustrated in Figure 279:

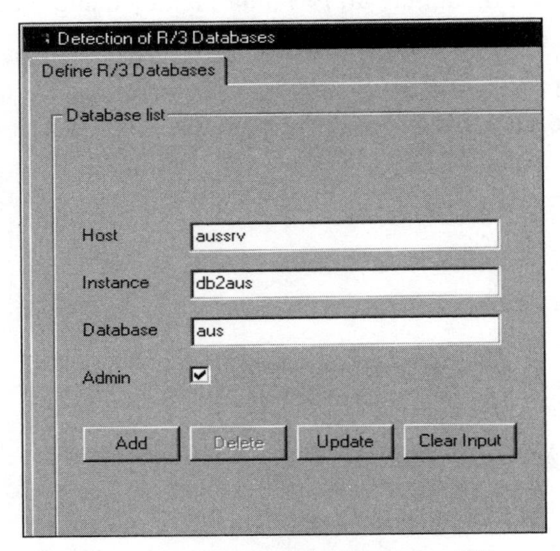

Figure 279. SAP-DB2admin DB Detection GUI

3. Click **Add** then click the **Save and Close** button.

8.2 DB2 UDB Logging Considerations

The DB2 UDB databases that R/3 uses may become unusable because of a hardware or software failure, so you should have a backup strategy in place to safeguard your R/3 system. The following items should be implemented:

- After installation, you should set the database parameters LOGRETAIN and USEREXIT to **on**. If these parameters are not switched on, the R/3 system database will not be recoverable, since the log files will not be available for a roll-forward recovery. When LOGRETAIN is switched on, the database will go into a backup pending state. See "Backing Up the R/3 Database" on page 342 for steps on how to backup your database.
- The R/3 system database <sid> should be backed up regularly. The frequency of these backups will be discussed later.
- You should check your backups by executing a restore under test conditions.

Although it is beyond the scope of this book to go into detail about how recovery and logging are implemented in DB2 UDB, certain important elements are discussed here in view of the fact that there is a great deal of inter-dependence between the R/3 environment and the DB2 UDB database.

8.2.1 R/3 Implementation of DB2 Logging

When the database is first activated, or the first connection established, DB2 ensures that the Primary log files are created and available. Secondary log files are created on demand during database operations. The maximum number of these log files is set by the database configuration parameter LOGSECOND. These log files are used if there are not enough LOGPRIMARY log files, such as during a long running logical unit of work (LUW).

Changes to data are recorded in the *online active logs* (SAP terminology) otherwise known as the *active logs*. At database first connect or activate, DB2 will search the log directory for these log files. The log directory is defined by the database configuration (db cfg) parameter LOGPATH, and is set to \db2\<sid>\log_dir during the R/3 installation process. We refer to this directory as the *log_dir* directory. If there are no log files available DB2 will create them. The number of log files is set by the db cfg parameter LOGPRIMARY and the size of the logs defined by the db cfg parameter LOGFILSIZ. These log files are shown in Figure 280 on page 339. These logs are used to recover from software or hardware errors. In combination with the database backups, they can be used to recover the consistency of the database up to the point in time when the error occurred.

When a log file fills up, the user exit supplied by R/3 archives (or copies) the active log to the archive directory, \db2\<sid>\log_archive\<sid>\node0000. We refer to this directory as the *log_archive* directory. The state of the log now becomes *online retained*. It is at this point that there are two copies of the log file; one in the log_dir directory and one in the log_archive directory. This state remains in force until there is no longer any reference in the buffer pools to the log pages in the online retained log file. At this point, the online retained log file is deleted (or reused by DB2 UDB), and the copied file in the log_archive directory becomes *offline retained*. See Figure 280 on page 339 for an example of this procedure.

It is recommended that you have enough space in your active log directory (log_dir) for 2 to 3 days worth of log files. This will give you room in the event that the user exit fails and the problem is not identified for several days. Furthermore, you should have enough space for the offline retained log files in the log_archive directory. This will depend on the type of activity going on and will be different for each installation of an R/3 System.

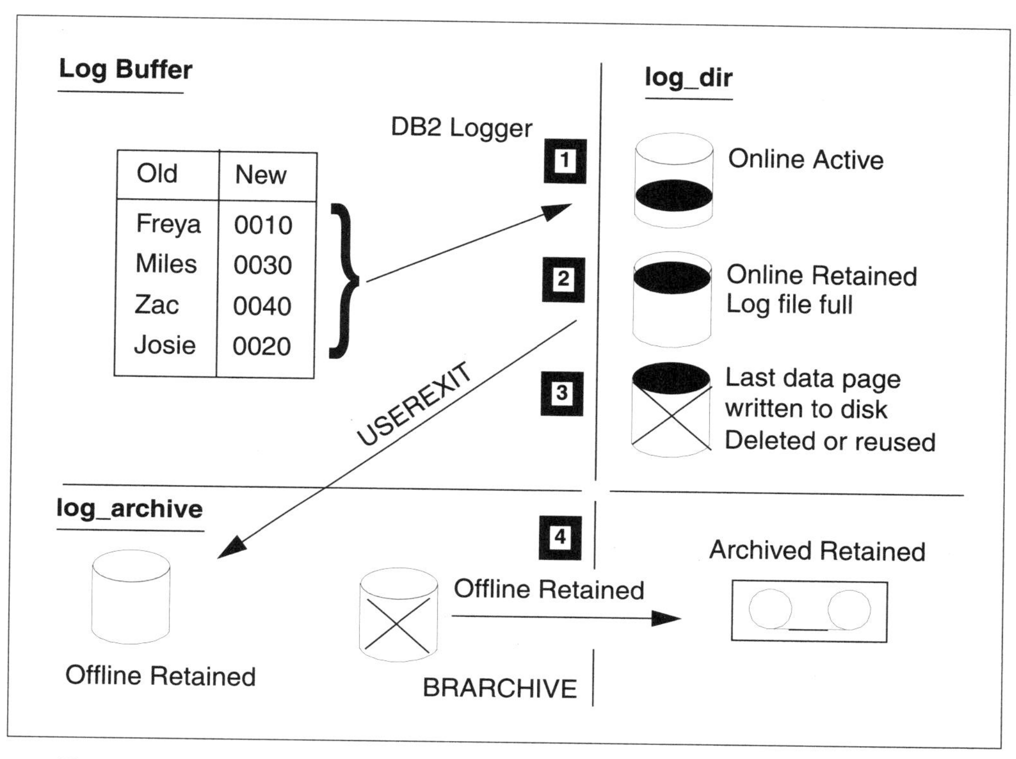

Figure 280. DB2 Logging with R/3 User Exit

The R/3 user exit described above allows for the unattended transfers of the logs from the log_dir directory to the log_archive directory. When a log file becomes full, DB2 calls the R/3 program **`db2uext2`**.

Note

The R/3 user exit supplied by SAP is tightly integrated into the R/3 system. Do *not* use the sample DB2 user exits.

The final step in the process is to copy the offline retained files to another media (usually tape) and remove them from the log_archive directory before this directory becomes full. After this step, these log files become *archived retained*. This process is described in "Moving Offline Log Files to Other Media" on page 356.

SAP and IBM's naming conventions differ in terms of the log files. The table below shows the comparisons.

Table 20. SAP and IBM Terms

SAP Terms	IBM Terms
online active	active
online retained	online archived
offline retained	offline archived
archived retained	n/a

8.2.1.1 Modes of Logging

DB2 can be configured to use one of two modes of logging for a database: circular or archival logging.

Circular Logging

Circular logging is the default for a new database. When this option is used, only full, off-line backups can be taken. The logs are re-used in a circular fashion. This means that this option does not allow for roll-forward recovery after restoring a backup.

Note

As it is not possible to perform roll-forward recovery with circular logging, this mode of logging must not be used for R/3 systems.

Archival Logging

Archival logging enables roll-forward recovery using both the active and archived logs to any point in time before a failure, or to the end of available logs. Active logs are kept and remain available to the DB2 system as *online archived logs.*To recover from a failure, you can restore the database from the last good backup and apply the desired logs, both active and archived.

8.2.2 Checking the R/3 Logging Environment

Details of your current logging setup can either be established using the Control Center interface or from the command line

In order to check the settings of the database configuration (db cfg) parameters related to logging in the DB2 Control Center, right-click on the database <sid> and select the **Configure** option. Select the **Logs** tab as illustrated in Figure 281. In this example, we have set the number of log files to 40 and the size of each log to 4095 4 KB pages. In addition, the Logs panel displays the location of the log files.

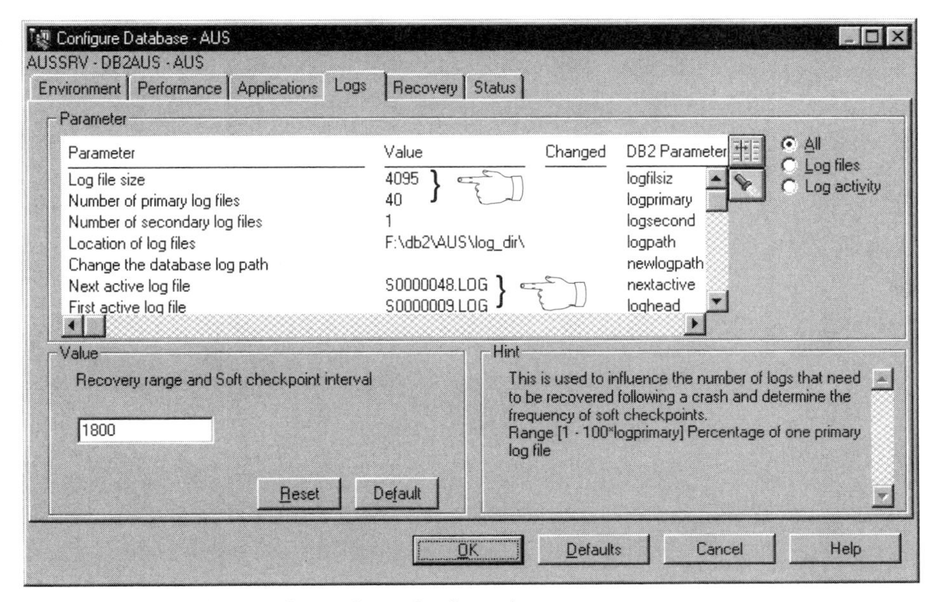

Figure 281. DB2 Control Center Logs Configuration

Alternatively, you can obtain the same information by issuing the following command from a DB2 Command Window or the DB2 Command Center:

```
db2 get db cfg for <sid>
```

The other logging parameters that should be checked are *Next active log file* and *First active log file*. These file names should match with the files in the log_dir path. In this example, by using the Windows NT Explorer, we can see that the first active log is S0000009.log and the next active log file is S0000048.log.

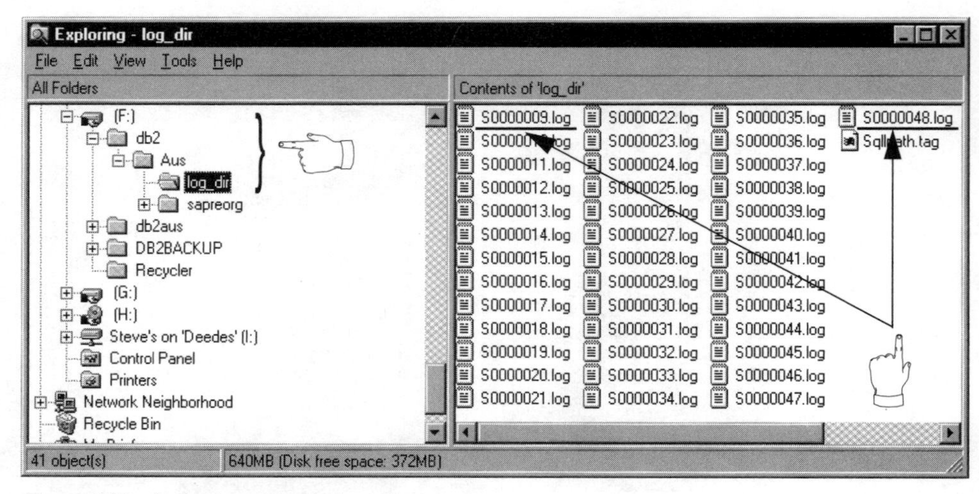

Figure 282. Active Log Files in log_dir

In the log_archive directory, there are 9 *offline retained* log files with names ranging from S0000000.log to S0000008.log. On Windows NT, the directory path is as follows: Drive:\db2\<sid>\log_archive\<sid>\Node0000.

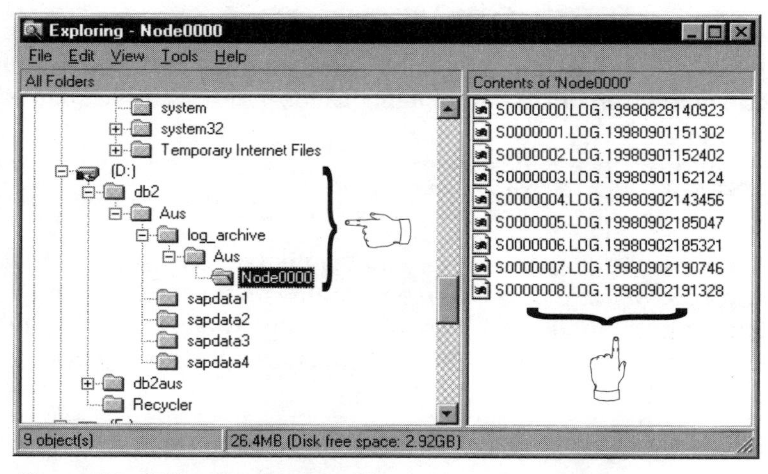

Figure 283. Offline Retained Log Files in log_archive directory

8.3 Backing Up the R/3 Database

In this section, we cover how to backup the R/3 database in offline or online modes. We show how to use the DB2 UDB Control Center to direct the backup to a tape device. We also cover the archiving of log files to tape.

8.3.1 Initial Backup

You should backup the R/3 <sid> database immediately after successfully completing the installation. First, you must change two database configuration parameters using the DB2 UDB Control Center.

You can do this either from the Administration Workstation (for an AIX or Windows NT R/3 server) or from a Windows NT R/3 server.

- Log retention must be enabled.
- The user exit option must be enabled.

On Windows NT, to make these changes, select **Start** -> **Programs** -> **DB2 for Windows NT** -> **Administration Tools** -> **Control Center**. Expand **Systems**, **Instances** and **Databases**. Then right-click on the database <sid>, select **Configure** and click on the **Logs** tab:

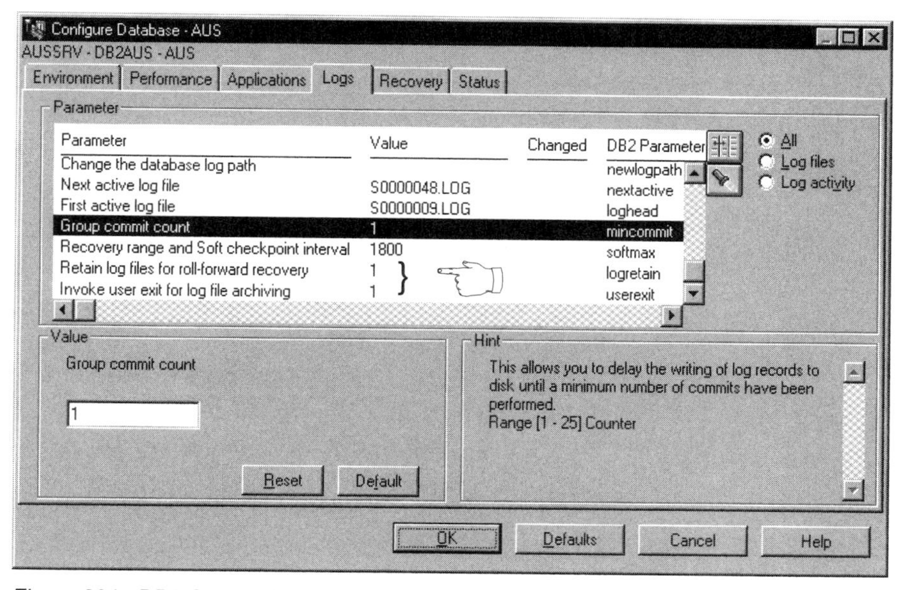

Figure 284. DB2 Control Center, Configure Log Options

Scroll down to Retain Log files and set the value to **1** (yes). Then set Invoke user exit to **1** (yes).

After you have confirmed your selection, a warning message will appear indicating that the changes will not come into effect until all applications have disconnected (Figure 285 on page 344). You are also advised to take a backup.

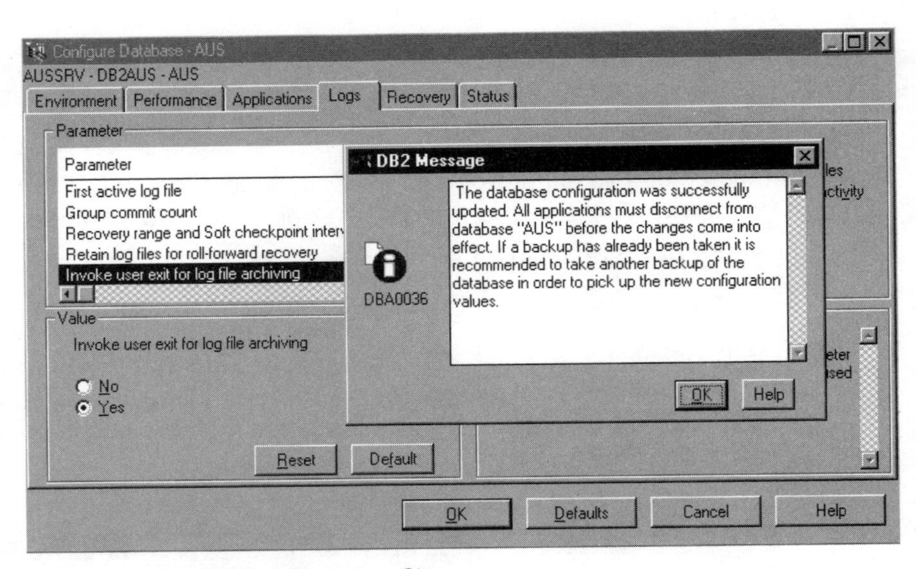

Figure 285. DB2 Control Center Log Change

To make this initial backup, from the DB2 UDB Control Center main panel, right-click on database <sid>. Select **Backup** ->**Database** and then select **Media type**. In this example, we took an initial backup to a disk on the Windows NT server. You will need roughly the same amount of disk space as is taken by the database itself to store the backup image file. You can use the **Browse** button to select this directory (see Figure 286). The directory must already exist.

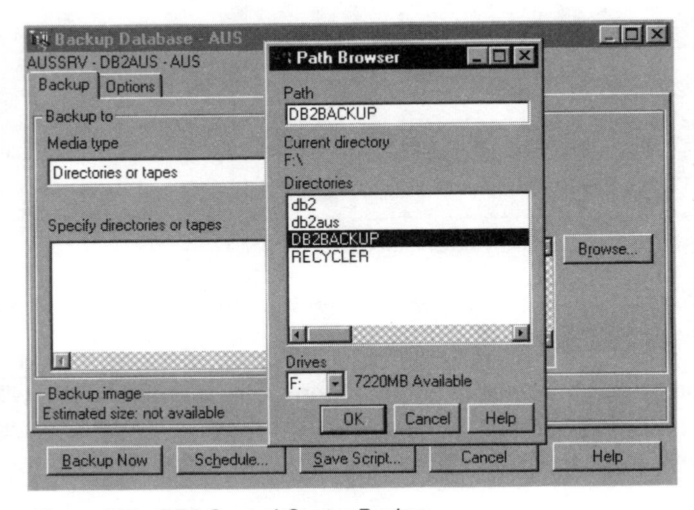

Figure 286. DB2 Control Center Backup

The full directory path of the backup image file will be further expanded by the system when the backup occurs:

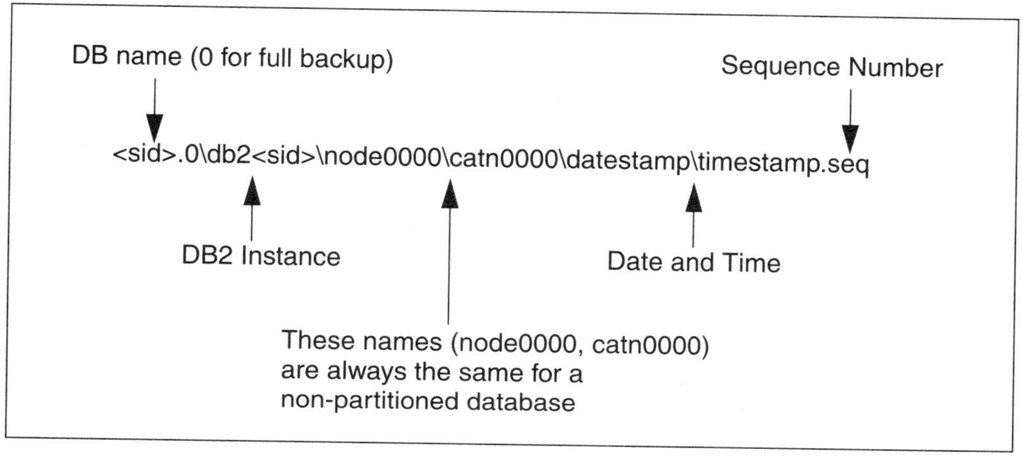

Figure 287. Windows NT Backup File Format

As shown in Figure 288, select the **Options** tab:

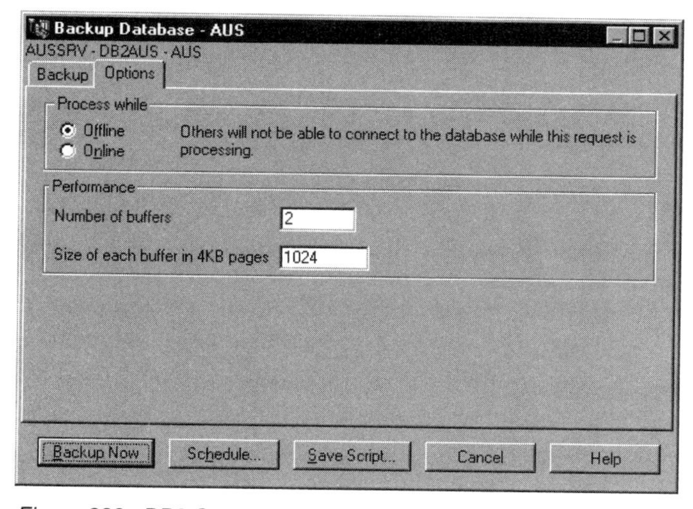

Figure 288. DB2 Control Center Backup Options

Select the **Offline** option and click on the **Backup Now** button. If prompted, enter a userid and password to connect to the database. This user must have SYSADM, SYSCTRL or SYSMAINT authority to perform the backup. You can use the DB2 instance owner user, db2<sid> (in our example, db2aus). You must also ensure that there are no connections to this database.

You will be presented with a message similar to the following, showing that a job has been created for this backup:

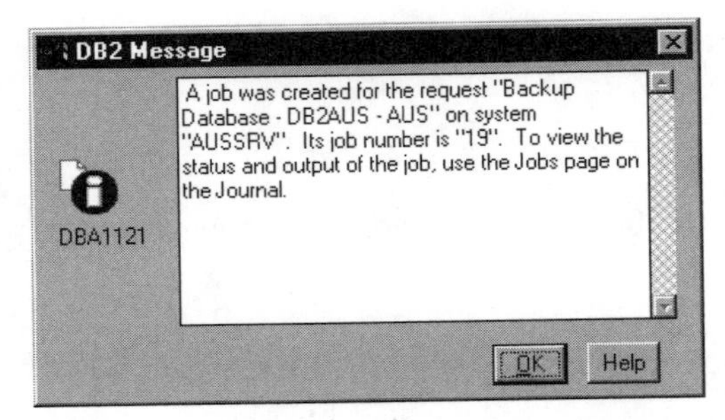

Figure 289. DB2 Control Center Journal Message

You can check the status of your backup job by using the DB2 UDB Journal. This is available from the Toolbar in the Control Center. Select the appropriate System Name and then select one of the following:

- Pending jobs
- Running jobs
- Job history

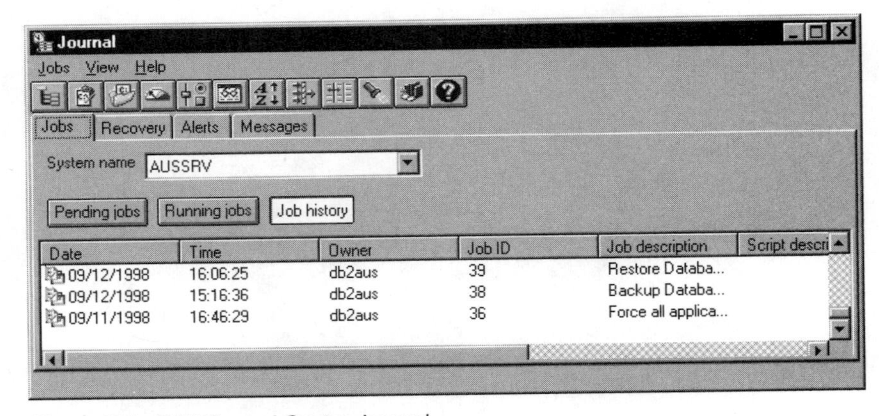

Figure 290. DB2 Control Center Journal

After the backup has completed successfully, you can check the status of the database to ensure that the changes to the database configuration parameters LOGRETAIN and USEREXIT have taken effect.

From the Control Center, right-click on database <sid>. Select **Configure** and then click on the **Status** tab. Scroll down to the two parameters and check that their values are set to 1.

8.3.2 Backup Strategy

After the initial backup has been done immediately after the R/3 installation, the administrator of the R/3 system should decide on a backup strategy. The possible scenarios are described below:

- Online backups

  With online backups, other applications or processes can continue to connect to the database while the backup task is running. Online backups are supported only if roll-forward recovery is enabled. The log files must also be archived.

- Offline backups

  With offline backups, only the backup task can be connected to the database. No other user or application can gain access to the database during the backup processing.

- A combination of the modes

  A combination of online and offline backups.

You must have SYSADM, SYSCTRL or SYSMAINT authority in order to issue the BACKUP DATABASE command. For the R/3 environment, you can use the db2<sid> user. The DB2 instance must be started in order to issue the backup command.

To perform offline backups, the RECONNECT parameter must be adjusted in the R/3 start profile, in order to allow for the R/3 System to remain running throughout the backup. Details on how to do this are explained in the section "Offline Backups" on page 353.

One suggested backup strategy for an R/3 system is to:

- Perform a complete online database backup each workday at a pre-determined time.
- Backup the offline retained logs each workday or less frequently depending on the amount of disk space available.
- Perform a complete offline backup once a week to tape or ADSM.
- Execute an additional offline backup when the structure of the R/3 system is modified or upgraded.
- Keep at least 3 generations of offline backups on tape including the offline retained logs.

8.3.3 Online Backups

Online backups can be performed to tape, ADSM or to disk and can either be executed from the R/3 Frontend or from the DB2 UDB Control Center. The following section describes how to take an online backup to disk using either the DB2 UDB Control Center or the R/3 Frontend.

8.3.3.1 Online Backups Using the DB2 UDB Control Center

To schedule an online backup to take place every weekday at 11:00 PM using the Control Center:

1. Select the <sid> database from Control Center's object tree.
2. Right-click and select **Backup** -> **Database**.
3. On the Backup page, select **Directories or tapes** as the Media type:

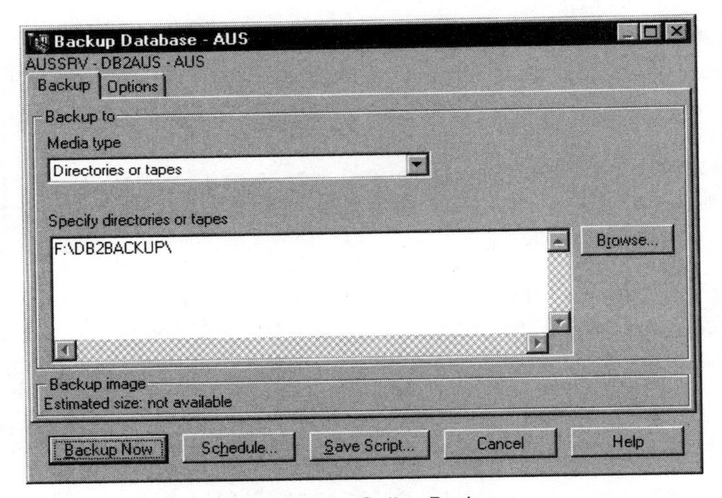

Figure 291. DB2 Control Center Online Backups

4. Select the directory and path for the backups using the **Browse** button if required. The directory must exist already.
5. Select the **Options** page:

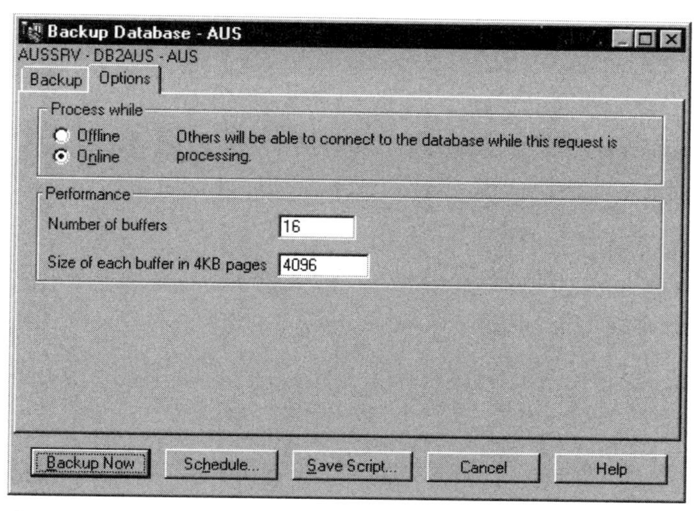

Figure 292. DB2 Control Center Options for Online Backups

6. Select the **Online** option.
7. Alter the performance parameters if required. Note that increasing the value specified for either parameter causes the backup operation to use more memory.
   - Number of Buffers

     Enter the number of buffers that are used for the backup operation. The default is 2. The valid range is from 1 to 65535. For our environment, we used a value of 16.
   - Size of each buffer in 4 KB pages

     Enter the size of each buffer in 4 KB pages. The current value is specified in the database configuration file. The default is 1024, and the range is from 16 to 524288. The recommendation is 4096.
8. Click on the **Schedule** button. The Schedule - Backup Database panel is displayed (Figure 293 on page 350).
   - In the Occurs panel, select **One or more times a week**.
   - Press the **Mon** through **Fri** buttons.
   - In the Owner section, enter the db2<sid> username and password.
   - Fill in the Start and End details sections.
   - Select **OK**.

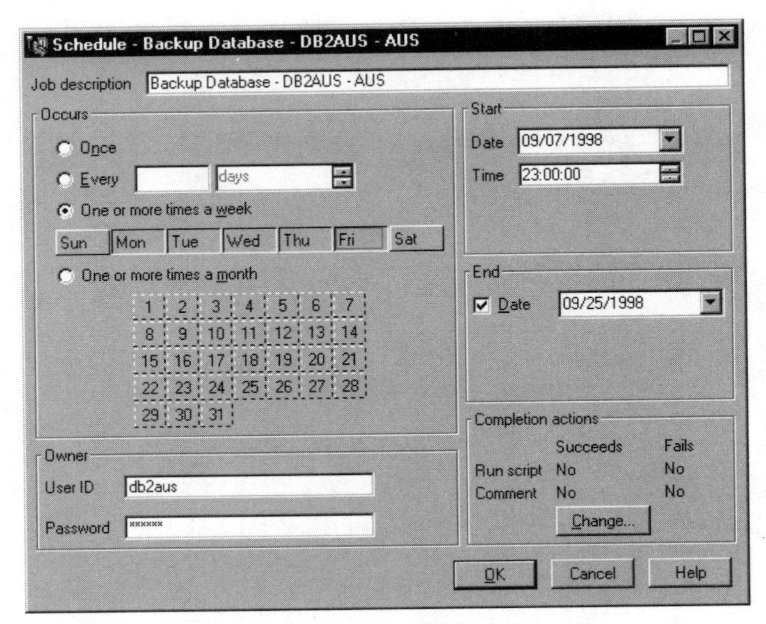

Figure 293. DB2 Control Center Schedule Online Backups

9. A job will be scheduled and can be viewed in the Journal option of the Control Center.

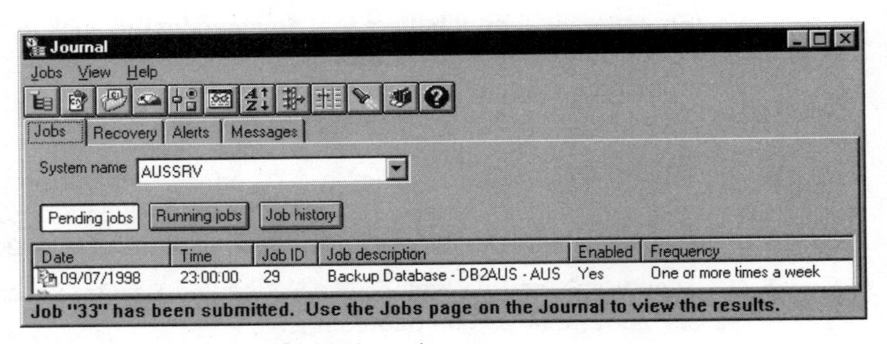

Figure 294. DB2 Control Center Journal

8.3.3.2 Online Backups Using the R/3 CCMS

In addition to running and scheduling online backups from DB2's Control Center, it is possible to start and schedule them from R/3's Computing Center Management System (CCMS).

1. From the R/3 Frontend, select **Tools** -> **CCMS**. Then select **DB Administration** -> **DBA scheduling** (Transaction **DB13)**.

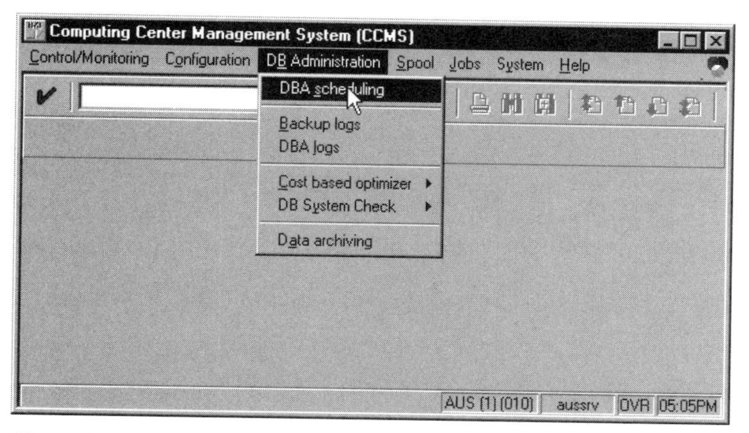

Figure 295. R/3 CCMS DBA Administration

2. Double-click on a date (either today's date or a date in the future) in the DBA planning calendar. The following window is displayed:

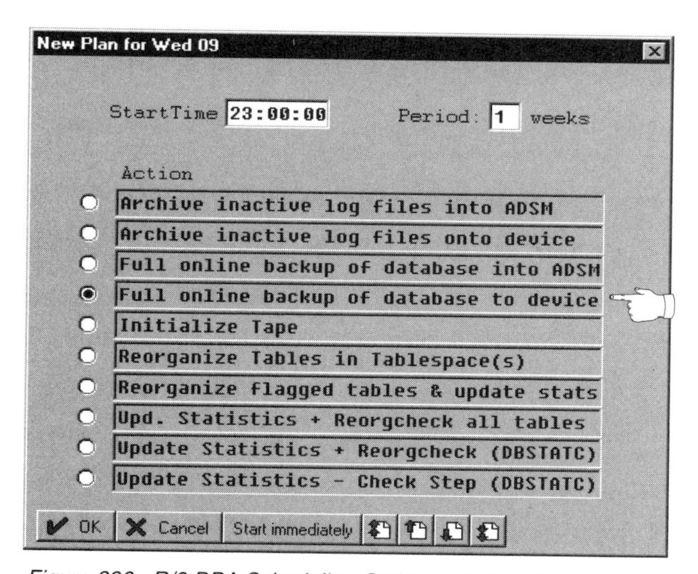

Figure 296. R/3 DBA Scheduling Options - Online Backups

3. Select one of the two options: **Full online backup of database**. You can choose to backup to ADSM or to a device. In this example, we will perform a backup to a device (tape or disk).

- The **Period** option refers to the number of times per week. In this example, we have selected 1, which results in an online backup being taken every

Wednesday at 23:00:00. In order to run an online backup every day of the week, you must select each day of the week and repeat the process.

4. Click **OK**. In the next pop-up window (see Figure 297), specify a path if you want to backup to disk, or a tape device to backup to tape.

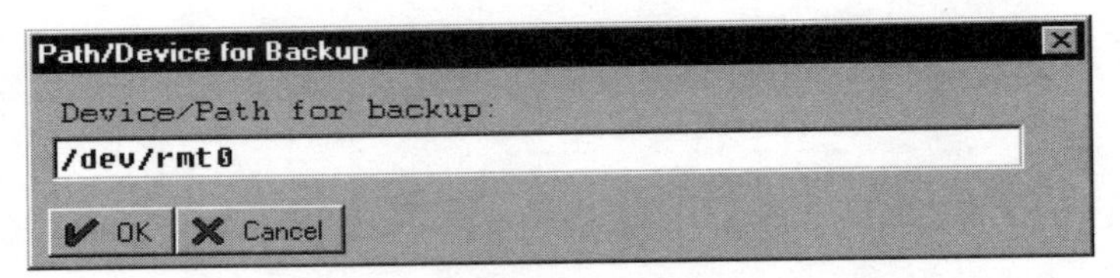

Figure 297. R/3 DBA Scheduling Options - Path/Device for Backup

5. Click **OK**. The scheduled batch jobs are displayed in the DBA Planning Calendar:

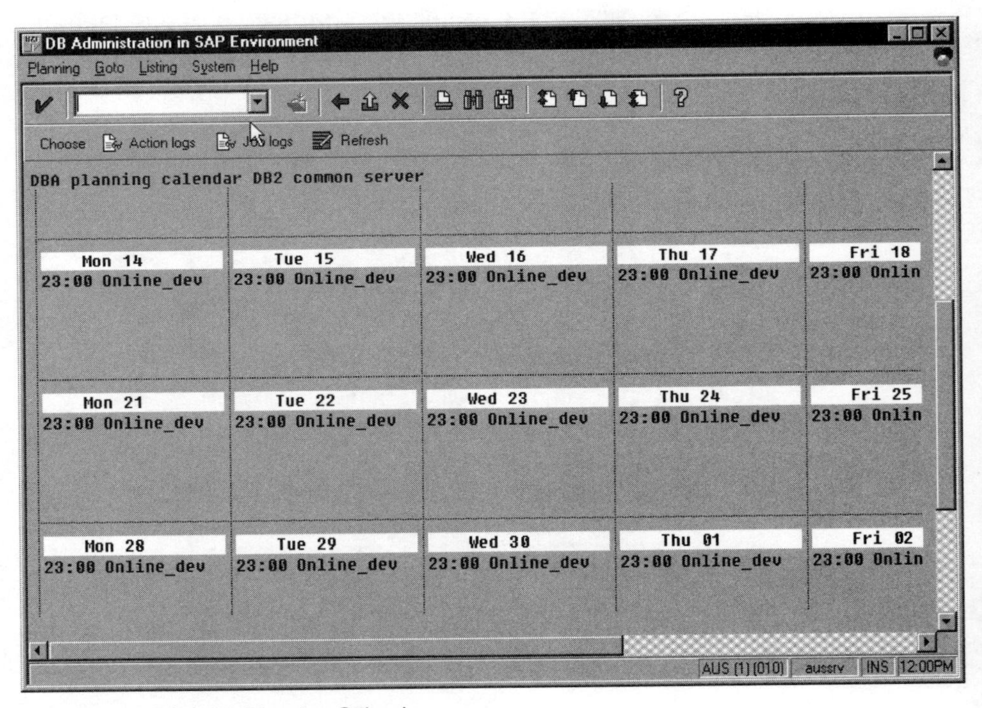

Figure 298. R/3 DBA Planning Calendar

The same information can be displayed by running the **SM37** transaction. If you wish to remove any scheduled jobs, you must use transaction **SM37** and not **DB13**.

8.3.4 Offline Backups

To take an offline backup, you must use the DB2 Control Center. You can not run offline backups using R/3's CCMS.

8.3.4.1 Offline Backups Using the DB2 UDB Control Center

As with online backups you can schedule or run immediate offline backups from the Control Center.

You use a similar process as described in "Online Backups" on page 348, however this time select offline as the mode. You can specify a tape device (identified on Windows NT as \\.\tape0 or on AIX as /dev/rmt0), a path for a file or alternatively offline backups can be directed towards ADSM.

An offline backup is normally taken less frequently than an online backup, since all applications must be disconnected from the database. For example, you might schedule an offline backup to run once a week so as to have the least effect on the users.

To ensure that the R/3 system remains running, although unavailable to the users, throughout the backup, you should set some R/3 parameters related to RECONNECT in the R/3 startup profile as follows. This will prevent the R/3 buffers from being flushed out thus avoiding performance degradation and will also prevent any delay in restarting the R/3 System.

1. Select transaction **RZ10**.

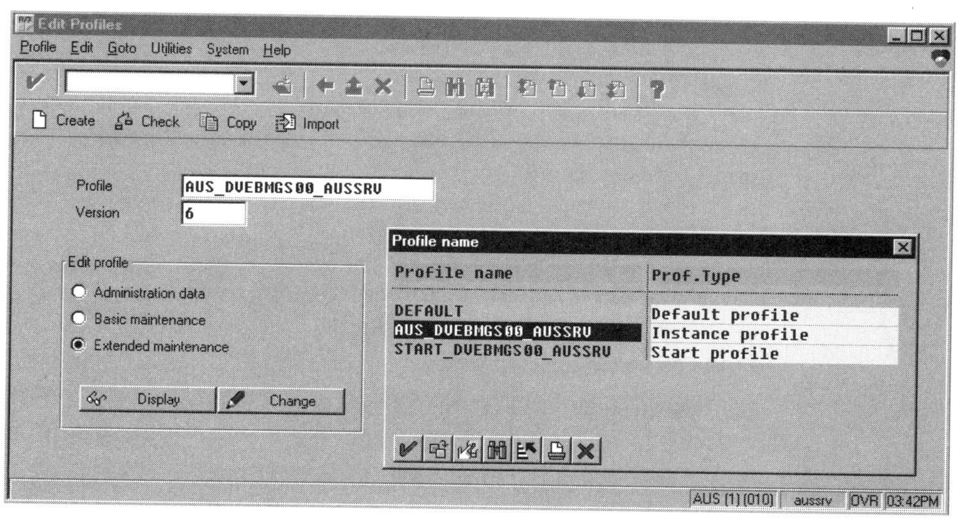

Figure 299. R/3 Edit Profiles

2. Choose the Instance Profile with **Extended maintenance** and click on the **Change** button.
3. Click on the **Create** button and add the 3 new parameters with their corresponding values as identified below.
   - rsdb/reco_sosw_for_db=OFF
   - rsdb/reco_trials=3
   - rsdb/reco_sleep_time=5

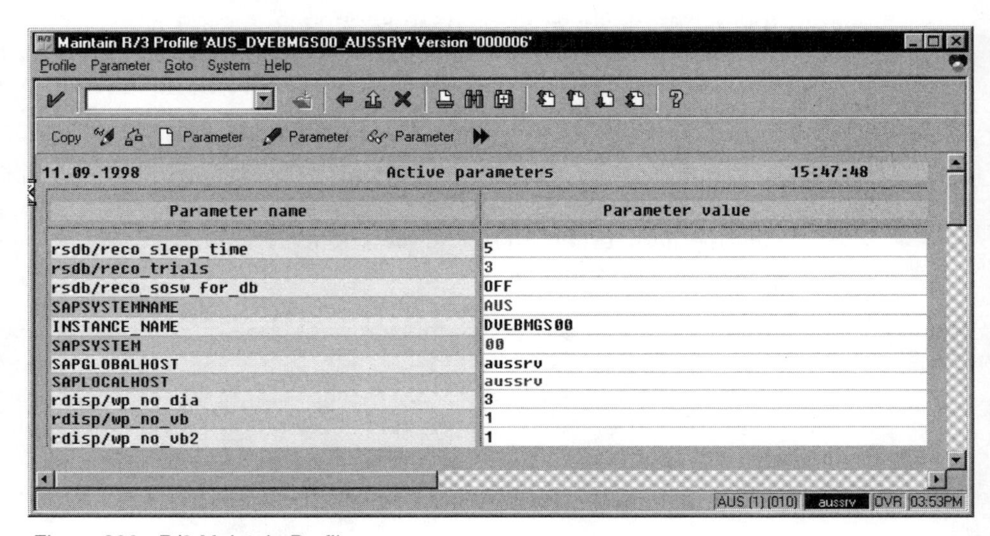

Figure 300. R/3 Maintain Profile

4. Save (or Copy) and reload the profile.

Prior to running an offline backup, you should make sure that no applications are connected to the database. You can do this using the `db2 force applications` command. Bear in mind that this command will rollback any in flight transactions. You can use the Script Center to schedule this task to run before an offline backup.

Create a Script to Disconnect all Applications

Start the Script Center either directly from the Start menu or from within the Control Center.

1. If you are already running the Control Center, click on the Script Center icon in the Toolbar. Otherwise, select **Start** -> **Programs** -> **DB2 for Windows NT** -> **Administration Tools** -> **Script Center**.
2. Select the System Name of the R/3 server from the drop-down list. In this example, this is AUSSRV.

3. Select **Script** and then **New** from the pull down menu.

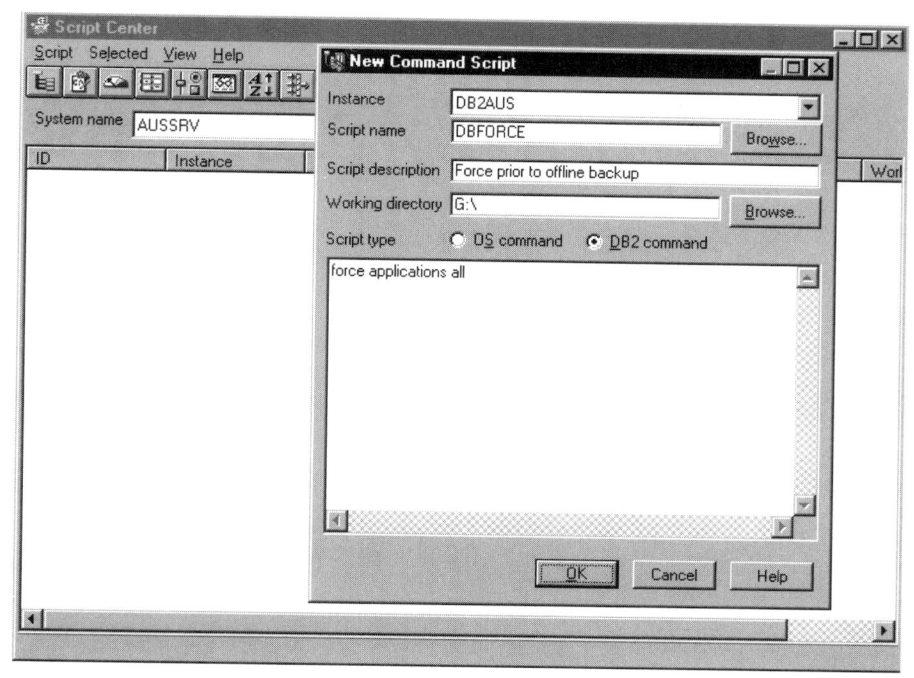

Figure 301. DB2 Script Center

4. Select the appropriate instance name (here DB2AUS) and enter a script name (here DBFORCE) and a description. The script type should be DB2 command. Enter `force applications all` in the command window. Click on **OK**.
5. You see a message indicating that the job has been created and displaying the job number.
6. To schedule the job, right-click on the job you have just created and select **Schedule**.

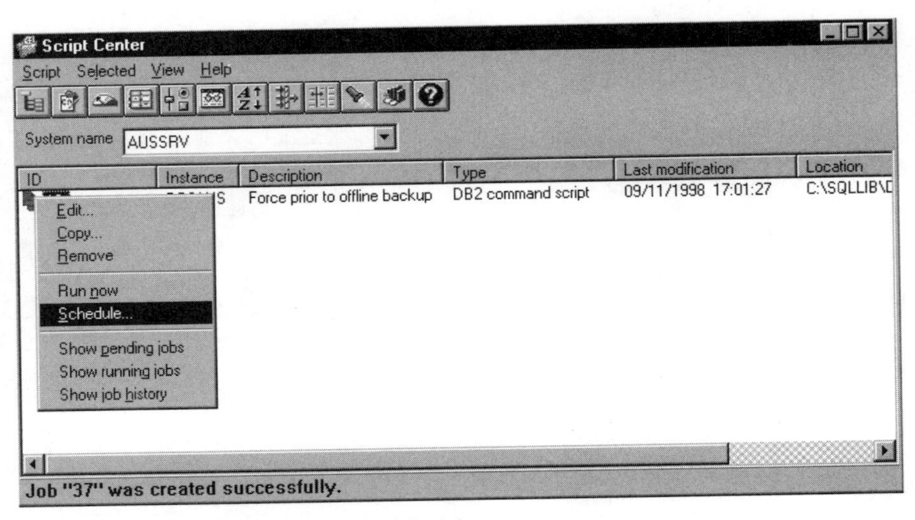

Figure 302. DB2 Script Center Schedule Job

7. Enter the scheduling information. The Schedule Panel is shown in Figure 293 on page 350. Make sure this job runs prior to the offline backup.
8. To verify the configuration, check in the DB2 UDB Journal. Select the name of the server and select the **Pending jobs** tab. You should then be presented with your offline backup job as well as your DBFORCE script.

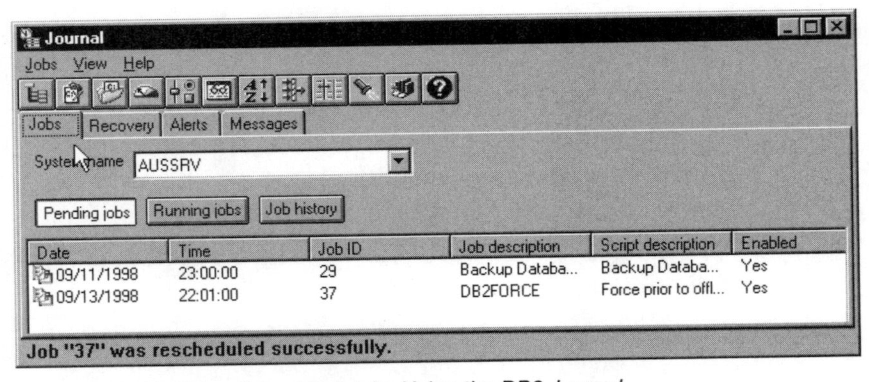

Figure 303. Verifying Scheduled Jobs Using the DB2 Journal

8.4 Moving Offline Log Files to Other Media

Details of how R/3 and DB2 UDB manage the log files has already been discussed earlier in this chapter, in "DB2 UDB Logging Considerations" on page 337. If offline archived log files (in DB2 terminology) are not moved to another media such as tape or ADSM, then you will eventually run out of disk space. You must also plan for the disk space needed by the log_dir and the log_archive directories. The log_dir directory must be large enough to hold the logs based on the number and size of log files. For example, if you have 41 log files, and each log file is 16 MB, then we need at least 656 MB as illustrated in Figure 304. If the log files are not moved out of the log_dir frequently, you should have more that this amount of disk space available.

41 logs
Each log = 16 MB } 16 MB x 41 = **656 MB**

Figure 304. R/3 log_dir Space Requirements

The log_archive directory must have enough space to hold the log files before they are moved to another media. If either of these directories become full then it will not be possible to complete transactions and the R/3 system will become unusable.

8.4.1 Initializing Tapes Using the DB2 UDB Control Center

Tapes must be initialized prior to a database backup or an archive of the log files. The SAP-DB2admin Control Center interface includes a tape management utility which interfaces with the SAP BRARCHIVE tool.

1. From the Control Center main window, right-click on the database <sid>.
2. Select **SAP-DB2admin: Tape Management**.
3. Select the **Tape contents** button to display the list of files on a used tape.
4. To initialize a new tape:
   - Select a tape name from the **Tape names** list, or enter a new tape name.
   - Select the **Force** option and then click on **Initialize tape**. If you select **Soft**, the tape will not be overwritten if it contains data.

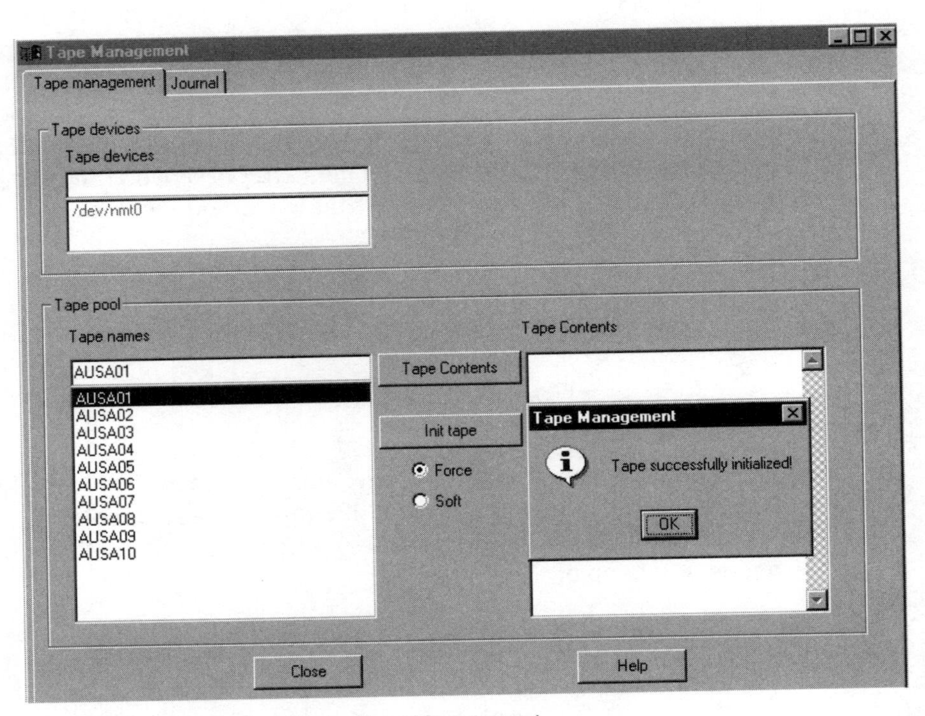

Figure 305. DB2 Control Center Tape Management

If you encounter any problems with tape initialization take a look in the **Journal** tab on the Tape Management panel (not the DB2 Journal). The BRARCHIVE output is captured and transferred to this journal as shown in Figure 306 on page 359:

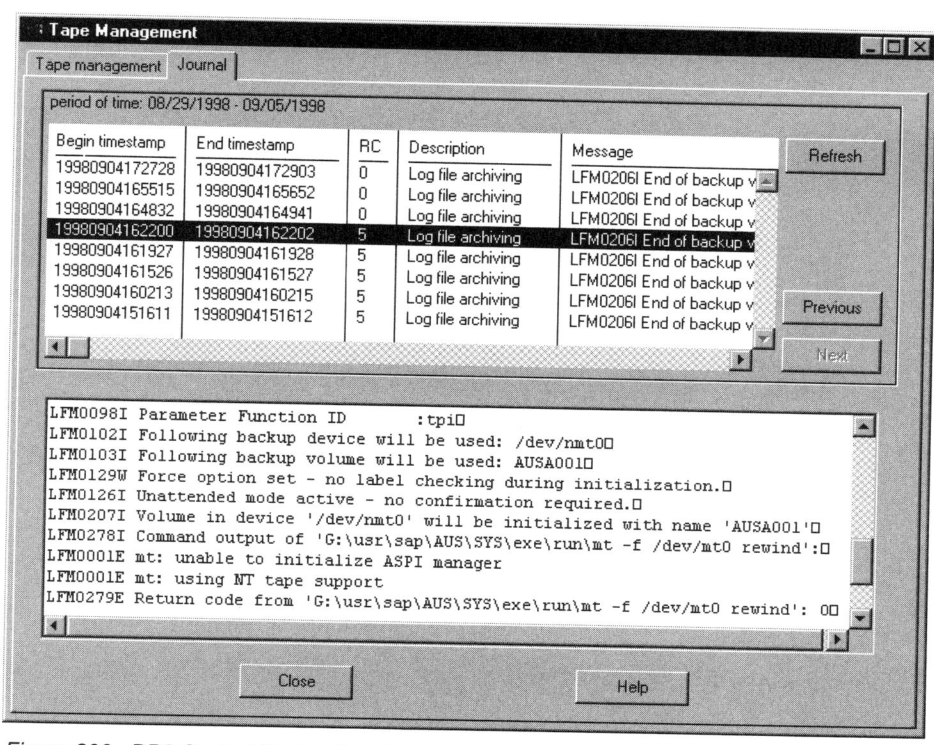

Figure 306. DB2 Control Center Tape Management Diagnostics

8.4.2 Initializing Tapes Using R/3

You can either use transaction **DB13** from the R/3 Frontend, or execute the BRARCHIVE command from a command prompt.

1. From R/3 Frontend, enter transaction **DB13**.
2. In the DBA Planning Calendar, double-click on any day. The following panel is displayed:

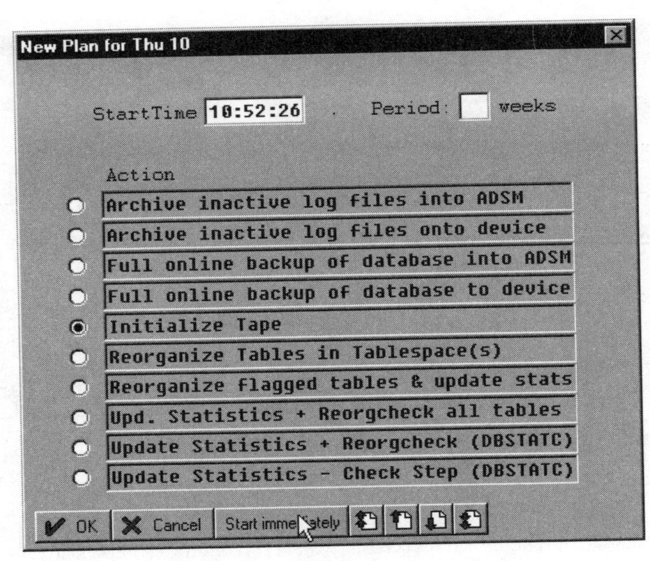

Figure 307. R/3 DBA Scheduling - Initialize Tape

3. Select the **Initialize Tape** option and click on **Start immediately**.
4. Accept the volume id and click on the **Yes** button to continue.
5. To verify that the tape initialization was successful, use transaction **SM37**:

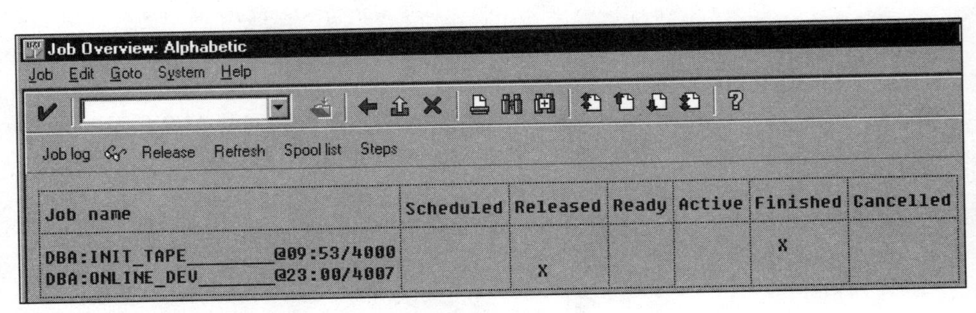

Figure 308. R/3 Job Overview - Tape Initialization

6. Double-click on the job name for a full list of messages.

Alternately, you can use the BRARCHIVE command. The syntax for the initializing a tape is the following, where AUSA10 is the volume name:

```
brarchive -i force -v AUSA10 -out
```

For more detailed information, use the help option:

```
brarchive -h
```

8.4.3 Archiving Offline Logs Using the DB2 UDB Control Center

To archive (or move) offline log files to another media using the Control Center:

1. From the Control Center main window, right-click on the database <sid>.
2. Select **SAP-DB2admin: Logfile Management**.
3. Select the **Archive** tab (see Figure 309 on page 362).
4. In the **Archive up to logfile** listbox, select the log file up to which you wish to archive. All the log files up to and including the one you have selected will be archived.
5. Select the **Delete logfiles** option. This will ensure that the log files are deleted from disk after they are copied to another media.
6. Specify if you want to archive to ADSM or to tape. In this example, we will use tape.
   - If you select ADSM, you have to accept the default value in the Management Class field. This can not be changed for the time being.
   - If you select the Tape option, select the **Tape device** and **Tape name** from the pull-down menus. Make sure the tape has already been initialized. See "Initializing Tapes Using the DB2 UDB Control Center" on page 357.
7. Click on the **Archive** button. You can not change the **Execution mode** for the time being. Synchronous execution means that archiving will take place immediately and that the Control Center will wait until the task is completed.

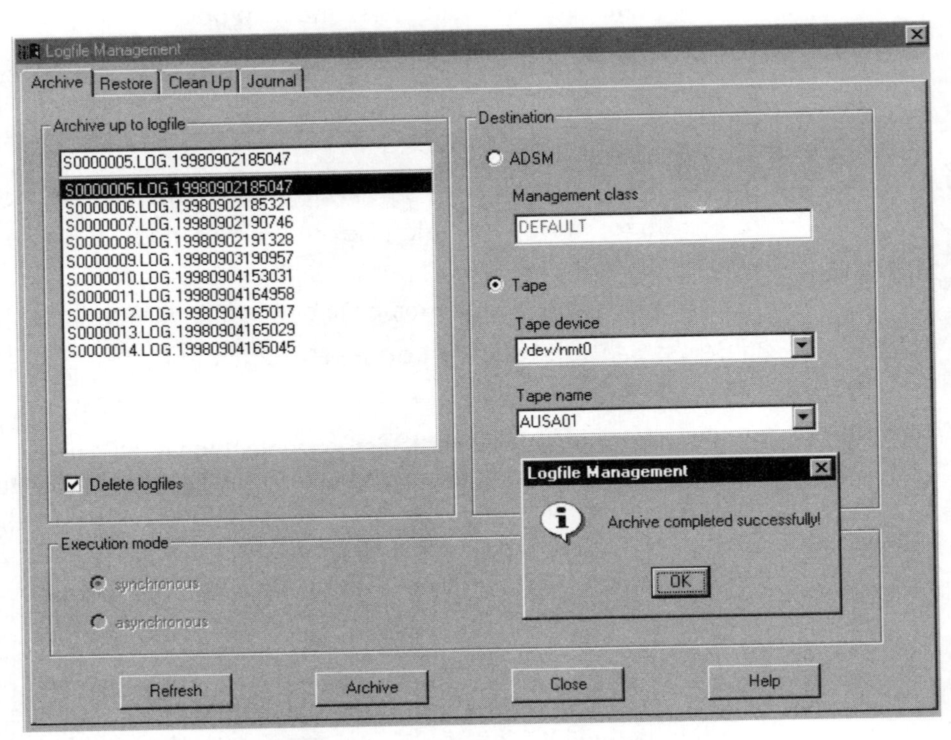

Figure 309. DB2 Control Center Logfile Management - Archive

If you have any problems, you should click the **Journal** tab on the **Logfile Management** panel for more details.

8.4.3.1 Using Clean Up

Optionally, you can choose not to delete the log files during the archive process. In this case, to free up the disk space, you should use the **Clean Up** option after the archive process has finished.

1. To delete the archived log files, select **SAP-DB2admin:Log file Management** from the Control Center after right-clicking on the database <sid>.
2. Select the **Clean up** tab (see Figure 310 on page 363).
3. The **Up to logfiles** listbox contains a list of all the log files that have been archived (moved to another media), but not yet deleted from disk.
4. Choose the last log file to be deleted. All the logs files up to and including the selected log file will be deleted.

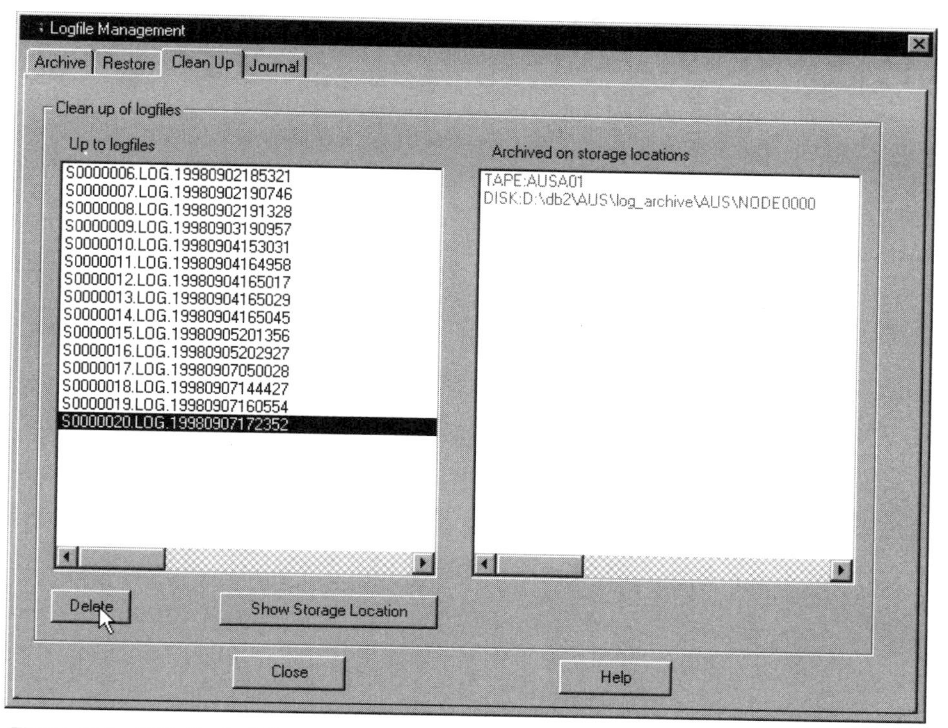

Figure 310. DB2 Control Center Logfile Management - Clean Up

5. Select **Delete**.

Note

Log files can only be deleted in the order that they were created.

8.4.4 Archiving Offline Logs Using R/3

Archiving offline log files from R/3 can either be done from the SAP Frontend using transaction **DB13** or from the command line. Both options are discussed here.

1. From transaction **DB13**, double-click on today's date or on a date in the future. You will be presented with a selection panel.
2. Enter an appropriate time and period and select **Archive inactive log files onto device**. Alternately, you can choose to archive these log files to ADSM.

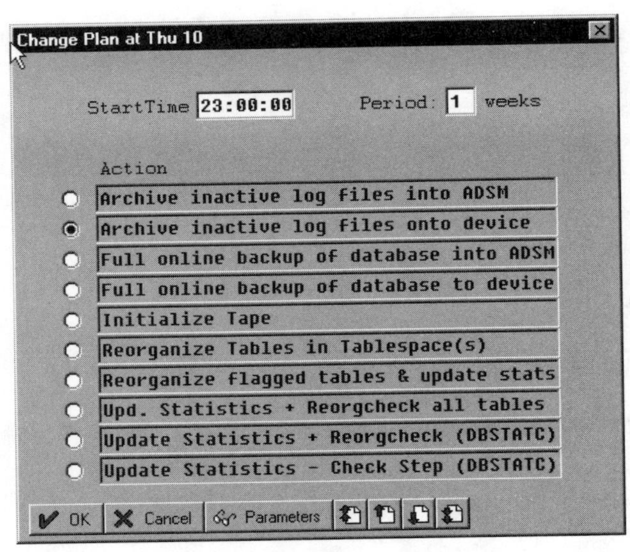

Figure 311. R/3 DBA Scheduling - Archive Inactive Log Files

3. Click on the **OK** button and select the volume you wish to use.
4. You will be asked if you wish to delete the logfiles after archiving. You may wish to delete the files now or at a later time. Select **OK**.

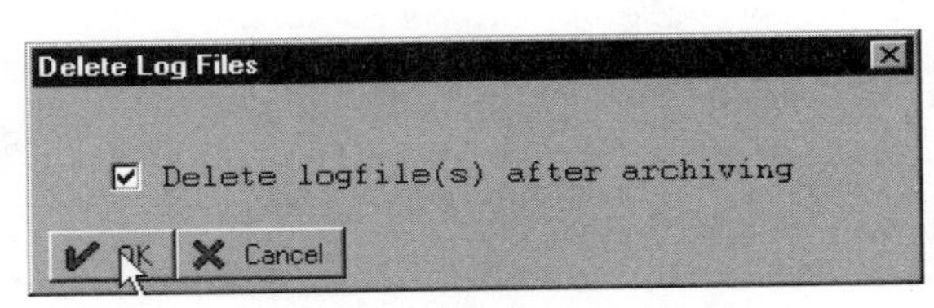

Figure 312. R/3 DBA Scheduling - Delete Logfiles

5. In order to check the successful completion of these jobs, use transaction **SM37**.

The command line option would be something similar to the one illustrated below where `-v` is the volume label and `-out` displays the output to the terminal.

```
brarchive -sd -v AUSA10 -out
```

The options for archiving the offline logs are:

`-sd` save (copy to another media) and delete archive logs

`-s` save archive logs

`-ds` delete saved archive logs

A sample output is illustrated below.

```
LFM0098I Parameter SID                  :AUS
LFM0098I Parameter Instance-Home        :D:\db2aus
LFM0098I Parameter Log_archive path     :D:\db2\AUS\log_archive\
                                         AUS\NODE0000
LFM0098I Parameter DB-Node              :NODE0000
LFM0098I Parameter Action ID            :acyfjvwb
LFM0098I Parameter Function ID          :lfa
LFM0098I Parameter cpio_flags           :-ovB
LFM0098I Parameter cpio_in_flags        :-iduv
LFM0098I Parameter rewind               :G:\usr\sap\AUS\SYS\
                                         exe\run\mt -f $ rewind
LFM0098I Parameter rewind_offline       :G:\usr\sap\AUS\SYS\
                                         exe\run\mt -f $ offlin
LFM0098I Parameter tape_size            :3500.000 MB
LFM0098I Parameter tape_address         :/dev/nmt0
LFM0098I Parameter tape_address_rew     :/dev/mt0
LFM0098I Parameter tape_pool            :AUSA01
LFM0097I Parameter expir_period         :6
LFM0097I Parameter tape_use_count       :100
LFM0011I 13 Log file(s) found for processing, total size 108.242 MB.
LFM0112I Files will not be compressed.
LFM0130I Archive device type: tape
LFM0102I Following backup device will be used: /dev/nmt0
LFM0103I Following backup volume will be used: AUSA10
LFM0126I Unattended mode active - no confirmation required.
LFM0208I Volume with name AUSA10 required in device /dev/nmt0
```

Note

If you are running SAP R/3 on NT, you have to issue the BRARCHIVE command at the NT machine where the R/3 database is located.

8.4.5 Backint

ADSM combined with BACKINT provides an integrated backup and recovery system for the SAP R/3 environment.

- ADSM supplements the existing R/3 utilities already mentioned above with a hierarchical storage management system.
- BACKINT provides the interface between the standard backup and recovery functions as supplied with R/3 and ADSM.

More information on BACKINT is available the IBM SAP Technical Brief, 'ADSM/BACKINT & SAP', produced by the International SAP IBM Competency Center,Walldorf, Germany. This document can be obtained through an IBM representative.

8.5 Recovery of the R/3 Database

In this section, we cover recovery from both offline and online backups, including reapplying log files.

8.5.1 Restoring Offline Backups

A database level offline backup provides you with a complete snapshot of the data at a fixed point in time. This is discussed in "Offline Backups" on page 353.

The advantages of taking an offline database backup are the following:

- You can recover the database from the backup with or without the archive log files.
- You can create a new database from an offline backup and change the definition of the table space containers using a redirected restore.

To recover from an offline backup without reapplying the archive log files:

1. Select the **Restore->Database** option from the Control Center by right clicking on the database in question.

2. On the first page, Backup Image, select the offline backup copy you wish to use (Figure 313 on page 367).

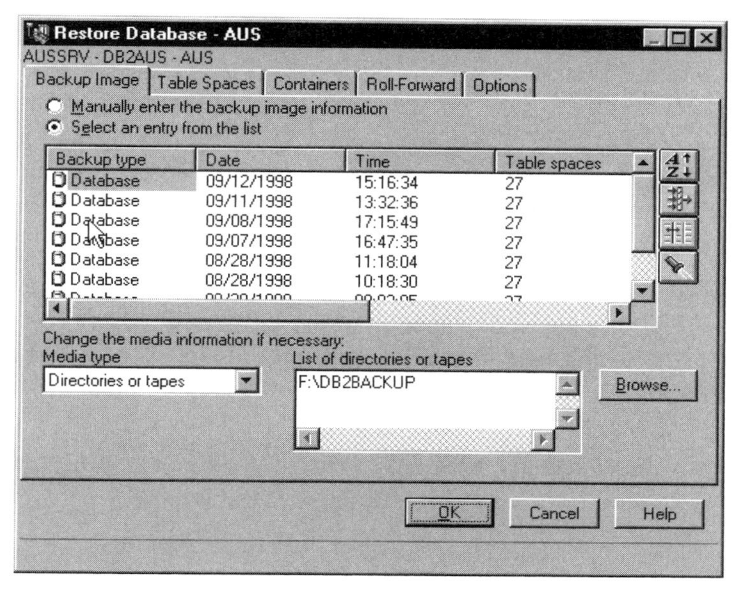

Figure 313. DB2 Control Center Restore Database - Backup Image

3. Select the **Roll-Forward** tab.

   You can restore the database to a specific point in time based on when the last offline backup was executed. Alternatively, you can reapply the logs as long as they still exist in the log_dir and log_archive directories.

   In this example, we simply restore back to the point-in-time the database backup was taken, without reapplying any log files.

4. On the Roll-forward page make sure that both the Roll-Forward and the Leave in roll-forward pending state options are left unchecked.
5. In the Options tab, you will be forced to do an offline recovery since you are doing a full database restore and not an individual table space restore.
6. Make sure the R/3 system has been terminated and that DB2 has been started.
7. Click on **OK** to start the restore.

Instead of using the Control Center interface, you could issue the following command in one step from the DB2 Command Center or a DB2 Command Window:

```
restore database aus from f:\db2backup without rolling forward
```

Alternatively, you can do the same task using the following two commands:

```
restore database aus from f:\db2backup
rollforward database aus stop
```

8.5.2 Restoring from an Online Backup

When restoring from an online backup, the database is not usable until the archive logs have been reapplied by performing a roll-forward operation. If any of these logs have been moved from the log_archive directory to tape or ADSM, you will first have to make these log files available. See “Restoring Archived Log Files” on page 369.

1. From the Control Center GUI, select the **Restore->Database** option.
2. Select the appropriate backup image and then click on the **Roll-Forward** tab.
3. Check the option: Roll-forward (reapply) the logs and select: Roll-forward to the end of the logs or Roll-forward to a point in time.
4. Ensure that Leave in roll-forward pending state is unchecked.

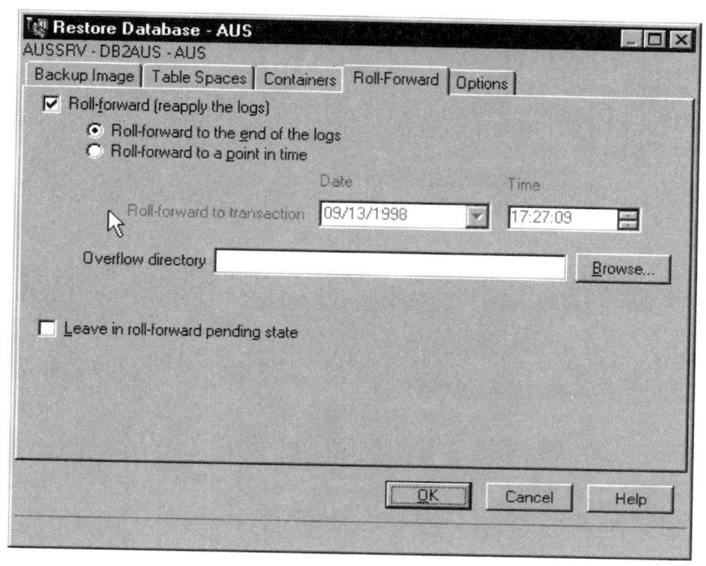

Figure 314. DB2 Control Center Restore Database Roll-Forward

5. Select the **Options** tab, making sure it is an offline recovery and click on **OK**.

The equivalent commands are as follows:

```
restore database aus from f:\db2backup
rollforward database aus to end of logs and stop
```

8.5.3 Restoring Archived Log Files

If any of the log files that you need for recovery have already been moved from the log_archive directory to tape or ADSM, you should restore the log files before performing the restore.

In order to first identify which logs are on which tapes you should:

1. From the DB2 UDB Control Center, select the **SAP-DB2admin:Tape Management** option (we want to scan the tape and list all the logs on the tape).
2. Click on a tape label.
3. Then click on the **Tape Contents** button. This will list all the logs that have been archived to the tape.

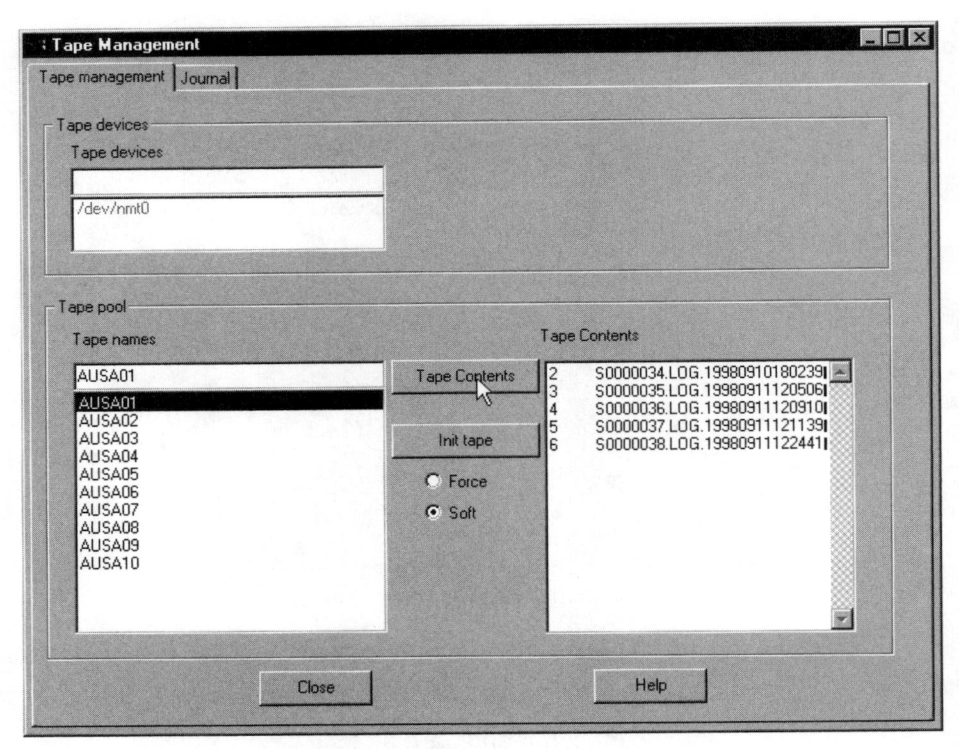

Figure 315. SAP-DB2admin:Tape Management

To restore these log files:

1. From the Control Center, right-click on the database <sid> and select **SAP-DB2admin:Log File Management**.
2. Choose the **Restore** tab.
3. Select the logs you need to recover.

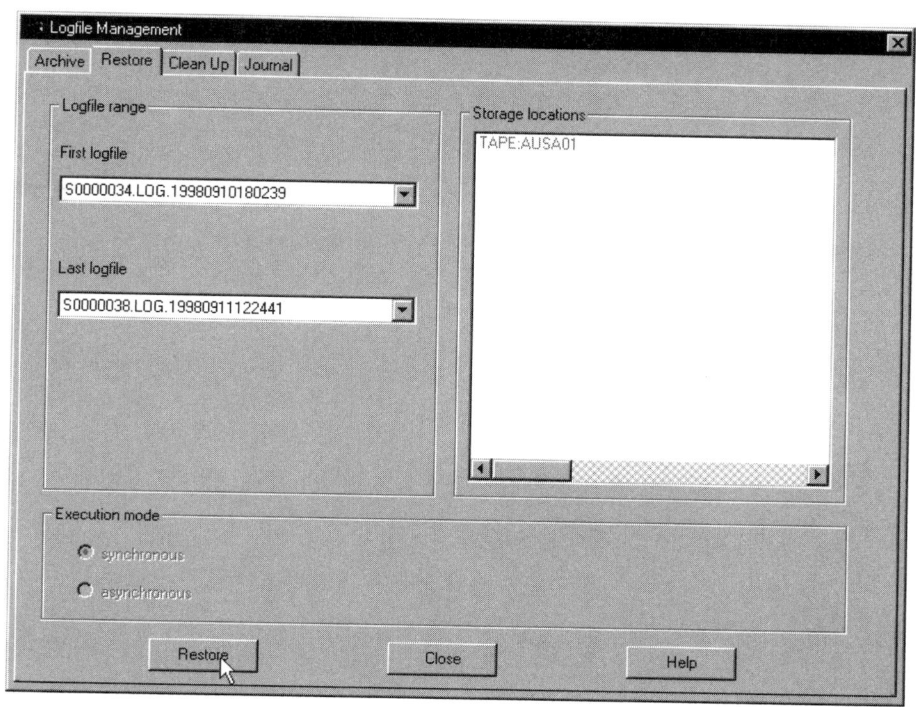

Figure 316. SAP-DB2admin: Logifle Management

4. The tape label should automatically appear in the Storage locations window.
5. Select **Restore**.

After the restore process has completed, you should verify that the restore has worked by clicking on the **Journal** tab in the Logfile Management panel:

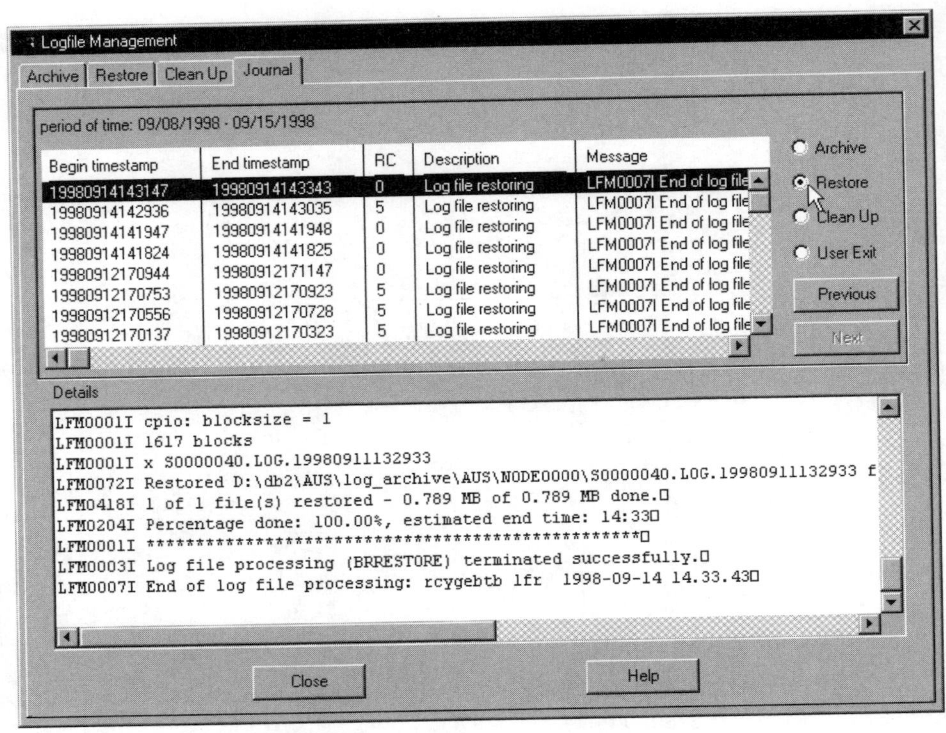

Figure 317. SAP-DB2admin:Logfile Management - Journal

8.6 Generating Statistics and Reorganizing Tables

Here we describe two procedures: generation of statistics (RUNSTATS) and table reorganization (REORG). First we describe these procedures from a DB2 UDB point of view, then we show how these procedures can be invoked from R/3. In an R/3 system, all RUNSTATS and REORG commands should be performed using the R/3 tools, as these tools implement additional features not available from the DB2 tools.

8.6.1 The RUNSTATS Utility

The RUNSTATS utility updates statistics in the system catalog tables to help with the query optimization process. Using these statistics, the database manager optimizer can formulate the best access plan to the data for an SQL statement. The RUNSTATS utility allows you to collect statistics on the data contained in the tables, indexes, or both tables and indexes.

Performing RUNSTATS is recommended in the following situations:

- When a table has been loaded with data, and the appropriate indexes have been created.
- When a table has been reorganized with the REORG utility.
- When there have been extensive updates, deletions, and insertions that affect a table and its indexes.
- Before binding application programs.
- When comparison with previous statistics is desired. Running statistics on a periodic basis permits the discovery of performance problems at an early stage.

8.6.2 The REORG Utility

The performance of SQL statements that use indexes can be impaired after many updates, deletes, or inserts have been made. In many cases, newly inserted rows cannot be placed in a physical sequence that is the same as the logical sequence defined by the index. This means that the database manager must perform additional read operations to access the data, because logically sequential data may be on different physical data pages.

In general, reorganizing a table takes more time than generating statistics. Performance may be improved sufficiently by obtaining the current statistics for your data and rebinding your applications. If this does not improve performance, the data in the tables and indexes may not be arranged efficiently, so reorganization may help.

The REORGCHK command returns information about the physical characteristics of a table, and whether or not it would be beneficial to reorganize that table.

The REORG utility can rearrange data into a physical sequence according to a specified index. REORG has an option to specify the order of rows in a table with respect to an index, thereby clustering the table data according to the index and improving the CLUSTERRATIO or CLUSTERFACTOR statistic values collected by the RUNSTATS utility. As a result, SQL statements requiring rows in the indexed order can be processed more efficiently. REORG also stores the tables more compactly by removing unused space.

Reorganizing your table data is recommended in the following situations:

- A high volume of insert, update, and delete activity.
- Any significant change to the performance of queries which use an index with a high cluster ratio/cluster factor.
- If running statistics (RUNSTATS) does not improve the performance of queries.
- The REORGCHK command indicates a need to reorganize your table.

To execute the REORG utility, you must have SYSADM, SYSMAINT, SYSCTRL or DBADM authority, or CONTROL privilege on the table.

If the REORG utility does not complete successfully, do not delete any temporary files, tables or table spaces. These files and tables are used by the database manager to roll back the changes made by the REORG utility, or to complete the reorganization, depending on how far the reorganization had progressed before the failure.

8.6.3 Using R/3 to Perform RUNSTATS and REORGs

The following functions are available from the CCMS in R/3:

- Update Statistics and Reorgchk all tables
- Update Statistics and Run Check Step
- Update Statistics and Reorgchk based on the Check Step
- Reorganize flagged tables and Update Statistics

We will cover each one of these options in turn.

8.6.3.1 Update Statistics, Reorgcheck All Tables

This option allows you to generate statistics and to perform a REORGCHK on all the tables in the R/3 database. To do this:

1. From the Computing Center Management System (CCMS), select **DB Administration** from the menu followed by **DBA scheduling**.
2. Double click on the current day in the planning calendar. You will be presented with a selection of DBA functions:

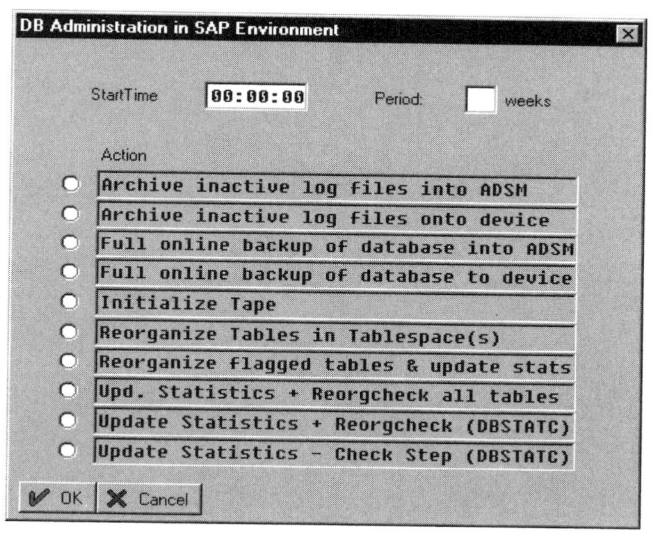

Figure 318. DB Administration from the CCMS

3. Select **Upd. Statistics + Reorgcheck all tables**.
4. Enter the **Start Time** and the frequency.
5. Accept the two further prompts as defaults.

   It is recommended to run this job on a regular basis when the system is not heavily used, for example, every Sunday evening. This job generates table statistics and produces a list of tables showing which tables need reorganizing. Due to the large number of tables in the R/3 database (approximately 16,000), it is usual for this job to take a considerable amount of time, depending on the resources at the R/3 server. For example, on our Windows NT R/3 server, this job took about 1 hour and 30 minutes.

6. In order to check the status of the job, use transaction **SM37**.
7. When the job has finished, to check the output, select the following from the SAP Frontend: **Tools** -> **CCMS**, **Control/Monitoring** -> **Performance**

Menu -> **Database** -> **Tables/Indexes**. Alternatively, execute transaction **DB02**. The following screen is displayed:

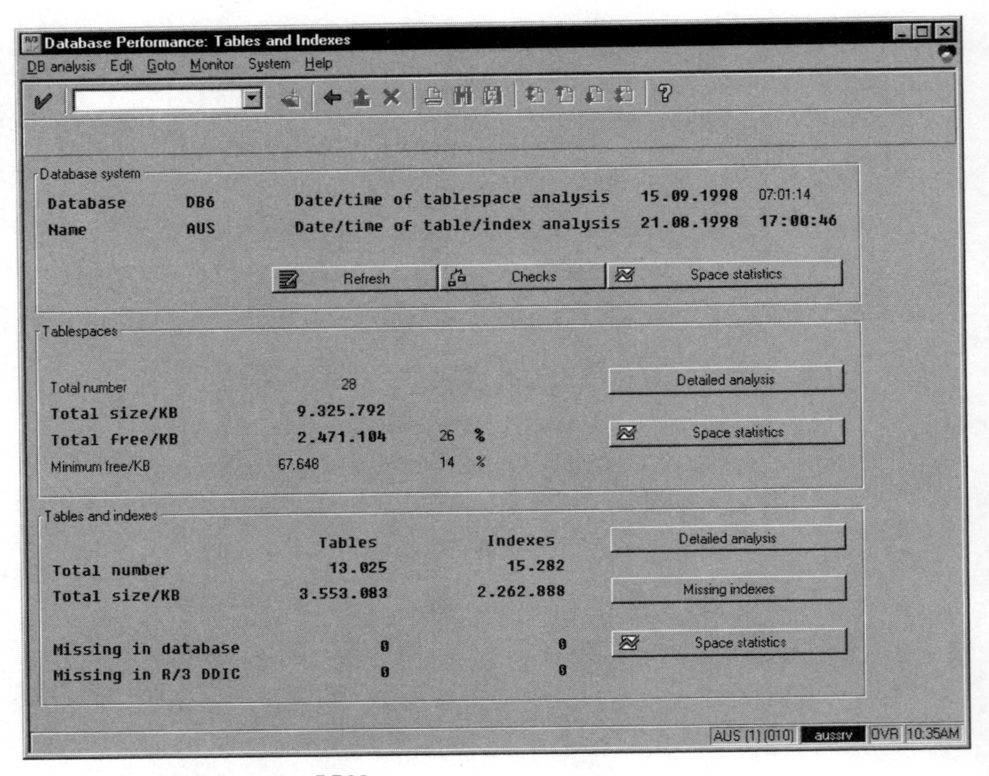

Figure 319. R/3 Transaction DB02

8. Select the **Detailed analysis** button in the Tables and Index section.
9. Once the list of tables is displayed (see Figure 320 on page 377), you can click in any of the data fields such as Table Size or Reorg Recommended and then click on the **Sort** button. You must make sure that the asterisk(*) is highlighted in the Reorg Recommended field before running the sort.

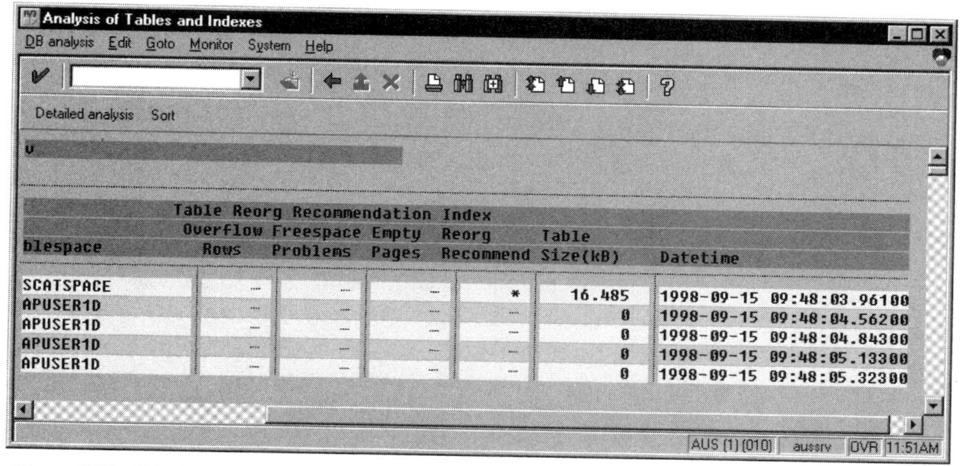

Figure 320. R/3 Analysis of Tables and Indexes

10.In the list of tables:

- If more than 5% of all records in the table are overflow records, an asterisk(*) is displayed in the field Overflow Rows. Overflow records can be caused by updates to varchar type fields.
- If the table size in bytes is less than 70% of the total storage allocated for the table, an asterisk is displayed in the field Freespace Problems.
- If more than 20% of the table's pages are empty, an asterisk is displayed in the field Empty Pages. An empty page can occur when objects such as clients have been deleted.
- If the index cluster ratio is less than 80%, an asterisk will be displayed in the Reorg Recommended field. This is an important indicator to watch out for since a unclustered index may lead to performance degradation. Note that a high cluster ratio for all the indexes on one table may not be possible.

11.In order to schedule a reorganization based on the information collected above, select the option **Reorganize Tables in Tablespace(s)** from the DB Administration panel shown in Figure 318 on page 375 and then select the appropriate table space.

Note

You cannot reorganize individual tables with this option. The section below explains how to reorganize individual tables and how to ensure you have space for a given reorganization task.

8.6.3.2 Update Statistics - Check Step (DBSTATC)

The R/3 database contains an table called DBSTATC. This table contains a list of about 400 tables for which statistics should be generated more often than once a week. These are the tables that R/3 recognizes as experiencing the most changes and for performance reasons need to not only have their statistics generated, but in addition their data may well require reorganizing. Instead of searching through the whole database (about 16000 tables), this job will only generate statistics for these 400 important tables and so reduce the time of a standard RUNSTATS considerably.

As with the *Upd. Statistics + Reorgcheck all tables* option, this job can either be executed immediately or scheduled to run at regular intervals. It is recommended that this job be scheduled to run on a daily basis.

8.6.3.3 Update Statistics + Reorgcheck (DBSTATC)

This job will take the information from the recently updated DBSTATC table and identify which tables, out of the 400 listed, should be reorganized. All invocations of the REORGCHCK command from CCMS updates R/3 tables such as DB6TREORG and DB6IREORG. If a REORGCHCK is run from outside R/3, these tables will not be updated.

Note

Unlike the backup and recovery tasks that can be executed from the DB2 Control Center, all RUNSTATS and REORG tasks for the R/3 database should be run from the R/3 CCMS.

As with the *Upd. Statistics + Reorgcheck all tables* option, this job can either be executed immediately or scheduled to run at a regular interval. It is recommended that this job be scheduled to run on a daily basis after the *Update Statistics - Check Step (DBSTATC)* job has completed.

8.6.3.4 Reorganize Flagged Tables & Update Stats

This option will use the information generated by the previous option, *Update Statistics + Reorgchk (DBSTATC)*. It will only reorganize those tables which have been marked for reorganization.

SAP

Note

The table REORGanizations are executed online and involve no outage of the R/3 System.

1. Double-click on a day in the DBA Scheduling panel and select the **Reorganize flagged tables & update stats** option.

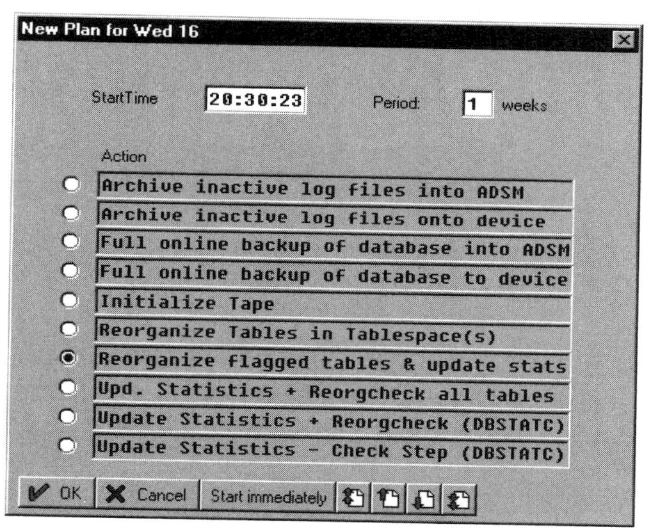

Figure 321. R/3 CCMS Reorganize Flagged Tables

2. You can either **Start immediately** or schedule it to run it later.
3. You will then be presented with a list of tables (from DBSTATC) from which you can either select individual tables to reorganize or select them all.

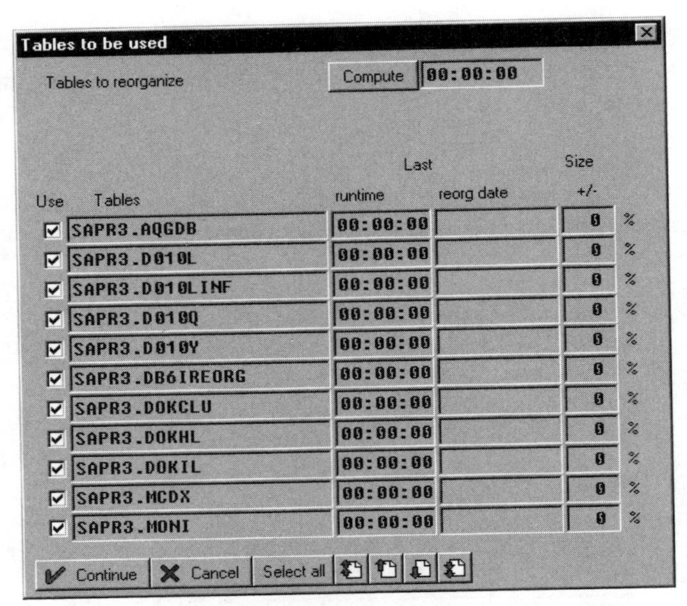

Figure 322. R/3 CCMS Tables to be Used for reorganization

4. The reorganization process uses the PSAPTEMP table space. You should make sure that the free space in this table space is at least twice the size of the largest table to be reorganized. To determine the free space in PSAPTEMP, run transaction **DB02**. Select **Detailed analysis** in the Table spaces section of the panel. In this example we have identified 127616KB of free space:

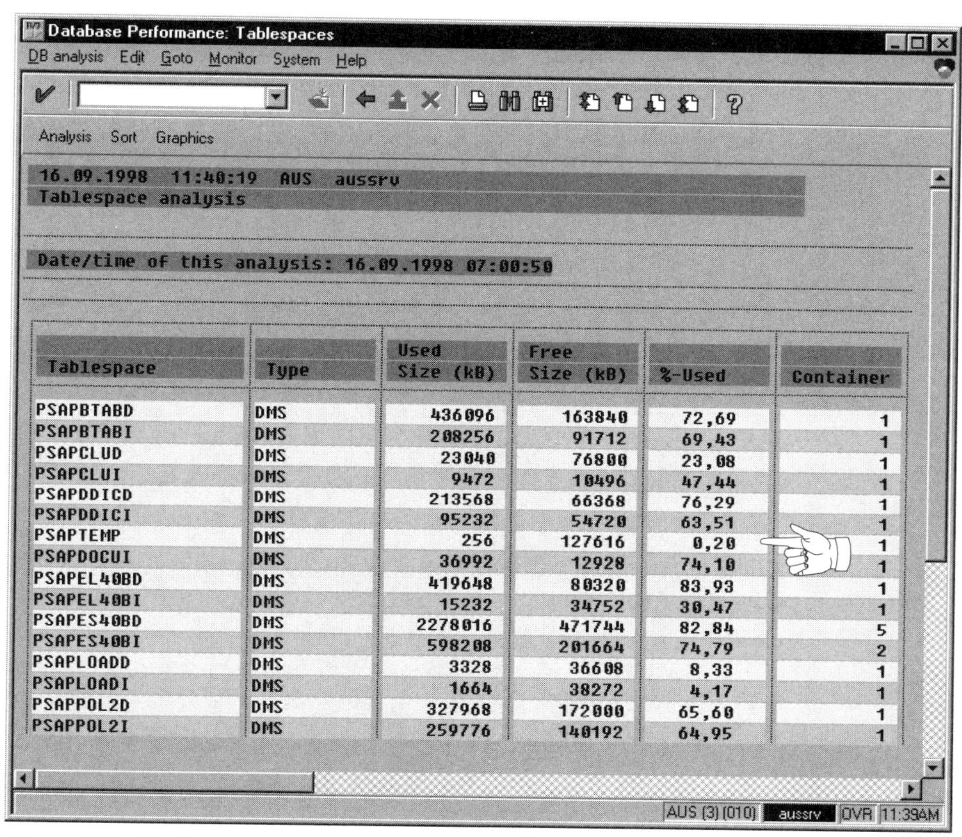

Tablespace	Type	Used Size (kB)	Free Size (kB)	%-Used	Container
PSAPBTABD	DMS	436096	163840	72,69	1
PSAPBTABI	DMS	208256	91712	69,43	1
PSAPCLUD	DMS	23040	76800	23,08	1
PSAPCLUI	DMS	9472	10496	47,44	1
PSAPDDICD	DMS	213568	66368	76,29	1
PSAPDDICI	DMS	95232	54720	63,51	1
PSAPTEMP	DMS	256	127616	0,20	1
PSAPDOCUI	DMS	36992	12928	74,10	1
PSAPEL40BD	DMS	419648	80320	83,93	1
PSAPEL40BI	DMS	15232	34752	30,47	1
PSAPES40BD	DMS	2278016	471744	82,84	5
PSAPES40BI	DMS	598208	201664	74,79	2
PSAPLOADD	DMS	3328	36608	8,33	1
PSAPLOADI	DMS	1664	38272	4,17	1
PSAPPOL2D	DMS	327968	172000	65,60	1
PSAPPOL2I	DMS	259776	140192	64,95	1

Figure 323. R/3 CCMS Database Performance Table spaces

5. To determine the size of the largest table, again from transaction **DB02**, select **Detailed analysis** from the Tables and Indexes section. You can either enter a particular table or table space or leave the prompts blank which will display space usage details of all the tables that exist in the R/3 System:

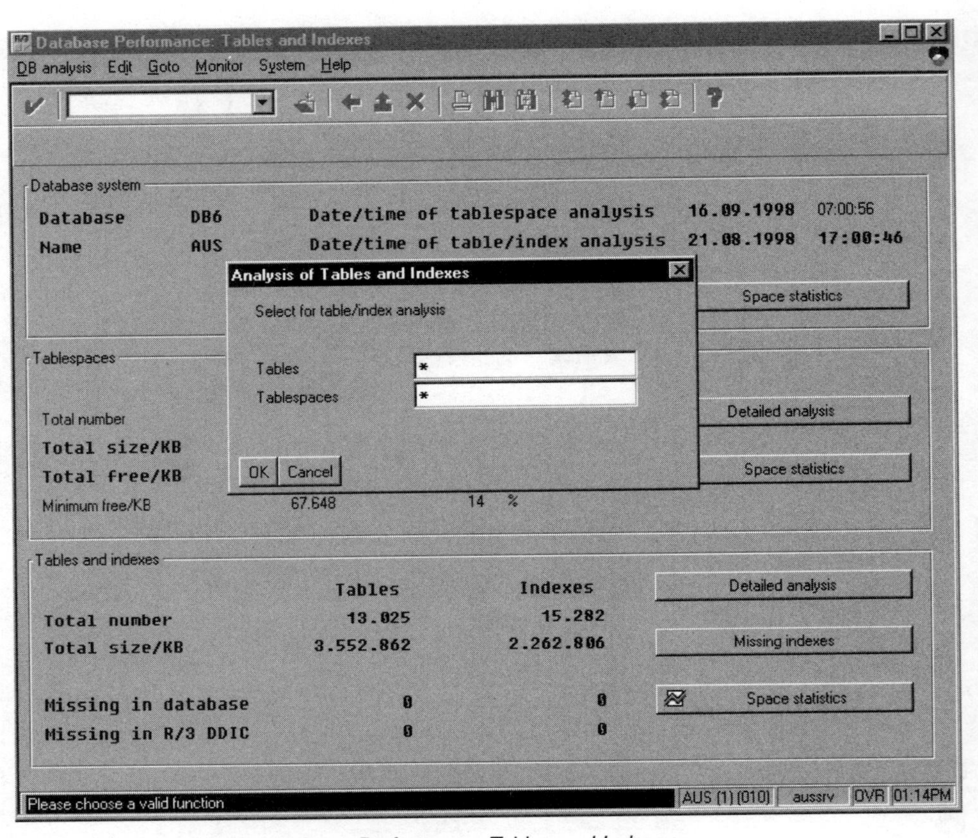

Figure 324. R/3 CCMS Database Performance Tables and Indexes

6. The output will look something similar to the following screen:

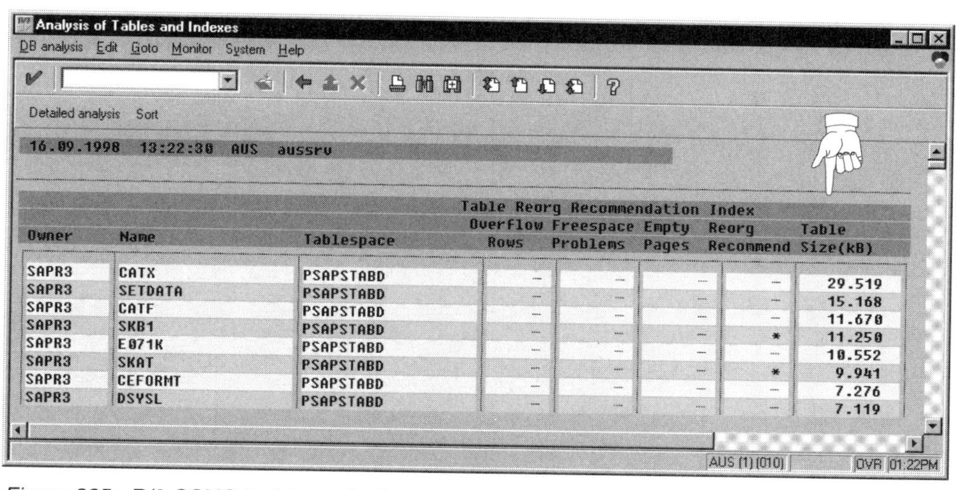

Figure 325. R/3 CCMS Database Performance Tables and Indexes Results

7. Once you have selected the tables you wish to reorganize and you have made sure there is enough space, select the **Continue** button from the *Tables to be used* window.
8. You can then start the reorganizations immediately or schedule them.
9. Use transaction **SM37** to check that the job has completed successfully.

8.6.4 Database Planning Calendar

In addition to scheduling the various individual jobs as described above, the R/3 Database Administration facility also includes a planning guide. You can either schedule the RUNSTATS and REORGs as detailed above or simply select the first and the last options from the DB Planning Strategy Patterns panel shown in Figure 326 on page 384.

1. Select **Planning** from the Database Planning Calendar menu, then **Planning Pattern**.
2. Select **Upd. statistics + reorg. check all tables (Sun.weekly)**.
3. Select **Check step, upd.statistics + reorg. check on DBSTATC (daily)**.

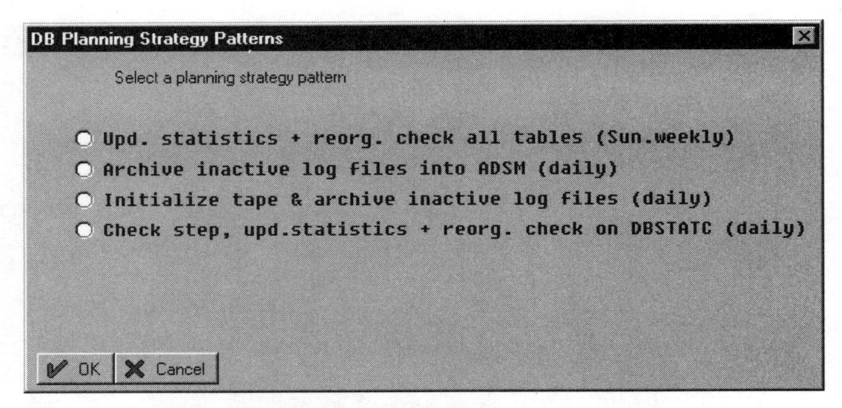

Figure 326. R/3 CCMS Database Planning Patterns

4. You will then be prompted for a time and a schedule:

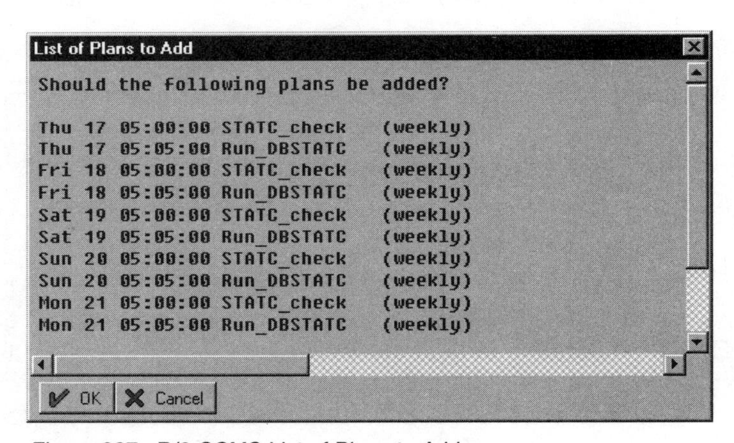

Figure 327. R/3 CCMS List of Plans to Add

Using this process to run the RUNSTATS and REORGCHK tasks on a regular basis is recommended by SAP. Note however, that you can not schedule REORGs using the R/3 CCMS planning pattern option.

8.7 Index Maintenance

You can use the transaction **DB02** to check on lost indexes.

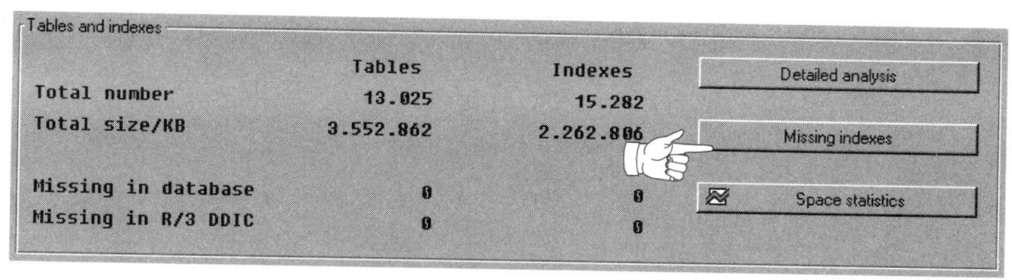

Figure 328. R/3 CCMS Missing Indexes

In R/3 terms, a lost index refers to an index that existed at one time. Every time an index is created against a table, its existence is recorded. System performance can be negatively effected if an index is missing. A table can lose an index under the following conditions:

- During a system update.
- After a reorganization.
- As a result of deleting an index.

8.8 Table Space Maintenance

This section describes how DB2 manages data, how to monitor this and how to maintain the table spaces.

8.8.1 Data Management

DB2 allows you to separate the data and any indexes from the same table into different table spaces. It is recommended to spread these table spaces across different devices in order to improve response times.

Table spaces use containers, which can be files, directories or raw devices, to store their contents. In addition, DB2 stores data in 4KB pages which are then blocked in *extents* of between 8 to 64 pages (based on DB2 UDB V5.0). These extents control how much data is written to one container before writing to the other.

When database objects grow, additional space is allocated by extents. If there is not enough free space, the allocation of new extents will fail and the database will become unusable. In order to monitor table space growth:

1. In transaction **DB02**, select **Detailed analysis** from the **Table spaces** panel.

2. Once the list of table spaces has been displayed, you can sort on the column **%-used** to identify those table spaces which are in danger of running out of free space.

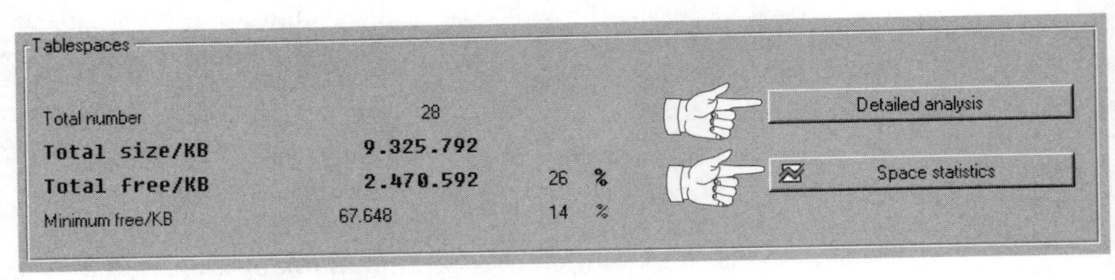

Figure 329. R/3 CCMS Table spaces Detailed Analysis.

3. To analyze the trends of table space growth, either double click on a table space as presented in the list. Alternatively select **Space statistics** from the Tablespaces panel.

8.8.2 Adding Table Space Containers

You are advised to use the DB2 Control Center for increasing the size of table spaces. You can extend a DMS table space by adding extra containers. You do not have to shut down the R/3 system. To add a container to a table space:

1. From the DB2 Control Center, click on the <sid> database to expand its contents:

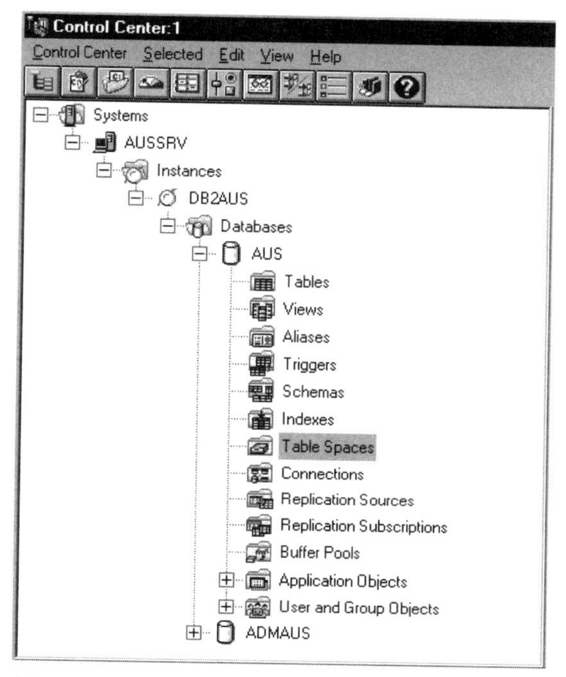

Figure 330. DB2 Control Center Database Tree

2. Click on **Table Spaces**. This will list all the table spaces in the contents pane.
3. Right-click on the table space that you wish to add a container to and select **Alter**.

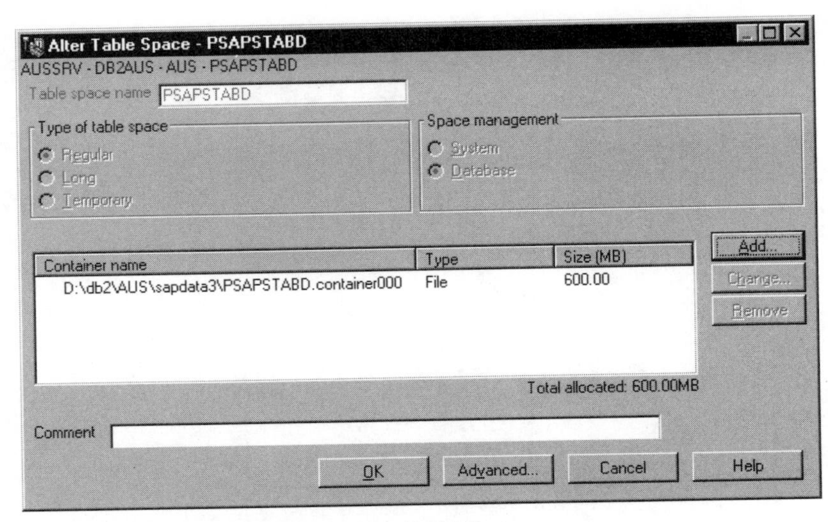

Figure 331. DB2 Control Center Alter Table Space

4. Make a note of the existing container name and then click on **Add**. It is recommended that you add containers of the same size as any existing containers.

5. In our example we will add a new container to the PSAPSTABD table space and will place it on a different device, F:\, with a container name of `PSAPSTABD.container001`.

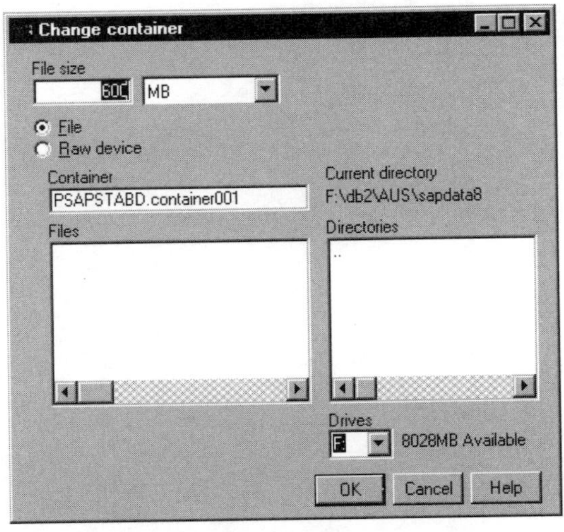

Figure 332. DB2 Control Center Add Container

6. Select **OK**. This will take you back to the initial Alter Table Space panel. At this point you can continue to add more containers or click on the **OK** button to execute the change.

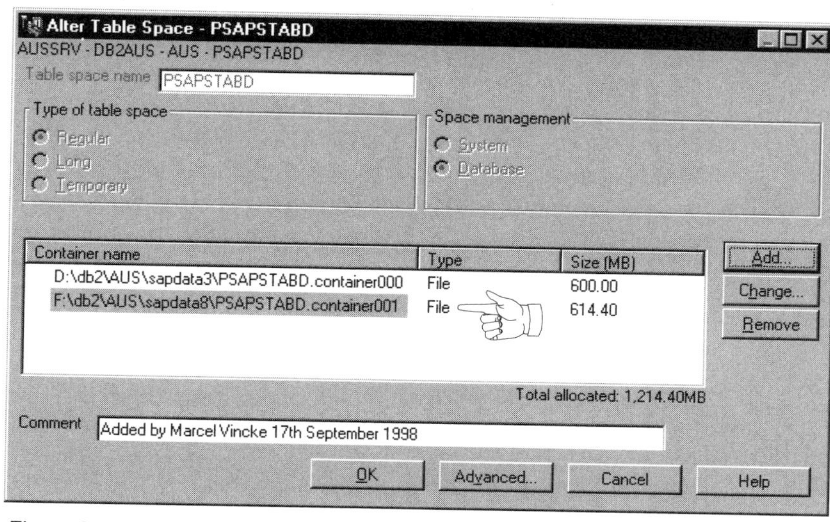

Figure 333. DB2 Control Center Alter Table Space

7. When a new container is added, DB2 will rebalance the table space in the following way:

   - It will first create the container and allocate the specified amount of pages to the container.
   - When the above allocation is complete, DB2 will begin to rebalance the original data across the new container(s).
   - For large table spaces, this process may take a considerable amount of time.

8. In order to confirm that the data has been successfully rebalanced, you can look in the db2diag.log file:

```
1998-09-17-13.56.23.710000   Instance:DB2AUS   Node:000
PID:174(db2syscs.exe)   TID:322   Appid:none
buffer_pool_services  sqlb_rebalance   Probe:2204

Rebalancer for tablespace 27 started.

1998-09-17-13.56.24.532000   Instance:DB2AUS   Node:000
PID:174(db2syscs.exe)   TID:322   Appid:none
buffer_pool_services  sqlb_rebalance   Probe:2876

Rebalancer for tablespace 27 completed successfully.
Last extent moved 998.

1998-09-17-14.00.59.397000   Instance:DB2AUS   Node:000
PID:174(db2syscs.exe)   TID:383   Appid:*LOCAL.DB2AUS.980917180059
buffer_pool_services  sqlbStartPools   Probe:0   Database:ADMAUS
```

In order to see the results of this change in the R/3 CCMS, you must use the **Refresh** button on the Database panel of transaction **DB02**:

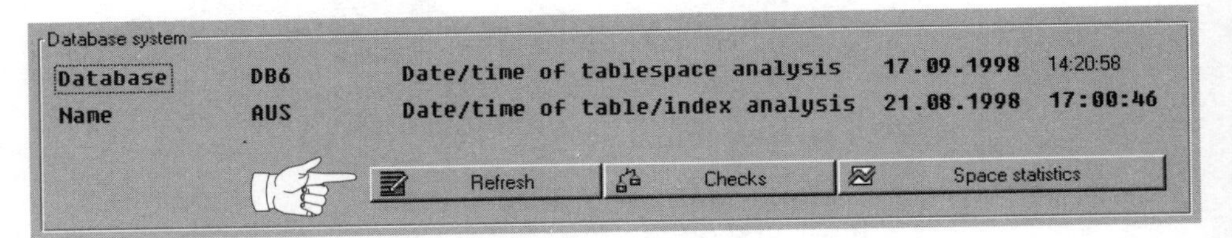

Figure 334. CCMS Performance Menu Database System

Chapter 9. Monitoring and Tuning the R/3 System

In this chapter we discuss some of the monitoring and tuning facilities available in both R/3 and DB2. This chapter is intended to acquaint you with the tools available in the DB2 and R/3 environment. This chapter is not intended to provide a definitive set of rules for tuning your SAP environment because R/3 configuration details can vary significantly from one installation to another. While there are many parameters that may be set to tune the DB2 database manager and the R/3 application server, learning to tune application queries by understanding SQL explains may be the area where you can most improve performance; we discuss this also in this chapter.

9.1 Monitoring the R/3 System

R/3 provides a variety of monitoring tools which are very useful to help you understand the behavior of the R/3 processing environment. If your R/3 system is operating at unacceptable performance levels, these monitors provide the proper tuning insight to enable you to make sure your R/3 installation is operating at peak efficiency.

The R/3 CCMS provides functions for:

- Checking system status and operation modes
- Locating and eliminating potential problems as quickly as possible
- Early diagnosis of potential problems, for example resource problems in the host or database system, that could adversely affect the R/3 system.
- Analyzing and tuning the R/3 system and its environment (host and database systems) in order to optimize the throughput of the R/3 system.

The CCMS provides graphical monitors for continuous runtime monitoring of the complete R/3 environment. The CCMS also provides list-oriented monitors for higher detailed analysis. You can generate comprehensive statistics for system tuning and for error analysis.

The CCMS also independently monitors other important components surrounding the R/3 system, for example, the operating system and network services, and the database system. It can also report potential problems automatically using alerts (alarm messages).

9.1.1 Maintaining Alert Thresholds Using R/3

Alert thresholds enable the administrator of the R/3 system to create a series of automatic checks on the system. For example, if a file system becomes more than 90% full, the entry for that filesystem in the Alert Monitor will be displayed in red.

Alert threshold maintenance is the first step before doing the monitoring and tuning. Initially, you can use the recommended SAP default values for the following thresholds:

- Database
- Operating System
- Performance
- Network
- R/3 Buffers
- System Log
- Others

You can also view the alert threshold settings for all servers or for each individual server in the R/3 system.

The Alert Threshold Maintenance tool enables you to easily change the system default alert threshold values, and also to copy sets of alert thresholds from one server to other servers.

9.1.1.1 Maintaining Alert Thresholds

To start the Alert Threshold Maintenance tool, from the R/3 main menu, select **Tools->CCMS, Configuration->Alert Monitor ->Thresholds (3.X)** or use the transaction code **RZ06**.

The Maintain Alert Threshold screen is displayed:

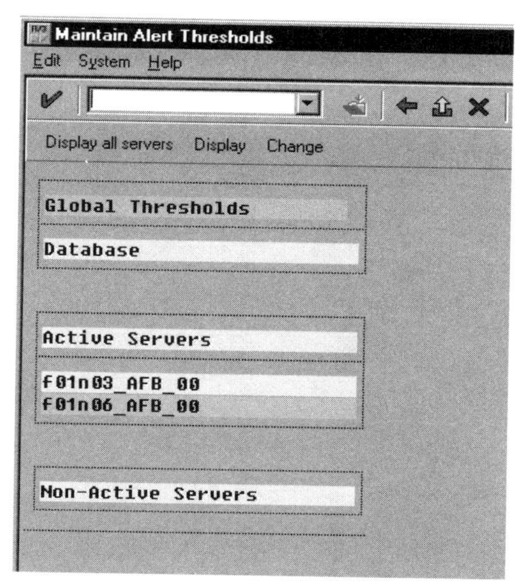

Figure 335. Maintain Alert Thresholds

A list of active servers and non-active servers is shown.

Changing Alert Thresholds for a Selected Server

To change alert thresholds for a selected server, perform the following steps:

From the Maintain Alert Thresholds screen (Figure 335), highlight the required server by clicking on it with the mouse, and click **Change**. In this example, the screen: *Alert Thresholds* for the server f01n03 is displayed:

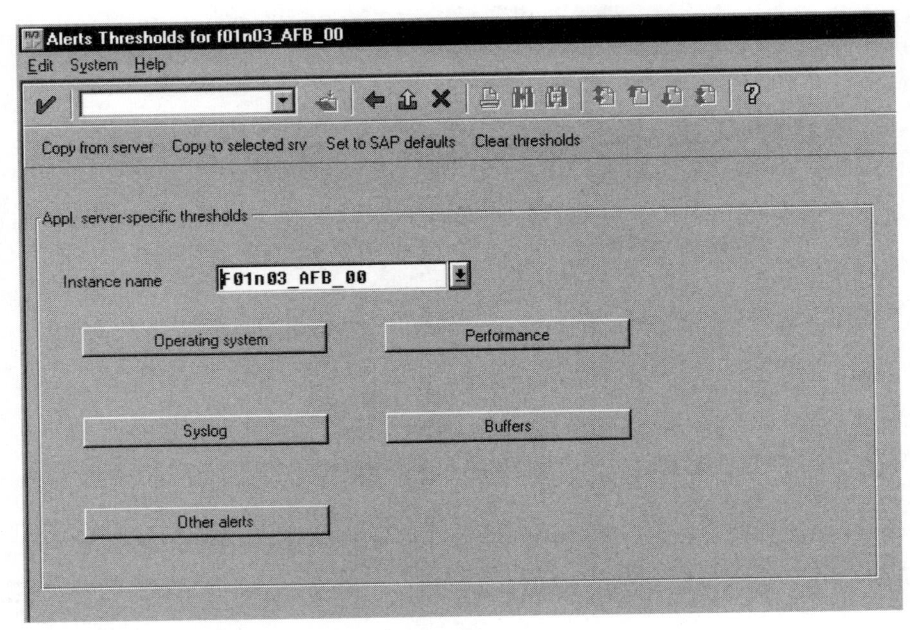

Figure 336. Alerts: Thresholds for f01n03_AFB_00

You have the following options:

- **Copy from server**

  Use this option to copy any existing alert threshold from any server or from the system default (indicated by *<Default>* or *<SAP Default>)* to the current server. If any of the Alerts thresholds are not defined, such as Operating System, Performance, System log, Buffers or Other, then the copy will not be performed.

- **Copy to selected servers**

  Use this option to copy the alert threshold values for the current server to one or more servers.

- **Set to SAP defaults**

  SAP recommends a set of alert thresholds for all types of alerts. When you select this option, all the alert thresholds for the current server will be set to the SAP default values.

- **Clear thresholds**

  Use this option to delete the alert thresholds for the selected server.

The following alert threshold values for all components were set to the SAP defaults as the first step:

1. **Operating System.** Here we see thresholds relating to the use of CPU, memory, swap space, disk, filesystems and network:

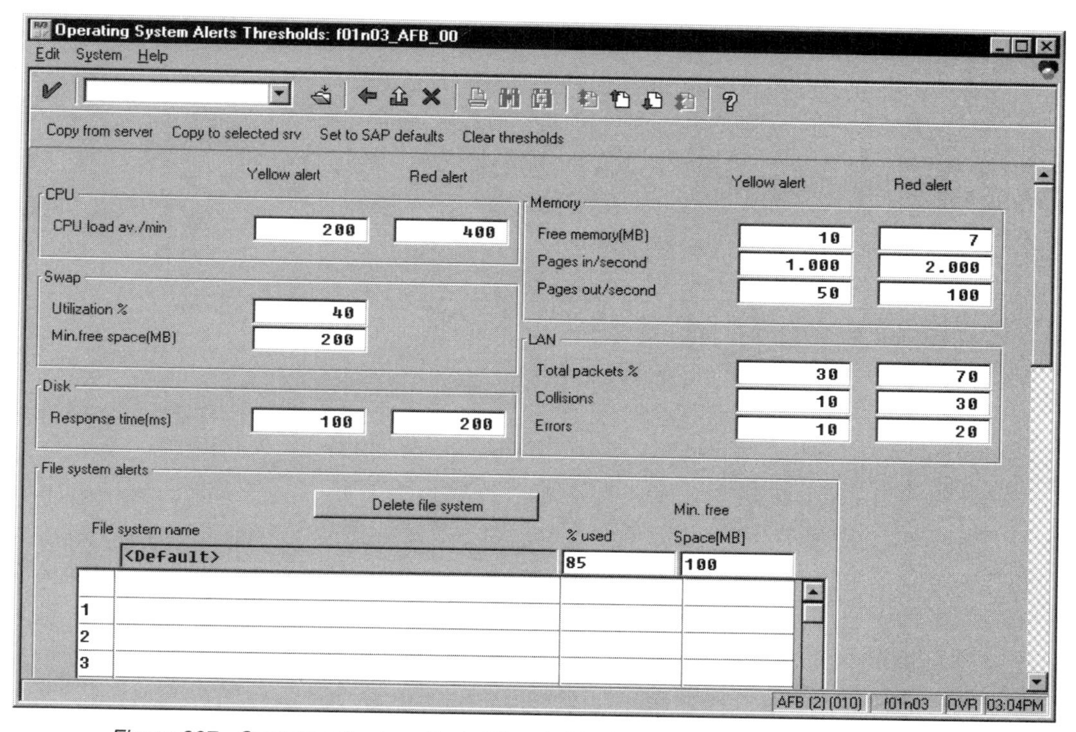

Figure 337. Operating System Alerts Thresholds: f01n03_AFB_00

Note that the format of the filesystem fields depends on the operating system. For example, for Windows NT: d:\db2\AUS\db2dump and for AIX: /db2/AFB/db2dump, where AFB or AUS is our <sid>.

2. **Performance**. Here we see thresholds relating to the use of the different kinds of R/3 work processes: dialog, update, batch and spool:

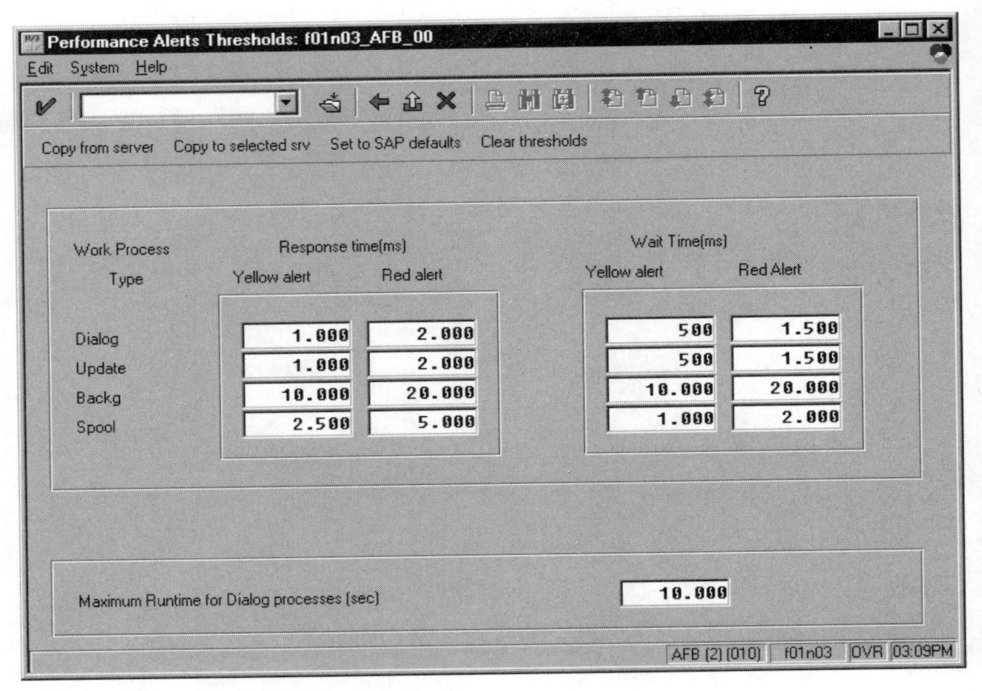

Figure 338. Performance Alert Thresholds

The last value, *Maximum Runtime for Dialog processes (sec)* means that the alert will be generated if the running time for a dialog process is greater than 10,000 seconds (or around 2 hours 45 minutes). Note that in this screen, a period is used as a separator between the thousands and units.

3. **Syslog**. Here we see thresholds related to R/3 syslogs, including a list of errors to exclude from being logged. You may choose to deal with a range of alert values or individual alert values:

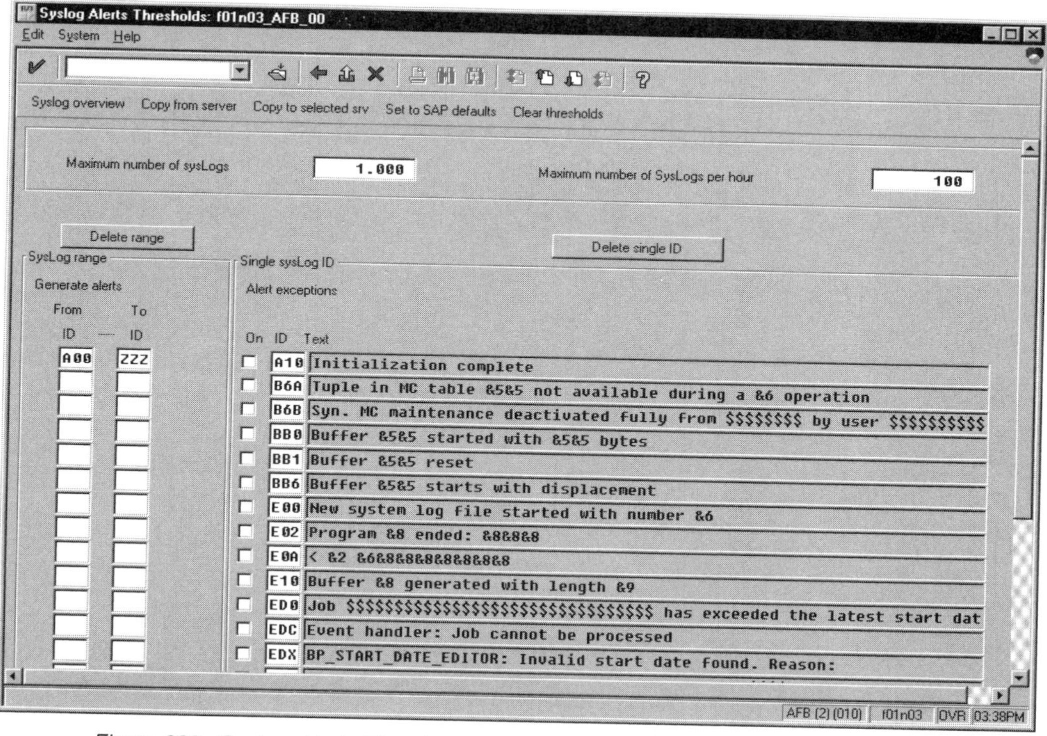

Figure 339. System Alerts Thresholds: f01n03_AFB_00.

4. **Buffers**. Here we see thresholds related to the different R/3 buffers, such as the Nametab and Table Buffers:

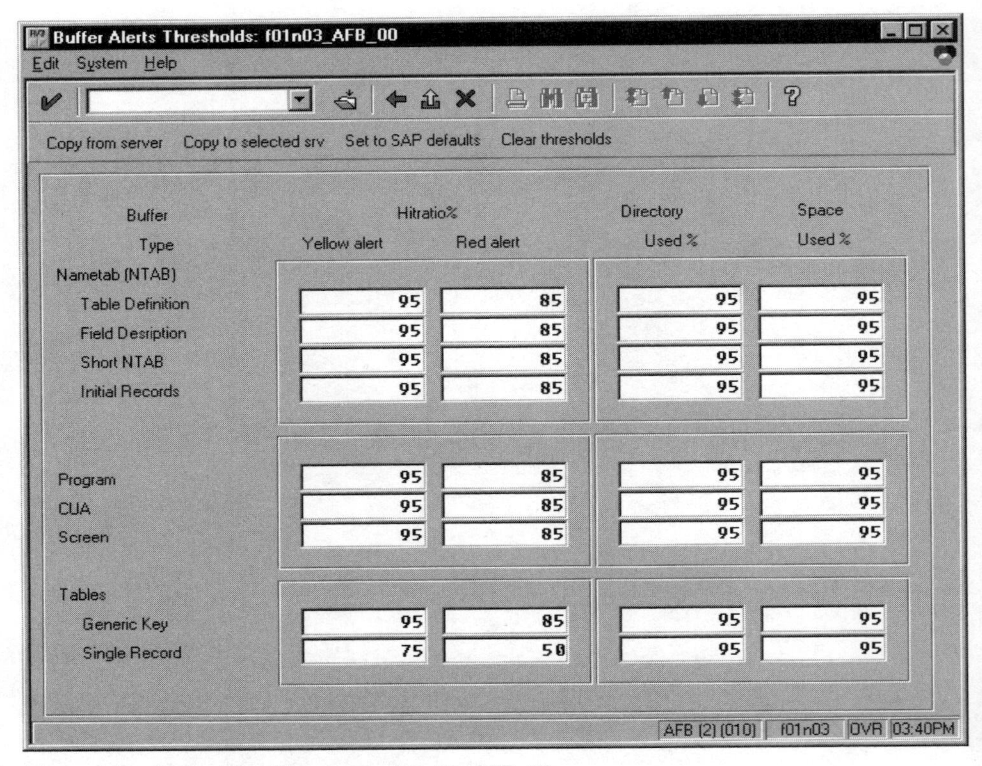

Figure 340. Buffer Alert Thresholds: f01n03_AFB_00

You can adjust these values according to your hardware capacity and tolerance of response time in such a way that you won't receive unwanted alert warnings or errors messages.

This panel gives you the flexibility to define alerts across **Hit ratio**, **Percentage of Directory used**, and a **Percentage of the space used.**

5. **Other Alerts**. Here we see thresholds related to the R/3 Roll File and the Enqueue and Dispatcher processes:

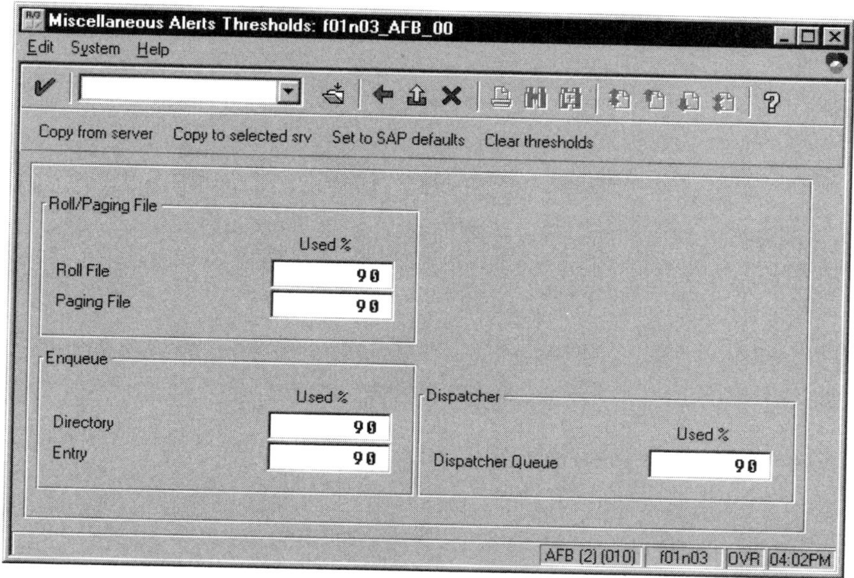

Figure 341. Miscellaneous Alert Thresholds: f01n03_AFB_00

The Dispatcher Queue should be close to 100% to keep wait times to acceptable levels.

6. **Database.** The procedure to access the database thresholds is a little different than other thresholds. You should start from the Maintain Alert Threshold panel as shown in Figure 335 on page 393. Click on the entry for **Database** to highlight it, and then click on **Change**:

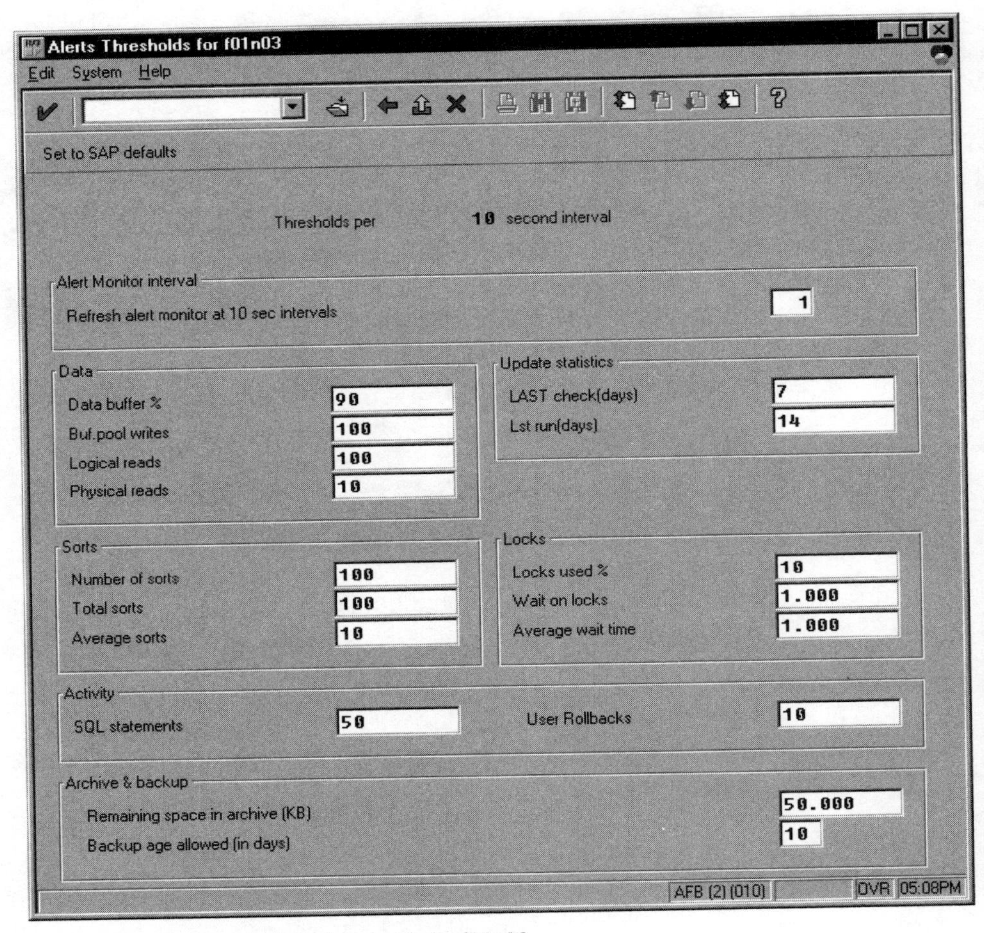

Figure 342. Database Alert Thresholds for f01n03

As shown in Figure 342, the Database Alert Thresholds are as follows:

- **Alert Monitor interval**:
  - Time interval in which the database alert monitor is refreshed. For example, if the value is 1, the Database Monitor will refresh the display every 10 seconds.

- **Data**:
    - Data buffer%: Indication of efficiency ratio of data found from buffers. It should be at least 90%. A higher value is better than a lower value.
    - Buffer Pool Writes: indicates the number of times a buffer pool data page was physically written to disk. If the threshold value overflows, it is advisable to start in increasing the number of buffer pool pages.
    - Logical reads: indicates the number of logical read requests for data pages that have gone through the buffer pool. If it is lower than the threshold, an alert monitor will be triggered.
    - Physical Reads: Indication of buffer quality. Physical reads occur if a read request cannot be accommodated by a buffer (i.e., the page is not found in the buffer). If the threshold value is exceeded regularly, the performance of the buffer is not good during high load or in other special circumstances (for example, full table scans). The goal is to have as few physical reads as possible.
- **Update Statistics**:
    - Last check(days): The number of days since the last time the database optimizer statistics check was run.
    - Last run(days): The number of days since the last time the update database optimizer statistics was run.
- **Sorts**:
    - Number of sorts (overflow): This indicator shows the number of overflow sorts that have occurred in the interval time. If it is higher than the threshold, the alert will show the in the database monitor.
    - Total sorts: Indicates the total sorts that have been executed during the interval of time. If this thresholds is exceeded, the alert monitor will trigger an alert.
    - Average sorts (in ms): If the average time of all sorts is longer than the threshold, monitor alert will be triggered.
- **Locks**:
    - Locks used%: Alert will be triggered if at any time the percentage of the locks used since database start-up exceeds this figure.
    - Wait on locks: If a thread waits for a lock for more than the time specified here, an alert will be triggered in the alert monitor.
    - Average wait time (in ms): If a thread holds a lock for more than the average time specified here, an alert will be generated in the lock monitor.

- **Activity**:
  - SQL Statements: Alert will be triggered if the number of SQL statements per second exceeds this figure.
  - User Rollbacks: Abnormal termination of a user transaction. If the threshold value is exceeded, you should check the system log to find out which transaction was the release mechanism and then carry out problem analysis.
- **Archive and Backup**:
  - Remaining Space in archive (KB): Triggered if there is less space than this value on disk for the log_archive location.
  - Backup age allowed (in days): If the most recent successful backup is older than this value, the backup alert is triggered.

This summarizes the database-related thresholds that are available from R/3. You can also use DB2 UDB to define alert thresholds on a large number of parameters as shown in “Maintaining Alert Thresholds Using DB2 UDB” on page 403.

9.1.1.2 Displaying Alert Thresholds for a Server(s)

To display alert thresholds for all servers:

1. In the R/3 main menu choose **Tools->CCMS, Configuration->Alert Monitor->Thresholds (3.x)**.
2. Click on **Display All Servers**.
3. Select the appropriate boxes for the alert threshold types you want to display. Click on **Continue**.
4. Alternatively, you can click on **Display All** to display a list of all the alert thresholds that are defined in the system.

To display alert thresholds for a selected server, highlight that server in the Active Servers list, and click on **Display**.

9.1.1.3 Resetting the Default Settings to a Servers settings

You can set the default settings to the settings at a particular server. To do this:

1. In the R/3 main menu choose **Tools->CCMS, Configuration->Alert Monitor->Thresholds (3.x)**.
2. Click on a server to highlight it.
3. Click **Change**.

4. Select **Edit->Copy to <DEFAULT>**.

9.1.2 Maintaining Alert Thresholds Using DB2 UDB

Alert thresholds can also be set using DB2 UDB via the Control Center. To do this, right-click on the <sid> database and select **Snapshot Monitoring->Show Monitor Profile**:

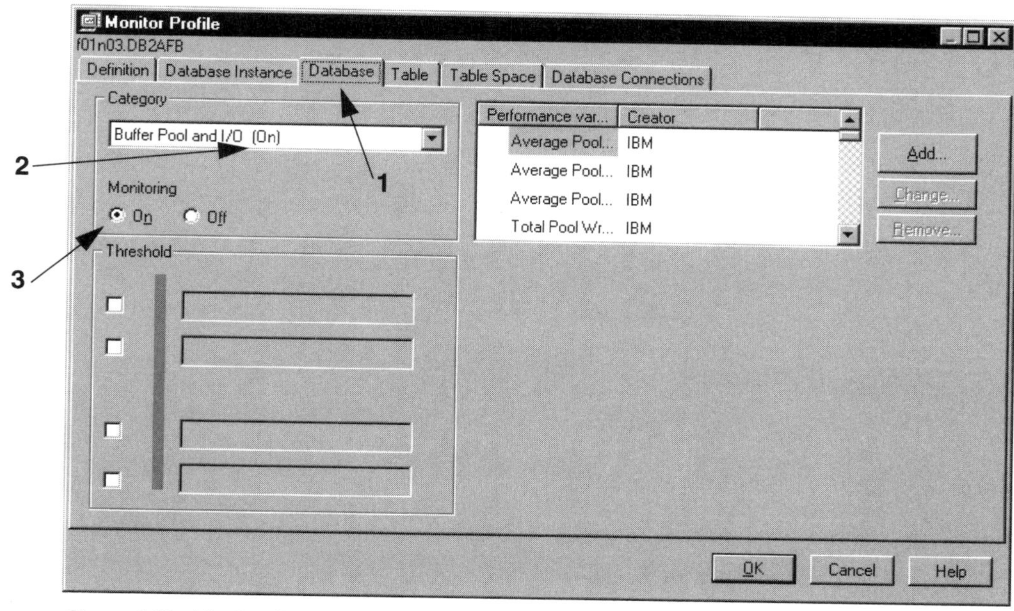

Figure 343. Monitor Profile

The database performance monitor, by default, collects data related to:

- Buffer pool and I/O
- Connections
- Locks and deadlocks
- Sorts
- SQL statement activity

In an R/3 environment, you can optionally restrict the amount of monitoring to items of particular interest. For example, we can turn off monitoring of Connections and SQL Statement activity. To do this, click the tab **Database** (1), click on the Category drop-down menu arrow from the category window (2) and select **Connections**. Select **Off** for Monitoring (3).

You should then select a performance variable and set its threshold limits. In this example, we choose Buffer Pool Hit Ratio Percentage, which is one of the

Buffer Pool and I/O performance variables. First, ensure that the Category is set to **Buffer Pool and I/O**, ensure it is set to **ON** in the Monitoring field, then select **Buffer Pool Hit Ratio (%)** from the list of Performance variables:

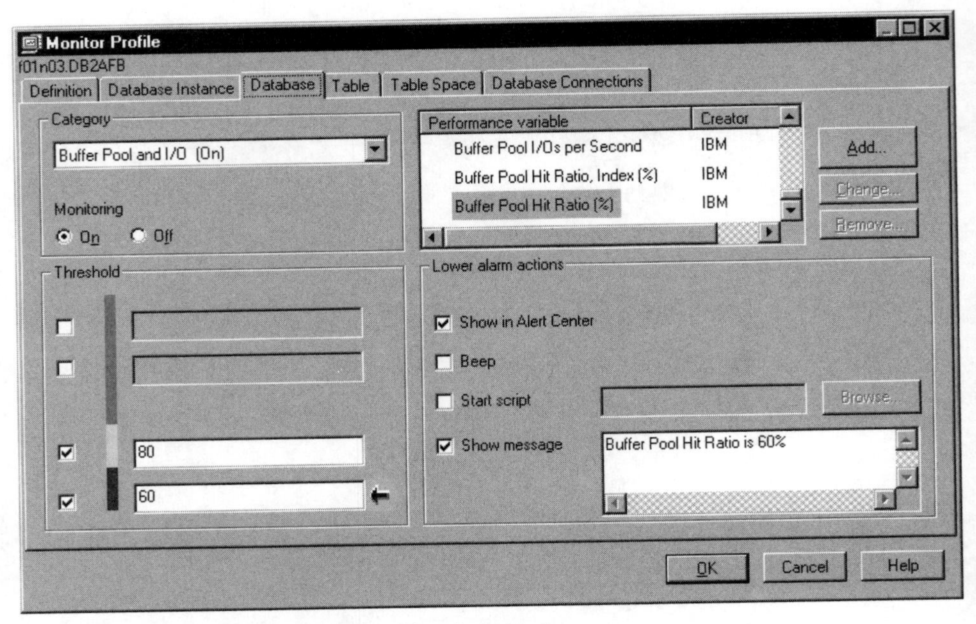

Figure 344. Monitor Profile - Defining Threshold Limits

Next click on the lower alarm entry box and enter 60. In this example, we have added a message in the Lower alarm actions box. This message will be displayed when this threshold is exceeded (that is, if the hit ratio drops below 60%). You can also optionally display an alert in the DB2 Alert Center, sound a beep or run a script. In this example we have also set a Lower warning threshold at 80. You can associate a separate set of actions with this warning.

For these DB2 Alert Thresholds to be enabled, we must start DB2 monitoring. From the Control Center, right-click on the R/3 database <sid> and select **Snapshot Monitoring->Start monitoring.** You will notice that the icon representing the <sid> database shows in light blue at the right side.

9.2 R/3 Alert Monitors

The R/3 Alert Monitors are designed as an early warning system. These monitors display both critical and simple warnings for all components in the R/3 environment. They consist of a series of graphical monitors, displaying red, yellow or green condition lights, and a single text monitor which displays the equivalent information in text format.

The use of these monitors can significantly improve the reaction time of the system administrator if potential problems arise. This in turn, can lead to higher availability of the R/3 system.

The alert monitors should be used on a daily basis and can help prevent:

- Performance problems
- Disk space problems
- Availability problems

They can monitor the following:

- R/3 system
- Database
- Operating system
- File systems

9.2.1 Global Alert Monitor

The Global Alert Monitor gives an overall view of the R/3 system. To start the Global Alert Monitor, select **Tools->Administration, Monitor-> Performance, Alerts->Global->SAP system** or enter the transaction **AL01**.

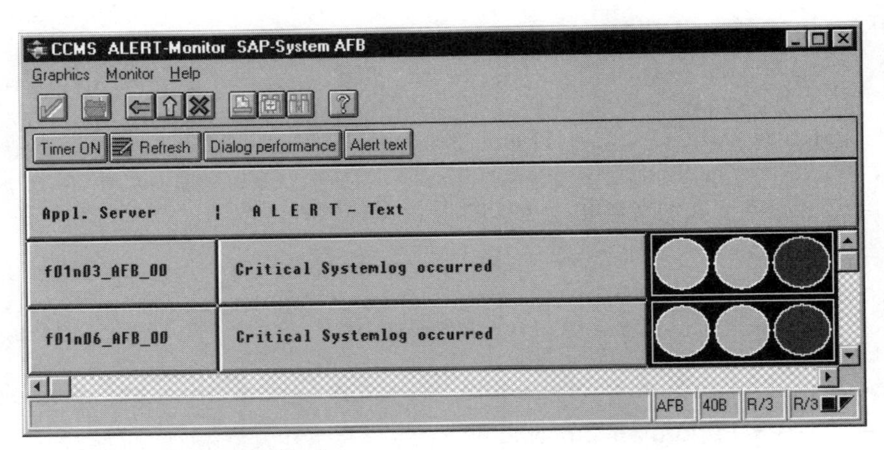

Figure 345. Global Alert Monitor

The Global Alert Monitor displays an alert message for each application server in the R/3 system.

- The left column of the monitor gives the name of the application instance server from which this alert originated. You can click on this column to log on directly to the server (instance) of interest.
- The middle column is a short text description of the alert originating from that application instance. You can click on this column to get a more detailed information screen.
- The right column shows the corresponding alert in the either red (critical alert), yellow (warning), or green (healthy).

To display views on Dialog, Update, Spool, and Job alerts, select **Monitor->Performance** from the menu bar of the Global Alert Monitor screen shown in Figure 345 on page 406 and then choose the option you wish to view. Alternatively, for Dialog processes, you can click on **Dialog Performance** from the tool bar.

To show the detailed view for an alert, click the middle column for a particular application instance server. The following screen is displayed:

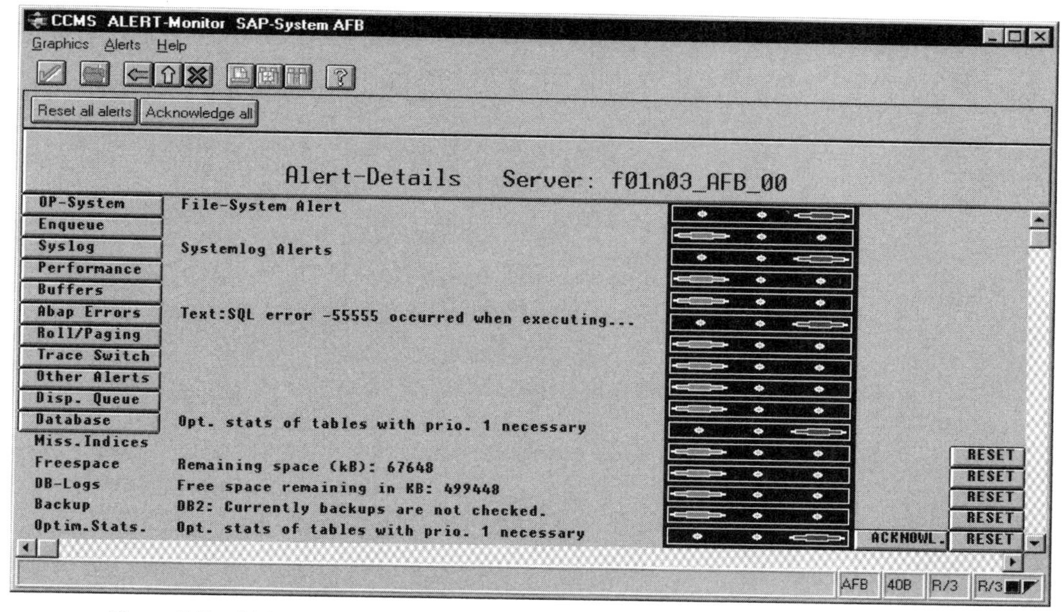

Figure 346. Global Alert Monitor - Detailed View

An overview of all the alerts for the instance is displayed. The alerts have the following color coding:

- Green (left side): No alert detected. The current value is beneath the threshold value. The system status is healthy.
- Yellow (center): A warning or non-critical event has occurred. The current value exceeds the threshold value, but this does not prevent you from working in the system.
- Red (right side): A critical problem, such as an update termination, may have occurred. The system requires attention.

From this screen, you can acknowledge or reset any alerts. The monitored areas on the left are push-buttons which you can select to get more detailed information.

9.2.1.1 Global Alerts in Text Format

You can also display the same information in a textual format. To do this, from the main R/3 menu, select **Tools->CCMS, Control/Monitoring->Control Panel** or enter the transaction **RZ03**. The following screen is displayed:

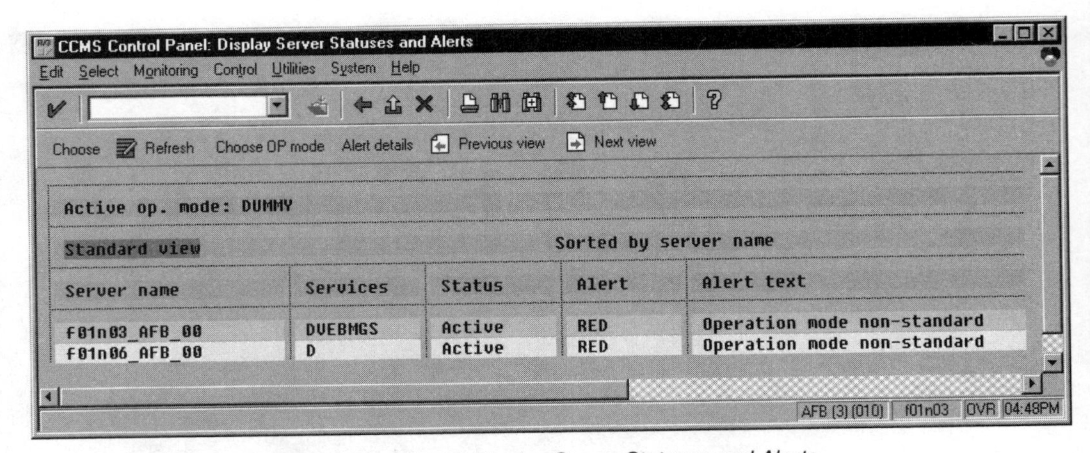

Figure 347. CCMS Control Panel: Display Server Statuses and Alerts

You can see the alert status of the application instances of your R/3 System in the Alert column. Each alert provides a short explanation of the cause of the alert along with technical information for error analysis. For more detailed analysis, other tools are also available, such as:

- The R/3 system log
- ABAP/4 runtime dumps
- Performance diagnosis tools (including transaction statistics)
- CCMS performance monitors

To get more details on an alert, double-click on an instance to highlight it. Then click on **Alert Details** from the tool bar. The Alert Overview is displayed for the server you have selected. For a given instance, the information displayed is the same as that displayed in Figure 346 on page 407, but in text format.

9.2.2 Database Alert Monitor

The Database Alert Monitor is used to check if any of the database-related alert thresholds have been exceeded. From the main R/3 menu, select **Tools->Administration, Monitor->Performance, Alerts->Global->Database System** or enter the transaction **AL02**.

The Database Performance Monitor screen is displayed:

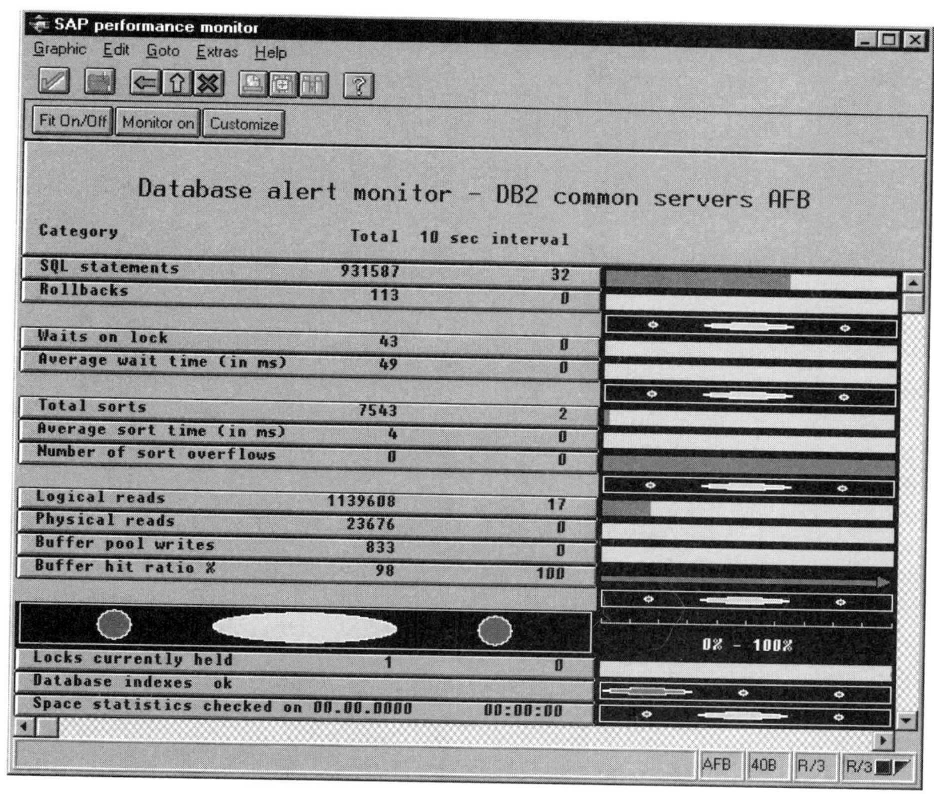

Figure 348. Database Alert Monitor

This screen shows the alert status of some database components. By default, the alert values are sampled every 10 seconds. Each alert provides a short explanation of the cause of the alert along with technical information for error analysis.

In the right hand column:

- A green bar: Under the threshold value, and starts from the left side to right side. This indicates that there are no problems.
- A yellow bar: Neutral.
- A red bar: Over the threshold value, and starts from the right side to left side. This indicates that there are problems.

Figure 348 on page 409 shows an arrow for Buffer hit ratio %. The arrow color changes from green to red when the value goes over the threshold setting.

9.2.3 Operating System Alert Monitor

The operating system alert monitor display alerts on the usage of components of the operating system, such as:

- CPU usage
- Memory and swap file usage
- LAN traffic
- Disk utilization

You can monitor either the machine that the SAP Frontend is connected to (known as the local application server) or another machine in the R/3 system (known as a remote application server). To monitor a remote application server, you must first add a remote RFC connection and add a SAPOSCOL destination (see “Monitoring a Remote Application Server” on page 412).

To start the Operating System Alert Monitor for the local application server, select: **Tools->CCMS, Control/Monitoring->Performance Menu, Alerts->Local->Operating system**, or enter transaction **AL16**. The following screen is displayed:

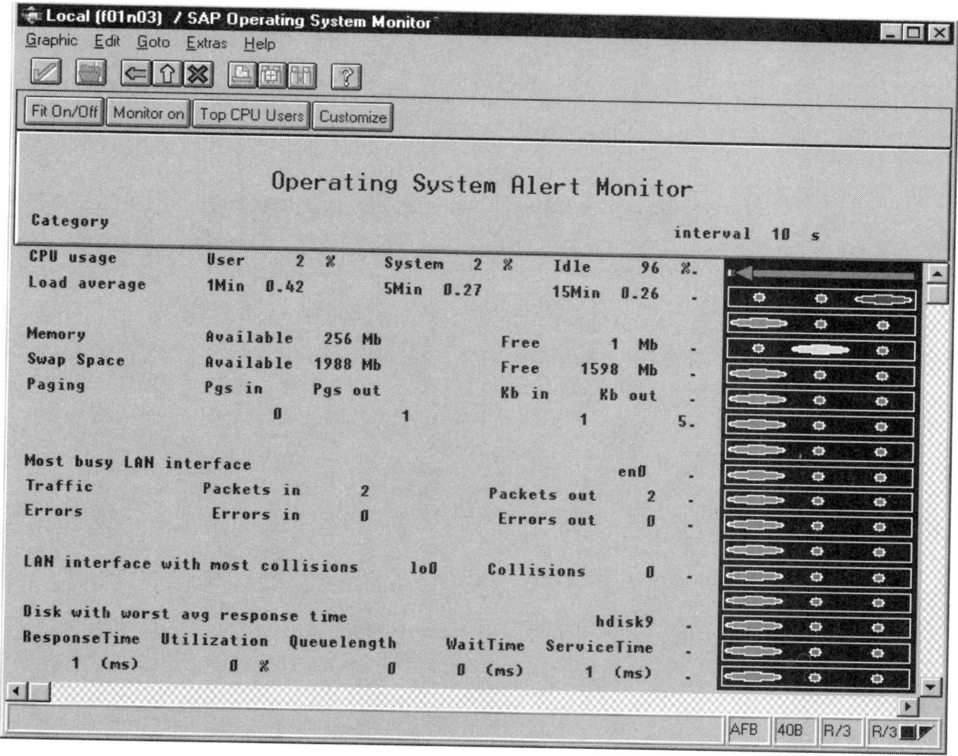

Figure 349. Operating System Alert Monitor

In this screen, traffic lights are shown in the right hand column. Within in this column, green lights are on the left side, yellow in the center, and red on the right side. The significance of these colors is the same as for the other Alert Monitors.

To start monitoring, click on **Monitor on** from the tool bar. To turn monitoring off, click on this button a second time (when monitoring is active this button will read **Monitor off**).

If you click on **Top CPU users**, the processes which are using the most CPU time are displayed in the form of a list.

You can modify the alert threshold values during the current monitoring session by clicking on **Customize** on the Operating System main panel. To permanently modify threshold settings, you should use the transaction **RZ06** as explained in “Maintaining Alert Thresholds” on page 392.

9.2.3.1 Monitoring a Remote Application Server

To monitor the operating system at a remote application server, you must first set up a remote function call (RFC) destination. Select: **Tools->Administration, Administration->Network-RFC Destinations** or enter the transaction **SM59**. The following screen is displayed:

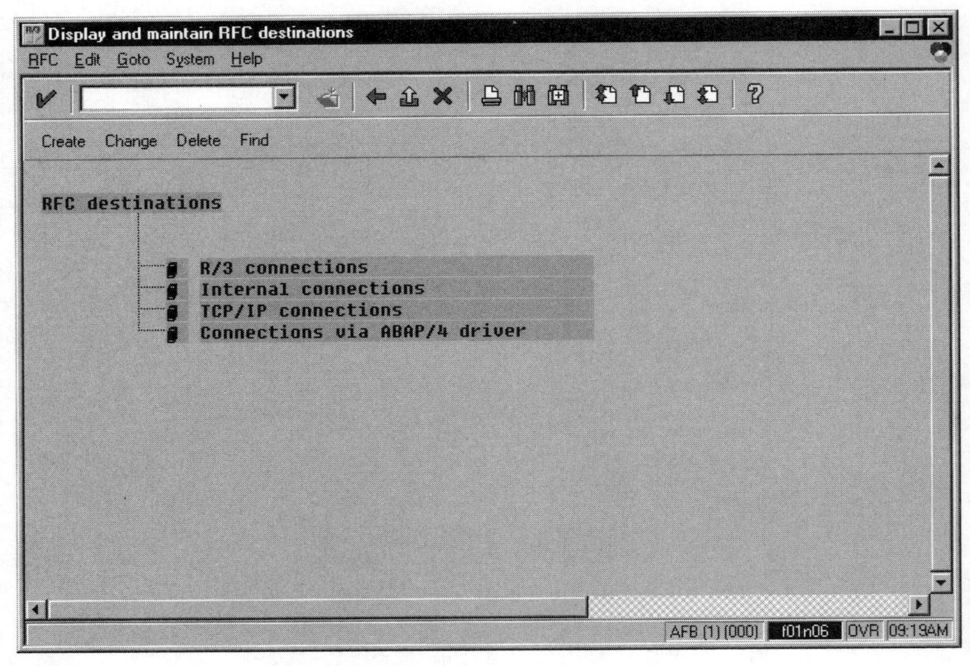

Figure 350. Display and Maintain RFC Destinations

To create a new RFC destination using TCP/IP, click on **Create** from the tool bar. The following panel is displayed:

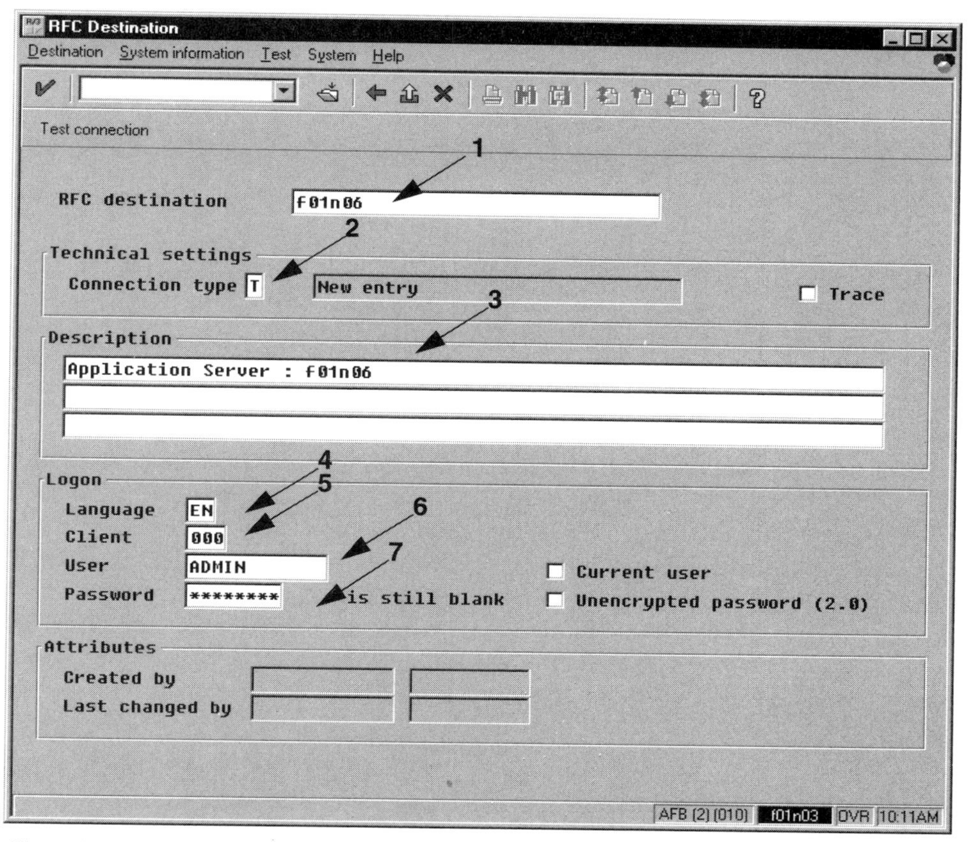

Figure 351. RFC Destination

Enter values in the following fields:

- RFC destination name (1): Enter the hostname of the application server
- Connection type (2): Select type T for TCP/IP.
- Description (3)
- Language (4)
- Client (5): Enter 000.
- User (6): Enter an R/3 administrator username,
- Password (7): Enter the password for the R/3 administrator.

Click on the Save icon (the folder symbol) in the tool bar to save this RFC destination name.

Next, you must add a SAPOSCOL destination by selecting **Tools->CCMS, Control/Monitoring->Performance Menu, Operating System->SAPOSCOL destination** or by entering transaction code **AL15**.

SAPOSCOL is an R/3 program that collects information about the operating system.

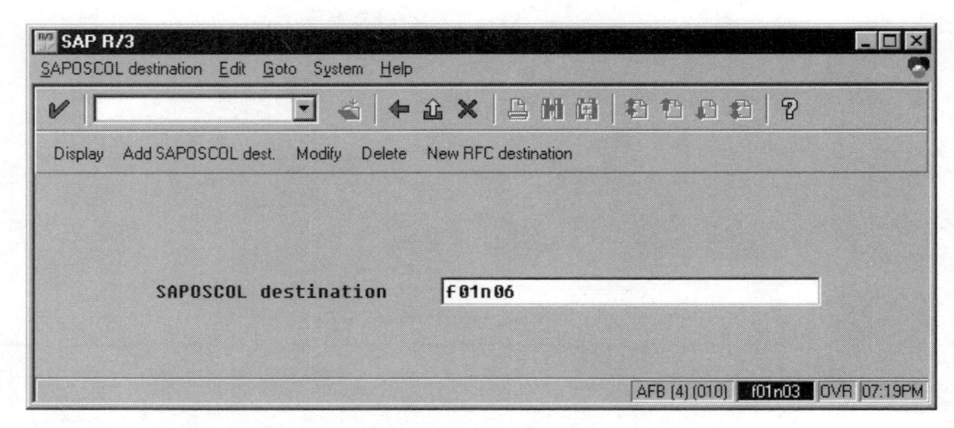

Figure 352. Adding a SAPOSCOL Destination

Enter the hostname of the application server in the SAPOSCOL destination field and click on **Add SAPOSCOL dest.** in the tool bar. This hostname must be defined in the local TCP/IP hosts file (AIX: /etc/hosts, Windows NT: \winnt\system32\drivers\etc\hosts) or at the TCP/IP Nameserver. You can then add a description in the Text field:

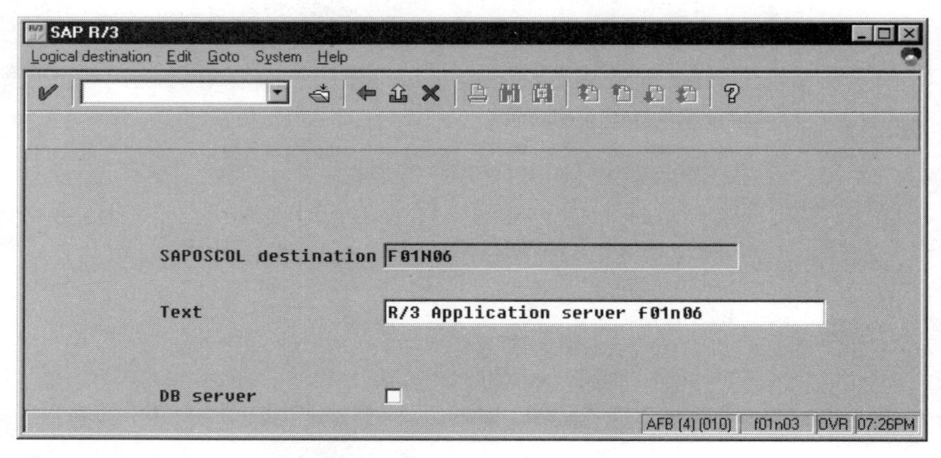

Figure 353. Customizing SAPOSCOL Destination

Click on the Save icon in the tool bar to add the SAPOSCOL destination.

To monitor the remote operating system, select: **Tools->CCMS, Control/Monitoring->Performance Menu, Alerts->Remote->Operating**

System or enter the transaction **AL17**. You are prompted to enter the SAPOSCOL destination name, then click **Continue**.

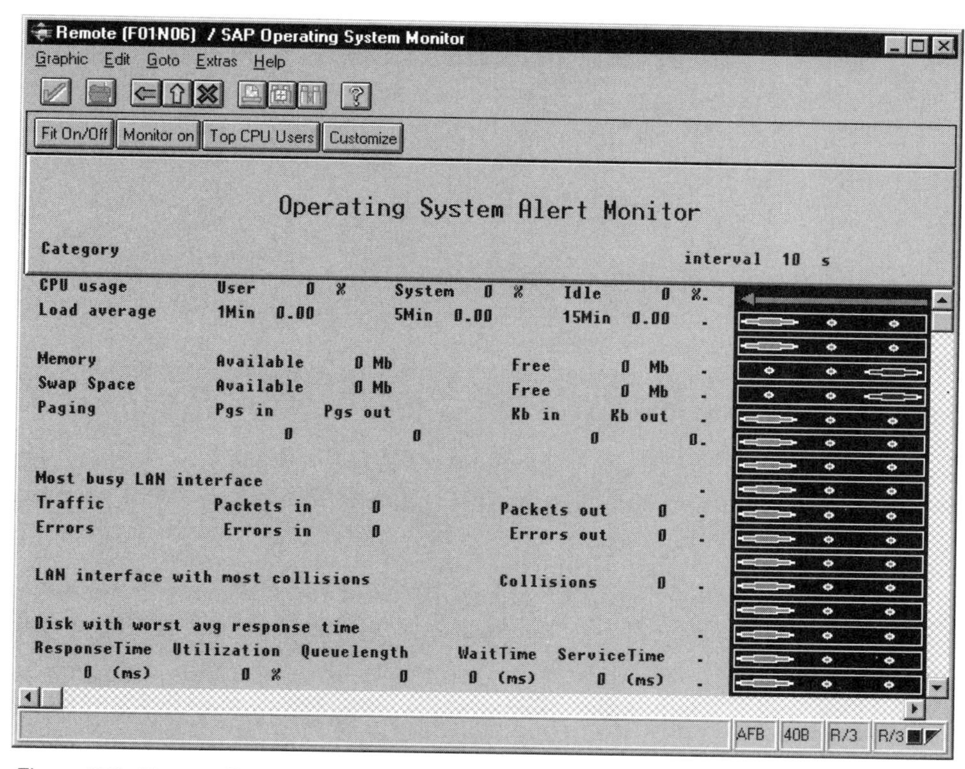

Figure 354. Remote Operating System Monitor

9.2.4 File System Alert Monitor

The file system alert monitor checks the space utilization of AIX file systems or Windows NT partitions. The file system thresholds are maintained using transaction **RZ06** as explained in “Maintaining Alert Thresholds” on page 392. For example, the thresholds settings on an AIX server might look like this:

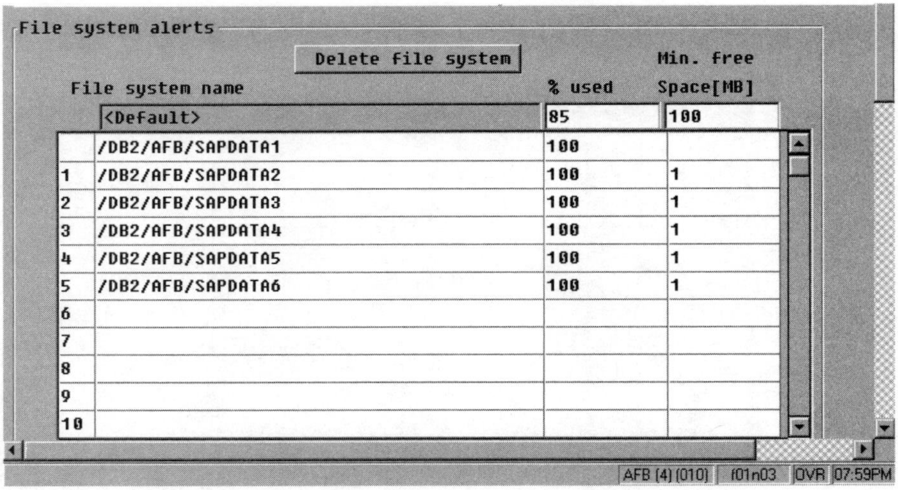

File system alerts

Delete file system

	File system name	% used	Min. free Space[MB]
	<Default>	85	100
	/DB2/AFB/SAPDATA1	100	
1	/DB2/AFB/SAPDATA2	100	1
2	/DB2/AFB/SAPDATA3	100	1
3	/DB2/AFB/SAPDATA4	100	1
4	/DB2/AFB/SAPDATA5	100	1
5	/DB2/AFB/SAPDATA6	100	1
6			
7			
8			
9			
10			

AFB (4) (010) | f01n03 | OVR | 07:59PM

Figure 355. File System Alert Thresholds

You can monitor either the machine that the SAP Frontend is connected to (known as the local application server) or another machine in the R/3 system (known as a remote application server). To monitor a remote application server, you must first add a remote RFC connection and add a SAPOSCOL destination (see “Monitoring a Remote Application Server” on page 412). Then run transaction **AL19**.

To monitor file system alerts for the local application server, select **Tools->CCMS, Control/Monitoring->Performance Menu, Alerts->Local->File System**, or enter transaction **AL18**. The following screen is displayed:

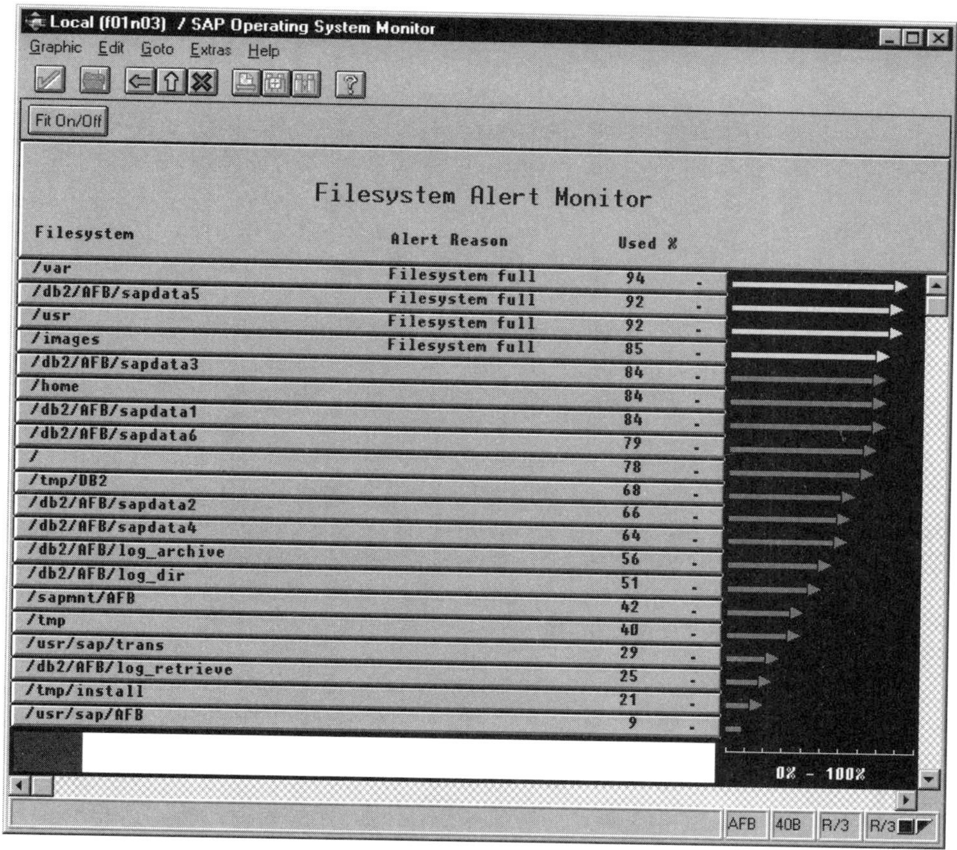

Figure 356. Filesystem Alert Monitor (AIX)

Figure 356 shows that the top 4 file systems on this AIX server have exceeded their threshold values and this results in Filesystem full messages being displayed.

Figure 357 shows the equivalent screen for an Windows NT server:

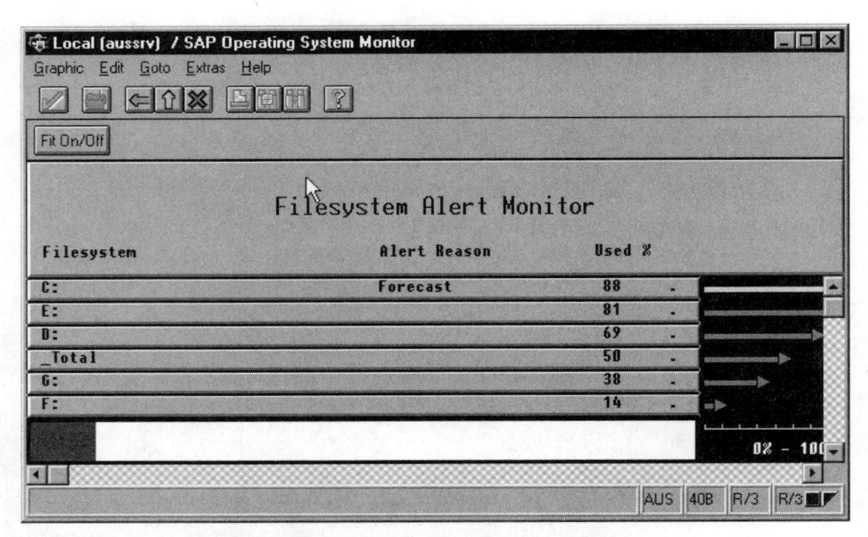

Figure 357. Filesystem Alert Monitor (Windows NT)

Figure 357 shows 5 Windows NT partitions: C:, D:, E:, F: and G: and the total space of all drives.

In either AIX or Windows NT, if you double-click on a filesystem/partition, a graph of the usage of the filesystem/partition is displayed:

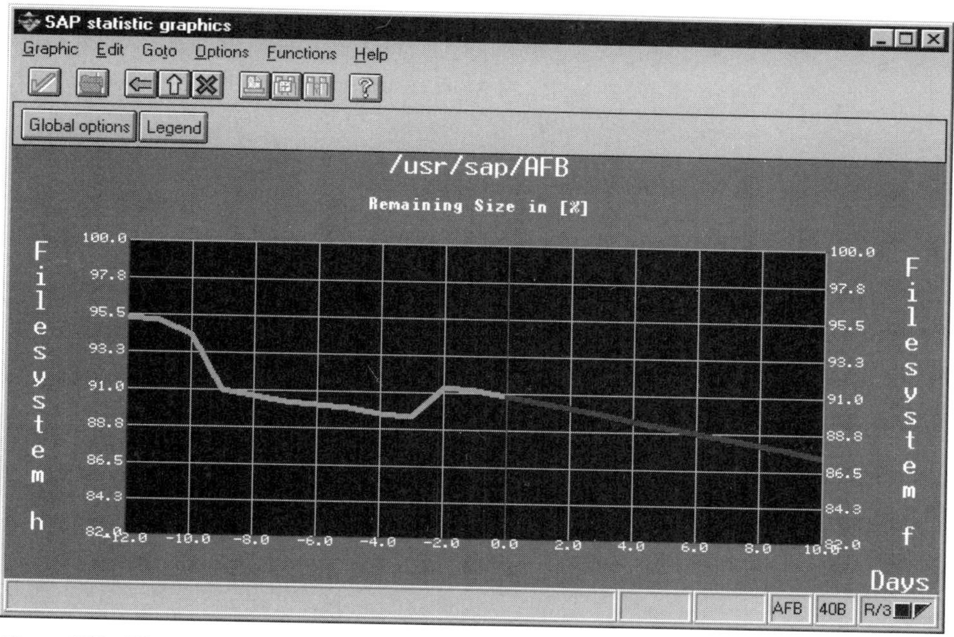

Figure 358. Filesystem/Partition Usage Forecast

In this graph, the horizontal axis shows time, with today (0.0) at the center. The usage values before today represent the actual usage of the filesystem/partition up to the present time. The usage values after today represent a forecast or estimation of the likely usage of the filesystem/partition in the future based on its past history. This example shows that in ten days, this file system will reach 86% utilization.

9.3 R/3 Performance Monitors

R/3 provides a variety of performance monitors. Each monitor supplies detailed statistics based on its individual component. These statistics enable you to do a healthcheck of your R/3 system, or help you decide how to optimize performance if your system is performing poorly. All statistics are kept in the database for the previous days, weeks or months and can be tailored to your requirements.

With these monitors you can:

- Check and analyze the status of the operating system(s)
- Check and analyze the status of the database system

- Check and analyze the status of the R/3 System
- Check and analyze the status of the network
- Activate additional alert monitors (if the host system provides the appropriate functionality)

To run the R/3 Performance Monitors, from the R/3 main menu, select **Tools->CCMS, Control/Monitoring->Performance Menu**, or enter the transaction **STUN.** The following menu is displayed.

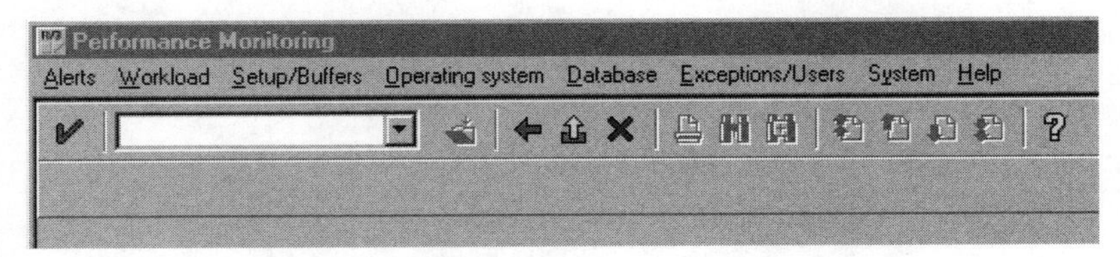

Figure 359. Performance Monitors

From this screen, you can access all performance monitors and their associated statistics.

9.3.1 Workload Monitor

When analyzing system performance, you should normally start by analyzing the workload statistics using the Workload Monitor. You can analyze workload statistics for:

- The server you are working on
- Another server
- All servers

You can use the Workload Monitor to find out how the workload is distributed over the servers and transactions. You can display the totals for all servers and compare the performance of individual servers over specified time periods.

You can display the following views of the R/3 statistics data:

- Workload for today or a recent period
- Daily statistics records
- Daily monitor response times
- Performance history for recent periods for all servers or users
- Performance history periods compared

You can display information on response times and resource consumption of any of the application servers in your R/3 System.

Use the Workload Monitor to display the following information:

- Number of configured R/3 instances
- Services supported by the R/3 instances
- Number of users working on the different instances
- The most frequently used transactions
- Response time distribution
- Differences between the response times for the different instances

9.3.1.1 Using the Workload Monitor

To run the Workload Monitor, select **Tools->Administration, Monitor->Performance, Workload->Analysis,** or enter transaction **ST03.** An overview of the active and inactive servers is displayed:

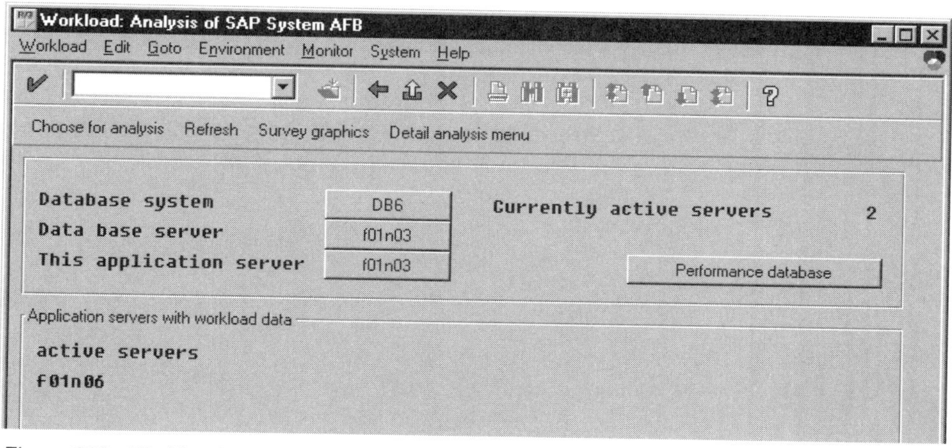

Figure 360. Workload Analysis of SAP System AFB

From this screen, you can access performance data on any listed server, or compare data from multiple servers. When you make a selection, you can specify constraints on what information is displayed.

9.3.1.2 Workload Overview for a Server

From the Workload analysis panel you can check R/3 performance in the following ways:

- Workload for Today
- Performance History
- Task Type Profiles
- Top 40 Response Times
- Workload Monitor Statistics

To display the workload overview for a server:

1. From the Workload Analysis screen (Figure 360 on page 421), click **Choose for analysis** in the tool bar, then select the server from the dialog box and click on the checkmark.

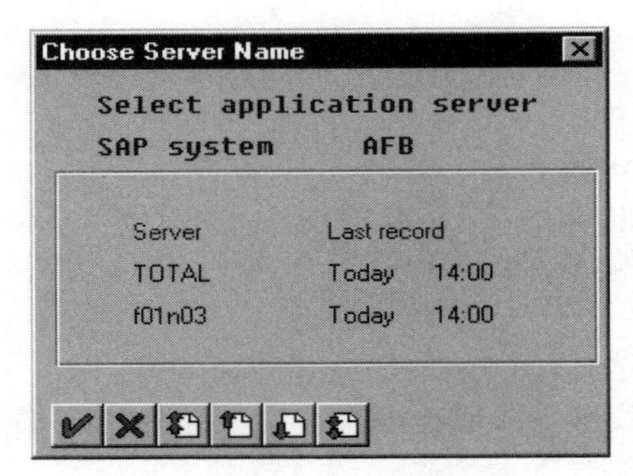

Figure 361. Choose Server Name

2. In the **Choose time period** dialog box, select the time period. You can choose daily, weekly or monthly statistics.

The following information is displayed:

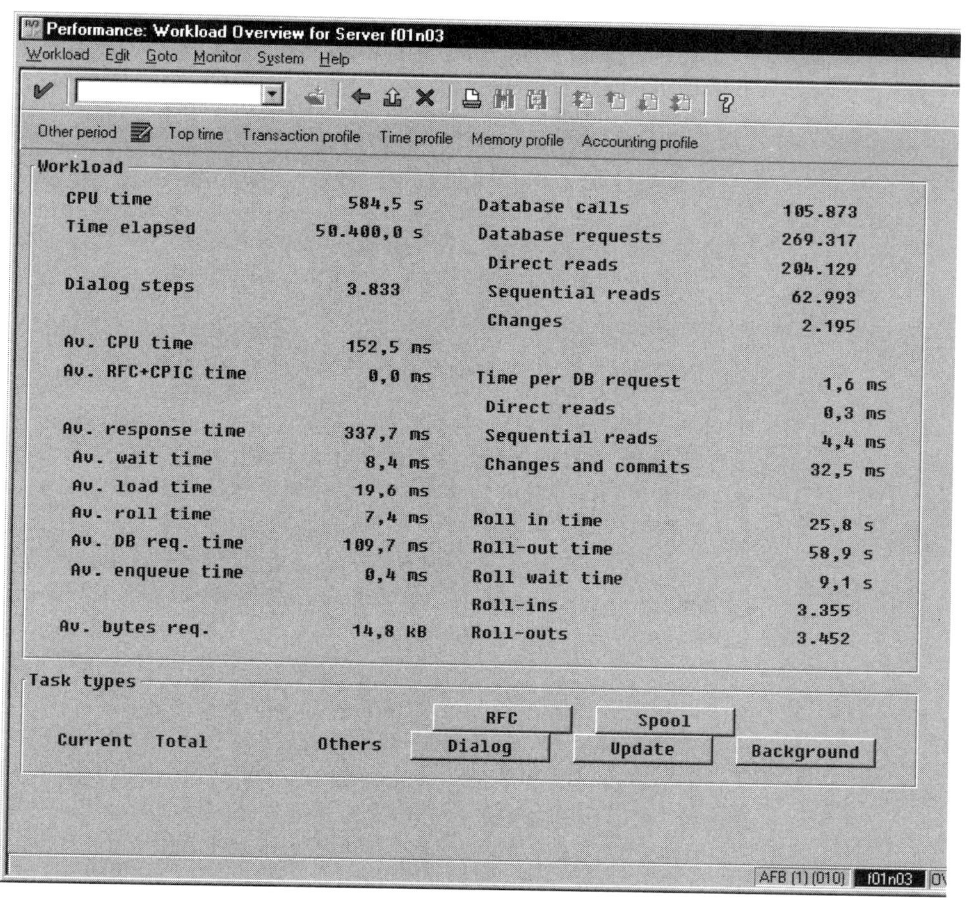

Figure 362. Performance: Workload Overview

Under Task type, choose between Total, RFC, Spool, Dialog, Update and Background. This allows you to restrict the analysis data to a particular task type. If you click on **Memory profile** in the tool bar, information on the memory usage of the user and transactions is displayed.

Here are some of the important fields in the Workload Overview panel:

1. Average response time

   Response time is measured from the time a work process is instructed by the dispatcher to perform the execution to the time the result is returned to the SAPGUI. The response time between the SAPGUI and the dispatcher is not included in this value.

2. Average wait time

The time an unprocessed dialog step waits in the dispatcher queue for a free work process. A high server workload could produce higher wait times.

3. Average CPU time

   CPU time used in the work process.

4. Average load time

   The time needed to load and generate objects such as ABAP/4 source code and screen information from a database.

5. Database calls

   The number of parsed requests sent to the database.

6. Database requests

   The number of logical ABAP/4 requests for data in the database. These requests are passed through the R/3 DB interface and parsed into individual database calls.

   The proportion of database calls to database requests is of interest. If access to information in a table is buffered in the SAP buffers, database calls to the database server are not needed. Therefore, the ratio of calls/requests gives an overall indication as to the efficiency of table buffering. A good ratio would be 1:10.

7. Average DB request time

   The logical database request time required for a dialog step. The time depends on the CPU capacity of the database server, network server and buffering, and on the input/output capabilities of the database server.

9.3.1.3 Performance History

Complete daily statistics are generated for the number of the days entered in the reorganization program for the performance database. On the basis of the daily statistics and the entered number of weeks and months, cumulative statistics are also compiled.

If you want to analyze performance developments, you can compare the performance development of a day, a week or a month for a certain time interval or for certain servers. These comparison statistics are less detailed.

To get a performance history, from the R/3 main menu, select: **Tools->CCMS, Control/Monitoring->Performance Menu, Workload->Analysis**, or enter the transaction **ST03**. Click on **Detail analysis menu** from the tool bar. From the Performance history box, click on **Compare recent periods**.

9.3.1.4 Real Time Workload

The real time workload enables you to check the current response time and see the distribution of time between different performance components. From the R/3 main menu, select:

Tools->CCMS,Control/Monitoring->Performance Menu, Workload->Analysis, Goto->Current Local Data->Alert Monitor.

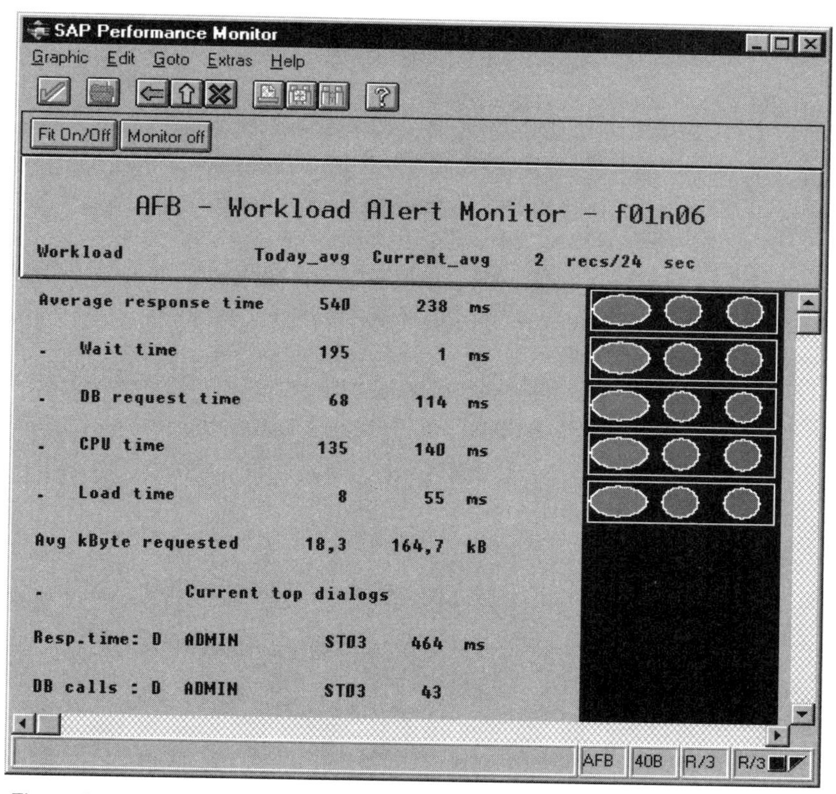

Figure 363. SAP Performance Monitor - Real Time Workload

9.3.2 Viewing Response Time Data

The R/3 Workload Monitor provides several ways to view data about response times, including the following:

1. Top Time: Response times of transactions or ABAP program ordered by time; with the longest first.
2. Top DB Request: Response times ordered by the most used request or ABAP Program.
3. Transaction Profile: Response time ordered by transaction.

4. Time Profile: Response time ordered by hourly intervals.
5. Task by Profile: Response time of type of work process type.
6. User Profile: Response time by each R/3 user.
7. Client Profile: Response time by each client of R/3.

In this section, we will look in detail at the second of these views, response time by top database requests. This view enables you to pinpoint the transactions that have the highest resource consumption.

1. From the R/3 Menu, select: **Tools->CCMS, Control/Monitoring->Performance Menu, Workload->Analysis**, or enter transaction **ST03**.
2. Click on **Choose for analysis** from the tool bar. Select the required application server from the pop-up window.
3. From the next pop-up window, select a time period. You can choose between: today, another day, this week, another week, this month or another month.
4. The Workload Overview screen is displayed. Select: **Goto->Hit lists->Top 40 DB requests**.

The system displays a list of the top 40 dialog steps ordered by the number of database requests (reads or changes):

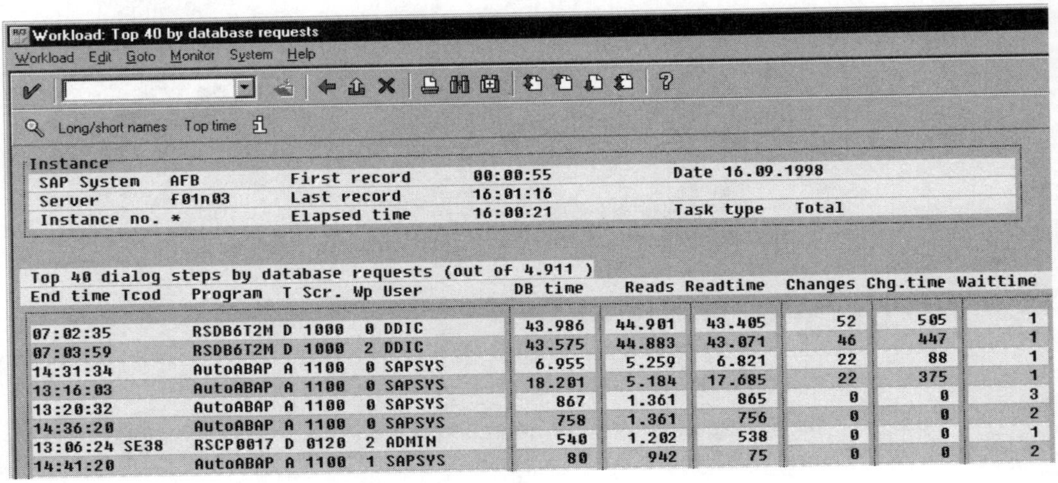

Workload: Top 40 by database requests

Workload Edit Goto Monitor System Help

Long/short names Top time

Instance
SAP System AFB First record 00:00:55 Date 16.09.1998
Server f01n03 Last record 16:01:16
Instance no. * Elapsed time 16:00:21 Task type Total

Top 40 dialog steps by database requests (out of 4.911)

End time	Tcod	Program	T	Scr.	Wp	User	DB time	Reads	Readtime	Changes	Chg.time	Waittime
07:02:35		RSDB6T2M	D	1000	0	DDIC	43.986	44.901	43.405	52	505	1
07:03:59		RSDB6T2M	D	1000	2	DDIC	43.575	44.883	43.071	46	447	1
14:31:34		AutoABAP	A	1100	0	SAPSYS	6.955	5.259	6.821	22	88	1
13:16:03		AutoABAP	A	1100	0	SAPSYS	18.201	5.184	17.685	22	375	1
13:20:32		AutoABAP	A	1100	0	SAPSYS	867	1.361	865	0	0	3
14:36:20		AutoABAP	A	1100	0	SAPSYS	758	1.361	756	0	0	2
13:06:24	SE38	RSCP0017	D	0120	2	ADMIN	540	1.202	538	0	0	1
14:41:20		AutoABAP	A	1100	1	SAPSYS	80	942	75	0	0	2

Figure 364. Workload by Database Requests

5. Note that you can change to a view ordered by response time by clicking on **Top Time** in the tool bar.

6. Double-click on an entry in the list for additional details. Click on **Task** in the tool bar to get information about the resources utilized by each task:

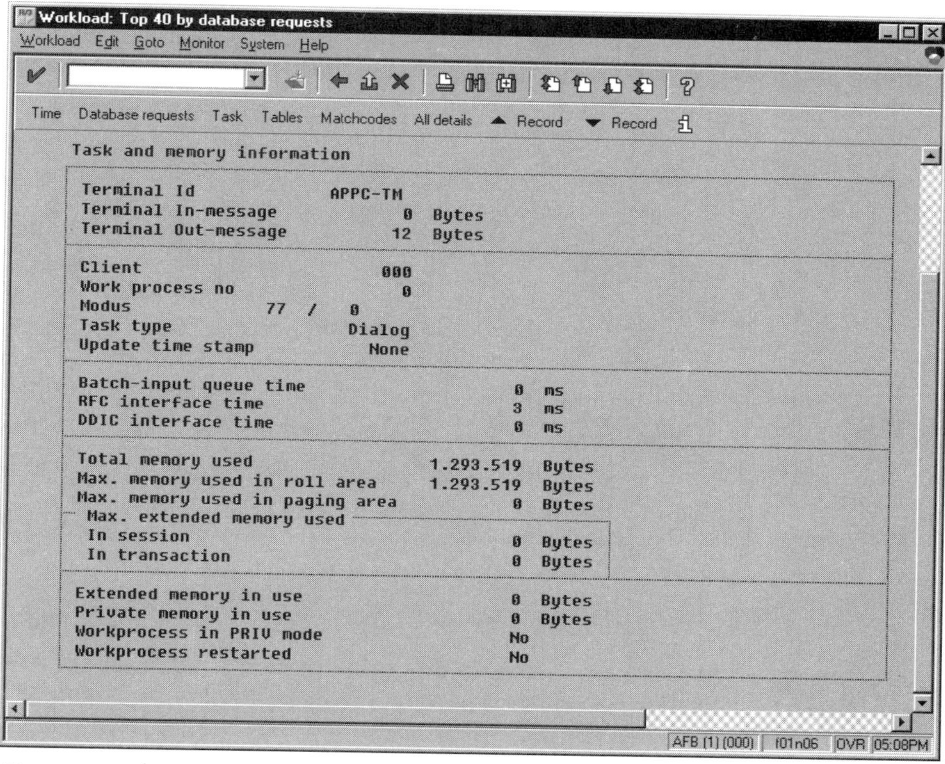

Figure 365. Workload Monitor - Task and Memory Information

7. If you click on **Time** from the tool bar, detailed time usage is displayed:

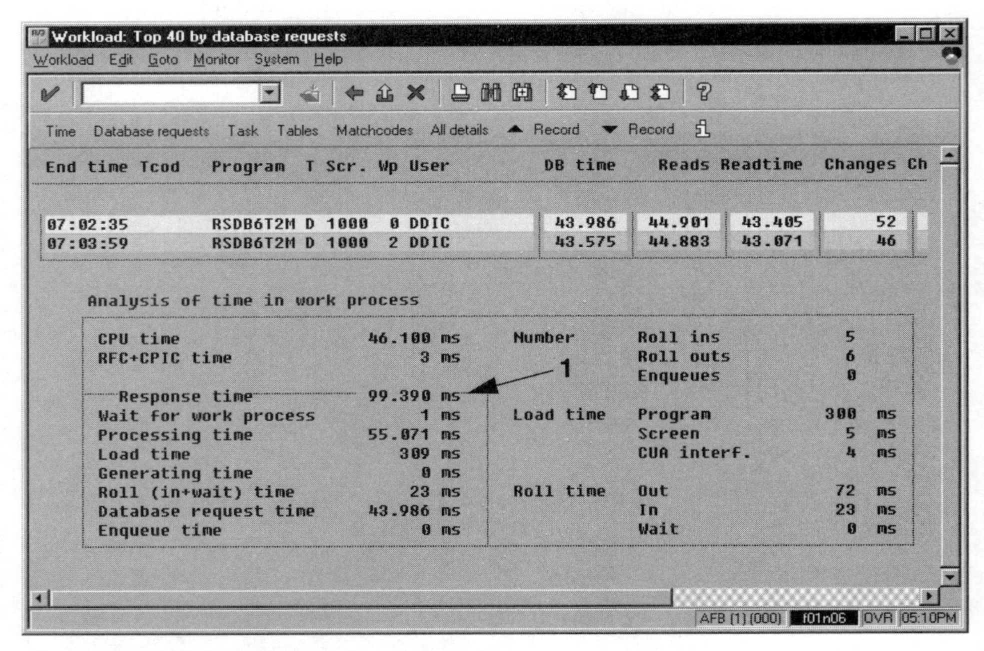

Figure 366. Workload Monitor - Time Information

To analyze this information, you should check the following:

- Is it always the same program that has a high response time? The response time (1) is shown in Figure 366.
- Is this program running at the same time in several sessions and locking work processes? You should look for repeated entries for the same program but with different users in the screen showing entries by response time (Top time).
- How many KB of information are transferred? This is found at the right of the screen showing entries by response time (Top time).

9.3.3 Analyzing Performance Data

The following table shows the rules of thumb for the different elements that contribute to the overall response time. You should use these rules as initial guidelines when analyzing response times:

Performance Data	Time
Average response time	Approx. 1 second (dialog), <1 second (update)
Average CPU time	Approx. 40% of average response time
Average wait time	<1% of average response time
Average load time	<10% of average response time
Average DB Request time	Approx. 40% of average response time

The operating system can affect these values by about 10%.

For database requests, these are some guidelines:

Database Requests	Time
Direct reads	<10 ms
Sequential reads	<40 ms
Changes	>25 ms

If you notice values higher than those listed in these guidelines, use the following table to help you find the cause:

Performance Data	Possible Reason
Load time	R/3 buffers may be too small May be caused by missing indexes
Wait time	Not enough work processes Long running transactions: all work processes busy
CPU time << Process time	I/O bottleneck, network problems, CPU bottleneck
DB request	DB server CPU has a heavy load Buffer hit ratio low, not enough memory, too many disk sorts, data is fragmented, catalog and/or package cache hit ratio is too low

9.3.3.1 R/3 Performance Analysis

To analyze the performance of your R/3 system in more detail, you should use the Workload Monitor. In this section, we will give details of some symptoms of bad performance together with some suggested actions. Use transaction **ST03** to display the Workload Overview screen for your selected server, as explained in "Workload Monitor" on page 420. The following screen is displayed:

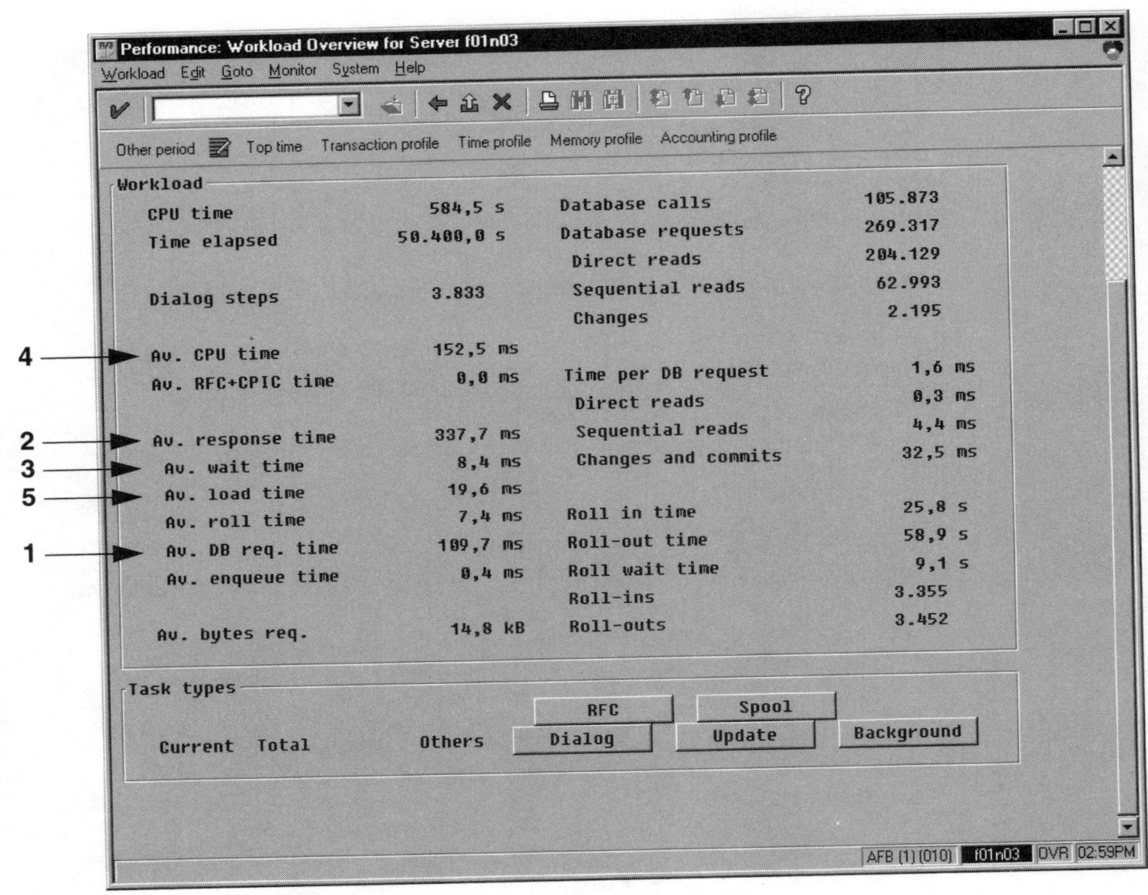

Figure 367. Workload Overview for Server f01n03

9.3.3.2 Average Database Request Time

As shown in Figure 367, the average DB request time (1) should not exceed 40% of the average response time (2). If it does, you should check the Database Performance Analysis panel to investigate the cause. From the R/3 main menu select **Tools->CCMS, Control/Monitoring->Performance Menu, Workload->Analysis** and click on **DB6**, or enter transaction **ST04**.

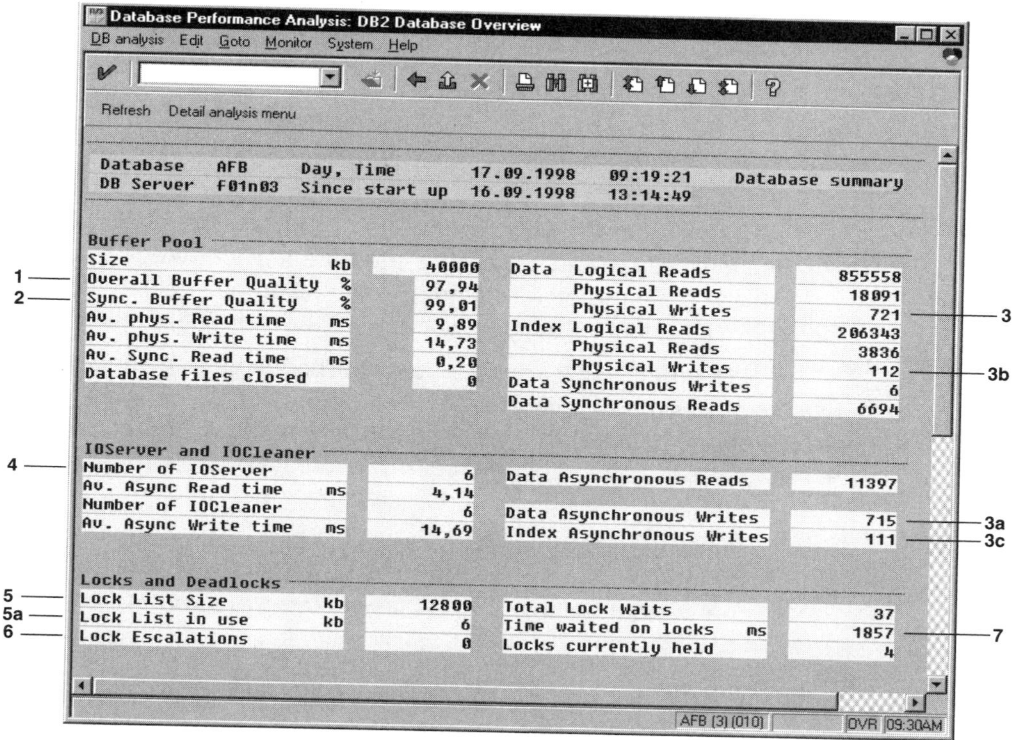

Figure 368. Database Performance Analysis: First Page

There are many potential causes for a high average database request time. The following points refer to numeric references in the above figure.

1. Overall buffer quality is lower than 97% (1 in Figure 368).

   The buffer pool hit ratio indicates the percentage of time that the database manager did not need to load a page from disk in order to service a page request. That is, the page was already in the buffer pool. The greater the buffer pool hit ratio, the lower the frequency of disk I/O. This includes both synchronous and asynchronous operations.

   - Action: Increase the size of the buffer pool by changing the DB2 database parameter BUFFPAGE. You should also ensure that pre-fetching of your data pages is activated within your DB2 UDB system.

2. Synchronous buffer quality is lower than 97% (2).

   This indicator is the similar to overall buffer quality (1) but it only applies to *synchronous* I/O operations.

- Action: Same action as for overall buffer quality (point 1).

3. Data physical writes (3) is much greater than asynchronous data writes (3a) or index physical writes (3b) is much greater than asynchronous index writes (3c).

   A *synchronous* write is performed when a buffer pool data or index page is physically written to disk.

   An *asynchronous* write is performed when a buffer pool data or index page is physically written to disk by either an asynchronous page cleaner or as a result of a prefetch request. A prefetcher may cause dirty pages to be written to disk to make space for the pages being prefetched.

   I/O Cleaners (also known as asynchronous page cleaners) write changed pages from the buffer pool to disk before the space in the buffer pool is required by a database agent. This means that the agents will not wait for changed pages to be written out before being able to read a page. As a result, your application's transactions should run faster.

   - Action: Increase the number of I/O cleaners by changing the DB2 database parameter NUM_IOCLEANERS until there is a balance between the number of pages written synchronously and asynchronously.

4. The number of I/O servers < number of physical disks (4).

   I/O servers are used on behalf of the database agents to perform prefetch I/O and asynchronous I/O by utilities such as backup and restore.

   - Action: In order to fully exploit all the I/O devices in the system, a good value to use is generally one or two more than the number of physical devices on which the database resides.

5. Lock list in use (5) > 10% of the lock list size (5a)

   The lock list in use indicates the total amount of memory (in bytes) that is being used for the lock list.

   - Action: Increase the size of the lock list by changing the DB2 database parameter LOCKLIST.

6. Lock escalations is greater than zero (6).

   Lock escalations indicates the number of times that an applications locks have been escalated from row locks to a table lock. When this occurs, you can decrease your concurrency on that table.

   - Action: Increase the setting of the DB2 database parameter MAXLOCKS. This is maximum percentage of the lock list one user can hold before their locks get escalated.

7. Total lock wait is high (7).

   Total lock wait indicates the total amount of time that applications or connections had to wait for locks.

   - Action: If the average lock wait time is high, you should look for applications that hold many locks, applications which are experiencing lock escalations, and applications which are not releasing locks frequently enough.

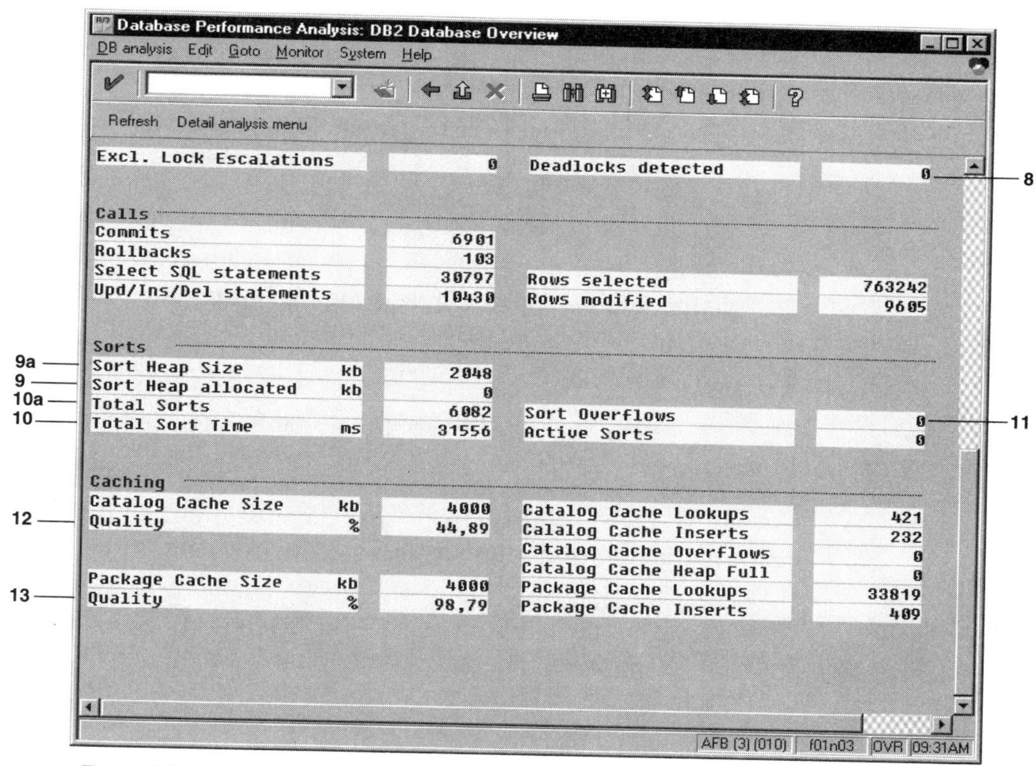

Figure 369. Database Performance Analysis: Second Page

8. Deadlocks Detected > 0 (8).

   This field shows the total number of deadlocks that have occurred. This indicates that applications are experiencing contention problems. These problems could be caused by contention for locks by processes using the database. As an example, two applications may hold locks on resources that they both need access to and the order they obtained the locks may be such that neither can complete their lock requests. This will cause a deadlock situation.

Action: Use the transaction **DB01** to look for any lock contention.

9. Sort heap allocated (9) close to 90% of sort heap size (9a)

   This indicates that the total number of pages allocated for sorts is close to the total sort heap size.

   - Action: Increase the DB2 database parameter SORTHEAP. You then need to increase the DB2 database manager parameter SHEAPTHRES to at least twice the value of SORTHEAP.

10. Total Sort Time (10) / Total Sorts (10a) is high.

    The average elapsed time for each sort is determined by dividing the total sort time by the number of sorts.

    - Action: Increase the SORTHEAP size as in point 9.

11. Sort overflow greater than 5% (11).

    This indicates that more than 5% of sorts are being performed on disk, not in memory.

    - Actions: Add appropriate indexes to minimize the use of the sort heap or increase the SORTHEAP size as in point 9.

12. Catalog cache hit ratio < 80% (12).

    The catalog cache stores table descriptors. A descriptor stores information about a table, view, or alias in a condensed internal format. When a transaction references a table, it causes an insert of a table descriptor into the cache, so that subsequent transactions referencing that same table can use that descriptor and avoid reading from disk.

    - Action: Increase the size of the catalog cache by changing the value of the DB2 database parameter CATALOGCACHE_SZ. You may also have to increase the database heap by changing the DB2 database parameter DBHEAP, as the catalog cache is part of the database heap.

13. Package cache hit ratio < 80% (13).

    The package and section information required for the execution of dynamic and static SQL statements is placed in the package cache as required. The package cache exists at a database level.

    - Action: Increase the size of the package cache by changing the DB2 database parameter PCKCACHESZ.

9.3.3.3 Average Wait Time

The average wait time is marked as (3) in Figure 367 on page 430. This should not exceed 1% of the average response time. If it does, then the possible causes include:

1. Not enough work processes available.

   Check this by entering transaction **SM50**, or select: **Tools->Administration, Monitor->System Monitoring->Process Overview**.

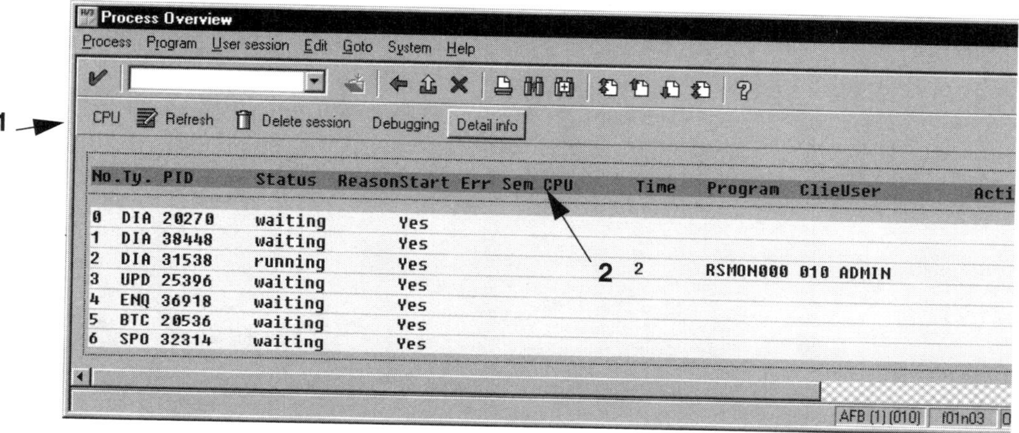

Figure 370. Process Overview

   Click on **CPU** in the tool bar (1 in Figure 370) to identify long running jobs.

   - Actions: Increase the number of work processes. Schedule the long running programs at another time. Investigate the program for problems.

2. Roll page area is too small.

   This is the case if the Sem column (2) continually displays 6.

   - Adjust the roll area using transaction **RZ10** to adjust the parameters:
     - ztta/roll_area
     - em/initial_size_MB
     - ztta/roll_extension

     For further details, read the OSS note: 33576 (Memory Management for UNIX and Windows NT.

9.3.3.4 Average CPU Time

The average CPU time is marked as (4) in Figure 367 on page 430. This value should not exceed 40% of the average response time. If it does, then you should:

1. Use ABAP trace on time-consuming transactions in order to analyze the efficiency of the code. Select **Tools->ABAP Workbench,**

Development->ABAP Editor or enter transaction **SE38**. Enter the program name and click **Debugging** from the tool bar:

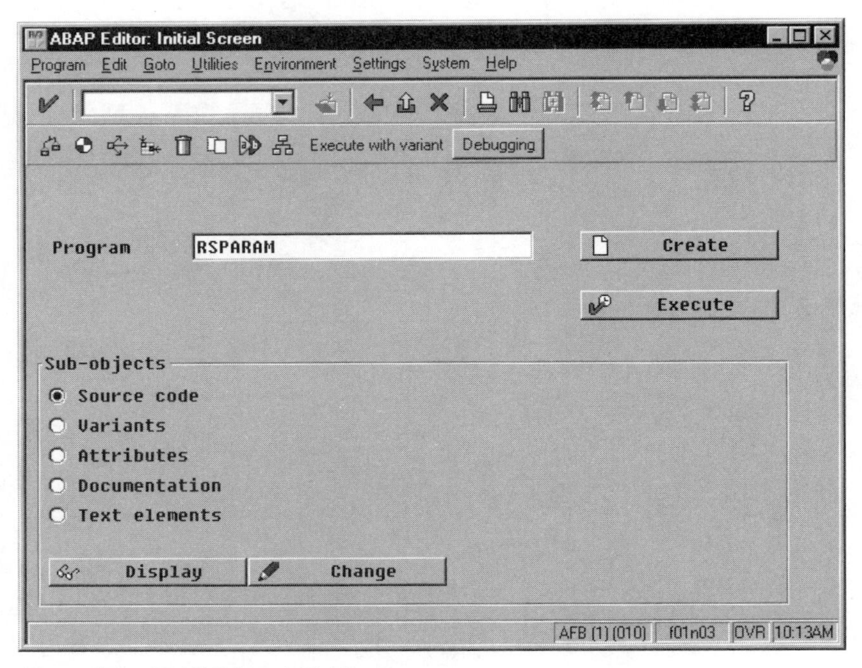

Figure 371. ABAP Editor: Initial Screen

2. Use other traces by selecting: **Tools->Administration, Monitor ->Traces**. You can choose to run:
   - An SQL trace, transaction code: **ST05**.
   - A System Trace, transaction code: **ST01**.
   - Developer Traces, transaction code: **ST11**.

9.3.3.5 Average Load Time

The average load time is marked as (5) in Figure 367 on page 430. This value should not exceed 10% of the average response time. If it does, then you should:

1. Check the R/3 buffers and indexes. From the R/3 menu, select: **Tools->CCMS, Control/Monitoring->Performance Menu, Setup/Buffers->Buffers** or enter transaction **ST02**.

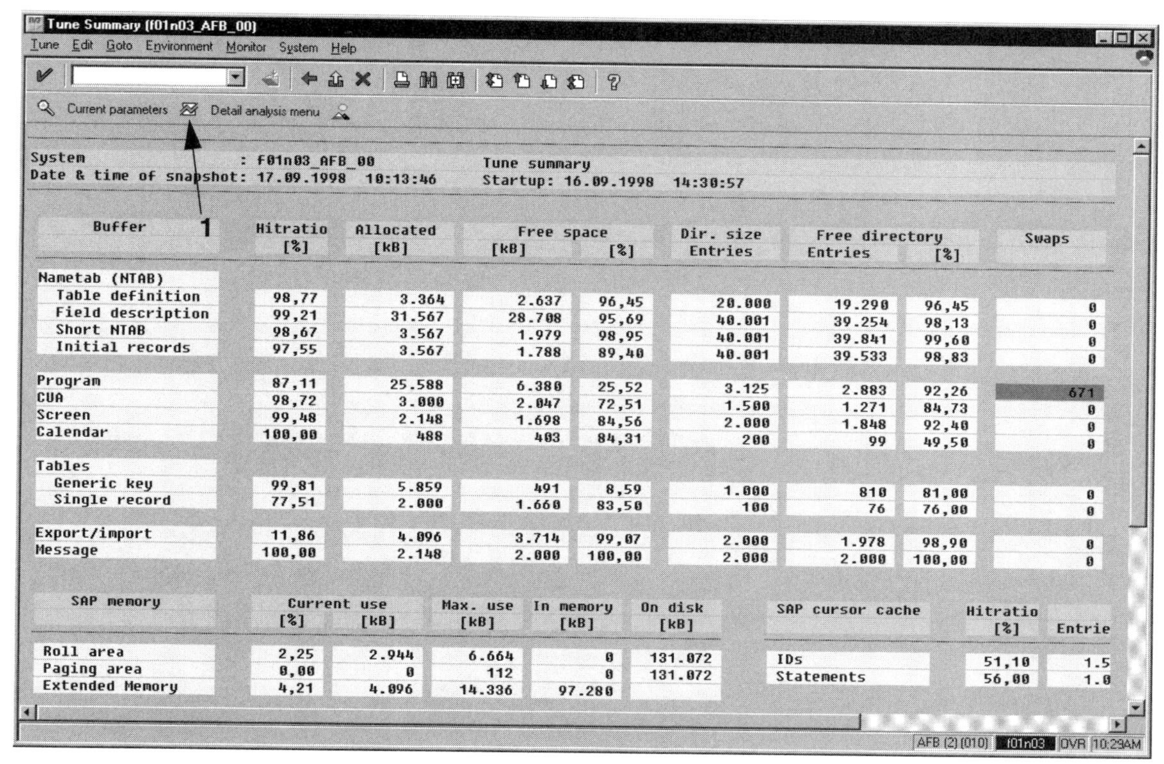

Figure 372. Tune Summary

Look for any entries marked in red under the *Swaps* column (the right-most column in Figure 372). This means that a buffer does not have enough storage.

Swapping occurs when the buffer is full, and R/3 has to load further objects into the buffer. When this occurs, objects removed from the buffer are lost and cannot be replaced until a new database access is performed, replacing what was lost. Objects in the buffer that were used least recently are removed.

There are two possible reasons for swapping:

- The buffer is too small. You should then increase the buffer size.
- There are no directory entries left. Although there is enough space left in the buffer, no further objects can be loaded because the number of directory entries is limited.

For the R/3 repository buffers, the number of directory entries is determined by the number of entry counts. All other buffers have their own parameters. For all other buffers you have to change the number of directory entries according to the change in buffer size.

2. Analyze Buffer Usage:

   Click on the **History** icon (1) in the tool bar to analyze the recent history of the usage of the various R/3 buffers:

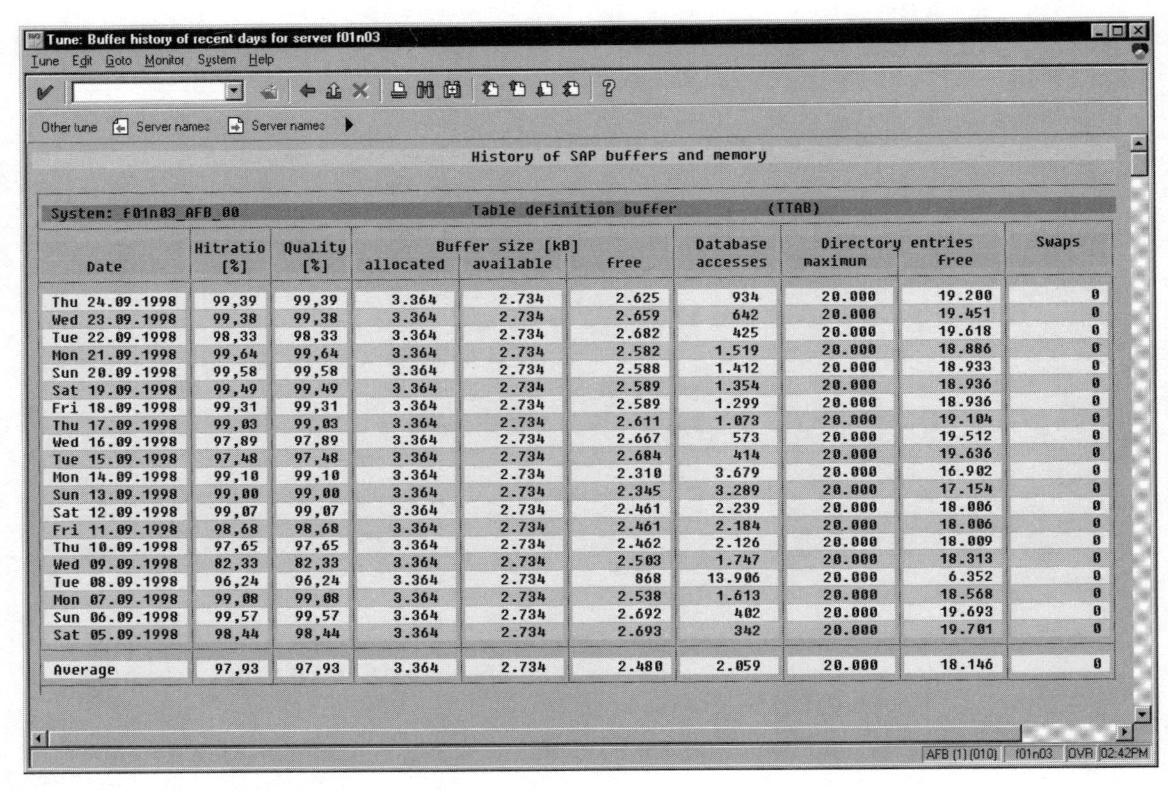

History of SAP buffers and memory

System: f01n03_AFB_00 — Table definition buffer (TTAB)

Date	Hitratio [%]	Quality [%]	Buffer size [kB] allocated	available	free	Database accesses	Directory entries maximum	free	Swaps
Thu 24.09.1998	99,39	99,39	3.364	2.734	2.625	934	20.000	19.200	0
Wed 23.09.1998	99,38	99,38	3.364	2.734	2.659	642	20.000	19.451	0
Tue 22.09.1998	98,33	98,33	3.364	2.734	2.682	425	20.000	19.618	0
Mon 21.09.1998	99,64	99,64	3.364	2.734	2.582	1.519	20.000	18.886	0
Sun 20.09.1998	99,58	99,58	3.364	2.734	2.588	1.412	20.000	18.933	0
Sat 19.09.1998	99,49	99,49	3.364	2.734	2.589	1.354	20.000	18.936	0
Fri 18.09.1998	99,31	99,31	3.364	2.734	2.589	1.299	20.000	18.936	0
Thu 17.09.1998	99,03	99,03	3.364	2.734	2.611	1.073	20.000	19.104	0
Wed 16.09.1998	97,89	97,89	3.364	2.734	2.667	573	20.000	19.512	0
Tue 15.09.1998	97,48	97,48	3.364	2.734	2.684	414	20.000	19.636	0
Mon 14.09.1998	99,10	99,10	3.364	2.734	2.310	3.679	20.000	16.902	0
Sun 13.09.1998	99,00	99,00	3.364	2.734	2.345	3.289	20.000	17.154	0
Sat 12.09.1998	99,07	99,07	3.364	2.734	2.461	2.239	20.000	18.006	0
Fri 11.09.1998	98,68	98,68	3.364	2.734	2.461	2.184	20.000	18.006	0
Thu 10.09.1998	97,65	97,65	3.364	2.734	2.462	2.126	20.000	18.009	0
Wed 09.09.1998	82,33	82,33	3.364	2.734	2.503	1.747	20.000	18.313	0
Tue 08.09.1998	96,24	96,24	3.364	2.734	868	13.906	20.000	6.352	0
Mon 07.09.1998	99,08	99,08	3.364	2.734	2.538	1.613	20.000	18.568	0
Sun 06.09.1998	99,57	99,57	3.364	2.734	2.692	402	20.000	19.693	0
Sat 05.09.1998	98,44	98,44	3.364	2.734	2.693	342	20.000	19.701	0
Average	97,93	97,93	3.364	2.734	2.480	2.059	20.000	18.146	0

Figure 373. Buffer Usage History

There are many different types of buffers. You can scroll down the screen shown in Figure 373 to see all the different types.

For these buffer types: table definition, field descriptor, short name table, initial record, generic buffer, single record, program, CUA, screen, calendar, export/import, and message; you should check for the following:

- Hit Ratio: The higher, the better.
- Buffer Quality: The higher, the better.
- Free Buffer Space: This should be above zero.
- Free Directory Entries: This should be above zero.
- Swaps: The lower the better.

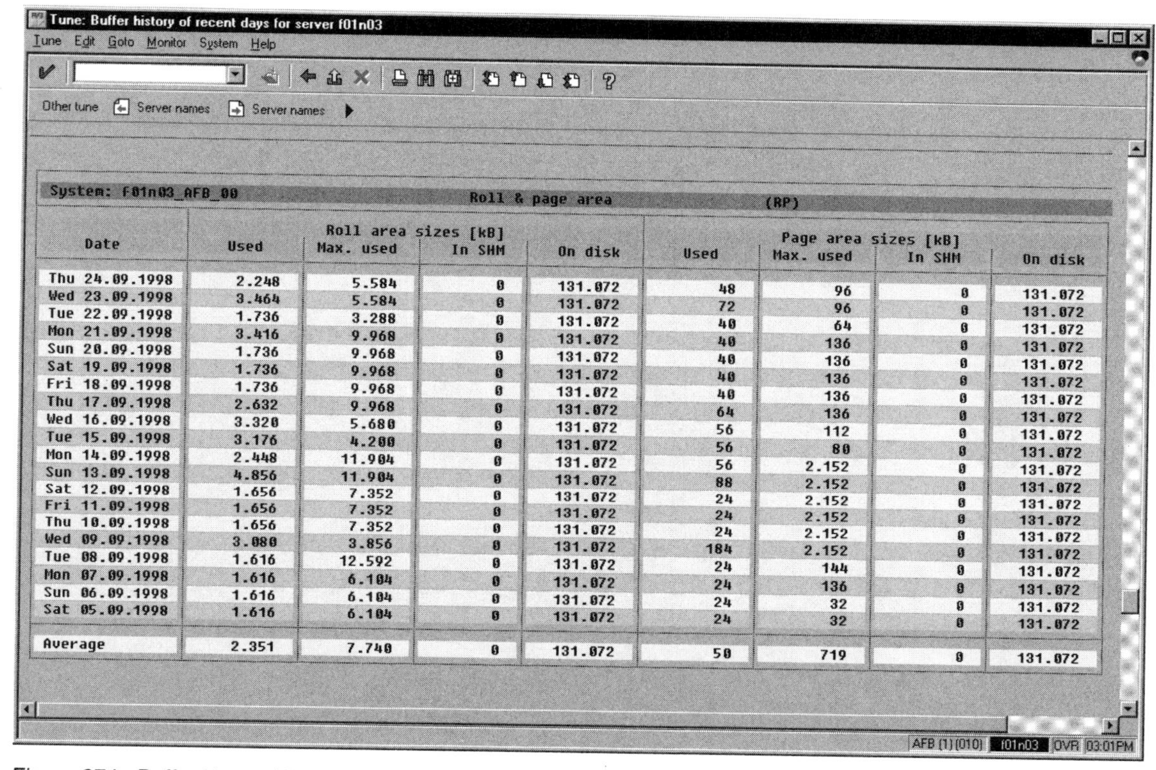

Tune: Buffer history of recent days for server f01n03

Tune Edit Goto Monitor System Help

Other tune | Server names | Server names

System: F01n03_AFB_00 — Roll & page area (RP)

Date	Roll area sizes [kB] Used	Max. used	In SHM	On disk	Page area sizes [kB] Used	Max. used	In SHM	On disk
Thu 24.09.1998	2.248	5.584	0	131.072	48	96	0	131.072
Wed 23.09.1998	3.464	5.584	0	131.072	72	96	0	131.072
Tue 22.09.1998	1.736	3.288	0	131.072	40	64	0	131.072
Mon 21.09.1998	3.416	9.968	0	131.072	40	136	0	131.072
Sun 20.09.1998	1.736	9.968	0	131.072	40	136	0	131.072
Sat 19.09.1998	1.736	9.968	0	131.072	40	136	0	131.072
Fri 18.09.1998	1.736	9.968	0	131.072	40	136	0	131.072
Thu 17.09.1998	2.632	9.968	0	131.072	64	136	0	131.072
Wed 16.09.1998	3.320	5.680	0	131.072	56	112	0	131.072
Tue 15.09.1998	3.176	4.200	0	131.072	56	80	0	131.072
Mon 14.09.1998	2.448	11.904	0	131.072	56	2.152	0	131.072
Sun 13.09.1998	4.856	11.904	0	131.072	88	2.152	0	131.072
Sat 12.09.1998	1.656	7.352	0	131.072	24	2.152	0	131.072
Fri 11.09.1998	1.656	7.352	0	131.072	24	2.152	0	131.072
Thu 10.09.1998	1.656	7.352	0	131.072	24	2.152	0	131.072
Wed 09.09.1998	3.080	3.856	0	131.072	184	2.152	0	131.072
Tue 08.09.1998	1.616	12.592	0	131.072	24	144	0	131.072
Mon 07.09.1998	1.616	6.104	0	131.072	24	136	0	131.072
Sun 06.09.1998	1.616	6.104	0	131.072	24	32	0	131.072
Sat 05.09.1998	1.616	6.104	0	131.072	24	32	0	131.072
Average	2.351	7.740	0	131.072	50	719	0	131.072

AFB (1) (010) f01n03 OVR 03:01PM

Figure 374. Buffer Usage History - Roll and Page Area

For the roll and page area buffers, you should check for the following:

- It is better if the size of the roll area is not greater than the roll area in SHM (shared memory).
- It is better if the size of the page area is not greater than the page area in SHM.

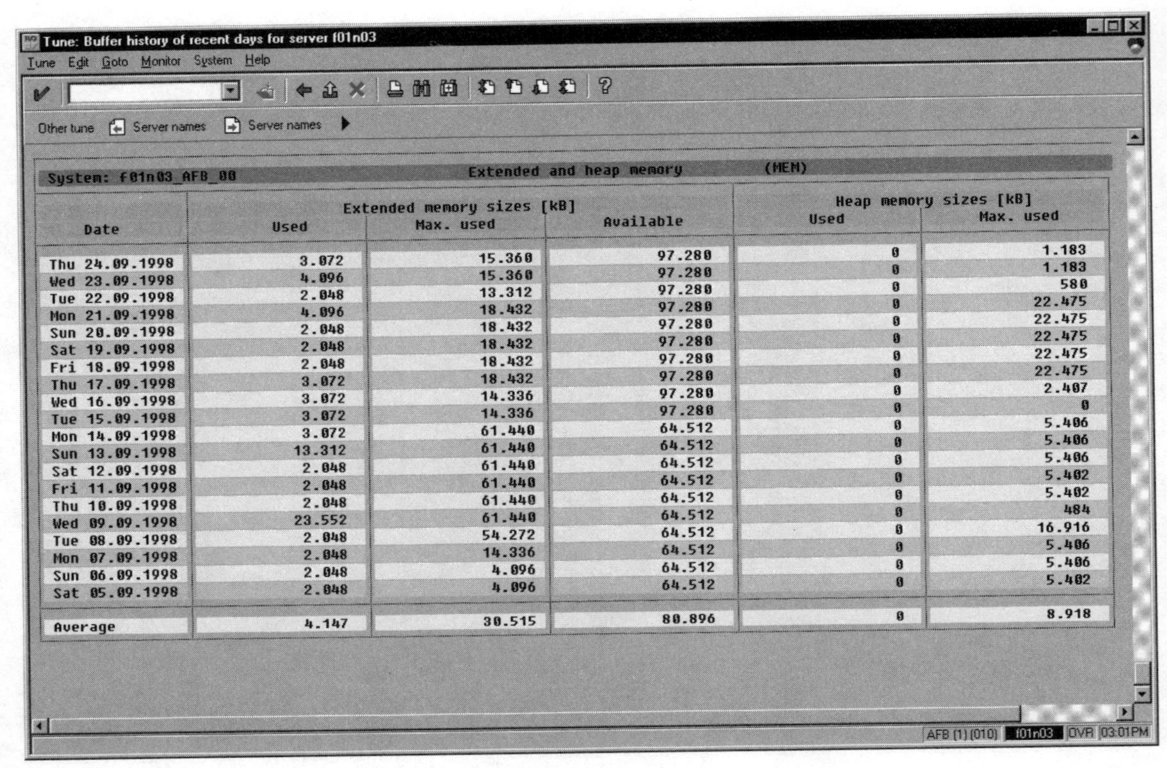
Tune: Buffer history of recent days for server f01n03

System: f01n03_AFB_00 Extended and heap memory (MEM)

Date	Extended memory sizes [kB] Used	Max. used	Available	Heap memory sizes [kB] Used	Max. used
Thu 24.09.1998	3.072	15.360	97.280	0	1.183
Wed 23.09.1998	4.096	15.360	97.280	0	1.183
Tue 22.09.1998	2.048	13.312	97.280	0	580
Mon 21.09.1998	4.096	18.432	97.280	0	22.475
Sun 20.09.1998	2.048	18.432	97.280	0	22.475
Sat 19.09.1998	2.048	18.432	97.280	0	22.475
Fri 18.09.1998	2.048	18.432	97.280	0	22.475
Thu 17.09.1998	3.072	18.432	97.280	0	22.475
Wed 16.09.1998	3.072	14.336	97.280	0	2.407
Tue 15.09.1998	3.072	14.336	97.280	0	0
Mon 14.09.1998	3.072	61.440	64.512	0	5.406
Sun 13.09.1998	13.312	61.440	64.512	0	5.406
Sat 12.09.1998	2.048	61.440	64.512	0	5.406
Fri 11.09.1998	2.048	61.440	64.512	0	5.402
Thu 10.09.1998	2.048	61.440	64.512	0	5.402
Wed 09.09.1998	23.552	61.440	64.512	0	484
Tue 08.09.1998	2.048	54.272	64.512	0	16.916
Mon 07.09.1998	2.048	14.336	64.512	0	5.406
Sun 06.09.1998	2.048	4.096	64.512	0	5.406
Sat 05.09.1998	2.048	4.096	64.512	0	5.402
Average	4.147	30.515	80.896	0	8.918

Figure 375. Buffer Usage History - Extended and Heap Memory

For the Extended and Heap Memory buffers, you should check for the following:

- It is better if the Extended memory size available is not zero.
- It is better if the Heap memory size used is zero.

3. Alter Buffer Size if required.

   To alter the size of a buffer, from the Tune Summary screen (see Figure 372 on page 437), select **Goto->Current Local Data** and choose the buffer type of interest. Click on **Current Parameters** from the tool bar:

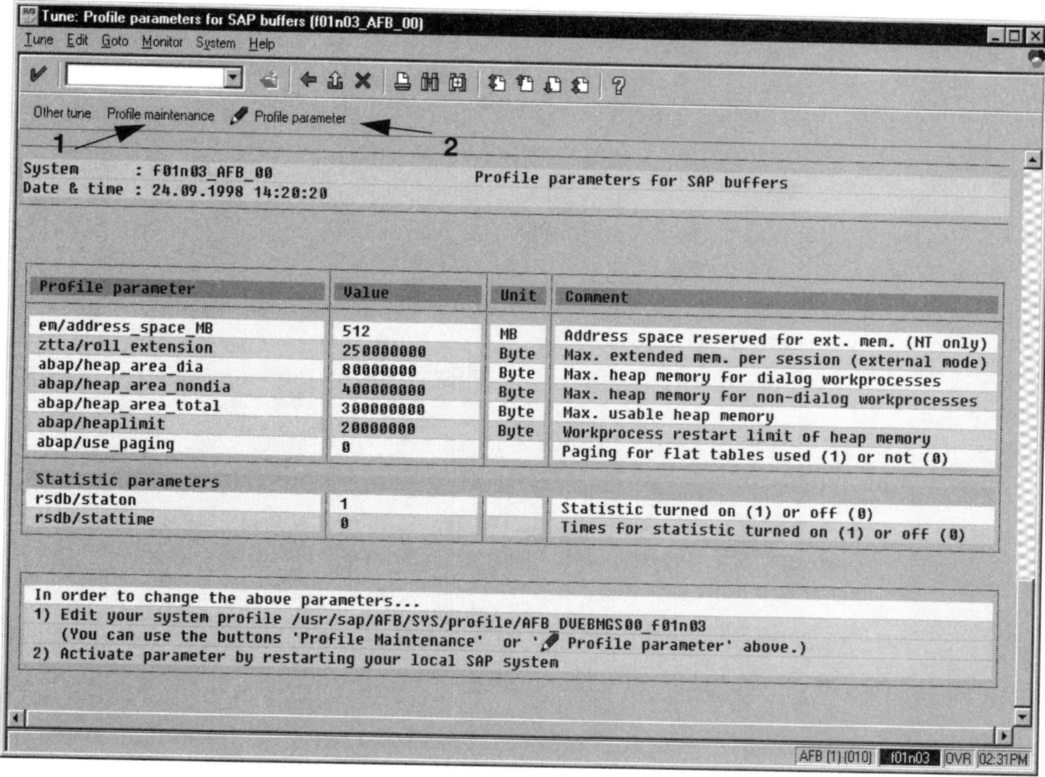

Figure 376. Profile Parameters for SAP Buffers

To modify multiple parameters, click on **Profile maintenance** (1) in the tool bar. To modify only one parameter, click on **Profile parameter** (2) in the tool bar.

Adjust the selected parameter by increasing or reducing its value until you get the desired effect.

9.4 Tuning SQL Statements

Tuning the SQL statements in your applications is an important step before going into production. Doing so will ensure that the applications execute in the most efficient way possible.

To examine the SQL statements used in your applications, you should use the R/3 SQL Trace tool.

9.4.1 Tracing SQL Using R/3

The R/3 SQL Trace tool allows you to examine the database calls in your applications. This tool shows you:

- The SQL statements that your application uses.
- Which values the system uses for specific database accesses and changes.
- How the system translates ABAP OPEN SQL commands (such as SELECT) into standard SQL commands.
- Where your application makes unnecessary database accesses or repeated accesses.
- Where your application positions COMMIT statements.
- What database accesses or changes occur in the update section of your application.

9.4.1.1 Running an SQL Trace

The system allows only one user at a time to create a trace file. If another user has already started a trace, the system notifies you.

Before you begin a trace, you should execute the program you intend to trace. Executing the program ensures that the database requests made by the program are buffered. When you execute the program again with the trace tool running, only the database accesses of non-buffered tables are recorded. Tuning the accesses for non-buffered tables has the most positive effect on your application's performance.

When activated, the SQL Trace records every database operation performed by the user or users. These measurements can affect the performance of the application server where the trace is running. To preserve system performance, you should turn off the trace as soon as you finish recording your application.

To start the SQL Trace:

1. Select: **Tools->Administration, Monitor->Traces->SQL Trace** or enter transaction ST05. The Trace Requests screen is displayed:

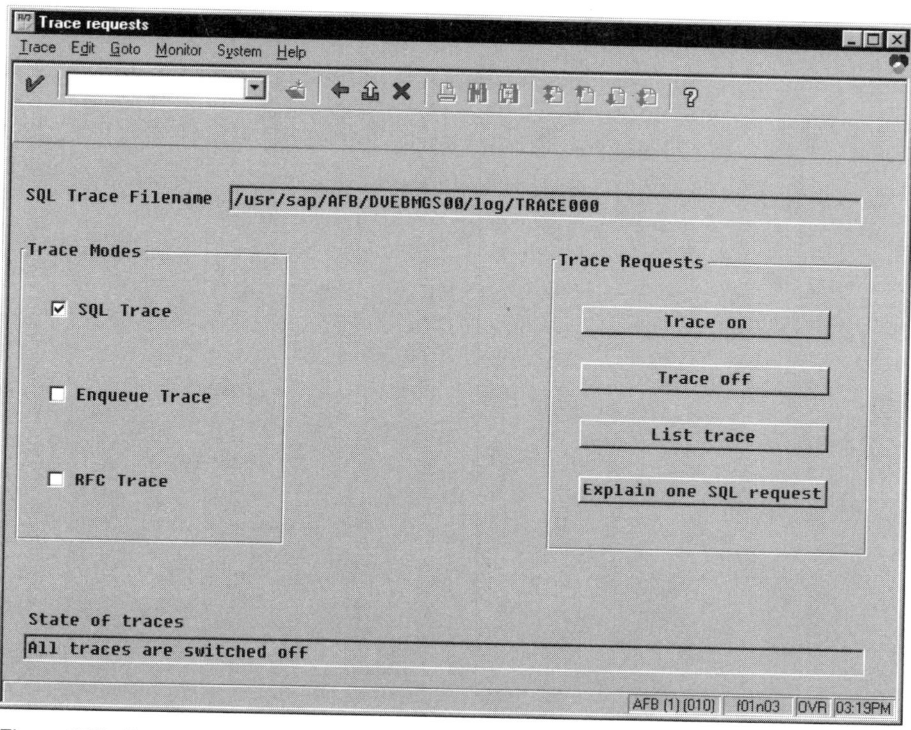

Figure 377. Trace Request

2. Make sure that the **SQL Trace** box is checked.
3. Click on **Trace on** to start the trace. The system will then prompt you for a username for the trace:

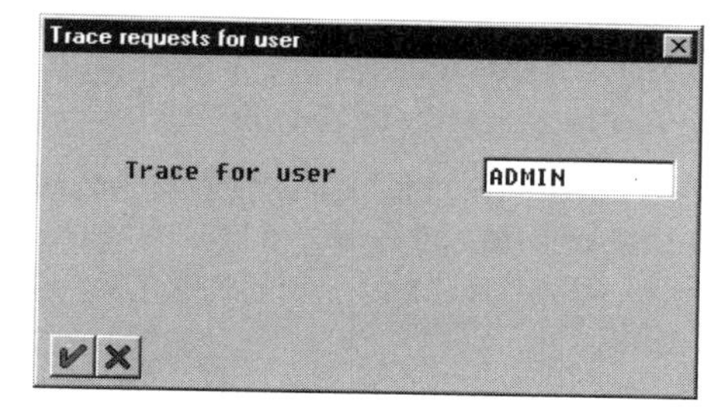

Figure 378. Trace Request for User

4. By default, your current user is selected. If you want to trace for all users, enter an asterisk.

5. Now that the trace is running, you should run the application that you want to trace.
6. When you have finished, turn the trace off by clicking on **Trace off** from the Trace Requests screen (see Figure 377 on page 443). The system confirms that the trace was turned off.
7. To see the SQL trace file that was generated, click on **List trace** from the Trace Requests screen to display this panel:

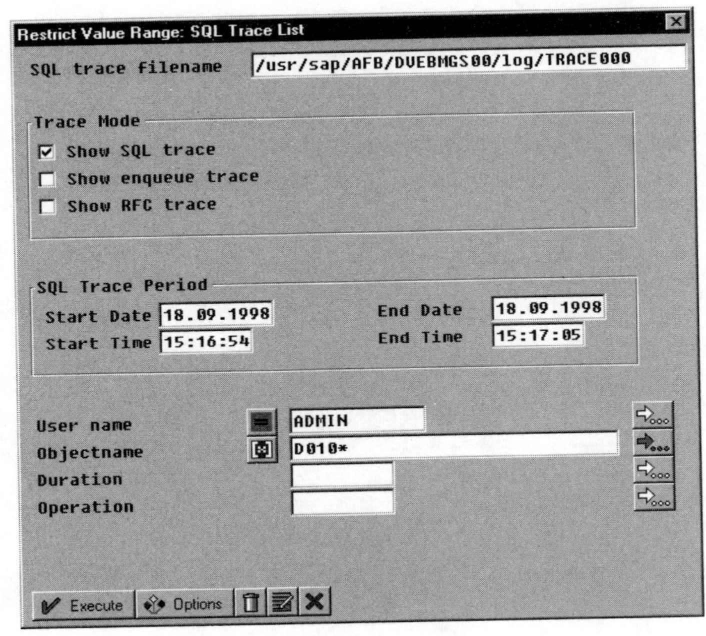

Figure 379. Restrict Value Range: SQL Trace List

8. The system prompts you to specify an SQL trace file name along with its directory. The last trace you ran is suggested as the default value.
9. If you ran a trace using an * (asterisk) for the user name, you must enter * (asterisk) in the User name field to retrieve the trace.
10. Click on **Execute**.
11. The system displays the chronological list of database requests captured for the duration of the specified trace:

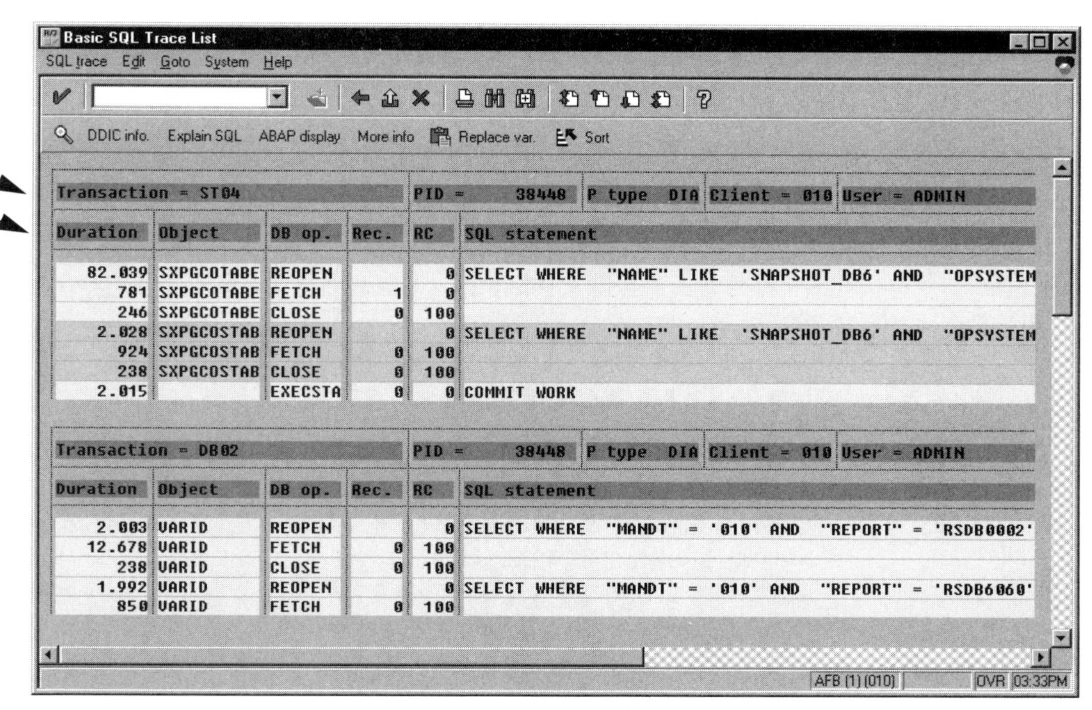

Figure 380. Basic SQL Trace List

The Basic SQL Trace List window shows the following information:

1. In the first title row (marked 1 in Figure 380): Transaction code, Process ID (PID), Program Type (Dialog, Update, Batch), Client, R/3 User ID.
2. In the second title row (marked 2 in Figure 380): Duration, Object name, Database Operation, Number of records, SQL Return code, SQL Statement

Here are some important things to check and do:

- Duration of Execution:

  The Duration column is one of the best indicators to analyze application performance problems.

- Repeated SQL Statements:

  The values in a WHERE predicate can help you decide whether or not to modify the application code to eliminate unnecessary repeated SQL statements.

- Viewing the Relevant Code:

You can use the ABAP Display function to view the relevant code for an operation. To use this function, place your cursor on a program in the Program column and choose **ABAP Display**. The system opens the program in the ABAP Editor at the point where an operation is defined.

9.4.2 Explaining SQL Statements Using R/3

The R/3 Explain SQL function provides you with an analysis of the strategy used to access tables in the R/3 database. You can use this analysis to identify the indexes used. You can explain a specific SQL statement in two different ways:

- From within the trace data file display, you can select a table and display details on the access method.
- From the initial screen of the SQL Trace tool, you can explain a statement by entering the statement using the SAP Editor.

To understand the information displayed by the Explain SQL function, you need in-depth knowledge of DB2 UDB.

9.4.2.1 Explaining SQL from a Trace Data File

To explain a statement from a trace data file, from the Basic SQL Trace List screen (as shown in Figure 380 on page 445), click on the desired SQL statement to highlight it, and then click on **Explain SQL**. The execution plan is displayed as follows:

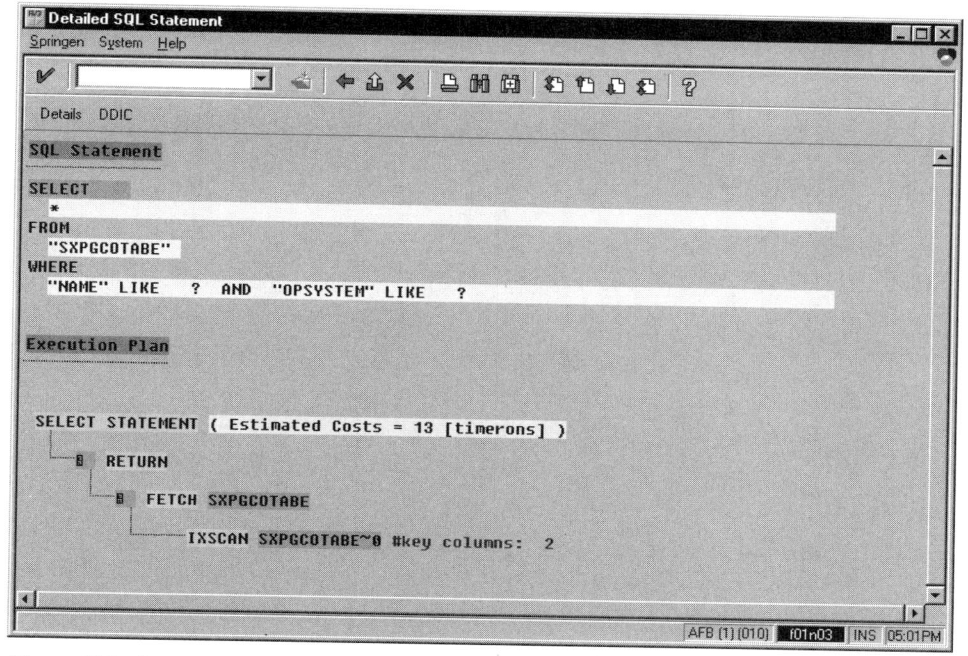

Figure 381. Detailed SQL Statement

To obtain further information about the table, click on **DDIC** in the application tool bar to display the following screen:

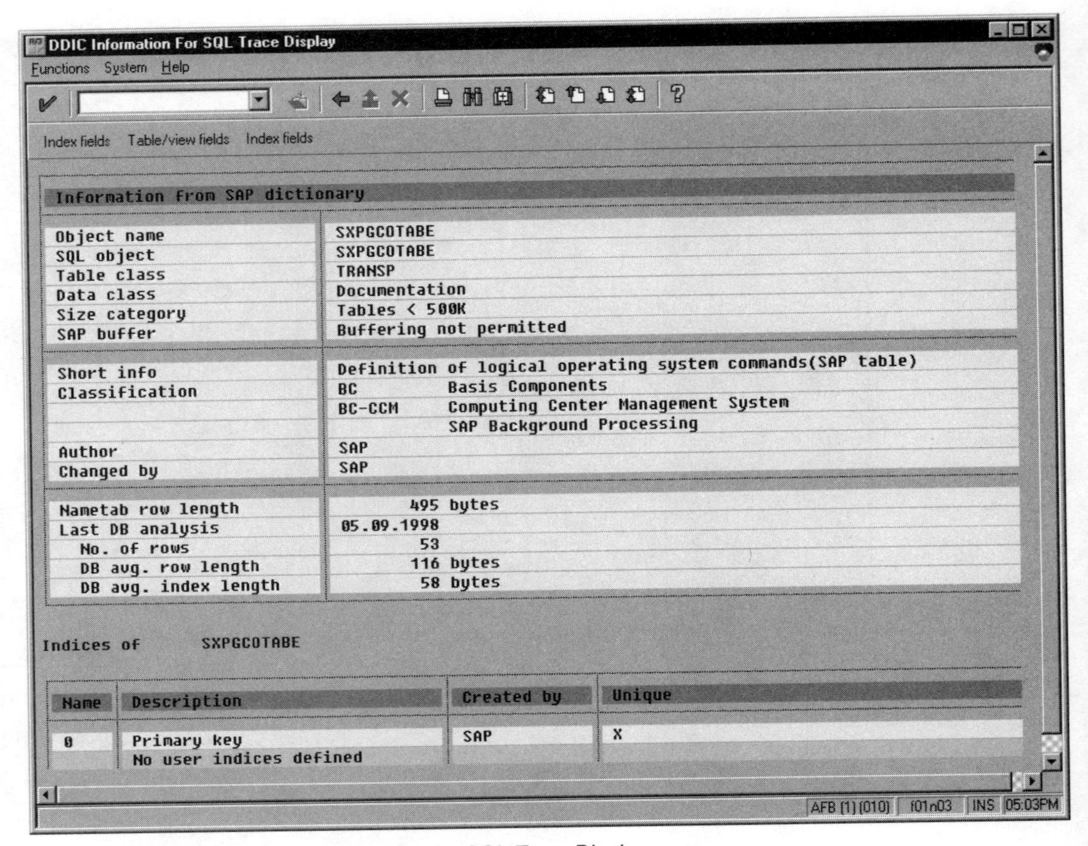

Figure 382. DDIC Information for SQL Trace Display

9.4.2.2 Explaining SQL using the SAP Editor

To explain a single SQL statement using the SAP Editor:

1. Click on **Explain one SQL request** from the Trace Requests screen (see Figure 377 on page 443). The following screen is displayed:

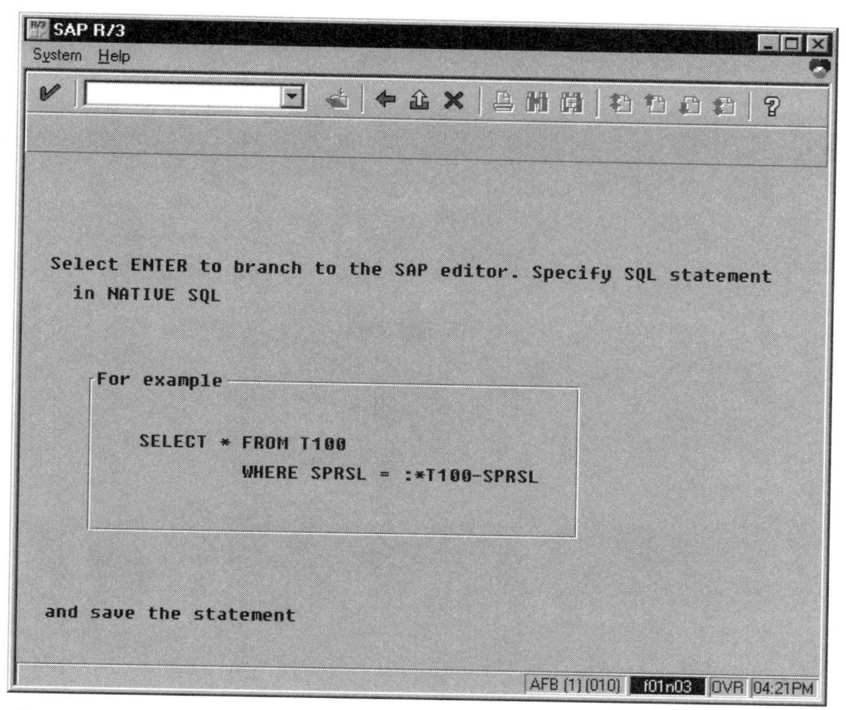

Figure 383. SQL Explain Using the SAP Editor

2. When you click on **Enter** (the green checkmark), the SAP Editor is started:

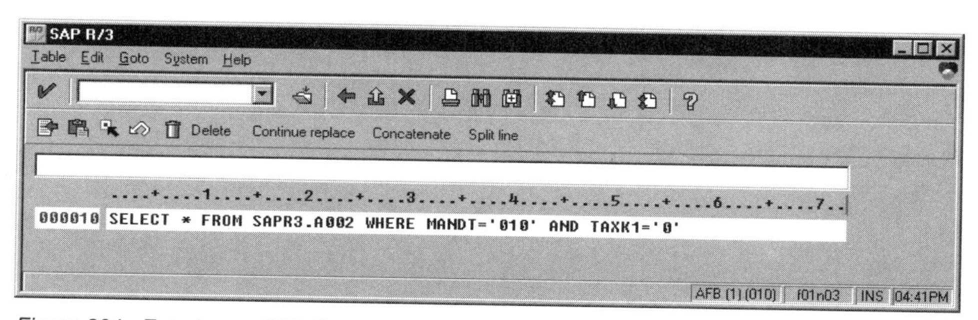

Figure 384. Entering an SQL Statement

3. Enter an SQL statement in uppercase.
4. Click on **Save** in the menu bar. The SQL statement is then explained and the output displayed as follows:

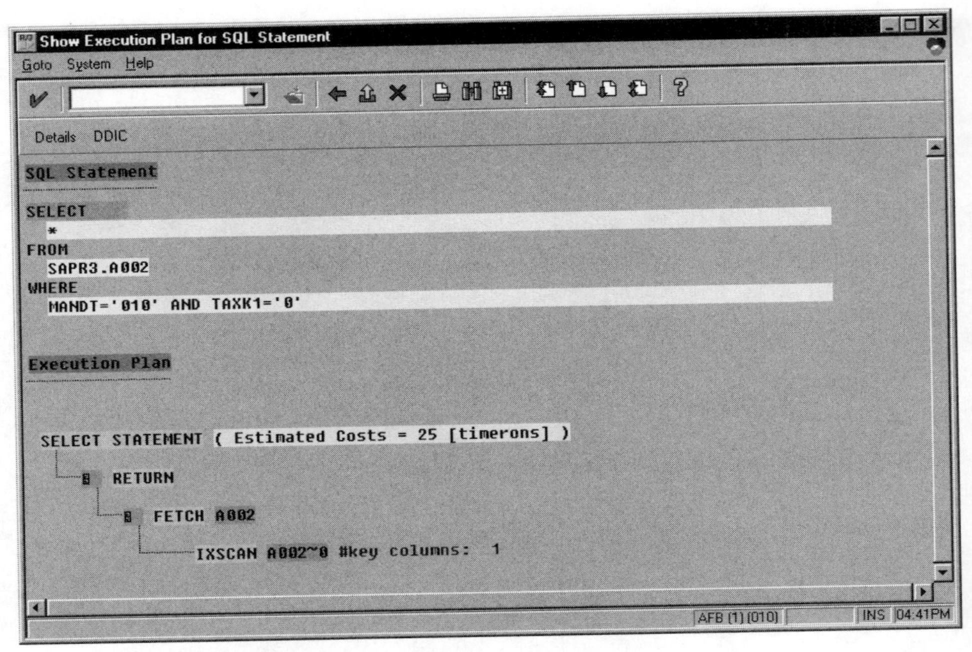

Figure 385. Show Execution Plan for SQL Statement

9.4.2.3 More Details about SQL Execution Plans

It is also possible to get more details on the access plan and other information used by the optimizer. To do this, click on **Details** in the application tool bar from the Show Execution Plan for SQL Statement window (see Figure 385 on page 450). Here is an example of the output generated:

```
Details from DB2EXFMT ---------------------
DB2 Universal Database Version 5, 5622-044 (c) Copyright IBM Corp. 1995,
1998 Licensed Material - Program Property of IBM
IBM DATABASE 2 Explain Table Format Tool
******************** EXPLAIN INSTANCE ********************
DB2_VERSION:          05.00.0
SOURCE_NAME:          SQLL3B0C
SOURCE_SCHEMA:        NULLID
EXPLAIN_TIME:         1998-09-21-09.50.36.966099
EXPLAIN_REQUESTER:    SAPR3
Database Context: ----------------
      Parallelism:          None
      CPU Speed:            7.714955e-06
      Comm Speed:           0
      Buffer Pool size:     10000
      Sort Heap size:       512
      Database Heap size:   8000
      Lock List size:       3200
      Maximum Lock List:    100
      Average Applications: 1
      Locks Available:      361600
Package Context: ---------------
      SQL Type:             Dynamic
      Optimization Level:   5
      Blocking:             Block All Cursors
      Isolation Level:      Uncommitted Read
---------------- STATEMENT 1  SECTION 397 ----------------
      QUERYNO:              20270
      QUERYTAG:
      Statement Type:       Select
      Updatable:            No
      Deletable:            No
      Query Degree:         1
Original Statement: ------------------
select *
from sapr3.fllog
```

Figure 386. Detailed Explain from R/3 (1 of 5)

```
Optimized Statement: -------------------
SELECT Q1.FLCODE AS "FLCODE", Q1.JETID AS "JETID", Q1.DAT AS
"DAT", Q1.DTIME
     AS "DTIME", Q1.ATIME AS "ATIME", Q1.DEPA AS "DEPA", Q1.ARRA
AS "ARRA",
     Q1.PLCODE AS "PLCODE", Q1.FLOWN AS "FLOWN", Q1.FCONS AS
"FCONS",
     Q1.PASSNO AS "PASSNO"
FROM SAPR3.FLLOG AS Q1
Access Plan: -----------
     Total Cost:          0.0771495
     Query Degree:           1
       RETURN
       (   1)
         |
       FETCH
       (   2)
      /---+--\
   IXSCAN  TABLE: SAPR3
   (   3)      FLLOG
     |
 INDEX: SAPR3
   FLLOG~0
     1) RETURN: (Return Result)
          Cumulative Total Cost:          0.0771495
          Cumulative CPU Cost:              10000
          Cumulative I/O Cost:            0
          Cumulative Re-Total Cost:       0.0771495
          Cumulative Re-CPU Cost:           10000
          Cumulative Re-I/O Cost:         0
          Cumulative First Row Cost:      0.0805827
          Arguments: ---------
          BUFFERS : (Required bufferpool buffers)
               1
          Input Streams: -------------
               4) From Operator #2
                    Estimated number of rows:       0
                    Number of columns:             11
                    Subquery predicate ID:         Not Applicable
                    Column Names: ------------
+PASSNO+FCONS+FLOWN+PLCODE+ARRA+DEPA+ATIME
                    +DTIME+DAT+JETID+FLCODE
```

Figure 387. Detailed Explain from R/3 (2 of 5)

```
2) FETCH : (Fetch)
        Cumulative Total Cost:          0.0771495
        Cumulative CPU Cost:            10000
        Cumulative I/O Cost:            0
        Cumulative Re-Total Cost:       0.0771495
        Cumulative Re-CPU Cost:         10000
        Cumulative Re-I/O Cost:         0
        Cumulative First Row Cost:      0.0771495
        Arguments: ---------
        BUFFERS : (Required bufferpool buffers)
            1
        MAXPAGES: (Maximum pages for prefetch)
            1
        MAXPAGES: (Maximum pages for prefetch)
            1
        PREFETCH: (Type of Prefetch)
            NONE
        ROWLOCK : (Row Lock intent)
            NONE
        TABLOCK : (Table Lock intent)
            INTENT NONE
        Input Streams: -------------
            2) From Operator #3
                Estimated number of rows:       0
                Number of columns:              2
                Subquery predicate ID:          Not Applicable
                Column Names: ------------
                +FLCODE(A)+$RID$
            3) From Object SAPR3.FLLOG
                Estimated number of rows:       0
                Number of columns:              10
                Subquery predicate ID:          Not Applicable
                Column Names: ------------
        +PASSNO+FCONS+FLOWN+PLCODE+ARRA+DEPA+ATIME
        +DTIME+DAT+JETID
        Output Streams: --------------
            4) To Operator #1
                Estimated number of rows:       0
                Number of columns:              11
                Subquery predicate ID:          Not Applicable
                Column Names: ------------
        +PASSNO+FCONS+FLOWN+PLCODE+ARRA+DEPA+ATIME
        +DTIME+DAT+JETID
```

Figure 388. Detailed Explain from R/3 (3 of 5)

```
3) IXSCAN: (Index Scan)
        Cumulative Total Cost:          0.0701289
        Cumulative CPU Cost:             9090
        Cumulative I/O Cost:            0
        Cumulative Re-Total Cost:        0.0701289
        Cumulative Re-CPU Cost:           9090
        Cumulative Re-I/O Cost:          0
        Cumulative First Row Cost:       0.0701289
        Arguments: ---------
        BUFFERS : (Required bufferpool buffers)
            1
        MAXPAGES: (Maximum pages for prefetch)
            ALL
        PREFETCH: (Type of Prefetch)
            NONE
        ROWLOCK : (Row Lock intent)
            NONE
        TABLOCK : (Table Lock intent)
            INTENT NONE
        Input Streams: -------------
            1) From Object SAPR3.FLLOG~0
                Estimated number of rows:       0
                Number of columns:            2
                Subquery predicate ID:         Not Applicable
                Column Names: ------------
                +FLCODE(A)+$RID$
        Output Streams: --------------
            2) To Operator #2
                Estimated number of rows:       0
                Number of columns:            2
                Subquery predicate ID:         Not Applicable
                Column Names: ------------
                +FLCODE(A)+$RID$
Objects Used in Access Plan: ---------------------------
    Schema: SAPR3
    Name:   FLLOG~0
    Type:   Index
            Time of creation:            1998-09-04-17.12.00.226941
            Last statistics update:       1998-09-05-10.28.04.651809
```

Figure 389. Detailed Explain from R/3 (4 of 5)

```
                number of columns:            1
                Number of rows:              0
                Width of rows:              -1
                Number of buffer pool pages:   1
                Distinct row values:          Yes
                Tablespace name:               PSAPSTABI
                Tablespace overhead:            24.100000
                Tablespace transfer rate:      0.900000
                Prefetch page count:           16
                Container extent page count:   8
                Index clustering statistic:    100.000000
                Index leaf pages:             0
                Index tree levels:           1
                Index full key cardinality:    0
      Schema: SAPR3
      Name:  FLLOG
      Type:  Table
                Time of creation:           1998-09-04-17.12.00.000366
                Last statistics update:      1998-09-05-10.28.04.651809
                Number of columns:            11
                Number of rows:              0
                Width of rows:              54
                Number of buffer pool pages:   1
                Distinct row values:          No
                Tablespace name:               PSAPSTABD
                Tablespace overhead:            24.100000
                Tablespace transfer rate:      0.900000
                Prefetch page count:           16
                Container extent page count:   8
                Table overflow record count:   0
-----------------------------------------------------------------------------------------
SQL Statement -------------
SELECT
  *
FROM
  sapr3.fllog

Execution Plan --------------
 SELECT STATEMENT ( Estimated Costs = 0 [timerons] )
  L--- RETURN
       |
     --- FETCH FLLOG
         |
         ------IXSCAN FLLOG~0 #key columns: 0
```

Figure 390. Detailed Explain from R/3 (5 of 5)

This detailed output includes information about:

- Database context: This describes important parameters such as the size of the buffer pool, sort heap and lock list.
- Package context: This describes the level of optimization used, blocking and isolation levels used for the SQL statement.
- Original and optimized SQL Statement.
- Access plan: More detailed information about the access plan that the overview explanation does not show.
  - Costs of CPU and I/O for each step of access plan access
  - Buffers used
  - Prefetching information
  - Locks on rows or tables
  - Input stream
  - Output stream
  - Objects used in the access plan; this describes the statistics information of index, table or other SQL objects that are being used by the access plan.

If you click on **DDIC**, you can obtain further information about the tables and indexes from the R/3 dictionary:

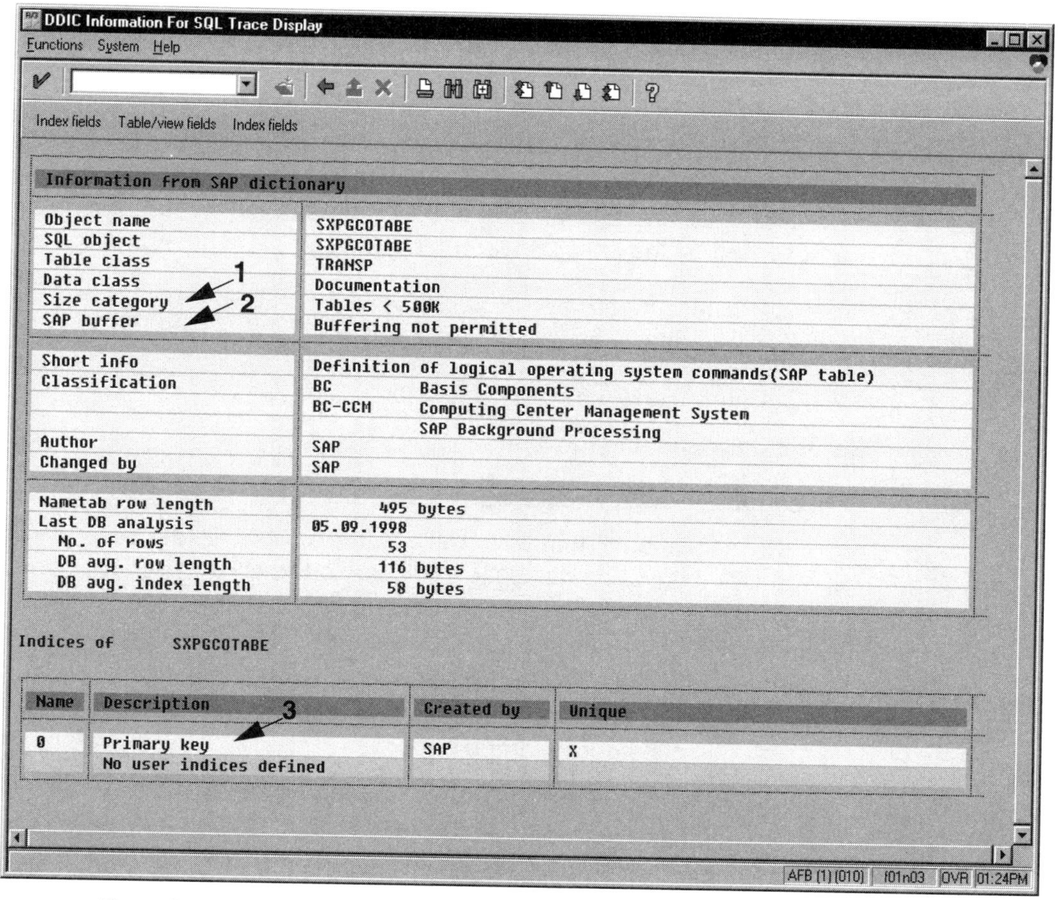

Figure 391. DDIC Information for SQL Display

Some of the important fields in this screen are:

1. Size Category: For example, this table is in the <500K category.
2. SAP Buffer: For this table, buffering is not permitted.
3. Indices: The indexes defined on this table.

9.4.3 Explaining SQL Statements Using DB2 UDB

You can also use the Visual Explain facility available in DB2 UDB to explain SQL statements. It supports both static and dynamic SQL statements and gives detailed optimizer information.

Visual Explain lets you view the access plan for explained SQL statements as a graph. You can use the information available from the graph to tune your SQL queries for better performance. Visual Explain also lets you dynamically explain an SQL statement and view the resulting access plan graph.

The optimizer chooses an access plan and Visual Explain displays the information as an access plan graph in which tables and indexes, and each operation on them, are represented as nodes, and the flow of data is represented by the links between the nodes.

From an access plan graph, you can view the details for:

- Tables and indexes (and their associated columns)
- Operators (such as table scans, sorts, and joins)
- Table spaces and functions.

You can also use Visual Explain to:

- View the statistics that were used at the time of access plan generation. You can then compare these statistics to the current catalog statistics to help you determine whether rebinding the package might improve performance.
- Determine whether or not an index was used to access a table. If an index was not used, Visual Explain can help you determine which columns should be considered for indexes.
- View the effects of performing various tuning techniques by comparing the before and after versions of the access plan graph for a query.
- Obtain information about each operation in the access plan, including the total estimated cost and number of rows retrieved (cardinality).

To explain an SQL statement using Visual Explain you can use either the Control Center or the DB2 UDB Command Center. To use the Control Center:

1. Right click on the R/3 database and choose Explain SQL
2. Enter your desired SQL statement in the SQL text input area and click on the **OK** button. The Visual Explain graph is then generated and displayed to you. Navigating through the Visual Explain output is the same regardless of whether the Control Center or Command Center is used.

To use the DB2 UDB Command Center, bring up the Command Center from the DB2 Universal Database for Windows NT folder:

1. Connect to the R/3 database by entering the SQL connect statement and pressing Ctrl-Enter:

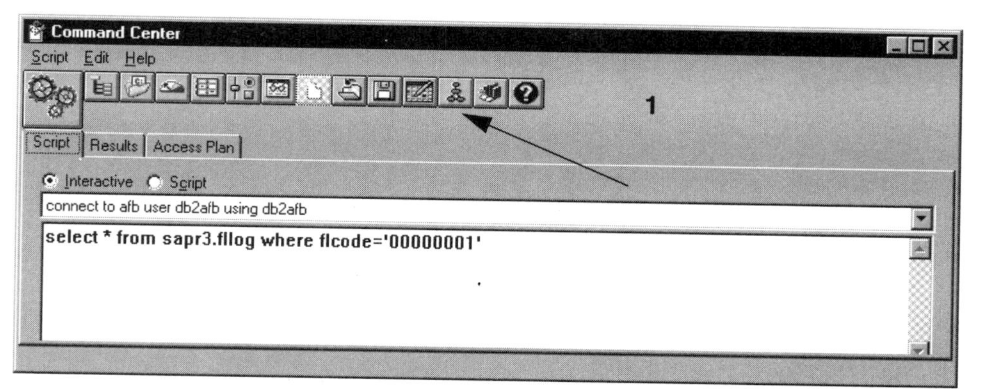

Figure 392. Command Center

2. Then enter the SQL statement you wish to have explained and click on the **Create access plan** icon (1) from the menu tool bar.
3. The access plan graph is displayed as follows:

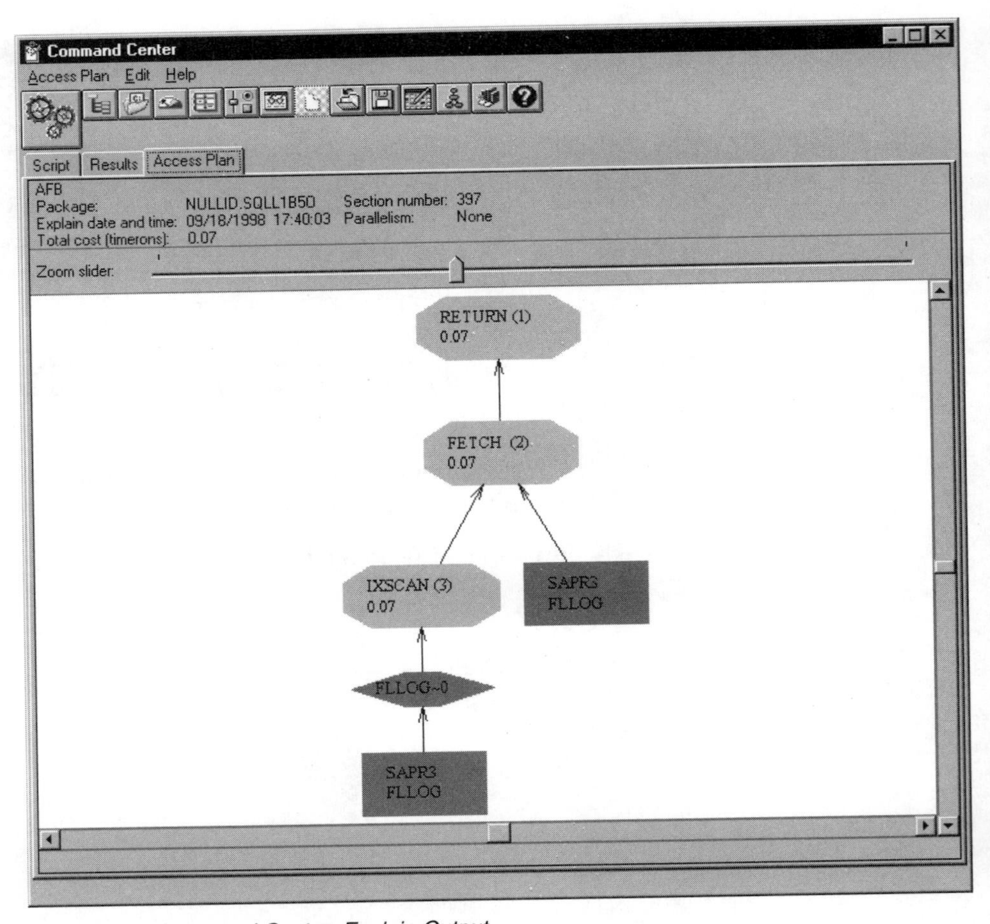

Figure 393. Command Center: Explain Output

The access plan chosen by the optimizer shows that the SAPR3.FLLOG table is accessed via the FLLOG~0 index using an index scan.

To get more detailed information, right-click on one of the objects shown in the access plan graph and choose **Show Details** or **Show Statistics** (depending on the object chosen). For example, for the SAPR3.FLLOG table, we see the following information:

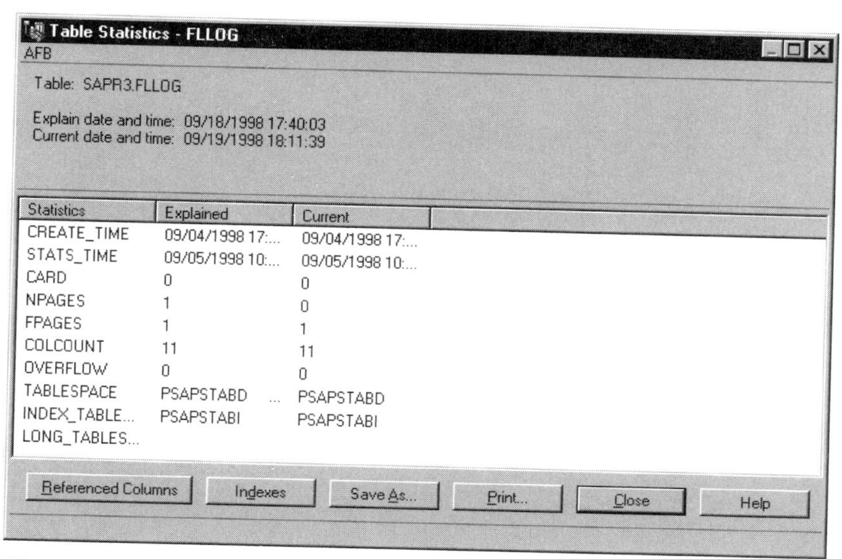

Figure 394. Visual Explain Table Statistics - FLLOG

The size of the table in 4 KB pages is given by the CARD entry. If there are a large number of overflow pages in the table (OVERFLOW), you should consider performing a reorganization of the table. A full list of these entries is given in the *DB2 UDB Administration Guide* under Catalog Views, SYSSTAT.TABLES.

The Index Statistics for the SAPR3.FLLOG~0 index are as follows:

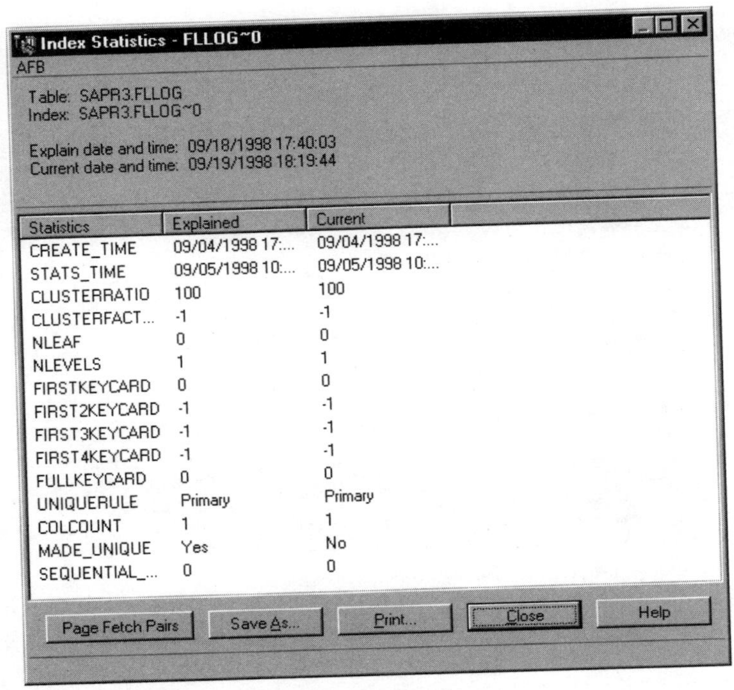

Figure 395. Index Statistics - FLLOG~1

You should make sure that the index has a clusterratio/clusterfactor near 100%. The FIRSTKEYCARD entry gives the number of distinct values for the first column of the index. The closer this number is to the number of table rows, the better the selectivity of access by this column. A full list of these entries is given in the *DB2 UDB Administration Guide* under Catalog Views, SYSSTAT.INDEXES.

By right-clicking on the IXSCAN operator, and choosing **Show Details**, the following screen is displayed:

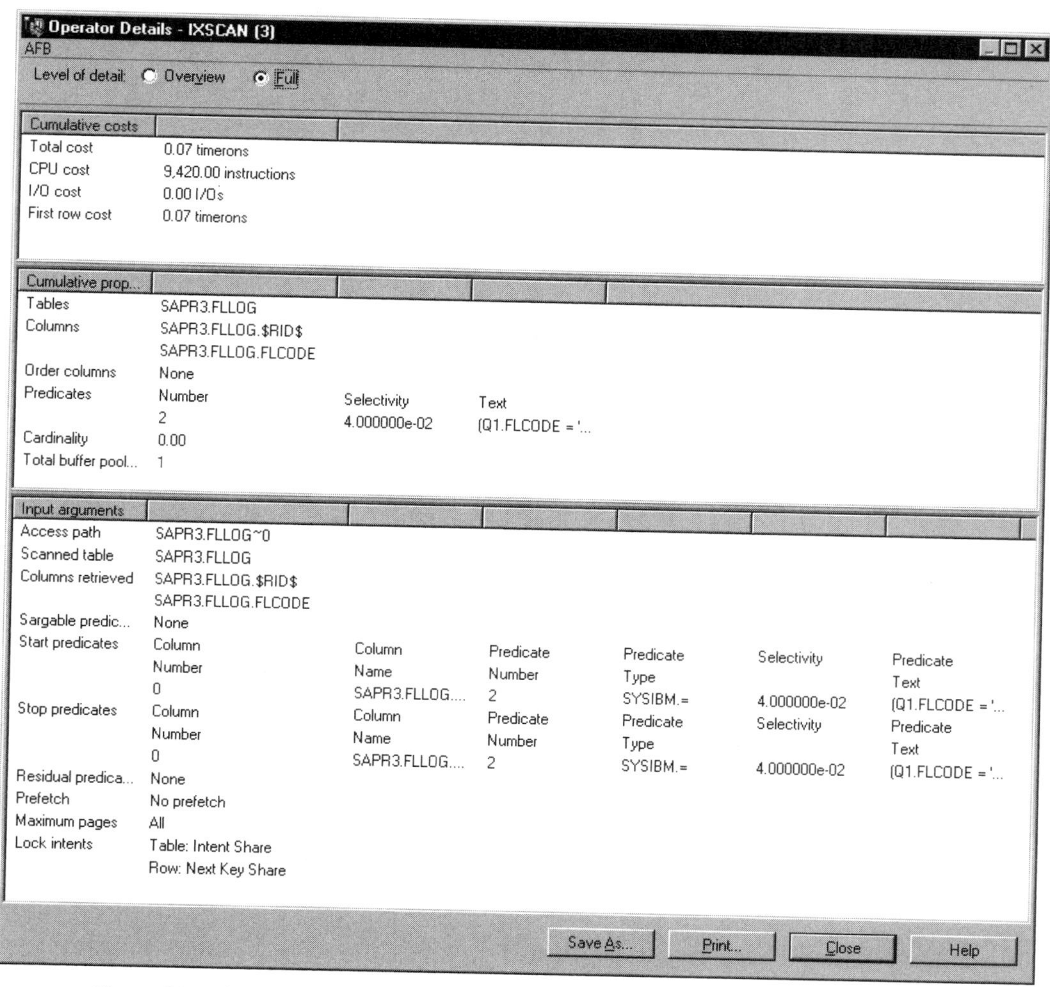

Figure 396. Operator Details - IXSCAN(3)

For more details about the information given in Operator Details, you should look in the *IBM DB2 UDB Administration Guide*, under SQL Explain Tools.

The optimizer can compute an accurate value for each explanation field only if the statistical information for each table is up to date. To enable the optimizer to compute accurate values for the above fields, you must ensure that up-to-date statistical information about the contents of relevant tables is available.

To update your information, use the R/3 Update Statistics function. Since the execution plan selected by the optimizer (for example, the use of a table scan versus an index scan) depends on this information, you should always ensure that it is kept as up to date as possible by regularly running Update Statistics. See “Generating Statistics and Reorganizing Tables” on page 373 for more details.

Chapter 10. Troubleshooting

This chapter is designed to help you determine the nature of problems that may arise in your R/3 system using DB2 UDB as its database. These topics are covered:

- DB2 and R/3 Information Resources
- DB2 and R/3 Logs
- DB2 and R/3 Traces
- DB2 and R/3 Common Problems

10.1 DB2 UDB Information Resources

The following DB2 UDB information resources are available to help you:

- The manuals in printed or HTML format. All the DB2 UDB manuals are available from a web browser.
- For a description of SQL codes and other messages, type **`db2 ? message`** from the DB2 UDB command line, where message is the SQL code or other message number.
- For a description and syntax of DB2 commands, type **`db2 ? command,`** where command is the name of the DB2 UDB command.

10.1.1 Web Site

Up-to-date bulletins and technical documentation are available from the DB2 Product and Service Technical Library on the World Wide Web at **`http://www.software.ibm.com/data/db2/library`**. The DB2 World Wide Web pages provide current DB2 news, product descriptions, and more. The DB2 Product and Service Technical Library provides access to frequently asked questions, fixes, books, and up-to-date DB2 technical information.

10.1.2 Internet Newsgroups and Forums

Newsgroups and forums are provided on the Internet or from on-line service providers. For example,

- comp.databases.ibm-db2, bit.listserv.db2-l

  These newsgroups are available for users to discuss their experiences with DB2 products and get assistance from other users.

10.1.3 Anonymous FTP Sites

The FTP site **`ftp.software.ibm.com`** has software fixes for DB2 UDB.

Note

You should **not** apply any DB2 UDB fixes from the IBM DB2 UDB anonymous FTP site unless SAP R/3 advises you to do so. SAP provides DB2 UDB fixes to address specific problems between DB2 UDB and R/3.

In the directory /ps/products/db2, you can find demos, fixes, information, and tools concerning DB2 and many related products.

10.2 R/3 Information Resources

SAP R/3 On-line Help has five components and covers all R/3 modules. The components are:

- Getting Started
- Glossary
- Implementation Guide
- Library
- Release Notes

The R/3 on-line help can be reached by one of three ways:

- By clicking on **Help** in the R/3 menu bar from any R/3 screen where you are working to get additional information about the fields in the screen.
- By selecting **Start->Programs->SAP On-line Help** from the Windows NT task bar.
- By positioning the pointer over the desired field in an R/3 screen and pressing **F1** to obtain additional information about the selected string or field.

You can also use the OSS as a source of information. For more details about OSS, see “Obtaining R/3 Notes from OSS” on page 41.

10.2.1 Web Sites

SAPNET at `http://sapnet.sap-ag.de` is the SAP R/3 World Wide Web site that provides current R/3 news, product descriptions, user groups, technical information, and much more.

10.2.2 Anonymous FTP Sites

R/3 software fixes are available from the R/3 FTP sites.

Note

FTP to the SAP servers only works when the customer has authorization to connect to the FTP sites: *sapservX* (where *X* is a number: 3,4,5,6 and 7) directly from your customer network.

To obtain fixes from the R/3 FTP server, you should log on as **anonymous**. Starting in the directory **/general**, you can download fixes, information, and tools relating to R/3 and third party related product fixes. The directory **/incoming** is the place to put your output traces for analysis by R/3 support. The directory **/specific** is the place where SAP provides non-official fixes and it is used to deliver specific solutions to customers.

10.3 DB2 UDB Logs

DB2 UDB logs information as errors occur using the facility known as First Failure Data Capture (FFDC). This information is written to the DB2DIAG.LOG file. This DB2 FFDC facilities often provides enough diagnostic information to solve a problem without having to reproduce a problem and take traces.

Diagnostic information is provided by DB2 in different forms depending on the target audience. Some information is intended for the database administrator and some for IBM service personnel. The information for the database administrator describes the reason for failure together with a detailed description of the error to help resolve the problem. IBM service personnel may need the descriptive information that is contained in the DB2DIAG.LOG file together with more detailed information, such as data from the database control blocks. This data is dumped into separate files, and is not contained in the DB2DIAG.LOG file.

There are two files that the R/3 DBA can monitor for DB2 problems, DB2DIAG.LOG and DB2ALERT.LOG. Both files are located in the /db2/<SID>/sqllib/db2dump directory on AIX and <drive>:\db2\<SID>\sqllib\db2dump on Windows NT. There is a DB2 database manager configuration parameter that you can set to control the amount of information written to these files. This parameter is DIAGLEVEL, and it has the following settings:

- 0 - No error logging
- 1 - Log severe errors
- 2 - Log severe and non-severe errors
- 3 - Log severe, non-severe and warning errors

- 4 - Log severe, non-severe errors, warnings and informational messages

The default setting is DIAGLEVEL 3. You can change the level with the DB2 UDB Control Center or the update database manager configuration command. For example, to change the DIAGLEVEL to 4:

1. Select **Start->Programs->DB2 for Windows NT->Administrative Tools->Control Center**. Right-click on the required instance and select **Configure**. Then click on the **Diagnostic** tab:

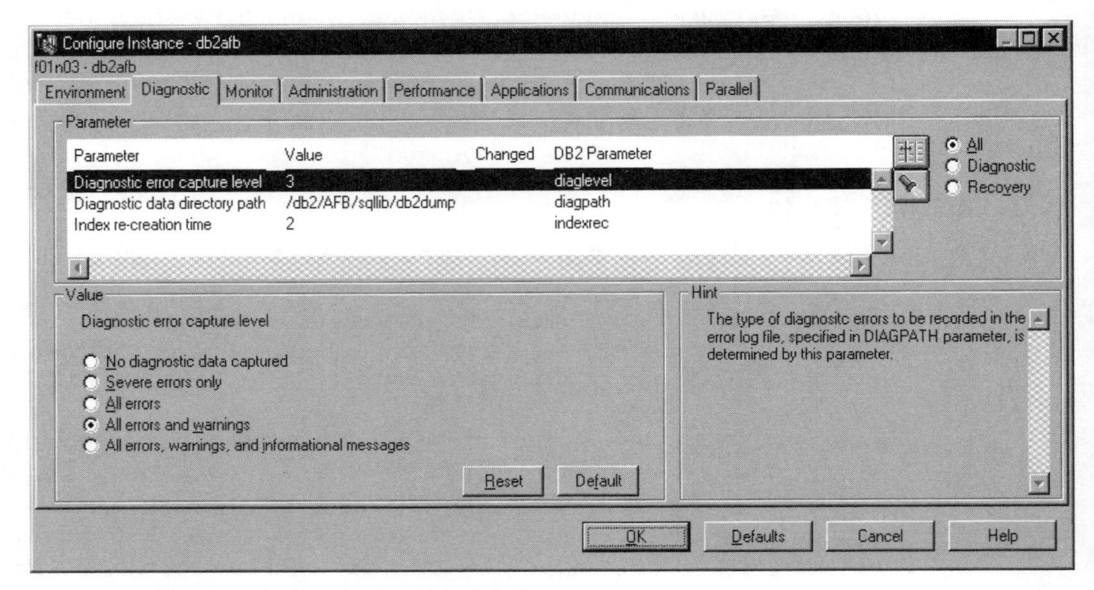

Figure 397. Configure Instance - db2afb

2. Select the Diagnostic error capture level from the list in the Parameter box.
3. Choose the diagnostic level in the Value box.
4. Click **OK**.

Remember that for any changes made at the instance level of DB2 to take effect, the instance must be stopped and restarted.

When an DB2 UDB error occurs, the DB2DIAG.LOG file is updated with information about the error (assuming DIAGLEVEL is set appropriately). If an error is determined to be an alert, then an entry to the DB2ALERT.LOG file is made and on AIX an entry in the syslog file is also made. You may notice other files in the sqlbin/db2dump directory. These files may be trap files (*.trp) or dump files (*.dmp). They are intended for IBM service personnel. If the problem is severe, you may need to submit these trap or dump files to IBM.

When you experience a DB2 error, the following steps should be performed:

- Check the online error message text by issuing the following command: `db2 ? pppnnn` (where ppp is SQL, DBA, or DBI and nnn is the error number).
- If the actions in the message text are insufficient to help you resolve the problem, examine the DB2DIAG.LOG error log. You can use any editor to view the file.
- Errors are appended to DB2DIAG.LOG as they occur, so you should examine the end of the log file for the most recent messages. You may find SQLCA information and/or diagnostic messages. These diagnostic messages are used to aid the description of the error. If any network alerts (SNA or SNMP) were generated, they will be recorded in the DB2DIAG.LOG file and the DB2ALERT.LOG file.
- If the problem still exists or you are unable to resolve it yourself, you should seek assistance from SAP and IBM service personnel.

Let's look at the contents of a sample DB2DIAG.LOG file with the components on separate lines for clarity:

```
(1)  1998-09-17-10.11.05.001160
(2)  Instance:db2afb
(3)  Node:000
(4)  PID:44829(db2agent (AFB))
(5)  Appid:*LOCAL.db2afb.980917101105
(6)  lock_manager
(7)  sqlplrq
(8)  Probe:111
(9)  Database: AFB
(10) DIA9999E A internal return code occurred. Report the following:
(11) "0xFFFFE10E".
```

Figure 398. Db2diag.log Entry

This entry from DB2DIAG.LOG shows the following:

1. A timestamp for the message.
2. The name of the instance generating the message.
3. The node number is only meaningful in DB2 UDB Enterprise-Extended Edition systems. For other versions of DB2 UDB, this value is always "000".
4. Identification of the process generating the message. In this example, the message came from the process identified by process id 44829. The name of this process is db2agent and it is connected to the AFB database.
5. Identification of the application for which the process is working. In this example, the process generating the message is working on behalf of a local application on the same machine with the ID *LOCAL.afb.980917101105.

   To identify more about a particular application ID, either:

   - Use the **`db2 list applications`** command to view a list of application IDs. From this list, you can determine information about the client experiencing the error, such as its node name and its TCP/IP address.
   - Use the **`db2 get snapshot for application`** command to view a list of application IDs.
6. The DB2 component that is writing the message.

7. The name of the function that is providing the message. This function operates within the DB2 subcomponent that is writing the message.

   To find out more about the type of activity performed by a function, look at the fourth letter of its name. In this example, the letter "p" in the function "sqlplrq" indicates data protection services. This includes the DB2 logger and the DB2 deadlock detector.

   The following list shows some of the letters used in the fourth position of the function name, and the type of activity they identify:

   - b - Buffer pools
   - c - Communication between clients and servers
   - d - Data management
   - e - Engine processes
   - o - Operating system services (such as opening and closing files)
   - p - Data protection (such as locking and logging)
   - r - Relational database services
   - s - Sorting
   - x - Indexing

8. Information on where within the function the message was generated.
9. The database on which the error occurred.
10. Diagnostic message indicating that an internal error occurred.
11. Hexadecimal representation of an internal return code. See the *DB2 UDB Troubleshooting Guide* for information on how to interpret these hexadecimal codes.

10.4 R/3 Logs

Here we examine the R/3 system log, which contains a log of errors generated in the R/3 system. We also cover ABAP dump analysis, which is used to find errors in ABAP/4 programs. This enables the user to find the line in the source code where the error occurred.

10.4.1 R/3 System Log

From the R/3 menu, select: **Tools->Administration, Monitor->System Log** or enter transaction **SM21**.

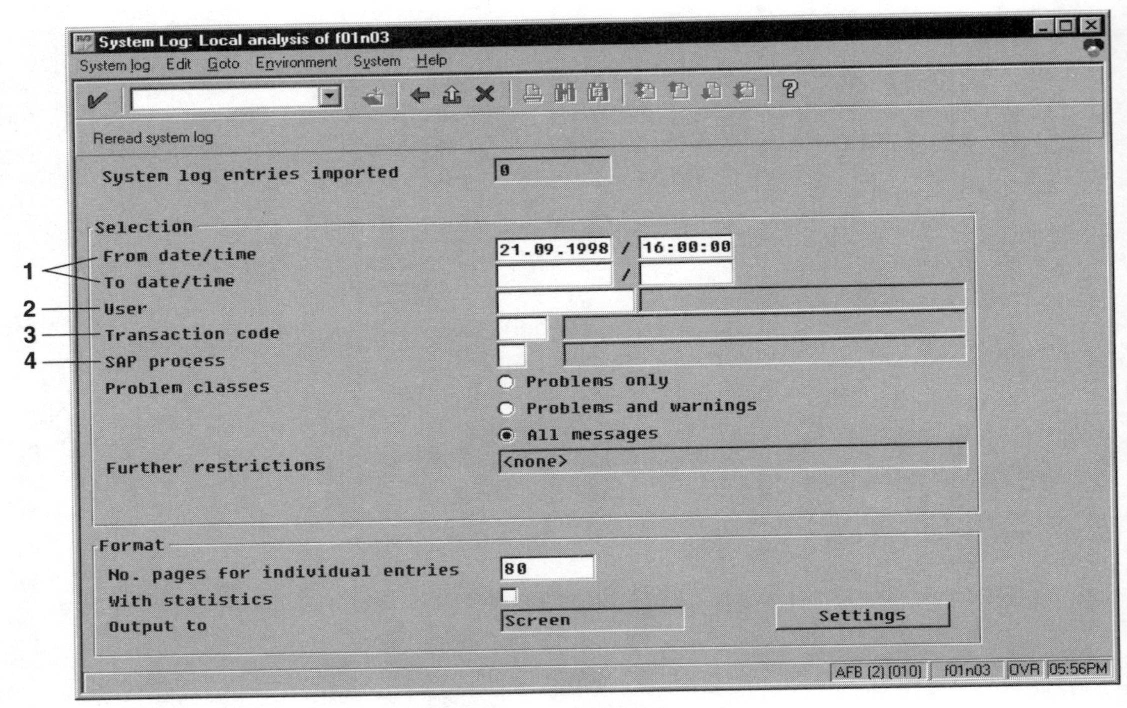

Figure 399. System log: Local Analysis of f01n03

You can restrict the output with the following criteria (among others):

- The time range using From/To date/time (1 in Figure 399)
- The user (2)
- The transaction name (3)
- The SAP process (4)

Click on **Reread system log** in the tool bar to display the contents of the system log:

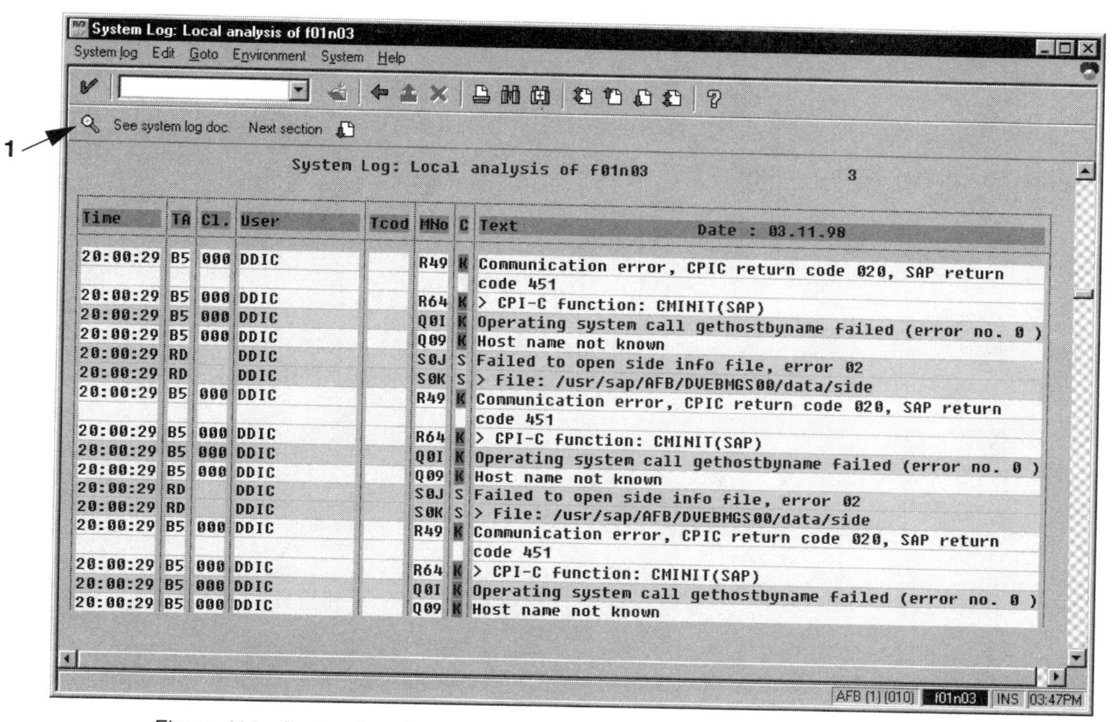

Figure 400. System log: Local Analysis of f01n03

To get more details about an entry, click on the desired entry and then click on the Details icon in the tool bar (1 in Figure 400). For example, if we display details for the first entry (Communication Error, CPIC return code 020, SAP return code 451), the following screen is displayed:

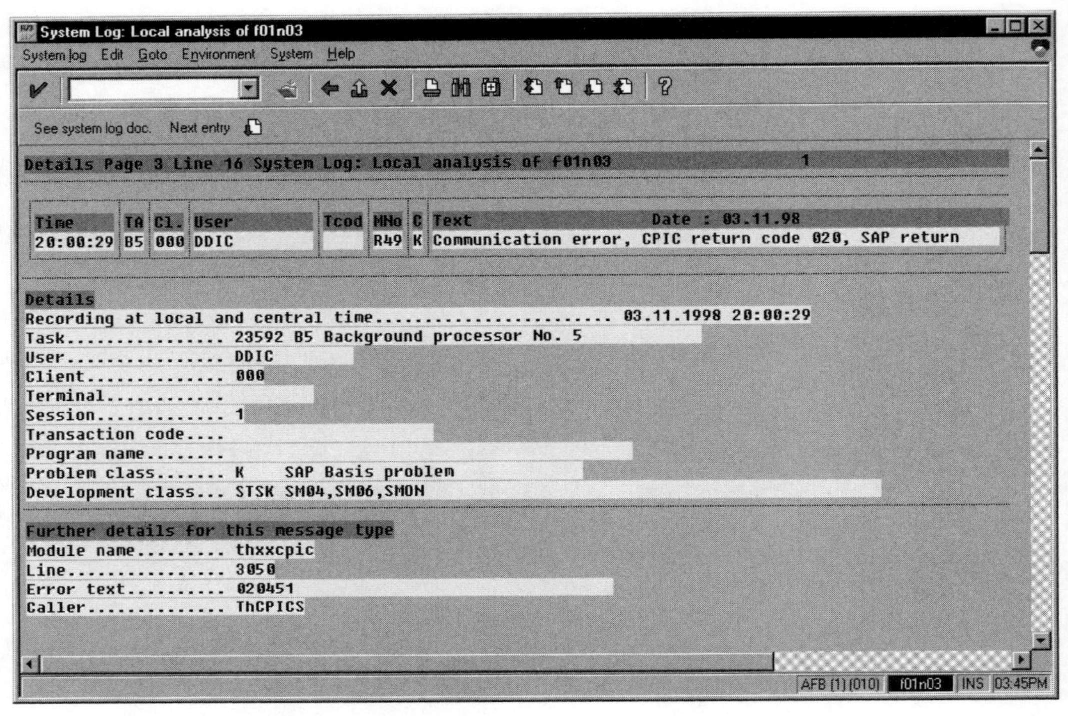

Figure 401. System Log: Detailed View

If you scroll down in detailed view, a long description of the message is given. For example:

```
Documentation for system log message R4 9 :
A CPIC function has failed.  The conversation ID and CPIC function are
specified in the system log entries.  Use the conversion ID to find
more detailed information about the error in the system log for the SAP
gateway.
```

Figure 402. System Log: Detailed View (2)

Further down, you can find the explanation of the SAP return code (in this case, 451, as shown by 1 in Figure 403):

2) Error in the CPIC interface:

450: No storage	451: No side-info entry
452: TP-START failed	453: No initialization
454: "getlu" failed	455: "signal" failed
456: Timeout during conn. setup	457: CMALLC failed
458: CMSEND failed	459: Prepare-To-Receive failed
460: "mc_flush" failed	461: CMRCV failed
462: Argument missing	463: "get_allocate" failed
464: CMDEAL failed	465: TP-END failed
466: Max.no.of conv. reached	467: "snaopen" failed
468: "snactl" failed	469: No flush in IBM environment
470: "snaclse" failed	471: Status error
472: No side-info entry	473: No conversation
474: Connection closed manually	475: Connection closed automatically
476: No partner found	477: Confirm failed
478: Confirmed failed	479: GWHOST not in side-info entry
480: GWSERV not in side-info e.	481: PROTOCOL not in side-info entry

Figure 403. System Log: Detailed View (3)

10.4.2 ABAP Dump Analysis

In order to get detailed information about dumped ABAP code, select **Tools->Administration, Monitor->Dump Analysis** or enter transaction **ST22**:

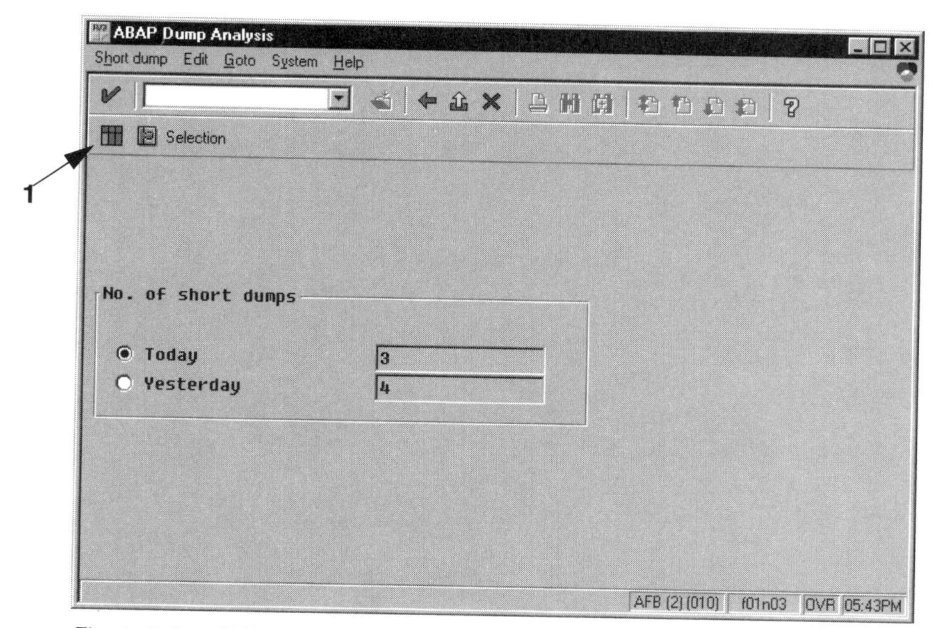

Figure 404. ABAP Dump Analysis

Click on today or yesterday, then click on the Display List icon (1 in Figure 404) in the tool bar to display the following screen:

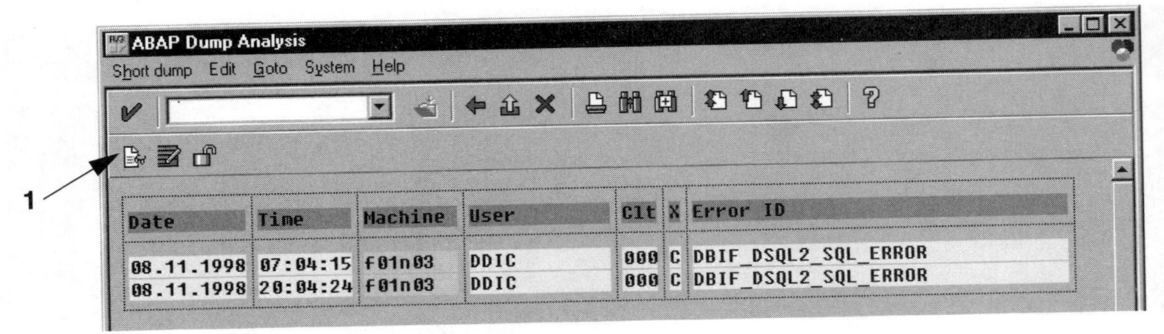

Figure 405. ABAP Dump Analysis (2)

To display detailed dump information for an entry, click on the desired entry, and then click on the **Dump Analysis** icon (1 in Figure 405) in the tool bar.

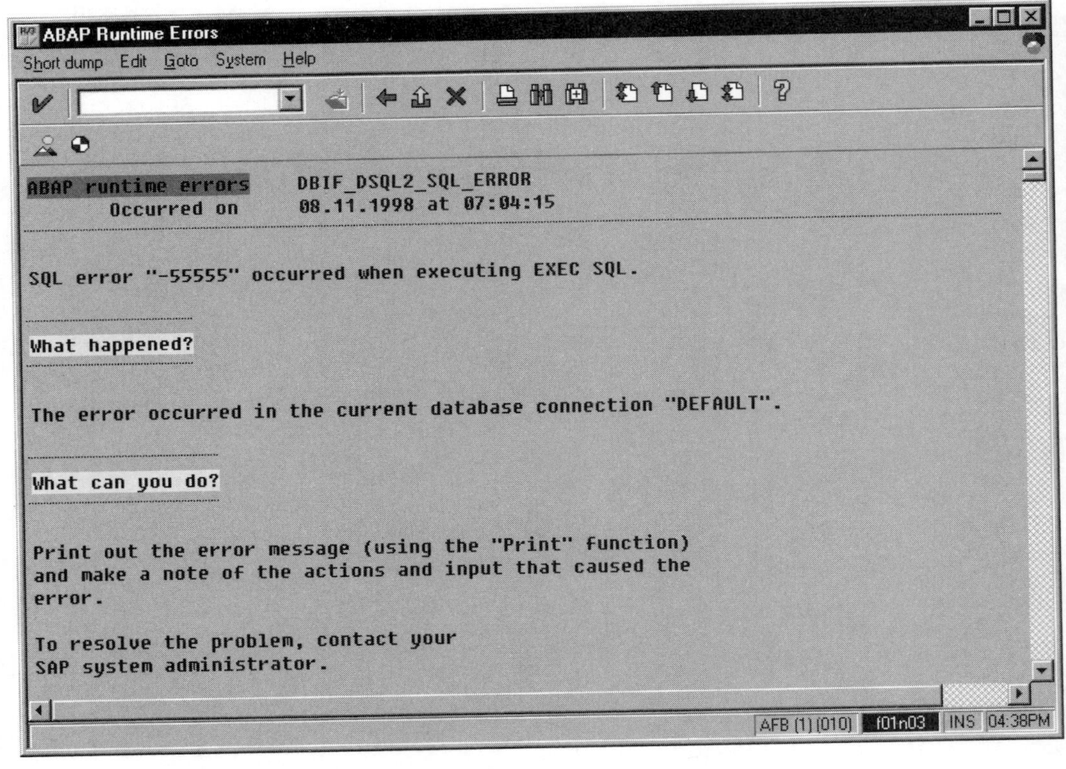

Figure 406. ABAP Dump Analysis (3)

Figure 406 on page 476 displays more details about the error, and gives suggested actions. If you scroll down a little further, advice is given on how to correct the error:

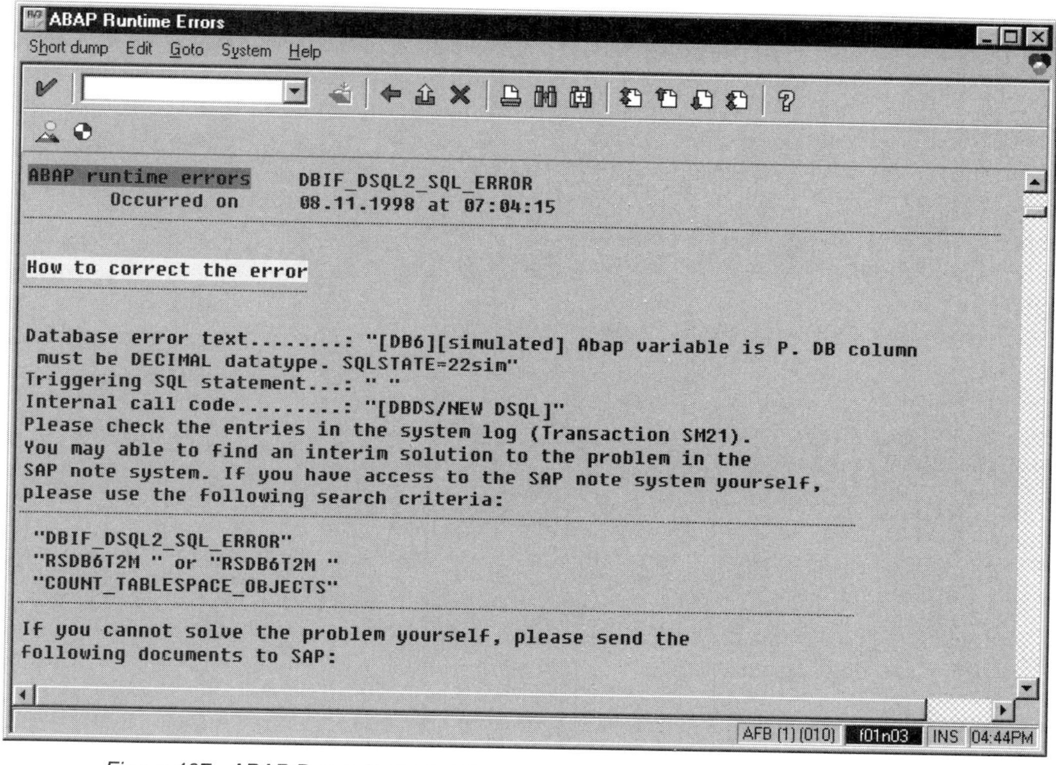

Figure 407. ABAP Dump Analysis (4)

As you scroll down still further, information on the following is provided (other information is also available):

- The system environment - The version of SAP, the operating system, and so on
- The user and transaction
- The ABAP/4 program where the error occurred
- An extract of the source code, highlighting the line at which the error occurred (1 in Figure 408):

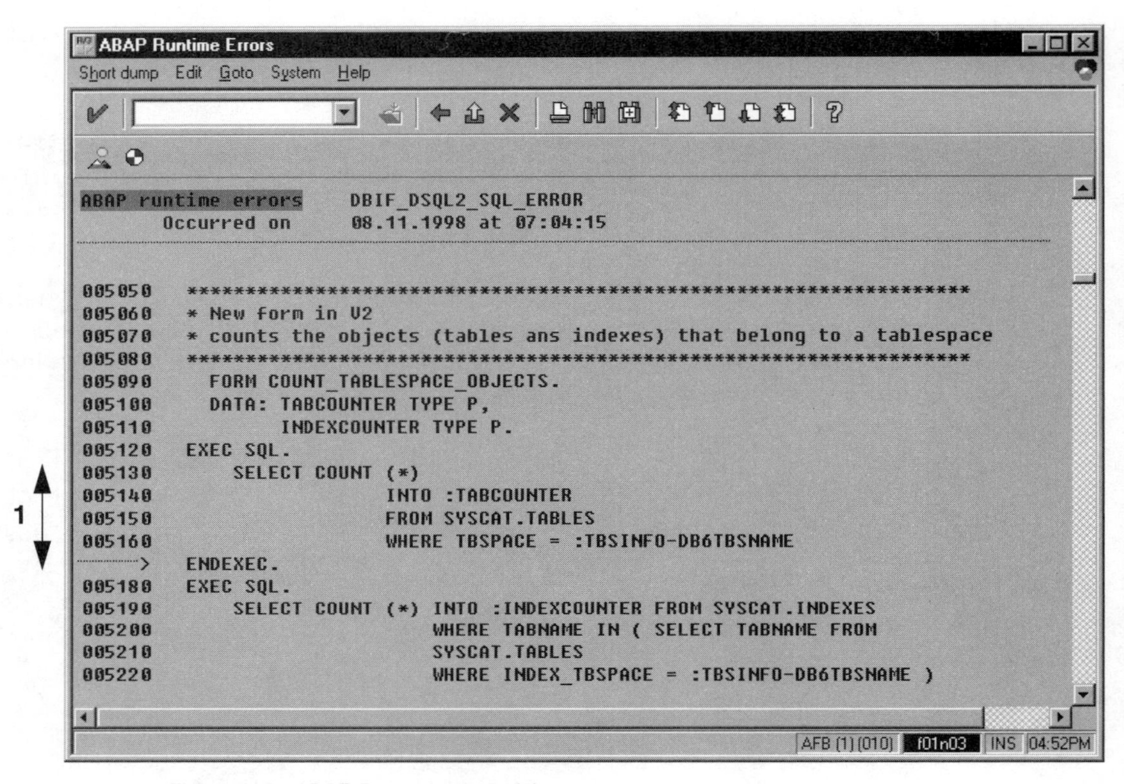

ABAP Runtime Errors
Short dump Edit Goto System Help
ABAP runtime errors DBIF_DSQL2_SQL_ERROR
Occurred on 08.11.1998 at 07:04:15
005050 **
005060 * New form in V2
005070 * counts the objects (tables ans indexes) that belong to a tablespace
005080 **
005090 FORM COUNT_TABLESPACE_OBJECTS.
005100 DATA: TABCOUNTER TYPE P,
005110 INDEXCOUNTER TYPE P.
005120 EXEC SQL.
005130 SELECT COUNT (*)
005140 INTO :TABCOUNTER
005150 FROM SYSCAT.TABLES
005160 WHERE TBSPACE = :TBSINFO-DB6TBSNAME
> ENDEXEC.
005180 EXEC SQL.
005190 SELECT COUNT (*) INTO :INDEXCOUNTER FROM SYSCAT.INDEXES
005200 WHERE TABNAME IN (SELECT TABNAME FROM
005210 SYSCAT.TABLES
005220 WHERE INDEX_TBSPACE = :TBSINFO-DB6TBSNAME)
AFB (1) (010) f01n03 INS 04:52PM
1

Figure 408. ABAP Dump Analysis (5)

10.5 The DB2 Trace Facility

If you have a recurring problem that you can reproduce, you may also wish to take a trace of the error. Unlike the DB2DIAG.LOG which captures information as the error is occurring, taking a DB2 trace requires you to reproduce the error. When taking a trace you need to be aware that you may be capturing information on a condition resulting from the original error, not the error itself.

Since the DB2 trace records the flow of control within internal DB2 functions, it cannot be interpreted by a database administrator. The DB2 UDB Support team may request a DB2 trace if the DB2DIAG.LOG file does not provide enough information to determine the source of the problem. In this section we will discuss the methods and considerations for taking DB2 traces.

DB2 trace information can be stored in memory or directly to disk. When DB2 trace collection is activated, the trace information is recorded in chronological order. Each entry in the trace file is called a *trace point* and is recorded sequentially.

The amount of information gathered from the trace will grow rapidly. The goal in performing a DB2 trace is to capture only the error situation. Any other activities, such as starting the database manager instance or connecting to a database that does not reproduce the error situation should be avoided. The goal in capturing trace information is to reproduce the *smallest, recreatable* scenario and capture it for further analysis.

Since the DB2 trace gathers information for every function within DB2 there will be a degradation in overall performance. How much degradation you experience is dependent on the type of problem and how the trace is being recorded (that is, in memory or on disk).

To perform a trace on AIX, use the **db2trc** command. On Windows NT, you may either use the **db2trc** command or initiate a trace though the Problem Determination Tools Folder. We will examine both of these methods.

10.5.1 The db2trc Command

The general syntax of the **db2trc** command is:

```
db2trc <subcommand> <options>
```

The complete syntax of the **db2trc** command can be found when the command is issued with the **-u** option. The following screen shows the subcommands of the **db2trc** command:

```
DB2 CLP
C:\>
C:\>
C:\>db2trc -u
Usage: db2trc <chg|clr|dmp|flw|fmt|inf|off|on> options

        chg|change
                change the trace mask, maxSysErrors or maxRecordSize
        clr|clear
                clear the trace
        dmp|dump
                dump the trace to a binary trace file
        flw|flow
                show control flow of the trace
        fmt|format
                format the trace
        inf|info|information
                get information on the trace
        off
                turn the trace off
        on
                turn the trace on

        For more information type db2trc <chg|clr|dmp|flw|fmt|inf|off|on> -u
C:\>
```

More detail for each of the different subcommands can also be found by issuing a subcommand and using the **-u** option. Let's have a closer look at the syntax of the **db2trc** command and its subcommands.

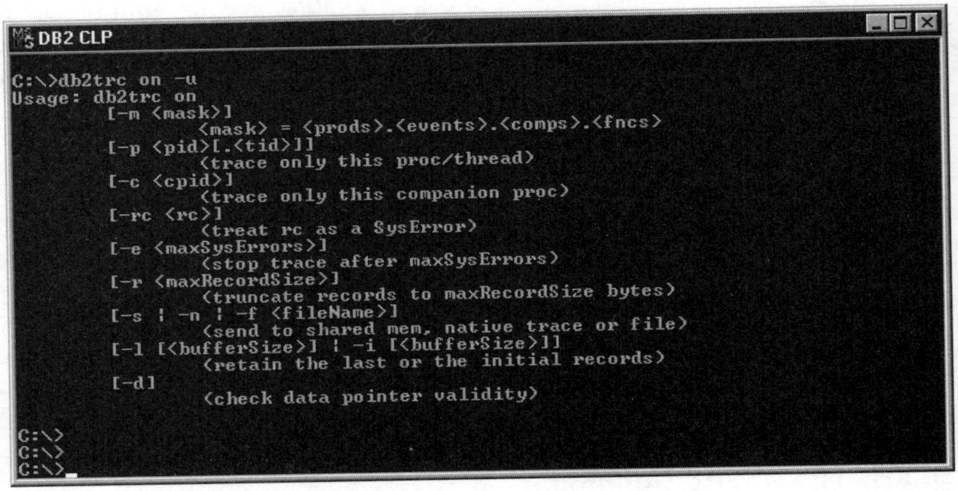

```
DB2 CLP

C:\>db2trc on -u
Usage: db2trc on
        [-m <mask>]
                <mask> = <prods>.<events>.<comps>.<fncs>
        [-p <pid>[.<tid>]]
                <trace only this proc/thread>
        [-c <cpid>]
                <trace only this companion proc>
        [-rc <rc>]
                <treat rc as a SysError>
        [-e <maxSysErrors>]
                <stop trace after maxSysErrors>
        [-r <maxRecordSize>]
                <truncate records to maxRecordSize bytes>
        [-s | -n | -f <fileName>]
                <send to shared mem, native trace or file>
        [-l [<bufferSize>] | -i [<bufferSize>]]
                <retain the last or the initial records>
        [-d]
                <check data pointer validity>

C:\>
C:\>
C:\>_
```

Collection of the trace information begins when **db2trc** is executed with the **on** subcommand. This will start the trace function and record the trace entries to a destination which may also be specified as part of the **on** subcommand. By default, trace entries are collected into *shared memory.* However, they can optionally be written directly to a file. Trace collection ends when **db2trc** is executed with the **off** subcommand.

10.5.2 Capturing Trace Information into Memory

Since writing to memory is much quicker than writing to disk, it is recommended that you use a memory buffer when taking a DB2 trace, unless absolutely necessary. We will now discuss the steps required to take a DB2 trace using a memory buffer.

In this command we will issue the **on** subcommand with the parameters **-e** and **-l**. These parameters are used to control:

- **-e** Specifies the maximum number of system errors allowed before trace collection is automatically terminated. If it is set to **-1,** as in this example, all errors will be collected until the DB2 trace is manually turned off.
- **-l** (note that it is a lowercase L, not the number one) indicates you wish to retain the latest entries into the trace buffer. The number specifies the size of the trace buffer in memory. It is expressed in number of bytes. In this

case we used a 4MB trace buffer (4000000 bytes). If you want to keep the initial trace entries use the **-i** parameter instead of **-l**.

```
db2trc on -e -1 -l 4000000
```

This will start the trace facility with a 4 MB buffer and the trace will run until manually stopped. The next step should be the recreation of the problem for which the trace is being collected. After you have reproduced the problem the trace information will need to be written to a file for analysis.

The subcommand to write the contents of the memory buffer to disk is **dump.** When dumping the memory buffer to disk you must specify the name of the file to write to. To write the contents of the trace buffer to the file named tracefile.dmp we would issue the command:

```
db2trc dump tracefile.dmp
```

It is very important that as soon as the collection of the trace is completed and the information that is contained in memory is written to a file that you stop the trace facility to eliminate the effect on the performance of the system. The trace can be stopped using the subcommand **off** as follows:

```
db2trc off
```

It is important to note that you must dump the trace buffer to disk prior to turning the trace off as the trace buffer is released when the trace is turned off. This trace dump file is a binary file and must be formatted for analysis by the DB2 UDB Support team. There are two methods of formatting the file for analysis:

You can issue the command

```
db2trc flow tracefile.dmp tracefile.flw
```

to format the events by process and thread, or:

```
db2trc format tracefile.dmp tracefile.fmt
```

to list the events chronologically, independent of process or thread.

10.5.3 Capturing Trace Information to a Disk File

In the event that the entire system hangs so that you cannot issue the **db2trc dump** command to write the contents of the memory buffer to disk, you will need to trace directly to a file.

In order to write to a file we need to specify the **-e**, **-l** and **-f** parameters. These parameters are used to control:

- `-e` Specifies the maximum number of system errors allowed before trace collection is automatically terminated. If it is set to `-1,` as in this example, all errors will be collected until trace is manually turned off.
- `-l` (note that it is a lowercase L, not the number one) indicates you wish to retain the latest entries into the trace file. The number specifies the size of the file. It is expressed in the number of bytes. In this case we used a 4MB trace file (4000000 bytes). If you want to keep the initial trace entries use the `-i` parameter instead of `-l`.
- `-f` Specifies the file name and extension of the file to which trace should be written. This file will be written to the directory from where the command is executed.

```
db2trc on -e -1 -l 4000000 -f tracefile.dmp
```

After the trace is turned on you will need to reproduce the error and then turn the trace off. You can stop the trace facility using the command:

```
db2trc off
```

You will find that there is a significant performance difference between tracing to shared memory and tracing directly to a file. A trace that is activated with the `-f` option will cause the system to be noticeably slower than the trace that is performed in memory.

The -f option of db2trc

The `-f` option of the `db2trc` utility is recommended when the error results in system hang situations such that you can no longer dump the trace file manually.

10.5.4 Using the info Subcommand

The `info` subcommand is used to look at information about the trace while it is occurring. It also gives you information about the environment and settings that were present when the trace was activated. The following screen shows you the syntax of the command and an example of the output of that command when tracing to shared memory.

```
C:\>
C:\>db2trc info -
Trace Version                :   3.01
Op. System                   :     NT
Op. Sys. Version             :    1.0
H/W Platform                 :  80x86
Version prod    1            :   3.01  (DB2)

Mask                         : *.*.*.*
pid.tid to trace             : all
cpid     to trace            : all
Treat this rc as sys err: none
Max system errors            : infinite
Max record size              : 32768 bytes
Trace destination            : SHARED MEMORY
Records to keep              : LAST
Trace buffer size            : 2097152 bytes
Trace data pointer check: NO

C:\>
```

10.5.5 Starting a DB2 Trace from the Graphical Interface

The task of starting or stopping a trace is made easier in DB2 UDB for Windows NT through the use of a graphical interface. Select **Start-> Programs->DB2 for Windows NT->Problem Determination->Trace**. This sequence will bring up the following window:

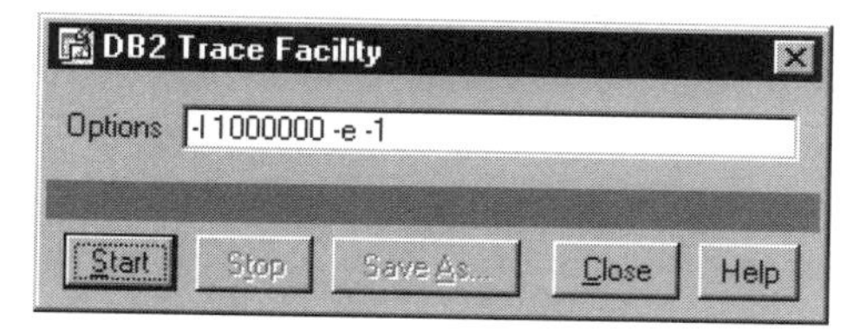

Figure 409. DB2 Trace Facility

You may start, stop, input any applicable parameters, and save to a file, just as you would if entering `db2trc` from the command line. Default options are already entered for you.

When you select the **Save As** push button, you may select a filename for the binary dump file. You may also select to format the output of your trace to ASCII files if you wish to verify the output. Select **Generate formatted trace file** if you want the full trace information, or **Generate control-flow trace file** if you want only the control flow of the trace information in a nested format.

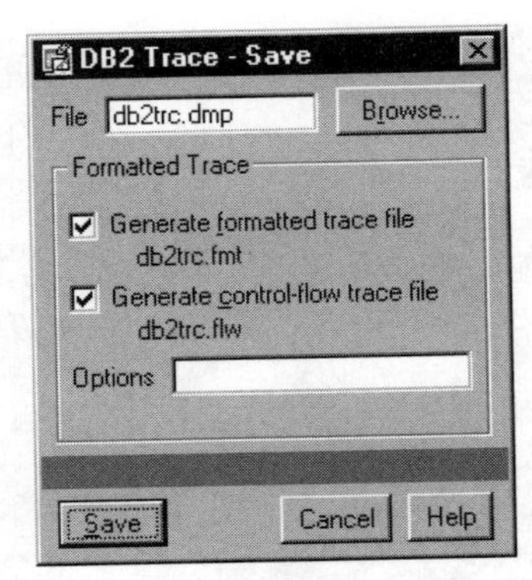

Figure 410. Trace Formatting Options

The following are valid options for trace formatting options:

-m mask	Specifies trace record types. The mask variable consists of four byte-masks that are separated by periods. The byte-masks correspond to products, event types, components, and functions, respectively.
-r	Output trace in reverse-chronological order.
-p proc ID[.thread ID]	Format only the trace records that belong to the specified process and thread.
-x single rec	Format only the specified record.
--x first rec-last rec	Format all records between the specified first and last record.

None of these options are mandatory. If omitted, the defaults are:

- Mask is as specified for execution.
- All records are formatted in chronological order.

10.5.6 Formatting the DB2 Trace

The trace file, whether it was written directly or was written from the memory buffer is a binary file and cannot be analyzed without formatting. The trace facility can format the trace in two different styles. To convert the trace dump file to a readable format you must specify the format or flow subcommand for db2trc.

- *flow* - Represents the flow of control and an overview of invoked functions and return codes (or error codes), and is broken down by process and thread.

* *format* - Represents each trace entry in formatted form in the sequence they occurred regardless of process or thread.

The following example is a fragment of the flow and corresponding formatted entries from the same trace showing some of the trace entries.

```
Flow:

1435      |sqlodelq   fnc_entry     ...
1436      |sqlodelq   fnc_data      ...
1437      | |sqlofmblk  cei_entry     ...
1438      | |sqlofmblk  cei_data      ...
1439      | |sqlofmblk  cei_retcode  0
1440      |sqlodelq   fnc_retcode  0

...

Format:

1435    DB2 fnc_entry      oper_system_services sqlodelq (1.30.15.196) ---------(1)
        pid 49; tid 1; cpid 0; time 197028; trace_point 0
        called_from 17DF6733

1436    DB2 fnc_data       oper_system_services sqlodelq (1.35.15.196) ---------(2)
        pid 49; tid 1; cpid 0; time 197028; trace_point 1
        0600 0000 0100 0100 50c4 3c0e              ........P.<.

1437    DB2 cei_entry      oper_system_services sqlofmblk (1.20.15.62) ---------(1)
        pid 49; tid 1; cpid 0; time 197028; trace_point 0
        called_from 17DF66EB

1438    DB2 cei_data       oper_system_services sqlofmblk (1.25.15.62) ---------(2)
        pid 49; tid 1; cpid 0; time 197028; trace_point 1
        c400 3c0e 50c4 3c0e                        ..<.P.<.

1439    DB2 cei_retcode    oper_system_services sqlofmblk (1.23.15.62) ---------(3)
        pid 49; tid 1; cpid 0; time 197028; trace_point 254
        return_code = 000000 = 0

1440    DB2 fnc_retcode    oper_system_services sqlodelq (1.33.15.196) ---------(4)
        pid 49; tid 1; cpid 0; time 197028; trace_point 254
        return_code = 000000 = 0
```

There are several types of trace entries shown in this example:

* Entry - Note that in the trace file, both **`fnc_entry`** and **`cei_entry`** denote an entry trace point.
* Data - This is where variable values are recorded at different trace points within a function and dumped to a trace file.
* Exit/Return - This is when the function ends and its return code is recorded.

- Error - While not shown above, this is where any additional information relevant to an error condition is recorded and dumped to the trace file.

10.5.7 The Format of a Trace Entry

Each trace entry contains information in a predefined format. Let's look at a sample formatted trace entry:

```
(1)339 (2)DB2 (3)cei_errcode (4)oper_system_services (5)sqloopenp (6)
(1.6.15.140)

(7)pid 44; (8)tid 11; (9)cpid 44;(10)time 500247;(11)trace_point 254

      return_code = (12)0xffffe60a = -6646 = SQLO_FNEX
```

- (1) Trace Entry sequence number. The trace entry is assigned a sequence number as it is recorded. The sequence always starts with one (1) and grows to the end of the trace file.
- (2) Product Indicator. (DB2)
- (3) Type of trace entry.
- (4) Component to which function being executed belongs
- (5) Function being executed.
- (6) Mask identifying (<Product>.<Event>.<Component>.<Function>) - This can be used to filter the trace collection, but only for specific Events, Components or Functions. Mask settings should be used as advised by a DB2 UDB Support analyst. The mask setting only affects the formatting of the trace. All entries will be recorded in the trace buffer/file no matter what mask is specified at format time.
- (7) Process Id of the process under which the function was executed.
- (8) Thread Id (if any) of the thread executing the function.
- (9) Companion Process Id - This is the process id of the process whose child is the process being traced. Frequently the companion process is a DB2 System Controller (DB2SYSC.EXE) process).
- (10) A time place holder. A parameter must be set to gather real time information. This slows down the system and is not recommended.
- (11)Trace point number - This entry uniquely identifies the trace entry within the DB2 UDB function itself. The DB2 UDB Support analyst having access to function source code can determine the exact line of code which reported this trace entry. This information is required if any data is written with the trace entry so that the analyst can decipher the data correctly.

- **(12)** The return code is represented as a hexadecimal value. This value must be analyzed the same way as return codes within the DB2DIAG.LOG file. First see if it is the correct order or is byte reversed. Once it is in the correct format convert it to decimal and see if it is a valid SQL code. If not a valid SQL code look up the hex value in the *DB2 UDB Troubleshooting Guide*, Appendix C. For some of the internal return codes, a symbolic name is also shown. Frequently, this symbolic name makes the identification of the problem much easier. In this example, `SQLO_FNEX` means File Not EXist (that is, the file does not exist).

10.6 R/3 Traces

R/3 traces contain ABAP/4 technical information, which can be checked if errors occur. In order to be able to use this information effectively, precise knowledge of the host system in which your R/3 System is running and of the R/3 System is required.

This type of trace is especially useful for analyzing problems which affect the operation of your R/3 System. For example, a trace of the disp+work process can show why it is not possible to generate work processes.

10.6.1 Activating R/3 Traces

To activate the R/3 traces, specify an option in the start profile for the machine of the R/3 instance. This file is called:

- START_<INSTANCE NAME><instance number>_hostname. For example on our AIX system, START_DVEBMGS00_f01n03.

This file is found in:

- /sapmnt/<SID>/profile on AIX
- <drive>:\sapmnt\<SID>\profile on NT

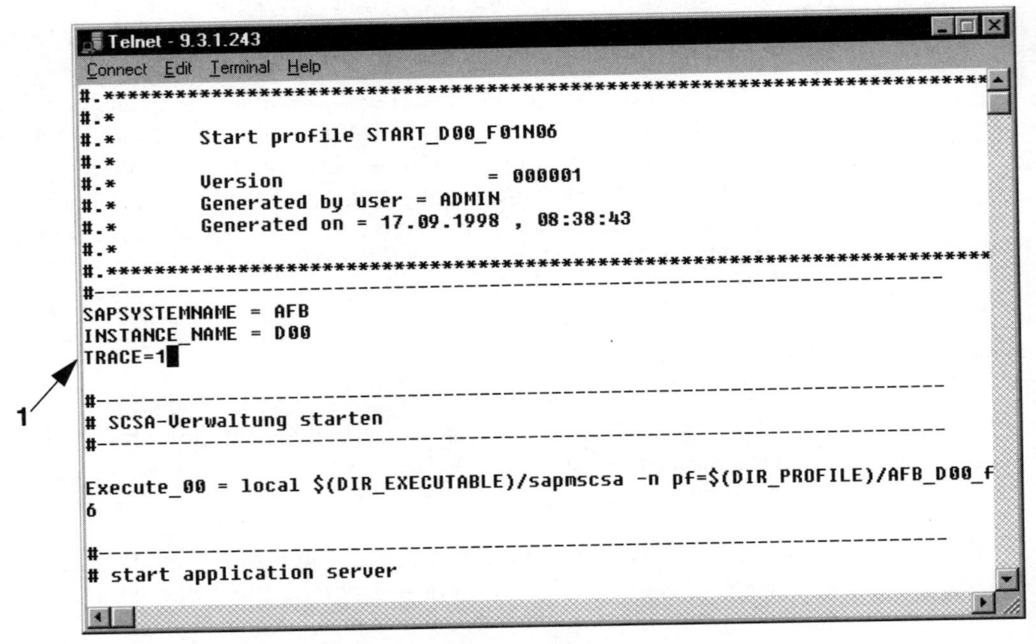

Figure 411. Trace option in: START_D00_f01n06

In this file (Figure 411), the following options are available:

- TRACE=0. No trace.
- TRACE=1. Write error messages to the trace file.
- TRACE=2. Full trace. The trace entries actually written vary according to the R/3 program being traced.
- TRACE=3. Also trace data blocks.

You also have the option of setting trace options for the instance by specifying an option in the instance profile. This file is called:

- <SID>_<INSTANCE NAME><INSTANCE NUMBER_HOSTNAME. For example on our AIX system, it is AFB_DVEBMGS00_f01n03.

This file is found in the same directory as the start profile listed above.

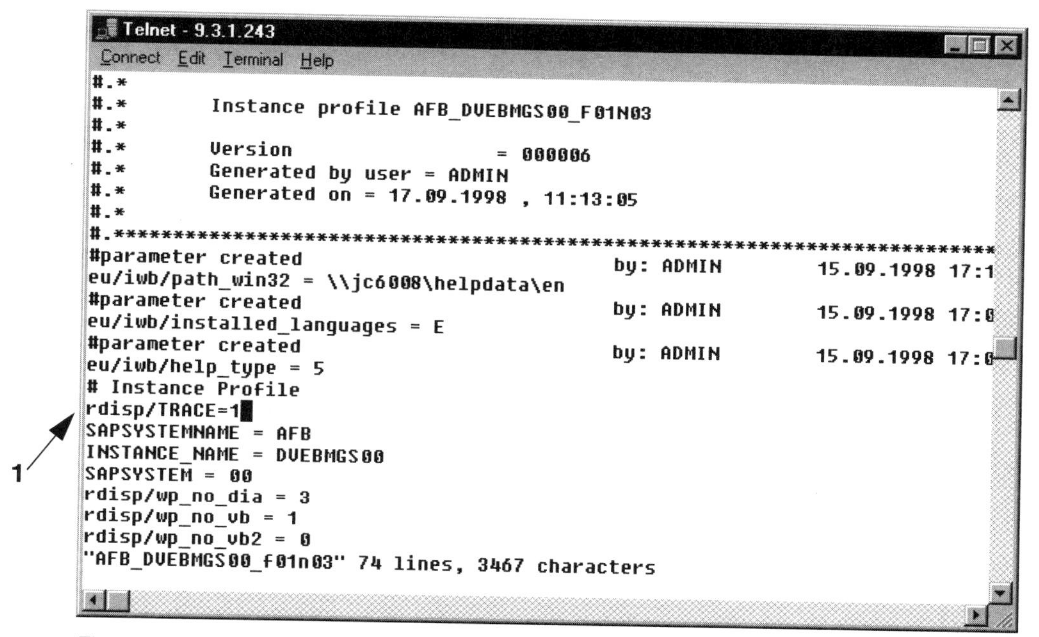

Telnet - 9.3.1.243
Connect Edit Terminal Help
#.*
#.*   Instance profile AFB_DVEBMGS00_F01N03
#.*
#.*   Version   = 000006
#.*   Generated by user = ADMIN
#.*   Generated on = 17.09.1998 , 11:13:05
#.*
#parameter created   by: ADMIN   15.09.1998 17:1
eu/iwb/path_win32 = \\jc6008\helpdata\en
#parameter created   by: ADMIN   15.09.1998 17:0
eu/iwb/installed_languages = E
#parameter created   by: ADMIN   15.09.1998 17:0
eu/iwb/help_type = 5
Instance Profile
rdisp/TRACE=1
SAPSYSTEMNAME = AFB
INSTANCE_NAME = DVEBMGS00
SAPSYSTEM = 00
rdisp/wp_no_dia = 3
rdisp/wp_no_vb = 1
rdisp/wp_no_vb2 = 0
"AFB_DVEBMGS00_f01n03" 74 lines, 3467 characters
1

Figure 412. The Parameter rdisp/TRACE in the Instance Profile

The parameter which affects trace settings is rdisp/TRACE. The values are the same as those listed above in the start profile.

10.6.2 Viewing R/3 Traces

To display these trace files, from the R/3 main menu choose: **Tools->CCMS, Control/Monitoring->Control Panel** or enter transaction **RZ03**:

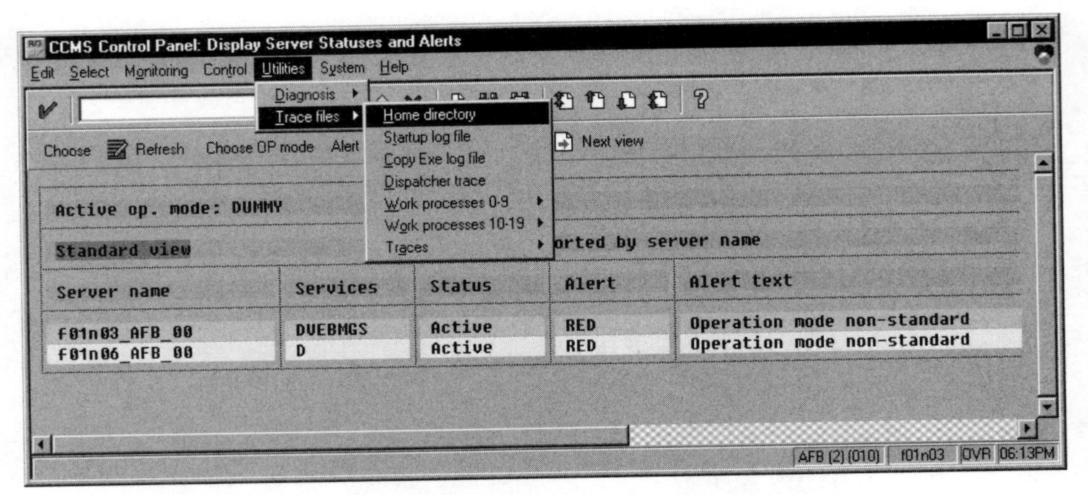

Figure 413. CCMS Control Panel: Display Server Statuses and Alerts

In the Control Panel, select an instance by double-clicking on it. Select **Utilities->Trace files** (Figure 413). You can then choose to display the trace file for the dispatcher or one of the work processes. For example, if you select Dispatcher trace, the following screen is displayed:

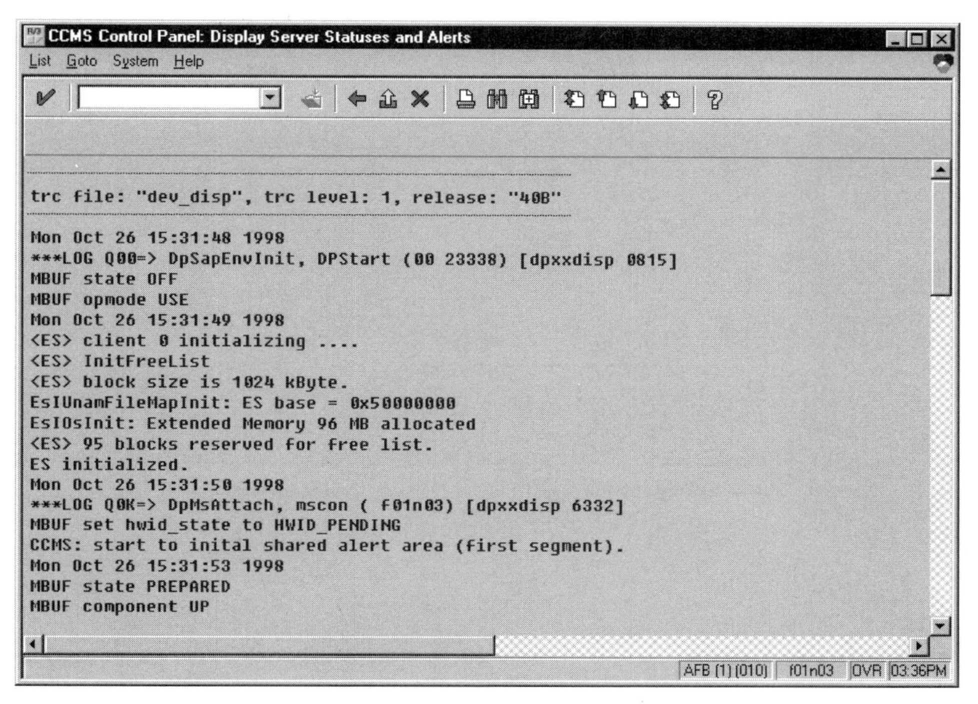

CCMS Control Panel: Display Server Statuses and Alerts
List Goto System Help
trc file: "dev_disp", trc level: 1, release: "40B"
Mon Oct 26 15:31:48 1998
***LOG Q00=> DpSapEnvInit, DPStart (00 23338) [dpxxdisp 0815]
MBUF state OFF
MBUF opmode USE
Mon Oct 26 15:31:49 1998
<ES> client 0 initializing ....
<ES> InitFreeList
<ES> block size is 1024 kByte.
EsIUnamFileMapInit: ES base = 0x50000000
EsIOsInit: Extended Memory 96 MB allocated
<ES> 95 blocks reserved for free list.
ES initialized.
Mon Oct 26 15:31:50 1998
***LOG Q0K=> DpMsAttach, mscon (f01n03) [dpxxdisp 6332]
MBUF set hwid_state to HWID_PENDING
CCMS: start to inital shared alert area (first segment).
Mon Oct 26 15:31:53 1998
MBUF state PREPARED
MBUF component UP
AFB (1) (010) f01n03 OVR 03:36PM

Figure 414. CCMS Control Panel: Display Server Statuses and Alerts (2)

Entries containing information on errors start with ***ERROR=> .
Entries containing system log entries start with ***LOG<message no.>.

An entry with error information contains the name of the calling function, the action that ended with an error, the error number (if a system call is involved) and the name and line of the C module that failed.

These trace files are found in the R/3 work directory, whose full path is:

- On AIX: /usr/sap/<SID>/<INSTANCE NAME><instance number>/work. In our example, this directory is /usr/sap/AFB/DVEBMGS00/work.
- On NT: <drive>:\usr\sap\<SID>\<INSTANCE NAME><instance number>\work.

The trace files have the following names:

Work process/Component	File Name
Dispatcher	dev_disp
Task Handler	Variable: depends on number of work process.
Dynp (Screen Processor)	dev_dy
Roll	dev_ro
Paging	dev_pg
DB Interface	dev_db
ABAP/4 Processor	dev_ab
Enqueue (lock)	dev_eq
Logging	dev_lg
Spool	dev_w
Message Server	dev_ms
SAPTEMU (Unix Presentation)	dev_st<logon name>
APPC Server (CPI-C Gateway)	dev_appc

10.7 DB2 UDB Common Problems

This section will discuss common DB2 UDB problems along with a recommended procedure to resolve each problem.

10.7.1 Archive Log Directory is Full

As long as there is still space in the archive log directory (*log_archive*), the database will continue to run. This filesystem should be monitored to ensure that it does not fill up. If it does, the R/3 database will become unusable until some space is freed up. In this case, you need make additional space available in the archive log directory by either adding more space to the filesystem or by backing up the archive log files and deleting them from this directory using the *SAP-DB2admin Logfile Management* facility in the DB2 UDB Control Center. Make sure you backup the archive log files as they are critical for recovery in the event of a database failure. Once the space is available, you will need to move the inactive log files from the log directory (*log_dir*) to the archive log directory. For a more details about log file management, see "R/3 Implementation of DB2 Logging" on page 338.

10.7.2 Table Space is Full

If a table space fills up, a message is recorded in the db2diag.log file. This file is in this directory:

- /db2/<SID>/sqllib/db2dump (AIX)
- <drive>:\db2\<SID>\sqllib\db2dump (NT).

Look for a message similar to this: Table Space 25(PSAPDOCUD) is full. You can also see error messages relating to full table spaces in the R/3 system log (use transaction SM21). If you need to increase the size of a table space, you should use the DB2 UDB Control Center. For more details, see "Adding Table Space Containers" on page 386.

10.7.3 Missing Archive Log File During Rollforward

When performing a roll forward of the database, you may experience the following error. Here is an example rollforward command:

```
db2 rollforward database AFB to end of logs and stop
```

This command produced this error:

```
SQL1273N Roll-forward recovery on database "AFB" cannot reach the
specified stop point (end-of-log or point-in-time) because of
missing log file "S0000034.19980910180704" on node 0
```

If you get a message like this, you need to make the log file available. First check that the log file is in the *log_archive* directory. If is not, you should recover it from a backup. This procedure is described in "Restoring Archived Log Files" on page 369.

10.8 R/3 Common Problems

This section discusses some common R/3 problems and the recommended procedure to resolve each problem.

10.8.1 Instance Crash

An instance is displayed red in the System Monitor, or ceases to be marked as active in the Control Panel if:

- The instance is not running any more
- The network connection to the instance is lost

Instance crashes are normally caused by external problems rather than by errors in programs. These external problems can be, for example, hardware problems or power failures, network problems, host system problems such as insufficient storage or hard disk space.

You can look for the cause of the crash in the following sources of information:

- System log:

  Once you have started up the instance again, you can log onto it and display the local system log. When the instance is down, you can display the central log from any other instance using **Tools->Administration, Monitor->System Log**. Alternatively, enter transaction **SM21**.

- Developer traces:

  If the developer traces were activated, you can look for the error in the dispatcher trace file and the trace files of the work processes. From the R/3 main menu select **Tools->CCMS, Control/Monitoring->Control Panel**. Alternatively, enter transaction **RZ03**. Select an instance by double-clicking on it, then select **Utilities->Trace files**.

You can activate traces for a complete instance using the system profile parameter *rdisp/trace*. You can also activate the developer traces separately for certain components, such as the background processing system.

Note

The contents of the trace are technical in nature and can normally only be analyzed in cooperation with SAP consultants.

- Start-up log

  To display the start-up log, from the R/3 main menu select **Tools->CCMS, Control/Monitoring->Control Panel**. Alternatively, enter transaction **RZ03**. Select an instance by double-clicking on it, then select **Utilities->Trace files->Startup log file**. In this file you can usually find an explanation for the instance shutdown and determine whether it was a normal shutdown or a crash.

10.8.2 Operation Mode Errors

Some common error situations related to operation modes are described here.

10.8.2.1 Operation Mode Switch Failed

If an operation mode switch does not function, the most frequent cause is inconsistencies in the instance definition. For example:

- For day operation, a different number of profiles are defined compared to the number for night operation.
- For day operation, a different number of work processes are defined compared to the number for night operation.
- A server was started with a different configuration than the configuration described in the instance definition.

If these problems occur, the message *Operation mode non-standard* or *Work processes non-standard* is displayed in the Control Panel.

You should analyze the problem, then make the necessary changes to the instance definition, or copy the current instance status to the instance definition.

10.8.2.2 Other Servers Cannot Be Started Remotely

If you cannot start servers from the Control Panel or the System Monitor, this is usually because the remote command (via rexec) could not be executed. This is often because the instance start-up user is not configured correctly.

Appendix A. R/3 and DB2 Userids

Table 21. List of R/3 and DB2 Userids

USERID	Definition	Standard	Example
<sapsid> also refered to as <sid>	R/3 System name	3 chars	aus
<sapsid>adm	R/3 Administration and Installation id	6 chars	ausadm
db2admin	DB2 Administrator Server Account	8 chars	db2admin
db2<sid>	Database Administrator	6 chars	db2aus
sapr3	SAP database owner	5 chars	sapr3
sapse<sid>	Standard SAP R/3 Service Account	8 chars	sapseaus
SAPService<sid>	SAP R/3 Service Account	13 chars	SAPServiceAus

Appendix B. R/3 and DB2 Installation Checklist

Table 22. R/3 and DB2 Installation Checklist (1)

Check List		Actioned
NT setup on Windows NT Server		
	Windows NT Version	
	Create Userids	
	Setup User Rights	
	Select Appropriate Hostname	
	Partitions	
	Virtual Memory	
	Optimize Network P	
DB2 UDB on Windows NT Server		
	DB2 Enterprise Edition	
	Service Pack	
	Drop DB2 Instance	
	DB2 UDB SAP R/3 Interface	
DB2 UDB on Administration Workstation		
	DB2 Client Application Enabler	
	Service Pack	
	DB2 UDB SAP R/3 Interface	
	Catalog R/3 databases with Control Center	

Table 23. R/3 and DB2 Installation Checklist (2)

Check List		Actioned
SAP R/3 Installation on SAP - Intial Copy		
	Temp Environment	
	Temporary directory	
	<sapsid> **UPPERCASE**	
	Logoff/logon	
SAP R/3 Installation on SAP - Central and DB Instance		
	<sapsid> **UPPERCASE**	
	SAP system number	
	Drive for R/3 code	
	NT Domain Name	
	SAP Transport Host	
	DB2 Encryption Key	
	db2<sapsid> userid password	
	Default DB path	
	DB2 diagnosis path	
	DB2 log archive path	
	SAP Reorganisation path	
	SAPDATA1 - SAPDATA6 path	
	sapr3 userd password	
	Default DB path	
	SAP TCPIP Message port	
	SAP TCPIP Service Port	
	SAPService<sapsid> userid password	
	SAP Kernal CD	
	SAP R/2 Connection	

Table 24. R/3 and DB2 Installation Checklist (3)

Check List		**Actioned**
SAP R/3 Installation on SAP - Central and DB Instance		
	Memory	
	DB2 Export CD 1 path	
	Reorganisation path for copying CD 1	
	DB2 Export CD 2 path	
	Report Load CD path	
	Parallel Processes for the installation	
	Platform specific	
	Default DB path	
	Default DB path	
	DB2 Export CD 1	
	DB2 Export CD 2	
	Report Load CD	
	MNLS support	

Appendix C. R/3 and DB2 Control Center Tasks

The following table identifies those tasks required for database maintenance and which tools should be used.

Note

This list is a summary of recommendations only. It possible to accomplish some tasks from either set of tools.

Table 25. R/3 and DB2 Control Center Tasks

Tasks	SAP R/3	DB2 Control Center
BACKUPS		
Initialize Tapes for Backups	NO	DB2admin CC
Offline Backups	NO	YES
Online Backups	YES	YES
LOGS		
Initialize Tapes for Log Archive	YES	DB2admin CC
Backup Offline Retained logs	YES	DB2admin CC
RESTORE		
Restore Offline Backup	NO	YES
Restore Online Backup	NO	YES
DATA MAINTENANCE		
RUNSTAT	YES	Possible
REORGCHK	YES	Possible
REORG	YES	Possible
Add table space containers	NO	YES
SECURITY		
Password Maintenance	NO	DB2admin CC

Appendix D. IBM and SAP Web Sites

The following table contains a list of websites that you may find to be useful in the support of your SAP R/3 system on an IBM DB2 UDB platform,

Table 26. List of Useful Websites

Name	URL
IBM	http://www.ibm.com
IBM/SAP Alliance	http://www.ibm.com/erp/sap/
SAP	http://www.sap.com
DB2 UDB	http://www.ibm.com/software/data
SAP Sizing	http://www.ibm.com/erp/sap/solutions/sizing.htm
RS/6000 Home Page	http://www.austin.ibm.com
Netfinity Home Page	http://www.pc.ibm.com/netfinity
IBM Redbooks	http://www.redbooks.ibm.com
DB2 On-line Manuals	http://www.software.ibm.com/cgi-bin/db2www/library/ pubs.d2w/report#udbpubs
IBM Software	http://www.software.ibm.com
SAP Ready to Run	http://www.ibm.com/erp/sap/technolody/readytorun.htm

Appendix E. Related Publications

The publications listed in this section are considered relevant as further information sources:

- *DB2 UDB Administration Guide*, S10J-8157
- *DB2 UDB Quick Beginnings for Windows NT*, S10J-8149
- *DB2 UDB Quick Beginnings for Unix*, S10J-8148
- *DB2 UDB Command Reference*, S10J-8166
- *R/3 Installation on UNIX/Windows NT*
- *R/3 Installation on UNIX - OS Dependencies*

Index

T